THE BLACKWELL COMPANION TO SOCIAL WORK

For Andrew and Roser, Paul and Pa

THE BLACKWELL COMPANION TO SOCIAL WORK

Third Edition

Edited by Martin Davies

BLACKWELL PUBLISHING
350 Main Street, Malden, MA 02148-5020, USA
9600 Garsington Road, Oxford OX4 2DQ, UK
550 Swanston Street, Carlton, Victoria 3053, Australia

First edition published 1997
Second edition 2002
Third edition published 2008 by Blackwell Publishing Ltd

2 2008

Library of Congress Cataloging-in-Publication Data

The Blackwell companion to social work/edited by Martin Davies. – 3rd ed.
p. cm.
Includes bibliographical references and indexes.
ISBN 978-14051-7004-8 (pbk. : alk. paper) 1. Social service–Great Britain.
I. Davies, Martin, 1936–

HV245.B53 2008
362.3′20941–dc22

2007025832

A catalogue record for this title is available from the British Library.

Set in 10 on 12 pt Sabon
by SNP Best-set Typesetter Ltd., Hong Kong
Printed and bound in Singapore
by Markono Print Media Pte Ltd

The publisher's policy is to use permanent paper from mills that operate a sustainable forestry policy, and which has been manufactured from pulp processed using acid-free and elementary chlorine-free practices. Furthermore, the publisher ensures that the text paper and cover board used have met acceptable environmental accreditation standards.

For further information on
Blackwell Publishing, visit our website:
www.blackwellpublishing.com

Contents

Contributors

Graham Allan is Professor of Sociology at the University of Keele.

Hugh Barr is Emeritus Professor of Interprofessional Education at the University of Westminster, Visiting Professor at King's College London, Kingston University with St George's University of London and at the University of Greenwich.

Rose Barton is Learning and Development Adviser at the East of England Regional Assembly in Flempton, Bury St Edmunds.

Neil Bateman is an author, trainer and consultant who specializes in welfare rights and social policy issues.

Peter Beresford is Professor of Social Policy and Director of the Centre for Citizen Participation at Brunel University and Chair of Shaping Our Lives, the national service user organization and network.

Jane Boylan is Lecturer in Social Work at the University of Keele.

Allan Brown was, before his retirement, Senior Lecturer in the School for Policy Studies at the University of Bristol.

Paul Bywaters is Emeritus Professor of Social Work at the University of Coventry.

Siobhan Canavan is Lecturer in Counselling Studies at the University of Edinburgh and a person-centred counsellor and supervisor in private practice.

Pat Collingwood is a Teaching Fellow in Social Work at the University of Stirling and independent trainer/facilitator/practice teacher and consultant within the South East Scotland Learning Network.

Viviene E. Cree is Professor of Social Work Studies at the University of Edinburgh.

Suzy Croft is senior social worker at St John's Hospice, London. She is a member of the Editorial Collective of the journal *Critical Social Policy*.

Brigid Daniel is Professor in Child Care and Protection at the University of Dundee.

Martin Davies is Emeritus Professor of Social Work at the University of East Anglia, Norwich.

Lena Dominelli is Professor of Applied Social Sciences at the University of Durham.

Mark Drakeford is Professor of Social Policy and Applied Social Sciences at the University of Cardiff and Cabinet health and social policy adviser at the Welsh Assembly Government.

Sally French is Associate Lecturer for the Open University and a freelance researcher and writer.

Sarah Galvani is Lecturer in Social Work at the University of Birmingham.

David Goosey is Principal Lecturer in Advanced Social Work at the University of Westminster and a partner with The Change Agency.

Nick Gould is Professor of Social Work at the University of Bath.

Gillian Harris is Senior Lecturer in Applied Developmental Psychology at Birmingham University, and Consultant Clinical Psychologist at the Children's Hospital, Birmingham.

Martin Herbert is Professor of Clinical and Community Psychology at Exeter University.

William Horder is Lecturer in Social Work at Goldsmiths College, University of London.

David Howe is Professor of Social Work at the University of East Anglia, Norwich.

Richard Hugman is Professor of Social Work at the University of New South Wales.

Cathy Humphreys is Professor of Child and Family Welfare at the University of Melbourne.

Beth Humphries is a writer and researcher with long experience of practising, teaching and studying social work.

Peter Huxley is Professor of Social Work at the University of Swansea.

Adrian L. James is Professor of Social Work at the University of Sheffield.

Hazel Kemshall is Professor of Community and Criminal Justice at De Montfort University.

David Leadbetter is Director and Programme Coordinator at CALM Training Services Menstrie, Clackmannanshire.

Karen Lyons is Honorary Professor of International Social Work at the University of Hertfordshire and London Metropolitan University.

Geraldine Macdonald is Professor of Social Work at Queen's University, Belfast.

Roger Manktelow is Course Director of the MSc in Social Work at the University of Ulster in Derry.

Deborah Marks is Lecturer in the Department of Psychology, Birkbeck, University of London.

Peter Marsh is Professor of Child and Family Welfare and Dean of the Faculty of Social Sciences at the University of Sheffield.

Eileen McLeod is Associate Professor in the School of Health and Social Studies at the University of Warwick.

Audrey Mullender is Principal of Ruskin College, Oxford and Professor in Social Work at the University of Warwick.

Teresa Munby is Tutor in Law and Social Work at Ruskin College, Oxford.

Kwame Owusu-Bempah is Reader in Psychology in the School of Social Work at Leicester University.

Jonathan Parker is Professor of Social Work at Bournemouth University.

Bridget Penhale is Reader in Gerontology at the University of Sheffield and Head of Research at the Institute of Health and Social Care Studies, Guernsey.

Alison Petch is Director, **research in practice *for adults***, Dartington Hall Trust, Devon.

Chris Phillipson is Professor of Applied Social Studies and Social Gerontology at Keele University.

Ian Philp is Professor of Health Care for Elderly People in the Institute for Studies on Ageing at Sheffield University and the National Director for Older People in the Department of Health.

Beverley Prevatt Goldstein has been Director of the Black Ethnic Community Organisations Network (BECON) and is a doctoral student at Bristol University.

Seamus Prior is Co-Director of Counselling Studies at the University of Edinburgh.

Carol Robinson is Regional Adviser for Valuing People Support Team and Programme Leader in Learning Disability Services, South West Centre of Excellence, Bristol.

Gwen Robinson is Lecturer in Criminal Justice at the University of Sheffield.

Tammie Ronen is Professor and Head of the Bob Shapell School of Social Work at Tel Aviv University.

Gillian Schofield is Professor of Child and Family Social Work at the University of East Anglia, Norwich.

Janet Seden is Senior Lecturer in Social Work, Health and Social Care at the Open University.

Ian Sinclair is a research professor at York University.

Kirsten Stalker is Reader in the Faculty of Education at Strathclyde University.

John Swain is Professor of Disability Studies at the University of Northumbria.

June Thoburn is Emeritus Professor of Social Work at the University of East Anglia, Norwich.

Neil Thompson is Professor of Social Work and Well-being at Liverpool Hope University and Director of Avenue Consulting Ltd.

Janet Walker is Emeritus Professor of Family Policy at Newcastle University.

Lorraine Waterhouse is Professor of Social Work at Edinburgh University.

Mary Webb is Principal Lecturer in Advanced Social Work at the University of Westminster and a partner with The Change Agency.

Jan White is an Independent Family and Systemic Therapist and Supervisor in Somerset.

All authors write in a personal capacity. Their expressed views do not necessarily reflect the policy of their employers.

Preface to the Third Edition

It has been a privilege to edit the *Blackwell Companion to Social Work* and to see it through three editions.

In this edition, there is a new Introductory chapter and additional entries on drugs and alcohol, migration, ethics, and assessment. The chapters on family/relationship breakdown, learning disabilities, counselling and research have new authors. All other chapters have been revised and some have been completely rewritten.

The contributors to this book are influential writers in their respective academic fields. I am grateful to each of them for making time available to provide an erudite framework of knowledge for the benefit of a new generation of social work students.

I owe a special debt to Mark Doel and Judith Phillips who gave valuable help in the process of updating two chapters.

Holly the collie kept me sane and kept me company during the lengthy business of pulling it all together.

Martin Davies
Norwich
June 2007

Introduction

Knowledge, Theory and Social Work Practice – An Easy Access Approach

Pat Collingwood and Martin Davies

Although we know that service users appreciate social workers who have positive human qualities like helpfulness, reliability and patience, we also know that high quality practice requires a depth of knowledge that can only come from learning about and absorbing a wide range of theoretical ideas and research-based evidence such as that contained in the chapters of this book.

To the beginning student the task of linking theory to practice can be challenging and feelings of apprehension may be fuelled by the fact that social work training courses are designed to cover material drawn, not just from one source, but from complex disciplines like psychology and sociology, social administration and politics, philosophy and law.

The process of becoming a social worker is exciting – but it involves a great deal of hard work. A detailed and reflective reading of the theories, facts and ideas that are outlined in the *Blackwell Companion to Social Work* will enable you to lay firm foundations for what lies ahead. But the most crucial step in the course of becoming a qualified social worker depends on you being able successfully to bridge the gap between the theory and knowledge that you learn during training and the way that you practise when you are working in the field with service users. Theory and knowledge, for example, are crucial components in ensuring high quality in the work that you do as you:

- prepare for each encounter with a service user;
- assess people and situations;
- decide how, when and whether to intervene;
- react appropriately at all times and to many different people;
- review what you have done and consider how the service user has responded;
- decide what to do next.

When you are qualified, your work will be judged neither by the marks awarded for essays nor by the quality of your contributions to seminar discussions but by the way in which you carry out your professional duties. Social work practitioners traditionally hold that social problems are solved or ameliorated by the application of ideas from a tried-and-tested body of professional knowledge. But as one student has commented, 'there are so many different theories and there doesn't seem to be any coherent way of identifying conflicts between them: why you pick one theory as opposed to another – or do you just randomly pick a theory?' (Collingwood, 2005).

In Chapter 2.1 of this book, Howe identifies five key points in his exploration of the importance of theory for social work practice:

- Social work theories help practitioners to make sense of complex and difficult human situations.
- Different social work theories generate different understandings of human behaviour and social situations.
- The social work process . . . describes a sequence and a structure which helps social workers to practise in a systematic way.
- Social workers who use theory to inform their use of the social work process are more likely to practise in a thoughtful and professional manner.
- The purposes of social work and the theories which support them vary depending on the cultural context in which social work finds itself.

A good theoretical base should equip the social worker with a high level of sensitivity to the needs and circumstances of service users and the skill to assess the relevance and impact of any situational context. It should suggest appropriate ways of intervening compatible with an agency framework. The methods which the social worker is likely to employ are usually drawn from sources that had their origins in humanist thinking, Freudian or post-Freudian ideas, developmental and social psychology or behaviourism. At times and in varying degrees in different fields of social work, significant ideas may come from Marxist theory, feminism, clinical psychiatry, evolutionary theory, educational psychology, law, criminology, the philosophy of ethics and pastoral or radical theology.

As Howe reminds us, 'there is nothing so practical as a good theory', but, with such a wide range of material to draw on, students will always need help as they develop their skill in deciding how best to make links between aspects of theory or knowledge and any particular piece of practice in respect of an identifiable service user. Student learning in this area has traditionally come through group discussion, role play, the viewing of video clips, analysis of transcripted case material and, above all, experience of real world practice in placements under the observation and guidance of skilled field professionals.

But recent research (Collingwood, 2005) has demonstrated that a pen-and-paper or on-screen tool can help students to focus their minds, think clearly, identify priorities, make choices and improve the level of their practice-related understanding. The model that achieves these objectives is the *three-stage theory framework*. It has been road-tested and has received positive feedback from students who have used it.

The Three-stage Theory Framework

The framework identifies three distinct stages that students need to go through when they are learning to access and apply the knowledge and theory that they require for social work practice. It is designed to have generic applicability.

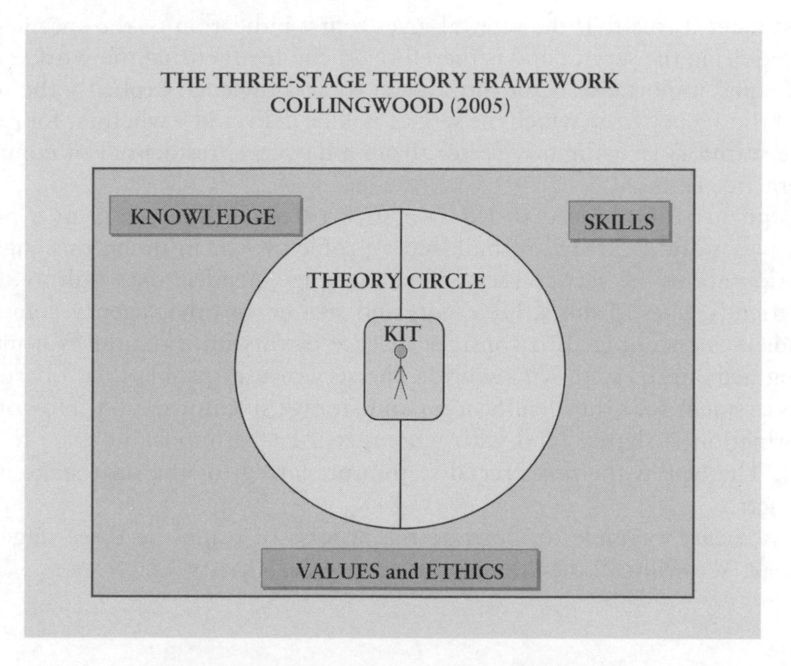

Figure 1 The three-stage theory framework

Stage 1: The service user profile

The first step is for the student to construct a service user profile, resulting in the creation of an identikit picture. For generic learning purposes, the service user becomes known as *Kit*. At this point the service user is gender, race, age and ability neutral. Students in groups may discuss together their respective *Kit*s and the issues that are raised by them as the profile emerges.

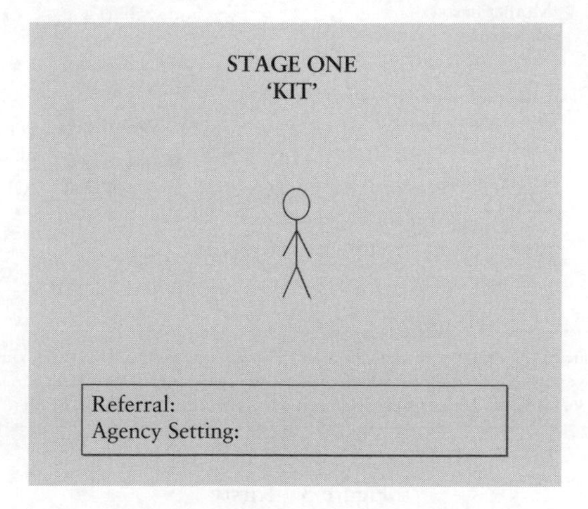

Figure 2 *Kit*

The student learns that the referral gives a first indication of the specifics of the person requiring the service and is therefore crucial for focusing the worker's attention. Of equal importance is for the student to acknowledge explicitly the role and nature of the agency from which the service will be delivered – whether, for example, from the statutory or voluntary sector, from a day care, residential or community-based practice team.

The student is introduced to *Kit* as a stick person in the centre of a prepared sheet of paper and is invited to build up a profile of *Kit*. In doing this, significant information about the service user will emerge: age, gender, race, culture, history, family, friends, likes, dislikes, life events and significant other agency connections. The student is encouraged to consider the use of this information as a means of becoming acquainted with *Kit*'s world. The service user profile (SUP) becomes an initial assessment tool for identification and storage of information. How much of the information is shared (and with whom) will be an important issue to discuss with *Kit*. The SUP is the first crucial step in preparing for the next stage in social work practice.

Here is a case example to illustrate the process of using the three-stage theory framework. We will call the anonymous service user Kirsty.

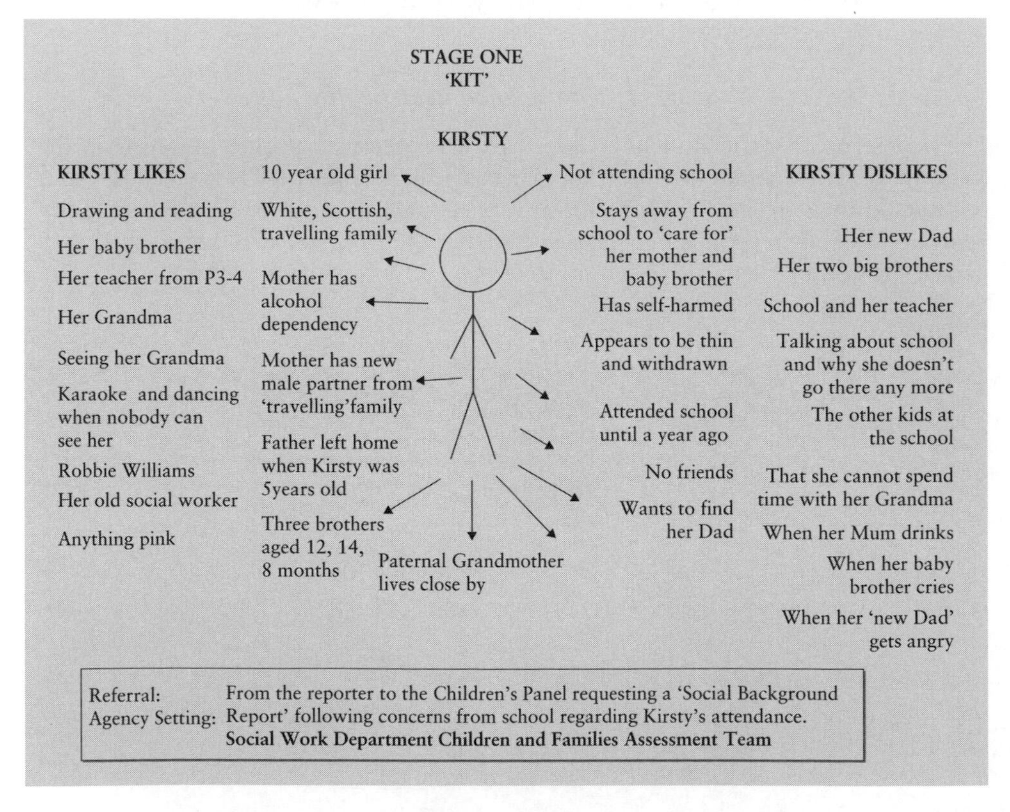

Figure 3 Kirsty

Kirsty is a 10-year-old white Scottish girl from a travelling family. She is referred to social work with a request for a social background report to be compiled following non-attendance at school.

Kirsty's home situation is difficult. Her parents have separated and her mother, who has an alcohol problem, has a new partner. Kirsty has two older siblings and a younger brother. She has a close relationship with her paternal grandmother who lives nearby.

She appears thin and withdrawn and there is some evidence of self-harm. She attended school regularly until a year ago.

Based on the information derived from the referral and having met with Kirsty the student is now in a position to move from the theoretical generality of *Kit* to the real-world specifics of Kirsty – as outlined in figure 3.

This information forms the basis for the initial assessment of Kirsty's situation and it enables the student worker to pinpoint what may be required before the process of drawing on theory can begin. One student who used the *Kit* approach commented at this stage, 'I have to go back and get more details from the client, I probably wouldn't have thought about, but when you do think about it and writing

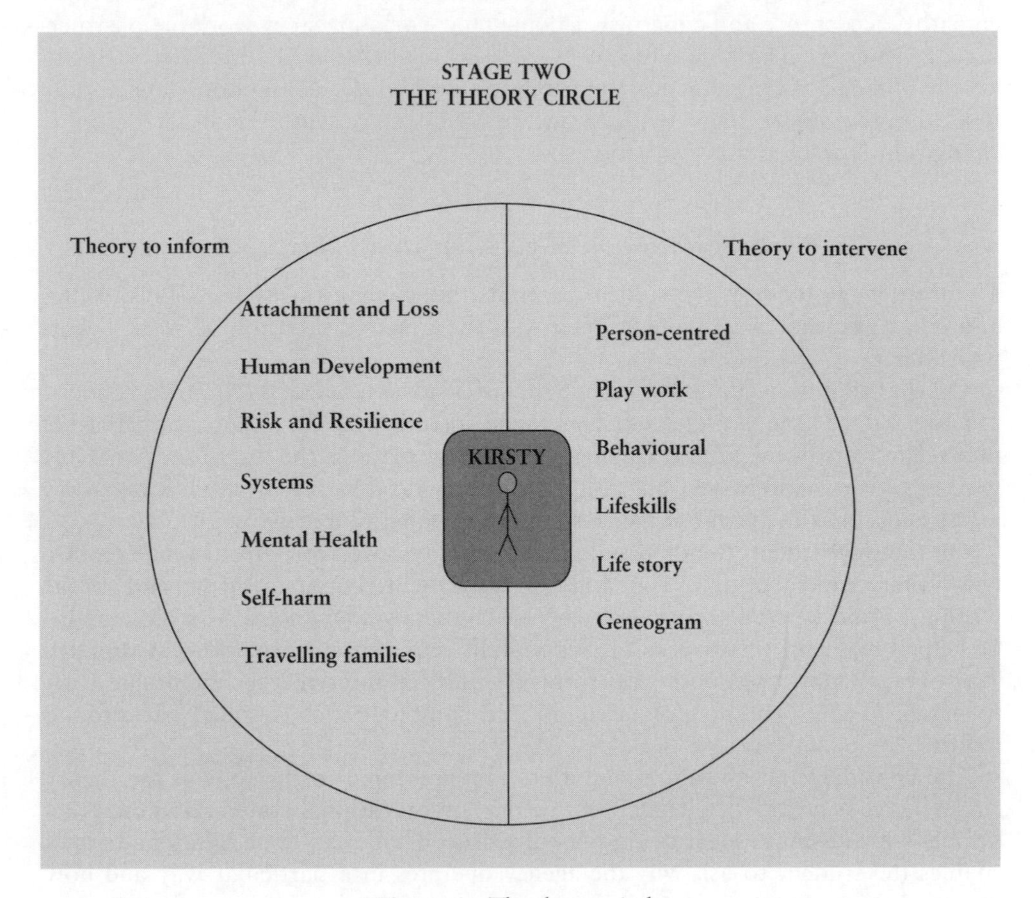

Figure 4 The theory circle

it down, you think "aha" I better check that . . . it makes obvious things I have maybe assumed or not thought about.'

Stage 2: The theory circle

The theory circle is divided vertically in two as shown in figure 4. The two halves signify the importance and interdependence of distinct strands of theory that can be drawn on to explain what may be going on in Kirsty's world (left half) and to think about what social work interventions might be appropriate (right half).

The left half of the circle encourages the student to be specific and to identify all the theoretical ideas and relevant writing that might help achieve an understanding of Kirsty and the environment she inhabits. In our example, relevant ideas can be drawn from attachment theory, human development, risk and resilience, mental health, self-harm and the sociological and social policy understandings of travelling people.

The theory entered into the left half of the circle will, of course, not directly enable social work intervention to take place. Only when the student moves into the right half of the circle can theories of intervention be considered for Kirsty. These might be underpinned by person-centred ideas about working alongside Kirsty with empathy, acceptance and congruence, doing play work, life story work or constructing a geneogram. Thinking which of these ideas might be used with Kirsty helps to lay the foundations for a tactical approach to social work intervention and helpfully links the assessment stage with the identification of potential goals or desirable changes for Kirsty and her situation.

Stage 3: Knowledge, skills and values

The third stage requires the student to think about what knowledge, skills, values and ethical considerations might enter into the practice situation as work begins with Kirsty.

On the left side of the theory circle (figure 5) the knowledge required for social practice with Kirsty is indicated. This might include specific organizational issues that relate to working with travelling families and schools, the legal framework for working with children, relevant policy and procedural information with regard to assessment and the availability of resources for undertaking the work.

On the right side of the theory circle the skills required for effective intervention with Kirsty are identified. The skills of assessment, communication and report writing, would be crucial for work with Kirsty. The student social worker can also be helped to identify the special practice skills required when working with a 10-year-old girl: play work and other forms of informal interview techniques in order to gather the information required for the completion of a social background report.

The consideration of values and ethics is represented at the foot of the theory circle. There is acknowledgement that theory, organizational context and the practitioner's professional identity are not value-free. Thinking about values and ethics enables the student to ask why the agency operates in a particular way and how this might impact on work with Kirsty; why a particular theory and theorist is

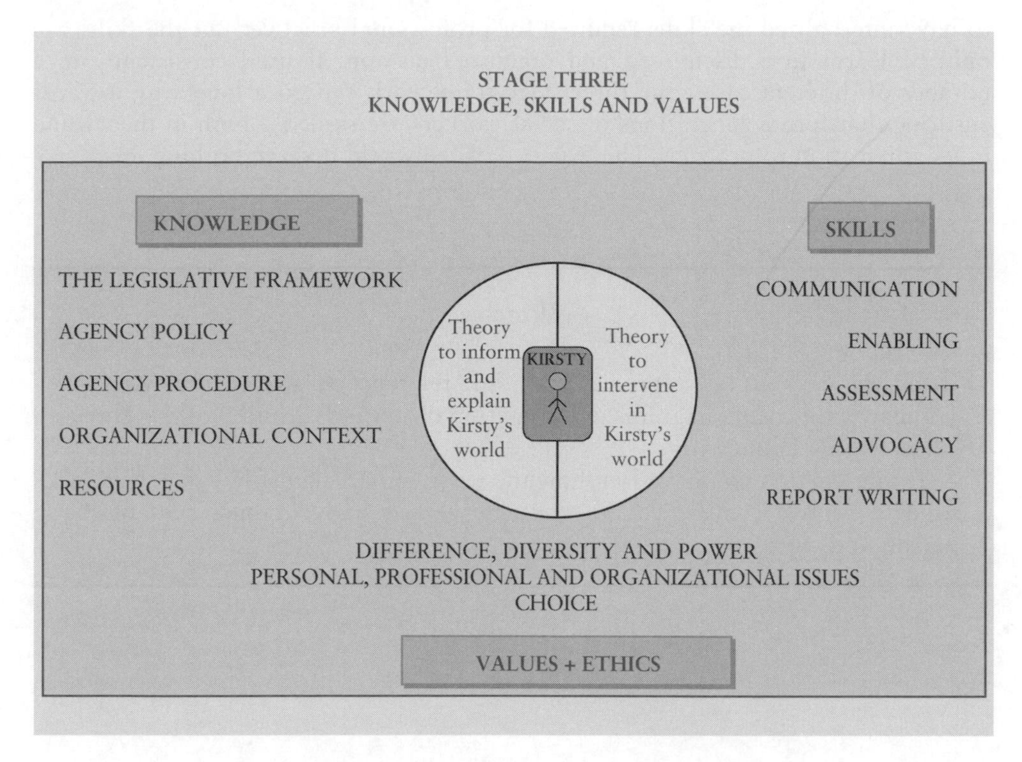

Figure 5 Knowledge, skills and values

chosen to explain Kirsty's experience; why a particular method was considered an appropriate choice. The student also brings his or her own personal and professional value base to working with Kirsty. (What preconceptions, for example, might the student have about the travelling community? How might the worker's age or gender affect the relationship?)

Practice choices are informed and underpinned by an amalgam of personal, professional and organizational value bases. Stage 3 gives opportunity for the student worker to consider issues of difference and diversity and to acknowledge the potential harming forces of oppression and discrimination for Kirsty. This could be about having an understanding of the issues relevant to Kirsty being a member of a minority ethnic group, her age, the impact of her mother's mental health and the consequences of the 'split' family situation.

Issues of power and powerlessness will require further consideration if Kirsty is to be understood in context and helped with her need for development in order to move on from this difficult period of her life.

Conclusion

As members of a profession social workers are trusted to practise autonomously. Because of the specialist nature of their expertise and knowledge, they are assumed to have internalized the skills required for professional practice. But the skills can only be learnt in a disciplined and organized fashion. If used consistently in a number of different cases, the three-stage framework can go a long way towards ensuring that future generations of social workers are skilled – both in theory and in its application to practice. The 'Kirstys' of the world deserve nothing less.

Exercise

Using the easy access approach and with reference to a case that you are familiar with, create diagrams in recognition of stages 1, 2 and 3 of the Three-stage Theory Framework.

Don't feel that you have to follow the Kirsty model slavishly – your outline needs to reflect sympathetically the age, gender and circumstances of the person and situation.

PART 1

Reasons for Social Work

CHAPTER 1.1

Family Disruption and Relationship Breakdown

Jane Boylan and Graham Allan

The demographic character of family life has been changing quite dramatically over the last 30 years. There have been significant increases in the number of people living alone, in the number of same-sex relationships, in the number of divorces occurring, in the numbers of people cohabiting, in the numbers of births to single women, and in the number of stepfamilies formed. At the same time, marriage rates have been declining and average age at marriage has been increasing. Overall it is evident that people are now choosing to construct their sexual, domestic and familial lives in far more varied and flexible ways than was common for much of the twentieth century. Moral values over issues of marriage, sex and childbirth have altered so that now far greater personal freedom is being exercised in patterns of family and household formation and dissolution. This chapter is largely concerned with the implications for social work practice of one aspect of these changes: marital separation and divorce.

Social work has long been concerned with problems in family relationships and behaviour. Such problems, including ones consequent upon family disruption, may become known to social workers through self-referral or through the concerns of other agencies. However, which family problems are considered to be relevant to social work practice is not a straightforward issue and in part depends on the agency that is providing the social work service. Moreover the 'content' of social work practice alters over time, both as a consequence of new social issues and problems emerging and because legislation and policy initiatives alter the ways different agencies come to prioritize their work. As a consequence, family problems that might have been deemed worthy of social work intervention and resources at one time may at another time come to be defined as personal matters over which there is no real need for social work professionals to become involved. In other words, what is regarded as pathological, damaging or symptomatic of familial disorder is at least in part a socio-historical construction rooted in normative understandings of how family relationships should be patterned.

As an illustration, consider births outside marriage. In the early and mid-twentieth century, such births were relatively uncommon, with illegitimacy, as it was then termed, being highly stigmatized and understood as morally, socially and economically problematic. Often mothers in this situation were seen as psychologically disturbed, unstable or weak, with the consequence that their children were routinely thought to be at potential risk and thus warranting a degree of social work vigilance. Similarly, divorce was quite highly stigmatized and readily seen as pathological, revealing as much about the character of those involved as it did about their marital experiences. Again, the implication here was that those children involved may be at significant disadvantage and warrant social work intervention (Gibson, 1994; Kiernan et al., 1998).

At the beginning of the twenty-first century, our ideas about single motherhood and lone-parent families have clearly altered. Being part of such a family is no longer of itself seen as necessarily symptomatic of other problems. Some of these families may face problems, especially ones associated with poverty and racism, for which social work intervention in the form of family support provisions under the Children Act 1989 may be appropriate. But equally, many of these families do not need such support. The fact that they live in family and household contexts which do not conform to standardized nuclear family patterns is no longer understood socially or professionally as of itself problematic.

Children and Family Disruption

So what are the changes in family and household formation and dissolution that are most relevant to social work practice? And what types of social work intervention might be beneficial and resource effective? Issues of partnership formation, whether marriage or cohabitation, are not generally seen as within the normal remit of professional social work practice. That is, whom adults choose to cohabit with or marry is usually understood as a private matter not requiring external overview. Similarly, aside from cases of domestic violence, matters of relationship termination are usually seen as outside the purview of social work when only adults are involved, although counselling or mediation services may be considered beneficial in resolving continuing conflicts. While some recent government initiatives in the UK have explicitly sought to provide relationship support for couples (see http://www.surestart.gov.uk/surestartservices/support/families/), statutorily, and in practice, it is when there are dependent children present that social work is most clearly recognized as potentially having a part to play.

Even here the tendency is to see social work involvement as more relevant at times of family/household disruption than at times of family/household formation. For example, while social work expertise is seen as necessary for fostering or adoption placements, it is not seen as relevant when lone parents re-partner and form new stepfamily households, unless there are specific concerns for the child's welfare as a result of the new relationship. (Nor for that matter are mediation or counselling services generally seen as pertinent for issues of re-partnering.) It is really only when children are involved in family disruption that professional involvement is considered to be at all warrantable. In part, this is because of the role that courts play in divorce proceedings, especially where agreement has not been reached over child care arrangements. Interestingly, official intervention in child care arrangements is far less common when (unmarried) cohabitations end (Silva and Smart, 1999).

However, as divorce has become more prevalent – and currently some 140,000 children under 16 experience parental divorce each year in England and Wales – the role of social work professionals in ensuring that children's best interests are protected is generally limited. Resources do not permit a social work service to be provided to all, even if it were wished or considered beneficial. If during the course of proceedings it appears to the court that a care or a supervision order might be appropriate it will direct the local authority under section 37 of the Children Act 1989 to make an investigation into the child's circumstances. How a child's best interests are determined and what response is most appropriate in particular cases remain difficult issues though. Our knowledge of the impact that parental separation and divorce have on children is imperfect, inevitably so given the range of variables involved in the complex psychological, social, economic and legal processes of separation and divorce.

Some children cope well in coming to terms with their parents' divorce (Hill, 2001). However, parental separation is typically experienced as traumatic, with children and young people often finding the familial and emotional disruption caused difficult to comprehend or accept. How they respond to the experience has been researched extensively and been shown to be influenced by many factors, some obvious, some more subtle. There is a significant body of literature outlining the negative effects family disruption can have for children and young people. (See Hill and Tisdall, 1997, and Rodgers and Pryor, 1998, for good discussions of these issues.) Social work practitioners do need to be acutely aware of the impact on and needs of children in the process and aftermath of parental separation and divorce. We know that in the short-run when parents separate or divorce, children and young people experience a strong sense of loss. They also share their parents' concerns about where they are going to be living, if there will be sufficient money coming into the household and what the future holds. There are also increased risks of adverse health, educational and behavioural outcomes in comparison to children and young people from similar backgrounds whose parents do not separate (Hill and Tisdall, 1997; Kroll, 1994; Hill, 2001).

The extent to which parents are in conflict with each other has an impact on a child's ability to come to terms with what has happened. The development of conciliation and mediation services aims to enable parents to resolve their disputes about issues of contact and residence. Family Court Welfare Services are provided under the auspices of the Children and Family Court Advisory and Support Service (CAFCASS). In private law proceedings – principally contested applications for residence and contact under section 8 of the Children Act 1989 – a children and family reporter may report to the court on matters pertaining to the child's needs and welfare. Though this person is not specifically the child's representative, they do influence court decisions. However, there is growing awareness of the need for some children to have access to separate representation in order for their views and opinions to be heard. It has been possible for a child to be made a party to the proceedings and a *guardian ad litem* appointed, under Family Proceedings Rule 9.5, but this has only been invoked in exceptional cases. In an important case, *Re A (Contact: Separate Representation)* [2001] 1 FLR 715, the court allowed the National Youth Advocacy Service to act as a guardian and it was noted that the influence of the Human Rights Act 1998 might mean that there are more cases in the future where a guardian might need to be appointed to ensure the child's view is heard by the court. Subsequently, the Adoption and Children Act 2002 has amended the Children Act 1989 so that section 8 applications are added to the list of proceedings where a children's guardian is appointed, particularly where there is an apparent conflict between the child's wishes and those of the parents.

The changes that children experience with separation are often not just changes in parental involvement or household composition. As well as developing a different relationship with the non-residential parent (usually the father), children's material circumstances are also liable to change. Female-headed lone-parent families frequently experience poverty; certainly there is likely to be less money in households following separation than there was previously (see Bradshaw, 2002). In addition, for some children, marital separation and divorce may result in moving home, neighbourhood and school, with implications for their friendships and other support networks. So too, partly depending on the character of their relationship with their non-residential parent, their relationships with that parent's family, especially the children's grandparents, may also alter. Moreover, the separation may be the first of a number of linked familial changes the child experiences, particularly if one or both parents re-partner – changes which some argue can have a greater cumulative consequence than the divorce alone (Rodgers and Pryor, 1998; Cheesbrough, 2003). Thus, the various changes following separation and divorce may have a continuing impact on children's lifestyles, over and above any immediate issues of parental disruption, conflict and loss.

Increasingly in Britain and elsewhere in the Western world, policy initiatives are now recognizing that it is generally in children's best interests to maintain positive relationships with both their parents, with divorce signifying the end of a partnership but not the end of parenting. While few children spend equal time living with both parents, the older perspective that children's interests are served best by a 'clean-break' with the non-residential parent is now discredited. Yet while sustaining positive parental relationships is in children's interests, it is not always easy for the parents to facilitate this in the aftermath of separation and divorce. The need for parents to cooperate with each other over contact and residence arrangements can be problematic when other aspects of their relationship are conflictual and adversarial. But it is clear that this is what children want; many children have a real concern that following separation and divorce they may lose contact with their non-residential parent. Indeed evidence suggests that a significant proportion of children do lose effective contact with their (non-residential) fathers following divorce, though less so with (non-residential) mothers (Bradshaw et al., 1999). Contact issues can readily become the focus for parental frustrations with each other. Many may wish to 'start afresh' and have no further contact with their ex-spouse, but find for the children's sake there is a need to continue their involvement (Simpson, 1998; Smart and Neale, 1999).

Giving Children a Voice

One factor that has become prominent in the research literature concerns the information children are given about the reasons for the separation and the consequences it will have for their lives. Often children are left in a void, not being told enough to allow them to understand what is happening. The adults involved are themselves struggling to cope, unsure of the future and seeking to 'shield' their children from the continuing disputes and uncertainties of the situation. Children are consequently often left in a state of 'unknowing', not able to make sense of their experiences and having little idea about what the future might hold. Increasingly, however, it is being recognized in both academic and policy contexts that not only do children need to be given better information but they also need to have their voice 'heard'.

Within academic research, new conceptions of children have emerged (James and Prout, 1997) in which the view of children as 'incomplete' adults or 'human becomings' has been rightly challenged (Lee, 2001; Boylan and Ing, 2005). Instead children are recognized as active citizens who shape and inform the world around them, including the private domain of the family. This has led to an increased awareness by parents and professionals working with children and young people of the importance of seeking children's views and involving children in the process of decision making. Similarly, developments in legal and policy frameworks have emphasized the importance of consulting with and listening to what children and young people have to say. Notably, Article 12 (1) of the United Nations Convention on the Rights of the Child 1989, and Article 8 of the European Convention on Human Rights and Fundamental Freedoms (incorporated into UK law by the Human Rights Act 1998), support children's rights as participants in decision making. The Children Act 1989 and the Adoption and Children Act 2002 also reflect these concerns.

In line with this, there is now increased awareness of the importance of listening and responding to children's and young people's accounts of parental separation and divorce. Historically, children's perspectives on these issues have either been ignored, or adult proxies used to identify the issues *they* feel are important *for* children, rather than listening directly to the accounts of children themselves. Yet children need a chance to understand post-separation arrangements and to have some input into decision-making processes, particularly though not only over issues to do with contact arrangements. Given the impact the separation has on their lives, children also need an appropriate understanding of why the separation occurred, though often they are presented with conflicting or incomplete accounts by parents who are themselves still working out their own versions / 'moral tales' of their separation (Hopper, 1993; 2001). Recent research which has drawn on children's narratives of divorce is illuminating here. For example, Butler et al.'s (2003) research provides a detailed and sensitive account of children's experiences of their parents' divorce, portraying children's experiences of 'being told' about their parents' separation, of the unhappiness children encountered, the questions they wanted to ask, and who children turned to for information and support. Hill (2001) notes that involving children and young people in mediation may go some way towards reducing their anxiety about their situation. Butler et al. (2003) argue forcefully for an inclusive approach that embraces children's participation, not as 'bystanders' but rather as key players who are trying to make sense of and come to terms with changes in their family lives.

Conclusion

A significant minority of children and young people in the UK and other Western countries now experience parental separation and divorce. However, the majority of these children will have no need for contact with social work services or professionals as a result of these experiences. Nonetheless, many social workers will have some level of professional involvement with children and families who are experiencing difficulties as a direct result of divorce or separation. As part of the day-to-day business of social work, in particular assessing need and providing appropriate family support, social workers will need to respond to many children, young people and parents who have their own stories to tell about the ways this experience has shaped and informed their lives. Importantly, these stories will not be uniform; each will have their own dynamic and their own history. It is therefore imperative that social work practitioners understand the ways in which divorce and separation impact on families in general and are able to listen to, hear and respond to the needs of children and young people.

Five Key Points

- The impact of parental separation and divorce for children and young people varies widely, depending in part on their post-separation experiences.
- Children and young people typically want to maintain a relationship with both their parents after parental separation and divorce.
- Children and young people need to be given as accurate information as possible about the reasons for their parents' separation and about the consequences it will have on their lives.
- Children's and young people's voices need to be heard in divorce matters, as in other areas.
- The main pieces of legislation relevant to social work input with children following divorce are the Children Act 1989, the Family Law Act 1996, the Human Rights Act 1998 and the Adoption and Children Act 2002.

Three Questions

? Under what circumstances should social work agencies be concerned with separation and divorce?

? What factors contribute to parental disagreement over post-separation arrangements for children?

? How as practitioners can you develop an approach that promotes children's participation and provides a 'space' for their accounts?

Further reading

1 Smart, C., Neale, B. and Wade, A. (2001) *The Changing Experience of Childhood: Families and Divorce*. Cambridge: Polity Press.
2 Butler, I., Scanlan, L., Robinson, M., Douglas, G. and Murch, M. (2003) *Divorcing Children: Children's Experience of their Parents' Divorce*. London: Jessica Kingsley.
3 Brammer, A. (2006) *Social Work Law*, 2nd edn. Harlow: Longman.

CHAPTER 1.2

Child Abuse

Lorraine Waterhouse

Child abuse and neglect cause personal misery for children and parents, raise public concern and require professional attention. In the UK, there is a nationally coordinated and procedurally administered system of managing child abuse cases. It is based on recommendations following an official inquiry into the death of Maria Colwell who died while in the care of social services. The publication of the Maria Colwell report in 1974 (Department of Health and Social Security, 1982) shaped the UK child protection system for the next 30 years. The system included local area review committees to coordinate policy and interdisciplinary cooperation. All local areas implemented child protection registers to identify children at risk of harm, multidisciplinary case conferences (normally led by social work/services) to identify children in need of registration, and local procedural guidelines for different professionals concerned with children's welfare.

The early years of the twenty-first century have seen further significant changes for dealing with child protection. In 2003 the Green Paper *Every Child Matters* was published (Department for Education and Skills, 2003), bringing together various strands of governmental work. Key outcomes are set for all children, and measures are outlined to protect children most at risk of falling short of being healthy, staying safe, achieving economic well-being and contributing to society. Barriers to implementing effective child protection procedures were identified in the Green Paper, including the need to revise existing legislation (Children Act 1989 Regulations and Guidance). The Children Bill was published in March 2004 and received Royal Assent to become the Children Act 2004. The follow-up publication *Every Child Matters: Next Steps* (Department for Education and Skills, 2004) came out at the same time. *Next Steps* outlines the government's plans for taking forward its proposals for the way in which children's services are planned, commissioned and delivered. Policies that focus on identification, early intervention and prevention in children's lives are central to these plans, the future of children's services and the child protection system.

Every Child Matters: Next Steps applies to England while legislative changes in the Children Act 2004 also apply to Wales. Under the Children Act 2004 each children's services authority must establish a Local Safeguarding Children Board to replace Area Child Protection Committees. The Boards must include partner agencies, including district councils, the police authority, and strategic Health Authority and Primary Care Trusts (in England) and other such relevant bodies. The Act introduces shared statutory duties, sharing of information on individual children across agencies and protecting children in private foster arrangements. The recommendations of the Victoria Climbié Inquiry (Laming, 2003), calling for better governance and accountability in local children's services, have been influential in shaping legislative reform in England and Wales.

In Scotland a review – *It's Everyone's Job to Make Sure I'm Alright: Report of the Child Protection Audit and Review* (Scottish Executive, 2002b) reported on an audit of 188 child protection cases. The views of children and parents with experience of the child protection system and of the public more generally were also sought. The review did not recommend legislative changes to the Children (Scotland) Act 1995. Instead it outlined multiple recommendations to improve the performance of agencies which have a role in protecting children. These included widening the remit of local child protection committees and developing linked computer information systems. The emphasis was on agency partnership and improvements in all children's services for the most vulnerable.

There remains no mandatory system of reporting or recording confirmed cases of child abuse in the UK. Local authority social workers and police have a duty to report that a child may be in need of care and protection. Local guidance may encourage other professionals (teachers, health visitors and other medical staff) to report as part of a professional duty, but they are not required to do so by law. The Council of Europe recommends mandatory reporting. The UK along with some other European countries remains cautious. Mandatory reporting is criticized for being inefficient and ineffective; it is argued that it would be better to spend the money on family support and other child care services.

Estimating Child Abuse

Estimates of the incidence and prevalence of child abuse depend on two main sources of information: child protection registration statistics and research studies. Child protection registers are 'not a record of children who have been abused but of children for whom there are continuing child protection concerns and for whom there is an inter-agency protection plan' (Home Office et al., 1991, 6.36). Registration statistics measure the incidence of child abuse as reported and recorded by official agencies. Research studies usually rely on specific samples of adults and sometimes children and young people. They try to establish whether an individual experienced abuse in childhood. General population studies suggest a higher prevalence of abuse than officially gathered statistics. It is not clear why this is. Using self-report to obtain information may contribute to higher reported levels than official statistics record. It is almost certain, however, that abuse remains undetected by professionals for some children.

The National Society for the Prevention of Cruelty to Children (NSPCC) in their 1986 survey of up to 2,000 children, 16 years or younger, placed on child protection registers in 11 local authorities in England and Wales (representing about 9 per cent of the child population) found some 15,000 children were abused (Creighton, 1994); 9,590 children were registered as physically injured by their parents, guardians or carers; a further 6,330 children as sexually abused. These estimates of incidence are based on the largest continuous survey of child abuse in the UK.

The prevalence of child abuse is estimated as between two to four children in every thousand, with one child per thousand under 4 years of age likely to be severely injured (Creighton, 1994; House of Commons, 1977; Gil, 1970). The rate of reported physical injury to infants under one year appears to be steadily increasing from 1.25 per thousand in 1979 to 1.82 in 1986 (Creighton, 1994, p. 38). The percentage of infants who are seriously or fatally injured, however, is declining. The reported re-injury rate has also fallen. There is almost no reliable data on the prevalence of emotional abuse.

The year ending 31 March 2005 saw 25,900 children in England and Wales on child protection registers (Department for Education and Skills, 2006a). This was 1 per cent fewer than the year before and nearly a quarter fewer than 10 years ago. A significant minority of referrals (121,800 referrals out of a total of 552,000 or 22 per cent) were repeat referrals made within the last year. Twelve per cent (3,000) of children on the registers were also looked after children by local authorities. Of these looked after and registered children the vast majority were in foster placements (79 per cent); 13 per cent were placed with their own parents. These statistics are important for two reasons. First, they suggest that some children or groups of children may be a source of continuing concern even when registered and/or a source of concern to multiple agencies. Second and somewhat surprisingly, most of the children on child protection registers are not looked after children. This raises an important question about the classification of children in child protection and child welfare systems. It also highlights that some children are common to both.

In England and Wales registrations for neglect are continuing to increase compared with registrations of physical abuse. The latter remains, however, the most common reason for registration in Scotland. Fisher et al. (1995) found in their study of case conference decision making that, despite the greater prevalence of child neglect, the child protection system is more sensitive to child physical and sexual abuse.

Cases involving neglect generally attracted less professional attention than might have been expected for the harm and unhappiness caused to the children. The parents were considered to be in need of significant help and support for the safer upbringing of their children.

Defining Child Abuse

There is no absolute definition of child abuse. Official definitions of child abuse identify kinds of abusive incidents, taking into account whether there is an intention to cause harm or failure to prevent harm by any person having care or custody of the child. Harm includes:

- physical injury;
- physical neglect and failure to thrive, for example, exposure to dangerous circumstances or starvation;
- emotional abuse where the health and development of the child is threatened; and
- sexual abuse where children under 17 years (England and Wales) have been involved in sexual activities they do not truly comprehend or to which they do not give informed consent.

The number of categories of abuse continues to increase to reflect better knowledge of child development and better understanding of situations and experiences that may cause children harm. The World Health Organization suggests that child abuse should include all forms of physical and/or emotional ill treatment including negligent treatment or commercial or other kinds of exploitation. They stress the harm caused by the abuse as affecting the child's health, survival, development and maturation or dignity. They identify the abusing agent as an individual(s) where there is a relationship with the child that involves responsibility, trust or power. This definition is helpful because it identifies core elements in child abuse and it can and should be adapted to the cultures of different individual countries.

Deciding a threshold where child abuse begins and normal control and discipline end is complex. Research (Department of Health, 1995a) suggests most cases coming to the notice of social work and other agencies involved in child protection fall between the extremes and involve children who are in need of support and protection but do not necessarily involve serious injury to the child. High public and professional tolerance of what constitutes cause for concern will reduce the numbers of children requiring investigation, registration and follow-up; low tolerance the converse. Whatever benchmark is employed, universal standards for bringing up children and accepted limits of 'good enough' parenting are likely over time to be affected.

Identifying Child Abuse

Children registered for child abuse are generally young. In Scotland, for example, 80 per cent of children on child protection registers in 2002 were under 11 years (2003–4, www. scotland.gov.uk/stats/bulletins/00369-00.asp). The average age for registration is 7 years with differences found depending on the nature of the abuse. Children who are sexually abused tend to be slightly older (average age of 10 years 2 months) and girls are more likely to be sexually abused than boys (Taylor, 1992, p. 40). Failure to thrive is most commonly found in infants. Cases of reported physical abuse mainly affect primary school age children (average age 6 years) and more often boys. Child protection statistics do not reliably record information about the ethnic background of the child.

Children who experience abuse may be subject to more than one type of abuse or neglect. The child protection audit and review (Scottish Executive, 2002b) concluded that the reason for registration, that is, the nature of abuse officially recorded, was not a good indication of the child's circumstances. Waterhouse et al. (1994), in a sample of 500 convicted child sexual abusers, found a significant proportion of the criminal offences against the children involved a form of sexual intercourse which was sometimes accompanied by violence or threats of violence. This also suggests an overlap between different categories of abuse, leaving children acutely vulnerable on multiple grounds.

The audit and review (Scottish Executive, 2002b) also drew attention to some very serious cases of neglect. The report stresses the importance of fully assessing the circumstances of children to take account of the possibility that abuse and neglect may both be present.

Explaining Child Abuse

There are numerous pathways to child abuse and neglect. Understanding causal links between family factors and risk of maltreatment remains a continuing challenge. The consequences and impact of abuse for children are increasingly linked to risks or factors that may influence a child's vulnerability or resilience in the face of adversity. Explanations of abuse have evolved from an initial concentration on single factors, for example, the presence of distinguishing psychological characteristics in parents of abused children to complex models of the interrelationship between multiple factors. Gelles (1987) and Browne (1988) stress the importance of an interaction between psychological, cultural and social factors and family relationships in family violence. Families already facing adversity (such as inadequate housing and unemployment where poor parent and child relationships routinely feature are considered more likely to resort to aggression in child upbringing.

Psychological studies (Sears et al., 1957) concerned with parenting style and child sociability suggest that highly punitive and highly permissive parents tend to have children who are aggressive. Parents who are aggressive to their children may, in turn, provoke aggression, contributing to a cycle of mutually antagonistic interaction. Parents who are highly permissive may fail to provide sufficient positive controls and support to children who may develop insufficient self-control. Pitcairn and Waterhouse (1993) found parents whose children were registered on child protection registers in Scotland were aware of facing difficulties in and of failing to discipline their children when they knew they should. Several studies (Roberts and Taylor, 1993; Pitcairn and Waterhouse, 1993) find that abused children score highly on standardized behavioural check-lists (Rutter, 1967; Richman et al., 1984) that have considerable predictive value in discriminating children with neurotic or antisocial behavioural disorders.

Parental substance misuse is considered a primary cause of the rise in reported child abuse and neglect in the United States (Massachusetts Citizens for Children, 2001). Recent statistics in Scotland suggest that between 40,000 and 60,000 children experience parental drug use (University of Glasgow, 2002) and between 80,000 and 100,000 experience parental alcohol misuse (Scottish Executive, 2002a). Hogan (1998) found evidence of an association between parental drug misuse and drug usage by their children. Increased awareness of domestic violence may also contribute to the rise in care and protection referrals in Scotland (Wallace and Henderson, 2004).

The Rowntree Inquiry into Income and Wealth (Hills, 1995) describes a cycle of 'poor parenting' in the poorest council estates in the country. This arises not only from poverty but also from high rates of family break-up; lack of understanding of the needs of children; social isolation; and universally high rates of unemployment among youth, many of whom were already parents. Five times the number of children were on 'at risk' registers from the poorest estates as in other parts of the same city (Hills, 1995, p. 35). A similar pattern in referrals to registers is noted by R. Clarke (1993) in Australia and Gough (1993) in Scotland. Gough questions whether registration is merely a means of identifying and monitoring children rather than positively assisting some of the most disadvantaged families.

Explanations of sexual abuse concentrate on the misuse of power by adults (mainly men) over children (more often girls), and have been highly influenced by feminist writing which examines the influence of gender on relations between men, women and children. Growing concern about sexual misconduct by women against children (especially boys) raises questions about the comprehensiveness of this explanation alone. Increased attention is turning towards young people sexually abusing children younger than themselves. Accounts of men convicted of sexual offences against children suggest that they first began abusing children younger than themselves when they were young.

It is not possible to identify the kinds of families most at risk of emotional abuse as a distinct problem because of its underlying presence in all types of abuse (Iwaniec et al., 2006). Multiple family factors are considered a better predictor of emotional abuse rather than any one single family or individual characteristic. In families where stresses exceed supports emotional child abuse is considered more likely (Belsky, 1993). This formulation – stresses exceeding supports – is helpful in thinking about children where their life balance is reaching tipping point and their environment one that contributes to children being abused.

Responding to Child Abuse

UK public inquiries into state failures to protect children from child abuse have been highly influential in determining child protection systems (Parton, 1985). Universal policies for child protection were formulated from these single 'hard' cases. Findings emphasized the investigation and surveillance of children who may be abused or neglected, especially by social workers who have duties in law to protect children from harm. Inquiries continue to influence UK policy as exemplified by the Victoria Climbié Inquiry (Laming, 2003).

Recent policy, however, differs in at least two important respects from that which has gone before. First, the protection of children who are especially vulnerable is seen in the context of key outcomes for all children growing up in the UK. *Every Child Matters* (Department for Education and Skills, 2003) focuses on measures to protect the most vulnerable children, within a commitment to provide universal services for children and to tackle child poverty. Second, the protection of children from harm is made a statutory responsibility across relevant agencies to combat compartmentalization of accountability for the child's welfare and safety. A core message underpinning child protection policy is the importance of reaching an agreed plan for the child and safeguarding their interests before the child is hurt or costly compulsory intervention is required.

Brown (1986) found that parents involved in child protection investigations feared their children would be removed from them and taken into public care. This is a serious misperception. Most children remain at home (Gibbons et al., 1995). Studies of child care decision making (Vernon and Fruin, 1986) suggest that social workers are reluctant to admit children to public care and instead adopt a 'wait and see' policy, hoping that admission to care can be avoided. Cleaver and Freeman (1995) point to the futility of parents covering up family troubles for fear of losing their children.

The importance of open communication is further reflected in Farmer's study (1995). Parents sometimes questioned the legitimacy of child protection intervention. Parents found investigatory procedures stigmatizing and blaming of them as failing parents. Brown (1986) discovered parents were unaware that a major part of social work intervention could be preventative and enabling rather than reactive and policing.

Magura and Moses (1984) found recipients of child protection services cited material deprivation as the major deleterious influence on their children's daily care. Poverty contributed to parental anxiety, stress and depression. More recent studies confirm that the majority of children on child abuse registers are children in need of child welfare services, only some of whom will prove in need of continuing protection for their personal safety. Fisher et al. (1995) note the lack of attention paid to the emotional environment in which the child grows up. This outlook may seriously inhibit accurate professional understanding of parent–child relations. Social workers and other professionals may fail to support parents by focusing narrowly on alleged abuse rather than the daily concerns of parents and the family environment in which the child is growing up.

Social workers can help children and their families by recognizing the potential impact of chronic adversity on parental morale and motivation; and by responding constructively to the concerns of parents and children. This is not to suggest that neglect or physical, sexual or psychological harm to children should be ignored: on the contrary, taking children and parents seriously is likely to improve assessment and to put resources where they count. Children on child protection registers have a strong claim and need for comprehensive and interdisciplinary children's services.

The Children Act 2004 in England and Wales and the Children (Scotland) Act 1995 encourage partnership between families and professionals. Procedural guidance which stresses detection and monitoring unless balanced by support and follow-up services may have the opposite effect. Parental confidence may be further affected by the growing capacity to store and access information electronically. One reason for this is to track children and to flag children where there are child welfare concerns and a child is known to agencies such as education or health. Public confidence in child protection systems will depend on striking the right balance between measures to safeguard children's safety effectively and respect for individuals' privacy.

Countries vary greatly in their social, legal, political and cultural values. These traditions influence child protection systems. Child protection systems may also influence these traditions over time. International comparisons, especially with respect to continental Europe, point to a greater emphasis on voluntary and confidential services for children and their families with compulsory intervention in family life a last resort. Mediation and problem solving are to the fore. All child protection systems have to find ways of getting the balance right between helping and controlling child and family life. The most important message in any child protection system is the need for all professionals to look for creative ways of reaching an agreed plan before the child is harmed and before compulsory intervention becomes necessary.

Five Key Points

- The management of child abuse depends on a nationally coordinated and procedurally administered system of child protection.
- Child protection policy is focused on better prevention and effective early intervention.
- Child protection systems vary widely between countries and are influenced by their different social, cultural and legal values. All systems recognize the importance of agencies and professionals working together to achieve key outcomes for child health, safety and development.
- Social workers need to recognize the potential impact of chronic adversity on parental morale and to respond constructively to the concerns of parents and children where abuse is alleged or proven.
- Social workers need to look for ways of reaching an agreed plan for the child involving the child and her/his parents and all relevant agencies before the child is harmed or compulsory measures becomes necessary.

Three Questions

? In what way do definitions of 'good enough parenting' vary over time and place?
? What are the main explanations for child abuse?
? What problems face the social worker in the search for a good balance between the provision of support for families and the protection of children at risk of abuse?

Further reading

1 Corby, B. (2000) *Child Abuse – Towards a Knowledge Base*. Buckingham: Open University Press.
2 Beckett, C. (2003) *Child Protection: An Introduction*. London: Sage.
3 Rustin, M. (2005) Conceptual analysis of critical moments in Victoria Climbié's life. *Child and Family Social Work,* 10, 11–19.

CHAPTER 1.3

Domestic Violence

Cathy Humphreys

Many social workers work with people affected by domestic violence, but only community sector women's organizations such as Women's Aid respond to women and children survivors as their core business. Intervention to support domestic violence survivors or to challenge domestic violence offenders may only be picked up when they fit into an agency's priorities under a different heading: mental health, substance abuse, child protection, criminal justice.

The 1990s saw renewed attention to domestic violence with an added focus on its impact on children. This move challenged the barrier between the practice focus on child abuse and services perceived to be for women – though Women's Aid refuges have always housed more children than women and employed children's workers from their inception. However, the process of gaining awareness of the needs of children affected by domestic violence has tended to marginalize recognition that domestic violence is a legitimate concern for social workers in adult services as well.

The Extent of the Problem

Problems arise in estimating the scale of domestic violence as it usually happens behind closed doors. Definitions and terminology are always contested, and the term 'domestic violence' has both strengths and limitations:

> *Domestic violence* typically involves a pattern of physical, sexual and emotional abuse and intimidation. . . . It can be understood as the misuse of power and exercise of control by one partner over the other in an intimate relationship, usually by a man over a woman, occasionally by a woman over a man (though without the same pattern of societal collusion) and also occurring amongst same sex couples. It has profound consequences in the lives of individuals, families and communities. (Mullender and Humphreys, 1998, p. 6)

Surveys show large numbers of women affected by domestic violence, usually citing one in four women affected over a lifetime. The British Crime Survey is the most comprehensive UK survey and showed that while many men report some form of abuse, women were overwhelmingly the most chronically abused and the most seriously injured. There were an estimated 635,000 incidents in 2001/2 in England and Wales, of which 81 per cent were attacks on women (Walby and Allen, 2004).

At its most serious, women die: almost two women a week in England and Wales die at the hands of a man with whom they are in or have been in an intimate relationship – accounting for almost half the women who are killed in the country. One-third have separated. It is far rarer for women to kill their male partners or ex-partners and accounts for only 9 per cent of male homicides.

The Effects on Children

The link between child abuse and domestic violence is now well established (Edleson, 2001). Research shows that children living in households where there is domestic violence are more likely to be abused themselves. This suggests that where domestic violence is occurring, questions need to be asked about whether children are also the subject of physical or sexual abuse, and conversely, where there is child abuse, the issue of violence particularly towards the child's mother needs to be explored.

However, the prevalence of direct abuse is difficult to establish. Studies vary widely from 30–66 per cent of child abuse cases (Edleson, 2001). Much depends on whether sensitive questions are asked about domestic violence. For instance, an early study by Gibbons et al. (1995) in an overview of 1,888 child protection referrals across several local authorities, found that in 27 per cent of cases, domestic violence was an issue in the family. However, later studies where staff had been trained to routinely ask questions about domestic violence indicate at least double this figure (Hester, 2006), with two-thirds of children who are the subject of case conferences affected by living with domestic violence (Sloan, 2003).

Similar issues arise in the exploration of child sexual abuse. Farmer and Pollock (1998), in an analysis of 250 children in substitute care who had been sexually abused or sexually abusing, found that 39 per cent came from families where there was domestic violence – primarily violence towards the child's mother. This rate rose to 55 per cent in a more detailed follow-up of 40 children.

Within the framework of domestic violence and post-separation violence, at its most serious, children also die. Child death enquiries, including those associated with deaths during child contact frequently show men who were violent to both the child and the child's mother. Recognition is growing that many children are seriously emotionally affected by living with violence and often witnessing the abuse of one of their parents, usually the mother. The tactics of abuse often represent an attack on the mother–child relationship by the perpetrator, undermining not only his fathering role, but also the mother's parenting abilities. Studies consistently show that children living with chronic domestic violence have two to three times the rates of cognitive and behavioural problems as comparison groups of children from non-violent families. Children who have themselves been physically abused while witnessing acts of violence consistently show the highest levels of behavioural and emotional disturbance. Problems for children can compound over time as developmental stages are disrupted (Rossman, 2001).

Some children, though, show high levels of resilience in the face of their difficult circumstances, and research points to the fact that children have the ability to recover from the effects of violence once they are in a safer, more stable environment. Children who have been most recently exposed to violence tend to show the most marked problems, while those who have moved on and are no longer living with violence may be much less disturbed, both emotionally and behaviourally. These findings have implications for child contact arrangements if violence and abuse towards the child's mother is ongoing.

In summary, then, children's responses to living with domestic violence cannot be predicted. Individualized risk and safety assessments of children and their circumstances need to be undertaken to ascertain the needs and the services which are required.

The Impact on Women

Social workers in mental health teams, disability teams, teams for older people and social workers in the substance use and health sector will all be in touch with women who are affected by domestic violence.

Studies of women and mental health illustrate the seriousness of the impact. Amongst abused women, depression, post-traumatic stress, suicide and self-harm are so prevalent that they can be referred to as 'symptoms of abuse' (Humphreys and Thiara, 2003). Stark and Flitcraft (1996) found that 65 per cent of women had been assaulted within six months of their first suicide attempt. Suicide rates amongst black and minority ethnic women in both the UK and the US are disproportionately high.

The level of problematic substance use (while not a cause of violence) is an issue for a significant number of perpetrators of violence, as it is for some of their victims, though the patterns of use are different. Men are more likely to drink prior to and during an incident and women following an incident often as a means of coping with the emotional and physical pain of abuse (Galvani, 2001).

Other work has highlighted the issues faced by disabled women. A Home Office survey (Mirrlees-Black, 1999) showed 12 per cent of disabled women aged 16–29 had experienced domestic violence in 1995 compared with 8.2 per cent of non-disabled women of the same age. The woman's difficulties in accessing appropriate help, combined with the losses she would incur if she were to separate and the ease with which she could be isolated, increase the power and control of the abuser and compound the impact of abuse.

Women with learning difficulties have been found to be highly vulnerable to domestic violence, and research on the abuse of older people suggests that a proportion of this abuse is the continuation of domestic violence into old age.

Social Work Responses to Domestic Violence

Social workers, particularly those employed in statutory child care, have often been taken to task for:

- ignoring violence towards the child's mother unless the child was directly harmed;
- minimizing the effects on children of witnessing domestic violence;
- focusing on the mother's 'failure to protect' or other problems rather than on the man's violence;
- being slow to recognize the link between domestic violence and child abuse; and
- paying little attention to the specific issues which black women may have in accessing help.

It is easy to blame front-line social work staff for insensitive responses, but accountability for these failings lies with organizations that fail to provide supervision, training and resources for this difficult area of work.

Social workers, like other professionals, have a strong tendency to minimize and avoid violence, and a number of practices have developed amongst social workers which consistently hide domestic violence: see the box below.

Hiding the reality of domestic violence

A study of case files in one local authority's children and families' teams (Humphreys, 2000) showed the ways that domestic violence is concealed:

- Professionals fail to report to child protection conferences known incidents of domestic violence.
- They inappropriately name violence, usually by the man towards the woman, as *marital conflict* or *arguments* so that the source of the danger is not identified and its impact obscured.
- They shift the focus of assessment to other issues such as mental health or alcohol abuse which, while also present, are not the cause of the danger and sometimes result from it.
- They name the mother's behaviour as a problem either equally or more serious than the man's violence, even when there is significant evidence in the file to the contrary.
- They identify the man as the 'cornerstone of the family' rather than challenging his violence towards his partner.
- They only name the most extreme forms of physical violence (the 'atrocity story') while ignoring other aspects of a pattern of emotional, physical and sexual abuse.

Significant organizational problems need to be overcome to develop more effective and safer intervention from social workers where domestic violence is present. Given that there are often both child and adult victim/survivors, policies involving adult and children's services should ensure that there is not an inappropriate focus on one at the expense of the other.

The impediments to women's help-seeking need to be recognized, particularly in relation to social work agencies. Women are often threatened by abusers with the loss of their children or construed as 'mad', bad or unbelievable. Proactive work needs to be undertaken by social workers to overcome discriminatory practices and to be alert to the danger of colluding with the abuser's definition of family problems which invariably invite minimization of the contribution of his violence and maximize the focus on the woman and her shortcomings.

As in many other areas of social work, interagency collaboration is essential. *Working Together* (Department for Education and Skills, 2006c) provides detailed guidance for multi-agency working in the area of domestic violence, while the Children Act 2004 provides the overarching legislative framework through which services to children and families are organized and delivered. A range of multi-agency plans exists in which domestic violence intervention should be featured, and these multi-agency collaborations can provide opportunities for social workers to provide a more responsive and safer service for women and children affected by violence. Attention to confidentiality and safety issues are crucial for good practice: inadvertent leaking of addresses and contact numbers to the abuser may be life-threatening, and concern about it could constrain women from trusting extensive inter-agency referral. Social work training that emphasizes working in partnership with parents may need to be re-thought in circumstances of domestic violence so that the safety of the victim (usually women) and children is not compromised.

It is not only the safety of women and children that needs to be considered. Workers are also at risk, particularly if they shift to a more challenging practice which does not collude with or ignore the perpetrator's violence. Organizations will need both policies and training to implement safety planning into practices of social workers in more self-conscious ways if work in this area is to be progressed.

Future Directions

While there are significant barriers that constrain effective intervention, the increased awareness of domestic violence has led to greater attention to the development of legislation, policy and practice.

A more effective legislative framework is in place with the passing of the Domestic Violence, Crime and Victims Act 2004 and the Protection from Harassment Act 1997. A further development in the UK has been the amendment to the definition of harm in the Adoption and Children Act 2002, which now includes 'impairment suffered from seeing or hearing the ill treatment of another'.

Police have been issued with a clearer mandate for action, including closer supervision of their decisions when called out to incidents of domestic violence. The area of child contact where there has been domestic violence remains problematic. Contradictions can develop between social workers on the one hand urging women to leave to protect their children, and family courts on the other ordering contact which is often unsupervised. Statutory social workers need to develop their practice to ensure that assessments and child protection conference recommendations relevant to private law contact proceedings are communicated clearly to family court practitioners and that women have copies of any relevant assessments, child protection conference minutes and reports.

The re-focusing of children and family services to strengthen family support should allow children and their families affected by domestic violence to have a claim on services (section 17, Children Act 1989). Unfortunately, this right is often tempered by limited resources. Nevertheless, many local authorities now provide funds for children's groups, women's groups, and occasionally for children's workers in refuges, children without recourse to public funds, and short-term payments such as taxi fares to schools and refuges.

Good practice will ensure that social workers are conscious of careful recording and enhanced evidence-gathering in cases of domestic violence. This will mean:

- screening for domestic violence at all stages of referral, investigation and assessment;
- recording in detail any information on domestic violence; and
- case advocacy to ensure that other agencies also document evidence.

A framework of good practice indicators for working with families affected by domestic violence has been developed through work with Women's Aid, social services and four children's charities (Humphreys et al., 2000).

While domestic violence features in the lives of a great many service users seen by social workers, policies and practice have been slow to develop. Numerous opportunities now exist for more sensitive, safer intervention which places this issue firmly on the mainstream social work agenda.

Five Key Points

- Domestic violence is a problem relevant to all areas of social work practice, though frequently the issue is invisible or marginalized as other service priorities take precedence.
- Children are affected by witnessing violence and are more likely to be physically or sexually abused than children living in families where there is no domestic violence.
- The two key principles for effective work in this area include: developing interventions which direct responsibility towards the perpetrator (usually the man) and his abuse; working with domestic violence survivors (usually women and children) attending to their separate needs as well as recognizing that the child's safety will usually be linked to their mother's safety.
- Screening for domestic violence by asking sensitive questions will significantly increase awareness of the numbers of individuals using the agency who are affected by domestic violence.
- Domestic violence intervention requires effective collaboration in and between adult and children's services, as well as a wide range of other agencies including police, housing departments, and the courts.

Three Questions

? What issues affect women's decisions to stay in or return to a situation of domestic violence?
? What issues could be covered in risk assessment and safety planning with (i) women and (ii) children affected by domestic violence?
? What local services should be available to create more effective domestic violence intervention?

Further reading

1 Mullender, A., Kelly, L., Hague, G., Malos, E. and Iman, U. (2002) *Children's Perspectives on Domestic Violence*. London: Routledge.
2 Calder, M. (2005) *Children Living with Domestic Violence: Towards a Framework for Assessment and Intervention*. Lyme Regis: Russell House.
3 Humphreys, C. and Stanley, N. (eds.) (2006) *Domestic Violence and Child Protection: Directions for Good Practice*. London: Jessica Kingsley.

CHAPTER 1.4

Ill-health

Eileen McLeod and Paul Bywaters

Significantly high levels of physical ill-health and inferior treatment or care when ill are endemic among service users. They have been recorded for looked after children and care leavers, mental health survivors, older people using community care services and people with learning disabilities. However, the association between service users' increased chances of illness and harsher treatment in ill-health and their adverse social circumstances, remains neglected as a focus for social work. It should constitute a key reason for practice because it represents a situation of social injustice lived out in individual pain and suffering.

Lifetime Damage

There is powerful evidence that social disadvantage is associated with increased chances of profound ill-health, reflected in the incidence of illness and reduced life expectancy. 'Those on the higher rungs of the socio-economic ladder are more likely to survive in good health; those on lower rungs are more likely to succumb to disease and premature death' (Graham, 2000, p. 2).

Relative poverty is deeply implicated in these processes. In the UK, the death rate for infants and children in social class V remains twice as high as for those in social class I (Office for National Statistics, 2001). Men in professional occupations can expect to live – on average – seven years longer than those in unskilled manual occupations (Office for National Statistics, 2004a).

Socio-economic differences in the risk of ill-health persist throughout the life course. Government figures on reported limiting longstanding illness show that men and women living in the most deprived areas in England spend twice as many years of their lives in ill-health than those living in the most affluent areas – 26 years compared to 12 years for women, and 22 years compared to 11 years for men (Office for National Statistics, 2005a).

Poverty interacts with other dimensions of structural inequalities such as racism and sexism. For example, Karlsen and Nazroo (2000) found that members of the Pakistani and Bangladeshi populations in the UK, four-fifths of whom live in relative poverty, were on average 44 per cent more likely to report only fair or poor health than the majority white population.

Similarly, the complex interaction of gender and poverty with physical well-being is reflected in damage to health through violence and suicide, as well as illness. Men in social class V are four times more likely to commit suicide than men in class I, with men three times more likely to commit suicide than women (Department of Health, 2002c). Almost a third of women will experience domestic violence at some point in their lives, which is not only associated with serious physical injury, but increased risk of self-harm and suicide (Humphreys and Thiara, 2003).

Service Users: At Risk

Service users are particularly vulnerable to such socially created inequalities in health chances, primarily because relative poverty is the most common problem confronting them. Individuals' efforts to obtain basic resources for warding off ill-health – adequate nourishment, shelter, warmth and social support – together with access to secondary resources such as screening, are circumscribed by relative poverty and discrimination. Yet poverty has remained largely undeveloped as a direct focus of social work action in the UK.

There is clear evidence that the low income which characterizes service users' lives will have health consequences. Care leavers identify safe, affordable accommodation as their major housing problem (Allard et al., 2004). Mothers parenting in poverty have commonly been found to go short of food themselves, to feed other family members (Seeley and Lobstein, 2004). Being unable to afford to heat their homes adequately remains a significant threat to older people, increasing both the risk of ill-health and current suffering (British Gas and Help the Aged, 2004).

Discriminatory attitudes and behaviour also undermine the supportive social relations which are essential to maintaining health. Institutionalized discrimination means that the experience of people who are lesbian, gay and bi-sexual remains a marginalized issue in social work discourse and practice, but there is disturbing evidence of the impact of homophobia on their physical well-being. A national survey of homophobic crime found that not only had two-thirds of respondents experienced homophobic incidents comprising intimidation, verbal abuse and physical assault, but that over 70 per cent were fearful of reporting such incidents (Wake et al., 1999).

Health screening programmes could be an important element in reducing service users' chances of ill-health, but social disadvantage is associated with generally lower rates of screening. This is reflected in the experience of people with learning disabilities. Even though it is known that they are more likely to have concurrent illnesses and lower life expectancy, they are screened significantly less for serious conditions such as breast cancer (Davies and Duff, 2001).

Ill-health: Unequal Treatment

Service users' unequal chances of ill-health and premature death are compounded by a further injustice: harsher social conditions in which to manage ill-health, and unequal access to good quality treatment and recovery. Socially constructed barriers may prevent people from getting to healthcare settings or accessing diagnosis and treatment. Internalized ageist assumptions about the inevitability of ill-health in old age can result in older people being disinclined to 'trouble the doctor' despite worrying symptoms. Members of minority ethnic groups are less likely (than the majority population) to get an appointment on the day they want and more likely to feel that the GP does not answer their questions (Office for National Statistics, 2004a).

The physical state of being ill, involving pain, malaise and debility, is also marked by social inequality, exacerbating the suffering involved. It is well recognized that effective assessment and management of pain in non-English speaking patients and patients from minority ethnic groups is undermined by failure to address linguistic requirements, and assumptions about cultural norms (Green, 2003).

As well as aggravating the rigours of being ill, social disadvantage can make recovery harder, creating heavier demands on personal resources. Expenses are likely to rise with the need for extra heating, a particular diet or as a result of being unable to shop for yourself. Extra domestic help may need to be organized and paid for or additional phone calls made. This is much more difficult to negotiate if you are unsupported, living on a limited income and perhaps have a pre-existing physical impairment. Unfortunately there is evidence that large numbers of older patients are still having to cope on their own with recovery after hospitalization, with inadequate material and social resources (Audit Commission, 2000).

Inequity when Dying

The pernicious health effects of social inequality persist even when people are dying; as a result they experience needless, intensified suffering. The serious and widespread consequences mean this should be the concern of social workers generally, not simply those practising in palliative care settings; and once more, the imprint of poverty is discernible in many ways. Population studies have found that where people are both terminally ill and poor, they are:

- often desperately worried about how they can provide for their dependants;
- more likely to be living in accommodation which is problematic for their care;
- less likely to be able to keep their home adequately heated or to be able to find the money for necessities;
- less likely to be referred for specialist home care which is associated with longer periods of survival;
- less likely to have what is most people's choice: the possibility of dying at home (McLeod and Bywaters, 2000).

Ageist discrimination also meshes with relative poverty in the course of terminal illness. The majority of older people will be dying in relative poverty, particularly older women in advanced old age, living alone. However, people aged over 85 are less likely to be admitted to hospice care, despite the adverse social conditions they are likely to be experiencing, together with a higher degree of physical impairment. Pain relief in nursing homes has been found to be inferior to that available not only in hospices, but also in hospitals, and with little specialist back-up palliative care available (McLeod and Bywaters, 2000).

Social Work: Making it Worse?

A key role for social work services in tackling inequalities in health has emerged in Government policy. This has primarily taken the form of the requirement that Social Services collaborate with other agencies such as Housing and Health Authorities and Primary Care Trusts to address deprivation on a locality basis. In addition, the Government has recognized the importance of social work's contribution in its own right (Bywaters and McLeod, 2001).

However, social work's record on health shows that current practice can contribute to the problems people face. For example, as we have discussed, relative poverty is a crucial factor in prejudicing service users' health, but directly addressing poverty remains marginalized in practice. Frequently, even assisting in maximizing benefit take-up is considered not to be core business. The failure to orient practice in a way which promotes primary prevention is compounded by the failure to ensure service users have access to needed medical services. Social Services have frequently failed to protect and promote the health of children in the care system (Broad, 2005).

Social work's inattention to the health dimensions of practice has been exacerbated by government under-funding of social services and the increasing policy emphasis on narrowly targeted, often means-tested, provision. For example, help with housework is now infrequently provided by local authorities as a preventative measure for older people suffering poor health. Informal carers continue to run an increased risk of long-term health problems, through inadequate levels of financial and direct homecare assistance (Carers UK, 2004).

Social Work: Making Things Better

There are powerful reasons for social work to recognize and address ill-health as a location of socially created inequality. Service users suffer from widespread, unjust suffering in the form – and course – of poor health, and social work itself is implicated in some of the processes involved. However, in incremental ways not confined to healthcare settings, social work can contribute to greater equity in the chances and experience of ill-health. Three examples reflect localized, possibly short-term initiatives but they redress some of the health-undermining tendencies in social work: they focus on addressing poverty, increasing domiciliary services and equalizing service users' access to healthcare.

For discussion

As a social worker in an outreach project working with homeless young people, you are in contact with Kerry who is living rough around the city centre. Kerry is 17, white European, and left care a year ago. Since then she has had a number of addresses including the lodgings she was first placed in, periods with a boyfriend who was living off her earnings as a prostitute and short-term stays with friends. She has also been quite a frequent attender at casualty as a result of asthma attacks and two occasions when she cut her arms. She weighs about 6 stone and smokes. Kerry attended special school and is described in her file as having 'mild learning difficulties'; she was rejected by her mother and father and taken into care when she became pregnant at 14. The baby was adopted. She is very reluctant to enter hostel accommodation.

In relation to this situation consider:

1 How are unequal social conditions implicated in Kerry's current experience and future risk of ill-health?
2 How can social work contribute to tackling the health problems she may face?

Addressing poverty

The potential for social work staff to contribute to anti-poverty initiatives is evident in a Birmingham-based drive to boost pensioners' take-up of benefits, organized by the Council's Welfare Rights and Money Advice Unit. Social workers in neighbourhood offices and front line social services staff in sheltered housing or day centres were integral to the inter-agency strategy. While existing social work services otherwise ran on as usual, 1,995 new claims were made by pensioners, involving £2.4 million in extra benefits, with clear health pay offs (Birmingham Voice, 2000).

Increasing domiciliary services

Work to secure extra domiciliary resources to improve health maintenance is illustrated in a locality based SSD scheme. The managers in question, aware of evidence that timely, low level preventative services could have significant benefits for older people, were concerned that scarcity of chiropody services was resulting in avoidable acute healthcare referrals. Working with the local primary care trust (PCT), they took the lead in drawing on NHS Partnership funding to increase foot care services for older and disabled residents. Interim findings indicate ready take-up by service users, confirming a more widespread need that shortage of funding had previously masked (personal communication, Area Manager, 2003).

Equalizing service users' access to healthcare

Finally, Age Concern's breast cancer screening campaign provides an example of anti-discriminatory practice to assist service users in gaining more equal access to healthcare. Through its local offices, workers and volunteers, Age Concern challenged the blatantly ageist discrimination which restricted automatic call up for NHS screening to women aged under 65 despite the incidence of mortality from breast cancer being highest among those over 65. Age Concern targeted older women directly through distributing an information booklet to encourage them to request screening. This led to its largest ever take-up of publicity (400,000 copies), followed by an increase of nearly 50 per cent in the numbers of older women requesting screening in the year following the campaign (McLeod and Bywaters, 2000). Finally, in 2000, the NHS Plan announced the extension of screening to the 65–69 age group (Department of Health, 2000d).

Conclusion

Physical ill-health as a site of social inequality needs to be a major issue in social work. Threats to health and the experience of ill-health characterize the lives of service users because of disadvantaged social conditions and interlocking dimensions to discrimination. As social workers we also need to be aware that our practice can exacerbate this situation. Nevertheless, the ultimate reason for this aspect of social injustice being a focus of practice is that social work can contribute to tackling service users' unequal chances and experience of ill-health.

Five Key Points

- Ill-health is a site of social injustice: social inequalities create unequal chances and experience of ill-health causing profound, widespread, needless suffering.
- Relative poverty cross cut by further dimensions to social inequality is centrally implicated in unequal chances and experience of ill-health.
- Because of the disadvantaged circumstances in which most service users live, they experience high rates of ill-health and often face inferior treatment and care.
- Social work policy and practice can compound inequalities in health to the detriment of service users' well-being.
- Across all settings, social work which explicitly targets inequality in ill-health and addresses unequal social conditions, can contribute to tackling service users' unequal chances and experience of ill-health.

Three Questions

? Why is ill-health described as a 'site of social injustice'?
? How is social inequality reflected in service users' experience of ill-health?
? How can social work contribute to a more equal chance of well-being in the course of ill-health?

Further reading

1 McLeod, E. and Bywaters, P. (2000) *Social Work, Health and Equality*. London: Routledge.
2 Barnes, M., Bauld, L., Benzeval, M., Judge, K., Mackenzie, M. and Sullivan, H. (2005) *Health Action Zones: Partnership for Health Equity*. London: Routledge.
3 Asthana, S. and Halliday, J. (2006) *What Works in Tackling Health Inequalities? Pathways, Policies and Practice through the Life Course*. Bristol: Policy Press.

CHAPTER 1.5

Physical Disability

Deborah Marks

When we think of physical disability, we tend to think of an impaired person using a particular technological aid, such as a young blind woman using a white stick or a young man with a spinal cord injury in his wheelchair. I have deliberately given a gender and age to these examples since they represent archetypal images of disability within contemporary Western culture. Images of disability within literature, charity advertising and movies, are replete with visual (gendered, racialized and ageist) stereotypes. Many impairments are used as short-hand signifiers of negative characteristics, portraying disabled people as malevolent (as in facially disfigured baddies in James Bond films) or vulnerable and helpless (as in so much charity advertising).

Whilst these representations are pervasive, they are not an accurate portrayal of the extent and nature of physical impairments in contemporary society. In order to go beyond visual stereotypes of physical disability, it is important to recognize that the meaning of disability is highly contested. Each definition of physical disability rests upon a set of theories about the body, society and the psyche. The kinds of theories we bring to bear have important consequences for the way in which we think and act in social work practice. This chapter explores medical, psychological and social models of disability. Then it attempts to show how each of these models may offer an important dimension to our understanding. Drawing upon these models, the chapter identifies some key concerns when working with physically disabled clients.

Theoretical Frameworks

Medical model

For a medical practitioner, a physical disability is a dysfunction or abnormality located within an individual person's body. Within medicine, there are different ways of categorizing disability; in terms of a specific medical diagnosis (e.g. asthma), the bodily system affected (nervous, visual, auditory, musculoskeletal) or the functional loss (paraplegia) (Olkin, 1999). Each of these forms of categorization provides different kinds of information. What unites these different classificatory systems is their focus on *pathology*. When we make even a cursory examination of the nature and variability of impairments, the distorting simplicity of our popular images of disability becomes clear:

- The most common disabling conditions such as heart disease, back problems and arthritis are not identifiable by simply looking at a person.
- The degree or experience of physical impairment cannot necessarily be predicted from gaining access to their medical diagnosis. The physical consequences of particular impairments will vary for different people. The age an impairment is acquired may shape the way it is cognitively, emotionally and physically experienced. The consequences of congenital blindness, for example, will be markedly different from losing sight in old age.
- The experience of an impairment may also vary within the same person. Physical states are rarely fixed and conditions may be progressive, relapsing, or otherwise changeable.

The problem of categorization

As well as impairments being highly variable both across populations and within an individual person, there are many boundary disputes regarding *who* comes to be identified as disabled. The process of rationing disability benefits and services is complex. Official definitions of disability may not coincide with a specific person's self image. Someone who, for example, has an official disabled parking permit, may see themselves as having difficulties walking far, but may not identify as a disabled person. By contrast, people who see themselves as physically disabled (for example, with a facial disfigurement) may not need or be entitled to benefits or services. Furthermore, there is great controversy regarding whether people who are ill should be categorized as disabled. For years, activists in the disabled people's movement have attempted to challenge the jurisdiction of medicine, which is concerned primarily with illness, over disability, which may affect healthy people (Barnes and Mercer, 1996). Thus the question of who is physically disabled is not a straightforward one, and for these reasons, learning about an abstract range of 'conditions' may offer only limited help in understanding the nature of physical disability. Even within what has come to be termed the medical model, states of impairment cannot be understood in isolation from getting to know about a specific *whole person* within a *particular context*.

Psychological models

Many, although by no means all psychological approaches to disability share with the medical model a focus on the individual. The problem psychologists have traditionally concerned themselves with, has been in helping a disabled person 'adjust' to their impairment. They may suffer from *learned helplessness*, which may compound the impairment. Therapeutic work (particularly if it is from a behavioural or cognitive perspective) may focus on improving *coping strategies*. Psychoanalytic approaches may use a *bereavement model* focusing on the importance of mourning the 'loss' of function, in order to come to terms with a new disabled self. The focus of such approaches is on the *individual* person's mental response to impairments.

Social model

In contrast to the medical and psychological models, the social model (Oliver, 1996) locates disability within society: in the *built environment* and the *values* and *social practices* which *discriminate* against people with certain differences. A distinction is made between impairment and disability. Although no-one is completely free of any 'impairments', only some kinds of impairment become disabling. For example, a wheelchair user in a fully accessible and inclusive environment, would, according to the social model, cease to be disabled, although they would still have an impairment. Thus, what is seen as 'disabling' changes in different cultures. In pre-Revolutionary China, the practice of foot-binding involved creating a functional impairment (breaking bones often caused infections and made walking difficult) but was not seen as 'disabling'. The converse was the case, since unbound feet could be constituted as an 'aesthetic impairment'. It is important to keep different cultural values and practices in mind when thinking about what kinds of physical differences come to be seen as disabling.

Social model theorists have been primarily concerned with challenging the discrimination and social exclusion suffered by disabled people. One of the key aims of this struggle has been to challenge the segregation of disabled people into 'special' institutions such as schools, residential homes and day centres and their exclusion from paid employment (Oliver, 1996). Disabled people should be treated as citizens with rights and responsibilities, rather than as recipients of care (Barnes, 1997).

The three models of disability

- The *medical model* views a physical disability as a dysfunction or abnormality located within an individual person's body.
- The *psychological models* (behavioural, cognitive or psychoanalytic) focus on the individual person's mental response to impairments.
- The *social model* locates disability within society: in the built environment and the values and practices which discriminate against people with certain differences.

Integrating dimensions of disability

It may be that the medical, psychological and social models of physical disability each contain valuable insights. Having the ability to learn from their client about the physical consequences of an impairment, having the capacity to empathize with cognitive and emotional experiences and finally having an understanding of the social policies and institutional contexts are *all* important aspects of social work practice. Here are some examples of experiences which have bodily, social and psychological dimensions:

- Having a physical disability or receiving hospital treatment may be physically painful and exhausting, may involve emotionally traumatic separations from loved ones (for example, for hospital treatments) and involve stigmatization and loss of social status.
- Whole families can be affected by the social barriers faced by an individual disabled member. It can also create anxiety and distress, in the form, for example, of guilt from parents who feel responsible or rivalry from a non-disabled sibling who feels her sibling is getting more attention. The pressures of intimate physical care between, for example, a husband and wife can undermine their sexual relationship. When such care is given by a parent to a young person, normal developmental moves towards privacy and separation can become confused. These are just some of the potential difficulties which can have not just an emotional toll on a family, but also make members more prone to stress-related illnesses.

Having an integrative approach to our understanding of disability may help us to remain in touch with these different dimensions.

Integrative theories of physical disability

There are different ways theorists have tried to integrate understandings of disability. Patterson and Hughes (1997), taking a *phenomenological perspective* have shown how social exclusion can be produced and reproduced at a *bodily* level. For example, conventional 'scripts' for communication may exclude people with impairments which affect their speech (such as people with cerebral palsy) because ordinary rules of interaction offer only a limited time for each speech 'turn'.

Another way of integrating social and emotional levels of understanding physical disability is through a *psychosocial* approach. Such an approach will bring together social factors, such as professional interests, class, gender and culture with an examination of unconscious investments (Marks, 1999). For example, we might ask why it is that certain professions involved in working with and caring for disabled people (such as nursing and social work) are so dominated by women?

To summarize, when we think about physical disability we are always thinking about *relationships* between people with different life experiences and social positions. An integrative approach may well be the most relevant one for social work practice, where work involves thinking about the whole of clients' lives, rather than just their body, psyche or social environment. The next section therefore examines some ways in which social workers may maximize the independence and enhance the lifestyle of their physically disabled clients.

Practical Steps in Working with Physically Disabled Clients

Checklists can be a useful way of fostering best practice. They can help workers identify common pitfalls which lead to the unintentional objectification and disempowerment of physically disabled clients. There are three key areas which need to be addressed to ensure good practice. These involve considering the *social*, *psychological* and *interprofessional* issues raised in working with physically disabled clients. Within all three areas, the checklist emphasizes critical *self*-reflection, because it is important to get one's own professional and personal house in order, before addressing the difficulties faced by clients.

Addressing social barriers

It is important to think not just about the needs of disabled social work clients, but also the needs of disabled social workers. Disabled people are more likely to face barriers in obtaining professional qualifications and in accessing the environments within which social work takes place. As a consequence, they are under-represented within social work. Also, physically disabled people tend to be socially constituted as *recipients* rather than *providers* of care. This has meant that social work departments have few staff members with direct experience of some of the barriers faced by their clients.

As with other socially disadvantaged clients, physically disabled clients may need to be informed of their rights or assisted in gaining access to and controlling their own benefits and services. Having an up-to-date understanding of disability legislation and social policies is therefore important.

Where clients suffer from low self-esteem, have learning difficulties or lack of access to relevant gate-keepers, social workers may need to become involved in undertaking advocacy work.

Disability equality training, ideally provided by physically disabled people, is important so that the culture of a social work service is one which treats physically disabled people – as employees or clients – with respect.

Addressing psychological factors

We all lie somewhere along an ability/disability continuum. For those who see themselves as able-bodied, they are only contingently so, since most of us will experience increasing impairment and disability as we enter old age. Furthermore, many of those drawn to work within areas which bring them into contact with a large number of physically disabled people will have personal experiences of physical disability, perhaps from a family member. For this reason, it will be important for all workers to examine their own thoughts and feelings about disability and to reflect on how this may shape relationships with clients (Obholzer and Roberts, 1994). A social worker who spends a lot of time trying to address the suffering of others may, for example, carry an unconscious sense of guilt or an unconscious identification with someone whom society sees as damaged. Attending to other people's 'dependency needs' may be a way of vicariously dealing with one's own unconscious needs. This carries the risk that a worker's response to a client may be based on assumptions which are more relevant to that person's own personal history, than to the real life concerns of the disabled person they are working with. Social workers might develop a self-reflective practice through keeping a diary or going into personal counselling or therapy.

Sometimes professional groups may mirror and even act out some of the difficulties faced by their clients. Reflective practice may help professionals appreciate the psychosocial context not just of their clients, but also of their own practice. This can be achieved at an institutional level, through the provision of regular supervision which has a supportive/listening aspect as well as a task-focused, educational and regulatory function. Having an experience of being heard is likely to help practitioners to develop sufficient mental space to be able to offer their clients a similar experience.

It is important for all social workers to have good listening and counselling skills. Many physically disabled people, unsurprisingly, suffer from low self-esteem, or what Mason (1992) calls 'internalized oppression'. The offer of a non-judgmental, empathic outsider, such as a social worker, may help families with a disabled member to manage some of the stresses of living in a disablist society.

Liaison work

It is important that social workers foster effective and genuine collaboration between themselves and service users (Beresford and Campbell, 1994). This may mean working alongside independent living groups and disability rights activists, who will be in a good position to represent the concerns of disabled people and therefore help support effective practice.

It is also important that social workers look at their collaboration with other professionals, such as healthcare workers and teachers. The management of case conferences is one key element in ensuring inter-disciplinary work. All too often, interprofessional rivalries, hierarchies, different professional languages may prevent working together, to the detriment of clients (Marks et al., 1995).

Extra-curricular activities

Social work practice with physically disabled people may be enriched if workers learn about disability culture outside the client–professional relationship. This may involve:

- Developing some familiarity with the burgeoning disability arts, literature and comedy. Listening to what disabled people say about professionals may offer an important mirror with which to view the profession. Narrative accounts by disabled people (e.g. Hockenberry, 1996) offer rich insights into the complexity, pain, amusement and frustration of living with a physical impairment.
- Becoming an ally within the disabled people's movement is another way in which social workers may increase their sensitivity to the concerns of physically disabled people.

These suggestions aim to bring a new dimension to understanding a range of experiences of physical disability.

Conclusion

Social workers are themselves often subject to disabling social barriers. They have only limited means to transform the wider educational, economic, political and cultural context of a disabling society. However, being aware of and willing to challenge social barriers, being sensitive to physical and emotional experiences and being willing to listen to disabled people rather than occupy a position of the expert can all play a key role in enhancing the lives of physically disabled clients.

Five Key Points

- Despite popular characterizations which treat physical disability as a metaphor for internal states, many impairments which come to be disabling in contemporary society are invisible.
- Categorizing disability is in many ways an arbitrary process, dependent on policies, institutions, culture and values within a society. What is disabling changes in different contexts.
- Disability contains bodily, social and psychological dimensions. Attempting to draw upon and integrate these different levels can give a more holistic understanding of the lives of specific physically disabled clients.
- Listening to and respecting clients must form a starting point from which to work with physically disabled people.
- Work with physically disabled people requires attention to one's own personal and professional experiences of and investments in disability.

Three Questions

? Where is disability located:
  - in the built environment, institutional policies and practices;
  - in the body of a person with a serious impairment; or
  - in the ability of that person to come to terms with and manage their difference?

  To what extent is it possible to integrate these models of disability?

? How might a social worker most effectively empower and enhance their disabled clients' quality of life?

? What issues might social workers take up both as individuals and as a profession to make their practice more inclusive for disabled people?

Further reading

1 Marks, D. (1999) *Disability: Controversial Debates and Psychosocial Perspectives*. London: Routledge.
2 Barnes, C., Oliver, M. and Barton, L. (eds.) (2002) *Disability Studies Today*. Cambridge: Polity Press.
3 Shakespeare, T. and Corker, M. (eds.) (2002) *Disability/Postmodernity: Embodying Disability Theory*. London: Continuum.

CHAPTER 1.6

The Frailty of Old Age

Chris Phillipson

Older people present a significant challenge and opportunity for social work. As a group they have moved from being a marginal concern (in the middle of the twentieth century), to one of central importance to the profession. A combination of forces associated with demography, social attitudes and legislative change have assisted this development. The first of these – demographic change – represents a crucial factor in terms of the rationale for social work with older people. The number of people in Britain over age 65 increased from 1.7 million to 8.8 million between 1901 and 1991, or from 4.7 per cent to 15.8 per cent of the population. By the year 2021, the respective figures will be 10 million or 17.2 per cent.

This ageing of the population reflects the convergence of two main factors: first, the downward trend in the birth rate, so that the proportion of older people is increasingly larger than the proportion of children in the population; second, improvements in life expectancy (an increase of 20 years over the course of the twentieth century in the case of Britain). For social workers, the absolute rise in the numbers of older people is probably less important than the growth in particular groups such as the very elderly (those aged 75 and over). In 1991, 44 per cent of the elderly population were aged at least 75, compared to one-third in 1951. By 2041 it is expected that for the first time the proportion of elderly people aged at least 75 will have exceeded 50 per cent.

The growth in the numbers of people aged 75 and over has important implications for the practice of social work. On the positive side, this is a group where there are significant numbers without major health and social problems: even amongst those aged 85 and over, around one-third of men and women do not have a long-standing illness or disability (Siddell, 1995). Conversely, the impact of ill-health does become a significant issue for most older people. For example, it is estimated that among those people aged 85 and over, one in five will have dementia (Jorm, 1990) and three in five a limiting long-standing illness such as osteoporosis or arthritis.

In terms of social relationships, it is the loss of close friends and relations which is such a striking feature of later life (for women especially). Unlike earlier generations, death is now clustered towards the end of the life course. Invariably, also, people experience death when their own personal resources of health and income may be diminished. Social work with older people, in these circumstances, is often inseparable from help in the context of bereavement and assisting people through the process of rebuilding their lives and social networks.

Family Support

Despite significant changes, the social world of older people is still closely associated with their immediate family. Clare Wenger's (1984, 1992) research showed that among those older people with children, residential proximity tended to increase with age, with widowhood resulting in a move closer to children. More than half of the parents in her study saw a child at least once a week, and this rose to three-quarters in the case of parents over 80.

Surveys in Britain based on nationally representative samples, have confirmed the existence of high levels of contact between older people and relatives and friends (Allan and Crow, 2001). At the same time, there is also strong evidence that this is translated into extensive care and support. Findings from the General Household Survey, to take one example, confirm the significance of spouses/partners and close relatives in providing help with domestic tasks (Rowland and Parker, 1998). Research also confirms the supportive role played by older people themselves, even into late old age (Phillipson et al., 2001).

Research has also highlighted the range of physical, social and financial costs associated with the type of care provided by partners, relatives and friends. The physical stresses of care may include the daily pressures associated with dealing with incontinence, lifting someone in and out of bed, manoeuvring a wheelchair; all of this carried out with limited help and alongside a range of other domestic and non-domestic tasks. Again, these activities have to be seen within the context of many carers themselves being in their sixties and seventies, with the likelihood of them also having a chronic illness or disability. The social costs attached to caring will include the isolation and possible loneliness associated with intensive care work, loss of friends and limited opportunities for holidays and regular breaks.

Levin et al.'s (1989) study of carers of older people with dementia identified a range of social costs arising from this kind of care. For example, only two-fifths of the supporters had taken holidays in the previous year and over half the others had gone without them for at least five years. Supporters who did most for their relatives, those who coped with incontinence and other major problems, were no more likely to have had a holiday in the previous year. Similarly, many carers experienced difficulties in getting to see friends on a regular basis and felt less free to initiate meetings with friends and relatives (Lewis and Meredith, 1988).

There is growing evidence that some of the stresses associated with informal care may lead to the abuse and/or neglect of the older person. One British researcher has suggested that around 500,000 older people in Britain (around one in ten) are at risk of abuse (Eastman, 1984; see also, Biggs et al., 1995). A study of caregivers of people with dementia found one-fifth reporting that they had, on occasions, recourse to shaking or hitting their elderly relative (Levin et al., 1989).

The social pressures facing carers may be reinforced by financial problems associated with the loss of earnings and promotion. Amongst sole carers (spouses or parents), Evandrou et al. (1986) note that a higher proportion are likely to be in poverty (as measured by those with an income on or below 140 per cent of the poverty line) in comparison with other groups of carers. Nearly one-third of sole carers were 'in' or 'on' the margins of poverty. In the case of carers with the dependant in the same household, 35 per cent had incomes 'in' or 'on' the margins of poverty.

The significance of the 'informal sector of care' indicates the importance of recognizing the kind of social networks within which older people are located. These may vary considerably in terms of the kind of help provided and their ability to respond to particular crises in old age (Phillipson et al., 2001). Moreover, there is also the issue of effective coordination between formal and informal sources of care, with the need for effective advocacy where appropriate both for the older person and the carer. Both these issues suggest an important role for the social worker, one which is likely to become of increased importance as community care evolves.

Divisions in Later Life

So far this chapter has discussed old age without reference to some of the key social, cultural and economic distinctions affecting older people. Bond and Coleman (1993), for example, suggest that social class is a much stronger predictor of lifestyle than age and argue that older people have much more in common with younger people of their own class than they do with older people from other classes. The importance of social class in influencing opportunities in old age is likely to increase, as the sources of income in old age become more dependent upon benefits such as private and occupational pensions.

Gender is a second major social division. The gender imbalances of later life are now well-established. Because women outlive men by an average of six years, there are 50 per cent more women than men amongst those 65 and over. The gender imbalance is even more marked in late old age: amongst those aged 85 and over, women outnumber men by three to one. 'The fact that over half of older women are widowed, whereas three-quarters of older men are married, has consequences for gender, identity, relationships and roles in later life' (Arber and Ginn, 1995, p. 11).

Race and ethnicity is another important division. In the early part of the twenty-first century, there will be a significant ageing of the black community as the cohorts of migrants of the late 1950s and 1960s reach retirement age (Blakemore and Boneham, 1994). Research suggests a significant role for social work in relation to older people from minority ethnic groups. Some key factors here are: first, the increased susceptibility to physical ill-health of this group because of past experiences such as heavy manual work and poor housing; second, greater vulnerability to mental health problems, a product of racism and cultural pressures; third, low uptake of health and social services; fourth, acute financial problems, with evidence

Old age is a concept that:

- legitimates age bars in the implementation of policy regulations and practice procedures;
- underpins a conceptualization of 'elderly people' which alienates *them* from *us*, often segregating them involuntarily in specially designated places (such as sheltered housing and day centres);
- sustains ageist perspectives on the life course which cause us all to fear our futures.

Source: Bill Bytheway (2000) Old age. In M. Davies (ed.), *The Blackwell Encyclopaedia of Social Work*, Oxford: Blackwell, pp. 236–7.

of elderly Asians being at a particular disadvantage. The problems faced by ethnic elders have been defined as representing a form of 'triple jeopardy' (Norman, 1985). This refers to the fact that ethnic elders not only face discrimination because they are old; in addition, many of them live in disadvantaged physical and economic circumstances; finally, they are likely to face discrimination because of their culture, language, skin colour or religious affiliation. All this suggests a key role for social work over the next 20 years, as the size of this group is substantially increased.

Reasons for Social Work with Older People

The context of ageing provides a number of suggestions about the purpose of social work with older people, and especially those in late old age.

First, social work has a major contribution to make in the area of 'anti-ageist practice' (Bytheway, 1994). Ageism may be defined as discrimination against older people merely by virtue of their age. Ageism affects many institutions in society and has a number of dimensions – job discrimination, loss of status, stereotyping and dehumanization. Ageism is about assuming that all older people are the same, despite different life histories, needs and expectations. Ageism not only affects the lives of older people, but like ageing itself, it affects every individual from birth onwards, putting limits and constraints on experiences, expectations, relationships and opportunities. These points underscore the importance of social work adopting a clear anti-ageist framework, recognizing principles such as the following:

- ageing as a period of normal development;
- the positive social and economic functions performed by older people;
- the importance of using the term older people not 'the elderly';
- the importance of talking about the rights and responsibilities of older people;
- the importance of listening to what older people have to say about their experiences and emotions; and

- the necessity of standing alongside older people, in some cases where there is conflict with carers – informal as well as formal.

Social work has a significant part to play in fostering greater awareness of the impact of ageism in society (and on the professions working with and for older people). The goal of working towards a society free of ageism should be as important as that of achieving a society devoid of racism and sexism.

A second important reason for social work relates to the provision and management of different kinds of social support to elderly people. This reflects the vulnerability of the old not just to losses which are inevitable (such as the death of a partner or friend), but also to events which reflect particular types of tensions and divisions in society (such as domestic violence or racist attacks). Elderly people experience problems which would be distressing at any point of the life course (and of course problems such as poor health or poverty affect the young as well as the old). But elderly people experience these changes when their own resources are invariably depleted. The resources social work has to offer may, therefore, be crucial in terms of helping people forward to the next phase in their lives.

Third, within this process of support, recognition of the strengths of older people is vital. It is relatively easy to highlight the problems of the old; and, indeed, this is important in terms of constructing different forms of social work intervention. Equally, though, social work has a major role in reaffirming the resilience and power of older people. Of course, elderly people have achieved this themselves through their writings and their political organizations (Curtis, 1993). Social work interventions can, however, be used positively (through forms of practice such as personal biography work and life review therapy), to enhance the process of individuals rediscovering a sense of purpose and identity in later life (Bornat, 1994).

Fourth, social work in the twenty-first century is closely concerned with advocacy for groups such as older people. The case for this reflects both social changes and the impact of social legislation. Dunning (1995) observes that changes in family structures, living arrangements and patterns of employment, mean that some older people might not have a partner or close relative who can provide support or speak out on their behalf. For others, family relationships may be poor and conflicts of interest are likely to arise. At the same time, greater emphasis is being given to the idea of consumer choice and user empowerment in the provision of services.

More specifically, social work and advocacy is important because of the likelihood of older people entering situations where their frailties may be exposed or enhanced. This may happen as people move into residential care, or are discharged from hospital, or embark on long-term domiciliary support. As events, these may lead to greater independence for an older person; equally, though, the elderly person may feel their autonomy undermined by professional carers taking key decisions on their behalf. This possibility underlines the importance of advocacy as a central social role in work with older people.

Conclusion

This chapter has noted, first, the increased importance of older people for the practice of social work; second, the pressures which they face through the loss of key relationships, this coming at a time when their own resources may be reduced; third, the possibility of frailty being enhanced within the context of developments such as a move into residential care.

Social work with older people needs to recognize both the actual and potential disabilities of later life and the possibilities for further growth and development even in very late old age. This points to the importance of the social worker adopting a clear anti-ageist framework, using this to guide the complex decisions which have to be made in the 'triangle' of user, carer and service provider. In the twenty-first century, social work with older people is fundamental to the profession and a central reason for wanting to assume the identity and practice of being a social worker.

Five Key Points

- Demography, changing social attitudes and legislation have all made older people a target group of critical significance for social work.
- Social work with older people often involves helping them to rebuild their lives following bereavement.
- Work with carers – many of whom are themselves no longer young – is a major task for social work.
- Social class, gender and ethnicity are all factors which need to be taken into account when considering the nature of social work with old people.
- Social work with older people must be anti-ageist; it must be supportive; it must recognize client strengths; and it must use advocacy.

Three Questions

? How might an anti-ageist practice be developed in work with older people?

? What sort of conflicts are likely to arise in the relationship between older people and informal carers?

? What are the issues that might be faced by particular minority ethnic groups as increased numbers move into late old age?

Further reading

1 Warnes, A. M., Warren, L. and Nolan, M. (2000) *Care Services for Later Life: Transformations and Critiques*. London: Jessica Kingsley.

2 Phillips, J., Ray, M. and Marshall, M. (2006) *Social Work with Old People*. Basingstoke: Palgrave.

3 Vincent, J., Phillipson, C. and Downs, M. (eds.) (2006) *The Futures of Old Age*. London: Sage.

CHAPTER 1.7

Mental Illness

Peter Huxley

Client groups may be defined by age or by contact with the criminal justice system, but the mental illness client group knows no such boundaries. Psychiatric patients are defined by contact with psychiatric services, but most mental disorder never reaches the psychiatrist. Mental ill-health is a major worldwide public health problem. Mental illnesses are among the most significant contributors to the global burden of disease accounting for almost 11 per cent of all Disability Adjusted Life Years (DALYs). In the UK in 1993, for example, 92 million working days lost (18 per cent of all working days lost) were due to mental illness, with a total estimated cost of £6.2 billion. Of this productive loss:

- 49 per cent was due to anxiety and stress;
- 27 per cent to depression;
- 16 per cent to psychotic disorders;
- 5 per cent to other psychiatric disorders; and
- 3 per cent to alcohol dependence.

Almost one in five days of certificated work incapacity are due to mental illness alone, and 40 per cent of reports of adverse health effects at work are attributed to emotional problems. Mental illnesses are common, disabling and expensive.

In the UK, it has been estimated that GPs assign a psychiatric diagnosis to six million people each year (1.2 million are over 65, and 300,000 are under 15), compared to cancer which affects two million people and AIDS about 2,000. Mental illness kills more than four times as many people as die in road accidents, and suicide is the second most common cause of death in young men. However, it is not simply the ubiquitous nature of mental illness which makes it an important reason for social work. Social factors play a crucial role in the causation of mental illness, in the course of the illnesses, in the outcome of treatment and care and in recovery.

In 1976, the first study of mental illness in social workers' caseloads was conducted in London. It examined the physical and mental health of clients referred to social workers in an outer-London borough. The research team rated physical and mental health from case notes and found that 45 per cent exhibited minor or major mental illness. Subsequent studies conducted using screening questionnaires, revealed that an even higher proportion of people receiving social work help experienced mental health problems, and these results were confirmed using standardized psychiatric assessments, which showed that the proportion of mental health problems ranged from 53 to 66 per cent (Corney, 1984; Huxley et al., 1988, 1989). One-third of the disorders were severe psychotic illnesses, and another 30 per cent were anxiety and depression.

Social workers, like GPs, do not identify all the instances of mental health problems presented to them by service users. Huxley et al. (1989) found that recognition varied by diagnosis; social workers recognized all of the people with a manic illness, but only half of those suffering from schizophrenia and less than half of those suffering from severe or psychotic depression.

One study (Isaac et al., 1986) suggests that the overlap between child care problems and mental health problems is very high. While none of the children entering care in this study sample had parental mental illness as an official reason, 84 per cent of the parents had received psychiatric care at some time. At the other end of the age spectrum a number of studies have shown that rates of mild and severe dementia and depression are between 30 per cent and 40 per cent in the residents of local authority homes for people over 65. Subsequent work has shown a strong relationship between problems in childhood and later mental health difficulties.

Knowledge about mental illnesses has undergone a major upheaval in the past thirty years. Diagnostic classifications based upon the treated population of patients are no longer regarded as adequate to describe the totality of mental health problems. Research has shown that the diagnostic systems themselves are not very reliable, except in the most crude sense, and diagnostic classifications are poor predictors of outcome and also of the costs of providing services. The discovery of the frequent coexistence of symptoms of anxiety and depression reduces the need to have categorical classifications of disorder for less severe conditions. Epidemiological research shows that the prevalence of mental illness is considerable, and that most people with symptoms consult their family doctor, and the family doctor sees and treats most mental illness. In two books (Goldberg and Huxley, 1980, 1992) we outlined the pathway to specialist psychiatric care in the UK. Subsequent research has confirmed important aspects of this model; and even in societies where the filtering mechanisms are dissimilar, the model acts as a useful template against which to examine rates of mental health problems in local populations.

The model consists of five levels, each one corresponding to a stage on the pathway to psychiatric care. The first level is the prevalence of disorder in the community (the data come from community surveys). The first filter is consultation behaviour or illness behaviour. Most people experiencing symptoms will present them to their family doctor, but the presentation is often of a somatic rather than a psychological complaint. Partly as a result, doctors vary in their ability to detect disorder and the factors which contribute to this variation are described in detail in the first book (Goldberg and Huxley, 1980); their ability to recognize psychiatric

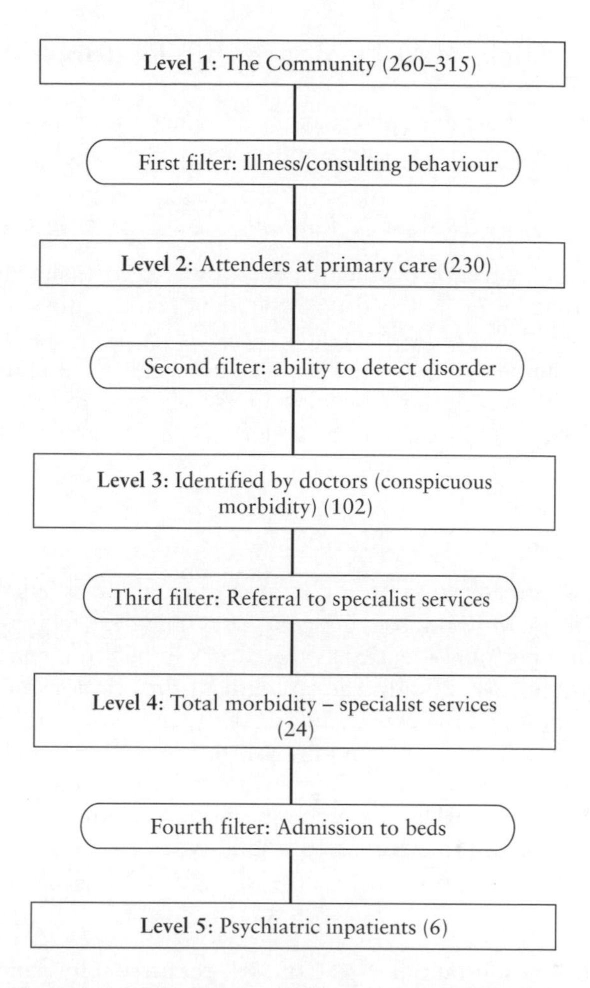

Figure 1 The Goldberg–Huxley pathway model

problems is the second filter. For cases which are detected, the family doctor decides to treat many of them and to refer the others for specialist psychiatric attention; the referral decision is the third filter. When the patient reaches the psychiatrist (level 4) they are treated as an outpatient, or admitted (filter 4) to hospital (level 5) (Figure 1 contains the rates at each level expressed per thousand population per year).

The mental illnesses encountered in community surveys are less severe than those admitted to psychiatric hospitals. Social dysfunction and clinical severity increase at progressively higher levels of the model.

Social and Demographic Factors

A number of social and demographic factors influence the rates of disorder which come to the attention of social workers and other professionals.

Gender

Female rates of mental health problems generally exceed male rates, although it should be noted that by including drug dependency and anti-social personality – where male rates greatly exceed female rates – greater parity is found. Jenkins (1985) has shown that if samples of male and female subjects are chosen who are closely comparable from the standpoint of social adjustment the difference in rates disappears. Women with children are a particularly high risk group for mental health problems.

Social class

Most studies show greater rates for common mental disorders in lower social classes. There is a growing interest in social psychological factors, social capital, social exclusion and personal identity as mediators in health inequalities (Office of the Deputy Prime Minister, 2004). The strength of the relationship between social class and mental illness and the consistency of the social class gradient in depression and anxiety appears to be greater than in physical illnesses. The social class gradient in mental ill-health may be influenced by specific social psychological and biological factors, experience of family disadvantage in childhood, and general vulnerability acquired through exposure to adversity of many types.

Unemployment

Unemployment has a substantial effect on self-reported physical health, anxiety and depression, and causes a decline in marital support (the number of weeks unemployed is related to the decrease in the quality of the marital relationship). Unemployment causes great financial strain which leaves people more vulnerable to the impact of otherwise unrelated life events. The effect of unemployment may be worse for those who have had little social contact outside the work setting. In the OPCS community survey, unemployment was the factor most strongly associated with the rate of mental ill-health (Jenkins et al., 2003).

Ethnicity

While black and minority ethnic groups are over-represented among involuntary hospital admissions and may use more emergency and in-patient services, the treatments given in hospital, compliance with depot injection clinics, and the prevalence of disorders in the community all appear to be unrelated to ethnicity. Hirschfeld and Cross (1982) found that differences between black and white rates of depression disappeared when social class was controlled. There continues to be an ongoing debate about the role of ethnicity in the onset, course and treatment of mental health problems.

Life Events

A variety of factors make an individual more susceptible to develop symptoms under stress, including: genetically determined emotional reactivity; personality; parental loss and early abuse; and social adversity such as poor housing and unemployment. These factors may act to increase the rate at which adverse life events occur as well as their impact. Good experience of early parenting and a good marital relationship act as protective factors against the rate (and impact) of life events. Goldberg and Huxley (1992) call the process of beginning to experience symptoms 'destabilization', and the process of losing symptoms 'restitution'. It appears to be the case that 'loss' events lead to depression, and 'threat' events lead to the development of anxiety, and combinations of the two to types of mixed anxiety–depression. Major life events are not all negative experiences, and some of the most stressful events are culturally accepted as positive experiences, the two most stressful being marriage and moving into a new home. In community surveys, restitution appears to be related to: a decrease in the rate of life events; positive or 'fresh-start' events; the presence of social support which is perceived positively and an absence of physical illness. In treated samples, restitution is associated with: better material circumstances; higher income; low expressed emotion relationships; an absence of negative self-concepts and satisfaction with levels of social support.

Though intimate close relationships are not universally positive in terms of mental health outcome, there is some evidence to indicate that social integration leads to better mental health. As the work of Brown and Harris (1978) shows, the existence of positive intimate relationships can be protective against depression. A substantial amount of research has also pointed to the importance of social ties in providing emotional and practical support (e.g. Harris et al., 1999).

Not all problems presented to the social worker are new episodes of common disorder, many are of long-standing psychotic illnesses which are re-occurring for the second or third time. The OPCS survey (Jenkins et al., 2003) found a prevalence rate of four per thousand of functional psychosis in the community. Schizophrenia is the major severe mental illness and it affects 1 per cent of the population. The onset is rapid or insidious (about half each), the course is episodic or continuous (also about half each) and outcome over the long term (more than 30 years) can be moderate or severe disability or full recovery (also about half each). Outcome tends to be better in Third World countries, which is said to be due to better community integration and more rapid return to a useful role. The recognition that serious illnesses can have very good outcomes in the long term, and some in the short term is an important factor in the development of the 'recovery' model (Roberts and Wolfson, 2004).

The rates of admission of severely mentally ill people to psychiatric hospital are higher in areas of high social deprivation. One of the major contributory factors to relapse of the illness is the level of expressed emotion in the family home; high-stress homes invariably producing relapse, and low-stress homes only doing so if independent stressful events occur. People suffering from schizophrenia show heightened levels of arousal which reduce in the presence of non-stressful relatives. A non-stressful social worker may have the same calming influence on the sufferer, and this may help them to maintain the client in the community.

People who develop long-term severe disorders are now cared for in the community where delivering the necessary coordinated health and social care is much more complicated than in a mental hospital. In the UK a legislative framework has been provided within which care can be focused on severely mentally ill people, and it appears that compared to ten years previously the clientele of community teams, on average, do indeed have more complex problems (Huxley et al., 2006). Highly publicized tragedies, such as the murder of innocent victims by severely disturbed patients, suggest that in the mid-1990s the policy was failing many of those it was designed to help. More recently however, prominence is being given to the fact that the number of homicides committed by people with mental health problems has actually been declining. Goldberg and Gater (1991) estimate that in a population of 100,000, there will be 2,600 people who will require planned, prolonged health and social care.

Case management was devised in the USA to provide this continuity of care (Ziguras and Stuart, 2000). When case management was adopted in the UK and transformed into care management, an inappropriate administrative, rather than a clinical or assertive model was used. All models include similar components: assessment, case finding, care planning, and monitoring and review, but in the assertive and clinical case management models direct face-to-face work is undertaken by the case manager. Research evidence (Ziguras and Stuart, 2000) suggests that assertive case management is successful with the most severely disabled people and that the administrative model is both unsuccessful and unpopular. A major reason is the need for a close personal working relationship (of a low expressed emotion variety) in order to sustain community living. This long-term clinical case management is also applicable to other client groups such as the older mentally ill person, and emotionally disturbed children and adolescents.

A welcome development in mental health services across the world is the focus upon the outcome of service provision and on 'recovery' models. The fundamental question arises, if people are no longer cared for in large institutions, or in psychiatric units in general hospitals, how can we be sure that community services provide them with a better quality of life and greater recovery opportunities? It is no longer good enough to assert that treatment in the community must be better, there is a need (arising from public accountability of services) to answer this question based upon sound and systematically gathered evidence. Quality of life (QOL) assessment gives social workers a systematic way of assessing the outcome in life domains which have meaning to service users, are consistent with recovery models and put user views at the centre of service provision and planning (Priebe et al., 1999). Results of the application of quality of life measures to community services show that community treatment is more popular and can improve mental health and social relationships.

A variety of models have been offered to explain the way quality of life is determined. One of the most useful is that originally produced by Campbell et al. (1976) – a revision of which is reproduced here as Figure 2 (Huxley and Evans, 2000).

Whatever the ultimate conclusions of the debate, there is little doubt that QOL assessment offers one opportunity to put the social dimensions that are crucial to recovery at the forefront of work on the outcome of care and treatment in the community.

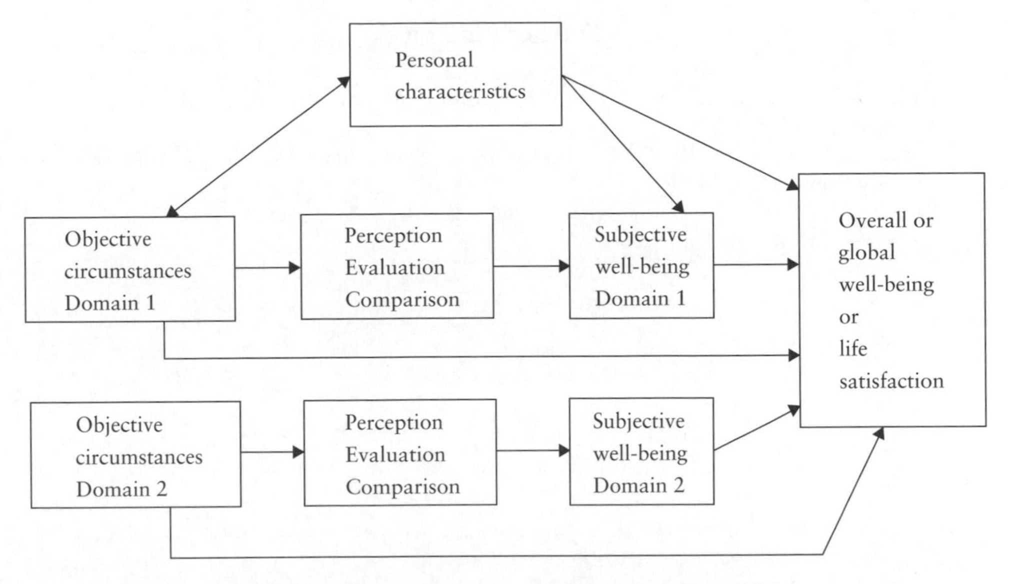

Figure 2 The Huxley–Evans model of quality of life

Five Key Points

- Fifty per cent or more of social work clients are suffering from mental disorder.
- Common disorders can be distinguished from severe disorders and the former more often fail to reach psychiatric care.
- Rates of mental illness in the community vary according to socio-demographic characteristics and social factors such as life events.
- In order for people with severe illness to survive in the community effective after-care and continuity of care must be provided and recovery emphasized.
- Quality of life measures reflect the social dimensions of severe mental illness, and can be used to assess recovery outcomes

Three Questions

? What are the main factors which contribute to the variation in the rates of mental disorder in the community?

? What are the main factors which contribute to more severe illnesses progressing to inpatient psychiatric care?

? How can systematic quality of life assessment of mentally ill people become part of the operational practice of social workers?

Further reading

1 Goldberg, D. P. and Huxley, P. J. (1992) *Common Mental Disorder: A Biosocial Model.* London: Routledge.
2 Social Exclusion Unit (2004) *Mental Health and Social Inclusion.* London: Office of the Deputy Prime Minister.
3 Warner, R. (2004) *Recovery from Schizophrenia: Psychiatry and Political Economy*, 3rd edn. London: Routledge.

CHAPTER 1.8

Learning Disabilities

Kirsten Stalker and Carol Robinson

This chapter begins by identifying the dominant theories and values informing social work with people with learning disabilities. It then outlines the relevant legal and policy frameworks across the UK and looks at numbers, needs, wants and services. Lastly, we summarize good practice principles in this important and rewarding area of social work.

The term 'learning disabilities' is now widely used in the UK, including by central and local government. People First self-advocacy groups have expressed a preference for the term 'learning difficulties' and we apologize for any offence caused to them. However, we wish to avoid confusion with conditions like dyslexia which, within education, are also referred to as 'learning difficulties' but do not necessarily involve cognitive impairment. 'Learning disability' is an umbrella term denoting a significant lifelong condition affecting an individual's development. It is applied to people with widely varying abilities, although most will need some level of support to understand information, learn skills and live independently.

Theoretical Frameworks and Value Base

Social workers engaging with people with learning disabilities need to draw on the same range of theories and models that apply to other areas of practice, tailored to individual circumstances. In particular, social workers are likely to use ideas derived from normalization (Nirje, 1980; Wolfensberger, 1972, 1983), inclusion (O'Brien, 1987; O'Brien and Lovett, 1992; Stainton, 2002) and/or the social model of disability (Oliver, 1990; Swain et al., 2004). Normalization and inclusion emphasize the importance of people with learning disabilities leading 'an ordinary life', having opportunities to exercise choice and control, and being meaningfully included in their communities through a network of valued roles and relationships. Recent thinking focuses on person-centred approaches and community capacity building (Charity Commission, 2000). The social model of disability identifies and challenges the material, social and economic barriers which disable people with impairments. Originally developed to explain the oppression of people with physical/ sensory impairments, the social model also has important implications for the civil rights of people with learning disabilities (Chappell et al., 2001, Goodley, 2004).

The numbers of people with learning disabilities

There is a shortage of reliable data about the numbers of people with learning disabilities in the UK population. The estimated number with mild to moderate impairment is 580,000–1,750,000 with a further 230,000–350,000 people estimated to have severe impairment (Foundation for People with Learning Disabilities, 2003). Recent work by Hatton et al. (2005) has suggested that 128,000 adults receive social services in England. In 2004, an estimated 22,369 people were known to Scottish local authorities (Scottish Executive, 2005) and just over 12,000 in Wales (National Assembly for Wales 2003). Between April 2004 and March 2005, 7,850 people with learning disabilities aged 16 and over were known to community health and social services trusts in Northern Ireland (Northern Ireland Department of Health, Social Services and Public Safety, 2005a) and a further 486 were recorded as resident in long-stay hospitals although data on two hospitals are missing (personal communication, Jenny Orr, Northern Ireland HSSPB). There are more men than women within the learning disability population. In addition, there is an increased likelihood of mental health problems, affecting an estimated 25–40 per cent of people with learning disabilities (Foundation for People with Learning Disabilities, 2003).

Legal and Policy Frameworks

Disabled people have a right to social care services under a range of legislation. The National Assistance Act 1948, section 29, permits local authorities to make arrangements for promoting welfare for disabled people while the Chronically Sick and Disabled Persons Act 1970 requires authorities to provide disabled people with information on relevant services in their area, to provide equipment and make provision for home adaptations. The Disabled Persons (Services, Consultation and Representation) Act 1986 places a duty on authorities to assess a person's need for services under the Chronically Sick and Disabled Persons Act and to consider whether a carer can continue to give a substantial amount of regular care. Under this law, councils should also be informed of disabled young people leaving special education in order to facilitate long-term planning and to assist young people in their transition to adulthood.

The NHS and Community Care Act 1990 placed greater emphasis on people being enabled to live as independently as possible in the community. It strengthens the idea of empowerment and the participation of disabled people in planning for their futures. Section 47 requires local authorities to assess people who appear to be in need of community care services to determine whether they are eligible for services, including those available under the Chronically Sick and Disabled Persons Act. Local authorities must keep service users at the centre of assessment, listening to their wishes, preferences and feelings and the care plan must address all eligible *risks* facing the person.

Since 2004, local authorities in England and Wales have had to apply Fair Access to Care Services criteria, whereby an individual is assessed as in 'critical' 'substantial', 'moderate' or 'low' need of services in order to preserve their independence (Department of Health, 2003c).

Wide-ranging anti-discrimination legislation is now in place throughout the UK. Social workers working with people with learning disabilities need to be aware of the provisions of the Disability Discrimination Acts, 1995 and 2005 and the Human Rights Act, 1998.

Strategic Frameworks

Following the establishment of the Scottish Parliament, the Welsh Assembly and the Northern Ireland Assembly, each jurisdiction within the UK has separate strategic frameworks relating to people with learning disabilities.

England

The White Paper, *Valuing People* (Department of Health, 2001e), was the first government policy document to be produced in accessible formats in England and to involve service users and carers in its development. The strategy encompasses services for children and adults and has at its heart the four key principles of civil rights, independence, choice and social inclusion. It aims to bring about improvements in all aspects of people's lives by providing new opportunities and better access to education, social services, health, employment, housing and support. Particular emphasis is placed on partnership working across a range of agencies, many of which previously had few dealings with people with learning disabilities. Learning Disability Partnership Boards, which must have representation from people with learning disabilities and family carers, were set up to promote this aim and, in particular, to ensure equal access to mainstream services such as leisure centres, health screening programmes and community housing. Implementation of this strategy has been promoted by a Valuing People Support Team made up of regional advisers, the development of a Learning Disability Task Force and Regional and National Forums of people with learning disabilities.

Wales

Whilst *Valuing People* was the first learning disabilities strategy document in 30 years in England, three policy documents have been published in a similar period of time in Wales. In 1983, the Welsh Mental Handicap Strategy (Welsh Office, 1983) articulated three principles relating to people with learning disabilities:

- The right to an ordinary pattern of life in the community.
- The right to be treated as an individual.
- The right to additional help and support in developing their maximum potential.

These principles were reiterated in the 1994 Guidance, which outlined how the objectives of the 1983 strategy should be met. Later strategy focuses on working with adults and older people with learning disabilities and emphasizes three key approaches to help people be regarded as full citizens with equal status – person-centred planning, a unified assessment process and partnership working. It helpfully identifies the service principles that should be in place and what actions should be taken in response (National Assembly for Wales, 2004).

Scotland

In 2000, the Scottish Executive published *The Same as You?* (SAY) the report of a 15-month review of services for people with learning disabilities (Scottish Executive, 2000b). It is based on seven principles: people with learning disabilities should be valued members of their communities, seen as individuals, consulted and given choices about services, supported to fulfil their potential, use local mainstream services wherever possible and specialist provision as appropriate. In addition, services should take account of people's age, abilities and needs.

Unlike *Valuing People*, *SAY* is not a White Paper and thus its 29 recommendations arguably have less force. There are broad similarities between the English and Scottish proposals, although one significant difference is the introduction to Scotland of local area coordination (LAC). LAC was developed in Western Australia to support families with learning disabled members living in remote rural areas: advocating for the family, developing informal support networks and building community capacity are key features of the role, along with a strong value base.

Northern Ireland

In September 2005, the Department of Health, Social Services and Public Safety published *Equal Lives: A Review of Policy and Services for People with a Learning Disability in Northern Ireland* (Northern Ireland HSSPB, 2005b). This report, which sets out a vision for developing services over 15–20 years, contains 74 recommendations. It is broadly similar to strategies elsewhere in the UK, although the Northern Ireland context has some distinctive features. The Province's joint Health and Social Services has avoided many of the difficulties in collaborative working experienced elsewhere (McConkey et al., 2004) but less progress has been made in terms of user involvement and inclusion. *Equal Lives* is based on five key principles of citizenship, social inclusion, empowerment, working together (meaning including people with learning disabilities and their families in planning and decision-making) and individual support. It proposes a 'new service model' designed to move people out of congregated, segregated services and promote integration, community participation and access to the full range of mainstream opportunities.

Personalized Funding

Across the UK, legislation exists to permit the use of direct payments by disabled adults, young people aged 16 and 17 years and families caring for a disabled son or daughter. To date, take-up among people with learning disabilities has been low, but local authorities must offer direct payments as an alternative to services for people eligible for support. In England, the Department of Health has promoted individualized/individual budgets and resource allocation systems, both of which are designed to allow people greater choice over how they get their support by allocating them a sum of money to spend (see Department of Health, 2005b; Prime Minister's Strategy Unit et al., 2005). It seems likely this approach will become increasingly important and may shift the role of social workers from assessors and care planners to facilitators of person-centred plans.

Wants, needs and services

As successive studies and consultation exercises have shown, people with learning disabilities want to be treated with respect, have opportunities to make choices, be included in local communities, exercise their civil rights, develop meaningful relationships – which for some will include having partners and children – have interesting and useful occupation, a reasonable income and, in some cases, their own tenancy or home. While family carers are likely to identify gaps in services, adults with learning disabilities are more likely to identify gaps in ordinary opportunities (Stalker et al., 1999). However, for inclusion to be successful, mainstream facilities must accommodate difference in a positive way by providing the right kind of support tailored to individual need: social workers can play an important role in promoting this process.

Principles of good social work practice

- Information giving in a way that enables people to make informed choices. This will require workers to have good knowledge about available options and be willing to research areas about which they have limited knowledge.
- Access to advocacy – workers will need to be aware of the ways in which individuals can get support to express themselves and be prepared to listen and act upon those views.
- Partnership working is required not only with the person with learning disabilities but also with family members and across a wide range of agencies to ensure that plans, both individual and strategic, reflect a wide range of views and can be achieved through joint ownership.
- An inclusive approach that promotes equality of access to local provision.
- A focus on achieving positive outcomes for people is essential.
- Keep an open mind – think about how things can change and try to anticipate new developments or ways of working.
- Act as an enabler not a 'gate-keeper'. If resources are hard to find, seek out alternative ways of helping people and 'sign post' them appropriately.

The paucity of accessible information about services and entitlements is a recurring finding of research, especially but not exclusively in relation to families from Black and ethnic minorities. Parents often talk about having to 'fight' for services. Families with learning disabled members value social workers who arrange practical help, provide information, act as a link to other support, take time to listen and allow users to remain in control (Stalker et al., 1999). It is important that social workers involve people with learning disabilities in making decisions affecting their lives, as far as possible using the individual's accustomed form of communication. Where individuals have little or no language, time can be spent observing their responses to different settings and services and garnering the views of relatives and staff who know the person well. This can lead to tension or conflict, where people have different opinions about what 'is best' for the individual, and these ideas may also differ from the person's own feelings. In these circumstances, it may be advisable to bring in an independent advocate to speak up for the person with learning disabilities or ensure they are supported to speak up for themselves. The social worker's overall aim, however, will be to work in partnership with all family members and colleagues from their own and other agencies.

As already indicated, social workers have legal duties to intervene or support people in certain circumstances, for example, planning transition to adulthood, conducting community care assessments, arranging direct payments or determining incapacity. They may assist in setting up regular support, such as short breaks or social and leisure activities, or they may intervene at times of family difficulty, such as bereavement or carer stress. The higher than average incidence of mental health difficulties among this population often calls for sensitive and skilled social work support.

People with learning disabilities are often perceived as being vulnerable to risk. Both family and professional carers may worry that individuals are open to abuse or exploitation: in some cases, they may also wish to protect a relative or client from relatively minor and/or unlikely risks, leading to unnecessary restrictions on an individual's activities. Social workers often face the difficult task of balancing their duty of care – ensuring adequate protection is available – on the one hand, while encouraging an appropriate degree of self-determination on the other. Sellars (2002) sets out good practice guidelines for assessing and managing risk with people with learning disabilities, including those with complex needs and/or behavioural difficulties who will need additional care and support.

Although social workers aim to promote inclusion by encouraging people with learning disabilities to use mainstream services, many individuals still rely on segregated services for much of their support. Residential provision, run by statutory, voluntary or private providers, ranges from so-called village communities located within or on the site of former long stay hospitals to supported living options where individuals own their own homes and have visiting or continuous support as required. The amount of time people spend in day centres is gradually shifting, as a wider range of work opportunities becomes available, ranging from open employment paid at the going rate to small amounts of voluntary work. Social workers are often involved in arranging short breaks for children and/or adults with learning disabilities. These can take many forms, ranging from ordinary family homes to institutional settings. Good short breaks offer a positive experience for the individual as well as a break for carers.

Five Key Points

- People with learning disabilities are not a homogenous group: they have the same range of needs, feelings and aspirations as anyone else.
- A person-centred approach that gives individuals an opportunity to express their wishes, needs and preferences is important.
- People with learning disabilities have repeatedly said they want more opportunities to work, have relationships and live where and with whom they choose.
- Risk aversive practice can result in unnecessary restrictions on individual lives. Some risk-taking is part of everyday life: wherever possible, it should be assessed and supported.
- Social workers must be familiar with the legal and policy frameworks which form an essential backdrop to practice.

Three Questions

? How can social workers promote inclusion for people with learning disabilities?
? What are the implications of user empowerment for social work practice?
? In what, if any, circumstances should the right of people with learning disabilities to self-determination be curtailed?

Further reading

1 Sellars, C. (2002) *Risk Assessment in People with Learning Disabilities*. Oxford: Blackwell.
2 Thomas, D. and Woods, H. (2003) *Working with People with Learning Disabilities: Theory and Practice*. London: Jessica Kingsley.
3 Grant, G., Goward, G., Richardson, M. and Ramcharan, P. (eds.) (2005) *Learning Disability: A Life Cycle Approach to Valuing People*. Maidenhead: Open University Press.

CHAPTER 1.9

Alcohol or Drug Problems

Sarah Galvani

For centuries people have sought to alter their physical or mental state. Humans of all ages have found natural and manufactured ways of changing the way they are feeling. Consider the children in the school playground who hold hands and spin round and round until they fall over. This is fun because it makes them feel dizzy and wobbly. Or the adults who subject themselves to potentially high risk leisure activities such as abseiling, parachuting or scary amusement park rides, because of the physical and mental buzz they get from doing so. People are creative in finding ways to alter their physical, emotional or mental state.

Using alcohol or drugs is another way of achieving this. Most people who use substances never develop problems. Some will use drugs occasionally at levels that do not create problems for them. However, like the activities described above, alcohol and drug use is not without its risks. For some people, alcohol and drug use becomes problematic in a number of ways: they may experience problems in their intimate relationships, friendships and family lives, problems with their work or studies, problems with their finances, problems with their mental and physical health, and problems with the law.

With such people, social workers are on the front line and can offer a way of working that operates from a social model of care: a perspective that takes a holistic approach to a person's life, rather than focusing on one problem alone.

Prevalence

Alcohol

In the UK, the General Household Survey is the main source of data on alcohol consumption in the general population. In the 2004/5 survey, 73 per cent of men and 58 per cent of women had drunk alcohol in the previous week (Office for National Statistics, 2005b). Of these, 22 per cent of men and 9 per cent of women were classed as heavy drinkers. This does not mean they have problems with alcohol; people experience problems at lower and higher levels of alcohol consumption depending on a number of individual factors, including pre-existing health or financial problems.

There are no reliable figures on the number of people receiving help for their alcohol problems. Even if there were, the figure would only represent the number of people that seek formal help from an alcohol service. Other people with alcohol problems may not want help or may be successful in reducing, or stopping, their alcohol problem by themselves.

Drugs

Estimates of the number of people in the general population who use illicit drugs are based on surveys of a sample of the population. Roe (2005) found that more than one-third (34.5 per cent) of people aged between 16 and 59 had used illicit drugs in their lifetime, 11.3 per cent had used in the last 12 months, and 6.7 per cent in the last month. People older than 59 use illicit drugs but there are no UK figures available. Simply using illicit drugs does not mean somebody will develop a drug problem, although they may get into problems with the law. Many people will try one or more drugs once or twice, or may use them more often during a particular period of their lives. Most will not develop a problem with drugs and will decide either to continue using at a controlled level or to stop using altogether. Some will continue to use drugs, increasing the amount they use and the frequency and this can lead to problems.

The number of people with drug problems is difficult to estimate because the illegality of drug use means that many people's drug use will remain hidden until they seek help or are deemed to be putting themselves or other people at risk. The National Drug Treatment Monitoring Systems (NDTMS) records the number of people receiving formal interventions for their drug problem. In 2004/5, 160,450 people were registered on the database as receiving structured treatment (National Treatment Agency, 2006). This is likely to be only a small proportion of the people who are experiencing problems.

Drug and Alcohol Use

The effects of drugs and alcohol will differ from person to person. People feel the effects because of the impact they have on the body's central nervous system (CNS). However, there is no 'one size fits all' effect as it depends on a number of factors including a person's mood, what other substances have been taken, beliefs about the substance and how used to taking it they are.

Substances are often grouped by the biological impact they have on the CNS. These groups are:

- Drugs that *depress* the CNS, e.g. alcohol, tranquillizers, solvents and gases.
- Drugs that *stimulate* the CNS, e.g. speed, cocaine, crack-cocaine, ecstasy, caffeine, tobacco.

- Drugs that *alter perceptual function* (hallucinogens), e.g. LSD/Acid, magic mushrooms, cannabis.
- Drugs that *reduce pain*, e.g. heroin, opium, methadone, codeine.

The way people use the substance determines how quickly and intensely the effects are felt: injecting a drug into the bloodstream will have a more immediate effect than smoking the same drug.

There are many useful websites that provide details of drugs, alcohol and their effects, including:

- Alcohol Concern – www.alcoholconcern.org.uk
- Drugscope – www.drugscope.org.uk
- Social work, alcohol and drugs – www.swalcdrugs.org.uk

Why people use

One person's motivation to use alcohol or drugs is likely to be different from the next person. What is the same for everyone is that *nobody starts using alcohol or drugs expecting to, or intending to, develop a problem.* Some of the reasons people will start, or continue using substances include:

- to experience something new;
- to take a risk;
- to feel better;
- to escape emotional or psychological pain or stress, including memories of abuse;
- to rebel, fit in, or to forget work/home problems;
- for medical purposes;
- to celebrate or commiserate;
- to conform with cultural norms;
- . . . and to have fun.

For people who have been using alcohol or drugs frequently and at high levels, one of the reasons to continue using or drinking is to avoid the uncomfortable, and potentially painful, physical and psychiatric symptoms that can accompany withdrawal. The withdrawal process needs to be medically supervised and the person may need prescribed medication to help them deal with the symptoms.

People tend to cut down or stop their alcohol or drug use when the problems associated with it outweigh the benefits. This may be when a relationship is in jeopardy, when they lose their job or business, or when their physical or mental health deteriorates. It may also be when statutory agencies become involved: for example, if there is trouble with the police, or social services become concerned about the care of children. Whatever the motivation for reducing or stopping substance use, it is important for the person to have adequate support in place to help them reach and maintain their desired goal. Social workers' holistic approach means that they are well placed to help put this support in place.

Importance of Social Work Involvement

All social workers work with people who *use* alcohol and drugs, some of whom have alcohol and drug *problems*. For some social workers alcohol and drugs work will be their chosen area of specialist practice. For others, working with people with alcohol and drug problems will be just one aspect of their specialist focus. For example, work with people experiencing mental ill-health will include working with people who have both mental health and alcohol or drug problems, or working with children and families will include families where there are child protection concerns based on parental substance problems.

There are few estimates of the number of people with drug and alcohol problems receiving social work interventions. Most estimates are based on research with a selection of social work teams working with children and families. Current research suggests that approximately 25 per cent of children on child protection registers involve parental alcohol or drug use (Advisory Council on the Misuse of Drugs (ACMD) 2003) while higher estimates have been found among parents involved with children and families services more broadly. Hayden (2004) in a review of this research found estimates ranging from 20 per cent to 78 per cent. Kearney et al. (2000) report that social workers estimated that 50–90 per cent of parents on their caseloads had drug, alcohol or mental health problems.

Research data shows the use of alcohol and drugs by people that social workers often work with:

- 44 per cent of people with *mental ill-health* use substances in harmful or hazardous ways (Weaver et al., 2003).
- Among *older people*, 17 per cent of men and 7 per cent of women (over 65) drink above recommended limits (Alcohol Concern, 2002).
- In one study of *adult offenders* 69 per cent of arrestees tested positive for one or more illicit drug while 36 per cent tested positive for 2 or more drugs; 38 per cent tested positive for opiates and/or cocaine (Holloway and Bennett, 2004).
- *Young offenders* have high levels of lifetime substance use although this varies according to the drug used. Alcohol, cannabis and tobacco are the substances used most (Hammersley et al., 2003).
- Among *young people aged 11–15*, research shows that the *amount* of alcohol they drink has doubled in the last 20 years (Institute of Alcohol Studies, 2006). Similarly young people have higher levels of illicit drug use than their adult counterparts: 19 per cent of secondary school children had used in the last 12 months, 11 per cent in the last month (The Information Centre, 2006).
- Of *young adults* (aged 16–24) 26.3 per cent had used drugs in the last year and 16.3 per cent in the last month (The Information Centre, 2006). For alcohol, 47 per cent of young men had exceeded the daily benchmarks as had 39 per cent of young women (Office for National Statistics, 2005b).
- There are no prevalence data in the UK on alcohol or drug use among people with *physical or learning disabilities* but US data suggest that 40–60 per cent of people in these service user groups use substances.

- There is a huge overlap between *domestic abuse* and substance use. Among women with substance problems estimates consistently suggest that approximately two-thirds of women have suffered domestic abuse in their lifetimes (see Galvani and Humphreys, 2005).

People who have problems with alcohol and drugs often have a *negative impact on other people in the family*, including partners, parents, siblings and children. Family members are at risk of psychological and physical harm but are often overlooked by alcohol or drug services which tend to focus on the individual alone. It is important that social workers identify and assess the needs of family members and offer them support in their own right. Research has shown that this helps to reduce their physical and psychological suffering and has a positive impact on the substance use of the person with the drug or alcohol problem (Copello et al., 2000, 2006; UKATT Research Team, 2005).

A social work perspective

Social workers work primarily with the social harms relating to alcohol and drug problems, although often these will overlap with health concerns. Social harms include the impact that alcohol and drug problems can have on a parent's ability to take care of the children, a young person's offending behaviour or a person with mental health problems whose substance use is putting themselves, or others, at risk of harm.

The impact of social context

Consider the difference between two people trying to reduce or stop their drug use:

- Trevor is a home owner in a middle-class neighbourhood, with a supportive partner, family and friends, no immediate financial crisis, and an employer who is giving him time off work to 'get himself sorted'.
- Roz is a single unemployed parent. She has been re-housed on an estate after escaping an abusive and violent partner. Both the domestic abuse and her drug use have left her isolated from her family and friends. The housing conditions are poor, there is a high crime rate and few local amenities. The children have nowhere to play because the playground is unsafe and repeatedly vandalized. Her only support is her drug using friends. She is in trouble with the police and social services have become involved after a neighbour became concerned about the children being left alone in the flat.

While both people face the same challenge of overcoming their drug problem, it is easy to see how the person's environment and social context is likely to help or hinder them during this process.

The social work approach looks at more than just the person's substance problem. It recognizes that the person may have a number of problems and is prepared to work with those too. A social work perspective should not view the person solely as an 'alcoholic' or 'addict'. Such terms are labelling and stigmatizing. They identify the person by a problem rather than as a person who has a number of identities – parent, colleague or friend. This distinction is important both for the person's sense of self-efficacy and their self-esteem. Using labels implies that addressing the alcohol or drug use will solve all the person's problems. This is not the reality as people with substance problems usually have other problems that predate their substance use and may have exacerbated it in the first place.

The importance of a supportive environment in helping someone overcome their alcohol or drug problem is portrayed by McCarthy's SCARS model (see Figure 1) (McCarthy and Galvani, 2004). It helps workers to analyse quickly what support a person has in place and where they may need help to plug the gaps. SCARS (or the Six Cornered Addiction Rescue System) uses a 'safety net' image to show that when a person has only one corner of the net supported, for example alcohol or drug treatment, the safety net is unlikely to support them. The more areas of a person's life that are stable or supported, the more likely it is that the safety net will hold them and help them to successfully reach their desired goal in relation to their alcohol or drug use.

The SCARS model operates from a perspective that problems are interlinked and, by meeting peoples' needs in a number of areas, their chances of successfully overcoming their problems will be maximized.

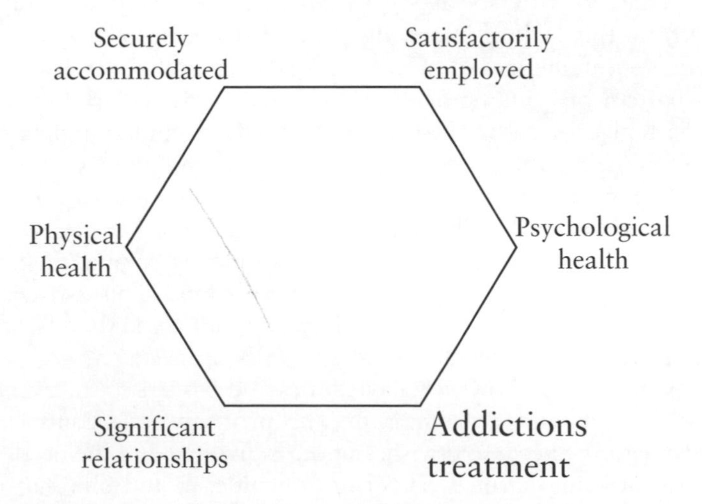

Figure 1 The Six Cornered Addiction Rescue System

Value Base

A lot of shame and stigma are attached to alcohol or drug problems. This is often exacerbated by media-enhanced stereotypes of the 'junkie' or 'alcy' that portray people as being weak-willed, liars and undeserving. The values and principles of social work reject such stereotypes and place emphasis on treating people with respect regardless of their circumstances.

People with alcohol and drug problems are used to being avoided and treated with suspicion. Anti-oppressive practice rejects such discriminatory behaviours; instead it respects people by working with them and understanding that each individual is the expert in their own lives and problems. It listens in a non-judgmental way and recognizes that the person's social, cultural and environmental context may need to be discussed in relation to what type of intervention or support they need.

People suffering alcohol or drug problems often report feeling out of control, not knowing who to ask for help or how to change their behaviour and the way they feel. Social workers are in a strong position to support someone in this situation due to the profession's commitment to working in an empowering way, helping the user regain a sense of power and control over problematic parts of their life, and so obtain increased confidence to make positive and healthy choices.

Challenges and Opportunities

Working with people with alcohol and drug problems provides both challenges and opportunities for social workers. One of the challenges is dealing with the frustration that the work involves. Social workers report a sense of frustration about how to intervene and work well with alcohol and drug problems. This is not helped by the lack of training they receive about alcohol and drugs on social work qualifying programmes. Nor does it reflect the prevalence of people with alcohol and drug problems in contact with social work services. The other frustration, which stems partly from this lack of knowledge, is that of seeing people with alcohol or drug problems repeatedly in and out of the 'revolving door' of services. Changing a long-term pattern of drinking or drug use is hard, particularly if people do not know what to replace it with. They can make many attempts to change their substance use before being able to do so. It is frustrating for the social worker to see the emotional, physical and psychological roller coaster that the individual and family go through during this difficult change process.

One of the important roles a social worker can play is helping them fill the void that reducing or stopping their substance use leaves behind. This is why a supportive environment is so important. Most people, however motivated they are, feel ambivalent about changing their substance use.

The social worker does, however, have duties and powers to intervene to protect vulnerable adults and children from harm. This protective and controlling role has to be balanced with the needs and wishes of the individual and the needs and wishes of those at risk of being harmed. This is a difficult task and one that needs to be made after consultation with service users and professional colleagues.

These conflicting demands are often mirrored in working relationships with alcohol and drug specialists. Historically, there has been a lack of mutual understanding between social workers and specialist alcohol and drugs staff, based on ignorance of each others' roles, priorities and referral and intervention procedures. In order to work well with other specialists it is important to understand the agencies' priorities as well as ask what they can and cannot disclose about their work with the person. It is also important to communicate what information or advice the social worker would like and why. Arranging joint interventions with the service user, social worker and specialist alcohol or drugs worker, as well as any individual meetings, is likely to be a more supportive and effective way of working with the individual and, where appropriate, their family.

A key challenge arises in working with someone who is denying their alcohol or drug problem or is unable to see the problems or harms related to it. It is unsurprising that people will not easily disclose their substance problems to a social worker because of the illegality of drug use, and the shame and stigma attached to problematic alcohol or drug use. Where the person has children, they may fear that they will be removed following disclosure of substance use. Overcoming this hurdle requires skilled communication and intervention on the part of the social worker. People are unlikely to disclose sensitive information if they feel threatened and defensive. The social worker needs to show understanding of the person's situation by listening to them, acknowledging and highlighting the person's strengths, and discussing the benefits the person gets from continuing their alcohol or drug use. The social worker is then in a better position to discuss openly and honestly their concerns, their statutory duties, and negotiate a way forward.

In spite of the challenges of working with people with alcohol and drug problems there are also huge personal and professional rewards. The nature of the work is never dull; every person and every situation is different. It involves working with and for a group of people who are often viewed as undeserving of help by professionals and public alike. At times, it involves protecting people from themselves and protecting others from the harm they may cause. Importantly, it is about supporting people who have a serious challenge ahead in terms of changing their problematic substance use. This means establishing what support they need to maximize their chances of success. It also involves an educative role that may be related to their alcohol or drug use, or may be about its impact on their children or their physical or mental health.

Social workers see people's lives turned around by working with people on their drug and alcohol problem and supporting them through the change process. Problematic substance use can affect every aspect of a person's life. Stopping or reducing their problematic use can have a hugely positive impact on their physical health and appearance, their psychological well-being and their social and family lives.

Conclusion

Social workers are ideally placed to work with people with alcohol and drug problems. Social work training and the principles which underpin the profession commit it to a holistic approach – working with the whole person rather than one aspect alone. A social work approach emphasizes the importance of a supportive environment to a person's ability to overcome their problems. Social workers recognize and build on a person's strengths.

The challenges and frustrations of working with people with alcohol and drug problems are outweighed by the rewards of seeing people regain self-esteem and personal control as they begin the difficult journey of changing their problematic substance use. Important, too, are the benefits this reaps for their children, family and friendships.

Five Key Points

- Don't be judgmental: nobody starts using drugs or alcohol intending to develop a problem.
- A social work model works with the whole person not just the person's alcohol or drug problem.
- Alcohol or drugs can be a way of coping with problems as well as potentially creating them.
- Helping people to develop a supportive social environment will help them overcome their alcohol or drug problem.
- Families and partners of people with alcohol or drug problems need support in their own right too.

Three Questions

? What are some of the reasons that people develop problems with alcohol or drugs?

? What are the key elements of a social work approach to working with people with alcohol or drug problems?

? To what extent can someone's environment or social context help or hinder their attempts to overcome their alcohol or drug problem?

Further reading

1 Barber, J. (2002) *Social Work with Addictions*, 2nd edn. Basingstoke: Palgrave Macmillan.

2 Petersen, T. and McBride, A. (2002) *Working with Substance Misusers: A Guide to Theory and Practice.* London: Routledge.

3 Stockwell, T., Greunewald, P., Toumbourou, J. and Loxley, W. (eds.) (2005) *Preventing Harmful Substance Use: The Evidence Base for Policy and Practice.* Chichester: John Wiley and Sons.

CHAPTER 1.10

Population Movement and Immigration

Beth Humphries

People across the world have always been on the move, and it is estimated that at any one time around 2 per cent of the world's population is in movement. In the late twentieth century and into the twenty-first, patterns of migration have changed as a result of globalization, which has brought new challenges for nation-states and for the concept of citizenship, bringing with it a growing international mobility, some of it voluntary and some of it forced. Contradictory trends have ensued. On the one hand, the boundaries of the nation-state are being eroded, as Castles and Davidson (2000, p. viii) point out:

> Millions of people have multiple citizenships and live in more than one country. Millions more do not live in their country of citizenship. Governments find that their power to control the economy, the welfare system and national culture is being eroded. Global markets, transnational corporations, regional and supra-national bodies, and a new pervasive international culture are all gaining in influence. The idea of the citizen who spent most of his or her life in one country and shared a common national identify is losing ground.

At the same time globalization has seen increased instability in a number of countries, resulting in ill-health, poverty and rising rates of child and mother mortality. Wars, ethnic cleansing and social disruption result in people fleeing from their countries of origin (Hayter, 2000). As a result many countries, especially in rich parts of the world, attempt to control their borders, to dictate who may come and go freely and who should be dissuaded or prevented from entering. In its extreme forms such control can involve high intensity lighting, high steel fencing, body-heat-and-motion-detecting sensors and video surveillance as at the USA/Mexico and the Spain/Morocco borders, and around Gibraltar (Nevins, 2002).

The European Union represents the formation of a regional market economy, characterized by the internal free movement of capital, goods and labour across member countries, but with heavily reinforced frontiers in a trend towards exclusion of non-EU citizens. Moreover, millions of people who have succeeded in gaining entry are disenfranchised because they cannot become citizens in their country of residence, and indeed in some cases are ejected from or starved out of it. Thus inequality is also a feature of globalization. Growing inequalities in wealth and health are apparent both between industrialized and 'underdeveloped' countries and amongst different social groups within countries. In summary, immigration controls exist both externally (through before-entry and on-entry border checks) and internally (through identity checks linked to work and benefits entitlements).

Immigration in the UK

Britain has always been a country of both emigration and immigration, and has benefited economically and culturally from people who came here from the New Commonwealth in particular (that is, former British colonies, mainly in Africa, the Indian sub-continent and the Caribbean), and from the Republic of Ireland. Immigration *controls* are a relatively recent phenomenon, with the first legislation at the turn of the twentieth century (although there had been a number of attempts to keep out 'undesirables' over several centuries). This was widely regarded as an attempt to prevent Jews from coming to Britain after fleeing pogroms in Eastern Europe (Hayes, 2002). After the 1939–45 war immigrants were welcomed as a valuable source of labour in the re-building of the country, especially in the new National Health Service and more generally in the Welfare State. Later, the perceived needs of the economy resulted in successively tighter restrictions, and by 1971 primary immigration from the New Commonwealth had largely come to an end. Since then, immigration for *settlement* was increasingly restricted and migrant workers have been recruited (mainly for restricted periods) to match labour requirements.

It is important to emphasize that not all prospective immigrants were targeted by immigration controls. Changes in the law on British citizenship during the 1970s and 1980s resulted in removal of an automatic right to British citizenship from mainly people who were non-white (but not from those with British ancestry such as many white Australians, Canadians, Zimbabweans and South Africans). Some immigration for the purpose of family reunion was allowed, provided the applicant could provide sufficient proof that the family was a genuine one. Throughout the history of immigration controls, the notions of 'race', nation and belonging have either been explicit or implicit themes in the debates.

From time to time in Britain and other European countries there is a shortage of skilled and unskilled labour, and special arrangements can be made to attract people from abroad to fill these gaps. Moreover, the flow has not been all one way. In the 1950s, 1960s and 1970s there was considerable return migration from Britain, resulting in a substantial net migration pattern during the twentieth century. It is well known that there has been a small increase in the UK population, and that over a third of residents are people over retirement age. This is balanced by over half of in-migrants being in the 25–44 age range (Office for National Statistics, 2004b), able to work to support an ageing minority. In these ways immigration continues to bring benefits to British national and economic life.

Asylum Seekers and Refugees

Although the topic of immigration is a much wider one than asylum seekers, encompassing people coming to work in the UK, to settle, to join family members, to visit, and so on, since the early 1990s immigration discourses have been dominated by the 'problem' of refugees and asylum seekers. The distinction of 'refugees' from 'asylum seekers' is a false one in that the people involved are all fleeing from inhuman conditions in their home countries. It is rather an administrative convenience to distinguish between those whose applications for asylum have been accepted, who have been granted leave to remain in the UK and therefore have 'refugee status'; and those whose application has been made but who have not yet received a decision, or have received a negative decision and are appealing or awaiting removal from the country.

The UK has an obligation under the 1951 UN Convention Relating to the Status of Refugees and its 1967 Protocol Convention, to grant refuge in the UK on humanitarian grounds to those with a 'well-founded fear of persecution'. The level of applications for asylum is largely determined by events in other parts of the world, so numbers fluctuate as crises erupt elsewhere. Only about 15 per cent of applications are successful. In the early years of the twenty-first century the estimate was of approximately 260,000 asylum seekers living in the UK (Humphries, 2006), and as a result of measures taken by the government to discourage applications, numbers have been falling consistently.

Although asylum seekers are people who are fleeing persecution in their home countries, they have become unpopular politically, and are perceived as an object of fear and suspicion, 'the luminous apparition at the foot of the bed' (Harding, 2000, p. 51). There is a wide assumption that most are 'economic migrants', their applications are 'bogus', that they come to benefit from generous health and welfare provisions, and that large numbers are in the UK illegally. This hostility is linked to other discourses about 'race' and the difficulties of 'race relations'. Most asylum seekers come from countries in Africa, Asia and Eastern Europe, and are black, Muslim or both, and they therefore are seen as 'not belonging' to the British nation. The focus on their experiences of torture, rape, war and murder is lost in a climate of Islamophobia, and they are treated with suspicion, resulting in their becoming an oppressed and marginalized group.

Asylum Seekers and Welfare

This climate of disbelief is reflected in social policies that impact directly on asylum seekers, which have become increasingly restrictive. At one time they were allowed to seek work after a period of being in the UK, but this provision has been removed (even so, amongst refugees who *do* have permission to work, the unemployment rate is likely to be more than 75 per cent [Humphries et al., 2004]). In terms of support, asylum seekers have since 1999 been removed from the normal systems of welfare, and are dealt with under a parallel and indeed inferior system. Asylum seekers who register with the National Asylum Support Service (NASS), operating under the auspices of the Home Office and not the Department of Health, the government department responsible for other aspects of health and welfare, are given accommodation and financial support, but are severely restricted in terms of the benefits they receive. No choice is offered to them regarding housing, which could be in any part of the country under the policy of dispersal. There are restrictions related to absence from the accommodation. Weekly income is worth around two-thirds of income support (regarded as the lowest possible subsistence level for families). They do not receive any benefits available to working or job-seeking families or core means-tested benefits of last resort (housing benefit, council tax benefit, a social fund payment), or family and disability benefits (child benefits, attendance allowance, disability living allowance, severe disablement allowance, invalid care allowance). Where they are supported by NASS, asylum seekers cannot seek support from local authorities under national assistance or children's legislation. They can be detained or tagged without a court order.

Local authorities do have responsibility for the care of some groups of asylum seekers. Community care legislation requires local authorities to undertake needs assessment for some groups such as disabled people, those with mental health problems or suffering the effects of old age, but *not* in cases where the need arises solely because they are destitute. Local authorities are also responsible for unaccompanied asylum-seeking children, and are expected to provide accommodation and education, and to support young people until the age of 18.

Criticism of the system has been widespread, including from respected organizations such as the Oxfam and Refugee Council (2002) and Save the Children (Stanley, 2001). Amnesty International (2000, p. 32) has commented that asylum is an area of UK law where the 'best interests' of the child does not play a part and where the protection of the child is not a paramount concern. Research for these reports found that young people often received only accommodation and no other services and were placed in unsuitable settings with older men. The Oxfam/Refugee Council report concluded that 'asylum seekers are forced to live at a level of poverty that is unacceptable in a civilised society' (p. 1).

Social workers and other state professionals have been faced with a number of ethical dilemmas in working in the area of asylum. They are required to report to central government anyone seeking services who is not entitled to them. They are expected to make judgments about eligibility to services of both adults and children, based on immigration status, rather than respond to need as it is presented to them. They are expected to decide on whether a person is 'destitute'. They have been drawn into age assessment of young people, an imprecise task at the best of times and the outcome of which has profound implications for whether a child receives support. Their decisions regarding which section of the legislation is appropriate have implications for leaving care support for a young person or on reaching the age of 18. With regard to families whose claim for asylum has been refused, benefits are withdrawn, and social workers are expected to take children into the public care where families are made destitute. This is one of the grounds the children's legislation was explicitly aimed at preventing. The Home Office has emphasized that all branches of the state should come together to prevent abuse of services, thus effectively pressing health and social work professionals into a policing role (Humphries, 2002). The British Association of Social Workers has protested at the imposition of this role, a sign that the social work profession is beginning to reconsider the authoritarian function expected of it, and to attempt to recapture its values of anti-oppressive and anti-discriminatory practice. Other professional organizations, such as those representing midwives, teachers, university lecturers as well as some trades unions, have all affirmed their opposition to immigration controls. In resolving to clarify the limits of their practice and their ethical responsibilities, and attempting to influence the direction of policies on immigration and asylum, health and welfare professionals will be deciding on their direction for the foreseeable future. The need for support to groups affected will not diminish for many years to come.

Five Key Points

- Movement of people is a normal occurrence, but globalization has accelerated the numbers forcibly displaced.
- Immigration and asylum policies are concerned with *control*, not necessarily *exclusion.*
- 'Race' is an ongoing sub-text in discourses about immigration and asylum.
- Asylum seekers in the UK are an oppressed and marginalized group who are given inferior levels of benefits, services and accommodation.
- Health and social care professionals have been drawn into internal controls in a number of ways, raising ethical questions about their role.

Three Questions

? What are some of the stereotypes of asylum seekers, and how have these affected services provided to them?

? What are some of the dilemmas for professionals in checking eligibility for services?

? What options do health and welfare professions have for resisting their policing role with asylum seekers?

Further reading

1 Cohen, S., Humphries, B. and Mynott, E. (eds.) (2002) *From Immigration Controls to Welfare Controls*. London: Routledge.
2 Segal, U. (ed.) (2006) *Immigration Worldwide*. New York: Haworth Press.
3 Hayes, D. and Humphries, B. (forthcoming) *Social Work with Asylum Seekers and Refugees*. Cambridge: Polity Press.

PART 2

Applying Knowledge to Practice

CHAPTER 2.1

Relating Theory to Practice

David Howe

In their day-to-day practice, social workers face a busy and complex world of human behaviour in a social context. It is a world in which relationships break down, emotions run high, and personal needs go unmet, a world in which some people have problems and some people are problems.

If they are to function in this confused mix of psychological upset and social concern, practitioners must begin to see pattern and order behind the tumult. They must try to understand and *make sense* of people and the situations in which they find themselves. Striving to make sense of experience is a fundamental characteristic of being human. If we are to cope with and be competent in social situations, we need to have ideas about what might be going on. This need becomes pressing in situations where need, stress and upset are present in large measure. Professionals who work in such situations develop more deliberate, systematic and formalized ways of making sense. It is these more self-conscious attempts to 'make sense' which we call 'theory'.

If social workers are to act clearly, competently and usefully in practical situations, they need to think theoretically. If we did not theorize, social life would remain a cauldron of unorganized experience and to all intents and purposes all practical action would be impossible. The join between theory and practice is a seamless one. And, it has often been said, there is nothing so practical as a good theory.

If practice is to be compassionate as well as appropriate, it is important that social workers retain a deep interest in people. The struggle to understand behaviour and relationships, actions and decisions, attitudes and motivations needs to be maintained at all times if practice is to be sensitive and effective. The more social workers think about, puzzle over and engage with people and the situations in which they find themselves, the more sense they will be able to make. The challenge is to remain curious about and thoroughly interested in people. The social worker needs constantly to ask herself the 'reason why' of things, to develop an active and enquiring mind. Why does this woman stay with her violent husband? Why is this four-year-old child so subdued and withdrawn? Why does this daughter feel so hostile towards her increasingly dependent 81-year-old mother? So, although there is no consensus about which theories best explain particular situations, there is agreement that practitioners who develop and offer coherent understandings of what might be going on are those best able to keep their professional bearings and sustain personal commitment. Both abilities are highly prized by the users of social work services.

The argument is that by analysing practice and reflecting on people's needs and relationships, social workers become clearer about their theoretical assumptions. However, it is also possible to turn this process around. As well as *induce* theory from practice and observation, it is also possible to *deduce* from theory what to do and what to see. The social worker in possession of a clear theoretical outlook finds that it guides and influences her practice in five key areas:

1 *Observation*: it tells her what to see and what to look out for.
2 *Description*: it provides a conceptual vocabulary and framework within which observations can be arranged and organized.
3 *Explanation*: it suggests how different observations might be linked and connected; it offers possible causal relationships between one event and another.
4 *Prediction*: it indicates what might happen next.
5 *Intervention*: it suggests things to do to bring about change.

Different theories, of course, lead to different observations and explanations. For example, in the case of a difficult toddler, the behaviourist notes that the young mother reinforces her child's poor behaviour by only giving him attention when he is naughty; the feminist practitioner is struck by the mother's stress, low self-worth and lack of support from her oppressive partner; and the social worker using a developmental perspective observes that the mother, who was neglected herself as a child, grows anxious and agitated when her son becomes too demanding and dependent. This is not to argue that these three observations are mutually exclusive. However, in practice it is often the case that a practitioner with a strong theoretical preference is inclined to observe, describe, explain, predict and intervene in a style and a language that is noticeably different from a social worker holding a contrasting theoretical outlook.

The Social Work Process

A simple but effective way of exploring the relationship between theory and practice is to ask a series of seemingly innocuous questions about a case or a piece of practice. By insisting on clear answers to these questions, the practitioner finds that she is able to reflect on matters at a surprisingly deep level. It is during this reflection process and the answer-giving stage that the relationship between theory and practice becomes explicit and available for discussion. Five questions can be asked of a case or piece of work:

1 *What is the matter?* This question helps the social worker define problems and identify needs. Supplementary questions might include: For whom is it a problem? Who benefits if the need is met?

2 *What is going on?* This is perhaps the most important question. It demands that the situation is assessed, analysed, diagnosed, interpreted or explained. The social worker makes sense of what is going on.
3 *What is to be done?* In the light of the assessment, goals are set, objectives identified, plans made and intentions declared.
4 *How is it to be done?* The methods, techniques, skills, services and resources needed to achieve the goals are chosen and deployed.
5 *Has it been done?* The outcome is reviewed and evaluated.

Different theories sponsor different answers to these five questions. But whatever the response, the answers and activities map out the basic features of the *social work process* with its five-stage sequence of: (1) the formulation of problems and the identification of needs, (2) the analysis of cases and the making of an assessment, (3) the setting of goals and objectives, (4) the design of methods of work and intervention, and (5) the review and evaluation of the involvement. This process describes a sequence and a structure to help social workers practise in a thoughtful and systematic way. It provides the basis of a disciplined and professional social work practice. It is also designed to overcome the tendency of social workers and their agencies to jump from problem to solution in one bound. Within the social work process, considerable importance is given to the stage of assessment. This is a time for reflection, enquiry and vigorous analysis. Assessments encourage practitioners to stop and think about what is going on. They provoke thought and liberate practice from the routine and humdrum.

Theories for Social Work

Things might be relatively simple and straightforward if social work was underpinned by one or two generally agreed theories for practice. In any one case the five questions of the social work process would receive a limited range of acceptable answers. Unfortunately, the theoretical world underpinning social work practice is a far from stable place. Because social workers deal with people in social situations, most of their theories, albeit adapted to the social work context, derive ultimately from psychology and sociology.

However, these primary disciplines have not established a consensus about the true character of human nature, individual development and social interaction. Although they strive to 'make sense' of people and society, the range of theories and understandings on offer are numerous and diverse. Sociology and psychology provide intellectual arenas in which fierce debates rage about the individual and society, the personal and the political, order and conflict, biology and culture, free will and determinism, causal explanation and subjective understanding. To the extent that social work's theories are based on psychological and sociological theories, they, too, will reflect the range, diversity and disagreements present in the parent disciplines.

So long as these epistemological disputes exist, there can be no universally agreed criteria by which to judge social work's theories and practices. This is not to say that some theories will not be preferred at certain times and in particular places.

Political and cultural factors also come into play and influence what is thought and what is done in the name of good social work. Nevertheless, social work theory remains a highly varied and contested activity. If the argument holds good that in practice there is no escape from theory, the social worker, denied an Archimedean point, needs to understand how and why different psychological and sociological theories vary as they do. Rather than bemoan the number and range of theories, the practitioner needs to acknowledge that the diversity reflects the subtlety and complexity of the human condition. Appreciation of the elegance and multi-dimensionality of these conceptual landscapes can be highly stimulating.

Types of Theory

Many frameworks and taxonomies have been developed to help practitioners find their way around social work's theories. The attempts to classify the theories rely on recognizing a limited range of key conceptual dimensions, various combinations of which help to define particular sets of related theories. At root, most of the classifications draw on discussions about human nature, the relative importance of biology, culture and experience in human development, and the social movements and ideological climates that define and shape human society (see Turner, 1996; Howe, 1987; Payne, 2005a). Mapping out social work's theoretical terrain helps practitioners locate themselves intellectually and invites them to explore new areas of thought and practice.

Although in some circles there is a coming together of psychology and sociology, these two disciplines still create one of the main divisions in social work theory between structural and psychological explanations of personal difficulty. Within the structural perspective, the focus is on the political, economic and material environment in which people find themselves. The approach includes anti-oppressive and anti-discriminatory perspectives. Poverty and inequality, the lack of opportunity and social injustice seriously disadvantage some people. The disadvantages induce stress, anxiety and 'poor social functioning'. Such problems bring them to the attention of society and its agents. However, structural theorists maintain that for these groups, the individual should not be seen as a problem for society, rather society should be seen as a problem for the individual. This outlook influences the way problems are defined, the type of assessment made, the goals planned and the social methods employed.

In practice, though, most social work theories remain heavily influenced by the more psychological approaches to human behaviour. There are many ways in which these psychological theories can be categorized. Most rely on making particular assumptions about human nature and the ways in which we learn, develop and respond. One simple division is to see whether a particular theory emphasizes either the client's emotional condition or his or her capacity for rational action.

Theories which pay most attention to the emotional side of people's lives and the quality of their relationships seek to understand present behaviour in terms of past experiences. The character of our relationship history influences our personality and social competence. As most social work clients experience or express difficulty in one or more of their key relationships (with partners, parents or children), it seems appropriate to try and understand the quality of their social and interpersonal development and how it might be affecting current behaviour. Understanding, support, nurturing, the meeting of emotional and developmental needs, containment and insight are present in many of the practices associated with these theories. By understanding past events, the client and the worker might be able to contain or make sense of current experiences. Making sense allows people to gain control of the meaning of their own experience and move into the future with a more robust, mature, independent and strengthened personality. Such a personality is likely to be more socially competent, and socially competent people handle relationships more effectively. Altering the meaning of experience brings about changes in behaviour.

Theories of this persuasion include all those which take a developmental perspective. They are person-focused. They consider people from the psychological inside. Psychoanalytic theory, attachment theory, theories of loss and separation, many forms of feminist theory and elements of the person-centred approach can all be placed within this broad category of developmentally orientated and relationship-sensitive approaches to social work practice.

Theories which appeal to clients' rational capacities and cognitive strengths tend to adopt a problem-solving approach. These approaches are based on the belief that people with problems can resolve them by the use of rational thought, cognitive understanding and behavioural advice. Practitioners work with clients in problem-solving partnerships. Typically, the approach involves:

- the identification, description and quantification of the problem;
- analysis of the factors, including the behaviour of other people, which maintain the problem;
- the selection of goals;
- the identification and implementation of those actions which will achieve the goals and resolve the problem.

Based on an analysis of present conditions, problem-solving approaches encourage clients to identify what steps they will need to take if they wish to move themselves into a problem-free future. Practice is often pragmatic, time limited and task-centred. People are viewed from the behavioural outside. The belief is that by changing behaviour, personal experience is improved.

Social work theories that fall into this category include task-centred approaches, cognitive-behavioural theories, many forms of family therapy, brief solution-focused therapy and some aspects of systems theory.

Theory and Practice in Social Context

One further layer of analysis has to be added if we are to gain a full understanding of the relationship between social work theory and practice. Social work takes place and is formed within a social and political context. It occupies and is defined by the space between the personal and the political in which the state relates to the individual and the individual relates to the state. So, although social work practices need the help of the psychological and sociological sciences if they are to make sense of people in social difficulty, the *purposes* of social work and its practices are defined by a different set of intellectual traditions.

In the broadest sense, the purposes of social work are determined by prevailing political values. These values influence welfare legislation, political policy, government guidelines, and the distribution and definition of resources. The politically defined purposes of social work also influence the psychological and sociological theories chosen by practitioners to help them 'make sense' and practise.

Political philosophies which emphasize collective responsibility and action also value harmony and cooperation, equality and interdependence. They support theories and practices which are more structural, developmental and therapeutic in their outlook. Psychologically healthy development occurs only if the individual is embedded in a good quality social environment. A sense of belonging and being wanted in a community of close personal relationships is essential if a secure and coherent personality is to form.

A case example

Anna is aged 10. She lives with her mother and two younger brothers, aged 5 and 3 years. Anna's mother suffers depression. The family live in a large apartment block in a very disadvantaged part of the city. The school authorities have expressed concern about Anna's increasingly poor school attendance record.

Think of as many reasons as you can that might explain Anna's school attendance problem. What is the theoretical basis of each explanation?

When the political pendulum shifts away from welfare collectivism towards neoliberal concepts of freedom, choice and personal responsibility in the context of a market economy, theories and practices tend towards the brief and the behavioural (Howe, 1996). The individual is seen as independent and free, disembedded from and unconstrained (and not limited) by his or her social environment. Such freedom and autonomy allows full scope for creative endeavour and the rational pursuit of what is in one's own best interests. Morally and psychologically, the individual must stand alone. Individuals are personally responsible for who they are and what they become, for what they do and how they do it. This represents a shift away from explaining people's psychological insides to measuring their behavioural outsides. The external performance, of both worker and client, becomes the unit of audit. *What* people do is more important than *why* they do it. Economic and political partnerships replace therapeutic relationships. The theories which come to the fore in this political climate are those which encourage brief, task-centred and behaviourally measurable practices in which the act rather than the actor becomes the focus of interest.

Summary

Practice, as defined by the social work process, varies as practitioners make use of different theories. Theories vary as they appeal to different understandings of human nature, personal development and society. And different theories come in and out of fashion as political values and social philosophies change with the flow of large social movements through history. Just as theory relates to practice, so practice relates to theory. Only the faint-hearted despair at the inordinate subtlety of personal experience and social life. So long as social workers retain a passionate interest in and concern for the quality of human experience, and so long as they strive to 'make sense', the relationship between theory and practice will continue to invigorate, fascinate and professionally uplift.

Five Key Points

- Social work theories help practitioners make sense of complex and difficult human situations.
- Different social work theories generate different understandings of human behaviour and social situations.
- The social work process of 'defining problems and needs – making an assessment – setting goals – carrying out methods to achieve those goals', describes a sequence and a structure which helps social workers practise in a systematic way.
- Social workers who use theory to inform their use of the social work process are more likely to practise in a thoughtful and professional manner.
- The purposes of social work and the theories which support them vary depending on the cultural context in which social work finds itself.

Three Questions

? How might different social work theories explain or make sense of the same case or social situation?

? What assumptions does a particular social work theory make about (a) human nature; (b) the influence of human biology, culture and social experience on personal development; and (c) appropriate political and personal values?

? In particular cases and situations, how do different social work theories influence the content of the social work process?

Further reading

1 Payne, M. (2005a) *Modern Social Work Theory*, 3rd edn. Basingstoke: Palgrave Macmillan.
2 Beckett, C. (2006) *Essential Theory for Social Work Practice*. London: Sage.
3 Coulshed, V. and Orme, J. (2006) *Social Work Practice: An Introduction*, 4th edn. Basingstoke: Palgrave Macmillan.

CHAPTER 2.2

Assessment, Intervention and Review

Jonathan Parker

The dynamic and complex arena of human need demands deployment of flexible, creative and negotiated responses from social work and social care services. At times, the mutable and constantly evolving nature of social life and interactions has militated against the development of sound scientific and systematized approaches to practice that build on evidence and provide a framework for social work practice which enables service users and their carers to engage in a clear process and assists practitioners in implementing structured and knowledge-based work with people. This is clearly untenable for a profession seeking to make a difference in the lives of people who are often vulnerable, marginalized and excluded. It is imperative that social work demonstrates the 'hows' and the 'whys' of its importance to contemporary society: in other words, showing its evidence base in a transparent way that also allows challenge and development to take place.

This chapter will introduce a systematic model for understanding some of the key processes involved in social work practice in a range of contemporary practice settings, namely assessment, intervention and review. Account will be taken of the complexities and challenges raised by working in human situations which are necessarily fluid, and the need for artistry and flexibility in applying the model and developing a clear evidence base will be stressed (Trinder, 2000).

Social Work: Its Roles, Tasks and Purposes

To a large extent the development of social work has been associated with the fragmentation of communities, a decline in the influence of traditional regulatory frameworks (whether political, social, familial or religious), and the anomie associated with social transition from agrarian to industrial economies. Its development, in modern forms, began in the West and has become embedded within the social and political landscapes associated with social regulation as much as it has with social change. This tension permeates social work thought and practice and provides the context for examining a systematic approach. The questions concerning the care and control functions and tasks of social work relate in part to questions of individual values, but also to the purposes for which agencies have been set up (their mandate), and to the legislative base which underpins the work. These aspects are built on wider social constructions that have been developed and generally concern social care and appropriate treatment of individuals, groups and communities. Social work practises within this context but has a broader professional perspective that enjoins with and promotes the principles of social justice.

Social work is a discipline that has unapologetically 'borrowed' many key concepts and theories on which it bases its practice. However, these are employed in particular situations with people at the margins of society with a view to assisting people to function, engage and challenge the structures that have led to their exclusion from society. In their work, social workers have developed and internalized a wisdom that is tacit and intuitive, built upon experiences and nuances within the social work relationship which cannot always be easily categorized and labelled. However, this 'artistic' approach to social work practice is not the whole story, and social workers need to develop the evidence base for their intuitions, for the practices they have developed, borrowed and repackaged if they are to convince their political masters and the general public who fund social services that they are valuable, if they are to justify their work to their agencies and teams, if they are to develop as practitioners and, most crucially of all, if they are to provide the best possible service to the people with whom they work. Some of the theories underpinning the processes of assessment, intervention and review within this chapter are taken from other disciplines but they have been modified in the context of social work practice. They are used in flexible and artistic ways drawing on practice wisdom but also grounded in established evidence-based practice that can be demonstrated as fit for the purpose for which they are deployed or to effect change.

A Systematic Model for Practice

There are different elements within the models that have been developed to describe social work practice. N. Thompson (2005) suggests there are five stages to the process – assessment, intervention, review, ending and evaluation. Elsewhere, I have suggested four stages to the process (Parker and Bradley, 2003; Parker, 2007) including planning as a separate stage, but in this chapter I follow Thompson (2005) in integrating planning with assessment whilst combining review and evaluation. In truth, the model is not linear and the component parts and stages merge into one another, and oscillate. Whilst assessment, intervention and review will be introduced and examined, a caveat needs to be introduced to indicate that the stages are not always so easily separated in practice and a degree of flexibility and interlinkage between them is important.

What Is Assessment?

Assessment is seen as the cornerstone of effective practice (McDonald, 1999) as it provides insight into the situation which is of concern or having an impact on the service user, or the person or agency making the referral. Middleton (1997, p. 5) describes assessment as:

> the analytic process by which decisions are made. In a social welfare context, it is a basis for planning what needs to be done to maintain or improve a person's situation . . . Assessment involves gathering and interpreting information in order to understand a person and their circumstances; the desirability and feasibility of change and the services and resources which are necessary to effect it. It involves making judgements based on information.

Assessment in the abstract is a neutral activity. However, it is important to note that in practice it always has political and value connotations depending on the reasons for assessment, the mode of assessment, the involvement of service users and others, and the attention given to questions of power. Smale et al. (2000) provide a useful model for assessment that describes the use of expertise without acknowledging the same in others, or the unquestioning following of procedures which characterizes some elements of social work practice, emphasizing that social workers must strive to engage with service users and seek a relationship based on exchange of information: a joint activity that guides the process. It may be asked whether a true exchange relationship can be achieved in the world of state social work and whether it should be attempted. However, whilst it is true that social workers necessarily follow given procedures and frameworks, the underlying spirit of assessment concerns engagement and exchange (Parker, 2007). The potential for exchange relationships is under constant attack, however, from the risk-averse bureaucracy and assessment culture emanating from the managerialist and actuarial approaches developed within neoliberalist society (Webb, 2006).

What Is Involved in Assessment?

Whilst there are a number of different models and types of assessment, they all follow a fairly similar pattern and include at least a variation of the following elements:

- Preparation, planning and engagement using the rapport and relationship building skills to work with people to introduce the need for assessment and decide how it should be carried out.
- Data collection and creating a perspective on a given situation using a range of means depending on age, understanding, abilities and the purposes of the assessment.
- Preliminary analysis and interpretation of data – testing out your thoughts and hunches with service users and carers.
- Deeper analysis after testing data – preparing an interpretation (which should be negotiated and shared).
- Construction of an action plan – together with service users.

Assessments may represent a perspective from a certain point in time and from particular points of view. It may be constructed for a given purpose such as a report to court or for a case conference or discussion. Whilst these represent important tasks in which social workers must develop high level skills, assessment is limited if seen purely as a means to an end. As part of the systematic process of social work it can be viewed as on-going and continuous, informing the working relationship and its evaluation throughout. In this the exchange becomes meaningful as specifically directed towards issues of concern and importance and reviewing where people are and what they have achieved.

How Do You Do It?

Social work skills in relationship building are as central to the assessment as they are to the systematic social work process. It is important to engage the person or people at the centre of the assessment, providing information about the reasons for the assessment, the uses to which it will be put, their role and involvement and the rights of those involved. However, alongside the interpersonal or people skills, and clear social work values, social workers need to be administratively competent in order to produce assessments that are meaningful, understandable and transferable.

One way of building the relationship and putting people at their ease within the assessment is to use drawing and charting techniques, producing genograms that will provide information about family networks, ecomaps that will show the strength of connections between people and places, and flow diagrams of life road maps that indicate important events in people's histories. Benefits of using these techniques include the fact that the physical act of doing them helps to provide a focus on a third object that can reduce anxieties; they also allow social workers and service users to explore issues in depth, to hold off or to correct mistaken impressions; and they provide information that can inform any tangible report that needs to be constructed (see Parker and Bradley, 2003).

A further way of assisting the process is to start from a wide perspective, gathering a broad social history that gives context and allows service users to construct ecological narratives before beginning to focus on more personal and individual issues and concerns. The pace of the assessment will determine the quality of the information provided. Service users may respond to service focused questions and set protocols but this is unlikely to get the rich detail of their lives which are central to effective planning, interventive work and the evaluation of change.

A good assessment allows the social worker to plan openly with service users what comes next, is likely to be a product or snapshot of a person's or family's life at a particular time and also a continuing process of narrative development. If the assessment is a negotiated process which is based on the relationship between the social worker who has a deep knowledge base about what works in what settings, with whom and how, and the service user and/or carer who is expert on their own situation, life and experiences, the power differentials can be mitigated. This acknowledges the importance of the social worker's knowledge and the importance of true exchange. The plan leads to the development of the intervention, the ways in which social worker and service user will work to meet goals and objectives agreed within the assessment and plan.

Intervention

Intervention is a contested term, raising for some the idea of 'doing to others' or imposing a level of expertise that is exclusive rather than inclusive. It need not be so, and can be understood as 'working together with people' in a systematic and planned way in an identified situation to make a difference. If social workers are to be effective in working with people and achieving identified goals – whether they be change or maintenance oriented – they will need to identify the evidence base from which they work. This is important in justifying the methods of practice employed or suggested to commissioners of social work, managers and supervisors and all importantly to service users themselves who are entitled to the best possible and most effective service. To be effective, social work practice should achieve what it claims it will. However, this does not in itself make it ethical or acceptable and the processes involved must be transparent as must the evidence base if service users are going to make informed choices about how to work together with practitioners. Of course, it might be argued that the knowledge base of social workers means they know best, and that the imperatives of practice – a child protection investigation, a mental health crisis, a discharge from hospital and so on – may lead some social workers to act rather than explain and take people with them. Social workers should have a command of the knowledge and theories underpinning the models they use if they are to be effective. However, the models used should fit the person and his/her lifestyle and choices if they are to work best. Intervention works best if it is engaged with by service users.

Types, Models and Theories

There are many different types of model and theory that can be employed in social work (Payne, 2005a). Sometimes social workers develop expertise in some areas as a result of personal preference, sometimes they elect to use an eclectic mix of theories and models. However, the driver for the model should always be the evidence base plus the active engagement, from a position of being fully informed, of the service user. Models for practice include individually focused work such as psychodynamic, cognitive-behavioural, crisis intervention and task-centred models; social approaches based on systems thinking, social psychology and social and community development; and socio-political frameworks including critical theories, feminist theories, anti-discriminatory and anti-oppressive practice. These approaches cover the wide variety of areas and settings in which social workers practise. Interventive models can be analysed and classified in various ways as coming from identifiable philosophical and political perspectives, and it is important that practitioners take a critical and analytic approach examining why they are using a particular model and the impact this may have on those with whom they are working. The analytic framework proposed by Payne (2005a), acknowledges that no theory can be defined by one category alone, but it is helpful in delineating the theoretical orientation and philosophical position of theories:

- reflexive-therapeutic;
- socialist-collectivist;
- individualist-reformist.

The importance of this analysis lies in its promotion of the purposes of social work as intrapsychic help, individualized and interpersonal assistance or social change. In practice all aspects interweave with one another as the individual constructs and is constructed by the social world, but such heuristic devices are important to our conceptualization of social work. Lymbery (2005) develops this understanding for work with older people.

How Do Social Workers Choose What to Use?

In order to make choices service users need to know what will work in what circumstances; they are entitled to the evidence and social workers have a duty to keep up-to-date with research and, indeed, to engage in their own practice research and development. The ways in which social workers themselves decide on which approach to suggest will be determined by a variety of factors. It cannot be divorced from the belief systems and value-bases of individual social workers but is likely to be guided more by the purpose of the agency and its underlying philosophy and the legislation and social policies underpinning it. As social services become more evidence-based in their practices and as social workers develop their duty to provide the best possible services to the people with whom they work, whether or not an interventive method achieves the outcomes it claims will be a fundamental influence on individual social workers' choices.

Many social workers choose to merge a variety of models, often resulting from a developing wisdom in practice gained from experience. Where it is subject to reflection and the tacit knowledge becomes framed as a model for working it can be seen as developing an evidence base which, although not always theorized consistently can begin to be justified. However, eclecticism may betray a lack of deep knowledge of models and their impacts on people and a lack of theoretical conceptualization serving as a powerful indictment of education which will need to be addressed in continuing professional development programmes. On the other hand, it may reflect a lack of time or opportunity to use models of intervention resulting from agency pressures and directives which indicates a need for review of the purposes and aims of the organization and team.

We noted earlier that Smale et al. (2000) constructed a three-fold model including expert, procedural and exchange approaches to understand assessment. This analysis can also be applied to ways in which intervention is approached by social workers. For instance, a social worker may develop a contingency management programme with a young person refusing to attend school based on expert knowledge of social learning theory and applied according to up-to-date research but ignoring the discrete situation in which this young person found him/herself. It may be, on the other hand, that the social worker's agency prescribes this particular method of working and a perfunctory approach to it is adopted. However, the exchange approach would seek to explain and share knowledge of the approach with the young person involved and seek to engage him/her actively in developing, implementing and evaluating that programme.

Review and Evaluation

The importance of review and evaluation can be neglected within social work but they are central to the furtherance of evidence-based approaches and key to developing transparent and open approaches to working with people. The two terms have some similarities but also a number of differences that need clarification.

Reviews can be informal in the sense of referring to a summation of work or discussion prior to continuing or ending a session. In a more formal sense, however, review relates to the statutory and procedural obligations social workers have to monitoring their work and preventing drift. For instance, there is a statutory requirement to review a care plan for a young person looked after by the local authority, for care plans developed for adults and so on. Reviewing the success of work undertaken, how a placement or care plan has proceeded and what needs to be done now may be considered wearisome by some but it is crucial to effective and ethical practice. Being involved in or responsible for reviewing social work practice demands a clear knowledge of legislation, models and theories for practice, and the individual care plan and people involved in the case. Social workers will also need to develop their interpersonal and communication skills to coordinate and chair reviews, and their administrative skills in keeping to timescales, ensuring good communication channels and keeping accurate records of the process.

Evaluation is more closely allied to research-mindedness and the inculcation of evidence-based practice, the two of which may be understood together. The models chosen for evaluation of practice will depend on and link with the methods of intervention chosen, which themselves will link to the assessment that was completed initially. The evaluation checks what has happened, whether plans have been achieved and provides evidence to demonstrate the achievement of agreed aims and objectives.

There are personal, professional, organizational and statutory drivers for conducting review and evaluation of social work practice (Parker, 2007). It is important that social work demonstrates to the government and to its employing agencies that it is doing what it is expected and created to do. However, the development of the profession alongside other disciplinary groups and the centrality of social workers' individual duty to provide best practice based on research demands the continued development and progression of practice by evaluating its success or otherwise. In this way it is much akin to reflective practice in which social workers consider what has occurred in a deep and critical manner looking at processes as well as surface issues and make hypotheses as to why and how practice has had the impact it has. This allows social workers to develop further their practice and maintain a critical edge whilst providing evidence that it is working.

Summary

The separation of assessment, intervention and review assists in developing a systematic approach to social work practice. However, the process is not a linear one and the stages merge with one another, or the relationship moves from assessment, intervention, review and further work at one or other stage. In a constantly changing and fluid world the model offers a way of guiding and conceptualizing social work that need not be constraining but facilitative of working together with service users.

Five Key Points

- Systematic approaches to social work require both evidence-based practice and person-centred artistry.
- Social work practice is concerned with the regulation of social life as well as promoting social change.
- Assessment, intervention and review are elements of systematic practice but do not necessarily follow a linear pattern.
- Assessment, intervention and review are politicized activities depending on the context of the work and agency and are mediated by the values of the social worker.
- Engaging openly and honestly with service users assists in making assessment, intervention and review more effective.

Three Questions

? How can social work practice be considered both an art and a science?
? The 'exchange' relationship is based on the social worker's appreciation of the service user as expert by experience. Describe how this model might be applied to assessment, intervention and review in social work practice.
? Explain why and how social workers might choose their models for practice and explore some of the possible implications arising from these choices.

Further reading

1 Adams, R., Dominelli, L. and Payne, M. (eds.) (2002) *Social Work: Themes, Issues and Critical Debates*, 2nd edn. Basingstoke: Palgrave.
2 Parker, J. and Bradley, G. (2003) *Social Work Practice: Assessment, Planning, Intervention and Review*. Exeter: Learning Matters.
3 Payne, M. (2005a) *Modern Social Work Theory*, 3rd edn. Basingstoke: Palgrave.

CHAPTER 2.3

Anti-discriminatory Practice

Neil Thompson

Social work theory and practice have changed and developed quite considerably since the mid-1980s when issues of discrimination and oppression started to receive serious attention. We are now much more aware of the need to see the individual in his or her social context. We are also much more aware of the need to see that context in a fuller and richer sense than is traditionally the case in social work literature.

The Need for Anti-discriminatory Practice

The field of anti-discriminatory practice is a broad one that encompasses a number of important issues. I shall address some of these here, but will inevitably omit discussion of many other important questions.

A basic feature of anti-discriminatory practice is the ability/willingness to see that discrimination and oppression are so often central to the situations social workers encounter. For example, the majority of social work clients are women, and yet the significance of gender in a male-dominated society is a factor that many practitioners can fail to take into consideration. That is, they adopt what is known as a 'gender-blind' approach.

Similarly, it is easy to remain firmly within an ethnocentric frame of reference – that is, to see situations from the perspective of the dominant culture without taking adequate account of the fact that we live in a multi-ethnic society. Social workers operate in a context of diversity, and forms of practice that do not reflect this are likely to undermine the importance of non-dominant cultural patterns, beliefs and expectations.

Consequently, parallel to the 'gender-blind' approach, we also have the 'colour-blind' approach, based on the false premise that 'all people are the same – members of one race with similar problems, needs and objectives' (Dominelli, 1992, p. 167). Such a view both denies the richness of minority cultures and ignores the reality of the experience of racism for very many people.

Other forms of discrimination, most notably ageism and disablism, can also be 'swept under the carpet' by an attitude that fails to recognize the destructive effects of oppression on marginalized social groups. This, then, is a fundamental principle of anti-discriminatory practice – the need to be sensitive to discrimination and oppression, to avoid the pitfall of becoming oblivious to their existence.

For staff schooled in traditional methods, the fact that social work clients are predominantly from disadvantaged groups is unlikely to be seen as a key issue. However, what anti-discriminatory practice teaches us is that discrimination and oppression are vitally important matters and, if we are not attuned to recognizing and challenging discrimination, we run the risk of, at best, condoning it and, at worst exacerbating and amplifying it through our own actions.

> There is no middle ground; intervention either adds to the problem (or at least condones it) or goes some small way towards easing or breaking such oppression. In this respect, the political slogan, 'If you're not part of the solution, you must be part of the problem' is particularly accurate.
>
> An awareness of the sociopolitical context is necessary in order to prevent becoming (or remaining) part of the problem. (Thompson, 1992, pp. 169–70)

In keeping with this line of argument, Giddens (1977) argued that power is intrinsic to all social interaction – we cannot escape the significance of power in our dealings with other people. This means that the potential for transforming structures of oppression is always a possibility for us. The power associated with human action can be used to challenge existing forms and patterns of discrimination. Alternatively, however, such power can be used to reinforce and legitimate structures of inequality. What cannot happen, then, is for our actions to be 'neutral' with regard to existing balances of power.

Of course, some people have more power than others, but we all have some degree of power in terms of being able, as Giddens puts it, to 'make a difference'. Social workers dealing with relatively powerless members of the community are therefore in a pivotal position. Social work interventions can contribute, to some extent at least, to empowerment and emancipation from oppressive circumstances, or can, in themselves, be oppressive. I shall discuss below some of the ways in which workers can seek to make their actions positive and consistent with anti-discriminatory practice.

A second fundamental principle of anti-discriminatory practice can then be identified as the need to recognize that social work interventions either condone and reinforce discrimination and oppression, or go some way towards countering and undermining them.

Anti-discriminatory practice is part of what Giddens (1991) called 'emancipatory politics':

> I define emancipatory politics as a generic outlook concerned above all with liberating individuals and groups from constraints which adversely affect their life chances. Emancipatory politics involves two main elements: the effort to shed shackles of the past, thereby permitting a transformative attitude towards the future; and the aim of overcoming the illegitimate domination of some individuals or groups by others. . . . Emancipatory politics is concerned to reduce or eliminate *exploitation, inequality* and *oppression*. (In Cassell, 1993, pp. 334–5)

From this he went on to identify three 'imperatives' of emancipatory politics: justice, equality and participation, and these are still highly relevant today. I shall outline each of these in turn:

- *Justice*. The notion of justice implies fairness of treatment, an assurance that we will not be exploited or denied our rights. There is a great deal of evidence to suggest that certain groups do not have the benefit of just treatment. For example, Marlow and Loveday (2000) discuss how black people can be treated far less favourably within the British criminal justice system.
- *Equality*. An important point to recognize with regard to equality is that it should not be equated with uniformity. To treat everyone the same is not to treat everyone equally, as this fails to take account of significant pre-existing differences and inequalities. For example, many people have specific needs (wheelchair access is a common example), and if these are not addressed, such people will be disadvantaged. That is, where people begin from a position of inequality, a uniform approach will serve only to reinforce such inequalities. In this respect, a failure to take on board different needs, circumstances and backgrounds is actually a barrier to equality, rather than a step towards it. Equality relates to rights and opportunities, and so we need to ensure that the focus is on equal outcomes, rather than uniformity of treatment.
- *Participation*. This is an important concept in social work at two levels. On a broader level, the concept of user participation is an important element in the development of anti-discriminatory practice. This refers to the involvement of service users in the planning, coordination, evaluation and so on, of services in order to (a) provide opportunities for empowerment and (b) ensure that the services provided are appropriate and responsive (Thompson, 2006a). At a narrower, micro level, participation is also extremely important in terms of interpersonal interactions within the context of social work interventions. At this level, the term 'partnership' is used to refer to the need to ensure that practice is premised on working *with* clients, towards mutually agreed goals, rather than doing things *to* them (Thompson, 2002). Partnership is a central theme of anti-discriminatory practice, and one to which I shall return below.

A further fundamental principle of anti-discriminatory practice, then, is the need to address the three imperatives of justice, equality and participation.

Countering Discrimination and Oppression

Jordan (1990) argues that the nature of social work tasks makes it necessary for social workers to exercise discretion and professional judgement: 'it is because situations are complex and susceptible to a number of interpretations that the judgement, discretion and skill of a trained person are required' (pp. 3–4). This introduces the need for what he calls 'moral reasoning', a level of analysis above and beyond simple technical reasoning. That is, social work is characterized by 'messy' situations (Schön, 1983) that require more than technical answers. This being the case, the scope for abusing professional power becomes an issue that needs to be addressed.

It poses a crucial question for practitioners: How can we ensure that the power inherent in the professional role is used positively, and is not allowed to become a force for coercion?

The remainder of this chapter seeks to answer this question, in part at least, by outlining a number of steps that can be taken to ensure that our moral reasoning is consistent with, and supportive of, equality and emancipation, rather than discrimination and oppression.

There are a number of ways in which traditional approaches to practice need to be changed if practice is to become genuinely emancipatory. Indeed, it can be seen as a basic principle of anti-discriminatory practice that we need to revisit traditional forms of practice and make them compatible with a spirit of countering oppression.

Social work practice has long placed value on the role of enabling as an important means of avoiding the creation of dependency. However, anti-discriminatory practice involves going beyond simply enabling to the point of *empowering* people. The concept of enabling is a very individualistic one. It implies helping people cope with, or adjust to, their circumstances. While this is a valuable notion in some respects, it does not succeed in going far enough. It does not take account of wider cultural and structural issues. This is where empowerment comes in. Empowerment involves helping people gain greater control over their lives and their circumstances. However, it also implies seeking to overcome the effects of discrimination and oppression. Oppression can be seen as an abuse of power, and so empowerment represents a means of using one's own power (and that of other people within a collective effort) to challenge or undermine the disadvantages experienced by being a member of a marginalized social group. This represents the legitimate use of power to challenge the abuse of power inherent in discrimination and oppression.

We can see, then, that enabling is quite a narrow concept that pays little or no attention to the broader social context of clients' lives. Empowerment, by contrast, shares the same emphasis on facilitating personal change, but locates this firmly within a context of structured inequalities (Thompson, 2006a).

Traditional social work has long been criticized for being a form of benign paternalism in which professionals help less fortunate souls to cope with their life demands (see, for example, Bailey and Brake, 1975; Thompson, 2006b). There has been considerable movement away from this form of practice over a period of years. However, anti-discriminatory practice has accelerated this movement by emphasizing the significance of partnership.

Working in partnership entails involving clients at every stage in the process:

- defining needs to be met, problems to be solved;
- deciding how best to meet the needs/solve the problems;
- implementing and reviewing such decisions;
- agreeing on bringing involvement to a close; and
- evaluating intervention.

This is an essential part of good practice in so far as any work done outside of a partnership relationship may be experienced as coercive.

Sometimes there is a conflict between a statutory duty and a client's unwillingness to cooperate with planning or intervention. However, although working in partnership may prove very difficult in such circumstances, we should be wary of abandoning our attempts to create a positive partnership. In some cases, it can take a great deal of time to develop the right circumstances for partnership work but the long-term success can often more than repay the efforts expended.

By working in partnership, we can seek to ensure that inequalities are not reinforced, and that relatively powerless people are given a voice. In this way, professional barriers can be dismantled, in part at least, and the tendency for social workers to be seen as a threat can be undermined.

One of the hallmarks of good practice in traditional approaches to social work has been a sensitivity to feelings. Social work interventions that take no account of feelings can be seen as potentially very dangerous indeed. For practitioners to intervene in people's lives without taking account of the emotional issues involved is clearly an example of bad practice, especially as such insensitive interventions can do considerably more harm than good.

We can now apply the same logic to anti-discriminatory practice. In direct parallel to the emotional dimension of practice, interventions that do not demonstrate a sensitivity to the experience of oppression and the role of discrimination in creating and sustaining inequality and disadvantage are also potentially very dangerous indeed. To intervene in people's lives without taking account of key factors such as race, ethnicity, gender, age, disability, sexual orientation and so on is contrary to anti-discriminatory practice. Such interventions can do considerably more harm than good.

There is also a direct parallel between learning how to deal with emotional issues and learning how to deal with discrimination and oppression. This applies at two levels. First, in both cases, no simple formulae can be provided for how to deal with specific situations. Both require considerable skill and sensitivity on the part of the worker. Good practice in both depends on building up knowledge and skills over a period of time, and both are likely to involve making a number of mistakes along the line.

Second, the emotional dimension of social work requires us to look critically upon our own responses, our own attitudes and values. Dealing with feelings inevitably involves our own subjective enmeshment, to a certain degree at least. A totally objective approach is neither possible nor desirable. The same is also true of dealing with discrimination:

- We need to look critically upon our own responses to oppression, our own attitudes and values – a certain amount of 'unlearning' is required in order to cast off the destructive stereotypes into which we have been socialized (Thompson, 2006c).
- There is inevitably a subjective dimension in terms of how we interact with people of a different background from our own, again reflecting the patterns of expectations into which we have been socialized.
- Attempting to be entirely objective is an unrealistic strategy. We need to recognize our own views and possible prejudices so that we are in a position to ensure that they do not stand in the way of good practice.

A further long-established hallmark of good practice is the recognition of the uniqueness of the individual. This is a practice principle that anti-discriminatory practice would not wish to challenge. However, we need to go beyond this to recognize that individuals need to be understood not in the abstract, but within the concrete circumstances of their cultural and social context. For example, consider the case of an older person being assessed for community care services. He or she would need to be recognized as a unique individual with specific needs, qualities and circumstances. However, it would also be important to take account of the person's 'social location' – where the person is situated in terms of class, gender, race, ethnicity and so on. In particular, in working with older people, we would need to address issues of ageism and consider how age discrimination plays a part in the client's life. To work with an older person without taking on board issues of the marginalization and stereotyping of older people as an oppressed group increases the likelihood of poor practice, practice inconsistent with their rights and dignity (S. Thompson, 2005). As Hughes and Mtezuka (1992) comment:

> Social work has not only failed to challenge ageism and its implicit assumptions of assumed homogeneity, it appears to have embraced these values. Furthermore, social work and social service provision have failed to identify the particular needs of the majority of old people – that is, older women – and, within that group, have not recognised the diversity related to social class, race and life history. (p. 233)

In short, then, to deny the uniqueness of the individual can be seen as a form of oppression in its own right, but to see *only* that uniqueness and not recognize common patterns of experience is equally problematic.

The quotation from Hughes and Mtezuka also introduces another important issue in relation to the development of anti-discriminatory practice. Different forms of discrimination – racism, sexism, ageism and so on – do not operate in isolation or independently of each other. They interact, and therefore act as different but related dimensions of the experience of oppression. We therefore have to be wary of seeing clients in terms of one form of oppression only. In many cases, clients are exposed to multiple forms of oppression, a fact that can produce a complex matrix of interacting factors.

This brings me to the next point I wish to emphasize – the importance of assessment. Assessment is the process whereby information is gathered in order to form a picture of what needs to be done. It is a key part in the social work process, as it forms the basis for intervention, review, ending and evaluation (Thompson, 2002).

Consider the major social divisions in society:

- Class
- Gender
- Disability
- Age
- Race

How do they impinge on social work practice?

Consequently, if a worker's assessment is characterized by stereotypical assumptions or, for example, a pathological view of black families (Robinson, 1995), then the scope for anti-discriminatory practice becomes very limited.

It is important that we are conscious of discrimination at all stages within practice, but the assessment stage can be seen as particularly crucial in terms of how it sets the scene for further involvement with the client. A clear assessment, developed in partnership with the client(s), which takes account of patterns of discrimination and the experience of oppression, is an essential first step in ensuring that subsequent intervention is not distorted by discriminatory assumptions or oppressive practices. Indeed, this can be seen as a further fundamental principle of anti-discriminatory practice – the need to ensure that assessment is non-discriminatory and anti-oppressive.

Conclusion

Discrimination and oppression are part of the everyday reality of a significant proportion of social work's clientele. Traditional social work practice goes some way towards recognizing the social context of clients' experiences, but the development of anti-discriminatory practice has shown that not enough attention has been paid to certain aspects of that social context, particularly those aspects to do with social divisions, conflict, power, discrimination and oppression.

This chapter has argued the case for making the countering of discrimination and oppression a central feature of good social work practice. One step towards that has been the 'reworking' of some aspects of traditional practice to make them more compatible with an ethos of countering oppression. This I see as a useful stepping stone from some of the strengths of established practice towards an anti-discriminatory practice that does not fall foul of the major weakness of such traditional practice – that is, a tendency to fail to recognize the role of structured inequalities in shaping the experience of social work clients in terms of the problems and deprivations that haunt them.

It is to be hoped that the reworking of traditional strengths can be one positive strand in the development of a truly anti-discriminatory social work practice. Alongside this, we are already seeing the development of new forms of practice (for example, in terms of user participation), new elements that have an important part to play in making sure that social work makes a positive contribution towards social justice.

Five Key Points

- We must develop a sensitivity to the existence all around us of discrimination and oppression.
- We must recognize that there is no comfortable middle ground – we are either part of the solution or part of the problem.
- We must address the three key imperatives of justice, equality and participation.
- We must revisit traditional forms of practice and amend them accordingly.
- Non-discriminatory and anti-oppressive assessment is a first step towards the achievement of anti-discriminatory practice.

Three Questions

? Does the organization where you work (or where you are a student) have policies on equality of opportunity and anti-discrimination? If so, are they actually followed or are they simply rhetorical statements? If there are no policies in existence, are any planned or currently being developed?

? Have you ever experienced discrimination or oppression? If so, how can you use this experience positively to guide your practice? If you have not, how can you develop an understanding of the experience of oppression?

? What positive steps can you take to ensure that you make a positive contribution to anti-discriminatory practice?

Further reading

1 Thompson, N. (2003) *Promoting Equality: Challenging Discrimination and Oppression*. 2nd edn. Basingstoke: Palgrave Macmillan.
2 Moss, B. (2006) *Values*. Lyme Regis: Russell House.
3 Thompson, N. (2006b) *Anti-discriminatory Practice*, 4th edn. Basingstoke: Palgrave Macmillan.

CHAPTER 2.4

Feminist Theory

Lena Dominelli

Feminist social work in the academy has developed from its beginnings in the early 1970s when 'women' were added onto the social work curriculum to having a body of theory and practice in its own right by the mid-1990s. This chapter outlines the key characteristics of feminist social work theory and practice, and evaluates its impact on the profession.

What is Feminist Social Work?

Feminist social work has a theory and practice which has drawn on a diversity of developments in feminism and the women's movement more generally (Tong, 1989). Beginning in the voluntary sector and in the field of community action, feminist social work has spread to both the statutory and the commercial sectors (Dominelli and McLeod, 1989), particularly in areas like counselling. It is perhaps ironic that a movement which looked to publicly funded provisions for the deliverance of women from oppression has been compelled by austerity programmes in the welfare state to engage in the 'dirty' world of profit making for its practitioners to offer a service aimed at empowering women and make a living. Much anguish has gone into the decision some feminists have made to 'go commercial'. Those who have done so have nonetheless sought to uphold feminist principles in the services they make available and the processes through which they engage 'clients'. They have addressed questions of access by having a sliding scale of fees which range from no payment for those who cannot pay to charging the 'market rate' for women holding highly remunerated posts. They have avoided stigmatizing people through means-testing by asking women to self-define their income status. Feminist counsellors and feminists providing women's health services have found 'going private' has also enabled them to practise unencumbered by the bureaucratic constraints stultifying statutory work (Judge, 1993).

Neither feminism nor feminist social work are monolithic entities subscribing to one version of 'the truth'. Rather, there exists a plurality of views – liberal, radical, socialist, anti-racist and postmodernist – which can be held by both black and white feminists: for example, white radical feminism, black socialist feminism (Collins, 2000). Each of the different schools of feminist thought has its own perceptions about the origins of the oppression of women and the task of how this is to be eradicated. Their variety reflects how feminists have attempted to respond to each other's critiques and given feminism a responsive and non-dogmatic basis. Nonetheless, they share a number of characteristics:

- upholding the right of women to be free from oppression;
- having women speak for ourselves in our own voices;
- listening to what women have to say;
- creating alternative lifestyles in the here and now;
- integrating our theories with our practice;
- seeking compatibility between the ends being sought and the means whereby these are achieved;
- seeking collectivist solutions which respect the individuality and uniqueness of each woman;
- valuing women's contributions; and
- using women's individual experiences to make sense of our social realities.

I write from a white anti-racist socialist feminist perspective. This position recognizes that alongside other social divisions, 'race', gender and class interact to differentiate one woman's experiences of oppression from another's.[1]

I define feminist social work as a form of social work practice which takes gendered inequality and its elimination as the starting point for working with women whether as individuals, in groups or within organizations and seeks to promote women's well-being as women define it. Rooted in women's experiences of reality and using research which attests to the presence of extensive and systematic discrimination against women, its immediate aim is to use helping relationships predicated on egalitarian values to enable women to develop the resources, skills and confidence necessary for taking control of their own lives. It also seeks to ensure that feminist insights are used to improve the well-being of children and men.

The fostering of women's self-esteem through a facilitating relationship between the feminist practitioner and the 'client'[2] encourages the woman to make her own decisions by playing an active role in assessing her situation, exploring alternatives, formulating plans of action and implementing them. The assessment process is likely to involve redefining the problem being considered from a feminist perspective. This removes it from the private realm of a personal problem for which the woman is solely responsible and lodges it in the public domain as a social problem which she is experiencing individually along with a number of other women.

Redefining the problem forms an important part of feminist social work intervention. It reduces the 'client's' sense of isolation and feelings of guilt by enabling her to see how her social role, position and status have contributed to her personally feeling powerless. Examining her insight into disempowerment from this perspective is empowering for the woman because:

- her experience is validated;
- she can make links with other women who are similarly situated;
- she can interpret her questioning of her position as one form of resistance marking the first step in the process of asserting greater control over her life.

A feminist practitioner assists in this development by placing her skills, knowledge and resources at the woman's disposal and sharing her expertise with her. In other words, a feminist practitioner can help the woman unpack the contingent realities in her situation and explore how she has used her knowledge and experience in both reproducing and rejecting her own oppression. Gaining self-knowledge enables the woman to more actively accumulate resources which will give her greater purchase over her circumstances.

In establishing a more egalitarian relationship with a 'client', a feminist social worker helps to unlock the 'client's' capacity for decision-making, self-validation and the acquisition of new knowledge and skills. The *process* of how they work together becomes as important as their meeting agreed objectives. Implementing a commitment not to disempower women means the feminist practitioner pays attention to how process shapes the quality of the professional relationship between them. Reducing power differentials arising from one's expertise by sharing this with the 'client' rather than seeking to restrict the flow of information and knowledge to maintain a professional superiority constitutes one means of achieving it. Changing the nature of the worker–'client' relationship and questioning the traditional notion of professionals as distanced neutral individuals characterize feminist facilitative working environments.

By challenging traditional professional paradigms in which the expert tells the 'client' what to do, the feminist social worker undermines the idea of the professional as the neutral uninvolved onlooker. Having rejected her own oppression as a woman, the feminist social worker can also use her own self-knowledge and experience of disempowerment as a basis for better understanding the 'client's' responses to her predicament. Thus, the feminist social worker's rejection of injustice helps her to gain the wisdom whereby growth and knowledge can be mutually promoted.

In the longer term, feminist social work practice has a role to play in fulfilling feminism's broader objective: transforming social relations in more egalitarian directions. It makes its contribution towards this by initiating less oppressive social relations within the worker–'client' relationship and reducing the oppressive nature of organizational policies and practices. It can also do so through campaigning activities and networks which tackle social issues that undermine the capacities of individuals to realize their full potential, for example, poverty, violence, sexual abuse. Through their work together, the woman 'client' begins to locate herself within her social context and make connections between structural inequalities and their impact on her life choices.

Feminist social workers' concern with the quality of people's lives and willingness to intervene in ways that promote the welfare of society's most disadvantaged groups make feminist social work a political form of social work and one that adopts a moral position which opposes injustice and oppression, including that perpetrated by women. And, in recognition of women's multiple identities, it condemns the prioritizing of one form of oppression over another. Feminist social work engages both the personal and the social by focusing on the whole person and examining the interconnectedness between people and the structures they live within. This helps to highlight the social nature of the exclusion women experience.

Feminism's main emphasis is on women as the major group whose needs are to be addressed. However, feminist social work practice is also relevant to children and men. Though rooted in women's experience of oppression, feminism's principles and methodologies are such that they can also be followed by men. Some authors have called men using feminist theory and practice 'pro-feminist' or 'feminist sympathizing' men (Pringle, 1995; Cavanagh and Cree; 1996; Orme et al., 2000). The use of feminist insights to work with men in practice is most evident in the probation service where men convicted of physical and sexual assaults against women are encouraged to consider how the ideals of hegemonic masculinity impact on their violent behaviours (Whitehead, 2002).

The Impact of Feminist Social Work

Feminism has placed gender issues on the social work map and transformed its gender-blind nature. But, given that social work is a profession composed primarily of women, its impact has not been as widespread as one would have expected. Indeed, Reynolds (1994) argues that feminism has had minimal influence on the social work curriculum and gives an account of the difficulties that she and her colleagues are encountering in getting sexism the same degree of attention that is given to racism. What she says about the problems which need to be overcome is familiar, but I am not as gloomy about either our current position or future prospects as Reynolds, although I think progress will continue to be an uphill struggle (Dominelli, 1997). Despite my frustrations with the obstacles to the advancement of feminist social work, there have been a number of significant improvements since the first generation of feminists 'added' women onto the social work curriculum.

Since that time, equal opportunities policies have become commonplace at least on paper, in both agencies and the academy. These now form a backdrop which facilitate the introduction of issues around women's unequal access to the workplace and the inadequacy of services agencies offer women. Feminist social work has become a part of the lexicon on social work courses and has become increasingly recognized as both a philosophical position and a practice method (Sibeon, 1991; Dominelli, 1997). There is a literature to which students can be referred covering: practice (for example, Hanmer and Statham, 1988; Dominelli, 2002a), policy (for example, Groves and McLean, 1991; Dominelli, 1991b, 1999) and theory (Dominelli, 1997). Practice placements which follow feminist principles are now options on social work courses although these remain primarily limited to one or two feminist agencies. However, both probation[3] and social services now have feminist practice teachers who secure opportunities for students to examine feminist practice in statutory settings.

Some of these practitioners have organized groups for mutual support in their workplaces and unions. Moreover, feminist social workers and scholars have opened up areas others have feared to broach, for example, demonstrating how unsafe the family can be for women, by virtue of their work on domestic violence (Gordon, 1986; Mama, 1989); and for children, through their work on child sexual abuse (Dominelli, 1986, 1989, 1991a; Wilson, 1993); making visible women's contribution to caring services, and raising their status (David and New, 1985; Ungerson, 1987); identifying the neglect of carers (Walby, 1990); and legitimating the valuing of difference (Lorde, 1984; Collins, 2000).

Of crucial significance, feminists have encouraged men to examine gender oppression not only in their relationships with women, but in their relationships with other men. This has led to the creation of men's groups on social work courses, and to men social workers and probation officers addressing issues of domestic violence and sexual abuse. In taking up this challenge across a range of activities, men have also organized men's groups to address particular types of male behaviour such as domestic violence. Considerable movement has occurred since Bowl (1985) exhorted men in social work to take feminism seriously. Masculinity has been redefined in feminist directions (see Connell, 1995; Whitehead, 2002).

Feminism, then, has had a profound effect on social work practice. It has raised gender as an issue and demonstrated how the oppression of women is structured into working relations and service delivery, even in a profession which is staffed largely by women workers and has a preponderance of women 'clients'. Feminists in social work have raised not only the position of women, but also that of children and men. They have highlighted the importance of child sexual abuse within the family and demanded that children's right to non-exploitative caring relations be upheld. They have also highlighted the problematic nature of masculinity, particularly in issues of both physical and sexual violence and demanded that it be redefined more in keeping with nurturing others and developed forms of intervention in keeping with this (Cowburn and Dominelli, 2001).

Whilst practice initiatives remain patchy and vulnerable, the impact of feminism on the social work academy has been more fundamental. Drawing on the work of feminist scholars more generally, it has encompassed the content of the curriculum in college and the agencies, the pedagogic processes and working relations on courses whether these are amongst students, between students and staff or amongst staff (McLeod, 1987; Reynolds, 1994). Feminism has:

- questioned the epistemological base of knowledge in theory and practice, and highlighted the invisibility of women's experience in traditional approaches to knowledge, including in social work (Marchant and Wearing, 1986);
- exposed the use of language as a way of putting people down and reinforcing relations of domination, and amended it (Spender, 1980);
- challenged the use of both practice methods and teaching techniques which encourage the passivity of those at the receiving end, and replaced these with more participatory ones (McLeod, 1987);
- rejected gender-blind research methodologies in favour of ones which acknowledge women's experience and developed a more active set of relations between researchers and the subjects of the research (Everitt et al., 1993);
- openly sought to use research to improve women's position in society and eliminate gender oppression (Kelly, 1988).

A gender dilemma

Research indicates that between 80 and 96 per cent of child sexual abusers are men. A number of child protection enquiries have revealed that most of the social workers who sexually abuse children are also men. Does this mean that men social workers should not work with children?

In short, feminism has demanded a transformation of long-standing and taken-for-granted principles and practices on social work courses.

Gendered Working Relations

Feminists in social work have highlighted how gendered relations are central to social work. These have been shown not to work to the advantage of women, even in a profession in which women form the overwhelming majority (Hanmer and Statham, 1988; Dominelli and McLeod, 1989). Although men are in the minority, they have collared the bulk of posts at the apex of the profession and senior managerial echelons rest predominantly in their hands (Howe, 1986; Hallett, 1990; Social Services Inspectorate, 1991). Meanwhile, the majority of front-line workers are women. Men, therefore, shape the parameters in which women carry out their practice through the decisions they make about policies and resource allocation. This situation is not new for social work; it has been a profession dependent on men and the state (dominated by men at higher decision-making levels) since its inception (Walton, 1975). Moreover, women have seldom been involved in decisions that multinational companies make that have an impact on the national economy, including elements in the social care sector.

Men's career structure in the profession is different from women's. In social services, even if they begin in the residential sector, men tend to leave it quickly for more prestigious child care posts and then move on to management (Howe, 1986). Women who start out in residential work are more likely to stay there, rising at most to head of home. These gendered dynamics are further complicated by racism which makes the progression of black women and black men different from that of their white counterparts. A handful of black men, but no black women have reached the rank of director of social services. Black women have been ghettoized in the residential sector, clerical jobs and cleaning posts (Bruegal, 1989). More research is needed to pin-point their experiences more specifically, but Ahmad (1992) has written of the impossible demands made of black women managers who wish to implement a different set of priorities to those which dominate social services agendas created by white men. Although the position has improved somewhat in the previous decade, women still made up only 20 per cent of directors of social services in 2004. And, they were mainly white.

The situation in the academy reflects this pattern. Although there may be more women professors in social work than in other disciplines, largely because its status in universities is constantly questioned and devalued as 'women's work', there is a preponderance of men at the senior levels. Yet, the majority of students and practice teachers are women. More recently, it seems that this trend has been reinforced by the elimination of the binary divide. The 2001 membership list of the Association of Professors in Social Work showed that the 'old' universities had 17 women professors out of 42 (or 40 per cent), while the 'new' universities had only five women professors out of 22 (or 23 per cent). The picture has improved somewhat in the intervening period and a trawl of social work websites in the UK revealed that women constituted 44 per cent of professors of social work in the old universities and 33 per cent in the new ones.[4] Despite this modest progress, we have witnessed the growth of 'Third Wave' feminism whose postmodern proponents claim that collective struggles on behalf of all women are unnecessary; women are better off making gains at the individual level (Baumgardner and Richards, 2000).

The Backlash against Feminism

Feminist gains in social work have always been vulnerable. To begin with, they have been considered oppositional and appealed to people who were not normally located in high powered positions. Moreover, oppressed people are drawn into (re)producing and (re)creating their own oppression by internalizing the dominant hegemonic group's values, norms and mores, and reproducing oppressive relations through their own interactive processes. In these, women's choices and options as individuals are shaped by the contingent realities of the position(s) in which they are located. Their access to power and resources, which provide a foundation for exercising choice, is limited. These constraints can turn resistance to oppression into a reinforcement of it, as Willis (1977) has admirably portrayed in the case of class oppression experienced by young white working-class men at school. This position should not be seen as 'blaming the victim'. Rather, it indicates the dialectical connection between being at the receiving end of oppression and questioning it.

The persistence of women's commitment and determination to continue resisting gender oppression has succeeded in limiting the damage which has been done to our capacity for independent action. However, opposition to feminist advances intensified during the 1990s as 'angry white men' took up cudgels in their own defence. In social work, the bulk of this 'backlash' was carried under the 'politically correct' banner and was aimed primarily against anti-racist initiatives, largely because anti-racism had been given a higher profile by the Central Council for Education and Training in Social Work (CCETSW) in documents setting out the requirements for the Diploma in Social Work (Dunant, 1994). This public attack against anti-racist initiatives in social work pulled other liberationist philosophies in its wake, and women students, practitioners and academics were forced into a retreat which made them fearful of exposing their feminist sympathies and/or credentials.

The shift was accomplished through a virulent attack on all 'isms' in social work conducted in the press during the summer of 1993, the promise of CCETSW through its Chair to get rid of 'lunatic tendencies' in social work and return it to its 'proper tasks', and the subtle and sophisticated interventions used to justify a more efficient use of scarce resources. This included getting rid of policies and practices which focused on specific 'isms' – primarily racism, sexism and heterosexism – and replacing them with more generalist ones which were said to cover all forms of discrimination. CCETSW's successor, the General Social Care Council (GSCC) has maintained a low profile on this issue. In local authorities, separate Race Equality Units and Women's Units were replaced with a single 'Equality Unit' with the remit of ensuring equal opportunities for everyone. In some ways, this was similar to the convention that claims 'he' includes 'she' and 'mankind' encompasses all 'humankind'. It is a form of unquestioned exclusion carried out in the name of inclusion. More importantly, feminist and anti-racist solutions which sought to encompass the collective group were turned into individualistic ones in which a grievance is associated only with a particular case and divorced from structural inequalities which affect a number of other individuals who are similarly placed.

What caused this response? White women and black people had questioned privileges which white men previously took for granted. Men who felt threatened by this turn of events sought to reassert their privileged position by blaming white women and black people for their declining influence. However, neither had caused the drop in men's fortunes. Men's privileges have been tied to their roles in the public domain which they have traditionally accessed through the labour market. The globalization of the economy and technological changes have led to substantial losses in men's full-time posts. Wide-scale redundancies in manufacturing have occurred as jobs have migrated to the 'Tiger' economies of Asia. There, women work for even lower pay than they do in the UK, concerns with health and safety issues are minimal and state-funded welfare provisions are limited. Full-time manufacturing positions have been replaced with part-time ones in the service industries, including the privatized parts of the welfare state. These are unattractive to white men, but keep capital's reproductive costs low and increase its profit-making potential.

White women, black women and black men have become convenient scapegoats for the displaced anger of white men who feel they have lost their place in society. Without his role as provider, the key allowing him access to the public sphere, the man becomes an inhabitant of either the streets or private domain of the home. The home as *his* space is not readily available. He now has to share it with women and children who are already ensconced within it in particular ways which do not easily accommodate themselves to his new set of demands. Thus, the home and the street as sites where men can create alternative lifestyles become contested terrains fraught with tensions. In other words, the loss of their role as provider has implications for men's relationships with women and children within the family as well as the workplace. Social workers and probation officers have yet to wrestle with the consequences of these changes for their practice.

Women have also supported men in opposing the advance of feminism. This reaction has to be recognized as women's rational response to the situations in which they find themselves and understood in terms of the multiple identities and realities in which men and women live. Some women benefit from the current configuration of social relations. Not only are women privileged vis-à-vis children through adultist relations which give both men and women power and authority over children that does not have to be justified in every interaction, some women enjoy privileging over other women. For example, white middle-class women, who rely on the availability of cheap labour provided by white and black working-class women to do the domestic chores, child care and elder care for their households, enjoy, along with those living with them, a privilege rooted in their position of having greater access to financial and other resources. That these women are oppressed vis-à-vis white men in their social grouping does *not* detract from that aspect of reality. Whilst it might give them a greater degree of understanding of the mechanisms and impact of oppression, they will not automatically transfer knowledge gained from that area into others. They have to put time, energy and work into achieving this. Thus, white middle-class women social workers cannot assume that they can automatically make connections with white working-class women 'clients' on the basis of a commonly shared gender oppression. Their experiences of it are completely different. The same holds true for white women vis-à-vis black women.

Women's multiple realities fracture the potential unity which could exist between us. Differences, therefore, cannot be assumed away. These must be understood and taken hold of as part of the social situations within which we work (Lorde, 1984). Working with differences means that these cannot be taken on board as 'deficits' or 'inadequacies' which are defined as such by those in positions of greater power. They must be valued equally alongside each other. Such valuing suggests that the acceptance of difference requires differentiated initial inputs to reach the same destination. So, discrimination against black women can be taken account of by redistributing power and resources towards black women so that they can have the same starting point as white women, for example. In other words, a level playing field has to be created, not assumed.

Conclusions

Feminist social work as a theory and a method has had a profound impact on both social work practice and the academic curriculum. However, its influence has not permeated statutory social work to the extent that its predominantly woman workforce and clientele would suggest. This is because resistance to the spread of feminist principles and methodologies by those who are privileged by the prevailing social order have been sustained and widespread. The task of safeguarding feminist social work, or as Giddens (1987) suggests achieving continuity over time and space, remains to be adequately addressed by feminists and pro-feminist men. Until this happens, feminist social work in the statutory sector will remain limited and vulnerable.

Five Key Points

- Feminism covers a number of different schools of thought each of which has its own features, although some general principles are shared.
- Feminism challenges many taken-for-granted assumptions in daily life: relationships between men, women and children; the nature and use of power; language.
- Feminism integrates theory and practice in ways that promote egalitarian relations in the here and now; emphasizes the connections between the content and process in interactions; acknowledges the interlinking of private and public lives; and recognizes people's multiple identities.
- Feminist social work seeks to promote the empowerment of 'clients' and the realization of their well-being, a feature that puts it in oppositional mode vis-à-vis powerful others in the profession, particularly white men.
- Feminist social work is vulnerable and under attack because it has failed to gain widespread support amongst privileged men and women.

Three Questions

? How can the dominant (managerial and policy making) positions white men hold in social work, a profession staffed primarily by white women, be explained?

? How can feminists relate to 'difference' in ways that are consistent with its egalitarian ethos?

? What is the nature of feminists' challenge to traditional professionalism?

Notes

1 I use 'race' in quotes to indicate its socially constructed rather than biological nature.

2 I place the term 'client' in quotes to denote its problematic nature and the lack of readily available alternatives. 'User' denotes an asymmetrical passive relationship in which the user is a consumer, not a creator of, services. The phrase 'the woman the feminist practitioner works with' is too cumbersome.

3 Probation was separated from social work in England and Wales in 1998; it remains linked in Scotland and many other countries.

4 Caution has to be used in interpreting these figures because I may not have accessed all the relevant websites because some professors of social work are not identified as such and some professors of social policy are responsible for social work courses in others. For this reason, I have given only the percentages and not actual numbers.

Further reading

1 Baumgardner, J. and Richards, A. (2000) *Manifesta: Young Women, Feminism and the Future*. New York: Farrar, Strauss and Giroux.
2 Collins, P.H. (2000) *Black Feminist Thought: Knowledge, Consciousness and the Politics of Empowerment*, 2nd edn. London: Routledge. First published 1990.
3 Dominelli, L. (2002a) *Feminist Social Work Theory and Practice*. London: Palgrave Macmillan.

CHAPTER 2.5

Task-centred Work

Peter Marsh

Task-centred practice has a high profile as a social work theory. It is reported by social work students as one of the most influential theories for their practice (Marsh and Triseliotis, 1996), and it is one of the very few approaches that is mentioned when practitioners are asked about the theoretical basis of their work. It has survived in social work through many decades of changing structures, developing practices and fashionable trends.

However, whether it is widely used in day-to-day practice is quite another matter. As one of the students from the study mentioned above commented, in her many years of experience 'before I went on the course, I thought I did task-centred work. Now I know more about task-centred, I don't think I do.'

Because task-centred work does have a clearly articulated model of practice, it may be that the approach is well known as a set of activities rather than as a theoretically based approach from which a set of activities flows. If tasks are undertaken then you are doing task-centred work. But going through the motions of task-centred work does not necessarily mean a task-centred approach.

Task-centred work is more than a set of activities. It is more than 'doing tasks'. It is an approach which is founded on a set of key elements and which needs, in its practitioners, a commitment to those elements.

The elements – for example, clarity about the voluntary and compulsory nature of work, a multi-service approach and a development of work by evaluation and research – have often been seen as lacking in social work practice (see, for example, a series of studies on child protection, Department of Health, 1995a, or research examining the difficulties of implementing partnership-based models of practice, Marsh and Fisher, 1992). Many social workers, before or after their course, probably think that they 'do task-centred social work' but actually they are carrying out a number of activities which do not hold together, and which will not necessarily lead to the successful outcomes that research has found in task-centred work. The emphasis in this chapter is on the main elements of the approach, and not on the detailed activities carried out within the model.

Task-centred Practice

The main elements of task-centred practice are best described as the building blocks which create the complete system. Each one is needed. Therefore each one needs to be understood, and to be integral to the worker's approach.

The overall approach

Task-centred practice is based upon a clear mandate for action from either the user, or the courts, or both. It may accommodate within it other approaches – for example, counselling or behavioural work. The agreement for work may be with individuals, groups or communities.

The purpose of practice is to move from agreed problems ('what is wrong') to agreed goals ('what is needed') in a set period of time. Goals are rarely complete solutions to problems.

Motivation is a key issue, hence the need to be clear about the mandate for the work: users must be concerned about the problems and want to achieve the goals. This still applies when the mandate is set in the context of legal processes that specify a number of concerns that users must address.

The movement from problem to goal takes place via tasks. These are undertaken by the users, by the social worker or by others. Tasks are at the core of the model. It is 'task-centred' social work. Tasks are the method of exploring motivation in more detail, of building on users' strengths, of holding workers to account, of generating change and of working in collaboration across services.

Negotiation is needed to establish the agreement, to specify goals and to develop tasks. If there is one key activity of a task-centred worker then *negotiation* is it. There is clear respect for users' cultures and views in this approach (Ahmad, 1990), and negotiation will help to make the mandate for work clear and the tasks as effective as possible.

A major requirement of a task-centred worker is to have a good knowledge of research as both a basis of practice and as part of the development of practice that is inherent in task-centred work. Task-centred workers use research and make a direct contribution to research. This stance fits well with the need to continue to develop evidence-based practice in social work (Alderson, 1996; HM Inspectorate of Probation, 1998).

Overall, task-centred practice is a highly structured model of practice, requiring substantial knowledge and good training. It is based on a number of building blocks which lead to a set of activities within the overall model. Workers negotiate with users, and then may agree that problems should be tackled, with success being indicated by a set of agreed goals. The movement from problem to goal is by tasks, which are as diverse and varied as the problems, goals, users and services which generate them.

A simple diagram may help to show the overall process of the work and emphasize the key role of the agreement that specifies problem and goals and the tasks that link the two. The model is described elsewhere (Doel and Marsh, 1992; Marsh

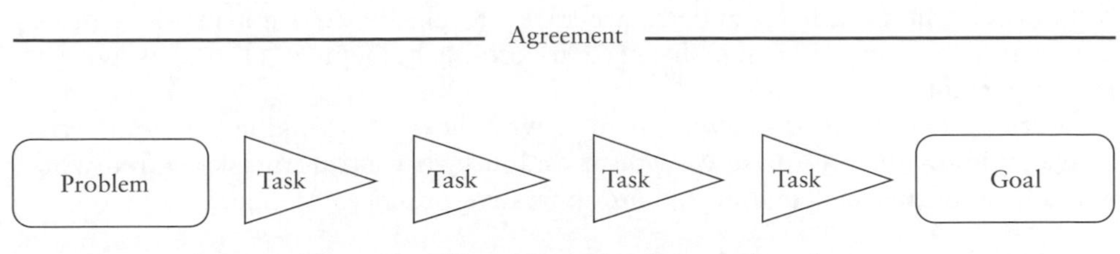

Figure 1 The process of task-centred work

and Doel, 2005; Tolson et al., 1994; and, in summary, in Marsh, 1991). The outline in Figure 1 covers the building blocks that underpin it.

Recognizing the voluntary and compulsory basis of social work

The users of social work often see themselves as subject to some form of compulsion. Most obviously, social workers and those who work within the criminal justice system have, from court orders, and legal processes, considerable powers to intervene in people's lives. Perhaps less obviously many users feel they have little alternative but to turn to social workers for help because they have few, if any, other options.

Task-centred practice is based upon a clear understanding of the basis of the work. To put it at its starkest, each time a task-centred practitioner enters into negotiation about service they should ask 'what right do I have to be engaging in this person's life?' On many occasions intimate details of families are discussed, on other occasions actions are taken by social workers with far-reaching implications for relationships and the well-being of users. These facts should lead to humility when beginning, continuing or ending work – it is often intrusive and it may be disruptive. Clarifying *what right a practitioner has to undertake the work at all* emphasizes the involvement and respect for the user.

The basis of task-centred work should, at the end of the day, be either the desire of the user to work on the problems outlined, or the clear mandate of the law to deal with the problems. On the other hand the pressure of neighbours, or the concerns of other professionals do not, in this approach, form a mandate for the work. They might, of course, strongly influence the user, and the skilled worker will, via negotiation, help the user to judge how they should respond to such influence.

It is important to note that the two bases of work – the wishes of the user, and/or legal powers – may co-exist. There might be full agreement to the legal order. There might be an order, and alongside this legally mandated voluntary problem, there might be some additional voluntary work. But if there is no agreement at all, then task-centred work cannot take place and the worker will need to proceed by some form of surveillance or monitoring.

The real world of social work practice will often make these definitions difficult to clarify, and there will be blurred edges. Indeed, social work has sometimes institutionalized a confused mandate, for example that deriving from the child protection conference, where the legal power of any agreed plan is negligible, but the plan could hardly be said to be voluntary (see, for example, the discussion of this 'third mandate' in Marsh and Fisher, 1992, pp. 21–9).

However the fact that mandates are tricky to clarify does not make them less important, nor does it make the need to establish them as clearly as possible less important.

Working hard to establish with the user why the work is taking place, and what is available for them to disagree with or establish, is central to task-centred work, and an important contribution to anti-oppressive practice (Ahmad, 1990).

Combining different services

Social workers may offer direct services themselves. For community-based staff this may, for example, be counselling or behavioural programmes, and for residential and day care staff this may also be different forms of service within their centre. On many occasions others will offer services, of education, health, justice or perhaps social care. It is fundamental to task-centred work that this range of services is considered and when needed offered, at both the initial stages and as work progresses.

Negotiation regarding problems and goals will often establish this need, as in other approaches to social work. The particular contribution of task-centred work is that tasks will allow the need for other services to be kept under review and demonstrated through actions rather than solely through discussions. Tasks act as a mechanism to allow workers to assess the need for other services, for example discussing which tasks might work best, or how a new service may help with a task which so far has been difficult to complete.

Other services and approaches are integral to the task-centred approach. The tasks themselves mean that there is regular review, and they allow a clear demonstration of the need, or the lack of need, for a particular service.

Work with individuals, families, groups and communities

Although some work will be solely with individuals, it is most likely that more than one person is involved in defining problems and in undertaking tasks. When considering relevant tasks, the willingness of the people concerned to undertake them will be important. When considering problems, and the mandate/agreement basis of work, the willingness of people to start off the work will be important. This is considered further below, but the question here is 'which people do social workers need to contract with?'

Is it the teenager in the family, or the parents as well? Is it the family with a child with disability, or the relevant support group as well? It must be clear which system is contracted with. The source of the mandate is the key issue. The focus of the legal order and/or the willingness to take part will be the bottom line for the decision about the primary system that is to be engaged with (Tolson et al., 1994, pp. 8–11).

This will not necessarily be the same as the focus of the tasks that are undertaken. For example, the work with the teenager may include the school staff in the tasks, but the teacher may not have been a partner to the agreement. Here again tasks will act as an indicator, this time of the way that the agreement for work may need to change to be based on a wider system. The work with the school may grow to the point where including them in the discussion of problems and goals becomes necessary.

Task-centred practice does not take as given the 'size' of system that should be engaged with at the start. It may be individuals or complete communities (for examples of the latter see Tolson et al., 1994, pp. 339–90). Negotiation needs to establish which system is contracted with, and tasks will clarify whether that decision should be reviewed.

Building on user strengths

Most, perhaps all, social workers will have thought that they personally could not deal very well with the difficulties and pressures that face many of the users of their services. Providing care for children, for example, while struggling with poverty and discrimination requires feats of ingenuity, and of sheer effort, that will often be remarkable. These feats and efforts will probably be extensive, and they will certainly be varied. It is inevitable that they will often be unknown to the practitioner.

Task-centred practice takes very seriously at least two consequences from these facts. The first is that users have a great deal of expertise in coping with their own circumstances. The second is that users understand their own circumstances in ways that workers, ultimately, cannot. Users would not be seeing social workers if there were no problems, but users are, at least in regard to the other areas of their lives, usually the 'primary experts'.

Task-centred practice is based on users' strengths. It is those strengths which will provide change, sometimes in directions that users clearly wanted, sometimes in directions that they have agreed to, however reluctantly, as a result of legal processes. Tasks use those strengths, and fill any gaps in strengths.

Task-centred practice should also acknowledge the reality of the users' day-to-day relationships. Attempts to involve family members, for example, will often founder on the lengthy history that has shaped their relationships. This complex reality is known best by the user, although of course it may not be clearly articulated in words. It may also change with the impact of social work practice. The grandmother, for example, who was previously a great support may become less so because of what she has learnt from the child protection enquiry.

Tasks will need to reflect the reality of users' relationships. Users will need to develop them in ways that are most likely to function in the circumstances of their own lives. Tasks may also provide a way to articulate social relationships, and can therefore add to discussion as a means of assessment or of change. Attempting to work with a grandmother on a task will demonstrate the nature of family relationships in a way that debating them in the office will not.

Change occurs in task-centred practice as a result of tasks. Tasks are founded on the idea of searching for strengths, recognizing the lack of them and developing ideas that reflect the actual reality of the users' relationships and lives.

Developing partnerships

Partnership between users and workers is an important element of social work practice (Lindow and Morris, 1995; Marsh and Peel, 1999; Masson et al., 1999;

Social Services Inspectorate, 1995). This does not imply an equality of power, nor an equality of work, and partnerships will come in all shapes and sizes. Users themselves have defined partnership, in one action research project, as 'a group of people who have agreed a common aim and who will pool resources in order to achieve it' (From Margin to Mainstream, 1995) and this working definition would form a suitable foundation for task-centred practice.

Finding a common aim by negotiation (with due respect for mandates), and then pooling the resources, of users, workers and others, via tasks: this is partnership in action in task-centred work.

Evidence-based practice

Task-centred work has been a pioneer of the linking of research, practice and policy. The importance of these links has been supported in major recommendations to the Department of Health (Department of Health, 1994a and 1994b; Richardson et al., 1990) and in significant projects attempting to develop evidence-based practice (Research in Practice, n.d.). Task-centred practice developed from research and this has been central to its continuing development (Bailey-Dempsey and Reid, 1996; Marsh, 1991; Naleppa and Reid, 1998). For example, early research suggested that goals without deadlines to meet them are much less effective, and therefore that time limits for the work are important (Reid, 1963; Reid and Shyne, 1969), and that longer-term work should be divided up into a series of shorter periods. Research has shown that there is a particularly effective approach to task development (Reid, 1975), that the use of tasks within sessions, as well as between sessions, is valuable (Reid and Helmer, 1985), and that there is an interrelationship of different task strategies with different problem areas (Reid, 1992).

But task-centred work's link with research does not depend solely on researchers. It also depends on practitioners and managers. It is developed through a research-like stance from those who practise it. They look for evidence of the links between their work and successful outcome. They ask users directly for their views about progress and their satisfaction about the work at each and every meeting. Tasks themselves are a miniature form of action research, trying different ways to achieve goals and learning from successes and failures.

A structured approach

Task-centred practice is a structured approach to social work. There is a clear model and a set of techniques within it. Development occurs within this structure. As such it can be replicated, improved and learnt. The evidence is that learning to *apply* the model, as distinct from learning *about* the model, is far from easy (Newton and Marsh, 1993; Reid and Beard, 1980; Rooney, 1985 and 1988; Tolson, 1985). All of the building blocks, including this one of structure, must be in place in order to carry out task-centred practice. 'Tasks' are not just activities carried out by the worker or user, they have meaning because of the overall structure within which they take place.

Discussion, action and change

Task-centred practice needs a firm base, a mandate for action from users or from legal process. On this base the notion of 'task' is central to the work, providing the means to link services, build on user strengths, develop partnerships, and develop the task-centred approach itself. It also provides an excellent example of the way the approach moves beyond the use of discussion as the basis of assessment and change. The idea that demonstration and personal experience are influential aspects of understanding is important to task-centred work.

Doing something adds to discussing something. Acting your way into a new way of thinking, may be easier than thinking your way into a new way of acting. This does not mean that major action is required for all tasks; simple activities can be powerful indicators of ability or the lack of it. Task-centred work is designed to provide indicators by both discussion and demonstration: indicators of need, of motivation, of lack of progress and of progress. It enables users to develop ideas about what they need and to call services to account, it enables workers to estimate their success.

Conclusion

Task-centred practice requires intellectual rigour, skilled practical application, serious commitment to respecting users and combating discrimination, and courage in specifying what social work is trying to achieve.

High quality professional practice needs a cogent and coherent theoretical base, accompanied by a relevant model and relevant techniques. The degree of genuine task-centred use and development may be one indicator of the state of health of social work as a professional activity.

Five Key Points

- Task-centred practice is based on user agreement, or user acknowledgement of a legal justification for action.
- Task-centred practice aims to move from problem to goal, from what is wrong to what is needed.
- Task-centred practice is based around tasks, which are central to the process of change and which build on user strengths as far as possible.
- Task-centred practice is open to other approaches and services, and can link with them via tasks.
- Task-centred practice develops and changes by continuing evaluation.

Three Questions

? Ethical, effectiveness, efficiency and user-satisfaction arguments all suggest that practice should respect and involve users' own views as far as possible. Is task-centred work's concern with this area a good reason to adopt the approach?

? How important is it to accommodate multiple services and multiple users (individuals, families, etc.) in social work practice? Does task-centred work do this particularly well?

? Task-centred work is dynamic, capable of responding to a research evidence base and to changing social values and policies – are other approaches? How important is this to the future of social work?

Further reading

1 Bricker-Jenkins, M. (1990) 'Another approach to practice and training – clients must be considered the primary experts', *Public Welfare*, Spring, 11–16.

2 Reid, W. J. (2000) *The Task Planner: An Intervention Resource for Human Service Professionals*. New York: Columbia University Press.

3 Marsh, P. and Doel, M. (2005) *The Task-centred Book*. London: Routledge.

CHAPTER 2.6

Care Management

William Horder

Care management is a system for assessing care needs and arranging services to meet them. It is a method for planning, organizing and delivering personal social services to vulnerable people through the negotiation of individualized care plans. In the UK since 1990 it has been a core structure for the planning, funding and delivery of personal social services to adults in need of care, especially older people. Care management aims to enable people to remain living in their own homes while also restricting the use of public funds to pay for residential care.

An example: Anna, a 70-year-old woman with multiple disabilities, was able to remain living alone in her own home as she wished, supported by her son and by a team of local carers who came in at different times of the day to do tasks she was unable to do for herself. The care manager helped her to arrange direct payments to fund this care and also to organize transport which enabled her to keep in touch with her work as an artist.

In this chapter the focus will be on care management in the UK context, but drawing on wider debates about case management and highlighting some of the inherent tensions.

What Is Care Management for?

Care management is a system designed to provide fair allocation of public resources for old people, for adults with physical disabilities, those with mental health problems, people with learning difficulties, people with HIV and those with drug and alcohol problems. These are groups for whom local authorities have powers and duties to fund residential care, day services and home-based care. Some of the principles of care management are relevant to social work with children and families, but in the UK care management is mainly applied to work with adults in need.

One of the strengths of care management is that it attempts to introduce equity into the provision of expensive services. There are probably few people who welcome the process of having their needs assessed by a care manager, but significant resources can be accessed following assessment. The care management process is helpful in blurring the boundary between public and private services and may help to reduce the stigma of public assistance. Care managers have to grapple with the tensions of a dual responsibility, acting as gatekeepers whilst also trying to ensure that needs are met.

Care management involves at least two people, the person in need and the person who makes an assessment, organizes and manages their care. The job title 'care manager' has in many places replaced that of 'social worker' and care management posts are open to nurses and occupational therapists but social work is the core profession. Some care managers have no professional qualification, an indication that work with older people is not highly valued. Confusingly, the term care manager is also used to describe service provider roles such as the management of residential care services; but these jobs do not involve care management as it has been defined above. The term *care* management was adopted in 1991 and is used in the UK in preference to *case* management, a term more familiar in the international context.

The introduction of care management in the UK was brought about by the necessity of controlling social security spending and reducing the number of admissions to private residential and nursing care, which had become easier for individuals to access and fund than home-based services. This was an issue of high priority for government because about half of all social security spending relates to older people. The personal social services were restructured so as to introduce a separation of purchasers from providers and to promote a mixed economy of private, voluntary and public services. The role of local authorities, as purchasers, was to commission new services and they were encouraged or required to contract out existing services. Providers were to have less influence on the pattern of services. These changes came at a time when public services and professional activity were under close scrutiny, with increased regulation and demands for accountability.

In the UK and other countries, case and care management systems have enabled community-based alternatives to hospital care to be planned and funded. Since most long-stay hospitals have closed, care management is applied to people already living in the community, as needs arise through age, illness or disability. Care management is in part an attempt to deal with problems arising from the long-existing structural divide between the National Health Service (NHS) and local government. It is primarily the responsibility of local authorities but there is a significant overlap with health services, with voluntary organizations and the private sector. Care management coexists with many other methods for delivering care, sometimes posing problems of overlap and duplication. For people with mental health problems, the Care Programme Approach is the main framework used by health and social services to provide support in the community, while care management enables local authority funding to be accessed. For people with learning disabilities, a system of Person Centred Planning may operate alongside care management. For people in hospital and needing help at home, care management is the system whereby hospital aftercare arrangements are made. Financial penalties may apply when there are delays in arranging hospital discharge. NHS staff contribute to care management processes, but they have many other roles and priorities and for the majority of the population, health services are more significant than social care.

The law for care management and community care policy is complex and fragmented, deriving from a number of different Acts of Parliament and many government guidance documents, interpreted through emerging case law (Mandelstam, 2005). For professionals to know what their powers and duties are, and for service users to know their rights, is not at all easy. In particular, whether a person in need has a right to receive services depends on many factors and may depend on varying interpretations of the law.

Rhetoric and Resources

The development of community care policy and practice has given prominence to adult care, often seen as a low priority for the personal social services. The goals of care management, underlined in a 2006 White Paper (Department of Health, 2006a), include the empowerment of users and carers and the promotion of choice and independence. But choice may in reality be quite limited. Care management involves, in many cases, the assumption of long-term financial commitments and local authorities have found it necessary to tighten eligibility criteria at certain times. Despite attempts to standardize assessment, the measurement of need is often subjective. Care managers operate in a constantly changing political environment, with ongoing debate about the role of government and the responsibility of families to care for their own.

Many writers have identified the contradictions between desirable goals of empowerment and choice and realities of rationing and risk management. Care management is 'the process of tailoring services to individual needs', but usually only within available resources. Tension between limited resources and unlimited needs has always been inherent in social work practice but the development of care management has accentuated this.

The Care Management Process

Care management is not defined in UK legislation but in official guidance following the implementation of the NHS and Community Care Act 1990. Section 47 of this Act outlines the duty of local authorities to assess people in possible need of services. The 1991 managers' and practitioners' guides supporting this legislation are the main source documents for care management. They outline seven core tasks:

- publicity;
- determining level of assessment and priority;
- assessment of need;
- care planning;
- implementation;
- monitoring;
- review.

This model envisages assessment and care planning as a cyclical process extending over time. But it should be remembered that the stages overlap, the tasks may be hard to distinguish in practice and it is unlikely that all of the tasks would be undertaken by the same person. In the sections below, four main stages of the cycle are discussed.

Publicity and screening

Local authorities are required to plan and publicize their services. This is to be welcomed because it may help to increase take-up and reduce unequal access – for example, in mental health, access to preventative services by black and ethnic minority people. 'Fair access to services' guidance specifies four levels of need and eligibility, an attempt to standardize the process of prioritization. Priority is given to those most in need; but this does mean that those in less need get less help. Eligibility criteria and response times may be published and these, together with complaints procedures, help to make agencies accountable. Rules on eligibility thresholds, though, are subject to change and may not be easy to understand. The range of possible services may be extensive but whether they are available is another matter. Publishing information may therefore be a form of tokenism but the requirement to do so is a spur to dialogue and openness, encouraging local authorities to take account of local needs.

Intake and screening systems have evolved to separate simple from complex assessments; access teams offering a single point of contact are efficient and helpful to the public but there is a disadvantage that assessment decisions may be prejudged and that qualified staff may be employed only for complex cases.

Assessment of need

Good assessment in social work has always been needs-led and one of the strengths of care management is that it focuses on need. Care managers are expected to assess needs before considering what services are available, a well-intentioned but sometimes difficult distinction.

The meaning of 'need' has come under much scrutiny in care management practice. Need can be understood in different ways. The care management process means that need is in most cases defined by professionals rather than by the person being assessed. Mandelstam (2005) points out the ambiguity and elasticity in UK community care law and that the rights of users are largely undefined in law. Care managers and their employing agencies hold much power and have to exercise their discretion in decision-making. They have to manage the conflicts that may arise when their view of need is different from the preferences of the person being assessed or those of relatives and carers.

The Carers Acts (1995, 2000 and 2004) extended the task of care management. Carers are entitled to an assessment of their own needs and may be eligible for some services to meet these. This important development in law and practice recognizes the differences which may exist between the needs of the service user and those of his or her carers, the majority of whom are women, and raises the question for whose benefit services are to be provided. Questions of professional judgement are central to assessment.

People with complex needs often have to be assessed by many different professionals. Government guidance on the single assessment process encourages health and social services to reduce duplication by encouraging them to collaborate and share assessments in work with older people.

Care planning and implementation

The formulation of care plans in partnership with the client is a principle of good social work practice which has been incorporated into care management. Anti-discriminatory practice involves awareness of power dynamics which may affect decision-making. The question of whether people in need have a right to services is rarely straightforward. Some needs have to be met by local authorities but many services are discretionary and in some circumstances lack of resources may be used as a reason to refuse services. Understanding and explaining the legal framework is a daunting task for care managers.

An unfortunate feature of care management is that it is often bureaucratic, involving form-filling, report writing, means-testing and hierarchical processes for authorizing expenditure. Delegation of budgets to care managers has been limited and financial decision-making is generally the responsibility of managers or local panels. Practitioners have to use their skills to make their dealings with users and carers empowering in the context of these procedural requirements and shortage of time. This is nothing new for social work but there has been concern that care management leads to impersonal, superficial and demeaning encounters and that organizational cultures may discourage sensitive and respectful interviewing.

Care planning does, however, offer scope for creativity in assembling packages of care which may draw together formal and informal sources of support to maintain people in their own homes. Care managers may act as brokers, finding and setting up appropriate services. The implementation stage requires skills in costing care packages, in contracting with providers and in balancing value for money against choice and quality of care, for example in purchasing services which could meet the cultural needs of a person from a particular ethnic group. Implementation of care plans may require negotiation skills of a high order.

Care managers usually have to explain the cost of services, information which may be confusing and discouraging to service users. Charges for residential care are mandatory on local authorities while other charges are discretionary. Some services are means tested, others charged at a flat rate, others free. Care managers have to keep up to date with the complexities of funding and charging systems which are subject to frequent change. The Direct Payments Acts (1996, 2000, 2001) enable disabled people to receive payment to organize and manage their own care. Although this option has been taken up by rather few people, it is of great importance, with much scope for development.

Monitoring and review

It is essential to monitor the quality and effectiveness of care services, especially in situations of risk. Some service systems, especially the Care Programme Approach for mental health, emphasize continuity of care, but this is not a feature of care management, which tends to downplay the significance of personal relationship and where long-term needs tend unfortunately to be dealt with through short-term processes.

Information systems for monitoring services and costs were slow to develop in local authorities but have become increasingly important with the proliferation of performance targets set by government. Efficient data collection and analysis is vital but may be a considerable burden for care managers. The gathering of data on unmet need is a politically sensitive but valuable part of the UK model. The importance of regular review is easy to see, as financial resources may be tied up in care packages which are inflexible while needs are continually changing. User involvement in reviews offers opportunities for empowerment but requires the commitment of professionals to make it more than a token activity. This part of the care management cycle may still be neglected, however important, as new referrals tend to take precedence.

Method and Theory

Care management has so far been defined as a structure and a practice. It is also a social work method in that it defines what practitioners should do and how they should go about their work. As a method, care management is not exclusive to social work but the process and stages are core social work activities. In the UK, aims and tasks of care management were clearly articulated in 1991 and belong to a specific political and organizational context. Since then there have been many further initiatives by central government and much local variation in delivery but the care management system has remained in place without fundamental change.

The ideological underpinnings of care management derive from liberal individualism, including belief in the discipline of the market, in consumer choice and in challenges to vested interests. Ideals of empowerment and user-centred practice also underlie care management but for disadvantaged people who lack buying power these may remain hopes rather than realities. The consumerist notion of 'packages of care' created an analogy with shopping which bears little relation to the reality of painful choices and emotionally charged situations. Care management is often viewed as an aspect of the 'new managerialism' in which ideas from management theory and practice have been applied to health and welfare work in order to improve efficiency and effectiveness. Other conceptual frameworks helpful for understanding care management are 'normalization' or the promotion of an ordinary life for marginalized groups, systems thinking and networking.

International Context and Research

Case management is long established in North America, applied especially to the coordination of long-term work with elders, in mental health and with children. Some versions emphasize clinical or therapeutic case management where relationship skills, counselling, advocacy and personal contact are core features of the work.

In the UK, however, an administrative model is more evident, emphasizing cost containment, resource management and coordination.

American experience led to a series of research projects in the UK, led by David Challis and others (Challis et al., 1998). These showed that intensive care management for people with complex needs could be very effective. Working with selected client groups, some – though not all – of the projects demonstrated improved outcomes for users and lower costs.

Influenced by these demonstration projects, the case management model was extended nationally but as the researchers warned it was not certain that these positive outcomes could be replicated on a national scale and in a watered-down form. Devolved budgets, autonomy in decision-making and protection of advocacy roles were some recommendations which have not been easy to implement on a large scale. The community care changes of the 1990s were envisaged as a long-term project, carrying the support of the main political parties in the UK. As a policy initiative it was successful in that cost-containment was achieved. Evidence about outcomes for users and carers is less easy to find and it is hardly possible that care management on its own could ensure better care; that depends on many other factors.

The Impact of Care Management on Service Patterns

The evolution of care management has been accompanied by growth in other occupational roles. Commissioning involves planning, contracting and negotiation to set up new services. Advocacy has emerged as a new specialism. Provider roles include those people, predominantly women, who provide direct care and have the most day-to-day contact with service users. Staff who know service users best are often unqualified and poorly paid. Unfortunately they may be allowed little or no part in assessment and decision-making processes.

Care managers are purchasers and are in a position of relative power which can be applied on behalf of users. There has, however, been concern that power has been exerted to ration care and drive down costs, putting the quality of provision at risk.

Other agencies and disciplines are involved in making referrals, contributing to assessment and review, and providing services. Care management has been implemented in the context of strong government promotion of inter-agency and

Criticisms of care management

In the view of some, there is a fundamental contradiction between a needs-based and a cash-limited system. They argue that care management is more about money than people and that commercial and managerial influences dominate. They also view it as an individualizing model whereby structural or political dimensions and collective needs may be neglected.

multidisciplinary work to prevent vulnerable individuals from falling through the net. While interprofessional collaboration is always desirable, there has perhaps not been sufficient recognition of its difficulties. Pressures on each agency to stay within budget may lead to tensions and encourage disputes over financial responsibility, while organizational structures and professional cultures may create barriers to communication.

Values

The values underlying care management are not very different from those traditional to social work. Care managers aim to empower people by working in partnership with them, identifying needs and making arrangements to meet these needs. This has to be balanced against the need to protect people from risk and harm; care managers act on behalf of the wider society with its changing norms. The Human Rights Act 1998 has highlighted the ethical responsibilities of care managers as public servants but putting values into practice is often far from simple. Values underlying care management include:

- equality of access to assessment and to services;
- priority to those most in need;
- partnership, participation, empowerment;
- individualized responses to need;
- a fair and open process with rights of redress.

There are some respects in which care management and social work values may diverge. Care management as a method is neutral as regards challenging injustice and inequality, taking for granted the existing societal context. Its individualistic basis means that issues of collectivity – the needs of groups and communities – may be sidelined. A value base such as that of social work seems therefore vital as an underpinning framework for care management.

Conclusion

Care management as adopted in the UK enshrines many elements of good professional practice. It was planned as an enduring structure and has proved to be so. Care management is a success from a governmental and organizational perspective. There are, though, some important limitations and criticisms of the system.

There is a fundamental contradiction between a needs-based and a cash-limited system. Funding is always insufficient and uncertain and care managers have limited scope to advocate for clients. Care management focuses on *individuals* in need with the result that structural or political dimensions and collective needs may be neglected. The measurement and flagging up of unmet need is not easy to do and the opportunity to identify gaps in services may not be taken.

The care management process can be impersonal. Care management implicitly downplays the significance of relationships, personal contact and continuity of care. Emotional needs of users may be ignored. The prioritization of those in most need may lead to early intervention or preventive work being neglected. Keeping vulnerable people at home is not always welcome to their families or their local communities and despite the Carers Acts, care management may not sufficiently address the burden on carers.

But care management shows significant strengths. Vital information may be made available and services may be responsive to local needs. A variety of providers may offer a choice and diversity of services. Assessment of need may be thorough and consistent and users and carers may be encouraged to be involved in the process of care planning or to manage it themselves. The possibility exists for intensive and imaginative arrangements for care at home. Inter-agency collaboration is a high priority, professionals are accountable and there is a reasonably fair allocation of limited resources.

Five Key Points

- Care management aims to enable people to remain living in their own homes, while also restricting the use of public funds to pay for residential and other care services.
- The assessment and care management cycle incorporates principles of good practice, including partnership and the promotion of choice, but it may be a bureaucratic and impersonal process.
- Care management emphasizes needs-led assessment but the concept of need is complex and the legal framework is confusing.
- A tension between limited resources and unlimited needs has always been inherent in social work and the development of care management has accentuated this.
- Care management provides a structure for fair allocation of public funds and has been successful in containing costs but improved outcomes for users and carers have not been demonstrated.

Three Questions

? Is care management social work?

? Is the care manager more accountable to the service user or the budget manager?

? Which is the most important of the stages of care management?

Further reading

1 Means, R., Richards, S. and Smith, R. (2003) *Community Care Policy and Practice*, 3rd edn. Basingstoke: Palgrave Macmillan.
2 Mandelstam, M. (2005) *Community Care Practice and the Law*, 3rd edn. London: Jessica Kingsley.
3 Thompson, N. and Thompson, S. (2005) *Community Care*. Lyme Regis: Russell House.

CHAPTER 2.7

Risk Assessment and Management

Hazel Kemshall

Risk assessment and management are key issues in social work, social care and probation. Responding to the risks posed by others, assessing and limiting risks to vulnerable clients, and managing risks to oneself as a worker are common place. Risk is often central to decisions to allocate resources, to intervene in the lives and choices of others, or to limit the liberties and activities of clients. However, there are different views on the nature of risk, how it should be assessed and managed, and the extent to which risk can be effectively managed and reduced.

What Is Risk?

Risk has traditionally been understood as an uncertain prediction about a future behaviour or event. For some, this means a 'chance' or 'likelihood' that something may happen, and where statistical calculations of likelihood are made (for example, in life insurance) the word 'probability' is often used. Whilst in gambling, risk can be associated with 'good risks' (for example, winning a bet at 25 to 1), in some aspects of contemporary use, risk is often associated with unwelcome, harmful and negative events or behaviours: for example, the probability of death from particular diseases, of car accidents, of prisoners re-offending after release from prison, or of child abuse in child protection work. In social work, social care and probation, risk assessment is usually of 'bad risks', harmful events and behaviours to be limited or avoided.

The idea of the probability of future harm is central to risk assessment, but what harmful event or behaviour is of concern? It is usually framed by the type of agency the practitioner works in. For the social worker in child protection, the concern is with the risk of sexual or physical abuse to children. For the probation officer, the concern is with the risk of re-offending posed by an offender on community supervision. In residential work, practitioners may be concerned with the risks of violence between residents, or of violence by residents on workers. The risk concerns of the nuclear industry are not the same as those of the Department of Transport, and neither are they the same as those presented to local authority social workers working in community care.

One way of analysing risks in social work is to separate them into two categories:

- those risks which people *pose to others*;
- those risks to which *people are exposed*; these are perhaps best understood as referring to people who are *vulnerable to risk*.

People who pose risks to others

The most common area in which risk is approached in this way is the risk assessment of offenders in probation work. The concern here is to identify and accurately assess the risks posed by offenders of re-offending either following release from custody or during the period of a community sentence. The assessment of re-offending has been paralleled by an increased concern with the assessment of likely dangerousness (Kemshall, 2001). Sex offenders, for example – especially paedophiles – have attracted increased regulation, risk assessment and management (Kemshall et al., 2005). Mentally disordered offenders and those with severe personality disorder have also been subject to increasingly formalized and rigorous risk assessment and community management (Home Office, 1999). The common features of such an approach are:

- the person assessed is seen as a poser of risk to others;
- risk is defined as harmful behaviour, with the harm directed at others;
- the desired outcome of risk assessment is accurate identification of risky persons and their likely behaviours;
- the desired outcome of risk management is the reduction or avoidance of risk to others;
- the rights, and to some extent the liberty, of posers of risk can be limited in the interests of protecting others and preventing future risks.

Vulnerability

Assessing exposure to risks – or a person's vulnerability – is central to assessment in social care and social work fields such as community care and work with older persons. Pritchard (1996) has argued that risk-taking is an important feature of all our lives, and that the wish and need to take risks is no less important for older persons. However, a key issue for workers, families and carers is often the risks to which the older person is exposed – whether in the home environment or in residential care. The key features of this approach to risk are:

- Identification and assessment of the risks to which the client is exposed. What risks are they likely to encounter and with what result?
- Determining whether such risks are acceptable or not. Should the risks be run?

- Balancing the desirability of reducing risk against the likely reduction of choice and the likely impact upon quality of life; for example, the reduction of risk to an older person through admission to a residential care home has to be balanced against their consequent loss of independence.
- Risk management strategies are generally informed by the desire to balance risk reduction with autonomy, quality of life and rights.

Is it that clear-cut?

In some cases, a person will both pose risks to others and also present as vulnerable: an example is of the mentally disordered person who, when acutely ill, offends harmfully against others. An individual's vulnerability may itself harbour the seeds of risk to others; for example, mentally ill persons who fail to comply with medication regimes are more likely to commit homicide and suicide than those who do (Boyd Report, 1994), and failures in community care provision to mentally ill persons have been associated with subsequent risk management failures (Blom-Cooper et al., 1995).

In such cases, risk assessment and risk management require a delicate balance between meeting the expressed needs of such individuals, respecting their autonomy and rights, and protecting the public and potential victims. Distinguishing between vulnerability and risk to others may assist practitioners in achieving clarity about this delicate balance of potentially conflicting objectives in risk assessment.

Risk Assessment: Key Components

Risk assessment can be understood as a calculation about the possible occurrence of a negative event or behaviour in the future. This usually involves a calculation of both likelihood, most often expressed in terms of *probability,* and the likely *impact* of the event or behaviour should it occur. Risk assessors are usually required to identify the consequences of any impact (for example, the likely extent of injury to a child), and who might be at risk should the risk occur. Risk assessments are usually made in order to inform decision-making on interventions, or *risk management strategies*. For example, the risks posed by a paedophile upon relocation into the community will inform the type and location of accommodation provided and the intensity of supervision carried out by the police and probation services. Risk assessment and management are inextricably linked.

Risk assessment in social care, social work and probation has the following key features:

- identification of the *risk of what?* – the behaviour or event of concern;
- calculation of its likelihood or probability;
- the conditions, situation(s) or circumstances in which the risk might occur;
- the likely impact of the risk;
- the consequences of the risk and who might be exposed to and harmed by the risk.

There are two basic assessment techniques used to assess risk: clinical assessment and actuarial assessment.

Clinical assessment

Clinical assessment is an individualized assessment method carried out by practitioners on a case-by-case basis and essentially a diagnostic technique derived from mental health and medical fields. It is an individualistic assessment of the personal and social factors deemed to be relevant to the risky event or behaviour, based upon case-based knowledge, personal contact and interviewing of the client and relevant others, and consideration of the individual circumstances of the client. The assessor uses this information to make a judgement of the risk that the individual poses or is exposed to. The process is highly dependent on assessor and client interaction and on interview and observation techniques designed to collect information on social, environmental and personality factors. As the clinical judgement of risk is individualized it is often not generalizable to other individuals. Whilst such assessments are often couched in the language of likelihood, they are not probability calculations.

Clinical risk assessment, particularly in the areas of offending, violent behaviour and child abuse, has a poor record of accuracy (Crighton and Towl, 2005). The method is plagued by various sources of bias and error and is highly dependent upon the subjective processes of interviewing, observation, and the self-report of the client whose risk is being assessed. The subjective bias of the assessor, particularly in cross-cultural situations, has resulted in high levels of inaccuracy (Milner and Campbell 1995). Two types of inaccuracies can result: false positives and false negatives.

- *False positive predictions* are those which predict that a risky behaviour or event will occur (for example, a violent offence) and it subsequently does not. This can result in people being detained in prison beyond their earliest release date, detentions under mental health legislation, removal of children in child protection cases, and over-intrusive responses in community care cases.
- *False negative predictions* are those which predict that a risky event or behaviour will not occur (for example, a child will not be abused by a parent) and it subsequently does. This can result in extensive harm to victims and public and loss of credibility for practitioners and agencies.

Naturally practitioners and their agencies wish to avoid both types of errors.

Whilst limited, clinical assessment can make an important contribution to risk assessment. Such risk assessments often have a low predictive accuracy, but can be useful in explaining behaviour, assessing motivation to change in risky persons, and in providing highly detailed information about specific situations and circumstances. Such assessments often aid practitioner understanding of risk and inform risk management strategies rather than predict with certainty probabilities of risk.

Actuarial assessment

Actuarial risk assessment has its roots in the insurance industry and is based upon statistical calculations of risk. Risk probabilities are usually expressed in numerical terms (for example, a 60 per cent probability of reconviction if released from prison, or a 1-in-3 chance of suicide under specified conditions). Such predictions are based upon aggregated statistical analyses of similar patterns of behaviour in similar circumstances. For example, car insurance for young male drivers is derived from statistical knowledge of the accident rates for that group of drivers. This method has been applied to the risk assessment of offenders, particularly in assessing the likely risk of re-offending if released from prison on parole.

Attempts have been made to apply the method to other social work risks such as child protection, but with limited success (Corby, 1996). Whilst more accurate than clinical assessment, the method is limited by the difficulty of transferring knowledge derived from groups to an individual. Statistical probability is flawed by the 'ecological fallacy' – that is, the use of knowledge about past behaviours relating to a particular group or type of behaviour and the presumption that this is knowledge of real events rather than an over-simplification of likely events:

> To put the matter bluntly, you will either die horribly in a road accident, or . . . you will not. After your eventual death, we can see retrospectively that the odds on this particular adverse event were 'really' either 1 or 0. (Heyman, 1998, p. 10).

A 60 per cent prediction of reconviction upon release from prison when applied to a particular prisoner means that the chances of being correct are 6 out of 10, little better than tossing a coin. Even in cases of high predictive accuracy, for example 90 per cent prediction, this still means that 1 in 10 predictions will be incorrect. Where life and liberty might be at stake this may be too high a false positive rate. Actuarial prediction is further limited by the difficulty in stating with any certainty which group an individual might belong to. Is an individual prisoner likely to be one of the 60 per cent who re-offend or one of the 40 per cent who do not?

The reliable application of statistical data is more difficult to obtain for infrequent behaviours in the population – such as child abuse or paedophilia. Even for those behaviours which occur more frequently (for example re-offending), the application of statistical aggregates to individual prediction is *inherently* limited. This problem is particularly acute around the probability range 40–60 per cent where most people will cluster and where chances are almost even.

In essence, the actuarial method is useful for the assessment and prediction of frequently occurring behaviours or events such as accident rates amongst young male drivers or the likelihood of death from heart disease, but the more infrequent the risk the less accurate the prediction will be.

Neither the clinical nor the actuarial method of assessment can guarantee 100 per cent accuracy, and, for this reason, the use of risk assessment to predict, particularly where liberty and civil rights are at stake has been heavily resisted (Wood, 1988). The moral and ethical issues involved in such predictions are seen as substantial (Walker, 1996), and, for some commentators and practitioners, they militate against the desirability of risk assessment in social work (Caddick and Watson, 1999). Psychiatrists have long eschewed the role of prediction, particularly in the court arena, not least because the accuracy of predictions is seen as unlikely to withstand either ethical or legal challenge (Monahan, 1993).

Holistic risk assessment: the 'second generation'

However, risk assessment is now a central feature of much social care, social work and probation practice, and this has fuelled research and practice responses to the dilemmas it presents.

Approaches to risk assessment which combine the best features of clinical assessment with actuarial prediction are now recommended (Kemshall, 2003). These combined methods are often referred to as 'second generation' tools (Monahan and Steadman, 1994). They combine the ability of clinical assessment to offer detailed explanations of risky behaviours and the circumstances pertinent to risky events in individual cases with the predictive accuracy of actuarially based risk factors. This has resulted in the development of methods utilizing aggregated and statistical data to establish base lines of risk; for example, previous offending is the best predictor of future offending, combined with detailed professional knowledge of individuals and their circumstances.

Such approaches are also seen as essential to the case planning and case management process, as combined methods highlight areas for significant intervention and change.

Risk Management

Risk management cannot guarantee to prevent risk. It can only attempt to reduce the likelihood that risky behaviours or events will occur, or reduce the impact of those behaviours and events should they happen. Minimization rather than reduction is the key, whether this be of self-harm or harm to others. The key objectives of risk management are:

- the reduction of the risk a person presents to others;
- the reduction of vulnerability or exposure to risk of an individual.

In both areas of risk work, practitioners are tasked with:

- identifying the factors which may lead to a risky behaviour or event (sometimes known as precipitating factors);
- working to remove or reduce them;
- reducing the impact of risky behaviours or events by improving the client's coping and/or choice mechanisms;
- reducing the impact of risky behaviours or events by implementing or strengthening the client's protective factors;
- providing and enhancing support networks to prevent situations and behaviours deteriorating;
- implementing strategies to protect potential victims and vulnerable persons 'at risk'.

Case study 1: Posing a risk

Frank is a white, middle-aged offender, currently on bail assessment in a local hostel. He has previous offences of sexual assault against children, and is awaiting a court appearance for similar offences. He is polite and cooperative in the hostel, and has assisted with clearing the garden. Hostel staff describe him as a model resident.

During his stay at the hostel Frank starts to extend his gardening activities to the front garden, and is often seen chatting to local residents and children in the road as they pass by. The hostel is located about a quarter of a mile from the local primary school, and on a busy road.

Hostel staff meet each week to discuss the risk of each resident.

- What factors do you think they should consider in respect of Frank and why?
- What risk do you think he presents, to whom and why?
- What risk management strategies should the hostel staff consider and why?
- What issues do you think would be crucial to a defensible decision in this case?
- Should Frank be relocated?

Case study 2: Vulnerability to risk

Freda is a 77-year-old white woman living alone in council accommodation. Her family have noticed that she is becoming increasingly forgetful, and that the household tasks she previously managed are increasingly difficult for her. Her son recently visited and found a gas ring on, and a saucepan boiled dry. Neighbours have complained about the smell of gas. Freda has always been fiercely independent, and resents any reliance upon family or 'interfering social workers'. However, her family remain worried and after monitoring the situation for some weeks feel they must refer her to the local social services department.

- What factors do you think Freda's family and the social worker should consider?
- What risks do you think Freda is exposed to?
- What risk management strategies should her family and the social worker consider and how can these be balanced with Freda's own wishes and her right to independence?
- What protective factors can be put in place and how can Freda's support network be strengthened?
- What do you think will be the crucial issues in a defensible decision in this case?

Risk management strategies are likely to become the subject of extensive scrutiny in those situations where 'things go wrong' and clients are either harmed or harm others – for example, child deaths in child protection work. Carson (1996) has argued that such situations are always subject to 'hindsight bias', or investigation of what went wrong with the benefit of hindsight. One implication of such bias, either in internal or external inquiries is that workers and their agencies must make 'defensible decisions'.

Defensible decisions

Carson argues that risk decisions are highly complex, based upon uncertain and incomplete knowledge and tools which cannot guarantee 100 per cent accuracy. In such situations 'errors' are bound to occur, and workers and their agencies may find themselves exposed to public scrutiny if not litigation for their decisions and actions. In effect, workers do not have to be 100 per cent accurate, but they do have to show that their decisions were the best that could have been made on the day, and are in line with the best current practice on risk assessment and management. This can be translated into minimum standards for risk decisions:

- Practitioners must work within and be trained in appropriate knowledge and skills for risk work, including clinical, actuarial and legal knowledge.
- Practitioners must base their risk decisions on appropriate information, including the questioning of significant others, and detailed investigative interviewing of the person either posing or 'at risk'.
- Practitioners must assess the likelihood and impact of the risk, based upon the evidence, and actively pursue relevant evidence and facts.
- Risk management plans should be well matched to the risks identified, appropriately resourced and delivered with integrity (adapted from Kemshall, 1998).

Conclusion

Risk is central to modern life. We are exposed to risks every day: food risks, crime risks, health risks, and life-style risks. Many of us are risk-takers, engaging in risky eating habits, smoking despite health promotion campaigns, or driving too fast despite speed restrictions and accident warnings. Social care, social work and probation are professions increasingly involved in risk assessment and management – either risks people pose to others, or risks people are exposed to. This requires highly skilled and complex decision-making in a climate where public and legal scrutiny of 'failed decisions' is likely to take place. Dealing with risk is itself a risky business, hence the trend towards combined and holistic methods and defensible decision making.

Five Key Points

- Risk concerns are framed by the type of work and the agency the practitioner works in.
- The range of risks facing workers can be divided into two key categories: clients who pose a risk, and clients who are vulnerable to risk.
- Combining clinical and actuarial risk assessment into second generation holistic tools provides the most accuracy.
- Risk decisions must be defensible.
- Risk management is about risk reduction and harm minimization, and not the elimination of risk.

Three Questions

? What do you understand by the term *risk*? What do you think are the key features of its assessment?
? Think about the last time you assessed risk either in your personal or professional life. What factors did you consider and why?
? Is your approach to risk assessment clinical, actuarial or holistic?

Further reading

1 Parsloe, P. (ed.) (1999) *Risk Assessment in Social Care and Social Work*, Research Highlights 36. London: Jessica Kingsley.
2 Kemshall, H. (2002) *Risk, Social Policy and Welfare*. Buckingham: Open University Press.
3 Titterton, M. (2005) *Risk and Risk Taking in Health and Social Welfare*. London: Jessica Kingsley.

CHAPTER 2.8

Welfare Rights Practice

Neil Bateman

Social care and social work are concerned with the protection and empowerment of people who have less power within society. And in a society which has great economic inequalities, a high potential for vulnerability and disempowerment inevitably accompanies life on a very low income. Welfare rights practice is one way of empowering and protecting people living in poverty. It is the area of social care activity which involves the worker taking on the role of adviser and advocate on social security, debt and/or housing rights issues on behalf of service users. It involves social care workers acting in a different but complementary way compared to their other roles.

Many welfare rights specialists may not have a social work background though they may be employed within social care organizations as well as by social landlords and the voluntary sector. They will have a specific role to act either as front line advisers or as second tier advisers providing training, consultancy and advocacy in complex cases as well as running initiatives to improve take-up of benefits by groups of people on low incomes. Such specialists may also have expertise in other areas of social welfare law – for example, employment, immigration or community care.

The welfare rights movement's history can be traced back through the history of formal welfare systems and there are examples of advocacy on behalf of paupers under the old English Poor Law. It was also a feature of the work of the Unemployed Workers Movement in the 1920s and 1930s and was a major part of the US Civil Rights Movement because of the blatant misuse of welfare rules by officials in the southern states of the USA against the predominantly African-American black impoverished populace. Indeed, the name 'Welfare Rights' was developed in the USA during this era, the word 'welfare' referring to the patchwork of state administered, discretionary, means tested income maintenance for the poorest people which still exists in that country today.

In the UK, there was a growth in welfare rights activities during the late 1960s and 1970s in which social workers and allied professionals played a key role. This development reflected the growing awareness of poverty. The 1980s saw a significant growth in welfare rights services, frequently located alongside social care services and was a response to the huge changes in inequality and joblessness of that era – unemployment rose from 1.07 million in May 1979 to over 3 million in May 1985 remaining above 2 million until November 1996 (sourced at www.nomis.co.uk). At the same time there were successive reductions in the real value of social security benefits, so welfare rights activity became not only a practical social care response to the growth of poverty but a way of challenging restrictions on entitlement and of highlighting the consequences of government policy.

Throughout history, a major driver behind welfare rights activity has been the experience of people on benefit and of those working on their behalf that welfare officials either deliberately or negligently misapply the rules and deny access to legally guaranteed benefits. This is still often the perception today and provides a strong rationale for the existence of welfare rights advocacy. Welfare rights advice and advocacy also acts as an important safeguard of constitutional rights for some of the most socially excluded members of a modern society who may not have ready access to formal channels of legal assistance to enforce such rights.

Social Work, Poverty and Welfare Rights

Most people who use the social care services are poor and there is clear evidence that poverty either causes or contributes to the issues handled by social care workers; for example, there are clear links between poverty and ill-health (see www.poverty.org.uk); poor people experience a higher rate of family breakdown (see Yeandle et al., 2003); and there are a disproportionate number of children from the poorest households in public care (see Becker, 1997). A more detailed discussion is contained in Bateman (2005).

And yet the relationship between social work and welfare rights practice has not always been an easy one and this is despite the nineteenth-century roots of British social work in the Charity Organisation Society which reflected a concern for the effects of poverty on people and a desire to respond to it.

Two key things have restricted the development of welfare rights practice in social work settings:

- the adversarialism implied in the role of an advocate may not rest comfortably with many social care organizations' expectations of their staff;
- the view that social work is about things other than money and that there is neither the time nor the skill to do welfare rights work.

This is despite the strong practical arguments for social care staff to be engaged in welfare rights practice and the urgings of much practice guidance – for example, in the *Mental Health Act 1983 Code of Guidance*, the *Framework for Assessment of Children in Need* (Department of Health, 2000b), the *Fairer Charging Policies for Home Care Practice Guidance* (Department of Health, 2002b) and the *National Service Framework for Children and Young People* (Department of Health, 2005c).

In trying to understand the ambiguous relationship between social work, welfare rights work and poverty, various writers have all drawn similar conclusions. Becker (1997), for example, says that

> many social workers have distanced themselves traditionally from the material and cash problems of their clients, which if they are acknowledged at all, are seen as the proper responsibility of other agencies, particularly the social security bureaucracies, or other specialists such as welfare rights advisers. While many social work users are claimants of social security, and many are also poor, this does not translate itself into prescriptions for social services policy or social work practice.

Becker further considers the focus of much social work practice:

> social services and social workers have largely managed poor families with children by defining them as dysfunctional families requiring individual or family treatment, rather than confronting and engaging with poverty as a structural and political issue. The social work 'mission' has centred on helping individuals to function more effectively in their social environment.

Concluding her observational study of attitudes to poverty among social workers, Dowling (1999) states that 'social workers appear aware of poverty in theory and acknowledge it is an indisputable part of social services users' lives. In practice the fieldwork has suggested they appear to find it difficult to translate attitudes into actions.' And Green (2000), when discussing the importance of poverty for social work practice, says that 'at the individual level, social workers appear to be suffering from collective amnesia as to why most of us came into the social work profession in the first place'.

The role of the social care worker as welfare rights adviser and advocate has been shaped by the international history of social work. In the USA, for example, state employed social workers are frequently engaged in aspects of income maintenance and the policing of welfare expenditure. Consequently much of the welfare rights activity in the USA has developed among voluntary organizations and among private attorneys funded through contingency fees. Social work practice in Sweden and some other European countries is often linked to income maintenance and generous income maintenance to behavioural expectations. This can compromise the social care worker's role as advocate on social security issues – even though effective operational protocols can minimize such conflict.

In the UK the drift towards social care organizations becoming income maintenance bodies because of gaps in the social security system or deliberate policy changes nationally has implications for the role of social care workers as welfare rights advocates. For example, the active involvement of social care services in providing income maintenance to care leavers and young people looked after under the Children Act, to destitute families under the Children Act, or to people cut off from the benefits system because of their immigration status, all have major implications for both the nature of care services and welfare rights practice. Similarly, the limited provisions of the Social Fund administered by the Department for Work and Pensions, have resulted in local authorities having to make up shortfalls in payments as well as spend time advocating for service users who have been refused. For a summary of research findings, see Craig (2006).

Since 2000 there has been a fixation among local authority services with obtaining 'stars' from government for good quality services. Very few of the criteria used for awarding stars have any relationship with tackling poverty. Local authorities have also displayed a marked reluctance to be publicly critical of central government social policies and the fall in headline unemployment has also masked underlying poverty.

Social Work and Advocacy

No work to empower disempowered people can be taken seriously unless its proponents are prepared to be advocates. Advocacy has a long history in the affections of social work, but there are signs that increasing managerialism and the workers' feelings of being under siege have encouraged people to avoid welfare rights work and the associated role of advocate. The use of eligibility criteria and the extension of charges for services both act to marginalize the welfare rights and advocacy perspective. Indeed, social care practitioners are now themselves increasingly likely to be on the receiving end of advocacy – particularly given the influence of the Human Rights Act 1998 and the development of litigation about local authority duties to provide community care services.

The General Social Care Council's Code of Practice for Social Care Workers requires care professionals to 'protect the rights and promote the interests of service users and carers . . . promote the independence of service users and carers . . . respect the rights of service users' (General Social Care Council, 2004). This requirement places advocacy at the heart of the social care worker's ethical obligations. The advocacy role can extend to that of whistleblower and has been given some statutory protection by employment legislation.

The ethics of advocacy

Because advocacy is always concerned with securing the best outcome for the service user, it involves a strong ethical emphasis on principles for practice. The advocate must always:

- act in the service user's best interests;
- act in accordance with their wishes and instructions;
- keep them properly informed;
- carry out instructions with diligence and competence (recognizing the limits of their knowledge and competence);
- act impartially and offer frank, independent advice;
- maintain client confidentiality.

In a classic social work textbook, Davies (1994) states that 'strategies of change in social work might sometimes need to be directed, not at the client, but at dysfunctional elements in the client's environment'. He goes on to describe two forms of advocacy in social work: personal advocacy and structural advocacy. Personal advocacy, he says, focuses on the individual's need and structural advocacy on a community or group. 'In either case, the assumption is that the social worker has skills and qualities or access to resources that are likely to tip the balance in the favour of those whose interests would otherwise be overlooked or over-ridden.'

The most common and successful form of advocacy in social work will be welfare rights work where the effects of a lack of an adequate income, often as a result of official error or interpretation, become pressing concerns in the lives of social work consumers.

The Importance of Welfare Rights Work

A great many arguments can be put for the case that social care workers should be engaged in welfare rights work:

- It is a practical response to the poverty of service users who will have money problems which need resolving so that they can survive in society.
- It eases the hardship which poverty causes and the consequent damage which creates a need for social work intervention.
- The additional income helps service users to lead more independent lives.
- The longstanding problems of poor levels of benefit take-up, poor standards of decision-making on benefit entitlement and the lack of widespread independent advice on benefits produces a clear need. 'It is not clear that the Department gives high priority to the quality of decision making' (Department for Work and Pensions, 2005).
- It builds a rapport with service users who will not be interested in nor respectful of a view that it is not part of the social care worker's role.
- The problem solving approach inherent in welfare rights work can be incorporated into task-centred casework methods.
- The alarmingly high error rate by the Department for Work and Pensions and other welfare bureaucracies means that one can neither rely on them as a source of consistent help and advice for consumers nor assume that people have been paid the correct amount of benefit.
- The need to sort out an external agency problem inherent in welfare rights work can put practitioner and service user on an equal footing – which complements empowering approaches to social work practice.
- The emphasis on rights to welfare reduces the potential for value based or discriminatory practice which may spread beyond financial problems, thus improving practice standards.
- An increase in income from benefits advice has proven positive effects on health and well-being, and higher levels of means-tested benefits increase babies' birth weights.

- Disability-related benefits are likely to be used by service users to buy-in additional care. For example, it has been estimated that the care component of disability living allowance to people on low incomes adds the equivalent of more than 25 per cent to community care budgets (Noble et al., 1997).
- The almost universal existence of charges for community care services means that service users whose income has been maximized are not only more likely to pay such charges, but the charge formulae frequently create additional revenue for social care services when service users receive particular benefits.
- It reduces unnecessary expenditure – for example, the creative use of the benefits system to subsidize supported housing, as an alternative to payments under the Children Act to destitute families, or to supplement payments to foster parents.
- An improved income reduces family stress.
- It increases the supply of money within low income communities thus aiding their social and economic regeneration.
- If properly supported and resourced, many social care workers find this an enjoyable area of work which contrasts with their other roles as social controllers and gatekeepers of services.
- Social care workers work with some very marginalized people, who may be unable to access or sustain contact with mainstream welfare rights advice services.

An important summary of the need for and effectiveness of welfare rights practice can be found in Wiggan and Talbot (2006).

Welfare rights work ranges from simple form filling through to complex legal argument and litigation. It is an ever-changing subject with numerous amendments to social security legislation each year. For example, the National Audit Office (2005) has observed that between 2000 and 2004 there were six Acts of Parliament and 364 Statutory Instruments affecting social security law.

A frequent response to such problems is to declare that the social work task does not extend to welfare rights work, but this response is not sustainable: because most social work customers are poor, they will require welfare rights help in some form, and unresolved money problems exacerbate and create other problems. Furthermore, an approach based on expecting external agencies to undertake welfare rights work (especially front-line advice services) frequently fails to meet the needs of the most marginalized and socially excluded people – the very people who are more likely to be the consumers of social work services.

It is possible to identify an appropriate level of competence in welfare rights practice for busy social care workers undertaking emotionally demanding work and which ensures that more complex issues are passed onto experts – indeed, one needs a reasonable level of knowledge in order to be able to identify when skilled help is necessary and a frequent complaint by welfare rights advisers is that all too often, even simple welfare rights problems which are having a detrimental effect on service users are not identified by social care workers and/or not referred on.

The nature of social care assessment lends itself to incorporating a welfare rights check. During an assessment, one is working at the service user's pace to build an all-round picture of social care needs. The process often involves gathering detailed information and evidence about material circumstances, ill-health or disability. It is easy to translate such information into a check on benefit entitlement – indeed, a typical community care assessment essentially collects the same evidence as is needed for a disability living allowance or attendance allowance claim.

The key to empowering social care workers to act confidently as welfare rights advisers and advocates is ready access to highly skilled, training, back-up and support. The back-up must be available *within* the organization, and many social care agencies have developed in-house welfare rights services to do this and some specialist provision is essential; for example, see Levy and Payne (2006).

It is also essential for there to be consistent messages from senior managers about the importance of welfare rights work and a commitment from them that social work includes advocacy. In this way the apparent complexity and time consuming nature of welfare rights practice is made manageable.

The specialist back-up service should provide training and consultancy support and a protocol for taking on the more complex cases; access to standard welfare rights textbooks and other written guidance is essential. Social care workers can then integrate welfare rights work with their practice, advise competently on benefit entitlement for service users, assist with the claiming process, deal with problems arising out of it and challenge wrongful and dubious refusals of benefit in the more straightforward cases.

Some Examples of Welfare Rights Practice

Welfare rights practice can involve work on behalf of both groups and individuals. At its best, it involves a strategic response to the issues raised in individual cases. A suitable level of competence for social care practitioners would be:

- Identifying benefit and tax credit entitlement in common situations.
- Helping people through the claims process, providing supporting evidence and resolving common problems which can arise.
- Acting as an advocate to resolve common problems and successfully challenging straightforward benefit refusals.
- Protecting clients from inappropriate questioning or investigation by benefit officials.
- Attempting to modify negative or stereotyped attitudes among benefit officials that they deal with.
- Supporting vulnerable service users through appeals, with representation being done by a welfare rights specialist. (Bateman, 2005, p. 61)

Here are some examples to illustrate the competences:

- Completing an *attendance allowance* application form for an older person, gathering supporting evidence for the claim and writing a supporting letter highlighting areas of strong entitlement. When the benefit is awarded, ensuring that the higher levels of means-tested benefits payable to people on attendance allowance were put into payment and backdated.
- Advising a parent with a child who has severe behavioural problems that they would be entitled to a *disability living allowance* and assisting with completing

the claim form and providing a letter illustrating the child's need for additional supervision; chasing up the Department for Work and Pensions if the claim is delayed; drafting a letter seeking a review if it is refused; and referring to the in-house welfare rights service to represent at an appeal tribunal if this was not successful.

- By negotiation and advocacy, securing a replacement payment of *income support* for someone whose benefit cheque was misplaced by the Department for Work and Pensions.
- Preparing a financial statement to persuade *creditors* that a service user is unable to pay unsecured debts and to obtain repayment of secured debts at an affordable rate. Seeking help if this is not successful.
- Advocating on behalf of a service user with a *learning disability* that they did not need someone to be an appointee who would therefore control their benefits.
- Challenging a housing official who did not take a *homelessness* application from a homeless person but instead offered advice about where to look for accommodation.
- Drafting a letter of appeal about a *benefit overpayment* with help from a welfare rights adviser over the phone.
- With support from the welfare rights service, undertaking a trawl of pupils in a *special school* to maximize benefit take-up.

An example of the knowledge and skills needed for welfare rights practice, including those appropriate for the type of welfare rights work undertaken by social care workers, has been published by the Scottish Executive as part of the suggested competences for Type I advisers in the *Scottish National Standards for Information and Advice Services*. It is available from www.communitiesscotland.gov.uk.

Knowledge and Skills for Advocacy and Welfare Rights Practice

A range of specific skills is needed for effective welfare rights work (Bateman, 2000 and 2005), including many which are used elsewhere in social work practice. They can be summarized as:

- Interviewing skills – especially in gathering relevant facts and evidence to support advocacy.
- Recording and report writing – especially important for any advocacy involving correspondence or in putting together a comprehensive and coherent argument in support of the service user.
- Skills in persuasion and assertiveness.
- Skills in negotiation – especially relevant where the law does not strongly support a service user's case.
- The range of skills associated with self-management and the effective use of one's time.
- Legal research skills and the ability to get a good grasp of the relevant and most favourable legal points in the service user's favour.

- Having a sufficient knowledge of social security law for the type of work being undertaken.
- Skills in litigation – in other words the ability to represent somebody at a hearing.

Central to being able to undertake welfare rights work as a social care worker, is a good grasp of the relevant legal framework of social security. As the level of expertise in welfare rights work is a continuum, there clearly has to be a cut-off point for the degree of knowledge required, but practice shows that it is not an impossible task to equip social care workers with the correct level of knowledge and skill in order to meet an appropriate level of competency – particularly if there is easy access to an in-house welfare rights support service.

Conclusion

Welfare rights practice is a combination of skills and knowledge which social care workers should include in their toolkit. It is a practical and empowering response to poverty which itself has major implications for social work and care practice. Welfare rights practice involves advocacy skills but it can be effectively carried out by busy practitioners provided the level of competence required of them is clear and if satisfactory support systems are in place.

For more information on welfare rights, visit www.neilbateman.co.uk.

Five Key Points

- Poverty has a major negative effect on many aspects of peoples' lives and it both creates and exacerbates the need for social care services.
- Welfare rights work is a practical and effective response to individual poverty.
- Welfare rights practice is a valid part of social work.
- Good back-up is essential to provide and support the knowledge base required by practitioners and to enable them to act as effective advocates.
- Social care workers often have an ambivalent response to poverty and to welfare rights practice.

Three Questions

? What are the implications of poverty for social care practice and service users?

? What is an appropriate level of competence in welfare rights for social care workers?

? What can employing organizations do to empower their staff to become effective welfare rights advocates?

Further reading

1 Bateman, N. (2005) *Practising Welfare Rights*. London: Routledge.
2 Child Poverty Action Group (published annually) *Welfare Benefits Handbook*, London: CPAG.
3 Disability Alliance (published annually) *Disability Rights Handbook*, London: Disability Alliance Educational & Research Association.

CHAPTER 2.9

Counselling

Janet Seden

Any discussion of counselling and social work has to consider a range of overlapping aspects of the relationship between the two areas of work. First, social work and counselling are two very different activities but often they are carried out in parallel. The same service user may require social work and counselling interventions. For example, Prior et al. (1999) studied the views and perceptions of children and carers involved in social work intervention in the area of child sexual abuse. They found that the participants in their study, despite some concerns, generally perceived the social workers to be helpful. When this was explored further, the carers and children most valued those social workers who provided emotional support, reassurance, information, explanation, well coordinated services and also helped them to find counselling or therapy.

Second, counsellors and social workers are trained differently but share similar skills, knowledge and values. Some practitioners have both social work and counselling training and experience. The carers and children in Prior et al.'s study valued those social workers who coordinated services well but also listened attentively and provided emotional support. Middleton (1998) shows that parents of disabled children value social workers who are proactive in arranging services but also offer supportive counselling, advice and listening. Often social workers have the skills to offer supportive counselling to their clients. Trotter et al. (2002, p. 126) describe how a social worker adapted social work skills to support the father of a young offender. The parent reported that:

> Prior to the counselling I was at my wits end as to how to cope with the situation my son and I found myself in regard to his offending, its effects on those around him, the grief it was causing . . . clearly these sessions could not be a cure all but they offered tools that could and did assist . . . I believe many families would value this kind of assistance.

Third, social workers and counsellors used to be employed in very different settings; nowadays counsellors and social workers often work within the same organizations in teams or in partnership arrangements. Examples are adult mental health teams, adolescent psychiatry services, post-disaster support work. The Buckinghamshire post-disaster team is a planning and training partnership led by social services but including voluntary counselling agencies (Smith et al., 2003). Over 12 years, through working together and responding to local crises they have developed joint practice wisdom on the efficacy of various ways of responding to human need in a crisis situation, using the insights of social workers, counsellors and others as needed.

However, it is still helpful to outline some of the differences between the role of the social worker and the role of the counsellor, in order to examine how their practices and skills are complementary.

Approaches to Counselling

In 2006 the website of the British Association for Counselling and Psychotherapy (BACP) defined counselling as taking place when:

> a counsellor sees a client in a private and confidential setting to explore a difficulty the client is having, distress they may be experiencing or perhaps their dissatisfaction with life, or loss of a sense of direction and purpose. It is always at the request of the client as no one can properly be 'sent' for counselling.
>
> By listening attentively and patiently the counsellor can begin to perceive the difficulties from the client's point of view and can help them to see things more clearly, possibly from a different perspective. Counselling is a way of enabling choice or change or reducing confusion. It does not involve giving advice or directing a client to take a particular course of action. Counsellors do not judge or exploit their clients in any way . . .

The key elements of the counselling process are:

- Service provided when you want to make a change in your life.
- An opportunity to make sense of your individual circumstances.
- Contact with a therapist who helps identify the choices for change.
- Support for the individual during their process of change.
- The end result leaving you better equipped to cope for the future. (www.bacp.co.uk)

The BACP definition applies to a range of different therapeutic counselling approaches, underpinned by diverse theorizing about the human personality and society. There are many counselling theories and methods – for example, feminist counselling or Gestalt – and an extensive literature which explores the thinking underpinning different approaches and applications (Corey, 1997; Egan, 1990; Heron, 1997; Jacobs, 1995a, 1995b; McLeod, 2003; Walker, 1995a, 1995b).The three most influential approaches have been person-centred counselling, psychodynamic counselling and cognitive / behavioural counselling. These are summarized next.

Person-centred counselling

Carl Rogers is the originator of what he called client-centred therapy. He believed that people have a 'self-actualizing tendency' and with the right support can trust their own feelings and thoughts to make their own decisions and life choices. The therapist's role is to create the conditions that allow growth to take place. The therapist's acceptance of the person shown through 'congruence', 'unconditional positive regard' and empathy provides a therapeutic environment where the individual who has been experiencing difficulties can achieve this new freedom. Therapists need the personal qualities, skills and values which enable them to create a facilitative relationship and this takes time and commitment. Fuller accounts of the person-centred approach and the training needed to practise are given by Rogers (1951, 1961) and Mearns and Thorne (1999, 2000).

Psychodynamic counselling

Psychodynamic counsellors build a positive therapeutic relationship based on trust and acceptance in a similar way to person-centred counsellors (Jacobs, 1993). However, psychodynamic counsellors work to understand the extent to which past childhood experiences affect the client's present difficulties. They draw from theories of human growth and development (Jacobs, 1988, 1998) to understand the psychological connections between developmental life events and the person's present situation. Psychodynamic theory derives from Freud's understanding of the structure of the personality (id, ego and superego) and the importance of the unconscious, seen in 'transference and counter-transference relationships' and 'defences' (Jacobs, 1988, 1991, 1998). The insight the person gains through the counselling sessions enables them to make changes and different choices for the future. The ability to practise this way is gained through training, including personal experience of psychodynamic therapy.

Cognitive approaches

Counsellors who work from this perspective assume that if someone changes the way they think about themselves and their situation and learn new and more positive ways of conceptualizing themselves and their lives they will resolve their difficulties. There are a range of different cognitive therapies (Beck, 1976; Ellis et al., 1997). Some cognitive approaches are combined therapies – for example, cognitive-behavioural, cognitive-analytic – but have in common the premise that behaviours and emotions are affected by faulty thinking. Therapy is usually on a short-term basis. The client is questioned about the problems and the therapist intervenes directly by suggesting ways of changing thoughts, feelings and behaviours. The client will be expected to practise new ways of thinking and behaving (homework) between sessions. This kind of approach is widely used in clinical settings and specialist therapist training is necessary to practise.

Finding the Right Counsellor

Sometimes therapists combine different theories to underpin the counselling they offer and it can be difficult for the service user, especially if they are feeling stressed or overwhelmed by their situation, to assess the usefulness of what is being offered, especially as free counselling therapy is in short supply. They may be under pressure to accept whatever is available, or recommended by a professional. It is helpful, therefore for social workers to understand the differences between the various counselling therapies and enable service users to find what is appropriate. They also need this understanding when they refer people to counselling services or purchase counselling for a particular service user.

Some of the more subtle differences make it difficult for someone to know what any particular kind of therapeutic counselling involves. If people are thinking about starting counselling and are to be truly empowered to make a realistic choice about what suits them, they may need advice about what is involved and the possible pitfalls as well as the benefits of counselling. Some counsellors specialize – for example, drugs counsellors – and research studies can show which kind of therapies are useful in specific circumstances.

Whatever the counselling therapy, the critical building block which enables the sessions is the relationship between the counsellor and the client, often called the working alliance (Jacobs, 1993). Another key element is that the client chooses to work with the therapist and is thus assumed to be motivated to achieve change. This can be different in social work where clients may be reluctant. However, the issues that lead people to become users of social work services and the compulsory nature of some of the work, means that social workers often meet people who might benefit from an in-depth counselling approach.

Social Work

Whatever agency a social work practitioner is employed by – voluntary, private, local authority, fieldwork or group care – the law provides a framework of roles and responsibilities for their work. Throughout their professional life social workers are expected to respond to complex and detailed changes in the law, policy and procedures. This is far less the case for counsellors both in private and public roles, where the aspect of law that might most closely concern them is deciding when to breach confidentiality because a client has disclosed an involvement in illegal activities. This will be rare.

Social workers' professional activities are embedded in government policy guidelines to which they are accountable. The work is also defined by the six key roles and national occupational standards which they have to meet in order to practice (TOPSS, 2003a, 2003b, 2003c). The international definition adopted in the requirements for the qualifying degree defines social work as a profession which

> promotes social change, problem solving in human relationships and the empowerment and liberation of people to enhance well-being. Utilising theories of human

> behaviour and social systems, social work intervenes at the points where people interact with their environments. Principles of human rights and social justice are fundamental to social work. (International Association of Schools of Social Work and the International Federation of Social Workers, cited in TOPSS, 2003a)

Social workers cannot just consider someone's personal and psychological goals, they are also involved in social action and improving social and material environments. They are often employed to carry out tasks which government mandates them to do – for example, child protection, criminal justice and mental health work. Sometimes the person they are working with hasn't chosen a service, doesn't really want a social worker and may be ambivalent, reluctant or hostile to the whole idea of state intervention in their lives. Some actions social workers take – particularly in mental health, criminal justice and child care, and recently asylum seeking – have profound implications for people's lives and liberties. Social workers also may have less choice than counsellors about the methods they use and who they work with, because of the expectation that they will follow government guidelines and meet relevant targets. So, even where counsellors and social workers can agree their codes of ethics, their roles give them different kinds of responsibilities.

Differences in practice, however, are not always clear cut. Motivation is sometimes created by the necessity of compulsion or containment and counsellees who leave therapy because it is uncomfortable can prematurely terminate useful work. Additionally, counsellors who are employed in similar agencies to social workers, such as NHS Trusts may find themselves equally challenged by the demands of business models as described by Harris (2003) which includes, among other things, contracting with the implication that the provider has to implement the purchaser's decisions, performance indicators which measure what is done against pre-set standards, and rationing.

Managerialism has influenced social work practice since the 1990s (Waine and Henderson, 2003). However, social workers have been tenacious about prioritizing relationships with service users. The same issues may now impact more on counsellors. Commissioning arrangements between the NHS, social services and counsellors, may mean that private counsellors, who used to be very self-determining with their clients about the nature of the work, will be subject to the scrutiny and wishes of purchasers. Counsellors in some settings may find that their managers ration the number of sessions any client may have.

However, people continue to appreciate practitioners who think relationships matter, as research into service user views into what makes a good social worker shows. For example, children (Department of Health, 2001b) value five main qualities in practitioners, reliability, practical help, support, time to listen and respond, seeing children's lives in the round. Service users want social workers to be good at practical parts of the role, but also to listen and build a relationship. In other words, they want them to be competent at their mandated role and carry it out using counselling type skills (Seden, 2005). Thus social workers and counsellors still hold much in common.

Some Commonalities

Shared history

The first social workers used mainly counselling and casework in their tasks (Hollis, 1964) and were trained from a literature and methodology very close to counselling training (Biestek, 1961). Over the years, social work has drawn from other sources of knowledge – especially sociology and social policy – and has actively prioritized advocacy, empowerment and combating social disadvantage through anti-oppressive practices (Braye and Preston-Shoot, 1995).

The result is a body of knowledge directly applied to the aims of social work (Adams et al., 2002; Davies, 1994;, Howe, 1987; Payne, 2006; Trevithick, 2005). There has also been increasing preoccupation with the means to deliver services – for example, through markets, commissioners and providers (Taylor-Gooby and Lawson, 1993). This has led social workers to a more bureaucratic and directive kind of work in contrast to the more personal kind of assistance given by counsellors.

However, social workers have remained concerned to relate well to people The use of counselling skills and some supportive counselling remains a critical component of the best practice (Seden, 2005; Trevithick, 2005). Many social workers are motivated by the wish to 'care', 'help people' and 'make a difference'. They work to a code of ethics which shares some principles with counselling ethics – for example, ideas about human rights, and service user voice and autonomy. Many social workers find the person-centred values of Carl Rogers useful, even if occasionally they have to step in to safeguard someone through a compulsory intervention.

Social work values include anti-discriminatory and anti-oppressive practice and counsellors have also become more aware of the potential for oppression in some approaches (BACP, 2006; McLeod, 2003). Counselling practice has been re-evaluated for its relevance to disadvantaged groups and to ethnic and other minority groups. Counsellors have also re-examined ideologies and practice, attitudes and values (Davies and Neale, 1996; Lago and Thompson, 1996). Increasingly both social work and counselling have sought to practise from a research-informed evidence base and there remains a creative synergy between the two disciplines.

Shared understandings of people

Social workers, like counsellors draw from person-centred, psychodynamic and cognitive behavioural theorizing to understand people and create methods for practice (Payne, 2005a; Trevithick, 2005). In the varied, everyday activities of social work it is impossible to function without engaging in some level of relationship and drawing from psychological as well as social theories about how to understand people and their lives. Social workers become involved with people needing support; protection from self or others; help to deal with disadvantage or injustice; in fact any combination of life-changing events depending on the particular circumstances. Developmental understandings of human growth and life course which are used to help people receiving counselling about a crisis, change, transition or loss are equally useful in social work and care (Seden and Katz, 2003) to support people through change and crisis.

Shared skills for communication and relationship

The counselling skills used to communicate and build relationships are central to social work and require practice and training opportunities to be effective. They are shown in the box below.

Basic counselling and communication skills:

- attention giving; active listening; non-critical acceptance;
- paraphrasing; reflecting back; summarizing and checking;
- ability to use different kinds of questions; minimal prompting; alternatives to questions;
- empathic understanding; linking; immediacy;
- challenging; confronting; work with defences;
- goal setting; problem solving; focusing techniques;
- knowledge about own and other's use of body language;
- avoidance of judging and moralistic responses;
- boundary awareness; structuring techniques; the ability to say difficult things constructively;
- the ability to offer feedback; techniques for defusing, avoiding the creation of and managing hostility.

Source: Seden (2005).

Such skills are essential for counselling, for interviewing and social work processes such as assessments, planning, carrying out and reviewing work and other core social work functions at the office, in care establishments and people's own homes and partnership working. Thus the skills overlap continues.

The Continuing Relationship between Counselling and Social Work

Brearley (1991) traces the historical interaction between counselling and social work and how the two activities influence each other in terms of skills, knowledge and values while at the same time have distinct identities and training pathways. She writes:

> A logical categorization of the counselling dimensions of social work would therefore be as follows,

- counselling skills underpinning the whole range of social work
- counselling as a significant component of the work, carried out in conjunction with other approaches
- counselling as a major explicit part of the job description. (Brearley, 1991, p. 30)

This remains the case, but increasingly multi-professional and inter-professional approaches to delivering services are being developed with social workers and counsellors in the same team. This creates a different set of relationships and debates about the ways in which counselling and social work interact.

Some social workers find themselves marginalized from the counselling role, as independent counsellors are commissioned to undertake therapeutic work. Valios (2000) quotes someone who retrained from social work to counselling because of 'my frustration with the way social work was going, it was increasingly about costs, budgets, and performance narrowly defined by managers and organisations.'

Managerialism and business methods have thus alienated some social workers from their jobs. However, there may be benefits to clients from having counselling provided by an experienced independent counsellor focusing on therapeutic needs. There may also be issues for the purchasing agency if those counsellors are unaware of the legal and practice issues around the work. The commissioner has to be clear about the counsellor's brief, in particular whether the session is completely confidential and independent, or whether there are limits to that or even expectations of feedback to the social worker if, for example, a child discloses problems about contact with a carer or other matter relevant to the social work. Many independent counsellors would not agree to disclose anything from individual sessions, while purchasers might expect the counsellor to have some allegiance to the funding authority. Such issues need to be clarified in each situation if the partnerships between social workers and counsellors are to be successful. It may be easier to debate and resolve when counselling services are more integrated with social work settings.

Counselling can be integrated into mainstream services effectively. Long (2000, p. 60) describes a counselling service for parents and children within a local authority family centre:

> The service is now approaching the end of its second year and the managers are committed to provide a therapeutic service which aims to intervene with vulnerable families who are having difficulties. The managers see it as cost effective and efficient as well as preventative. The counselling service is now become an integral part of the family centre and the hours the service provides have been extended to include some work on early assessment of young children's development where there are mental health problems in the family.

As the organizational framework for practice changes, and social workers and counsellors are working together in multidisciplinary and multi-agency structures, they may be subject to similar organizational constraints and dilemmas. They will also need more than ever to appreciate the boundaries of each other's roles, to understand each other's contributions to the well-being of people using services and to understand their own roles in the particular organization.

There will also need to be clarity in some key areas such as values and policies and practices regarding confidentiality. Where teams are set up with professionals who are dual qualified in social work and/or counselling or psychotherapy the team can jointly decide the boundaries on confidentiality. This is particularly important for those working in children's services, as with children there can never be total confidentiality and no-one can be sure that something will not be said to a counsellor by a child which is a child protection issue. Working closely in multidisciplinary teams provides an environment where such issues can be clarified and decisions made, such as separating the person in the role of therapist for the child from a key role in investigation.

In a mixed economy of contexts for service provision, professionals from different backgrounds will need to know enough about counselling roles and the similarities and differences to their social work roles to be able to deliver an effective response to human need and make the necessary referrals and partnership arrangements that benefit the people who need the service. For example, counsellors working independently will continue to have a freedom of contract with clients, subject to BACP regulation and codes of ethics, which social workers rarely have, even when working in the voluntary and private sector. The challenge will be to review understandings of the commonalities and difference between the role of counsellor and the role of social worker and to know what and how each person might contribute to any particular person's well-being.

Five Key Points

- Counselling and social work are different activities, but can happen in parallel.
- Counsellors and social workers share some skills, knowledge and values.
- Social workers must understand the different counselling therapies to help people find the therapy they need.
- Service users value relationship skills and supportive counselling from all practitioners.
- New organizational arrangements for delivering services are changing the relationships between social work and counseling.

Three Questions

? What are the main overlaps in skill knowledge and values between social workers and counsellors?

? What are the main differences between social work and counselling roles?

? What counselling skills do service users value from social workers?

Further reading

1 McLeod, J. (2003) *An Introduction to Counselling*. Buckingham: Open University Press.
2 Seden, J. (2005) *Counselling Skills in Social Work Practice*. Maidenhead: Open University Press and McGraw Hill Education.
3 Trevithick, P. (2005) *Social Work Skills*. Maidenhead: Open University Press and McGraw Hill Education.

CHAPTER 2.10

Anger Management

David Leadbetter

Describing it as one of the most talked about and least studied emotions, Novaco (1975) defined anger as 'an effective stress reaction to provocation events'. It is an emotional state encompassing mild irritation to intense fury. It has no diagnostic classification, yet given the popular perception of ever-increasing levels of stress and frustration in modern society, it has the potential to impact on the lives of all. Human service workers, in particular, may be brought into direct and regular contact with a diverse range of people for whom the inability to regulate and manage anger, and its behavioural corollaries, may impair the quality of their own lives and erode the emotional and physical well-being of others.

The human infant's undifferentiated feelings of distress coalesce into recognizable anger as early as four months.

Anger can play a facilitative role in social interactions, counteracting feelings of helplessness, promoting self-assertion, energizing the victim and, in many situations, may serve a constructive 'potentiating function' (Novaco, 1976). However, the historic perception has been of a negative force, a *passion* which grips, assails and possesses the individual, sitting in opposition to reason. Such a view detracts from our understanding of the emotion, preventing us from seeing its socially constructed nature and the influence and durability of underlying cognitive structures which determine what receives attention and how events are appraised.

Anger is significantly associated with a wide range of physical health problems, such as raised blood pressure, cardiovascular disorders, tension headaches and mental health disturbances including disorders of personality, childhood and adolescence organic syndromes, paranoia, depression and post-traumatic stress. The relationship between anger and violent behaviour is not simple, nor is anger an essential precursor to aggression. However, anger is likely to increase the likelihood of violence, and it is the association between anger and interpersonal violence that has tended to dominate research and clinical agendas.

Anger may impair an individual's social functioning due to its severity, duration or frequency. Whilst Averill (1982) suggests that violence is a very low frequency response to anger in the general population, the individual's failure to develop effective self-regulatory mechanisms and skill repertoires for responding to perceived provocation is recognized as a key variable which can contribute to dysfunctional and abusive behaviour.

Links have been demonstrated between anger and violent conduct in a number of different contexts:

- learning disability (Benson et al., 1986);
- aggressive children (Dodge and Frame, 1982);
- young offenders (McGuire, 1995b);
- manslaughter (Averill, 1982);
- rape (Groth, 1979);
- domestic violence (Dobash and Dobash, 1979);
- child abuse (Gardner and Gray, 1982).

Human service workers may be required to support or act as change agents to service users for whom the inability to maintain self control is a powerful and longstanding component of dysfunctional or dangerous behaviour. Whilst the distinction between the treatment and management of aggression must be recognized, the operational ability to engage constructively with such problems demands the development of a range of effective intervention strategies supported by a practice milieu which promotes personal safety.

The Information Processing Model

A range of remedial approaches to anger management have emerged within different theoretical frameworks. For example, behaviourist approaches have tended to focus on the reinforcers which maintain behaviour. From a *constructional* or *skills deficit* perspective, anger is seen as a result of poor social skills and an inability to express emotion appropriately. Such perspectives have concentrated on the construction of repertoires of social skills, utilizing methods such as instruction, role-play, modelling, coaching and feedback, aimed at enabling the individual to manage previously aversive situations. But the most important development has been in our understanding of the influence of subjective interpretations and appraisals of events in the genesis of anger. These have emerged from the broad church of cognitive behaviourism, which represents a collection of assumptions about disturbance and a set of treatment interventions in which human cognitions are assigned a central role.

Exploring the processes through which the growing child develops the ability to regulate his or her own behaviour, the Russian psychologist, Luria (1961), charted a process of self-regulation of internal impulses, in which the child's dependency shifts from external adult verbal cues and speech to their own overt speech, until finally behaviour is governed largely by covert or internal speech between the ages of 4½ and 5½. In reviewing studies on the role of verbal mediation, Goldstein and Keller (1987, p. 40) conclude that 'there is considerable evidence to support the belief that self control develops largely as a function of a child's development of internal language mechanisms'. Meichenbaum (1971) demonstrated the link between inner speech and impulsive behaviour in 4-year-olds: reflective youngsters who took their time over tasks tended to use their private speech in a more instrumental, self-guiding fashion whilst the private speech of impulsive children had a greater self-stimulatory content.

The emergent emphasis on the regulatory role of inner speech reflects a key principle within cognitive behaviourism: there is a reciprocal relationship between the three modalities of thoughts, feelings and behaviour; change in any one effecting change in the others.

Various studies have confirmed that individuals prone to anger and aggression often suffer from specific information processing problems and attributional bias. 'Ample research has demonstrated that the appraisal of events as provocation stimuli (direct or indirect threats or aversive stimuli) influences the magnitude of aggressive behaviour' (Feindler and Ecton, 1986, p. 3) which may lead to a thinking style, described by Howells (1982) as *aggressonogenic.*

Predisposed individuals may be inclined to attend selectively to aversive cues. Shelley and Toch (1968) found that men with violent case histories were more likely than non-violent prisoners to interpret presented experimental scenarios as violent. Similar conclusions have emerged from studies on children (Naseby et al., 1980) and adolescent males (Lochman, 1984). McGuire (1997, p. 73) has suggested that aggressive children demonstrate specific processing errors: they 'encode a narrower range of environmental cues; selectively attend to aggressive cues; attribute hostile intent to others, especially in ambiguous situations; more readily label internal states as anger; generate fewer alternative solutions to problems; select action orientated rather than reflective solutions; possess a more limited range of interactional skills; and manifest an "egocentric" perspective in social problem solving'.

Attributional errors and biases tend to overemphasize person-based explanations (for example, personality and intention) and minimize situational variables (for example, environmental pressures) within the individuals' interpretative judgements. Thus, in the clichéd scenario, a drinker may be inclined to interpret the spilling of his pint as an intentional or malicious act, rather than an accident caused by jostling in a crowded bar situation, and may retaliate accordingly.

A *false consensus* may further influence attributional judgements. The incorrect assumption that one's own behaviour is typical or normative may erode empathy – a crucial component of effective communication – and restrict the ability to understand the perspective of others. Reliance on first impressions may create an *anchoring effect* in which initial impressions carry disproportionate weight and become resistant to change by subsequent events, a processing error which arousal is likely to reinforce. Such errors are likely to result in enduring patterns of behaviour (schemata or 'cognitive scripts') which assist the individual to understand and manage new events. However, where such scripts oversensitize the individual to provocation, and immobilize them within an egocentric worldview, they may also promote misinterpretation and a disregard for others, in which the appraisal of events and actions as provocative or intentional is likely to be a powerful spur to confrontational behaviour.

Emergent research (for a review see Palmer, 2003) has clarified the socialization processes underpinning the development of such cognitive distortions, and the link between parenting style and the development of conscience. As originally outlined by Kohlberg (1969) and elaborated by Gibbs (2003), this involves a transition through successive stages in which egocentricity diminishes in favour of empathy and perspective taking, as the adolescent develops mature moral reasoning. The use of inductive discipline, in which the child is offered explanations of behavioural transgressions (Palmer and Hollin, 1996, 1997; Speicher, 1992); enhanced parental warmth; and low levels of perceived rejection (Boyes and Allen, 1993; Janssens and Dekovic, 1997) appear to be associated with enhanced levels of moral reasoning in children.

In the seminal model of anger management the American psychologist, Ray Novaco (1975, 1976) proposed that, as an emotional state, anger consists of three principal and interrelated components:

- the *physiological* component – cardiovascular and endocrine activation and muscular tension;
- the *cognitive* component – antagonistic thought patterns, labelling, and destructive impulses;
- the *behavioural* component.

Novaco suggests that no direct link exists between external events and anger (see Figure 1), and proposed that 'a basic premise is that anger is fomented, maintained, and influenced by the self statements that are made in provocation situations' (1975, p. 17). Citing previous evidence (May and Johnston, 1973) that private speech

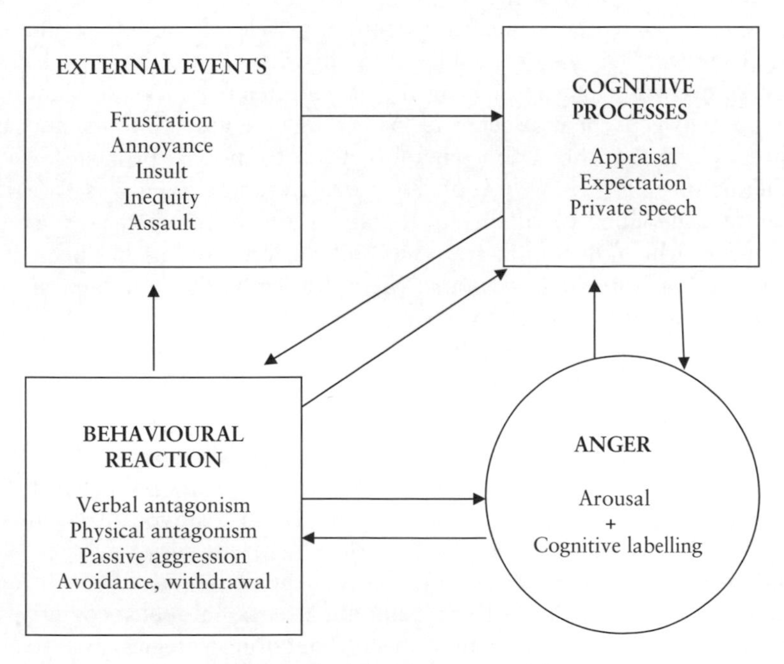

Figure 1 The Novaco model

produces measurable autonomic effects, he viewed such appraisals as the key initiator of heightened arousal and consequent anger.

> Anger is thought to consist of a combination of physiological arousal and a cognitive labelling of that arousal as anger . . . Anger arousal results from particular appraisals of aversive events. External circumstances provoke anger only as mediated by their meaning to the individual. (Novaco, 1975, p. 252)

Within Novaco's model it is anticipated that anger-prone individuals are more likely:

- to anticipate or predict problems;
- to make negative appraisals of events;
- to carry a limited expectation of their own ability to cope with aggravation.

They may effectively 'look for trouble'. They may carry unrealistic or inflexible notions of how others *should* behave and may react aggressively when these internalized *rules* are transgressed. In essence, negative expectations and appraisals produce heightened arousal, leading to impulsive behaviour, which, in a feedback loop, interacts with external events.

Treatment Approaches to Anger Control

Cognitive behavioural approaches are primarily concerned with achieving a *cognitive restructuring* – the development of a thinking style which, whilst endorsing the legitimate expression of anger, enables the individual to develop more functional appraisals of events, primarily through the development of an understanding of the relationship between their anger and preceding events, thoughts and resulting behaviour. Covert self-instruction remains central to most approaches.

Meichenbaum's (1977) method of *self-instructional training* was an early intervention model, designed to enhance self-control and promote the ability to 'stop, look and listen' which, in combination with relaxation training, has been developed into a general *stress inoculation model.* Metaphorically, the individual is helped to develop *cognitive anti-bodies* to aversive events.

Novaco's treatment approach is the principal model of anger management. It is based on a *stress inoculation approach* and falls into three stages:

1 An *educational stage,* in which the subject explores the functions of anger, personal patterns and triggers and the behaviours which contribute to the pattern of escalation. This process is assisted by the use of a standardized provocation inventory, diaries and the identification of a hierarchy of triggers.
2 In the *skill acquisition stage,* the subject is helped to develop strategies for dealing with thoughts and feelings including attentional focus, cognitive restructuring skills, problem-solving and arousal-reduction strategies, assertiveness and communication skills.

3 In the *application stage,* the previously developed skills are tested through gradual exposure to real life situations through role-play and eventual exposure to previously aversive situations.

Building on Novaco's work, Eva Feindler (Feindler, 1979; Feindler and Fremouw, 1983; Feindler et al., 1984, 1986) developed a ten-week anger control programme in which the use of a diary or *hassle log* is an important feature. The programme sequentially explores five elements of the anger chain:

- *Triggers* – the events and appraisals which instigate anger.
- *Cues* – the physiological and kinaesthetic experiences which signify anger.
- *Reminders* – self-instructional means for modifying anger.
- *Reducers* – strategies for reducing anger.
- *Self-evaluation.*

A diversity of generic and population-specific anger control programmes have been developed: for offenders (Schlichter and Horan, 1981), police officers (Novaco, 1977) domestic violence (Moran and Wilson, 1997), learning disability (Gardner and Gray, 1982; Benson et al., 1986; Gardner and Cole, 1987), delinquent adolescents (Feindler et al., 1984, 1986) and child abusing parents (Denicola and Sandler, 1980; Bank et al., 1987, 1991). In summary, results appear generally, if not universally, positive (Little and Kendall, 1979; Rimm and Masters, 1979). *Instrumental* or *incentive based* anger and aggression presents particular problems for cognitive-based approaches. Accurate assessment of underlying pathology and client motivation remains an essential prerequisite for treatment. Multimodal approaches which combine anger management techniques with other approaches such as assertiveness and social skills training seem to offer the best prospect and widest potential application (Feindler et al., 1986; Goldstein and Keller, 1987).

Building on our enhanced understanding of their inter-relationship, more recent clinical models, such as Aggression Replacement Training (ART; Goldstein et al., 1998), actively address the links between cognitive distortions, delayed moral reasoning and impaired social skill development. ART comprises three concurrent interventions involving 'skillstreaming to address the social and interpersonal skill deficits associated with aggression, anger control training to address emotion regulation, impulsivity and anger control problems; and moral reasoning training to address egocentric bias and moral development delay' (Palmer, 2005). Recognizing the powerful impact of peer influence on behavioural change the parallel EQUIP (Equipping Peers to Help One Another) programme (Gibbs et al., 1995) also seeks to achieve a 'climate for change' by application of these approaches in a group format.

Many anger management programmes involve complex systematic interventions requiring considerable clinical knowledge and support. Nevertheless, understanding anger as a problem of information processing and habitual thought patterns may help a broad range of practitioners to assist service users to understand and address chronic anger problems and correctly locate the responsibility for their anger.

Five Key Points

- The growing child's ability to exercise behavioural self-control is highly dependent on the development of effective, regulatory internal speech.
- The nature of a person's inner speech will affect how they interpret and respond to events.
- The thinking of people with chronic anger problems may be impaired by bias in their thinking and social interpretations – they may interpret events and the intentions of others inaccurately.
- Working with the person to explore and understand dysfunctional patterns of thinking is crucial to altering chronic anger related behaviour.
- Other people do not make you angry. *You* do!

Three Questions

? How can a cognitive behavioural understanding of chronic anger problems assist you in your work?
? What potential problems are generated in working with chronic anger problems?
? What organizational, clinical and support structures need to be in place as a prerequisite of such work?

Further reading

1 Goldstein, A. P., Glick, B. and Gibbs, J.C. (1998) *Aggression Replacement Training: A Comprehensive Intervention for Aggressive Youth* (rev. edn). Champaign, IL: Research Press.
2 Beck, A. T. (1999) *Prisoners of Hate: The Cognitive Basis of Anger, Hostility and Violence*. New York: Harper Collins.
3 Acton, R. G. (2001) *Angry Parents: A Group Psychotherapy Manual for Aggression Management Training*. Calgary: Acton House.

CHAPTER 2.11

Family Therapy

Jan White

Social work is concerned with the relationship between individuals and their social context. The way that an individual constructs his world and his sense of self is mediated through a variety of large and small social groupings, including family, school, neighbourhood and social agencies. Intertwined with these social realities are the unique meanings that we put upon them, which will be influenced by personal history, religion, culture and race. Family therapists are concerned with the most primary of these social groupings, literally, that which is most 'familiar'. Families are socially constructed units, based upon relationships of kinship, obligation and intimacy which exert a powerful socializing influence on the behaviour and understandings of their members.

It is rare for families to present themselves for therapy. Much more commonly an individual will be presented as 'having a problem'. The worker using a family therapy approach will view the individual's 'symptom' as part of an interactional pattern, and herself as a facilitator, enabling the family to harness its own strengths and flexibility towards a solution. For example, it is common for young people to be referred to the Child Mental Health Service with 'separation anxiety', which may prevent them from attending school or nursery. A family therapist would be interested in the child's history of relationships, as well as current factors at school and at home which might make them anxious either about being in school, or about leaving home. Within this model, interventions to prevent marital violence, or support a parent with mental health difficulties may be a key consideration in releasing the young person from crippling worries.

Family Therapy and Systems Theory

Family therapy draws upon two traditions: psychoanalytic practice and systems theory. During the 1950s psychoanalytically orientated psychiatrists such as Bell and Jackson (Bateson et al., 1956) observed that improvement in schizophrenic patients was often accompanied by a crisis in another family member. In seeking an explanation they looked to the anthropological theories of Gregory Bateson, who was interested in two ideas: how society and groups within it maintain a state of balance, and how they may escalate towards instability and change.

Jackson related their work to families, which he saw as developing over time a pattern of predictable relationships or 'homeostasis', governed by implicit or explicit rules. Rules may open or close options; for example, the Victorian saying 'children should be seen and not heard' served to support the strict rules of social behaviour in upper class England but limited parents' understanding of children's experience and behaviour.

Bateson also contributed the idea of 'circular causality' according to which, each person's behaviour influences and is in turn influenced by the other, and behaviour thus becomes self reinforcing.

The search for a 'cause' – and by implication the allocation of blame and responsibility – becomes irrelevant. Pattern and process acquire new importance as the worker seeks to tease out habitual patterns of interaction, and, where they contribute to distress, aims to interrupt the cycle. Patterns may exist intergenerationally, and it has been said that families keep an 'unconscious ledger' through the generations which may be balanced to the advantage or disadvantage of each succeeding generation; for example, the parent who felt unloved by her parents may compensate with devotion to her own children, or she may expect unconditional love from them to compensate for her own deprivation.

Family styles of problem-solving will relate to their habitual patterns. The family which repeatedly solves child care problems by having the child received into care will be matched by the social work agency which cites this as evidence of the family's inability to cope. In this way, agencies may become part of a repetitive cycle.

Byng-Hall (1995) developed the notion of *family scripts*, collections of stories and ideas which family members construct over time about themselves and each other. These stories may support resilience ('We are strong and can cope with anything') or close down options ('She is damaged by her early experiences and doesn't cope with change').

The idea of the family as an 'open system' allows us to consider its relationship to other social and belief systems. The family becomes a powerful mediator of internal and external influences (see Figure 1). It is continually creative, renegotiating roles and responsibilities and acting upon its environment to find a comfortable enough fit.

Professional help may be sought when a family has been unable to move forward in response to changed circumstances. The adolescent who seeks increased independence and begins dating, may find himself out of fit with parents who continue to respond to him as a dependent child. Further complexity may be introduced if the family have migrated from another culture which accentuates family responsibility above individual needs, and where religious mores do not support 'dating'. Moreover, part of that family's response may be a protective one to shelter their child from the experience of racism.

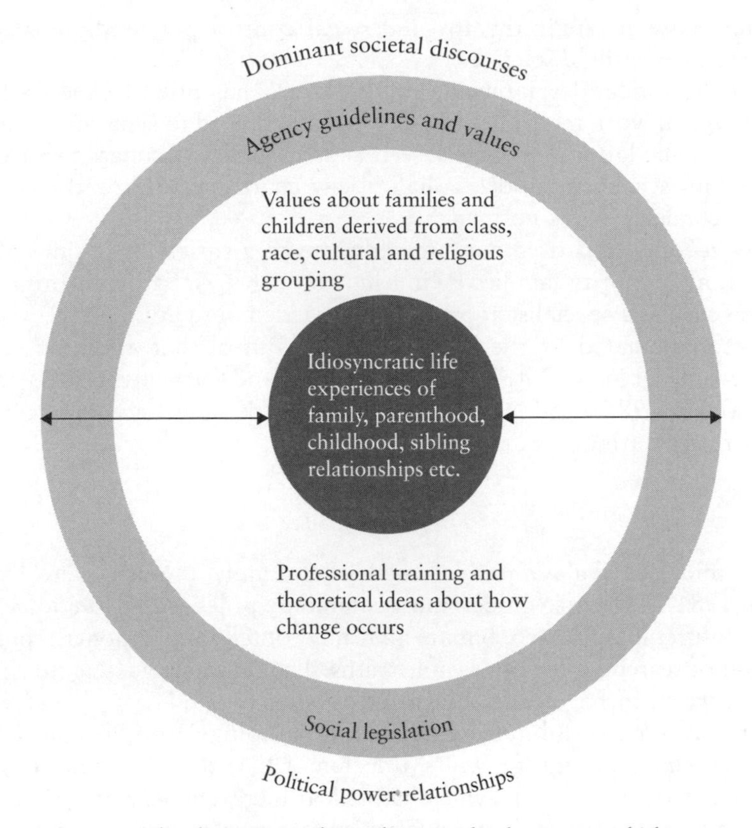

This diagram may be used to consider the ways in which your own background and context may be influencing the assumptions that you make when meeting with families.

Figure 1 Factors influencing the social worker's family assessment

Historical Development and Key Ideas

In recent years, family therapy has become established as a profession in its own right. At the same time, changes in social policy which emphasize care in the community, family preservation and choice for individuals and families have led to the employment of family therapists in a range of settings, including fostering treatment teams, mental health and disability. Structural changes to the way services are delivered, including the development of integrated children's services and NHS and Social Care Trusts, have broken down traditional boundaries between social work, social control and psychological therapies, and enabled the development of new interprofessional groups focused on developing and delivering family therapy. Family therapy has been identified by government as a means of reducing youth offending and substance misuse, and of preventing (rather than meeting) the need for public care for the young, the old and those mentally or physically disabled. This closer relationship between family therapy and social control potentially enables social workers to embrace the discipline.

During its historical development, family therapy has often lacked credibility as a legitimate social work model because of a perceived need to separate social control from therapy. The latter was largely seen as a specialist occupation for clinicians working within a medical model. I shall briefly chart key ideas and developments which have challenged this notion.

Pioneers in America carried out family therapy in a variety of settings often with poor and ethnic minority families (Minuchin et al., 1967). Sadly, in Britain, family therapy was seen as a specialist approach to be carried out within prestigious clinical settings uncontaminated by the issues of social control that are central to social work. It was only with the contributions of Treacher and Carpenter (1983), Dimmock and Dungworth (1985), and Dale et al. (1986) that the relevance of family therapy to social services settings was recognized.

Therapist style

Up to the mid-1980s a number of models of family therapy were elaborated (Hoffman, 1981). The three models most commonly practised – *structural*, *strategic* and *Milan* – differ in approach, but are all firmly rooted in the 'modern' philosophical tradition of searching for observable truths. The therapist as 'scientific observer' is expert, carrying in her head a blueprint of what *is* and what *should be*. She is thus able to make powerful judgements about 'pathology' and 'dysfunction'.

Within *structural family therapy* (Minuchin, 1974) the blueprint consists of a healthy 'family structure' – one which has a clear hierarchy in which parents are in charge of children and flexible boundaries exist between individuals allowing for individuation whilst retaining open communication. Problem behaviour relates to faulty structure. The therapist intervenes powerfully to block 'dysfunctional' interactional patterns, and coach the family in new behaviours.

Strategic therapists (Haley, 1980) went further, often using their power covertly to force change. Strategies were employed to address the family's 'resistance', the most simple of which was the prescription of 'no change' for the time being. Continued resistance required the family to change.

The *Milan Associates* (Palazzoli et al., 1978) proposed a different therapist style, that of 'neutrality'. Unlike the structural family therapist who is principally interested in changing behaviour in the room, their aim was the discovery of the meanings and beliefs underlying problem behaviour. They carefully elicited each person's position and ideas in relation to the problem, giving equal weight to all views. The Milan Associates considered the relevant system to be therapist-and-family, and said that the process of therapy itself exerts an influence upon events. A consulting team, which remained outside the therapist/family system behind a one-way screen, was responsible for devising interventions, sending powerful 'expert' messages to the family.

Common to these approaches was the belief that change can occur out of the understanding or control of family members. This expert, medical approach ran counter to the traditions of facilitation and empowerment more familiar to social workers.

Power and empowerment

Early family therapy literature has been justly criticized for its failure to understand the nature of power relationships, both within the family, and between family and social agencies. The blueprint of the 'healthy' family which emerges is firmly rooted in white Western culture and fails to consider gender relationships or differences of power within and between diverse races, cultures and classes.

For social workers, a central discourse is the relationship between therapy and social control. Dale et al. (1986) were influential in addressing this in the context of child protection work. Where statutory authority had hitherto been seen as a drawback to therapeutic work, they turned it to advantage. Typically they worked with families where the child was the subject of care proceedings, making explicit use of their authority to negotiate change in family structures and behaviour. Support for such approaches waned following the publication of research (Department of Health, 1995a) indicating the need for a lighter touch.

Social services agencies developed from the traditions of alleviating poverty and policing social behaviour, and their underlying principles sat uncomfortably with the 'treatment' orientation of early family therapy.

In approaching these important questions, I shall consider some more recent contributions to theory before considering the social work context in more detail.

Social Constructionism

The social constructionist approach signals a move from the 'modern' philosophical position. A postmodern approach recognizes the importance of joint exploration of problems. Central to this is the attribution of meaning and belief: it is impossible for a family to hear what I say in exactly the same way as I intended it, because their understanding will be mediated by the unique meanings and beliefs which they put upon it. The worker must find ways to understand the 'sense' that the family make of their own situation. This is particularly crucial in the context of differences of gender, race, culture and belief between therapist and family.

Anderson (1987) proposed a *reflecting team* approach, whereby the team of workers meet with the family after the initial part of the interview, not to deliver 'expert' messages, but to offer tentative observations upon what they have heard. The family is then invited to comment on the sense that they make of what is offered.

The most important contribution of social constructionism is the idea of joint exploration and developing choice, and the removal of the 'therapist as expert'. This fits with philosophies of client empowerment and partnership. However, it also carries with it a problem for social workers. Taken to its logical extreme, it assumes that 'anything goes', that the family's story is the only important thing. As such it has little to say about justice, ethics, or collective ideas of right and wrong. Social workers dealing with domestic violence and child abuse are left with no yardsticks against which they can judge behaviour. Feminist writers (for example, Jones, 1993) have made significant contributions in this area.

The Question of Power and Injustice

Traditionally, power in family therapy has been thought of in relation to complementary roles, with a focus on the way in which the roles reinforce one another. The notion of 'no blame' can come dangerously close to denying injustice. However, 'there are differences between individuals and their ability, within a particular systemic pattern, to influence the outcomes of actions and interactions in that pattern' (Jones, 1993, p. 144).

Jones cites the example of the incestuous abuse of a young girl by her father. The worker needs to be clear about the differences of choice, responsibility, influence and independence of father and daughter. Each will be influenced by social attitudes (obedience to parents, the myth of male uncontrolled sexual drive) as well as family and personal events and beliefs, but to assume equal responsibility in the therapeutic work is to guarantee further abuse of the child. To be 'neutral' is to be partial. Boyd-Franklin (1989) similarly refers to the family worker, working with a black family, who does not consider the possibility of racism as an important organizing principle in the family's thinking and behaviour. This could be construed by the family as condoning their experiences of persecution.

Walters (1988) demonstrates the importance of the 'gender lens' in reconstructing some important ideas from structural family therapy. For instance, in considering 'enmeshment' (a pathological state of over-closeness), she points out that women more frequently seek greater intimacy, seeing this as a valued experience of connectedness. Women tend to see relationships as more consensual, less hierarchical than men. Goldner et al. (1990) note that women often seek 'second order' change, at the level of meaning and belief: for example, 'I want my relationship to my husband to be closer'; whereas men seek first order, behavioural instructions: 'What exactly do you want me to do differently?'

Family therapists need to consider ways in which gender-patterning may contribute to difficulties, and be prepared to encourage both women and men to increase their range of behavioural choices. They must be prepared, where necessary, to *selectively empower* members of the family, to enhance their safety and well-being, whilst encouraging powerful members to try out different behaviour.

Whilst feminist approaches made a significant contribution to thinking about gendered power relations, they remained limited by their location within a Western white middle-class perspective. A broader-based critique, able to encompass the power relations of culture, class belief and ability was required.

Foucault described the process by which dominant discourses in society hold the power to marginalize whole social groupings (White, 1995). These discourses are reflected in social policy, such that, for instance, lone parents and stepfamilies are evaluated, using a deficit model, as less able to meet the needs of children. Family therapists using a 'narrative' approach emphasize the need for individuals and families to create new and more affirming stories about themselves, emphasizing resilience and healing over the medical notions of pathology and treatment. Healing lies in recapturing the subjugated stories or unique 'local' knowledges which support survival and hope. Linked to this is the idea of cultural competence. By this is meant the ability to perceive not only that behaviour may be understood with reference to wider cultural patternings, but also that the particular way in which each family and individual relates to and interprets cultural values will be unique. Within this understanding, the worker is expected to arm herself with cultural knowledge, yet avoid stereotyping on the basis of it.

Self-knowledge has become an increasingly important aspect of family therapy training. The worker who carries an awareness of her own cultural and belief system can more easily put aside assumptions and work with the family's own frame of reference.

Putting the Family Back in the Centre

A central discourse within family therapy, is how best to share power with families in a way which allows them to take responsibility for their own choices, but retains safety for all members. Power should be reframed as the responsibility to create a safe environment within which the family can find its own solutions. The worker should use her expertise in systems theory and family relationships to get alongside the family, help them to make sense of their world, and explore differences and alternatives available to them.

Reimers and Treacher (1995) make proposals for 'user friendly' family therapy based on consumer research. They advocate the provision of clear information in written and verbal form prior to the commencement of work. The first interview should be used to discuss the method of work rather than to begin an assessment. The use of technology and the size of the team should be kept to a minimum, video being used only for specified and explained purposes (for example, for training or for the family to review progress). Where supervising teams are used, members should be introduced to the family, their composition should reflect a gender balance, and their workings should be explicit to the family. My own experience is that working in this way enables the family to make a relationship with, and feel contained, by the whole team.

Reimers and Treacher emphasize the central importance of the 'therapeutic alliance'. The most important consideration is to find a 'fit' with the family. Some families will seek understanding; others will seek advice and clarity. Some cultures and individuals will prize hierarchy and instruction, others will value equality and exploration. Above all, it is important to act ethically, and to do so means being client- rather than technique-centred.

The Social Work Context: Family Therapy or Systemic Practice?

While family therapists are increasingly being employed to work therapeutically alongside social workers in the community, the climate is also ripe for social workers to use systemic skills in a range of everyday social work activities. The emphasis is shifting from a focus on assessing risk to mobilizing the energies and resources of family and community. Hence, in the child protection context, Turnell and Edwards (1999) advocate that workers look for 'signs of safety' – positive parental behaviours which can form the building blocks in a partnership entered into with carers towards future safety. A *family group conference* (Tunnard and Atherton, 1996) may form part of this approach; here, family and kin are themselves encouraged to make a safe plan on behalf of a member considered at risk. 'Local knowledge', often not available to professionals, will inform their decisions.

Similarly, *care planning meetings*, convened to consider future plans for older people or those with disability are increasingly mobilizing the resources of family and community. Within mental health, *care in the community* is being supported by services to families coping with the early onset of psychosis and the long-term effects of enduring illness. Here, a combination of family management and systemic approaches has been found helpful (Burbach and Stanbridge, 1998).

Social workers habitually work with the relationships between systems. For example, within fostering and adoption, they may be working with relationships between sibling groups, birth family, foster family, schools, a range of other welfare professionals and their agencies. A systemic approach enables them to consider the habitual patterns which exist in these relationships, and to intervene more effectively.

Conclusion

Taken together, family therapy and systemic practice form important social work tools. Family therapy has developed from its early emphasis upon clinical expertise, to a more gentle, power-sharing approach focusing on the family's own style and choices. In so doing it has come into line with social welfare principles of partnership and empowerment and has acquired the flexibility to survive contemporary changes in the nature of families and kinship systems.

Five Key Points

- 'The family is a self-governing system which controls itself according to rules formed over a period of time through a process of trial and error' (Palazzoli et al., 1978).
- Each family is unique in structure and beliefs. The first aim of the worker should be to find a therapeutic style which makes sense with this family.
- Consumer research amongst family therapy users suggests the need for clear information about the method of work, and keeping technology and team size to a minimum.
- Family therapists aim to expand upon strengths and, through the introduction of difference, to increase the range of choices available to families to think and act creatively in relation to their circumstances.
- A systemic perspective increases the effectiveness of a range of social work practices, management and inter-professional relationships.

Three Questions

? How can we usefully decide who to invite to a 'family therapy' session?
? What approaches best enable a social worker to join with families different to him/herself in race, gender, class, culture, ability or sexuality?
? What aspects of social work training, and work context enable family therapy, and what might be the obstacles to working in this way?

Further reading

1 Carr, A. (2000) *Family Therapy: Concepts, Process and Practice*. Chichester: Wiley.
2 Dallos, R. and Draper, R. (2000) *An Introduction to Family Therapy: Systemic Theory and Practice*. Milton Keynes: Open University Press.
3 Walker, S. and Akister, J. (2005) *Applying Family Therapy*. Lyme Regis: Russell House.

CHAPTER 2.12

Groupwork

Allan Brown

Groupwork is recognized as a mainstream method of social work practice because it offers different kinds of opportunities from those available in other approaches. It also has some problematic aspects which may explain why it is not always used as widely and consistently as might be expected. We therefore need to understand what groupwork can offer and how the extent and quality of its use is affected by four key variables: the context, small group dynamics, the individual group member and the groupworker's role and skills.

Theoretical understanding about small group behaviour has been influenced by social psychologists. Their work has taught us about the effects of group size and composition, the stages of development in the life of a group, the 'leadership style' of the worker(s), and the powerful ways in which individuals can be influenced by their peers. Sociologists have stressed the importance of the influence of social context and structural factors on behaviour in the small group, and psychodynamic and behavioural theorists contribute understanding of the individual group member in the group.

Building on these theoretical foundations, and equally on the grounded experience of groupworkers and group members, social groupwork has developed in the last 40 years towards becoming a discipline in its own right. There is now a considerable groupwork literature available; note especially Garvin et al.'s encyclopaedic *Handbook of Social Work with Groups* (2004) and Doel's *Using Groupwork* (2006). The establishment of two groupwork journals (*Social Work with Groups, Groupwork*) has been a critical factor, not least in model building and the articulation of practice developments.

A continuing issue is whether or not groupwork is best regarded as a separate social work discipline requiring specialization both in training and in practice. The approach in the UK has favoured a generic methodology with some specialization, but the trend towards providing specialist services for different categories of service user has created more demand for method specialists.

The Characteristics of Groupwork

Groupwork applies to the whole range of ways in which the small group can be instrumental in the achievement of social work purposes. Thus the aims, agendas and methods of groupwork are as diverse and ubiquitous as those of social work itself. We can, however, identify some of its distinguishing characteristics.

- *Being with others who in at least one important respect associated with group purpose are similar to oneself*. This feature offers myriad opportunities for sharing, learning, supporting, challenging, joint action, role-modelling, relationship building and so on. A common fear in groups is of labelling and shared stigma, and of being 'taken over' by others. This can happen, but the paradox is that for many the first time they experience themselves as an individual with their own identity is when they are in a group with similar others. In the family each person's identity is largely defined by the family group system, as usually there is no one in the same position with whom that individual can make a direct comparison. In the one-to-one relationship of service user and social worker, the inherent role and power differences set limits to self-definition.
- *The opportunity for individual empowerment, and growth in self-esteem and self-confidence*. The opportunity to be a 'helper' as well as a 'helped', and to get positive feedback and support from one's peers – as well as the worker – creates the conditions for personal growth and development. Dependence, whether on family, agencies or drugs, disempowers. In a group an ethos of interdependence can enhance personal empowerment and self-esteem. Many group members have internalized the oppression they have experienced in the wider society; and in a peer group – say of other women, or other disabled people – they can begin to relieve themselves of that burden and put it back where it belongs in the oppressive social structures from which it derives.
- *The opportunity for change*. The power and collectivity of the group creates options for change – for individuals to change their behaviour/feelings/attitudes, for a group to take on a change of direction, or for action to be taken to change things external to the group, perhaps in the neighbourhood or in the way services are being delivered.
- *A resource for learning*. The personal learning opportunities in groups are extensive. Whilst didactic teaching has a limited place in social groupwork, the essence is what emerges from the social interaction between members and between members and workers. Skills can be rehearsed in the safety of the group, and a rich resource of ideas and advice can be offered by other members who face similar life stresses, which may not be in the experience of professional workers or other family members.

The Context of Groupwork

What are the factors which determine whether a group can be established, and if it is, whether it can create optimum conditions for the realization of its potential? The importance of context cannot be overstated.

- Overshadowing everything else is the prevailing *socio-economic-political* climate. This impacts in some obvious and many less obvious ways. It determines the allocation of resources to agencies and to individuals; it shapes prevailing values and attitudes and it determines the distribution of wealth and power. The less obvious impact stems from the group itself being a social microcosm of the wider society. Social attitudes, relative status and the oppression and discrimination experienced by certain populations, will be imported into the group as a major influence on process – unless or until countervailing steps are taken.
- The *agency* itself is a powerful influence both on the extent to which groupwork is encouraged and resourced, and in determining the purposes it is expected to achieve – be these control, change, empowerment or learning. Contrast agency influence on a probation group for violent offenders with that on a community group for adult survivors of sexual abuse.
- The *setting* of the group can have a profound effect on what happens. This includes its physical location, and whether there is adequate space and comfort. Group living settings in day and residential establishments affect every group all the time because the participants – particularly in residential care – experience a whole range of organized and informal group contexts, each affecting and being affected by the others.
- The *community* from which the group membership is drawn is another contextual factor. This may be a community of interest (as in a group for those with an alcohol problem or a carers' group), or a neighbourhood/locality community. In each instance the culture and ethos associated with that particular community will be imported into the group, and the exported impact of the group will be mediated by the environment. From the group members' perspective, both kinds of communities develop 'received wisdom' about the positive or negative value of local group services.

The agency and the workers have to try and create a facilitative environment for groupwork practice. Whether or not they do so may make all the difference between 'success' and 'failure' of a groupwork programme. Some agencies regard groupwork as a peripheral rather than a mainstream method of service delivery – an attitude sometimes associated with an individualistic orientation, and/or apprehension that group power may become a threat to managerial control.

The Small Group

There are many ways in which a group forms; it may form spontaneously as some self-help groups do, it may be part of an agency programme of groups, or it may follow the initiative of an individual worker or be a response to pressure from service users. The members may have joined freely, or there may be a degree of coercion and involuntary membership. There may be a careful, long, drawn-out planning process, or the group may form very quickly with little or no period of preparation. Whatever the history of a group's creation, the subsequent group process will be affected by it.

Research confirms personal experience that the size and composition of a group has a big impact on group process (Brown, 1992, pp. 46–55). In larger groups, some individuals will get 'lost' unless the group is structured to ensure participation by all. Redl's 'law of optimum distance' (1951), that groups should be 'homogeneous enough to ensure stability, and heterogeneous to ensure vitality', is a useful guide to optimum group composition. However, in practice this often cannot be achieved, and the group then needs to take steps to compensate for an 'unbalanced membership'. This may mean, for example, ensuring that any individual who is in a minority (perhaps being the only black member) is actively supported and helped to avoid isolation/marginalization, and to get as much benefit from the group as that enjoyed by 'majority' members.

Every group functions at both the task level (what the group aims to achieve) and the process level (the feelings and relationships that develop between the people in the group). Sometimes group process takes over to the detriment of task, as in protracted conflict between two members; sometimes the group is so task-focused that personal feelings of members get ignored. Neither of these is healthy for group development, which requires effective group maintenance work to reinforce and sustain the task.

Theorists have identified various models to describe the stages of development of a group, and some also suggest the corresponding tasks of the worker and the group to navigate successfully the particular stage characteristics through which the group is passing (Henry, 1992). These models reduce to linear, spiral and cyclical in basic format. Groups with open and therefore changing membership are particularly likely to have uneven patterns of development as membership changes and re-forming is needed.

Most groups negotiate 'ground rules' to set the basis on which members agree to work together within the overall contract and purpose. These 'rules' typically refer to such issues as confidentiality, equal treatment and participation for all, opting out and anti-discriminatory practice. In some groups the agency itself sets ground rules which apply to all agency activities, for example, no violence, no racism, no sexism.

The small group is a dynamic system in which whatever happens in any part of it, needs to be understood in the context of the group as a whole (and the external context). A group perspective is therefore essential for the worker and for group members if they are to understand what is happening and to respond positively.

Another dimension is the means by which the group attempts to carry out the task and achieve its aims. This usually includes talking, but may include a whole range of activities like artwork, role-play, games, exercises, going places, telling stories and inviting visitors.

The time-frame of a group needs to relate to the purpose, varying from a block of a few days for an intensive experience, to single meetings once a month for a support group.

The Individual Member

The first group most of us experience is the family group(s) we are part of in childhood. The kind of roles we experience in that formative grouping may set an initial expectation of role-taking in subsequent groups. Thus the family 'scapegoat', 'isolate', 'internal leader' or 'mediator' may find themselves unconsciously taking that kind of role-expectation into peer groups at school and in 'formed groups' at work and leisure activities. Equally, if not more influential, will be the structurally determined oppression and marginalization many experience because of their sex, the colour of their skin, their disability or their sexual orientation.

An individual thus enters a group with a whole range of expectations based on these earlier and current experiences, combined with whether they have joined voluntarily and enthusiastically or under some form of duress. It can be a great relief when entering a new group to find someone you already know, or at least someone who seems rather like yourself and with whom you experience a feeling of rapport. On the other hand, some group members prefer 'stranger' groups because this both protects confidentiality about the past, and offers more freedom of choice of behaviour and role-taking in the group.

Groups which develop a caring and collective ethos offer many opportunities to individuals both psychologically (for example, to increase self-confidence and self-esteem), and in practical ways (new ideas and ways of solving practical problems and difficulties). Group support and solidarity can also be a source of strength. By contrast, groups can be destructive and disempowering. Someone may leave a group with more difficulties than those they faced on entry. This points out the special responsibility the groupworker has to help create a facilitative environment and group culture.

The Worker(s)

Working with a group is more complicated than working with one other person. There is the need to relate simultaneously to each individual and to the group as a whole, not to mention keeping a firm eye on the task. It is easy to lose sight of task or process or group or individual or some individuals. For this reason, among others, it is commonplace in Britain to have more than one worker to share all these facets. Co-working has its advantages and disadvantages, but the apparently daunting task of the worker when seen from the perspective of worker-as-leader, looks rather different when seen from the perspective of worker-as-facilitator. This latter role conceptualizes the worker as the person not who runs the group, but who helps the group to run itself.

Different models of groupwork suggest different roles for the worker. In group psychotherapy the worker is leader and holds much of the expertise. In social action groupwork, the worker's task is to help the members identify external objectives which they then tackle collectively. In mainstream social groupwork, the assumption is that whilst the worker may start the group as 'central person', their task is to move out of that role as the group members gradually take responsibility for the running of their group. The choice of model obviously depends in part on the type of group and membership, but a core value in social groupwork is that all group members, whatever the extent of any personal difficulty or impairment, have it within them to contribute to group development and goal achievement.

A qualification to a value base of empowerment applies to groups whose primary function is to work with the perpetrators of harm to others – and/or themselves – where the aim is to try and change behaviour to protect others. For example, it is well established that many sex offenders have no intrinsic motivation to change their behaviour. Left to their own group devices they might simply reinforce each other's offensive and offending behaviour. The worker in this type of group needs a much more controlling challenging role, although ultimately the individual himself still has to develop some personal motivation for change to be effective.

The groupworker needs both process and task skills, and an understanding of how the former can facilitate the latter. She or he also needs to have a clear understanding of the issues of power – including their own – which affect group process and the behaviour of group members. This includes the conscious use of role modelling of group and personal behaviour. For example, if the worker expects members to be frank and open, then he or she needs to role-model this behaviour by being appropriately open and self-disclosing.

Co-working is a highly skilled activity in its own right. Working together effectively with another person first requires checking out for mutual compatibility and a shared approach to the forthcoming group. Lack of careful preparation of the co-working relationship can lead to all kinds of confusion in the group, and failure to provide the safe environment which many groups need, and which the members are entitled to expect. Co-working is an opportunity to model an equal relationship, which is particularly important when the social expectation may be of an unequal relationship, say between a man and woman or a white and black person.

Self-help groups do not, by definition, have a designated worker. Leadership may be shared by the group as a collective, or individual members may be given specific roles – for example, chairperson or convenor – by the group, perhaps on a rotation basis. 'Workerless' groups have all the properties of groups generally, which may include dynamics which are disempowering and marginalizing for some members. Thus people who are not used to being in small groups – whether self-help or worker-led – need help in learning about group dynamics and how to manage themselves as group members. Workers who are experienced in groups can easily underestimate how intimidating being in a group may be to those new to groups and groupwork.

For discussion

Identify a particular group – real or imagined – that you and a colleague have been asked to establish to meet a specific service need in your agency. Then discuss some of the key group membership issues you might face, including:

- Membership self-selection versus worker selection of members.
- Size of the group: implications for group dynamics and the group programme.
- Open versus closed membership.
- Issues of inequality and discrimination which may arise, given the group's membership and co-workers.
- Particular issues you identify as potentially problematic for a group with this (projected) membership.

Some Groupwork Issues

Three issues among those common to groups and groupworkers will now be considered.

Package versus process

A fundamental question in any group is how much to plan before it starts, and how much to let the 'programme' evolve as the group develops. The answer obviously depends in part on the type of group and the aims. Groups with a strong educational purpose, for example a social skills or alcohol education group, often have a largely predetermined programme. However, a fundamental of social groupwork is what Papell and Rothman (1980) were referring to when they said 'spontaneous and meaningfully evolving group processes are the instrumental means for realising group purpose' (p. 8). This cannot be achieved if the content and method of the group is largely determined beforehand by the worker(s).

This issue is becoming increasingly important as groupwork 'packages' become very popular. They are popular with agencies because they are tangible and fit the prevailing ethos of competencies and the contract culture. They are popular with stressed practitioners because they provide a ready-made resource for running a group, requiring minimal preparation time and effort. They may even be quite popular with some group members because they take away much of their own membership responsibility.

However, packages put severe limits on the rich resource of social groupwork which is what is generated by the interaction between the members. Furthermore, there is a real danger that the 'package' approach is not responsive to the needs of group members. They are being fitted into the method, rather than the method being responsive to them – a not unfamiliar scenario in social work generally. There is, however, a middle way, which is to use packages as an available resource to be drawn on flexibly and creatively as the needs arise. Group members themselves can express an opinion on what they would prefer and find most helpful.

An anti-oppressive empowering approach to groupwork

Small groups are a microcosm of the wider society from which the membership is drawn. They will tend to replicate those inequalities of power, status and influence that are prevalent in the external community and social institutions. Thus group members will tend to give higher status to members who are middle class, white, male, heterosexual and without physical or learning disabilities. Those who are working class, black, female, lesbian/gay or with a disability, may experience stereotyping and active discrimination in the group, similar to that which they experience outside.

These oppressive phenomena pose a challenge to the groupworker and the group members, raising questions about group composition and group skills. For some purposes, particularly those associated with personal identity, discrimination and the raising of self-esteem, a homogeneous group confined to those who share the same oppression will often be the preferred option. Lee (1991) has written about an empowerment group for disadvantaged and disempowered black women, which aims both to relieve their internal oppression, and to generate group strength to tackle external disempowering institutions such as housing agencies.

In practice, for all sorts of reasons, groups will often not be homogeneous, and will require the active use of deliberate strategies and skills to counteract inequality and oppression. Brown and Mistry (1994) make some suggestions, including having a clear explicit value-base and ground rules, and being ready to respond actively to any unacceptable behaviour in the group.

The worker's use of self

How a social worker uses herself or himself as a person is probably more significant than any other aspect of their knowledge and skills. Personal and professional selves cannot – and in my view should not – be wholly separated. This applies whatever the setting and method, and particularly in groupwork where workers are in a minority, and often under pressure to be 'one of the group'. For example, in exercises where group members are expected to share something personal, the groupworker has to decide whether or not to join in and do likewise. If they always decline they distance themselves from the members; if they participate in everything as though a member they risk moving out of the worker role. Neither of these options may be helpful to the group. The skill lies in being secure enough to disclose personal matters when this is likely to be helpful, whilst retaining the distinct worker role of assisting group members to achieve their individual and group goals.

Conclusion

Groupwork is the 'natural' social work method for empowering practice because it is predicated on the strengths and active contribution of every individual group member. It has a firm theoretical and research base to support it, and has much to offer to both members and workers. It is also a potentially radical approach when group members are given full reign to determine the nature and scope of 'their' group.

Five Key Points

- The small group is a social microcosm, and is likely to replicate patterns of social inequality, unless countervailing steps are taken.
- The essence of groupwork is how the social interaction between group members is harnessed to the achievement of group purpose.
- Groupwork is a uniquely empowering method of social work because all are potential 'helpers' as well as 'helped'.
- Groups are powerful instruments for change, whether of individuals, groups or environments.
- Four key variables influence what a group can offer: context, group dynamics, the individual members and the worker's role and skills.

Three Questions

? What kind of balance needs to be struck between task and process for effective groupwork?
? What are the prerequisites of empowering anti-oppressive groupwork?
? What particular demands does groupwork make on the workers' 'use of self'?

Further reading

1 Doel, M. and Sawdon, C. (1999) *The Essential Groupworker*. London: Jessica Kingsley.
2 Garvin, C. D., Gutiérrez, L. M. and Galinsky, M. J. (eds.) (2004) *Handbook of Social Work with Groups*. New York: Guilford Press.
3 Doel, M. (2006) *Using Groupwork*. London: Routledge/Community Care.

CHAPTER 2.13

Cognitive–Behavioural Therapy

Tammie Ronen

Cognitive–behavioural therapy (CBT) is a dynamic mode of intervention – both subjecting itself to a constant process of change incited by our developing society as well as guiding therapists to modify their thinking and adapt their methods to the changing needs of individual clients. CBT's main role – helping people change – can be realized only by combining new theoretical knowledge with empirically tested interventional approaches that account for the cultural, social, economic and political transformations typifying modern life.

CBT constitutes a way of thinking about human functioning and needs, and a way of operating within the environment in order to achieve the most effective means for accomplishing one's aims (Ronen, 2003). Being a cognitive–behavioural therapist necessitates dynamic thinking, considering that no one correct approach or intervention exists for treating the variety of clients encountered in social work. The therapist always makes decisions adapting available techniques to specific client-related factors – the individual client and problem – and to therapist-related factors – the service setting and the therapist's abilities, knowledge and skills.

The Dynamic Nature of CBT Theory

The behaviourist approach in psychology emerged in the 1920s when Watson (1970) brought together concepts and methods of conditioning research developed in Russia. Psychologists attempted to contest psychiatrists' medical intervention model by proposing a scientific theoretical foundation for human disorders rooted in behavioural principles. The theoretical base for behavioural therapy has since undergone a continuous process of change as new knowledge enabled new explanations of human behaviour and, later, as behavioural theory was integrated into cognitive theory. Behaviour therapy thus saw a dynamic evolution from its original conceptualizations: these were based on laboratory study and the theory of learning, branching in three directions: classical, operant and social learning or modelling.

Classical conditioning as demonstrated by Pavlov's study of dogs' digestion depicted the connection between stimulus (food) and response (salivating). Classical learning principles soon became the basis for explaining human habits, behaviours and disorders and the source from which relaxation training and desensitization techniques were developed (Wolpe, 1982). The latter are still considered an important contribution to the treatment of anxiety disorders. Yet these concepts – stimuli, response, conditioning – were used to analyse behaviour without relating to the person as a human being.

Skinner's contribution (1938) of the notion of consequences triggered the development of operant conditioning, giving a specific role to the environment and focusing on the ability to modify a behaviour by changing its consequence. Behaviour eliciting positive outcomes would continue, whereas behaviour eliciting negative outcomes would be eliminated, decreased or made extinct. Operant conditioning pinpointed the need for environmental change, emphasizing techniques such as positive and negative reinforcement, extinction and punishment, and more complex programmes such as contingency contracts, token economies and exposure techniques.

The inability of classical and operant conditioning to yield explanations for all kinds of learning (for example, for gender roles or social skills) led to a third learning theory: social learning, or modelling. Bandura (1969) demonstrated that learning can occur as a result of observation and in the absence of reinforcement either to the model or to the learner. His social learning theory and his notion of vicarious (observational) learning provided the basis for conceptualizing the person–environment relationship as a reciprocal process of influence. People are perceived as active participants in their own learning.

Through the 1970s, psychologists' interest in cognition, memory, perception and motivation was reflected in behavioural theory by extending it towards cognitive learning. Bandura's (1997) identification of the role of expectancies and self-regulation in the control of behaviour as key concepts in vicarious learning provided new information serving as an incentive for an increase in cognitive therapy. Research began to focus directly on the alteration of covert behaviour and the role of cognitive processes in different populations. Ellis's (1973) idea of irrational thinking as the main source of human disorders and the work of Beck et al. (1979) on cognitive therapy for depression demonstrated the clinical utility of mediational models of human behaviour. Clinical implications of cognitive theory included:

- identification of thoughts;
- awareness of emotions elicited following those thoughts;
- the link between thoughts and emotions;
- the view of behaviour as the outcome of a process combining thoughts and emotions.

Rosenbaum and Ronen (1998) pinpointed seven basic features of cognitive therapy:

1 therapy as a meaning-making process which helps the client to develop new and often more complex meaning systems of what they define as problematic areas;

2 systematic and goal-directed therapy;
3 focusing on practising and experiencing elements rather than on 'talk therapy';
4 collaboration between client and therapist;
5 focusing on the client rather than on the problem;
6 facilitating change processes by the therapist;
7 empowerment and development of the client's independent functioning.

Behaviour therapy had become transformed into cognitive–behavioural therapy, with a multidimensional focus on changing overt as well as covert behaviour such as imagery, thoughts and emotions.

Adding cognition to the earlier basic learning model placed the *person* rather than the *pathological response* at the centre of therapy. CBT moved in the direction of helping people to help themselves. Theories of self-control sought to explain human functioning, noting the role of language as an important mediating feature in the natural acquisition of self-control (Ronen, 2005). Self-control was described as a shift, from being directed by others' talk to the development of self-talk aloud, and finally to the capacity for silent self-talk (thoughts). Being in control of oneself was seen as facilitating: coping with stress, pain or disturbing emotions; delaying temptation; and establishing criteria and targets for conducting one's own life. Self-control was conceived as the way new behaviours need to be learned and as necessary when choices have to be made or when habitual response sequences are interrupted or prove ineffective (Rosenbaum, 1990, 1999).

Several assumptions have characterized basic cognitive–behavioural theory since its inception:

1 The theory is a scientific approach relying on empirical studies of human behaviour.
2 Human behaviour is seen as being in a constant process of change; people are always able to render changes in their behaviour.
3 The same rule explaining normal human behaviour can explain deviations: people who learn to be aggressive can learn to behave themselves.
4 An interaction exists between behaviour and environment; therefore, change can be achieved by changing either the environment or the individual.

During the 1990s, CBT, which shifted from traditional behaviour theory to more cognitive theory, has moved towards constructivist theory. Constructivism focuses less on immediate cognitive or behavioural change and more on emotional processes. The person is viewed as a scientist who actively formulates personal hypotheses and then refines, revises or elaborates them in the course of ongoing experience. People are responsible for making their own realities by the way they construe and reconstruct their life events and how they attribute meaning to their personal experiences (Mahoney, 2003).

Recently, other developments in CBT have included techniques emphasizing the need for acceptance of problems rather than a focus on overcoming and coping (Hayes et al., 1999). In addition, mindfulness techniques have been integrated into the process of intervention (Hayes et al., 2004).

Replacing Diagnosis with Assessment

CBT has replaced the traditional meaning of *diagnosis* (as a rigid concept emphasizing the medical model where common pathological characteristics of disorders are identified before treatment) with the dynamic notion of *assessment* that continues throughout the therapeutic process. The therapist is interested not in rigid definitions like 'depression' but rather in how the problem manifests itself: for example, the person does not leave home, is not involved in social activities, does not eat or smile, cries often.

Assessment concentrates on contemporary determinants of behaviour rather than on early life events or the client's past; throughout the therapeutic process, it focuses on the *what?* and *how?* and not the *why? How* does the client learn to act this way? *What* maintains the behaviour?

Objectives, target behaviours and appropriate methods of measurement are carefully identified. The therapist aims to construct a behaviour profile of the client based on a series of questions: How do you behave today? What disturbs you regarding this behaviour? How do you behave when you face your difficulties? What do you think influenced your behaviour in the past? What interferes with you trying to overcome your problem? What would be better if your problem was solved? How should the therapist know that the problem is over? Why do you wish to solve this problem? Imagine your life without the problem: how would you like it to look? Who are the people who can help you fight the problem?

Therapy: Trick or Treatment?

There is a misconceived tendency to look at CBT as a collection of magic tricks that the therapist performs to solve human disorders and maladaptive behaviours. Instead, CBT comprises a very careful, continuous assessment process that attempts to analyse the client's needs, our knowledge of the specific problem and the client's skills and abilities, to determine the treatment of choice. The same problem could be treated differently as a result of decision-making related to personal, environmental and behavioural considerations.

To illustrate the link between theory and therapy, Table 1 describes the explanation and treatment of social phobia.

Most therapists today are cognitive–behaviourally oriented, meaning that they apply principles derived from research in experimental and social psychology for the alleviation of human suffering and the enhancement of human functioning, with systematic evaluation of the effectiveness of these applications and a commitment to an applied science of clinical treatment. The field of CBT espouses direct links between theory, assessment, intervention and evaluation (Ronen, 1994, 2003). CBT interventions are devised empirically on the basis of behavioural assessment outcomes and are constantly evaluated. The targeted change of CBT is overt as well as covert behaviour, and thinking is considered by today's therapists to play an important role in the aetiology and maintenance of disorders.

CBT advocates the selection of intervention strategies with: a high probability of success; sequential steps that match available skill levels; clear, relevant means of monitoring progress; practice opportunities; and maintenance and follow-up periods

Table 1 *Development and treatment of social phobia (fear of participating in social events) according to different CBT theories*

Learning theory	*Phobia aetiology*	*Suggested treatment*
Classical	Repeated experiencing of fears while attending social events caused a contingency between the event and the response	Disconnect the fear from the event by desensitization and relaxation
Operant	Repeated positive reinforcement of the avoidance behaviour; punishment while exposed to the feared event	Gradual exposure to the feared event and positive reinforcement for successful exposure
Modelling	Repeated exposure to an admired model who fears social events caused vicarious learning of avoidance	Presenting a new model who is not afraid of social events and is reinforced for attendance
Cognitive	Negative expectancies and automatic negative thoughts on the result of attending social events elicit stressful emotions and avoidant behaviour	Changing negative thoughts, developing positive expectancies, and teaching coping skills

(Gambrill, 1990). Homework assignments are considered an integral part of most CBT interventions because of the need to apply knowledge from the intervention setting to the natural environment. The therapeutic setting is not limited to time sequences (once a week, for example) but is linked to role accomplishment: 'We will meet again when you complete your homework assignment.' Therapy is terminated not when the problem decreases but only when clients prove their ability to maintain their achievements and generalize them to other settings and problem areas.

As CBT theory develops, new intervention modes and new techniques are supplied to aid the therapist. Treatment techniques moved from Wolpe's (1982) desensitization methods in the early days of CBT to the modern treatment of anxiety disorders through self-exposure. Instead of the therapist conditioning clients to relax, clients are instructed in the importance of exposing themselves to unpleasant feelings and are encouraged to select their own assignments and exposure targets.

Self-control theory is an example of the cognitive self-help evolution. Rosenbaum (1998) described three types of self-control to elucidate different behavioural problem areas. *Redressive* self-control is required when one's behaviour is disturbed and one needs to overcome existing concrete difficulties (for example, a woman wants specific techniques to help her lose weight before her anniversary in a month's time; she needs to learn self-talk, imagination and relaxation to overcome her wish to eat). *Reformative* self-control is needed to change one's whole way of life, eliminate poor habits, and set up new targets and expectancies (for example, the problem is not an immediate weight loss but rather the poor eating habits that caused her to eat when she was tired, frustrated, angry or bored; she needs to learn how to change her eating patterns and entire way of life). *Experiential* self-control targets one's ability to let go of control and expose oneself to new experiences (for example, the eating stems from avoiding social activities, low self-image, and poor self-esteem; she needs to learn to accept herself and her body and stop avoiding social activities, in order to change her appearance). Ronen (1997) applied these three self-control types to the understanding and treatment of different behaviour disorders. In general, the *redressive* type denotes therapy, *reformative* implies a preventive model, and *experiential* suggests the development of self-fulfilment and personal potential. Table 2 presents the

Table 2 *Types of self-control*

	Redressive	*Reformative*	*Experiential*
Aim	To solve existing problems, decrease disruptions	To change lifestyle, improve coping	Opening up to experiences
Target	Homeostasis	Heterostasis	Heterostasis
Time	Present	Future	Present, future
Problem's setting	Environment	Person	Person
Targeted behavioural classification	Under-controlled, externalizing	Over-controlled, internalizing	Over-controlled, internalizing
Client behaviour problems	Aggression Anger Conduct disorders Delinquency Disruptiveness Fears Hostility Hyperactivity Phobias Sociopathy Stress	Anxiety Apathy Depression Impulsivity Inhibitions Sensitivity Shyness Submissiveness Withdrawal	Anxiety Avoidance Depression Mental retardation Shyness Special education Withdrawal
Treatment setting	Therapy, educational	Therapy, educational, practice in natural environment	Primarily natural environment
Techniques	Self-instruction Imagination Relaxation	Criteria establishment Relaxation Problem solving Resisting temptation	Exposure to new experiences Relaxation Exposure to music, etc.
Methods	Modelling Role playing Rehearsal Record taking Discussions Written manuals	Homework assignments Practice exercises	Exposure to hobbies, youth groups, art, music, etc.

adaptation of Rosenbaum's three types of self-control to intervention with children (Ronen and Rosenbaum, 2001).

Learning to Think Like a Cognitive–Behavioural Therapist

The CBT therapist's role has changed over the years. Therapists in the past were conceived as being in charge of the entire intervention process from planning to method selection and pace. Whereas most of the literature in the 1960s and 1970s suggested effective procedures for therapists' intervention, the 1980s saw more attention given to the therapist's role as an educational, therapeutic trainer and an increased focus on the process of therapy. In the 1990s therapists were seen as enabling experiences and providing a safe setting for practising skills. Safran and Segal (1990), for example, presented most of their therapy in the context of the client–therapist relationship. Now the CBT intervention process has become an educational, therapeutic process aimed at teaching, practising and applying new skills, knowledge and coping strategies, and offering an experiential setting. Treatment focuses on emotional processes and on methods for helping clients let go of control and accept and live with problems rather than constantly trying to overcome them.

Kanfer and Schefft (1988) suggested six rules summarizing the cognitive–behavioural therapist's way of thinking:

1 *Think behaviour.* Often, therapists concentrate on the client's problem, making assumptions and interpretations regarding its causes. The cognitive–behavioural therapist defines the problem in terms of behaviour rather than insecurities, anxiety or similar constructs. Action is the main dimension on which interchanges in therapy are focused.
2 *Think solution.* Often, therapists devote more time to thinking of difficulties and problems than to finding solutions. A full problem description requires knowledge, not only of the current situation or state, but also of a more desirable future end-state and some indication of how to achieve it.
3 *Think positive.* Just as therapists help the client to think positively and to focus on small changes and positive forces rather than on difficulties, they must themselves also aspire to positive thinking. CBT reinforces positive outcomes and strengthens any strategies, plans or actions that make these outcomes more likely.
4 *Think small steps.* Although clients are usually interested in the major, significant changes in their lives, extreme changes are difficult to obtain. Targeting small gradual changes reduces fears, motivates clients and helps therapists to observe and pinpoint difficulties. An accumulation of many small changes constitutes one large and significant change.
5 *Think flexible.* Sheldon (1987) accused therapists of falling in love with the methods they use, arguing that this precludes them from asking questions about effectiveness or from negotiating the best method for particular clients. *Think flexible* challenges therapists to be creative, modify their traditional

interventions, and try to adapt themselves to the clients' needs. Gambrill (1990) suggested that therapists look for disconfirming evidence (which points to alternatives), try to understand other people's point of view, use language carefully, watch out for vivid data, move beyond the illusion of understanding, complement clear thinking skills with knowledge, and ask about accuracy.

6 *Think future.* Many therapeutic approaches focus on the past and its role in the client's present. CBT challenges therapists to think towards the future, predicting how their client will cope and how they themselves would like to be different or better in the future.

As therapy is a planned process, much attention has been given to the construction of intervention. The most familiar procedure for intervention, Gambrill's twelve steps (Gambrill et al., 1971), has provided guidelines for social workers and other therapists as well as for students learning to conduct the process of intervention. Each step comprises three components – its objective, rationale and means of operation (Table 3).

Clients, Problem Areas and Important Concepts in CBT

A major change in the main concepts of therapy has occurred, with CBT moving from *doing something to* people towards *working with* them, and from teaching people how to *overcome* problems towards teaching them to *live with, cope with and accept* them.

In the early days of behaviour therapy, the focus was mainly on psychiatric disorders, on children with severe handicaps in institutional settings, and on mental retardation and autism. Over the years, health attitudes and modern science have highlighted the importance of helping people remain in their natural environments. As a result, CBT began to focus its attention on open clinics and day care centres and started treating less severe problems such as anxiety and depression. Another change was extending interventions to non-clinical populations and environments. CBT nowadays tries to work with large ranges of the whole population: different cultural influences, children, adults, families and organizations.

During the 1970s and the 1980s much attention was given to the treatment of social anxiety, fears, phobias and depression (Beck et al., 1979), whereas the late 1980s saw a move towards hysterical disorders, post-traumatic stress disorders, obsessive-compulsive disorders and social skills training. Social changes raised new social problems, focusing attention on abused and neglected children, abused women, drugs and alcohol, homosexuality and the treatment of AIDS. New medical developments expose people to new problems: the ability to live longer necessitates helping elderly clients get the most out of their lives; surgical techniques such as transplants necessitate helping people live with their changing bodies; and coping with new treatments for illnesses such as cancer, diabetes and anorexia facilitates the generation of new intervention techniques. One focus of modern life is the urge to improve life quality, as reflected by the development of interventions in institutions, work organizations and individual therapy.

Table 3 *Gambrill's twelve steps in the intervention process*

Step		*Objective*	*Rationale*	*Means of operation*
1	Inventory of problem areas.	Obtain the whole spectrum of problems.	Helps draw the problem area profile.	Accumulating full descriptions of presenting problems.
2	Problem selection and contract.	Reach client/therapist agreement on problem areas selected for change.	Stimulates client cooperation and involvement.	Conversing about the problem list and negotiating the selection.
3	Commitment to cooperate.	Obtain client agreement to cooperate with the process.	Facilitates compliance.	Providing explanations, reading the agreement, and seeking agreement.
4	Specification of target behaviours.	Specify details about the selected problem.	Demonstrates what maintains and reinforces the problem.	Using samples of problem behaviours and desirable alternatives.
5	Baseline of target behaviour.	Obtain pre-intervention frequency and duration of the problem.	Provides a concrete basis for judging change.	Charting, estimating.
6	Identification of problem-controlling conditions.	Learn the conditions preceding and following the problem's occurrence.	Demonstrates the importance of discriminatory stimuli affecting the problem.	Charting incidents before, during and after the problem's occurrence.
7	Assessment of environmental resources.	Identify possible resources in the client's environment.	Enlists environment's help, without which change is difficult.	Asking the client or interviewing significant others in the environment or mediators.
8	Specification of behavioural objectives.	Specify the behavioural objectives of the modification plan.	Elicits the client's terminal behavioural repertoire.	Using baseline and assessment.
9	Formulation of a modification plan.	Select an appropriate technique.	Enables selection of most efficient programme for change.	Reviewing information in previous steps, and examining available interventions.
10	Implementation of modification plan.	Modify behaviour.	Focuses effort on change.	Conducting specific intervention techniques.
11	Monitoring outcomes.	Obtain information about the effectiveness of intervention.	Gives feedback on effectiveness.	Data-gathering techniques.
12	Maintenance of change.	Achieve maintenance and stabilization.	Helps prevent relapses.	Using the environment for maintenance or specific plan.

The Adaptation of CBT to Social Work

Cognitive–behavioural therapy has gained a prominent position in clinical social work – probably because of its relevance to social work concepts, purposes, ethics and intervention modes (Ronen and Freeman, 2007). Social work as a profession is built on the notion that theoretical knowledge can be translated into skills and practical know-how in order to achieve change, with clearly defined objects for change and clear, concrete and well-defined targets (Gambrill, 1983, 1990). CBT puts the client in the centre of treatment by focusing on action and change, examining a person's behaviour, emotions and thinking style, in light of her/his strengths, weaknesses and goals (Ronen, 1998, 2003).

As social work involves weak populations, empowerment constitutes an important interventional goal. Instead of instituting long-term dependent relationships between therapists and clients, social workers aim to assist clients to become independent and help themselves. The purpose of CBT is to help individuals find their own resources, learn to recognize and use their own wisdom, and discover personal methods for self-help. These can lead them towards greater independence, self-trust and capability for self-change.

Five Key Points

- Cognitive–behavioural therapy is a direct application of behavioural and cognitive theories.
- Cognitive–behavioural therapy is a dynamic model for helping people change and acquire self-help skills.
- The process of change is an active process designed to give clients knowledge and skills and to facilitate practice and application of the newly acquired skills.
- Cognitive–behavioural therapy involves changing people's way of thinking, feeling and behaving.
- Cognitive–behavioural therapy aims to help people identify their automatic thoughts, become aware of their emotions, link their thoughts and emotions to behaviour and change their automatic thoughts to more adequate ones.

Three Questions

? With so many similarities between social work and cognitive–behavioural therapy, why has CBT not become the treatment of choice for social workers?
? How does CBT's development towards the future affect social work interventions?
? What modifications need to be undertaken in order to adapt CBT to social work's specific clients and targets?

Further reading

1 Alford, B. A. and Beck, A. T. (1997) *The Integrative Power of Cognitive Therapy*. New York: Guilford Press.
2 Bandura, A. (1997) *Self-efficacy: The Exercise of Control*. New York: W. H. Freeman.
3 Ronen, T. and Freeman, A. (2007). *Cognitive Behavior Therapy in Clinical Social Work Practice*. New York: Springer.

PART 3

The Practice Context

CHAPTER 3.1

Social Work with Children and Families

June Thoburn

There are few, if any, countries which do not have some form of state or local authority child and family welfare service, the scope of which will vary depending on the extent of more universalist provisions in the field of housing, income support, healthcare, education and local community services. In England and Wales the Children Act 1989, the Adoption and Children Act 2002 and the Children Act 2004 require local authorities to provide a range of services for children and young people under the age of 18:

- who are 'unlikely to achieve or maintain, or have the opportunity of achieving or maintaining, a reasonable standard of health or development without the provision of services' by the local authority;
- whose 'health or development is likely to be significantly impaired or further impaired without the provision of such services'; or
- who are disabled (Children Act 1989, section 17).

Local authorities have a corporate responsibility to meet the needs of such children, which means that all the relevant departments (including housing, education and leisure services), working in partnership with health trusts and schools, must jointly plan and provide services. There are some differences in the detailed requirements for service delivery between England and Wales; the Children (Northern Ireland) Order (1995) provides for broadly similar services, and there are major differences in legislation and service provision in Scotland under the Children (Scotland) Act 1995. In England the Children Act 2004 requires the appointment of a Director of Children's Services, who is accountable both for the education and children's social services functions of the local authority, and is required to lead multi-agency children's trust arrangements that draw up an agreed Children and Young People's Plan. In drawing up and working to achieve these plans, children, parents and their carers and representatives of the voluntary sector must be consulted. The particular circumstances in any local authority which may lead to children being 'in need' or at risk of significant harm have to be researched and strategies and services devised to help such children and their parents. These services must then be publicized in a way which makes the information accessible to any parents, carers and children who may need them.

As with other local authority personal social services, there is encouragement in the legislation for a 'mixed economy' of child welfare services. Services are to be provided by the voluntary/not-for-profit and private sectors alongside local authority services. However, the more rigid 'purchaser/provider' arrangements developed for community care services for adults have not taken hold in children's services, and by far the largest number of child and family social workers still work in local authority teams. Although the terms 'care manager' and 'case manager' are sometimes in evidence, it is most likely that the term 'child and family social worker' will be used for registered social workers employed in this area of practice.

Child and family social workers mainly work in one of six settings:

- the community child and family social work team (sometimes referred to as an 'area team' and sometimes divided into intake, assessment, family support, long-term or child protection teams);
- a family placement team;
- a day care resource such as a family centre;
- a residential (group care) setting;
- service centres set up for a particular clinical or therapeutic purpose and often as part of a multidisciplinary team;
- a team working with a particular group of children or young people such as disabled children, young offenders or children leaving care.

Social workers may also be 'outposted' or 'attached' to organizations largely comprising and managed by other professionals such as extended schools, children's centres providing day care and other services for the under fives, or specialist health services for disabled children.

The Community Child and Family Team

The majority of child and family social workers work in community teams managed by children's services departments. Some of these may work from the same premises (are 'co-located') as other children's services professionals, allowing for closer integration with aspects of the health or education services such as special educational needs assessment. Some voluntary child care agencies provide an outreach service to children and families in their own homes, mainly from a family centre base alongside group and community development activities. Because it is virtually impossible to uncouple the legal mandate to provide a protection and care service alongside family support services, the private (for profit) sector has not, to date, become involved in the provision of community child and family social work services.

Parents and older children may refer themselves directly to children's services teams for assistance, or the referral may come from another agency. Once contacted, a social worker must assess whether any child in the household is 'in need' under the terms of the legislation and, in consultation with family members, work out how best the identified need can be met. In most cases, social workers will (with the permission of parents and older children, unless to seek permission might be harmful to the child) consult other agencies who may be working with or have relevant information which can assist the assessment. In so doing they are guided by the *Assessment Framework* (Department of Health, 1999b – a set of guidance materials, research digests and schedules to aid assessment practice, published, together with a set of training materials). The *Common Assessment Framework* (Department for Education and Skills, 2006a) and provisions for sharing information between professionals when a cause for concern is identified (Department for Education and Skills, 2006b) provide guidance for community support staff who wish to refer families to the children's social work teams.

A second group of children, smaller in number and included within the broad definition of 'children in need' but making the greatest demands on social work time, is the group who are suspected of being in need of protective services. This may be because of maltreatment by a parent or carer, or because the parent is unable to protect the child from accidental or deliberate harm by a relative, neighbour or stranger. Protective support and therapeutic services are also provided for children who have been abused by carers in day care, residential or school settings, even when there is no question of parental fault. In the UK the child protection system has four interlocking parts.

In the first instance, the Children Act requires child and family social work teams and colleagues in other agencies and schools to seek to prevent children from suffering maltreatment by use of the family support provisions available to all children in need.

Secondly, there is a complex *formal* child protection administrative system which has been put in place over the years to facilitate a coordinated multidisciplinary response to children who may be suffering significant harm as a result of maltreatment. *Working Together to Safeguard Children* (HM Government, 2006) provides detailed guidance on how the different professions should coordinate their efforts to protect children. These arrangements replace the previous system that operated from the 1970s based on the *Child Protection Register*. However, the multidisciplinary child protection conference, bringing together family members and professionals to agree appropriate protection plans in each case, and the careful recording and monitoring of such plans by 'core groups' are still central to this service. Although there is no clear evidence that more children are maltreated in the UK now than was the case in the recent or more distant past, a series of well-publicized cases in which children have been killed by their parents or sexually or physically abused in the family or children's homes has led to a concentration of social work time and resources on the investigation of cases of suspected child abuse. The formal system has developed from being a coordinating process for protecting children from violent assault or life-threatening neglect to one which encompasses children harmed in a variety of ways. Neglect and emotional abuse of children past infancy whose emotional rather than physical development is threatened increasingly figure in the child protection statistics. Thoburn et al. (1999) found that of 701 children under the age of eight referred to three local authorities, 51 per cent were seeking a family support service. Of the 49 per cent referred because of child protection concerns, under a third were in respect of physical or sexual maltreatment, with the largest number being about neglect.

Thirdly, if it becomes clear that compulsion is required to protect the child, the social worker may apply to a Family Court for either a supervision order or a care order.

Fourthly, action may be taken against the alleged perpetrator in the criminal courts. This is the responsibility of the police and the Crown Prosecution Service, although the social worker may be required to give evidence or facilitate the collection of evidence from the child.

The role and tasks of child and family social workers have been described, monitored and evaluated by many researchers. Those most relevant to area team social workers have been summarized in four documents: *Patterns and Outcomes in Child Placement* (Department of Health, 1991a); *Child Protection: Messages from Research* (Department of Health, 1995a); *The Children Act Now: Messages from Research* (Department of Health, 2001b); and *Supporting Parents: Messages from Research* (Quinton, 2004).

These studies identify children who regularly receive social work services as broadly fitting into three overlapping groups. First those who have been on the receiving end of neglectful or abusive parenting. The second 'volunteered' group are those whose parents request services because they are unable to adequately meet the needs of their children as a result of some combination of personal or interpersonal stresses, deprivation or disability, and who sometimes request that their children be 'accommodated' away from home (Children Act 1989, section 20). These children tend to be either in the younger age ranges or to have behaviour problems or disabilities. The third group comprises troubled and troublesome older children who cause concern to the authorities as well as to their parents because of their challenging behaviour, delinquency, non-school attendance or other anti-social activities.

Research has shown that these are overlapping characteristics and that there is considerable scope for the social worker making the initial assessment to exercise discretion as to whether, for example, a case should be seen as a child protection case or one in which the parent is under stress and seeking assistance and support (Brandon et al., 1999; Packman and Hall, 1998). Similarly, an adolescent with challenging behaviour and some delinquency may be perceived as 'troublesome' (and perhaps referred to a youth offending team) or 'volunteered' in that the troublesome behaviour might be attributed *either* to wilful misbehaviour *or* to stresses in the family necessitating additional support. A *Family Group Conference* (an extended family based way of identifying ways of helping parents and children pioneered in New Zealand) may also be part of the assessment and case planning process (Marsh and Crow, 1998).

Research shows that the children assessed as 'in need' of additional child welfare services tend to come disproportionately from certain groups in society. Amongst those who are over-represented are children from single parent or reconstituted families; those who are badly housed and living in deprived areas, and those whose families subsist on incomes below the recognized poverty line. The parents and children tend to have more physical, mental health and addiction problems than the general population. Intimate partner violence has been recognized as having a significantly negative impact on children's development by an amendment to the Children Act 1989 (Adoption and Children Act 2002, section 120) listing 'seeing or hearing the ill-treatment of another' as providing evidence of harm that might lead to a care order. Although the statistics are complex, it seems that children of African Caribbean heritage and those of dual white and African Caribbean heritage tend also to be over-represented amongst children receiving a service, whilst children with two parents of South or East Asian descent may be under-represented both amongst those receiving a service in their own homes and those looked after by the local authority (Thoburn et al., 2005).

The Services Provided to the Family Home

Alongside their duty to assess the needs of children and to ensure that they are protected from significant harm, area team social workers provide a package of help to the child in need and members of his or her family. Once a child is assessed as being 'in need', services may be provided to any member of the family, provided that there is benefit to the child in need. For example, a holiday or play scheme may be provided for the sibling of a child with a severe disability. There is a strong emphasis in law and guidance on multidisciplinary assessments and multidisciplinary family support and (if necessary) child protection plans. The area team worker usually retains the case management role (in child protection cases referred to as the key worker role) and provides a social casework service for as long as the case remains 'open', drawing in other statutory, voluntary or private sector services as needed. In some cases the 'key worker' role may be retained by a 'lead professional' from another agency already known to the family. Child and family cases are often complex and reassessments and changes in services are frequent. Some follow a pattern of case closure and reopening (referred to in Thoburn et al., 1999 as *revolving door* cases), whilst others remain open cases for years, with the intensity of services provided varying according to stresses in the family. This is especially the case if it is necessary to provide long-term accommodation for a child or seek a care order through the courts to protect a child from significant harm.

There are many ways of looking at the range of services available. They may be considered in terms of therapeutic or supportive relationships; deeds or services; and words or therapy (Thoburn, 1994). There is much evidence from adult mental health as well as child care research that the availability of emotional support is associated with lower levels of stress and more competent parenting. Ideally this will come from partners, family or friends but, if these sources of support are not available, the area team worker may wish to link the parents with a volunteer or a self-help group or to encourage a relative to play a supportive role (Ghate and Hazel, 2002).

Research with parents whose children were in need of services has shown that a family casework service involving continuity of relationship with a social worker as well as the provision of practical help, and in some cases therapeutic work designed to achieve change, is particularly valued by parents and older children (Department of Health, 1995a).

A range of social work methods may be appropriate and effective if care is taken to match the social work method used with the needs and wishes of the family members. If a parent is not requesting a service, as may be the case when an allegation of maltreatment is made which a parent denies, ensuring that a child is safe, keeping the family fully informed of the protection process, and giving clear information about what may happen and the powers available to the agency, is likely to be the most effective approach. For those who seek help to make changes which they know to be necessary, a combination of a trusting relationship, practical help and the skilled use of appropriate social work methods will be needed. In more difficult cases where there are multiple and overlapping problems, short-term methods are unlikely to be successful unless they are provided episodically in the context of a longer-term relationship either with an individual worker or a team of workers. In the USA and a small number of pilot projects in the UK, 'family preservation services' in which the provision of a short-term but intensive relationship with a social worker plays an essential part, have been found to have positive results with some families in crisis whose difficulties were severe (Maluccio et al., 2000).

The Children Act 1989 lists the services which should be available to support families whose children have been assessed as 'in need'. They include the provision of day care and out-of-school care; help with recreational activities and holidays; the provision of respite accommodation in appropriate cases; practical help in the home, and assistance with laundry, for example if a child has a severe disability involving incontinence. Surveys have shown considerable discrepancy in the way in which these provisions are implemented. Some authorities have adopted a minimalist approach, whilst others provide a much wider range of services, from help to community groups to setting up Credit Unions or food or clothing cooperatives on the one hand, to the provision of respite care or accommodation schemes at the other end of the continuum. Research and consumer surveys report considerable satisfaction with the provision of practical assistance, day care, and voluntary befriending schemes.

An essential arm of a child welfare service is the provision of out-of-home care. In 2004–5, 24,500 children started to be looked after by local authorities, most of them (67 per cent) under voluntary agreements with parents and remaining for periods of weeks rather than years. Around 30 per cent come into care each year as a result of court orders, and they tend to stay longer. In March 2005 there were 60,900 children looked after, 31 per cent at the request of parents (the term used is 'accommodated') but well over three-quarters on care or emergency orders or remanded into care. Only 13 per cent of these were in children's homes, boarding schools or secure accommodation and just under 6,000 were placed back home with parents under the terms of the care order. The majority were in foster family care, 68 per cent in March 2005, with 7,500 (12 per cent of all looked after children) being placed with relatives or friends approved as foster carers for that particular child. The Children Act 1989 makes it clear that the provision of accommodation should be seen as an appropriate family support service in some cases. A further 11,400 were looked after during 2004–5 for a series of short-term placements, usually to provide respite as part of a family support package. Respite care schemes for children with disabilities have been well established for some years, but the provision of this service for families under stress for other reasons is a comparatively recent development and provision is patchy despite some evidence of effectiveness and parent and child satisfaction with the service. Aldgate and Bradley (1999) show that parents under stress greatly value this form of support and assistance and offer suggestions about how respite care can best be arranged to maximize the benefits and minimize any distress to the child.

Area team workers liaise with family placement workers (discussed in the next section) in order to match the child to the placement (though a chronic shortage of foster parents means that all too often there is little or no choice). They continue to provide support to the parents and the child, make arrangements for continued contact between family members and seek to return the child safely home. If this is not possible, a reviewing process involving parents and child, chaired by an independent reviewing officer (employed by children's services but not otherwise involved in the management of the case) will consider what sort of longer-term placement is needed and in some cases may recommend placement for adoption.

Thus, the daily work of a child and family area team social worker will be a mix of assessment, social care planning, and the direct provision of a social casework service (including practical help) to parents, children and close relatives. The mix will vary in each case. The social care planning role requires the worker to be particularly skilled as a negotiator, mediator and advocate. Increasingly the child and family social worker needs team leadership and chairing skills as they will be working closely with support workers and other professionals in networks formed around individual children and families. The ability to work directly with children of different ages, and with parents who have a range of problems from material deprivation to mental ill-health or learning disability, is essential. It is particularly important in such cases to work closely with colleagues in adult services/community care teams for adults, to ensure the provision of coordinated assistance to parents in need of a community care service and to their 'in need' children. Recent organizational changes resulting in greater separation between services to adults and services to children may make it harder to achieve this aim. The recruitment, training and support of volunteers, who may provide support or advocacy, has become an increasingly important part of the work, the skills for which are close to those required for the recruitment and support of foster carers.

It can be seen that the exercise of professional discretion is central to the work of child and family area team social workers. They are the 'general practitioners' of the child welfare system and retain responsibility for the assessment and reassessment of the needs of the child and family, and for the provision of a varied and flexible casework service. The results of their decisions may be life enhancing or life threatening. Although the decision as to whether to remove a child from home or return a child back home will usually be supervised or sanctioned by the courts, the research makes it clear that it is social workers, through their day-to-day practice, who have the major influence on these decisions.

The Family Placement Team

In most agencies there will be specialist resource teams responsible for recruiting, preparing and supporting the families who provide respite care, short- or long-term foster care or adoptive homes. Sometimes adoption and foster care work is undertaken by a single 'family placement' team. In other authorities one team recruits and supports short-term foster carers and a 'permanence team' is responsible for adoption and long-term fostering. Foster care services are regulated by the Children Act 1989 and the accompanying guidance.

During the last two decades of the twentieth century, the proportion of children in foster care increased as children's homes were closed. This, and the improvement in family support services, resulted in the children in foster care being older and experiencing more serious difficulties. Foster care has come to be seen as a skilled task for which training is required and often a fee for service paid on top of the maintenance element of the allowance.

Some foster carers take a succession of short-term children, whilst others, in the course of a fostering career stretching for 20 or more years, take only three or four children (either concurrently or sequentially) until it is safe for them to go home or they reach adulthood. Others may take one or more children into their home on a permanent basis, planning to bring the child up as a member of the family until adulthood. In almost all cases an important part of their role will be to facilitate comfortable contact between the children and their birth parents, other relatives and siblings (Cleaver, 2000; Sinclair, 2005).

The role of the family placement team is to publicize the need for foster and adoptive families in a way which encourages a wide range of families to come forward. On top of the other social work skills, team members need to be able to work with the media and with community groups. The Children Act 1989 requires that strenuous efforts be made to ensure that children are looked after by families of their own ethnicity, language, culture and religion. Managers of family placement teams, like their counterparts in area teams, try to ensure that team membership reflects the community to which they provide a service, and this diversity has helped in the recruitment of foster families from diverse communities. Matching in terms of ethnicity is important for short- as well as long-term placements since there is a growing trend (encouraged by research findings of positive outcomes) for children to remain permanently with their short-term carers if they cannot be safely returned home.

The approval process for potential foster parents usually involves the checking of references and a series of interviews in the family home (referred to as a home study). At the same time, most families attend a series of group meetings where they learn more about the rewards and pressures of fostering. Groupwork and educative skills have to be part of the toolkit of the family placement worker. The final stage is the writing and presentation of a detailed report to the foster care or adoption panel which makes a recommendation to a senior manager of the agency either to accept or decline the application. Once approved, the family placement worker becomes the 'link worker' for the family, discussing their training needs, sorting out any problems with payments, providing support over and above that provided by the child's worker if a placement is particularly problematic. The most useful account of the role of the family placement worker with short-term foster carers is that of Triseliotis et al. (1995).

Although the majority of foster carers still contract directly with local authority social services departments to provide a service, there has recently been a growth of private or not-for-profit foster care agencies, referred to jointly as the 'independent sector' (Sellick and Howell, 2004). The service they provide usually includes social work support to the foster carers and children and sometimes special education and therapy. Foster carers' remuneration tends to be considerably higher than the local authority foster payment. However, the children placed often have even more problems than those in local authority foster families, though this is not invariably the case since some authorities are so short of placements that they turn to the independents to help them out with children who do not have special needs or behaviour difficulties.

Adoption services are provided by voluntary sector adoption agencies as well as by local authorities. The number of children adopted in England and Wales fell from 25,000 in 1965 to just over 4,000 in 1999. If adoptions by stepfamilies are taken out, the decline is even greater. In the 1960s, most of the adoptions were of infants relinquished by their birth mothers and placed with childless couples. In 2004–5, of those adopted 3,800 were children in care, and most were adopted against their parents' wishes. Although 97 per cent of these were under the age of five when they started to be looked after, only a small minority were infants. Another big change is that the 'closed', secret model of adoption has been replaced by much more open arrangements which result in between 80 and 90 per cent of adoptive families maintaining either indirect or (less frequently) face-to-face contact with birth parents, other relatives and siblings placed elsewhere (Neil and Howe, 2004).

There are big differences between adoption in the UK and adoption in most European countries where large numbers of infants are adopted each year from overseas, but very few are adopted from care. Family placement social workers are responsible for providing home study reports to the Foreign Office to enable British families to adopt from overseas, and for providing post-placement support as required by the Children and Adoption Act 2006.

Following mounting concern about maltreatment of children in care, the Prime Minister commissioned a review of adoption services which concluded that adoption should be more closely linked with the child care services and encouraged local authorities to think of adoption as a route out of care for more children who cannot return home. However, the scope for increase is limited, in large part by the ages at which children come into care, since most adopters want to adopt children under five (47 per cent of those who started to be looked after in 2004–5 were aged 10 or over and only 17 per cent were under the age of 12 months). Also, some children do not wish to be adopted and in other cases there is no evidence to justify dispensing with the consent of the parents. Others are so troubled that there would be a high risk that the placement would break down, causing even more damage to the child and considerable distress to the adoptive family. In an attempt to improve the success of adoption for children with complex needs, the Adoption and Children Act 2002 requires children's services to assess the support needs of adopters and those who take on the legal guardianship of looked after children (under the new 'special guardianship' provisions). However, it seems likely that foster care will remain the main family placement for children looked after. Fortunately, when placements of similar children are compared, the success rate for adoptions and 'permanent' foster placements is similar (Fratter et al., 1991; Sellick et al., 2004; Beek and Schofield, 2004).

Residential Child Care and Day Care Settings

This type of work is often called 'group care' because much of the social work practice takes place with a group of residents or day care attenders. A proportion of the staff will be qualified social workers and others will have qualifications as teachers, youth workers, nursery nurses, play therapists, occupational or physiotherapists or nurses (usually for specialist facilities for children with disabilities or severe mental health problems). However, the majority still have no professional qualifications, a matter of considerable concern to enquiries on abuse within residential care.

Residential child care has declined in a dramatic way since the 1970s. This started well before the reports of maltreatment in children's homes, but these have hastened the rate of decline. However, the 2005 figure of just over 8,000 children resident in children's homes or other 'group care' settings at any one time underestimates the role they still play. Although they tend not to stay long, many more young people pass through, placed in an emergency if they are evicted from their families or their foster or adoptive placement breaks down. The Utting (1991) report into abuses in children's homes concluded that, as well as their short-term functions, they were still needed to provide longer-term homes for children who:

- have decided that they do not wish to be fostered;
- have had bad experiences of foster care;
- have been so abused within the family that another family placement is inappropriate;
- are from the same family and cannot otherwise be kept together.

The independent sector has traditionally played an important part in the provision of residential child care. There are indications that the fall in numbers has bottomed out and that small, highly staffed specialist establishments are being opened again to cater for some of the very damaged children who need help in preparing for independence or, at the younger end, need a 24-hour-a-day therapeutic environment to help them recover from the trauma which led to care and to move on to an adoptive or foster family. The Department of Health overview, *Residential Child Care: Messages from Research* (1999c) provides a good way into the research literature on this subject.

Day Care and Family Centres

The Children Act 1989 encouraged the growth of day care resources, usually called family centres, as sources of support to parents and children living in stressful circumstances. The voluntary/independent sector plays an important part in family centre provision. Holman (1988) gives an account of their history and provides a broad classification in terms of their breadth of focus.

'Client focused' or 'referral' centres are at one end of the spectrum, working only with families referred to them by another agency because of identified problems, and often where there are concerns about maltreatment. The workers in these centres become involved in child protection assessments or may supervise contact meetings for children looked after. Parenting education is often a part of their work.

- Neighbourhood centres tend to have 'drop-in' facilities and members of the community are encouraged to see themselves as 'members' rather then 'attenders' or 'customers' (Gibbons et al., 1990). Activities such as credit unions, work skills training, Internet facilities and welfare rights advice will often run alongside parenting classes and activities for the children.
- The community development model might involve similar activities but may also encourage pressure group activities.
- In the late 1990s the *Sure Start* programme saw the expansion of community-based services, including child care and parent support, for children under five living in areas of deprivation. As part of the *Every Child Matters* agenda these have been incorporated into mainstream services, with plans for a children's centre, including day care, accessible to all families. Tunstill et al. (2006) conclude that, although children's centres and extended schools have an important role to play in early prevention of family problems, there is still an important role for the smaller and more intimate neighbourhood family centre.

Leaving Care and Youth Offending Teams

These have been grouped together because both involve work with adolescents.

Leaving care teams help to prepare for independent living those young people in care whose foster placements break down and who cannot return to their birth families. Their work is governed by the Children (Leaving Care) Act 2000. The work involves a combination of counselling, advice giving and practical help to find lodgings or make sense of the benefits system. Social workers often work closely with volunteer 'mentors' or 'befrienders'. They also act as mediators to help build bridges between young people and their birth relatives or adoptive or foster families or to support those foster families continuing to provide a home beyond 18. Stein (1997) has summarized the research in *What Works in Leaving Care*. Researchers are critical of the tendency to concentrate on practical skills (independence training) at the expense of social and relationship skills which prepare for 'inter-dependence'. The implementation of the Act has brought this type of work into greater prominence since it made Social Services Departments responsible for providing income maintenance, accommodation and a range of practical, emotional and educational support services to all young people who are looked after on or after their sixteenth birthday, in some cases to the age of 21.

The Youth Offending Teams were established by the Crime and Disorder Act 1998 to work with young people aged between 10 and 18 (and even younger) who have become or are at serious risk of becoming involved in criminal activities. The growing use of anti-social behaviour orders (ASBOs) has increased the number of social workers employed in this type of work, with some being attached to housing authority teams. They are multidisciplinary teams comprising social workers, probation officers, healthcare workers, representatives of education departments and the police. They work closely with drug action teams and with social workers in all other settings. Their work tends to be short term, with group and individual work based on cognitive–behavioural methods being major tools used to help a young person turn away from criminal activity.

Principles for Practice

To work effectively, child and family social workers must apply the values, knowledge and skills required of all social workers to fulfil the specific requirements of the child care task. The principles for practice required by the Children Act 1989 and its guidance notes (Department of Health, 1989b) are congruent with social work's values of respect for individuals, families and communities, with a commitment to maximize the rights and freedoms of children and parents and to give them as much choice as possible about the services to be offered. From these come five pointers for positive practice (see box).

These principles apply to work with colleagues in other agencies and professions; with self-help and interest groups within the community; or with parents and children in need of a service and their carers. The Children Act's emphasis on attempting to work in partnership with family members is congruent with social work's ethical requirement to treat people with respect and to maximize their opportunities for making their own decisions.

The Knowledge Base and Organizational Issues

The knowledge required by child and family social workers in order to provide the most appropriate package of support, therapy and services is extensive (Thoburn, 1994). If the case comes to court or the child needs long-term out-of-home care, the social worker will require research-based knowledge of the likely outcomes of alternative placements, since the court may not make an order unless convinced that the outcome of the plan proposed by the worker, if an order were made, would be

Five pointers for positive practice

1. Prevention of family disintegration by using flexible approaches to practice.
2. Protection of the child and other vulnerable family members.
3. Permanence – the importance of the child's sense of this.
4. Partnership with family members and colleagues in own and other agencies.
5. Preparation of both the social worker and family members before important meetings, courts, etc.

likely to be better for the child than if alternative measures were taken. The Department for Education and Skills produces summary *Quality Protect Briefings* and the Social Care Institute for Excellence produces a series of *Knowledge Reviews* to help the busy practitioner keep up-to-date.

In developed as well as in developing countries the need for family support and child protection services is greater than the resources available. The child and family social worker must therefore engage with the difficult question of prioritizing or rationing scarce resources. In some agencies priorities are determined by managers. Most often, cases where there is any question of parental maltreatment will take precedence over other cases, with the unfortunate result that some children who are likely to suffer significant harm from other causes than parental maltreatment remain unhelped. These might include children who have been seriously assaulted but where the abuser is no longer living in the household, or even children in care who, for whatever reason, cannot return home. Unless a skilled social worker is allocated to help them to maintain links with their original family, and to work to secure an appropriate long-term placement for them, their chances of avoiding serious harm are very poor. This has been documented by recent reports on the over-representation of young people who were in care amongst the homeless and prison populations (Utting, 1997). The response of the Government was to launch *Quality Protects* and *Choice Protects,* a programme to improve the life chances of all children assessed as 'in need' but with a particular emphasis on children looked after away from home.

Another group whose needs are not being prioritized at the moment are children who care for seriously ill parents or parents who have a mental health problem, addiction or other disability. Recent UK legislation requiring social services departments to assess the needs of carers, including children who care for a parent or other dependent adult, should ensure that their needs are given a higher profile through community care legislation, which will necessitate close cooperation between children and families teams and adult services teams.

Conclusion

Child and family social work started in the UK as a service for the placement of children who were orphaned, maltreated or for some other reason unable to live with their parents or extended family. The logical move in the 1960s was to develop preventative strategies to avoid the need for out-of-home care. Initially the emphasis was on prevention of a range of hazards which led to child placement or family breakdown. However, the emphasis soon shifted to the prevention of delinquency, shortly followed by a change in emphasis to protection from physical and sexual abuse. A realization that children in care could be abused by carers or by the care system designed to protect them led in the 1970s and 1980s to a child rescue philosophy and the move to place more children permanently in adoptive families. However, research indicating that somewhere between 80 and 90 per cent of children who start to be looked after will eventually return to their parents or home communities, pushed the emphasis in the Children Act 1989 back to prevention, now reframed as 'family support'. As a consequence of this move, child care social workers and managers are encouraged by government to reorder their priorities. This is not without opposition from child and family workers themselves who have grown up during a period when professional value and status was more likely to lie in competence in therapeutic methods, such as family therapy, or specialist aspects of the work, such as child abuse investigation. The Children Act partnership principles require the skilled delivery of therapeutic and protection services but also emphasize negotiation skills, and take away some of the power of the professional worker to determine the methods to be used. The clear message from research, backed by legislation and guidance, is that the skilled technician must also be a skilled communicator, negotiator and advocate. Child and family social work went a long way along the path of technical competence and practice dominated by official procedures. Abuse enquiries, consumer and outcome studies have once again shown clearly that neither will succeed either in engaging families or in achieving positive outcomes for children without the accurate empathy, warmth and genuineness which have long been known to be associated with effective social work practice.

Five Key Points

- Child and family area team social workers are the 'general practitioners' of the child welfare system and are responsible for the provision of a flexible casework service. They work closely with colleagues in family placement teams and in day care, residential and specialist settings.
- Whatever the setting, the work will be a mix of assessment, social care planning, and the direct provision of casework, group work or support services to children and families. There is a strong emphasis on working jointly with other professionals.
- Parents or children may request services to alleviate stress or tackle specific problems; they may be referred because of child protection concerns; or a young person's challenging behaviour or delinquency may result in referral or request for service. The services will be provided by the public, voluntary sector and private agencies.
- Child protection and family support are two key objectives in this field.
- Good practice today requires the social worker to operate in partnership with parents, children and substitute carers; the skilled helper must also be a skilled negotiator.

Three Questions

? How and why has the emphasis of child and family social work practice changed in recent years?
? In what way has child care policy been influenced by research?
? How far can the principle of partnership be taken in social work with parents and children?

Further reading

1 Department of Health (2001b) *The Children Act Now: Messages from Research*. London: The Stationery Office.
2 Quinton, D. (2004) *Supporting Parents: Messages from Research*. London: Jessica Kingsley.
3 Thomas, N. (2005) Social Work with Young People in Care: Looking After Children in Theory and Practice. London: Palgrave Macmillan.

CHAPTER 3.2

Social Work and Schools

Karen Lyons

Social work in relation to schools in the UK is primarily though not exclusively undertaken by staff in the education welfare service – in some places renamed the education social work service. The service has a long history but an ambiguous position, structurally and professionally, in relation to education and the personal social services.

The origins of the education welfare service date from late nineteenth and early twentieth century legislation: this aimed to ensure basic education for all children and recognized that social conditions might affect children's ability to benefit from school. Nationally, ensuring education was a part of a wider process of securing a literate, disciplined and healthy workforce. The tensions between the goals of individual development and meeting the needs of the economy persist and are, to some extent, still reflected in the expectations and roles of education welfare officers as well as schools.

Service development has mainly been in the context of local education authority powers and provisions and always had an important 'control' element with its involvement in the regulation of school attendance and youth employment. However, early voluntary initiatives also resulted from concern about the material needs and moral welfare of school children and young people and these elements have been incorporated into current service provision by different education authorities to varying extents.

The twentieth century saw the establishment of health, psychological and psychiatric services for students, as well as statutory child care provisions (also under the auspices of local authorities) and social work with families or young people by a range of voluntary organizations. The need for effective liaison between professionals in various departments and agencies, and the role of the school as a possible focus for preventative or remedial actions, are therefore long-standing. In the twenty-first century, policy and organizational shifts are changing the landscape within which education social workers operate and, potentially, the relationship which other social workers might have with schools and related education services.

These shifts include the transfer of responsibility for children and family work and child protection services from Health to the Department for Education and Skills, with commensurate organizational changes at local level, and the extension of services offered by some schools (for instance, provision of breakfast and/or after school clubs), as well as appointment of new staff (such as education mentors).

Historical roots and persistent ambivalence about the organizational base and required training of social workers in relation to schools are factors in the differences within this field of activity in the UK and relative to some other countries. In the USA, for instance, different history and organization have resulted in school-based and professionally trained social workers having a well-established role in providing a wide range of preventative and treatment programmes for children and young people in schools (Allen-Meares, 2004). In the UK the implementation from 2003 of a specific qualification for education welfare officers (EWOs) through the National Occupational Standards project has decreased the extent to which a social work qualification might have been seen as desirable for this area of work.

Key Areas of Practice

The potential range of social work activities in relation to the school population is wide, particularly if preventative strategies are included. Some aspects of the work carried out by education welfare officers have a statutory basis, notably in the regulation of school attendance and youth employment. School attendance, in particular, has been a consistent and dominant area of intervention, often with children at the secondary school stage, perhaps to the detriment of development of other tasks, including work with younger children or a more active role in the life of particular schools.

Atkinson et al. (2000a, 2000b) investigated the range of work carried out by education welfare officers with the results shown in the box.

However, the paring back of all local authority services to statutory functions and the devolution of budgets to schools have had a significant impact on the education welfare service (Blyth and Milner, 1999), and a more limited role is suggested by a recent description on the *Every Child Matters* website (http://www.everychildmatters.gov.uk/ete/agencies/welfare; accessed February 2007). This states that 'enforcing school attendance' is the main role of EWOs and identifies five other core areas (see below). The emphasis on attendance can be viewed in the context of concerns about social exclusion and levels of educational attainment, as reflected in school league tables and individual achievement, as well as in increases in youth crime and school exclusions.

Poor school attendance takes various forms and is a complex issue affected by a number of factors. *Truancy* was traditionally attributed to the problems of individual students or their families, but there has been increasing recognition of the role the school may play through its organization, culture and curriculum. Truancy can also be related to wider community norms and societal expectations (Blyth and Milner, 1999). The causes of individual attendance problems therefore require careful assessment, and a range of responses are needed. These may entail direct work with individuals, families or groups, as well as the establishment of whole

The range of work of education welfare officers

Main areas of work (*percentage of respondents citing activities*)

School attendance	99	Looked after children	21
Child employment	69	Education other than at school	16
Child protection	68	Welfare issues	16
Exclusions	47	Prosecutions	15
Child entertainment licensing	35	Youth crime	12
Special educational needs	23	Pupil and family support	9

Liaison and referral work

For the local education authority		*Other services*	
Educational psychology	69	Social services	95
Special educational needs services	45	Police	74
Behavioural support services	30	Health	41
Admissions	24	Voluntary agencies	35
Advisory services	19	Probation	23
Youth services	17	Youth justice	15
Hospital and home tuition	15	Youth justice teams	14
Pupil referral unit	14	Careers services	12
Pupil support services	12	Housing services	12
Schools	12	Mental health	8
Inspectorate	10	School nurses	8
Learning support services	10	Child and family services	8

Source: adapted from Atkinson et al. (2000a).

school programmes – for example, where bullying or racial harassment is thought to be a possible cause. Non attendance may be the reason for another of the core roles identified, namely, 'advising on children being educated otherwise than at school'. While this provision was initially primarily for medical reasons, there has been some growth in 'home tuition', including by parents who see this as a positive educational choice.

It seems likely that the imposition of a national curriculum and the stress on school examination results have in some cases increased the barriers for vulnerable pupils and have discouraged schools from devising alternative programmes or taking back pupils with a poor record. Meanwhile, government policy has reinforced the notion of individual or family failure through stressing 'parental responsibility' as a key device for tackling behavioural problems and deviance, including school non-attendance. Skilled and imaginative interventions, possibly involving collaboration between schools and other professionals, are needed in this area.

Concerns have been expressed that recent government thinking has undervalued the experience of the education welfare service (Taylor, 2000) but there have also been occasional reports of imaginative and apparently successful new initiatives (Reid, 2004).

Although one of the identified core areas of work, the framework for the regulation of youth employment is outdated, and the task tends not to have been given a high priority relative to other demands on the education welfare service (Whitney, 1998). Given the poor employment prospects of some school leavers, it is ironic that there is apparently a rise in the illegal employment of juveniles and that this is therefore an area of renewed concern. It has come back on the agenda in the context of changing attitudes to children's rights and increased attention to family poverty in the UK, together with concerns about child labour internationally.

There are differing views on the risks and benefits of paid work undertaken by school students; these relate to the nature and hours of work and the extent to which such employment can be viewed as exploitative and damaging or contributing to the healthy personal development of individuals. The family circumstances which give rise to the pressures on some students to work may also be a factor to be taken into consideration in decisions about whether and how to intervene.

The work of education welfare officers in relation to child protection is identified as another core area and illustrates the important place which EWOs have in liaising between schools and child protection services (whose social workers have the responsibility to investigate cases of alleged child abuse or neglect). The significant role of the school in monitoring the well-being of students, particularly those thought to be *at risk,* has been recognized by many. Education welfare officers participate in case conferences about individual students and sometimes contribute to the training of teaching staff and the maintenance of school policies in respect of child protection.

The education welfare service also has a recognized role to play in respect of students with 'special educational needs'. Debates about the extent to which such children can and should be accommodated in mainstream schools (rather than special schools) have been wide-ranging: policies vary and are contested. EWOs play a part in the provision of advice and advocacy for students with special needs and their families as well as in contributing to school policies and to individual assessments. This is a significant area of responsibility among school social workers in the USA, but, despite being identified as a core area, its development as a distinct area of practice in the UK has been patchy with possible input sometimes limited to 'helping prepare reports . . . as part of the statementing process' (Every Child Matters website, 2005).

An area of work not specifically mentioned as a core area, unless assumed under the attendance related duty, 'helping to arrange alternative educational provision for individual pupils', concerns school exclusions. The threefold rise in the number of students excluded in the 1990s, (not least older black pupils, predominantly male), and the possible link with social exclusion in adult life, became a focus of government concern (Social Exclusion Unit, 1998) and has continued to be problematic. To some extent the increase in the number of school exclusions may be seen as another consequence of the pressure on schools to secure conformity and good results, though clearly there are other factors at work in particular schools, neighbourhoods and individual cases. Some would see the rise in unruly and dangerous behaviour – the formal basis for exclusion – as attributable to breakdowns in family relationships, causing personal unhappiness and 'acting out', although a public culture in which there is little respect for education and the teaching profession also suggests a climate in which indiscipline in the school context is harder to manage.

In some services education welfare officers mediate between home and school to try to prevent exclusion by ensuring communication between students, their parents and teachers about problems, or, if exclusion occurs, to assist parents in understanding procedures, including their rights of representation and appeal. However, this is far from a widely agreed role for the education welfare service and there is some concern that, at times, procedures may not be followed and exclusions could be unjustified (ACE Bulletin, 2000).

Finally, students who are accommodated by local authorities under child care legislation are very susceptible to problems of various kinds in school (Jackson, 1998; NCH, 2005) and, although not identified as a core area of work, some services include in their remit liaison with residential homes. However, this is an area in which field and residential social workers should also engage constructively with schools. While any kind of inter-agency or inter-professional activity raises important issues of confidentiality and ethics, good communication at practice level and agreed strategic goals and policies between agencies are not only in line with government thinking about 'joined-up' services, but are also recognized by professional bodies as necessary for efficient and effective intervention (Harker et al., 2003).

The foregoing examples of work carried out under the auspices of the education welfare service all suggest a form of social work that involves reacting to individual problems – generally as defined by schools or the wider society – and, in reality, an individual focus predominates. However, there have periodically been imaginative groupwork programmes, including ones sometimes run by social workers in other agencies or by volunteers operating in cooperation with schools, to provide more systematic schemes designed to prevent problems or to address them before they take hold (for example, Bourne, 1999). Such programmes are sometimes related to the needs of selected pupils seen as vulnerable, while others address the risks or stresses which all children might face.

Looking to the Future

There is considerable scope for the practice of social work in schools, even if there is disagreement about who should undertake it, the appropriate organizational base and the necessary qualifications. In many ways the problems to be addressed suggest the need for a range of skills and knowledge familiar in other areas of social work practice, while the values of respect for service users and practice aimed at empowerment are essential. Additionally, as with social work in other secondary settings (like prisons or hospitals), knowledge about the organizational context and skill in relating to the key occupational group (teachers) and other professionals involved in educational policy and provision are necessary, suggesting the value of an ecological approach (Allen-Meares, 2004).

The Children Act 2004 (requiring integration of education and children's social services) lays the basis for new ways of organizing services and collaboration across professional boundaries. Additionally, in line with other broad government concerns and priorities, three more locally based developments indicate possible new directions for social work in relation to schools:

- an increased emphasis on early intervention (at the pre- and primary school stage) with a view to improving parenting skills and reducing 'disruptive behaviour';
- schools can now provide services and employ staff directly (including possibly education welfare officers) to encourage attendance, well-being and attainment;
- *personal advisers* (sometimes schools-based) employed in the Connexions Service aim to avert social exclusion and crime through coordinated approaches to the school–work transition stage.

These developments, together with other factors, such as the recognition of the potential role of schools in promoting positive mental health, suggest a climate in which there are considerable opportunities for social work activities in relation to schools, including preventative work. They also suggest that the current reorganization of services and relocation of children and family social workers may be timely. Whatever the training and role of education welfare officers, social workers also have a legitimate interest in this area of practice. In any new developments there are things to be learned from continental Europe and elsewhere about social pedagogy and about school social work as a specialism (Huxtable and Blyth, 2000).

Social work in relation to schools is a demanding role in which professional identity, allegiances and skills are challenged and the focus of intervention is varied. All social workers concerned about practice and policy in relation to children and young people should recognize the significant role of schools in students' lives and the impact of 'school failure' on their future prospects. Social workers in this field need a general orientation to the idea that education is or can be an empowering experience and that all children and young people have an entitlement to the best that can be offered. As in other settings, it is sometimes the responsibility of social work to contribute to the achievement of this goal.

Five Key Points

- Social work in relation to schools in the UK, as provided by the education welfare service, has a long history but an ambiguous position structurally in relation to both education and the personal social services.
- The organization and provision of services to school children varies considerably, both within the UK and between the UK and other countries.
- While two aspects of the role of education welfare officers have some statutory basis, there is no agreed universal role, and new developments suggest the possibility of new models of organization and intervention.
- Although maintenance of school attendance has been seen as a core activity of education welfare officers, the range of services which might be provided is very wide, particularly if social workers hope to develop preventative strategies.
- The knowledge, skills and values required for effective practice in the school social work setting are basically the same as for other forms of practice, with the addition of specialized knowledge and skills in relation to schools as organizations, educational policy, and the needs of particular categories of pupils.

Three Questions

? What are the factors which have militated against the development of a clearly identified social work service to schools and their students in the UK?

? How might the existing education welfare service personnel respond to significant changes affecting the education and personal social services sectors, the people who work in them and the users of these services?

? How might social workers work with schools to:
- improve attendance rates;
- reduce the number of exclusions; or
- increase levels of attainment of looked-after pupils?

Further reading

1 Blyth, E. and Milner, J. (eds.) (1999) *Improving School Attendance*. London: Routledge.

2 Huxtable, M. and Blyth, E. (eds.) (2000) *School Social Work Worldwide*. Washington: National Association of Social Work Press.

3 Allen-Meares, P. (ed.) (2004) *Social Work Services in Schools,* 4th edn. Boston: Pearson.

CHAPTER 3.3

Social Work, Divorce and the Family Courts

Adrian L. James

Social work in the context of family breakdown and divorce has seen major changes in recent years, reflecting shifts in the social and the legal contexts of divorce. However, there has also been a fundamental reconceptualization and reorganization of court welfare work, which has been only partly in response to these developments.

The Social, Legal and Historical Context of Divorce

A complex web of social, demographic, economic and political factors contributed to rapid changes in British society during the second half of the twentieth century. Surrounding marriage and the family are powerful images and ideologies, which serve to shape attitudes towards these important social institutions and towards marital breakdown and divorce, and which have also had an impact on both the changes and the often heated debate that has accompanied them (Coote et al., 1994; Cretney, 2005).

Such processes are reflected in changing patterns of family formation and an increasing diversity of household structures (Alcock et al., 2004; Utting, 1995). These are partly a consequence of the rate of divorce which is one of the most obvious effects of this continuing social upheaval. This increased more than fourfold from 38,000 decrees absolute granted in England and Wales in 1965 to 158,700 in 1991, since when there has been a slight decline to 153,339 in 2004, figures that take no account of the simultaneous increase in the number of relationship breakdowns between unmarried couples. Such changes have had major implications for social work practice, which increasingly has had to address the broader issue of family breakdown rather than just divorce.

From the 1930s, largely by an accident of history, the probation service was the main statutory provider of social work services to the courts and to families experiencing marital breakdown. Since then, there have been a number of significant changes in the law relating to divorce (Cretney, 2005). The current legal framework for divorce was introduced by the Divorce Reform Act 1969. This introduced 'irretrievable breakdown' as the sole ground for divorce, based on the proof of one or more of five facts – adultery, cruelty, desertion, two years' separation with the respondent's consent, and five years' separation. However, partly because it became evident that court hearings in such cases served no obvious function, but also and perhaps more importantly out of a desire to reduce the growing burden on the civil legal aid budget of matrimonial costs, a streamlined 'special procedure' was introduced by the Matrimonial Causes Act 1973, and was eventually extended to all undefended petitions, with legal aid being restricted to disputes over ancillary matters. These changes probably did more to alter the nature of the divorce process than any substantive legal changes introduced by the 1969 Act since as a consequence the process became primarily an administrative one for the majority of divorcing couples.

Simultaneously, dissatisfaction was growing with the constraints imposed by the legal process on addressing the social and psychological impact of relationship breakdown. The adversarial nature of the legal process, particularly with the increasing use being made of allegations of unreasonable behaviour to substantiate claims of irretrievable breakdown in order to secure a swift divorce, was coming under increasing attack for exacerbating the conflict between couples seeking divorce, thereby inflicting even greater damage on children unfortunate enough to be caught up in the process (James, 2003).

Against this background, and as a consequence of a growing interest in the concept of conciliation – helping couples to reach agreements in order to reduce the conflict associated with divorce – first mooted by the Finer Committee in 1974, a process of redefining substantial elements of both the legal process of divorce and the social work contribution to this began (Parkinson, 1997). With the growing interest in and development of voluntary conciliation services (drawing extensively on the experience of mediation in the USA), family court welfare officers (FCWOs – probation officers with special responsibilities for such work) also increasingly began to question the limitations of a role defined solely in terms of 'investigating and reporting' and to experiment with some of the ideas and practices being developed by conciliators and family therapists working with divorcing families (James and Hay, 1993).

Although in some areas, with the encouragement and cooperation of courts, conciliation was formally offered as a service by FCWOs, this was not a universal development and wide variations in local practice began to emerge. This was partly because of a wide range of local initiatives by practitioners, but also because of a general lack of management of such developments at a time when probation managers were preoccupied with managing the changes in their work with offenders. In addition, a particular problem faced by FCWOs was the absence of any statutory responsibility for or authority to undertake conciliation. As a consequence of this, and occasionally in the face of trenchant judicial criticism of perceived failures of welfare officers to investigate adequately and to provide courts with the information they required, much of this settlement-seeking work was covertly incorporated into the report writing function.

In the wake of these changes and following proposals from the Law Commission (1990), a Green Paper and a White Paper (Lord Chancellor's Department 1993 and 1995), and a heated debate in Parliament, 'no fault' divorces, with irretrievable breakdown as the sole ground, were introduced by the Family Law Act 1996. These changes chimed with the move towards a more informal, administrative system of divorce, whilst the Act also endorsed the development of mediation by introducing arrangements for the public funding of mediation, along with improved provisions for dealing with domestic violence. Resistance to the removal of fault-based grounds for divorce, however, meant that the Act's provisions to alter the grounds for divorce have never been implemented.

These many and diverse developments were reflected in the work of the probation service (James and Hay, 1993). Its marriage-guidance work plummeted whilst the number of requests from courts for reports on the welfare of children steadily increased, a total of 35,531 welfare reports having been prepared in 1998 (Home Office, 2000).

The Welfare of the Child and the Children Act 1989

The Children Act 1989, which led to major changes in the legal context of social work with families experiencing divorce, remains the primary piece of legislation shaping this area of practice. The Act took a significant step towards creating a family jurisdiction, although it fell short of creating a family court *per se*.

Under the Act, children's issues, such as residence and contact with parents, can be dealt with in magistrates' family proceedings courts (FPCs), county courts or the High Court, while undefended divorce petitions and related children's issues, which constitute the large majority of divorce cases, are dealt with mainly by the county courts (see Figure 1). The Act also made it possible for more difficult cases to be transferred from the FPCs to the county courts. Thus the majority of the cases concerning children's issues which require social work intervention are brought before local magistrates' and divorce county courts.

More importantly, the Act is based on clearly articulated principles (see box), all of which endorsed in various ways the development of approaches that sought to preserve family autonomy and to maximize parental responsibility, involvement and agreement, in order to minimize harm to children. Thus, even though section 1(3) of the Act makes explicit the criteria by which the welfare of children is to be judged (which FCWOs must therefore consider when preparing reports), which has resulted in greater prominence being given to children's wishes and feelings, where parents are in agreement the principle of family autonomy prevails over the paramountcy of the child's welfare (Parry, 1994).

Increasingly, therefore, the social work contribution to the judicial task of ensuring the paramountcy of children's welfare in divorce has come to be defined in terms of reducing conflict and encouraging parents to agree about the arrangements for post-divorce parenting (James, 1995). As research has revealed, however, one consequence of this has been the marginalization of children's voices in divorce proceedings (James et al., 2004), in spite of the provisions of the Children Act 1989 and Article 12 of the United Nations Convention on the Rights of the Child (which gives children the right to have their views heard in such proceedings). Such findings represent a major challenge for social workers.

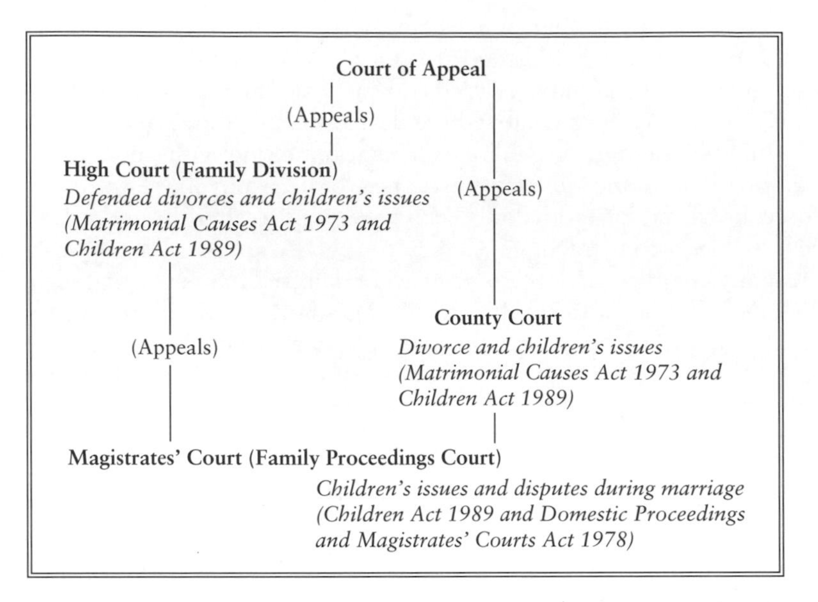

Figure 1 Courts dealing with divorce and children's issues in England and Wales

Principles underpinning the Children Act 1989

- *The welfare principle* – courts must treat the child's welfare as the paramount consideration in all questions about his or her upbringing.
- *The principle of parental responsibility* – in the interests of the child, parents retain responsibility for their children, even after separation.
- *The principle of parental involvement* – in exercising their responsibilities, parents should be as fully involved as possible in making decisions relating to the upbringing of their children.
- *The principle of positive intervention* – courts shall not make orders unless satisfied that they will be a positive contribution to the interests of the child.
- *The principle of minimal delay* – delay in court proceedings is generally harmful to a child and must be kept to a minimum.

It is worth noting in passing that the Children Act 1989 also confirmed the existing powers of the courts to involve other social work agencies. Under section 7, for example, courts may ask for a welfare report to be prepared by the probation service, the social services department, or any other agency which the court thinks appropriate, whilst family assistance orders may also be made under section 16 to either the probation service or to the social services department. There is no evidence to suggest that such arrangements are common, however.

Recent Developments

As a consequence of growing political dissatisfaction with the effectiveness of social work with offenders in the 1990s, coupled with a marked shift towards a more explicitly punitive and controlling agenda in relation to dealing with offenders in the community, the continued involvement of the probation service with the social work activities and values implicit in its divorce-related work became increasingly anomalous.

In 1999, therefore, following a review of the work of FCWOs, guardians *ad litem* (GALROs) and the Official Solicitor (Department of Health et al., 1998a), the Government announced the formation of a new Children and Family Court Advisory and Support Service (CAFCASS), combining these services into a single organization under the oversight of the Lord Chancellor's Department. This severed the links between the family courts and the probation service, but also those between GALROs and local authority social services departments. This new service, a non-departmental public body which was to be accountable to the Lord Chancellor, was introduced by the Criminal Justice and Court Services Act 2000 with the remit of providing all of the child welfare services required by the family courts and the Children Act 1989.

CAFCASS (http://www.cafcass.gov.uk/index.htm) was launched in 2001, amidst high hopes that a unified agency, dedicated to 'putting children and young people first' (the motto that appears on the cover of all its publications), would bring about an improved service, which would receive higher priority and better resourcing than it did as the Cinderella of the probation service. The new organization had a difficult start, however. Within a year, as a result of complaints about lack of resources, poor management, the problems of achieving an integrated workforce, and increasing delays in the preparation of reports in both divorce and child protection proceedings, it was the subject of a full-scale inquiry by the House of Commons Select Committee on the Lord Chancellor's Department (2003). As a result of this, sweeping changes were made, including a transfer of accountability from the Lord Chancellor to the Minister for Children, Young People and Families in the Department for Education and Skills. Other changes, introduced by the Adoption and Children Act 2002 and the Children Act 2004, have placed increasing emphasis on children's participation. However, the increasing priority being given by CAFCASS to dispute resolution, and plans to shift resources away from the writing of reports, suggest that this might not be so easy to achieve in practice.

Main Themes and Issues

The development of social work in divorce has been complex, reflecting changes in both the social and legal contexts of divorce. However, certain trends are apparent which seem likely to continue to shape these developments.

The first of these is the shift away from the notion of parental rights over their children to that of parental responsibility for them (Piper, 1993). This has brought with it a growing concern about children's rights and the need for social workers to take full account of their wishes and feelings when preparing reports for the courts. It should be noted, however, that active lobbying from fathers' rights groups in recent years has seen a re-emergence of debates about rights.

Secondly, and closely associated with this, has been the increasing equivalence between securing children's welfare and reducing parental conflict. This has resulted in a decline in the investigative approach to welfare reporting and the growth of family-focused dispute-resolution as the favoured social work approach, both for obtaining information for the courts and for addressing the best interests of the child.

Thirdly, the changing nature of the social work role in divorce must now be understood in the context of the massive organizational changes that have resulted from the introduction of CAFCASS, including the continuing influence of budgetary constraints and the drive towards dissolving the traditional boundaries between social work practice in child protection proceedings and those in divorce.

The fourth theme, which has permeated many of these developments, has been the shift towards a less formal and primarily administrative divorce process. This has been heavily informed by the need to reduce the costs associated with the increasing divorce rate. It seems unlikely that there will be a sudden or substantial reversal of recent divorce trends and since the costs associated with divorce will continue to be high, the search for the cheapest methods of delivering divorce and related social work services seems likely to continue.

The fifth trend, which reflects the impact of the others, is the redefining of the role of social work in family breakdown and divorce. This has increasingly been reconstructed in terms of dispute resolution, with a focus on the welfare of the children and not just the adult parties to the divorce. However, the continuing increase in the number of family proceedings, coupled with growing concerns about how best to deal with post-divorce conflict (Department for Constitutional Affairs et al., 2005), suggests that other approaches to the provision of social work services in relation to family breakdown and divorce will need to be developed in the context of CAFCASS.

Five Key Points

- There has been a transition from thinking about parents having rights over their children to their having responsibilities for them.
- There has been a change of focus for social work from marriage-saving to that of child-saving.
- There has been growing concern, evident in successive changes in the law and procedures relating to divorce, about the increasing burden of the costs associated with family breakdown and divorce.
- There has been a fundamental reconstruction of the concept of children's welfare in divorce and of divorce court welfare, with increasing emphasis on resolving disputes over post-divorce parenting and reducing conflict between parents, and its harmful effects on children.
- The establishment of the Children and Family Court Advisory and Support Service (CAFCASS) has created a completely new context in which social work services are provided to the courts and to those families who use them.

Three Questions

? Who are the service users in the context of divorce court welfare work? The parents? The child(ren)? The family? The courts?

? What support services should be available for parents and children during and after family breakdown and divorce and how should these be provided?

? To what extent should social workers actively support children's rights to express their views and to be heard in divorce proceedings?

Further reading

1 Walsh, E. (1998) *Working in the Family Justice System: A Guide for Professionals*. Bristol: Family Law/Jordans.

2 Day Sclater, S. and Piper, C. (eds.) (1999) *Undercurrents of Divorce*. Aldershot: Ashgate.

3 Bainham, A., Lindley, B., Richards, M. and Trinder, L. (eds.) (2003) *Children and Their Families: Contact, Rights and Welfare*. Oxford: Hart.

CHAPTER 3.4

Social Work with Adult Service Users

Alison Petch

Social work practice with adult service users requires recognition of a number of key dimensions. These include:

- the definition of need and the judgement as to which of these needs should be met;
- perceptions of dependency and the ways in which independence can be maximized;
- acknowledgement of the variety of responses that can be put in place for individuals with similar needs.

For many adult service users in the UK the provisions of the NHS and Community Care Act 1990 are a major feature. This Act, together with its associated guidance and directions, provided the framework within which current arrangements for service provision for adult service users were developed. More recently the Green Paper, *Independence, Well-being and Choice* (Department of Health, 2005b), and the subsequent White Paper, *Our Health, Our Care, Our Say* (Department of Health, 2006a), together with a cross-department strategy document *Improving the Life Chances of Disabled People* (Prime Minister's Strategy Unit et al., 2005) have set out the agenda for adult social care.

This is based on the principle that service users should be able to have greater control over their own lives, with strategies that deliver personalized rather than uniform services – this is referred to as 'personalization'. Service providers are being urged to consider outcomes, the impact of what they provide on the lives of the service users. The White Paper identifies seven key outcome areas: improved health and well-being, making a positive contribution, economic well-being, freedom from discrimination, improved quality of life, choice and control and personal dignity. Within this framework, providers are being urged to ensure in particular that the outcomes identified as important by service users (user-defined outcomes) are achieved.

This chapter will address in particular social work provision for older people, including individuals with dementia, and adults with learning or physical disabilities.

Organizational Arrangements

Traditionally there was considerable variation in the organizational arrangements for working with adults. Many local authorities distinguished work with adults from work with children and established separate teams. In some areas, particularly more rural areas, these teams were generic community care teams, embracing both older people and adults with a range of disabilities. Other local authorities developed more specialist structures, for example separate teams for older people, people with learning disabilities and people with physical disabilities. Alternatively, depending on the size of population covered by teams, there might be individual specialists within a single team. Care has to be taken with any specialist team structure to ensure that individuals do not get lost at the boundaries; for example, should the needs of an individual with dementia be met by the mental health team or the older people's team?

In 2006 there was a radical reorganization in service delivery in England (but not Wales or Scotland) with the separation of children's and adults' services and the creation of a distinct adult care service with a Director of Adult Social Services for each authority. The Director has strategic responsibility for the planning, commissioning and delivery of adult support services, and as part of their remit is charged with promoting well-being and preventing social exclusion. Several authorities have taken the opportunity to create wider community service departments, embracing other responsibilities that contribute to the well-being of adults, for example leisure or library services. Partnership working more widely, particularly with health, has also been strongly promoted, a recognition of the need for what has come to be known as a 'whole systems' approach. The Health Act Flexibilities, section 31 of the Health Act 1999, have enhanced such opportunities with provision for pooled budgets across health and social care, lead commissioning, and integrated provision.

Another important development in recent years has been the emergence of multidisciplinary teams, providing within a single team the range of professional skills which may be required by an adult service user. Community learning disability teams and community mental health teams have been gaining increasing prominence. Again there can be a range of organizational arrangements. A key distinction is whether the team is single agency (for example, local authority or health) or whether it is not only multi-professional but multi-agency, bringing together professionals across agency boundaries. Such teams will most often bring together professionals from health and social work agencies – community nurses, occupational therapists, social workers and social work assistants, home care workers – but may also embrace wider specialisms, for example housing or welfare rights. An important consideration in any multidisciplinary or multi-agency team is the management structure; does the team have a team leader with authority across the range of professionals or do individuals report through line management structures specific to each profession?

Organizational arrangements for work with adults may also be affected by the mechanisms adopted for the purchase and provision of services. Following the 1989 White Paper, *Caring for People,* and the subsequent NHS and Community Care Act, local authorities have shifted from being major direct *providers* towards enabling the *purchase* of services from a range of independent sector (voluntary and private) providers. This move towards a purchaser/provider split and the related emphasis on commissioning and contracting has had a number of consequences for social work with adults. At the macro level it has led to increased diversity of service provision, both in terms of providers and content; it has introduced features related to the contracting process, for example approved providers lists and service level agreements; and it has led some authorities to adopt internal structures designed to meet the demands of commissioning and contracting. At the micro level, the role of purchaser is key in the original formulation of care management which is the focus of the next section.

Care Management

The intention of the community care reforms of the 1990 Act was that the response to adults with physical or learning disabilities or to older people should be needs-led. Rather than individuals being slotted, somewhat arbitrarily, into services already available within the community, the basis for any response should be a holistic, preferably multidisciplinary, assessment of the particular needs of each individual. This assessment should be conducted free of any consideration of available resources. Once the assessment has been completed, the most appropriate way(s) in which to meet the needs of the individual – the 'care package' – should be agreed. Although often highlighted separately, the process of assessment is most accurately included as one of the seven stages of the care management process.

The concept of care management was endorsed by the Government following evidence of its effectiveness in a series of demonstration projects in the 1980s evaluated by the Personal Social Services Research Unit. It was promoted as 'the cornerstone of community care', the key to the delivery of effective support to adults with a range of needs. The seven stages of the care management process are identified as:

- publishing information;
- screening;
- assessing need;
- care planning;
- implementing the care plan;
- monitoring;
- review.

Core elements in the original formulation of care management were, first, that the care management process was targeted on those with more complex needs and, secondly, that the budget for the purchase of support services was devolved to the individual care manager.

Implementation of care management in practice has been highly variable (Lewis and Glennerster, 1996; Petch et al., 1996). The term *care manager* is used to signify a wide variety of practices and it is therefore essential that any individual engaging in discussion of care management clarifies how the term is being employed. Where the model is well developed, there will be a mechanism for the aggregation of unmet need from the individual assessments, and an ability to commission, both for individuals and more extensively, specific services or support arrangements to alleviate the unmet need.

Assessment

The process of assessment is the key to work with adults, establishing the nature and breadth of issues that require to be addressed for the individual. These will vary widely, and may include the availability of appropriate accommodation and access to regular healthcare, access to money whether through employment or the benefits system, assistance with personal and domestic care tasks, attention to individuals' recreational and social needs and response to particular circumstances such as the need for bereavement counselling or befriending networks. Assessment of an individual referred for the first time to the adult services team is likely to be much more comprehensive than the response to a family well known to the department who may be requesting a week of respite care.

Community care assessments were first introduced in the 1990 Act. Many authorities spent extended periods in the early years seeking to design the perfect assessment tool, arguably somewhat of a 'holy grail'. Some opted for highly structured 'tick-box' formats, lengthy or more concise, whilst others adopted a more discursive, narrative style. More recently the emphasis has been on ensuring that assessments are as holistic as possible with Scotland introducing a single shared assessment for all groups from 2002 (Scottish Executive, 2000a) and England requiring a single assessment process for older people as part of the National Service Framework (Department of Health, 2001d), subsequently transformed into a Common Assessment Framework for all groups.

The need to ensure that assessments address the range of an individual's needs in a holistic fashion is exemplified by the apparent neglect of the health needs of individuals with learning disabilities. A number of studies have demonstrated that, in hospital and community settings, both generic and specific health needs are inadequately addressed (Kerr, 1998). It is important therefore to ensure that opportunities for health screening and for health promotion are accessed and that opportunities to respond to identified health needs are pursued.

Two particular issues should be highlighted in respect of the assessment process. The first is the extent to which the needs of any informal carer are addressed independently. Since 1996, the Carers (Recognition and Services) Act has imposed a duty on social work departments to assess the needs of carers independently of those of the person they support. Initially there was no requirement to respond beyond the identification of needs, but the Carers and Disabled Children Act 2000 and the Community Care and Health (Scotland) Act 2002 imposed a requirement to consider how these needs might be addressed.

The extent to which individuals are enabled to participate in the assessment process (and more generally) can be enhanced though the role of advocacy. Advocacy can take a variety of forms; the common intent, however, is to ensure maximum input of the views of the individual service user, whether, according to individual circumstance, this be through direct participation or whether the advocate represents the interests of the individual. A key distinction is between the professional (paid) advocate and the advocate who undertakes the role as a volunteer. Citizen advocacy, developing in the main longer-term one-to-one relationships, is a major focus of voluntary advocacy, pursued in particular with individuals with learning disabilities. In contrast, professional advocates often work short-term on individual cases, or may coordinate unpaid individual or group advocacy. A particular focus for advocacy in recent years has been the closure of long-stay hospitals, with advocacy projects established for the duration of the closure process in an attempt to ensure that individual preferences are recognized.

The development of advocacy is but one aspect of a practice environment which seeks to maximize the empowerment of the individual. In practice this interprets as the individual determining to the maximum extent possible the nature of any support they may require and the ways in which such support should be delivered. Practically there may be considerable variation in the mechanisms for support between the individual with major physical disabilities and the individual with complex learning disabilities or later stage dementia; the underlying principles of maximizing independence and choice, however, are the same.

The concept of independent living, emerging initially amongst individuals with physical disabilities, epitomizes the ideals that individuals wish to pursue (Kestenbaum, 1996). Progress was accelerated with the development of the Independent Living Fund and the creation of a number of Centres for Independent Living. Developments were in tune with the emergence of the social model of disability and the acknowledgement that barriers were external to the individual. Nonetheless, there is often ambivalence amongst social work authorities towards the support of individuals with physical impairments. Some would argue that they are very much the 'Cinderella group'.

Person-centred Planning

The principles initially developed amongst people with physical disabilities have emerged more generally in recent years in the concept of *person-centred planning*. Person-centred planning requires a conscious effort to put the person at the centre of the assessment and planning process. This has been translated into a number of specific applications including *Essential Lifestyle Planning* and *Individual Personal Plans*.

The general requirement, however, is that key basic principles are applied in the course of assessment and care planning. These can be encapsulated as:

- put the individual at the centre of the process at all times;
- start with the individual, their current situation, and their current support network;

- recognize the universal set of needs common to all individuals;
- provide as much information as possible on the process itself and on the options and opportunities that are available;
- ensure that they are enabled to participate and to express their views, with access to advocacy if appropriate;
- make provision for any specific communication needs;
- clarify any particular cultural requirements;
- take time to explore the particular needs and ambitions of the individual;
- in partnership, think creatively and imaginatively about alternative ways of responding to the needs of the individual;
- discuss fully the possibilities around different options;
- operate in a culture of rights and entitlement rather than dependency and constraint;
- provide details of any financial constraints and how they impinge on available options;
- ensure that the selected support package most closely fits the individual's needs and preferences; where there are shortfalls ensure that unmet need is recorded and activated;
- ensure the individual knows who to contact about their support package;
- clarify the process for monitoring and review and ensure that the individual knows how to initiate the process;
- specify longer-term goals to ensure that the process does not become static.

Assessment of Risk

The key challenge for the social worker of assessing risk is particularly acute in work with adults. A balance has to be sought between the right to individual autonomy and self-determination and intervention to avoid what may be deemed undesirable outcomes. Situations are, however, often complex; additionally, there may be conflict between the individual and their informal carer. A son may be anxious for his mother who has developed dementia to move into residential care. She lives on her own and has been found on a number of occasions in the vicinity of the house, uncertain as to her whereabouts. The mother, however, is adamant that she wishes to remain in her own home and has in the past reacted with horror to any discussions of residential care. Another familiar scenario is the young person with physical or learning disabilities who seeks to move from the family home but whose parent(s) are either unwilling or are uncertain that their child will be able to live more independently.

A somewhat different aspect of risk is the situation where there are concerns that a vulnerable individual may be at risk of abuse, whether from an informal carer, support worker or from the wider community. Sensitive but rigorous practice is essential in order to ensure that situations of abuse are identified. Increasingly there will be local procedural guidelines, preferably inter-agency, to be followed, while the Protection of Vulnerable Adults Scheme is designed to list those excluded from the support workforce.

Support Packages

Once an individual's needs have been determined through a community care assessment, the social worker must decide on behalf of the local authority whether the needs call for support services to be provided. The fact that a person's needs have been assessed does not in itself give the individual a right to have that need met. If, however, there is a right to a service because of other legislation this will be easier to enforce if the need has been established in a community care assessment. In order to maximize entitlement, it is suggested that if a 'disabled' person is being assessed they should also be assessed under the provisions of the Chronically Sick and Disabled Persons Act 1970. The Act specifies a range of welfare services which must be supplied by a social care department to a person who needs them and comes within the provision of the Act, namely is 'chronically sick', 'disabled', or a person with mental health problems or a learning disability. These services include:

- practical help at home, such as help with dressing or cooking;
- access to recreational facilities or help in using educational facilities;
- help with transport to local authority or similar services;
- home adaptations or other facilities;
- holidays;
- meals at home or at a day centre.

There are other services which the local authority has a legal duty to provide, including adequate domiciliary services and suitable training and occupation for people with learning disabilities who are over school age, together with adequate transport to the sites of training or day care. Despite the legislative framework, however, the detail of social work provision for adults is largely determined outwith the detailed legal requirements. Legal challenges in the form of judicial review are rare and it is likely that many local authorities could be criticized on the extent to which this legal duty to provide welfare services is fulfilled.

It is appropriate at this point to make reference to what is termed 'the Gloucestershire judgment'. This judgment in the House of Lords in 1997 confirmed that local authorities may take their resources into account when assessing a person's need for the services of the CSDP Act as listed above and deciding what services to arrange. Authorities cannot, however, arbitrarily change a service without reassessment against revised criteria; moreover they have a duty to arrange the listed service once they have decided it is necessary in order to meet needs.

From April 2003, councils in England have been required to apply the Fair Access to Care Services framework of eligibility criteria (Department of Health, 2003c). This is designed to balance needs and risk and specifies four eligibility bands as presented in the box below.

This focus on risk management as the mechanism for allocating scarce resources is significant and chimes with the argument of Waterson (1999) that there has been a shift in social work for adults from responding to need to reducing risk.

Fair Access to Care Services: eligibility criteria for adult social care

Critical – when

- life is, or will be, threatened; and/or
- significant health problems have developed or will develop; and/or
- there is, or will be, little or no choice and control over vital aspects of the immediate environment; and/or
- serious abuse or neglect has occurred or will occur; and/or
- there is, or will be, an inability to carry out vital personal care or domestic routines; and/or
- vital involvement in work, education or learning cannot or will not be sustained; and/or
- vital social support systems and relationships cannot or will not be sustained; and/or
- vital family and other social roles and responsibilities cannot or will not be undertaken.

Substantial – when

- there is, or will be, only partial choice and control over the immediate environment; and/or
- abuse or neglect has occurred or will occur; and/or
- there is, or will be, an inability to carry out the majority of personal care or domestic routines; and/or
- involvement in many aspects of work, education or learning cannot or will not be sustained; and/or
- the majority of social support systems and relationships cannot or will not be sustained; and/or
- the majority of family and other social roles and responsibilities cannot or will not be undertaken.

Moderate – when

- there is, or will be, an inability to carry out several personal care or domestic routines; and/or
- involvement in several aspects of work, education or learning cannot or will not be sustained; and/or
- several social support systems and relationships cannot or will not be sustained; and/or
- several family and other social roles and other responsibilities cannot or will not be undertaken.

Continued

Low – when

- there is, or will be, an inability to carry out one or two personal care or domestic routines; and/or
- involvement in one or two aspects of work, education or learning cannot or will not be sustained; and/or
- one or two social support systems and relationships cannot or will not be sustained; and/or
- one or two family and other social role and responsibilities cannot or will not be undertaken.

It is useful to reflect on the nature of the resources that care managers or other social workers may seek to access following the assessment process. These can include:

- a range of housing resources or adaptations;
- referral to access a variety of healthcare elements;
- domiciliary support at different levels of intensity;
- day activity, whether the more traditional day centre or more innovative integrated provision or employment opportunities;
- specialist advice in areas such as finance or (re)training;
- assistance with the establishment of social contact.

Housing

A key directive of the community care reforms was that individuals should be supported to live in their own homes or in settings as 'homely' as possible. Care planning will vary depending on whether an individual is currently living within their own home or whether a new community base is being sought following extended institutional care or a move from a family setting. For older people for whom increasing frailty or immobility has become an issue or for an individual with a newly acquired physical disability the initial assessment will often be of the extent to which their current accommodation is amenable to modification and the provision of aids and adaptations. Repeated research evidence has demonstrated the preference of the majority to remain within their own homes. Liaison with housing providers and specialist schemes such as care and repair is essential, together with the use of assistive technology such as falls detectors or remote control devices.

At other times the involvement of social work will be with individuals where the challenge is to create a new housing and support structure; for example, for an individual with acquired brain injury on discharge from hospital or for an individual who has major physical disabilities following accident or other trauma.

Encouraged on the one hand by concerns for social inclusion and on the other by financial structures more favourable to the individual, current provision for those with fairly intensive support needs tends to separate the components of housing and support. The housing with support model accesses housing benefit to pay tenancy costs – for example, to a housing association or local authority – while support, funded through individual living and disability benefits, is provided by a support agency. A variety of configurations have emerged in the provision of what may often be intensive support; for example, for individuals with complex learning and physical disabilities who traditionally would have spent all their lives in long-stay hospitals.

Core and cluster models allow for support staff to work across a number of houses within a given locality and for varying intensities of support to be managed from the core base. Alternatively a house for three or four people may have a dedicated staff group, or an individual within a single tenancy may be supported by staff from either a specialist support agency or a more generic domiciliary support provider. Good practice now suggests that individual tenancies should be granted to individuals within housing and support arrangements of this type. Although housing and support models most often involve tenancies, ownership should not be precluded if an appropriate financial package can be compiled. Specialist agencies (for example, Ownership Options) have developed expertise in this area.

For older people, a traditional model has been sheltered housing, local authority or housing association provision offering low-level support through a warden structure. The demand for traditional sheltered housing has declined; more recent developments have focused on providing much more intensive support, including very sheltered provision for individuals with dementia. Imaginative schemes have sought to combine the independence of individual units, supported by a range of community professionals, with access to communal resources, such as a daily meal and 24-hour cover (Oldman, 2000).

Traditionally the smaller-scale housing and support models outlined above have been developed for individuals with learning and physical disabilities or mental health problems. For older people the response has been large-scale development of residential and nursing homes, ironically a model now rejected on the grounds of scale for these other groups. Thought needs to be given as to the extent to which, for example, smaller scale housing and support provision can also be pursued for older people with dementia, as exemplified in Cox (1998) and Vallelly et al. (2006).

Domiciliary Support

Despite the resources and energy which necessarily have to be focused on the development of housing and support models, the majority of support to adults is focused on their own homes. Local authorities were traditionally the main providers of home-based care in the guise of home helps offering primarily domestic support. Recent years have seen major changes in this service. Increasingly support is provided for personal care rather than domestic tasks alone. Moreover the local authority is often no longer the major provider. Instead the local authority, often the individual care manager, has become the purchaser, sourcing appropriate provision within the independent sector.

A study by Henwood et al. (1998) suggests that satisfaction or dissatisfaction with home care is determined by two core features: the nature of the relationship with the home care staff and the manner in which care is delivered. Key factors, with major implications for practice, include staff reliability and continuity, kindness, cheerfulness and understanding shown by care workers, competence to undertake specific tasks, knowledge of the needs and wishes of the user and carer, and information about the services to be provided. By contrast, dissatisfaction is generated by a failure to provide help with specific tasks, inability to provide help out of hours, disruption to services through change of contracts or changes in home carer, inflexibility, incompetence and unreliability.

It has been argued that much of the potential for intensive domiciliary support remains unfilled (Curtice et al., 2001) and that frail older people are often admitted to residential or nursing care without consideration of more intensive home-based packages. It is extremely important that both social workers and the wider multi-professional team are apprised of the range of support possibilities that are currently available within any locality. GPs in particular, a major source of information for older people, may be unaware of more recent developments in augmented or intensive home care. At the other end of the spectrum, it has been argued that it is important to recognize the preventative value of low intensity support (Clark et al., 1998), the need, for example, to initiate the social contact that may avoid the development of isolation and depression, to access a mechanism for small-scale repairs, to acknowledge the importance to morale of maintaining domestic standards.

The nature of tasks carried out by domiciliary support workers has been discussed following the deliberations of the Royal Commission on Long Term Care (1999). In particular, the recommendation that both personal and nursing care should be provided free of charge to the individual (implemented only in Scotland) has provoked close scrutiny of the nature of support tasks and their performance by different professionals. Extensive debates have taken place on the boundaries between health and social care tasks (the ubiquitous medical and social bath), although increasingly such debates are being superseded by the recognition that the more appropriate response to individual need is often some variant of the generic worker model, a single professional able to carry out both personal and domestic tasks and simple nursing tasks. While such debates may preoccupy the statutory agencies, they are generally less relevant to independent sector providers who are often able to be much more flexible in the provision of staff.

A particular requirement for some individuals will be assistance in accessing respite support. The range of respite opportunities needs to be appreciated, both based within an individual's own home, support offered within another domestic setting, or temporary placement in some form of group living. Informal carers are often ambivalent about the resources for respite provision, particularly if they have experience of less than satisfactory placements in the past. The issue must be approached with sensitivity and recognition of the potentially somewhat different requirements and perceptions of the individual with support needs and the informal carer.

Activity

While the provision of housing and support is a prerequisite, social work provision with adults must respond as necessary to the full range of identified needs. The form of assistance in respect of an individual's day activity may vary widely. For an individual with a physical disability in full-time employment, the prime requirement may be assistance to determine the most effective transport arrangements. For an adult with a learning disability the most appropriate response may be the creation of a varied programme of activity, including induction into training opportunities at a local college. For an individual with early onset dementia the challenge may be to find, faithful to the person-centred directive, alternative activity to the local day centre which may be neither age nor activity appropriate.

For both worker and individual the challenge is often to have full knowledge of the work, training and leisure opportunities that are available. Workers need to maximize access to resource listings and other local sources which will maximize the pool of opportunities from which individuals can make or be assisted to make their choices. Likewise, transport resources and schemes, where appropriate, for befriending or the development of social networks, need to be accessed.

The need to develop imaginative care planning cannot be underestimated. Judgments will vary as to the extent to which the traditional service-led response, slotting people into available services, has been consigned to history. Certainly, however, there remains considerable potential for creating individual packages designed to respond to the particular needs of the individual and attuned to their preferences and choices. The strength of the devolved budget is the ability it affords to readily purchase a preferred option, avoiding hierarchical bureaucracies. Leat and Perkins (1998) discuss the creative juggling and dealing which is necessary to construct the responsive care package.

An important feature of the care management process is the opportunity to aggregate from the individual assessments the component of unmet need. Provided that there are adequate local mechanisms for the accumulation of the individual records of unmet need, this provides an invaluable resource for the planning of service provision for the locality. The availability of a dedicated budget to more immediately put in place provision responding to the unmet need is a further asset.

Financial Resources

It is increasingly important for practitioners to be aware of the financial structures within which they are working. This has two main implications. First, it is usually necessary at some stage for there to be a financial assessment detailing the capital and income resources of an individual. Authorities vary in their practice; in some, this financial assessment will be completed in conjunction with the community care assessment, in others, the two processes will be conducted by different individuals. Whatever the process, good practice would ensure that the opportunity was taken for income maximization, ensuring that the individual is accessing all the financial and benefits in kind to which they may be entitled. In more complex situations, specialist welfare benefits or other financial advice may be accessed.

The second dimension in respect of resources is the need to be aware of the cost of the support package that is being accessed. Where care managers are purchasing from a devolved budget this will be a daily routine, assembling packages on the basis of unit costs. Where budgets remain more centralized, a variety of mechanisms may operate with shadow costings or notional budgetary allocations. Ascertaining the costs of packages to different parties has increased in complexity with the widespread introduction of charging for domiciliary support and, increasingly, its spread also to various forms of day activity. Unlike nationally determined benefit rates, there is wide variation in the charges that are imposed by local authorities, a source of considerable inequity.

Care Home Provision

Financial considerations may gain particular prominence in consideration of whether an individual should move into a care home. This will most often, but not exclusively, involve an older person where frailty or dementia has prompted debate as to how and where their support needs should be met. Alternatively the assessment may have been provoked by the illness or death of an informal carer or admission to hospital following an acute medical episode. Under the provisions of the NHS and Community Care Act, responsibility for the funding of residential and nursing home places was transferred from central government to local authorities, with access for those requiring state funding restricted to those whose community care assessment demonstrated the need for such provision.

Those paying for their own place can, of course, seek a residential or nursing home place independently of any community care assessment. Good practice, however, would suggest that, certainly for those likely to require statutory support in the future, a community care assessment should be completed to ensure that individuals do not find themselves at a future date requiring assistance with the payment of fees but not deemed to require residential or nursing care.

More generally, social work has a critical role in any decision making process surrounding entry to any form of institutional care. Individual workers may be a primary conduit for information; they may be the only source for direct accounts of what institutional care may comprise, and they may be the key route to the exercise of choice in selection between different homes. Most particularly, however, they may be agents for the interpretation of any policy within the authority on financial limits to community based packages. It can be difficult to ascertain the extent to which individual authorities impose ceilings on the costs of packages which they will fund within the community. For older people in particular, however, many authorities, although they may not have a specific policy statement, will question packages which exceed the weekly cost of residential care on a long-term basis. For younger people, individuals with a physical or learning disability, higher weekly costs are often acceptable, an issue which many would argue raises questions of ageism.

Direct Payments

The Community Care (Direct Payments) Act 1996 came into force from April 1997. This gives local authorities the discretionary power to make direct cash payments to individuals in lieu of the support services they have been assessed as needing. Individuals can then use the payments to secure for themselves their preferred support arrangements, although regulations preclude the employment of relatives. Initial eligibility for Direct Payments was restricted to disabled people under the age of 65, including (though rarely in practice) individuals with learning disabilities. In 2000, Direct Payments were extended to people over 65, while the Carers and Disabled Children Act 2000 grants entitlement to parents and guardians of disabled children, informal carers, and 16- and 17-year-olds.

Publicity on the extended availability of Direct Payments masks a fairly limited uptake (Leece and Bornat, 2006). Following initial work by In Control (Duffy, 2005), individual budgets were being piloted across 13 sites from 2006, with an intention in the White Paper that this mechanism for resource allocation, tapping into six income streams, should become mainstream.

Five Key Points

- A person-centred approach should be key to work with adult service users.
- Practice should be guided by the principles of the maximization of independence and choice.
- Assessment of individual need should be holistic, with a shared assessment across all agencies and professionals.
- The creation of responsive care packages should be assisted by the availability of budgets devolved to care managers.
- Dissemination of adequate and accurate information is essential, to both service users and informal carers and between professionals.

Three Questions

? To what extent can assessment of need be independent of resource considerations?
? What is the scope for support packages to be more imaginative?
? Are Direct Payments a route to empowerment?

Further reading

1 Kemshall, H. and Littlechild, R. (eds.) (2000) *User Involvement and Participation in Social Care*. London: Jessica Kingsley.

2 Bytheway, B., Bacigalupo, V., Bornat, J., Johnson, J. and Spurr, S. (2002) *Understanding Care, Welfare and Community: A Reader*. London: Routledge.
3 Leathard, A. (ed.) (2003) *Interprofessional Collaboration: From Policy to Practice in Health and Social Care*. Hove: Brunner-Routledge.
4 Barnes, C. and Mercer, G. (2006) *Independent Futures: Creating User-led Disability Services in a Disabling Society*. Bristol: Policy Press.

CHAPTER 3.5

Social Work in Healthcare Settings

Bridget Penhale

A number of changes in the provision of healthcare services in the UK have taken place in recent years. There have been:

- changes in hospital-based care – smaller bed numbers, shorter lengths of stay;
- changes brought about by the implementation of the Patients' Charter;
- changes in primary care and the shift towards a primary care led health service;
- changes linked with a shift towards the provision of intermediate services;
- changes caused by the rising number of non-elective and emergency admissions.

Several models of social services work relating to social care provision have arisen in response to these developments – particularly in the wake of the changes affecting primary care. Other developments in the very nature of hospital social work have arisen, in part, from transformations in hospital-based care but are particularly linked with developments in the provision of intermediate services and changes in emergency admissions.

The Primary Care Led National Health Service

In October 1995, a debate was launched by the Secretary of State for Health about the future of primary healthcare. There had already been changes following the introduction of new technologies, different ways of working (including GP fund-holding) and developments in patterns of care. Following a consultation exercise (National Health Service Executive, 1996) five principles were outlined. Primary healthcare, it was concluded, should:

- be comprehensive;
- provide continuity of care;

- be properly coordinated so that it is effectively delivered;
- be the gatekeeper to secondary (hospital) care; and
- address the health needs of local communities as well as those of individuals.

Offering care close to the person's home has to be reconciled with the requirement of clinical effectiveness. The setting for primary care is often the GP practice, although the focus is generally on the primary healthcare team rather than solely on the doctor. Not surprisingly, social services departments were perceived by the Department of Health as having an important part to play in the provision of primary care (National Health Service Executive, 1996).

Policy changes have led away from a concentration on secondary and tertiary (specialist) forms of hospital care towards a focus on the increase of provision for patients in their local communities. Nonetheless, the availability of acute hospital care, when needed, continues to form an important part of secondary healthcare. While more care is being provided at community level with routine pre-admission screening for elective admissions and post-discharge check-ups being conducted locally at health centres, the hospital is still a central focus.

Health-related Social Work Provision

Traditionally, there have been a number of models of social work provision to GP practices including attachment and liaison services. Generally, these have worked to the benefit of clients, health and social services staff. Social work liaison schemes, where the social worker is not based in a health centre (as is the case in attachment schemes) but works from a social services office, appeared to have been the more common approach in the UK prior to the implementation of community care. There is an impression that such schemes have decreased in number since 1993 because of the increase in other demands on the time of district-based social workers/care managers in adult social care. Nevertheless, attachment schemes have become more accepted and valued in the early years of this century.

Attachment and liaison schemes remain, however, an area of potential development, and one that continues to be explored by social services departments: Nottinghamshire, for example, ran a successful pilot attachment scheme basing social workers in health centres rather than in district offices (Lymbery and Millward, 2000). When each social services district covered large numbers of separate GP practices or health centres, the notion of basing social workers/care managers in each one was not feasible, but, given the shift towards fewer primary care group clusters, the idea of attachment schemes has become more feasible.

An alternative model exists in some rural social services departments where social workers/care managers are viewed as an increasingly specialized and expensive resource that cannot be afforded in the majority of situations that arise in primary healthcare settings. In this model, a variation of the liaison scheme, referral and reception team workers link with a particular health centre and may run sessions based there once or twice a week. Callers are seen by appointment (generally arranged by the health centre receptionist) or on a 'drop-in' basis. Referrals from the primary healthcare team members are screened and filtered by the practitioner

A case study

'Grace' was 82 years old and was referred to the day hospital by her GP for attention to her leg ulcers and her immobility due to arthritis. During her visits to the hospital she began to talk to one of the nurses about her fear of a son who had been living away but had recently returned to the area in search of work. Grace had been physically assaulted by this son several years previously. The son had a history of alcohol abuse and relationship problems; his employment record was patchy. On his return to the area he had renewed contact with Grace and had begun to threaten her, especially concerning money.

At this point the nursing staff referred Grace to the social worker based in the hospital. Grace was keen to find out what options were open to her. Because of her immobility, she was virtually housebound, so arrangements were made by the social worker for the local community policeman to visit Grace at home. In the event, he spent an afternoon with Grace and another son discussing what might be done about the situation. Grace decided that she did not wish to pursue a legal remedy at that point but was pleased to have had the chance to talk. Following the assessment, a slight increase in Grace's home care provision was made. This was initially for a temporary period and helped Grace feel more secure but also provided much needed support at home. As part of the care plan for Grace, the social worker contacted the local volunteer bureau which found a visitor to call on Grace at home once a week. When she was well and mobile enough, alternatives to the day hospital were found for her. The locks to her bungalow were changed via assistance from the local Age Concern group. Contact with the community policeman was maintained, and this helped her to feel more secure at home. Once Grace had been discharged from the day hospital and her care plan had been reviewed, the case was transferred to a community team covering the area in which Grace lived, for ongoing monitoring and support.

and only those referrals meriting a fuller response are taken back to district office for further action and allocation to a social worker or occupational therapist for an assessment. The development of such a model provides an innovative attempt to link more effectively with primary care and to provide earlier assistance to individuals in need.

Hospital Social Work Provision

The provision of social work services to hospital patients is based on a long historical tradition. Indeed, 1995 saw the centenary of health-related social work in the UK and the origins of modern day social work are said by some to be rooted in the tradition of social work within hospital settings (Baraclough et al., 1996). It is noteworthy, however, that whilst social workers have been based in hospitals for over a century, their particular contributions in relation to healthcare, where social work may be marginalized (McLeod and Sanden Eriksson, 2002) and perhaps especially in relation to the wider profession of social work, have never been fully recognized.

Moreover, the full range of hospital social work services has not been subject to national review by the Social Services Inspectorate of the Department of Health for some years, although attention has been paid to discharge from hospital (Department of Health, 1995b, 1998a). The focus on discharge appears to have resulted from a perceived increase in the use of social workers in discharge planning following the implementation of the NHS and Community Care Act 1990. This followed the government's emphasis on the need for agreement between health and social services departments about discharge planning and their joint involvement in assessment for nursing home provision where public funding was necessary.

Beyond involvement of social workers/care managers in discharge planning, other aspects of hospital social work provision remain relatively uncharted.

Much has been written about the problems surrounding discharge from hospital and the transfer of care across the health and social care divide. Recent changes in inpatient care (especially in acute care settings) and the resulting reductions in the length of hospital stay for individuals have led to people being discharged 'quicker and sicker' with higher levels of dependency and disability than before (Victor, 1992). The difficulties surrounding discharge can be summarized as follows:

- poor two-way communication and information flow between community and hospital teams, before, during and after discharge from hospital;
- a lack of adequate assessment and planning for discharge;
- failure to identify individuals and carers who have special needs or who may be vulnerable;
- the perception of over-emphasis on the needs of the hospital in effecting early discharge, rather than a focus on the needs of the individual;
- a lack of service provision and subsequent reliance on informal support systems;
- inadequate discussion with and involvement of patients and their carers, including insufficient notice of discharge.

Hospital social workers/care managers are heavily involved in those sections of care having a high number of older patients in need of assistance with regard to discharge planning to enable a safe and early discharge home. Other patients with different kinds of complex needs – for example, in neurology, HIV/AIDS, traumatic injury, intensive care, oncology and accident and emergency – are also covered by hospital social workers/care managers. Additionally, specialist workers are actively employed within hospice and palliative care settings. The provision of social work in some specialist areas is sometimes provided through joint financing agreements with charities like the Macmillan Fund (cancer). This is because a more traditional hospital social work service (including the provision of counselling) is likely to be required rather than a primary focus on assessment and discharge planning.

The implementation of the NHS and Community Care Act in 1993 was intended to assist adult service users to remain at home for as long as possible. There was a shift in emphasis away from institutional care towards the ideal of offering more choice and flexibility of provision. The ideas of *working in partnership* and the *empowerment of service users* were highlighted, together with the need to ensure that account was taken of resource constraints and that *best value* was achieved. The idea of partnership working primarily referred to the relationship between service user and professional, but it also applied to arrangements for liaison between professionals from different disciplines. The legislation did not, however, specifically require people to work together; this was included in related guidance material instead of within the legislation.

There has been much discussion about the importance of multidisciplinary working between groups of professionals together with exhortation from successive governments about the need for professionals to work together, but the professions have been left to work out the detail of such arrangements for themselves. Multidisciplinary team working (including social workers) in hospital settings has existed for years. Teams in psychiatric settings or those that focus on the care of older patients within general hospitals have been the most successful and are well established.

But multidisciplinary working does not exist in all specialities. Medicine and surgery are areas where the exigencies of the market place appear to prevail above all else. It is in these areas where the holistic approach to the individual patient may in effect be given scant regard despite the efforts of nursing staff and where the decision of the consultant may well hold sway.

It is some time since the notion of (female) ward staff acting as 'handmaidens' to (male) doctors was developed; the idea was also said to apply to medical social workers in hospitals (Rushton and Davies, 1984). Yet even in the twenty-first century it is still apparent that in most hospitals clinicians defend their power base that revolves around the decision-making that affects individual patient outcomes; to an extent they are supported in this by the requirement of applying the principles of the economic market to the healthcare setting.

In 1999, the Health Act was passed. This included sections that refer specifically to the need for professionals to work together and for collaborative work between organizations to be part of normal practice. The possibility for there to be shared financial budgets between health and social services, was also included for the first time, indicating a welcome move to eliminate, or at least reduce the major division that existed between the centrally funded NHS and locally run social services (Lewis, 2001a). In 2000, the NHS Plan discussed the need for health and social care services for older people to be more integrated. Indication was also made in the Plan that partnerships between health and social services departments should be strengthened and that there should be shared budgetary arrangements and improved communication between organizations. This has begun to happen with the development in some authorities of integrated care teams and pilot schemes involving the development of Care Trusts, which integrate the commissioning of health and social care for older people (Rummery and Coleman, 2003).

Although the NHS Plan referred to community settings rather than specifically to a hospital environment, such developments mean that multidisciplinary working in hospital settings is given new impetus and that the role of social workers/care managers within hospitals has been emphasized. Furthermore, integrated teams for other service-user groups (for example, mental health or learning disability) have also been developed in a number of social services departments across England and Wales. These usually include both health and social care professionals and allied health professionals such as occupational therapists, working as a multidisciplinary team from the same location, accessing a single budget for provision.

Intermediate Services

The NHS Plan also introduced the concept of intermediate services: a new level of service provision that enables older people to continue living at home or that provides care after illness and treatment. In many respects, the future of hospital social work concerns the development of these intermediate services, and one development of intermediate services has revolved around the provision of rehabilitation services at more local, community-based levels. This includes both medium-term rehabilitation for older patients (recovering from strokes, for example) but also some longer-term provision for severely disabled younger adults (who have progressive illnesses or head injuries, for instance). The development of rehabilitation services within community settings is considered to be consistent with district-based care managers providing continuity of provision for disabled adults but linking with specialist hospital social workers/care managers as necessary.

If older people are transferred at an early stage from acute settings to intermediate centres for further recovery and/or rehabilitation, key aspects of the multidisciplinary teamwork and discharge planning process take place in that intermediate setting. A high proportion of people transferred to such settings have complex needs for assistance and for assessment and care planning by a social worker/care manager. This is therefore more likely to be successful through the provision of social work within the community hospital setting, as the hospital based social worker can maintain continuity throughout the individual's hospital stay, no matter how long it takes. Although time pressures hold less immediacy in intermediate settings, care managers not based in the hospital setting can find it difficult to maintain continuity with other professionals. This is particularly so in relation to the need for the frequent and continuing communication that takes place within multidisciplinary settings.

Research has indicated that on-site social workers in hospitals are much more effective than those visiting the hospital from a district base (Connor and Tibbitt, 1988; Department of Health, 1992). Additionally, the presence of hospital-based social work/care management staff specializing in work with older people and able to participate in the work of the multidisciplinary team proves invaluable to older patients and their relatives; this was the finding of a Social Services Inspectorate study of hospital social work provision even before the implementation of the community care reforms in the UK (Department of Health, 1993).

Although a few social services departments, mostly in the London area, have reduced in number or withdrawn altogether their hospital social workers, the majority of local authorities still have social workers/care managers based in hospitals, and many have increased their number since 1993 (Department of Health, 1998b). The role of the hospital social worker has developed, however, to reflect the shift towards their increased involvement in discharge planning, especially in relation to older people (Davies and Connolly, 1995; Rachman, 1995).

Basing the assessment task of care management in community or intermediate centre settings could lead to a perception within the acute hospital setting that social work provision is only accessible in those locations; however, the presence of a core of social workers based in the acute setting counteracts that perception. The role of social workers/care managers in such acute care instances may be more focused on either specialist provision or on the speedy discharge planning that is necessary for those people able to return home from hospital rapidly with some assistance. Additionally, locating social services personnel in Accident and Emergency and Admissions Units can help prevent unnecessary admissions to hospital (McLeod et al., 2003); to be effective, such provision would require round the clock presence in A&E or at least easy availability outside normal office hours. This has been an area of some discussion (Department of Health, 1999a, 2005a).

Inter-professional Relations

The multidisciplinary team consists of people with different training and professional bases and requires a high degree of internal cooperation; team functioning may be affected by a number of factors including differences in status and power. In research that examines the perceptions of and relationships between the 'semi-professions' involved in multidisciplinary teams (Reed, 1993) it is suggested that the healthcare semi-professions are still governed by an implicit acceptance of the medical model and that this does not help in the development of collective and cooperative working practices.

Further work on ways of improving interdisciplinary relationships is clearly of benefit in the endeavour to achieve effective team-working. Ward staff, in particular nurses, can be empowered to successfully challenge doctors over their decisions where necessary and to work more conjointly with them; they may be helped in this by the supportive and facilitative role of social workers/care managers within the team. Multidisciplinary teams of paramedical staff *can* work together without medical input in order to discuss and determine potential outcomes and present them to the clinician for approval or affirmation.

Some have suggested that social workers in hospitals can become marginalized and that it is important for them to maintain a strong view of the social model of health (Bywaters, 1986). This is also of benefit when working with healthcare professionals whose education and training focuses on the holistic needs of individuals, as the introduction of the social model at appropriate points will help to ensure that a holistic view is maintained.

A willingness to share power and to empower others – particularly individual patients and their carers or families – is needed within healthcare systems and must be encouraged; involvement in the process from the beginning maximizes the participation of individuals and their carers (Rachman, 1993). Decision-making that is shared by all involved in the process and that leads to a flattening of the hierarchical structures within healthcare organizations may also be helpful.

The centrality of the user and the promotion of the holistic approach to the person is of crucial importance. A reframing of the situation to empower, enable and to allow for participation, partnership, development and choice is essential to the whole endeavour. Social workers/care managers in such settings have a key role to play in this respect. While there is clearly a need to promote team working and to develop partnership arrangements between professionals, it is also necessary to encourage and promote a cultural and attitudinal shift away from the 'team knows best approach'. There should always be full participation by patients and their families. (See also Chapter 3.8, 'Social Work in Collaboration with Other Professions'.)

Two Objectives

There is a tension between the need:

- to make the best use of resources and be effective within the constraints of the market; and
- to promote user-centredness and individual choice for service users and patients.

It is debatable how far these distinctive objectives can ever be reconciled: to allow for user involvement and choice takes time, but time may never be a totally realistic or appropriate commodity in economic terms in the acute sector. It is not easy to design and implement systems that will incorporate both objectives, particularly when the language used in each system is so different and culturally distinct. We need to deal with these tensions creatively and social workers in healthcare settings can make a constructive contribution. This is also why the contribution in longer term and intermediate care settings is so necessary.

If agreements between health and local authorities are to be truly effective and if the NHS Plan is to succeed, the two objectives must be reconciled. We have to find ways of ensuring that people participate fully within healthcare systems – ways that do not patronize or otherwise demean them and which are wholly sensitive to their needs. Professionals need to work together and to collaborate fully, and multidisciplinary team working, when effective, is the best way of achieving this. Social workers within healthcare settings have a key role, and look set to continue their distinctive contribution. But the most critical challenge must be how to empower individuals within such processes and how to involve them more centrally. This challenge is ongoing and social workers can positively assist in meeting and overcoming this challenge.

Five Key Points

- Social workers contribute effectively within a number of healthcare settings.
- Multidisciplinary team working is an essential aspect of collaborative working.
- Health-related social work is becoming increasingly important with the development of primary care.
- Developing partnership working with service users involves moving beyond the 'team knows best approach' in order to empower individuals.
- Discharge planning has become a key element of hospital-based social work since the implementation of the NHS and Community Care Act 1990.

Three Questions

? Will social workers continue to be based in acute hospital settings?
? Should social workers linked with primary care settings always be members of an integrated, multidisciplinary, health and social care team?
? What should be the principal focus for the social worker in an intermediate care setting?

Further reading

1 Baraclough, J., Dedman, G., Osborn, H. and Willmott, P. (1996) *One Hundred Years of Health Related Social Work 1895–1995: Then, Now, Onwards*. Birmingham: Venture Press.
2 Department of Health (1999d) *Working in Partnership: Joint Working between Health and Social Services in Primary Care Groups*. London: The Stationery Office.
3 Bradley, G. and Manthorpe, J. (eds.) (2000) *Working on the Faultline*. Birmingham: Venture Press.

CHAPTER 3.6

Mental Health Social Work

Roger Manktelow

There is now general concern about rising rates of depression, widespread prescribing of psychotropic drugs, vigorously promoted by the pharmaceutical industry, and increasing diagnoses of mental disorders in children and young people. If we examine closely the cause of our mental health problems, we will find a social component at the root. This reflects the findings of the classic study of the social origins of depression in working-class women in south-east London (Brown, 1996) which provides a blueprint for the prevention of mental ill health by social work and social action.

Mental health social workers now operate in a range of locations including social services fieldwork offices, primary care health centres, hospitals and specialist team settings. Epidemiology is the study of the pattern of the distribution of diseases in the general population and is focused on their prevention. The epidemiological model consists of three levels of intervention and can be applied to mental health social work practice:

- At the primary level of prevention, problems are common to many vulnerable groups and intervention is aimed at localities and communities as well as individuals and their families. Mental health social workers are found in primary care settings such as health centres and community resource centres where they work with groups who are at risk of mental health problems to promote positive mental health.
- At the secondary level, the client who is in acute crisis is the target for help and the focus is on individual and family work. Mental health social workers working at the secondary level are located in crisis intervention services, day hospitals, psychiatric units in general hospitals, psychiatric hospitals and specialist settings such as child, adolescent and family psychiatric services.
- At the tertiary level of prevention, intervention is aimed at the client with long-term disabilities. Mental health social workers in rehabilitation programmes, assertive outreach teams and recovery services work at this level to reduce the negative effects of institutionalization and to promote social integration.

Since the mid-1980s, the provision of care and treatment of people with mental illness has been transformed to the extent that hospital admission can be an unlikely occurrence. The halving of the number of hospital beds has resulted in shorter admissions and an apparent increase in the number of admissions probably largely explained by frequent readmissions of a core of 'revolving door' patients unable to manage in the community (Lester and Glasby, 2006).

The mixed economy of care and the purchaser/provider split has meant that mental health services are now provided by a variety of agencies from the private business world, the not-for-profit (voluntary) sector as well as the statutory health and social services trusts. Community-based facilities aim to meet the needs of people with mental illness for treatment and therapy, health and social care, occupation and self-fulfilment and social integration. Drug treatment and electro-convulsive therapy are delivered within the National Health Service. Mental health professionals, private practitioners and specialist voluntary groups offer counselling help and a wide range of 'talking' therapies. Non-governmental organizations (NGOs) and private businesses, for the most part, provide health and social care in a wide range of respite and residential schemes offering varying levels of support. Occupational needs are met by retraining schemes and job placement into the wider workforce and creativity and self-fulfilment by purposeful programmes located in community settings. The need for social integration is provided for by drop-in centres, social clubs and befriending schemes. Mental health social workers can be involved in the planning and delivery of all these services.

The stigma attached to mental illness remains a deterrent to users of mental health services (Rankin, 2005). Although public attitudes are now generally more enlightened than in the past, a negative image of people with mental illness is reinforced by media publicity of violent attacks committed by individuals suffering from acute mental disorder (Stanley and Manthorpe, 2001). Nevertheless, care in the community offers the possibility to break down these negative stereotypes by providing opportunities for people with mental illness to take part in the activities of everyday life and meet the general public in normal, non-stigmatizing situations (Manktelow, 1998a). Mental health social workers must challenge stigma and prejudice by anti-discriminatory practice to counter discrimination based on class (Rogers and Pilgrim, 2005), gender (Prior, 1999), race (Fernando, 2003), and religious identity (Manktelow, 1998b).

Multidisciplinary Teams

A distinguishing feature of mental health social work is the extent to which it takes place in multidisciplinary teams. These teams consist of a number of different disciplines each having a particular ideology and understanding of mental illness.

First, medicine is represented by a medical hierarchy: the consultant psychiatrist as the team leader; the registrar specializing in psychiatry; and the senior house doctor on placement for a limited time period. The medical model of mental illness posits that mental illness is similar to physical illness in that it has physical causes which respond to treatment. Doctors have as their first concern the diagnosis of mental illness and for this purpose they use the International Classification of

Websites for mental health

www.mentalhealth.org.uk
www.mind.org.uk
www.niamh.org.uk
www.mental-health-matters.com
www.rethink.org
www.rcpsych.ac.uk
www.carersuk.org
www.scmh.org.uk
www.namli.org.uk
www.openuptoolkit.net

Mental Diseases (ICD 10; World Health Organization, 1992) or the Diagnostic and Statistical Manual of Mental Disorders (DSM-IV; American Psychiatric Association 1994). On the basis of their diagnosis, doctors decide treatment which is often the prescription of some form of medication but can also involve counselling or forms of physical treatment, principally electro-convulsive therapy.

Secondly, there is a nursing hierarchy of nursing manager, sister/charge nurse and state registered nurses. Nursing is a profession allied to medicine (PAMs) with a philosophy of *tender, loving care* and principal concerns with the improvement and monitoring of individual health and well-being through medical treatments. The primary role of community psychiatric nurses (CPNs) is to make short, purposeful visits to administer long-acting injections of major tranquillizers at regular intervals to people with enduring mental illness living outside hospital and to monitor their individual mental states. More recently, CPNs have also undertaken psychological and social therapies and this role mixing has caused some professional friction with mental health social workers.

The third discipline represented in the multidisciplinary team is psychology, in the person of the clinical psychologist. At one time, the work of the clinical psychologist was restricted to the administration of psychometric tests to individual patients such as personality tests, intelligence tests and tests of disordered thinking. Their role is now primarily with individuals and couples to provide therapeutic interventions such as behaviour modification, cognitive behavioural therapy and counselling, particularly to people suffering addiction problems and common mental health problems. Their work style is clinical: appointments are booked; sessions are held in an office; and a planned programme of intervention is followed.

The fourth professional group consists of occupational therapists (OTs) whose responsibility is the assessment of daily living skills to determine the functioning level of the individual patient in and out of hospital. OTs provide didactic training programmes to individuals and groups in occupational, recreational, social and life skills in order to improve personal, social and economic functioning.

Social workers work with representatives of each of these four disciplines in:

- hospital ward rounds which are clinical in format and which decide treatment care plans;
- care management procedures which are bureaucratic in format and which coordinate the written assessments of professionals into a costed care package of community services;
- case conferences which are driven by statutory duties and which determine risk assessment and management.

In these settings, each of the team members promotes their professional ideology, sometimes vigorously, generating considerable heat and dissension. A collegiate model is an effective method of team working where each team member is aware of and respects the role and function of team colleagues. Key worker systems are advocated to improve team liaison and accountability although such arrangements blur professional roles. Dual team membership and accountability to both the multidisciplinary team and the mental health social work team may be an area of further potential difficulty (Payne, 2000).

The Social Model of Mental Disorder

The bio-psychosocial model is a holistic approach, now widely accepted, which combines the biological (medical), psychological and social models (Tyrer and Steinburg, 2003). A contemporary paradox is that at the same time as new areas of modern life are medicalized, there is a recognition of the value of a spiritual life for positive mental health (Scott Peck, 1990) and a growing popularity of alternative and complementary therapies (Graham, 1999).

Social workers utilize a range of interventions based on a social and interpersonal understanding of mental disorder which emphasizes social factors and interpersonal relationships as explanations for behaviour. Our search for an explanation of psychiatric breakdown takes place on the family and society level as much as on the individual. At a macro-societal level, structural and environmental factors such as poverty, inadequate housing and unemployment are identified as causes of stress and disorder. At a micro social-interactional level, the quality of social networks, partner relationships and family life are investigated as sources of emotional distress. When families report their experience of hardship, discrimination and relationship breakdown, these are identified as the aetiological factors in the onset of mental illness. Unfortunately, because people with mental illness are often patients in hospitals or clinics they are consequently divorced from their social and family backgrounds and the impact of their social contexts is all too easily ignored. The social perspective corrects this distortion of reality.

There are four distinct components to the social model of mental disorder (Cockerham, 2000). Each of these theoretical perspectives has a particular focus which contributes a unique understanding of the social process of being mentally ill.

1 The first theoretical strand is *positivism* which looks for the social causes of mental disorder – for example, the theory that the rate of suicide in a society is determined by the level of alienation in that society was developed by the

founding father of modern sociology, Emile Durkheim, at the end of the nineteenth century.

2 The second theoretical formulation is *functionalism*, which looks at the function of mental disorder in maintaining equilibrium in society – for example, how the sick role is a set of privileges and obligations. Talcott Parsons, a 1950s American sociologist, formulated the sociological theory of functionalism.
3 The third theoretical strand is *symbolic interactionism,* which focuses on the social interface between people with mental illness and others – for example, the effects of stigma and social interaction. Erving Goffman is essential reading on this perspective.
4 The fourth theoretical formulation is *labelling*, which concentrates attention on societal reaction or the action of others in defining mental disorder. It was Thomas Scheff who was a key proponent of the social construction of mental disorder.

Help-seeking Behaviour

One of the great advantages of the medical model is that it absolves the individual sufferer of responsibility for his or her illness. But this can also be a disadvantage because it can disempower the individual who must depend on professional experts for recovery. It is also important to remember that the level of tolerance of ill-health – and therefore the point at which outside help is sought – varies greatly between individuals and families. The symptoms of mental illness are often denied by the sufferer and this lack of insight can lead to a delay in referral resulting in a rapid deterioration in behaviour and well-being, psychiatric emergency and compulsory hospital admission. A study of the paths to psychiatric hospitalization (Manktelow, 1994b) revealed that family relatives were most likely to seek medical help for the mental illness of the sufferer rather than the sufferer him/herself.

It is not the task of the mental health social worker to diagnose mental illnesses but there is a useful division between different types of mental disorder. In the first place, there are common mental health disorders, such as anxiety, depressive feelings and phobias, which are most commonly seen in primary healthcare by the general practitioner (Goldberg and Goodyer, 2005). Alternative mental health techniques using a self-help strategy, such as meditation, affirmations, positive thinking and visualizations, can play an important part in overcoming such emotional distress. In the second place, there are the 'real' severe mental illnesses which are often enduring, most frequently requiring periods of hospitalization, and to be treated by long-term medication. These include schizophrenia, manic depression and endogenous (severe) depression (Pritchard, 2006).

Roles of the Mental Health Social Worker

Therapist

The mental health social worker may be trained in a range of therapeutic interventions. These will include grief and loss counselling for the bereaved, cognitive therapy and debriefing for the traumatized, motivational interviewing for the addicted, codependence therapy for the victims of dysfunctional relationships and brief therapy for practical problem solving.

Social biographer

The role of social biographer is a key function which is formalized in the social history, the chief vehicle for highlighting personal, family and social factors. The social worker meets with the nearest relative to collect this account and presents it to the multidisciplinary team as an important contribution to the diagnostic task. Taking a social history is an opportunity for beginning a working relationship between social worker and family which will continue through treatment, discharge and follow up. Under mental health legislation the mental health social worker is also required to submit Social Circumstances Reports to statutory bodies such as the Mental Health Commission and the Mental Health Review Tribunal.

Link professional

The mental health social worker is ideally placed to provide the link between hospital, clinic or specialist services and the individual's home and social environment. The social worker helps the family to cope with the impact of hospitalization which may be felt in a number of ways. The diagnosis of mental illness is likely to have repercussions for the whole family and members must be helped to accommodate these changed circumstances. Help may be needed to renegotiate family relationships. The social worker may also be required to link with the individual sufferer's employers and, as illness reduces family income, it is the task of the social worker to assist with benefit advice to ensure income maintenance. The mental health social worker will play a central role in being a key informant to other professionals.

Coordinator

The social worker acts in a key capacity to plan the provision of a care package which meets the individual needs of each user of mental health services. At case meetings, discharge plans are discussed and, following team agreement, it is often the responsibility of the social worker to coordinate the provision of the services required. For clients with a high level of needs, care management procedures will have to be followed. These needs include health and social care, housing, income maintenance, occupation and social inclusion.

Educator

It remains a source of considerable concern that users of mental health services are not provided with sufficient information about their diagnosis, the prognosis of their condition and their treatment, in particular the side-effects of major tranquillizer medication (Rogers et al., 1993). Using everyday, non-medical language, the mental health social worker can provide a safe and confidential space in which the fears and worries of the sufferer and relatives can be shared and explored.

Planner

Mental health social workers have played and must continue to play an important role in the development of community alternatives to hospital psychiatric services. If such resources are to prevent psychiatric hospital readmission then a range of services are required, providing different levels of support targeted at groups of users with similar needs. Such services must be carefully located in neighbourhoods with a degree of tolerance to groups with special needs.

Specialist adviser to other social workers

Mental health problems occur across all social work programmes of care and mental health social workers have an important role as specialist advisers to colleagues. The need for mental health social work in child protection has been highlighted by the work of Sheppard (1997) which revealed that up to one-third of mothers of children on child abuse registers suffered from depression, a factor which had often not been recognized by their child care social workers. Mental health problems occurring in other programmes of care are: in older people, problems of depression and dementia are common; in criminal justice, significant numbers of offenders have mental health problems; amongst the learning disabled, dual diagnosis of learning disability and mental illness is frequent; and in medical social work, physical illness is often accompanied by mental distress.

The statutory mental health social worker

Mental health legislation in England and Wales (Department of Health and Social Security, 1983), Scotland (Department of Health and Social Security, 1984) and Northern Ireland (Department of Health and Social Security [NI], 1986) provides substantial statutory powers to mental health social workers who are trained and appointed to act as approved social workers. Approved social workers may apply for the compulsory admission of a mentally ill person to hospital against her/his will if the individual is suffering from a mental illness which requires hospitalization, if hospital is the least restrictive alternative and if there is a substantial likelihood of physical harm to her/himself or others. Outside hospital, approved social workers can apply for guardianship on welfare grounds to determine place of residence, occupation and daytime activity and attendance for treatment (Manktelow et al., 2002).

There has been an extensive period of consultation to review and redraft current mental health legislation although a final way forward is still to be agreed. The most contentious proposal is the compulsory administering of medication to individuals outside hospital under a proposed Compulsory Treatment Order. However, such legislation must not breach individual human rights as protected under the European Convention on Human Rights. It is likely that approved mental health professionals will replace approved social workers and the role will be extended to include mental health nurses, occupational therapists as well as social workers. Discussion has been overtaken by new mental incapacity legislation which defines incapacity and the circumstances in which individual decision-making can be taken over by an appointed agent.

Working with Service Users

Surveys of service users' experiences have revealed a negative picture of poor hospital care, a lack of services outside hospital and a failure to hear their opinions (Rogers et al., 1993). As a result, there has been a recent emphasis on user and involvement in the planning and delivery of mental health services. Our knowledge and understanding of mental illness has been dramatically increased by heartfelt accounts from sufferers, most famously Janet Frame and Sylvia Plath amongst others. The collective voice of service users has been heard in radical groups such as 'Survivors Speak Out' and a scheme of independent advocates, who may themselves be former users, is proposed in the new legislation.

Basic needs such as accommodation and income are the first priority of the mental health social worker. Many people who are mentally ill are at risk of homelessness and similarly many homeless people are at risk of mental illness. Enduring mental illness is a disability and sufferers require long-term social work intervention. In order to feel safe and secure, they need sheltered accommodation with a regular income and adequate domiciliary support with cooking, washing and shopping.

The need for love and belonging for many of us is provided by our families. However, one of the most upsetting consequences of mentally ill behaviour is that it is often directed at relatives who have to cope with the disruption and disturbance, sometimes over a prolonged period. As a result, the family can become estranged from the sufferer who is left without family contact. Because of the stigma of mental illness, there is often little scope to develop new friends and acquaintances to replace family. Moreover, the disabling effect of mental illness on the ability to interact and socialize increases isolation. It is therefore necessary for the mental health social worker to actively foster social networks for sufferers of severe mental illness. Without social contacts, the sufferer will become preoccupied, withdrawn and relapse and readmission will follow.

Working with Carers

In dealing with mental illness, families play three important roles: they must experience disturbed behaviour; they must judge this behaviour; and they must act to seek outside help (Manktelow, 1994a). Caring can be a debilitating experience affecting physical and mental health, the finances and the social lives of carers. Moreover, it has been found that, whilst the disruptive behaviour precipitated by the so-called 'positive' symptoms of delusions and hallucinations may create acute apprehension and stress for the family, it is the negative symptoms resulting in social withdrawal, apathy and self-neglect that cause more long-term conflict and disruption (Atkinson and Coia, 1995). A recent study in East London revealed the dominant emotions for families to be those of shame, grief and guilt (Jones, 2002).

The mental health social worker must provide the family with help, advice and support to develop coping strategies in the following important areas: managing medication; maintaining personal hygiene; dealing with aggressive behaviour; coping with delusions and hallucinations; and responding to suicidal behaviour (Lefley,

1996). Carers' experience is often one of lonely isolation with infrequent social work contact. In these circumstances, carers' groups are an essential form of support offering a safe opportunity to share worries and fears, and the potential to form a consumer campaign to demand improved services.

Five Key Points

- Mental health social workers intervene with individuals, families and communities at three levels: the primary, secondary and tertiary.
- Mental health social workers are members of multidisciplinary teams including a psychiatrist, nurse, occupational therapist and clinical psychologist.
- Mental health social workers offer a unique perspective emphasizing the importance of social factors in mental disorder.
- Mental health social workers work to meet the needs of people suffering emotional and mental distress.
- The primary focus of work for the mental health social worker is the family who are often the main carers of people with enduring mental illness.

Three Questions

Outline an appropriate social work intervention with (1) the individual, (2) the family and (3) the community in the following case:

P is a middle-aged single man with a history of mental illness. He is diagnosed as suffering from schizophrenia and is prescribed long-term medication. On medication, he no longer experiences delusions or hallucinations. Since his mother died five years ago P has lived alone but does not look after himself properly. He is in receipt of statutory benefits but is always penniless. Although his mother was very strict with him, he misses her a great deal. He is lonely and isolated but when in company he drinks to cover his nervousness, often to excess. As a result, people shun him, which makes him morose and preoccupied.

Further reading

1 Rogers, A. and Pilgrim, D. (2005) *A Sociology of Mental Health and Illness,* 3rd edn. Buckingham: Open University Press.
2 Lester, H. and Glasby, J. (2006) *Mental Health Policy and Practice*. Basingstoke: Palgrave Macmillan.
3 Pritchard, C. (2006) *Mental Health Social Work: Evidence-based Practice*. Abingdon: Routledge.

CHAPTER 3.7

Social Work in the Criminal Justice System

Gwen Robinson

The main statutory agencies responsible for the administration of criminal justice in England and Wales are:

- the Police Service;
- the Crown Prosecution Service;
- the criminal courts (magistrates' courts; the youth court, with responsibility for under 18s; the Crown Court and the higher courts of appeal);
- the Prison Service and the National Probation Service (jointly known as the National Offender Management Service since June 2004). Together these constitute the core elements of the *penal system*.

Scotland and Northern Ireland have separate systems for the administration of criminal justice.

The sentences available to the criminal courts fall into three main categories: custodial, community and monetary penalties.

The objectives of criminal justice include retribution, incapacitation, deterrence, rehabilitation and reparation, with the proportions of these 'ingredients' varying at different points in time. Cavadino and Dignan (2007) have described three broad strategies for criminal justice policy: (1) the *highly punitive* approach embodying 'law and order' ideology and the attitude that offenders should be dealt with as severely as possible; (2) the *managerialist* strategy, which emphasizes the smooth running and cost-effectiveness of the system; and (3) a strategy which seeks to minimize punishment and protect and uphold the *human rights* of both offenders and victims of crime. This strategy, which most closely reflects the traditional values of social work, is a broad one which includes:

- the *restorative justice* movement, which seeks to respond to crime with positive measures whereby offenders make amends for the harm they have caused;
- those who favour attempts to *reform* or *rehabilitate* offenders; and
- those who espouse a philosophy of *just deserts* whereby punishment is strictly proportional to the seriousness of the offence.

Social Work and the Criminal Justice System: A Brief History

Three broad phases in the history of social work in the criminal justice system can be identified, reflecting changing views about the role of the state in relation to the problem of crime.

In the second half of the nineteenth century, criminal justice policy was highly punitive, emphasizing retribution and deterrence; imprisonment was the standard punishment. The welfare of the offender – in common with the welfare of the poor, the aged, the sick and the unemployed – was specified as outside the domain of the state, and therefore a matter for the 'private agencies of moralization' in the field of charitable practice. This tradition of *penal philanthropy* (Garland, 1985) constituted a positive counterweight to the negative, repressive penal institutions and the poor law. A particular concern of penal philanthropists in the latter half of the nineteenth century was the number of prosecutions for drunk and disorderly behaviour; the appointment of police court missionaries by the Church of England Temperance Society from 1876 aimed to tackle this problem by persuading magistrates to bind individuals over into their 'reformative' care rather than sentencing them. Thus did the notion of the supervision of offenders emerge. By the time the Probation of First Offenders Act 1887 was passed, court missionaries were undertaking 'social enquiries' about offenders in order to identify those individuals for whom *probation*, as it was now called, might be appropriate.

The second phase, neatly captured in Garland's (1985) notion of *penal-welfare*, came into being around the turn of the century. The notion of penal-welfare was part of a broad reconceptualization of the role of the state in social and economic affairs, whereby issues such as criminality and poverty came to be understood as *social problems*, warranting the interventions of experts employed by the state. The 1907 Probation of Offenders Act transformed the previously *ad hoc* practices of penal philanthropy into a statutory provision which established a non-custodial, supervisory sanction for both juveniles and adults. Central to the penal-welfare system, which was dominant up to the 1970s, was the notion of reformative or rehabilitative treatment. From the 1920s, religious and moral notions of reform gradually gave way to the more psychological, scientific-sounding idea of rehabilitation; the methodology of *social casework* moved probation practice firmly into the realm of social work.

During the 1960s and early 1970s the probation service began to work with more serious and prolific offenders, taking on responsibilities for work with prisoners, including parole supervision, whilst passing much of the responsibility for young offenders to local authority social workers. These developments led some to argue that the traditional welfare philosophy of probation was being compromised, such that the balance between 'care' and 'control' in social work with (adult) offenders was favouring 'control'. Nevertheless, throughout this period the probation service continued to be viewed predominantly as a welfare-oriented organization, sharing the values, skills and practices of other social workers.

From the late 1970s the legitimacy of social work with offenders was increasingly threatened for a number of reasons. First, research evidence indicated not only that rehabilitative treatments were having little impact on rates of reoffending but also that the welfare-oriented interventions of social work with young people were actually accelerating rather than halting their criminal careers. Secondly, law and order became an important political issue, and an increasingly punitive stance towards offenders was adopted. Probation came to be viewed not only as ineffective, but also as being 'soft on crime' and too closely aligned with the interests of the offender. Over the next two decades, the government introduced a raft of legislative and other measures which would essentially 'toughen up' the image of the service and reorientate it toward the principle of *public protection.* This effectively meant thinking about offenders in terms of the potential risks they posed to members of the public rather than the welfare or other needs they presented, and being much stricter about the enforcement of orders. This transition was reinforced by resource cuts, which meant that the more obviously social work tasks such as throughcare, voluntary after-care, 'welfare' work with lower risk offenders and community-based work came to be reluctantly redefined as secondary to the 'core tasks' of providing reports to the courts and offence-focused work with statutory orders. The government's hostility to the idea of social work with adult offenders was brought home in 1995 when it repealed the need for probation officers (in England and Wales) to hold a social work qualification.

Meanwhile, and ironically perhaps, the 1990s also witnessed a revival of optimism about the possibility that probation intervention could demonstrate effectiveness in terms of reducing reoffending (McGuire, 1995a). This optimism centred on the development of offence-focused cognitive-behavioural programmes and risk/needs assessment instruments to identify those offenders most likely to benefit from such interventions. These programmes and assessment instruments were based on a new distinction between the *criminogenic* and *non-criminogenic needs* of offenders. Criminogenic needs, defined as those needs or problems which research has shown to be directly related to the risk of reoffending, were the focus of the new 'effective' programmes, whilst non-criminogenic needs came to be defined as largely outside the remit of statutory supervision.

There is little doubt that the probation service has, since the mid-1990s, taken on the mantle of a 'law enforcement' agency, seeking to distance itself from its social work roots. To what extent this shift reflects significant changes in practice as well as changes at the level of policy and the service's public image is, however, a matter for debate. The probation service has certainly been criticized for paying scant attention to the personal and social problems faced by offenders, in favour of an almost exclusive focus on their 'offending behaviour' (e.g. Farrall, 2002), but the service has not completely lost sight of its traditional focus on offender rehabilitation (Raynor and Robinson, 2005). It is arguable that recent trends in probation practice simply reflect the changing profile of social work more generally, and that social work in common with probation is increasingly dominated by the assessment and management of risk; based on a case management rather than a casework model; and driven by resource considerations. In support of this argument it is worth noting that in Scotland, where a separate probation service ceased to exist in 1969, developments in *criminal justice social work* tend to reflect many of the changes in probation practice in England and Wales.

The Role of Non-statutory Agencies

Looking beyond the statutory domain, however, it can be argued that social work in the criminal justice context is still very much alive. Since the 1960s the 'normality' of high crime rates in most contemporary Western societies has led to a fundamental rethink of the role of the state in relation to the problem of crime. In short, the idea that the state agencies of criminal justice should assume sole responsibility for crime has become increasingly untenable. Crime has come to be defined as a problem not just for the state but for *communities,* the resources of which should be mobilized to provide a broader and more effective set of defences and responses to the problem of crime. Thus, for example, the Home Office has, since 1979, provided substantial financial support to the national independent organization *Victim Support*, which offers practical help and emotional support to over one million victims of crime every year. More recently, attempts to increase lay involvement in crime control have included the establishment of *community panels* in the context of new sanctions for young offenders (e.g. Crawford and Newburn, 2003) and *circles of support* (commonly drawn from faith-based communities) to support sexual offenders in the community. A further example is New Labour's 'Respect' agenda, which assumes the active participation of communities – alongside police and local authorities – in its quest to reduce anti-social behaviour (Home Office, 2006).

This reconceptualization of the problem of crime has had important implications for the profile of social work in the criminal justice system. As the focus of the statutory agencies which had traditionally undertaken social work with offenders has gradually shifted toward structured interventions focused on criminogenic need, responsibility for other types of work has shifted to *non-statutory agencies*. In short, there has been a *dispersal of social work* in the criminal justice context, such that non-statutory organizations play an increasingly important role in the provision of 'social' services for offenders (e.g. assistance with financial, accommodation, employment and other social problems). Similarly, as the statutory social work presence in prisons has diminished, prisons, too, have begun to contract out social work services. Non-statutory agencies are also central to the delivery of specialist services for offenders with drug and alcohol problems, both in prison and community contexts.

Local Authority Social Work and the Criminal Justice System

There are a variety of ways in which local authority social workers can become involved in the criminal justice system. Most commonly, however, local authority social workers come into contact with the criminal justice system in the context of *multi-agency* working.

One example of multi-agency working in the criminal justice context relates to the care and management of *mentally disordered offenders*. Another is in the arena of child protection. The exchange of information about offenders who have been convicted of offences against children (often referred to as *schedule one offenders*) and participation in child protection case conferences are well-established elements of the routine work of both social workers and probation officers, and child protection work has necessitated close working relationships with the police when civil or criminal proceedings are sought. More recently, Multi-Agency Public Protection Arrangements (MAPPA), established in England and Wales in 2001, have introduced a statutory framework for inter-agency cooperation in assessing and managing the risks posed by violent and sexual offenders. Under these arrangements, social services are among the agencies which work alongside the police, probation and prisons to facilitate information exchange, risk assessment and supervision planning in relation to high-risk offenders in the community (Kemshall et al., 2005).

Another key example of *formalized* multi-agency working in the criminal justice context is the establishment, under the Crime and Disorder Act 1998, of *Youth Offending Teams* (YOTs), which involve social workers, probation and police officers, and education and health staff, with scope to involve the voluntary sector. YOTs exist to prevent offending by children and young people, and to ensure that appropriate youth justice services are available for young offenders aged 10–17. Social workers employed within YOTs provide court services in the Youth Court (e.g. the preparation of Pre-Sentence Reports) as well as supervising a range of community-based orders.

The reform of the youth justice system has attracted both praise and criticism. Whilst many of the principles associated with reform (e.g. a renewed emphasis on helping young people stay out of trouble, and the introduction of principles of *restorative justice* into the youth justice system) have generally been well received, the implementation of these principles has not been unproblematic. For example,

The social work role in prisons

Work may be undertaken individually or in group settings, and in liaison with other professionals such as prison officers, governors, chaplains, psychologists and teachers, and outside community groups and service providers. The social work task has to be juggled with the administrative demands of the prison, and social work values may at times conflict with the demands of security and risk management. For these reasons, prison-based social work is best undertaken by experienced, self-confident and committed staff who are equipped to cope with the role strain involved in balancing the various demands upon their time, and managing value conflicts in practice.

Source: Brian Williams (2000) Prison-based social work. In M. Davies (ed.), *The Blackwell Encyclopaedia of Social Work*. Oxford: Blackwell, pp. 268–9.

some have questioned the 'fit' between restorative justice principles (which imply voluntariness, remorse and a desire to make amends for wrongdoing) and a compulsory court order or final warning (e.g. Gray, 2005). Further, research on some of the new orders indicates that victims are not routinely involved in and rarely benefit directly from 'restorative' processes (e.g. Crawford and Newburn, 2003). The development of demanding programmes of 'intensive supervision' for prolific offenders, often involving multiple interventions and restrictions and with a high likelihood of imprisonment on breach, have also prompted fears about the acceleration of young offenders 'up the tariff' before they have had a chance to 'grow out of crime' (Cavadino and Dignan, 2007).

Concerns have also been raised about the propensity of a variety of 'preventative' orders and interventions to stigmatize and label young people and potentially accelerate their entry into the criminal justice system. For example, *anti-social behaviour orders* (ASBOs), introduced by the Crime and Disorder Act 1998, are civil orders designed to deter and prevent the escalation of anti-social behaviour, but breaching the conditions of an ASBO does give rise to criminal proceedings and penalties. Whilst not specific to young people, the majority have been passed on those under the age of 21.

Social Work and Other Criminal Justice Agencies

A 'dispersal of social work' has already been noted, whereby non-statutory, community-based agencies are increasingly providing services which were formerly undertaken by social workers employed in the probation service, both in the community and in prisons. A final observation is that, whilst probation may be moving away from social work, other criminal justice agencies – namely the police and prisons – are arguably moving towards it. For example, the police have become much more involved in issues traditionally addressed by the caring professions, particularly in relation to their handling of vulnerable groups, such as mentally ill offenders, women who are victims of sexual assault and cases of child sexual abuse. The delivery of reprimands and final warnings based on principles of restorative justice, and the growth of police-led 'restorative conferencing' in some parts of the country (e.g. Hoyle et al., 2002) are cases in point, as is the secondment of police officers to multi-agency YOTs.

Similarly, it could be argued that the prison service is moving closer towards social work and welfare needs, through recent initiatives such as the appointment of 'personal officers' to inmates and the involvement of prison officers in the delivery of offending behaviour programmes and services for drug users. The notion of prison as a positive good has been reinforced by the revival of faith in rehabilitative treatment discussed above, and is clearly evident in the establishment of the National Offender Management Service, which seeks to promote closer collaboration between prison and probation services. However, significant cultural differences between the probation and prison services remain, and the notion of prison as a positive environment remains highly controversial, not least because such a view potentially legitimates the passing of more and/or longer prison sentences.

Conclusion

Questions about the role of social work in the criminal justice system are hampered by changing conceptions of what it means to 'do' social work in the twenty-first century. If we accept a broad definition of social work as working in the interests of individual and community welfare, we are by no means witnessing the death of social work in the criminal justice system. However, that is not to say that its *profile* is not changing. First, whilst the probation service developed as the 'social work arm' of the criminal justice system, the relationship between probation and social work is an issue for debate. Has probation practice become completely detached from social work; or has it simply adapted to reflect the changing agenda of social work more generally? Leaving this question aside, social work in the criminal justice context clearly continues in the work of non-statutory organizations. Finally, social work, broadly defined, can arguably be found in criminal justice agencies other than those traditionally associated with social work.

Five Key Points

- The profile of social work in the criminal justice system is highly dependent upon changes in criminal justice policy.
- Until recently the probation service was commonly understood as the 'social work arm' of the criminal justice system.
- There has been a 'dispersal of social work' in the criminal justice context. As in other areas of social work, non-statutory organizations currently deliver many of the services which were formerly the responsibility of state agencies.
- The involvement of local authority social workers in the criminal justice system is increasingly in the context of multi-agency working.
- Police and prison service culture is arguably becoming less controlling and more caring.

Three Questions

? To what extent is the objective of 'public protection' consistent with the practice of social work with offenders?
? Does it matter that, in the context of criminal justice, much 'social work' is not delivered by social workers?
? To what extent do you think social work will be evident within the criminal justice system in ten years' time?

Further reading

1 Garland, D. (2001) *The Culture of Control.* Oxford: Oxford University Press.
2 McIvor, G. and Raynor, P. (2007) *Developments in Social Work with Offenders,* Research Highlights in Social Work. London: Jessica Kingsley.
3 Cavadino, M. and Dignan, J. (2007) *The Penal System: An Introduction,* 4th edn. London: Sage.

CHAPTER 3.8

Social Work in Collaboration with Other Professions

Hugh Barr, David Goosey and Mary Webb

Such was the suspicion with which the first almoners were viewed by doctors, nurses and administrators at St Thomas's Hospital in London that they were instructed to walk outside instead of along the corridors to avoid being noticed (Willmott, 1996).

A hundred years later, Henkel wrote about the 'incorrigible marginality' of social work at the interface between the life-world and social systems, between private and public domains. Interpreting the needs of disadvantaged groups to other professions, officials and institutions set social workers apart. Working mainly in social services departments, they were separated from other professions, separation reinforced as legal and managerial values supplanted those of social work and rendered it less professional in the eyes of others. This had forced social workers into a position where they had become the instruments of others. Government intervention had damaged the identity of social work. So too had ambiguity about boundaries and ambivalence about the pursuit of professional and graduate status which, together with the emphasis upon competency-based outcomes, had detracted from the academic base of social work and made its position tenuous in higher education. Even so, Henkel agreed with Lorenz 'that a profession placed socially and politically on the boundaries between so many divisions in society should be in a position to take a lead in conceptualising and facilitating the crossing of new frontiers in a period of change' (Henkel, 1994, 1995; Lorenz, 1991).

The Post-Seebohm Years

The Seebohm Committee (1968) believed that social work would gain corporate strength and enhance its professional standing by coming together in a single local authority department. Henkel was not alone in questioning whether those goals were achieved. Doctors had long argued that the creation of the departments had distanced them from social workers and hampered inter-professional working

(Kessell, 1986). Social workers practising in healthcare had fought to escape from being regarded as ancillary to medicine, but many were as distressed as were the doctors when their inclusion in the new departments drove a bureaucratic wedge between the two professions (Baraclough et al., 1996).

Seebohm had drawn attention to long-standing tensions between social workers and GPs and had recommended that the new departments should make determined efforts to develop teamwork between them, out-posting social workers to practices, although social services departments showed no enthusiasm for this despite positive reports of such initiatives in the past (Huntington, 1981).

The rapid expansion in the number of social work posts following the formation of social services departments had called for recruitment beyond traditional middle-class sources. Riding high at that time in public esteem, social work was seen to be an attractive career and gained popularity amongst first generation graduates. It also offered a second chance to people in mid-life who had missed out on opportunities for higher and professional education, women re-entering the labour market and those opting for or obliged to seek second careers. Prior qualifications were not required and the prospect of secondment to qualifying courses was appealing.

Whilst the social composition was similar to that in nursing, with whom social work was building closer links, it differed increasingly from the established professions such as medicine which remained essentially middle class. Doctors and social workers no longer came from much the same social backgrounds. Diverse routes into social work enabled different groups of entrants to access patterns of qualifying education best suited to their circumstances. A non-graduate level of qualification was retained, in parallel with graduate and postgraduate levels, in the belief that this would keep the professional award within reach of those social workers who lacked educational credentials for graduate entry. But parity of access led to disparity of outcome, leaving some social workers at a disadvantage relative to others, even though all received the same professional award that conveyed the status of qualified social worker. Retention of non-graduate awards also denied social workers the coveted status of an all-graduate profession on a par with, say, the professions allied to medicine, who had narrowed the educational gap between themselves and medicine.

Social work education was coming under fire for emphasizing generalist studies at the expense of specialist, although the 'generic movement', which had driven the Seebohm reforms, began to fall into disrepute by the late 1970s. In part, this was a recognition that only specialist social workers could command the respect of specialists in other professions.

Changes in the objectives and content of courses influenced perceptions of social workers. Psychodynamic teaching, which had long been the bedrock of social work education lost ground to sociology as courses entered the mainstream of higher education. Explanations for problems came to be found more in society than in the individual, as the rising generation of social workers became more politically aware and more assertive on behalf of the poor and the oppressed. The price that social work paid was to be scapegoated along with them as politicians, public and established professions came to regard social work as too left-of-centre for its own good. Social work, for its part, prided itself on its value base which it saw as its distinguishing mark, albeit at the risk of some tension in relations with other professions.

Nowhere was this more evident than the stand taken by social workers on anti-racism and anti-oppression, a stand that at first strained relations with other professions, but, according to Pierce and Weinstein (2000), began to win their support.

Some in the new generation in social work were reluctant to adopt conventional professional norms. Elitism was challenged in social work and, by implication, in other professions. Holding fast to their egalitarian values, social workers tended to identify more closely with their clients than with other professions. Professionalism in social work was further weakened when the British Association of Social Workers (BASW) compromised its standards by admitting unqualified members. Meanwhile, professional representation on the council of the validating body for social work education (CCETSW) was reduced as it became increasingly subject to government intervention and to control by employers.

Preoccupied with these problems, social work educators may have done less to prepare students to work with other agencies and professions than the situation demanded, although opportunities were increasing for experienced social workers to share post-qualifying studies with other professions, opportunities often built around specialist studies. Shared qualifying studies, however, remained the exception and were mostly confined to social work and nursing students in the field of learning difficulties. Learning with nurses rather than doctors established the status of social workers in the NHS hierarchy.

Collaboration in Adult Services

The case for putting health and social services together was revisited repeatedly over the years (Department of Health and Social Security, 1973) with guidance on joint care planning (Department of Health and Social Security, 1976), although the Royal Commission on the National Health Service (Department of Health and Social Security, 1979) concluded that no radical solution would command general support. Both the Audit Commission and Parliamentary Committees were critical about lack of progress. The 1987 Griffiths Report did little to help when it recommended the purchaser-provider split and a mixed economy of welfare as a more efficient means to deliver health and social care services (Department of Health 1989a).

Implementation of the NHS and Community Care Act 1990 served only to institutionalize divisions within and between health and social services, even though the role of care manager was introduced as a means to coordinate packages of care. These were to be purchased from statutory and private providers across health and social care, but allowing market forces play which, according to Langan (1993), had become an internal organizing principle throughout the state sector. Working together came to be seen more as a means to increase efficiency than to improve services as central government control sought to ensure that provision of community care services was held within affordable limits.

Much has subsequently been written about 'deprofessionalization' and the threat to social work values resulting from the imposition of managerialism and budgetary controls in place of social work discretion. The care management role was carried by whomsoever senior management chose to assign from a range of professional backgrounds or none, with inescapable implications for the role of the social worker in the care of adults and their relations with other professions. Some argued in vain that successful care management required a user-centred approach (Lloyd, 2000; Lloyd and Taylor, 1995) with the care manager being prepared to advocate vigorously for the user to ensure the development of appropriate services, in short a social work approach.

Paradoxically, nowhere were relations to become more fraught than between social workers and doctors in mental health where their role was most strongly enshrined in law. Tension was much in evidence, despite the provision of mechanisms under the Mental Health Act 1983 for collaboration between 'Approved Social Workers' (ASWs) and doctors. The Act required that two medical doctors make recommendations for the compulsory detention of a patient in hospital, but only following an application by an ASW. The scene was set for a struggle for ownership of the patient or client between social work and medicine.

The need for closer collaboration was reasserted by the Labour Government elected in 1997 which was determined to build more effective bridges not only between health and social care for adults, but also education and social work for children.

The Department of Health (1997) argued that many people had complex needs spanning health and social services, but found themselves in a no man's land caught between 'sterile arguments about boundaries'. Repeated assessments, often by different agencies, and complex navigation round the care system were incompatible with a quality service. The system was too fragmented with too many organizational boundaries getting in the way (Department of Health, 2000c).

The Department called upon the NHS and local authorities to forge partnerships to break down organizational barriers. Incentives would encourage joint working to improve all aspects of health through pooled budgets, lead commissioning and integrated provision (Department of Health, 1998c and 1998d). These relatively modest measures were overtaken by the publication of the NHS Plan (Department of Health, 2000d). Social services should in future, it said, be delivered in new settings (*sic*) such as GPs' surgeries, as part of a single local care network. Rapid response teams made up of nurses, care workers, social workers, therapists and GPs should provide emergency care at home. Integrated care teams should ensure that people received the care that they needed following discharge from hospital, while health and social care professions would employ a common assessment framework.

The first primary care trusts had already been established. These were creating opportunities to foster closer working between health and social services. Care trusts would, said the report, go further. They would commission and deliver both primary health and community care. Some would be established jointly by health and social services authorities of their own volition; others would be imposed by the Department of Health where local arrangements for collaboration were found wanting. Incentive payments would encourage and reward joint working. Old divisions between health and social care would be overcome, although new ones soon took their place, for example, when legislation required local authorities to make a payment if an older person's continued stay in hospital was considered to block a bed for another patient (Community Care [Delayed Discharges, etc.] Act 2003, section 6).

Collaboration in Child Care

Measures to improve collaboration in child care proceeded in parallel. Successive enquiries during the 1980s into child abuse (for example, London Borough of Brent, 1985; Secretary of State for Social Services, 1988; Staffordshire County Council, 1991) criticized professions, notably social work, for failures in communication and collaboration contributing to the abuse and sometimes death of children.

The 1989 Children Act seemed to herald a new dawn for social work with children as it came once again to be seen as a technically stretching task emphasizing inter-professional and inter-agency work. Delivering family support services necessitated working with other professionals, notably from schools but also from a range of new services, such as Sure Start, developed since 1997. Child protection required social workers, whether as employees of local authorities or guardians *ad litem*/children's guardians, to collaborate with an ever-expanding group of professionals including lawyers. Child care practice came under closer judicial oversight and regulation (Langan, 1993) as social workers found themselves required to account to the courts and accept direction by them. Although overturned later by the House of Lords,[1] two Court of Appeal cases in 2001 set precedents for elements of final care plans being starred by the judiciary for continued oversight beyond the making of the Care Order.[2] The waiting rooms of courts became the arena in which local authority social workers and the lawyers did battle whilst the courtroom itself was the place of ritual social work slaughter (Dickens, 2006), although guardians fared much better, probably because their experience and independence was recognized.

For too long social workers had been left to plough their own furrow, compounded by reluctance on the part of the other professions to engage with child protection and tacit relief that social services children's teams had the primary responsibility. The Laming Report (2003) ended that. The death of Victoria Climbié and the subsequent inquiry gave rise to a radical re-organization of social work with children (Children Act 2004). Children's services were now to be located in 'super' departments with Education Services. Many children's services traditionally delivered from social work offices would in future be delivered from school premises. But social work services would be dwarfed by schools, prompting fears that they might become poor relations within the new departments.

There were, however, signs of an increasing recognition that the duties and responsibilities attendant upon the integration of children's social work within education had implications for all staff. There was an acknowledgement that some education staff did not know what they had a duty to know, driving moves towards collaboration with new found social work colleagues. The Children Act 2004 (section 11) also placed a duty of safeguarding children on health, probation, youth justice and police services which, together with a similar duty imposed in education services in the Education Act 2002 (section 175), meant that social services for children shared a principal activity with other agencies. The new Children's Services Authorities promoted cooperation between local agencies with a view to improving the well-being of children.

'Corporate parenting' provided the umbrella under which children's services were beginning to group together as elected members came to grips with their enhanced role. The subsequent development of Children's Trusts saw the joining of health and voluntary sector/not-for-profit organizations with these local authority services.

Establishing Frameworks for Collaboration

Policies to improve collaboration focused on outcomes for service users. These were enshrined in the National Service Frameworks for Older People (Department of Health, 2001c) and for Children and Maternity Services (Department for Education and Skills and Department of Health, 2004). Both documents set out ten-year programmes for service development and emphasized the need for the professions to collaborate. However, the wide-ranging introduction of performance indicators (incorporated into the National Service Frameworks) introduced an element of competition when central government compared local authorities. Pressure to meet targets could distort practice.

For their part, service users and carers expected a joined-up response from the professionals to match the complexity of their needs, but what made good sense to them has proved to be a major challenge in practice. They have long been clear that what they wanted was a 'one stop shop', which local authorities had persistently failed to provide.

The new emphasis on service user involvement called for collaboration within and between professions. Sure Start required that parents, who would ultimately benefit from early intervention programmes, be involved in the management and delivery of each local programme. On the whole, professionals benefited from this (Department for Education and Skills, 2005).

The meaning accorded to 'collaboration' has changed radically over the years. Preoccupation with relations between social work and medicine has given way to a wider appreciation of the spectrum of professions with whom social workers collaborate (Whittington and Bell, 1991). This may reassure those social workers who have long resented imputations that social work had escaped from medical oversight – in any case a historical inaccuracy save for the minority in psychiatric and medical social work.

We have drawn attention to some, but by no means all, of the extensive network of relations between social workers and others, but conscious that we have neglected those, for example, with housing, police and supplementary benefits officers. Nor have we done more than touch upon relations between social workers, their managers and policy-makers.

The scene seems set to bring the panoply of inter-professional relationships into a coherent whole. Or does it? Whatever the merits may prove to be in combining education with children and family work, a wedge has been driven between social work with adults and with children, threatening to split the UK profession. Reinforcing the corporate identity of social work is now critical, encouraged by reports of growing numbers joining BASW for the first time in many years.

Social workers, whether working with children or adults, will from now on be co-located with other professions with profound implications for respective roles and relationships. Housing many professions under the same roof may resolve some long-standing difficulties in collaborative working, although there is no guarantee. Each will have to surrender some autonomy. Respective roles will be renegotiated and redefined within iterative relationships during the course of everyday work. Readers may be better placed than we are to weigh how the roles of social workers have changed, and may continue to change, within reorganized adult and children's services. At issue is whether social work will hold together as a single and coherent profession.

Fortunately, organizational reforms have been underwritten by educational reforms, led by the creation of the General Social Care Council (GSCC). These are clearly designed to reassert and reinforce the corporate identity of social work, a process that had begun earlier following a review of the content of training courses by JM Consulting (1999), who had argued that social work should establish the attributes of a profession, even though 'a few interests may resist the idea'. But it needed to develop a more flexible and inclusive structure than more established professions. 'Multi-discipline, multi-agency working' called for more attention. Students, said JM Consulting, should become familiar with working in and across organizational and professional boundaries on placement, through joint learning and being taught by teachers from other professions.

The 20-year campaign to establish social work as a registered and graduate profession was finally achieved with the establishment of the GSCC. Qualifying courses were no longer acceptable at non-graduate level and the first students from the new social work degree programmes graduated in 2006. School-leavers with A levels were encouraged to apply for these courses as well as the older, more experienced and no less academically able candidates. Certificated proficiency in maths and English was now a prerequisite for acceptance on to a qualifying course. In addition, a new post-qualifying framework began in 2007 comprising postgraduate courses located in universities. Requirements for, and outcomes from, pre- and post-qualifying education were now putting social workers on a par with many other professions.

An explicit emphasis on collaborative working with other professions underpinned qualifying and post-qualifying courses. National Occupational Standards for Social Work provided the scaffolding for the social work degree, with Unit 17 requiring qualified social workers to be competent in working with other professionals. Similarly, the Revised Postqualifying Framework for Social Work Education and Training set standards for the development and implementation of effective ways of working in networks across organizational, sectoral and professional boundaries.

Inter-professional education can, however, never be more than part of a qualifying course in social work. Students need to find their identities as social workers, and to develop a distinctive body of knowledge and skills to bring to their work with other professions. This is essential before they will be ready for the fuzzy world of practice, especially in multidisciplinary teams where roles are often flexible and subject to constant redefinition – for example, between the social worker and the clinical psychologist, community psychiatric nurse or occupational therapist.

In Conclusion

We began by painting a sombre picture of the problems besetting social work over many years and the price paid in its working relations with others. We end on a more optimist note, but tempered by caution.

Reliance on single 'solutions' – organizational, educational or professional – has been replaced by a composite strategy in which reforms in services are complemented by reforms in the education and regulation of social work. The package signals support for social work's resurgent professional aspirations, guided by the GSCC, informed by employers' expectations, outward looking and committed to closer collaborative relations with others.

The future for social work seems to be set fair with the organizations, regulatory mechanisms, awards, educational systems and professional institutions deemed to be the hallmarks of a profession. It has left behind its self-destructive debates about professionalism. Parity has been established with social work in other countries and with other professions at home. Status differentials are narrowing with more established professions.

Social work has restrained its radical tendency. Restoration of long-standing professional objectives that survived throughout the post-Seebohm years is in sight. Social work values are being strengthened and reinterpreted for our times, espousing a model of professionalism grounded in public accountability and user-centred service, which others may emulate.

But far-reaching reforms have carried social work into deep and uncharted waters, where roles and relationships are in flux and change sometimes threatening. The need for inter-professional learning opportunities is accordingly more pressing than ever to provide a safe and neutral environment where all the parties can review the impact of change and explore afresh ways to work together.

What would those almoners have thought?

Five Key Points

- Seebohm is history.
- Collaborative practice responds to complex needs and users' expectations.
- Co-location helps but is not enough to ensure effective collaboration.
- Collaboration embraces an ever-widening spectrum of professions.
- Collaborative working relationships are always in flux.

Three Questions

? How are roles and relationships changing when social workers are co-located with other professions?

? How can the tension be held between profession-specific identities and roles and collaborative working?

? How can interprofessional learning best pave the way for collaborative practice?

Notes

1 *Re: S (Minors) (Care Order: Implementation of Care Plan) and Re: W (Minors) (Care Order: Adequacy of Care Plan)* [2002] 2 AC 291.

2 *Re W and B, Re W (Care Plan)* [2001] EWCA Civ 757, [2001] 2 FLR 582.

Further reading

1 Loxley, A. (1997) *Collaboration in Health and Welfare: Working with Difference*. London: Jessica Kingsley.

2 Glasby, J. and Littlechild, R. (2000) *The Health and Social Care Divide*. Birmingham: Pepar Publications.

3 Low, H. and Weinstein, J. (2000) Interprofessional education. In R. Pierce and J. Weinstein, *Innovative Education and Training for Care Professionals: A Providers' Guide*. London: Jessica Kingsley, Chapter 13.

4 Meads, G. and Ashcroft, J. (2005) *The Case for Interprofessional Education in Health and Social Care*. London: Blackwell.

PART 4

Social Work and its Psychosocial Framework

CHAPTER 4.1

Social Work and Society

Viviene E. Cree

Social work and society are caught in an intense and changing relationship. Just as social work seeks to influence society (and individuals and families within it), so society in its many guises seeks to control social work, by setting limits on what social workers can and should do. Social work is situated in the middle, pulled between the individual and society, the powerful and the excluded, negotiating, and at times in conflict with both.

This chapter examines social work and society from the perspective of a history of social work in the UK. This does not presume that the UK is the only country which might offer insight into this topic. Instead, it is argued that the UK provides a useful case study example for exploring the changing relationship between social work and society over time. Nor is it to suggest that this is the only 'true' history of social work in the UK. There are many possible ways of presenting history, and many voices which have often been excluded from social work histories, such as the voices of the many people who have used social work services. This account should therefore be regarded as one attempt to do justice to the histories of social work in the UK, demonstrating as it does the complexities and contradictions at the heart of the relationship between social work and society.

What Is Social Work?

There have been many attempts to define social work in recent years. One definition is widely quoted:

> The social work profession promotes social change, problem solving in human relationships and the empowerment and liberation of people to enhance well-being. Utilising theories of human behaviour and social systems, social work intervenes at the points where people interact with their environments. Principles of human rights and social justice are fundamental to social work.

This definition was negotiated and adopted at separate meetings of the International Federation of Social Workers (IFSW) and the International Association of Schools of Social Work (IASSW) in Montreal, Canada in July 2000, and then agreed as a joint definition in Copenhagen in May 2001. The definition has not been without its critics. For some, it is aspirational rather than practical; it tells us little about the realities of social work practice, especially in government agencies where the focus may be more on social control and safeguarding the public than on personal liberation. For others, it is seen as relying too heavily on 'Western' ideas about rights and justice. Interestingly, the IFSW website provides a rider to the definition: 'It is understood that social work in the 21st century is dynamic and evolving, and therefore no definition should be regarded as exhaustive.' This captures well the contested and changing nature of social work, as does the story of the historical development of social work.

Historical analyses demonstrate that social work has always been subject to competing claims of definition and practice; it is only by exploring some of the discourses within social work that we can begin to understand what social work is and what it might be (Cree, 1995, p. 1). Social work cannot be separated from society – we cannot explain or understand social work without locating it within society.

What Is Society?

The Oxford English Dictionary suggests that society is 'the aggregate of people living together in a more or less ordered community'. But what is an 'aggregate of people'? How many people must this include for it to be considered a 'society'? Does the definition assume a homogeneous or a heterogeneous group of people? What is a 'community'? What does it mean to be 'more or less ordered'? Most importantly, whose answers should we accept, and what are the implications of holding a particular position?

Classical sociologists had no problem in defining society. They worked from the assumption that 'society' (sometimes presented with a capital as 'Society') could be examined and analysed, much as any material object could be investigated in a laboratory. As the physical sciences studied the physical world, so sociology was the 'science of society'. In the late nineteenth century and early twentieth centuries in Western Europe and the USA, sociologists' main priority was to examine and explain what they saw as the new, 'modern' society in which they were living. Industrialization and urbanization had brought a new way of life: society had shifted from a feudal, agrarian, 'simple' society to a capitalist, industrial, 'complex' society. Sociologists saw this positively: the 'modern' world signified progress, scientific reasoning and enlightened thinking. They were also concerned, however, about the negative consequences of modernization, including the loss of traditional values and social networks. They therefore sought to find ways of ameliorating the worst aspects of industrialization and so create a better society. Capitalism and socialism represented two very different ways as to how this might be achieved.

In more recent years, the idea of society as a single entity has been severely criticized. Pluralist approaches present society as a mosaic of competing worlds.

Table 1 *Conceptualizations of society*

Pre-industrial society	*Modern society*	*Postmodern society*
Feudalism	Capitalism	Global capitalism
Agrarian	Industrial	The information society
Rural	Urban	Decentralized
Simple	Complex	Fragmented
Religious	Secular	Pluralist
Faith	Science	Scepticism/relativity
Superstition	Reason	Diverse beliefs/ambivalence
Tradition	Universal truths	Contingencies/contradictions

Postmodern analyses have taken this further, emphasizing the contingent nature of existence and the chaotic, unexpected characteristics of late capitalist society. Society is here perceived as being complex and fragmented: just as we all have more than one identity, so we live and move in many diverse societies. The different ways in which society has been conceptualized is illustrated in Table 1.

The history of social work in the UK offers unique insight into the social, economic and political changes which have taken place in the past and are being lived through in the present. It provides a window onto the modernization process; we can see at first hand the social changes which led to the emergence of 'modern' social work and the struggle within social work to professionalize and live up to the 'modern' ideal. An examination of social work's current position throws postmodern ideas and analyses into sharp relief. The complexities and uncertainties which seem to be endemic in social work are inevitable given the dynamic and contested nature of post/late modern/risk society.

Social Work and 'Pre-industrial' Society

There have always been those who need help from others, though this help was not always called 'social work'. In pre-industrial society, poverty was widespread. However, there was no notion at this time that the state should have any part to play in alleviating hardship. It was accepted that it was the family's responsibility to care for those in need. The 1601 Poor Law Act confirmed this:

> It should be the duty of the father, grandfather, mother, grandmother, husband or child of a poor, old, blind, lame or impotent person, or other poor person, not able to work, if possessed of sufficient means, to relieve and maintain that person.

Beyond this, churches and monasteries provided residential services for older and infirm people without family support through almshouses, infirmaries (for the care and treatment of the sick), and hospitals (literally 'hospitality' for the poor, especially the old, and for travellers in need of temporary shelter). At the same time, landowners gave extra help (sometimes financial and often in kind) to tenants and their families at times of sickness or poor harvest.

The social and economic changes known as the 'agrarian revolution' changed established systems of social support for ever. The process of enclosure which converted arable land to pasture led to mass unemployment for rural labourers, rural depopulation across vast areas of the countryside, and a decline of traditional obligations between landowners and tenants. Simultaneously, the dissolution of monasteries destroyed the provision of institutional social care services and led to hundreds of older and disabled people being thrown out onto the streets. Fears of social disorder led to the passing of the 1601 Elizabethan Poor Law Act (England and Wales). The Act reaffirmed the principle of family responsibility, while authorizing parishes to levy rates on property to pay for services for the poor and needy who had no family support. It also determined what help should be provided:

- the 'impotent poor' (the aged, chronic sick, blind and mentally ill who needed residential care) were to be accommodated in voluntary almshouses;
- the 'able-bodied poor' were to be set to work in a workhouse (they were felt to be able to work but were lazy);
- the 'able-bodied poor' who absconded or 'persistent idlers' who refused work were to be punished in a 'house of correction' (Fraser, 1984).

Parishes were never able to raise sufficient funds to make this a realistic programme of social support. Nevertheless, what the Act demonstrates is a series of propositions about a new relationship between the individual and society. First, it recognized that individual and charitable efforts were no longer sufficient to meet need; the state must therefore intervene to provide services. Secondly, it formalized the notion that there were different types of poor people, requiring different kinds of intervention. Finally, it presupposed the idea that the state's responsibility should be limited to the control, punishment and deterrence of the 'bad' poor, whilst 'good' poor people would be helped by voluntary agencies. Subsequent legislation and social welfare policy built on these ideas, with significant implications for the development of social work practice.

Social Work and 'Modern' Society

If the agrarian revolution of the sixteenth and seventeenth centuries marked the beginnings of a transformation in the relationship between individuals and society, it was the social crisis known as the 'industrial revolution' in the eighteenth and nineteenth centuries which consolidated this shift across Western Europe and North America. Social work emerged as a response to this crisis, and as a compromise between different views about what form that response should take.

The industrial revolution brought with it rapid industrialization and urbanization which changed forever the lives of all people, rich and poor alike. Social problems that had been dispersed and largely invisible in the countryside (for example, poverty and overcrowding, poor housing, ill-health and disease, alcohol and drug abuse, prostitution, unsupervised children) became more concentrated and more visible in the new towns and cities. Working-class freedom and social deprivation spelt danger to the middle-class city dwellers who clamoured for something to be done to contain and control the threat from the 'dangerous classes'. This is clearly illustrated in the following excerpt from a sermon preached by the Reverend Thomas Chalmers in 1817:

> on looking at the mighty mass of a city population, I state my apprehension, that if something be not done to bring this enormous physical strength under the control of Christian and humanised principle, the day may yet come, when it may lift against the authorities of the land, its brawny vigour, and discharge upon them all the turbulence of its rude and volcanic energy. (quoted in Brown, 1997, p. 95)

Something *was* done. The nineteenth century saw the introduction of a vast array of social welfare initiatives, including the establishment of new social work agencies. These initiatives were promoted by a range of stakeholders: public bodies, voluntary agencies, and private individuals, often, but not exclusively, members of the new urban middle class.

Statutory (public) initiatives in the nineteenth century

At the statutory or public level, there was innovation in the nineteenth century across many spheres of life. Schemes for public sanitation, education, policing, prisons, juvenile correction, public workhouses and mental asylums accompanied legislation governing working conditions and the treatment of children as well as new mechanisms for recording population change. The social welfare initiatives demonstrate both continuity and change in thinking about the relationship between the individual and the state.

The Poor Law Amendment Act of 1834 (England and Wales) divided the poor into two groups:

- the 'deserving poor' (e.g. elderly, sick or disabled people, orphans and widows) who were to receive financial and practical support (often home-based) from charitable or voluntary organizations;
- the 'undeserving poor' (e.g. able-bodied unemployed men, single mothers, prostitutes) who were forced to turn to the state, and thus to the workhouse, since there was to be no poor relief outside the institution (Mooney, 1998).

The Act thus built on the distinctions created in earlier Poor Law legislation, confirming the separation between the 'deserving' and 'undeserving' poor and furthering the idea that it was the state's job to exclude and discipline the 'residue' (the 'underclass' in today's language). They were to be removed from society, in common with those others who did not have a place in the new, modern, industrial society: those with mental health problems, disabled people and offenders.

The nineteenth-century initiatives also illustrate new ideas about the role of the state. For the first time the state was to take action to set social conditions for *all* people, not just those who had transgressed society's rules. Free education was to be available for all children up to the age of 11 years; public sanitation would benefit all classes of people; employment legislation would control the economic and work practices of all factory and mine owners. And legislation allowed the state to intervene in the heart of private lives, that is, the family. The 1889 Prevention of Cruelty and Protection of Children Act for the first time made cruelty towards children illegal and introduced provisions for children to be removed from their families to a place of safety.

This new conceptualization about the role of the state was not reached easily, and was not accepted by all. Individuals and groups fought against state encroachment into individual liberty and the right to live (and work) without statutory interference. Dissenters were often the new middle classes who bore the burden of rising taxes to pay for social improvements (Brown, 1997). Scotland showed marked reluctance to go down the road of statutory intervention. Although Scottish parishes had been permitted by a Poor Law Act of 1579 to raise taxes through rates, few did, and the chosen means of support remained the church or the estate (Levitt, 1988). Where relief was given, it was targeted at those who could not work (the 'destitute' and 'disabled'); financial support of the 'able-bodied', by either voluntary or public agencies, was discouraged.

Voluntary (philanthropic) initiatives in the nineteenth century

There was an explosion of voluntary activity in the nineteenth century, with the creation of hundreds of new philanthropic agencies. These included police court missionaries; rescue societies for 'fallen women'; housing associations; university settlements; children's charities; hospital almoners; caseworkers from the Charity Organization Society (COS) and other relief agencies; visitors on behalf of churches of all denominations and many other secular visiting organizations. Large numbers of middle-class people and some working-class people were involved in some form of philanthropic effort, either as fund-raisers, visitors, managers or activists. Some philanthropists restricted their involvement to small-scale action, such as visiting people at home. Many others were also involved in large-scale campaigning work. They saw no contradiction between 'personal troubles' and 'public issues' (Mills, 1959). Instead, their work with individuals and families was a key part of their mission to change society. Helen Bosanquet, a COS District Secretary for many years, expressed this as follows:

> What we aim at in all social work . . . is that both the whole community and every member in it shall be progressive, on the rising scale. We shall not be satisfied if the community as a whole can show a momentary increase in wealth, or learning, or culture, unless all classes within it are partaking intelligently in the social life, sharing in its progress, a source of strength and not of weakness. (Bosanquet, 1902, pp. 5–6)

Much of the philanthropic work took place on the margins of public agencies; the workers saw their task as mediating between individuals and the state (J. Clarke, 1993). They also, however, frequently sought to set limits on the state's involvement in the lives of individuals, by working as both Poor Law Guardians and 'friendly visitors', or by passing on information about individuals' circumstances to Poor Law boards. Most philanthropists believed passionately that statutory measures encouraged dependency and that the only way people could be helped to help themselves was through the reciprocal relationship between an individual and a trained volunteer. Octavia Hill, manager of a large number of Housing Associations in London, wrote in 1886:

> The more I watch the more the action of the public puzzles me. By rashly pouring vast sums into new largely advertised, wholescale schemes, their feverish excitability is creating a body of thriftless, ungracious, mendicants, living always on the brink of starvation, because taught to look to what may turn up. And those who love and know the people have to stand sadly aside, feeling that all giving is fatal until such rushes be over . . . (reprinted in Whelan, 1998, p. 93)

Octavia Hill's words show that philanthropy was not envisaged simply as a neutral alternative to state intervention; it was a deliberate attempt to hold back the increasing role of the state. From this perspective, philanthropy (and later social work) was not an apolitical, private intervention into social problems but was a 'deliberately depoliticising strategy for establishing public services at sensitive points midway between private initiative and the state' (Donzelot, 1980, p. 55). It offered a way of intervening in the lives of individuals and families to 'fit' them for the new industrial society without undermining individual responsibility and the role of the family (Parton, 1994a).

The principal actors in this new sphere were middle-class women. While men busied themselves with political and economic affairs, and in the management of charitable organizations, it was largely women who performed the visits to people at home and in institutions. A survey carried out in 1893 estimated that approximately 500,000 women worked 'continuously and semi-professionally' in charitable activity, with another 20,000 employed as paid officials in philanthropic organizations (Prochaska, 1980, p. 29). These women brought to their voluntary work specific (middle-class) ideas about class and gender, family and work, age and sexuality. They believed that their own, bourgeois culture and beliefs were superior to those of working-class people; their goal was to make them more 'middle-class'. They also believed that men and women had different 'natural' qualities and abilities; that as women, they had a special contribution to make to the management of poorhouses and workhouses, school boards and prisons, as well as to the daily household management of poor families.

There was a fundamental contradiction here. Middle-class women, through educating the working-classes in domesticity, also freed themselves from their own domestic confinement. Philanthropy brought opportunities for useful work, recreation, and creativity to middle-class women excluded from the world of paid employment. As Florence Nightingale declared: 'Charity work, free from chaperons and prying relatives represented deliverance from the stitch-stitch-church-stitch routine of female existence. It was adventure' (quoted in Prochaska, 1980, p. 11). The 'private' world of the working classes was thus the point of entry for middle-class women into the 'public' world of work and politics. At the same time, the 'private' work carried out by working-class women in middle-class households (as domestic servants, cooks and nannies) gave middle-class women the leisure-time they needed to indulge in charitable work with the working classes (Summers, 1979).

Social Work in the Twentieth Century

It has been stated already that the nineteenth century witnessed the introduction of a wide range of social support initiatives, instigated by both statutory and voluntary agencies. In the twentieth century, social work services became increasingly incorporated into the state, either carried out directly by the state, or by the voluntary sector on its behalf, and statutory agencies became responsible for regulating and controlling the voluntary sector, through funding and inspection arrangements. As social work became progressively a more legally defined, narrowly prescribed activity, so the social reform agenda within social work became marginalized.

So how did this change come about? We have already seen in the previous centuries a growing acceptance of the idea that the state should intervene to provide services and set conditions (to a limited extent) on behaviour. Digby and Stewart (1996) assert that the twentieth century witnessed a fundamental change in the role of the British state. Liberal reforms at the beginning of the twentieth century were followed during and after the Second World War by a massive programme of social legislation which promised to tackle outright the five giants of 'Want, Disease, Ignorance, Squalor and Idleness' (HMSO, 1942) and remove all trace of the stigma attached to the Poor Law. The principal systems of provision included social security and pensions, the National Health Service, education, family allowances, housing and planning, child care and national assistance. The aim was to end social inequality for all; the task of social work was to pick up the small number of people who fell through the welfare net and rehabilitate them so that they could again play their part as full citizens. Three separate local authority departments were set up in 1948 to meet social work needs: children's departments targeted children deprived of a 'normal' family life; welfare departments were set up to work with older, physically handicapped and homeless people; and local health departments were created to provide services for mentally ill and handicapped people. According to this new standard, the voluntary sector was complementary and supplementary to the state, filling in gaps and experimenting with new forms of help.

But it would be wrong to assume that arguments against the increasing role of the state had been defeated for all time. The tide of social democratic optimism and new confidence in central planning measures that followed the Second World War may have muted the voices against state encroachment, but, as Stewart (1999) argues, they did not disappear. The limited funding made available to the new social work departments in the post-war period demonstrates that they were never expected to be a central arm of the welfare state in the way that health and education services were. A key aspect of social work practice – child protection services – remained in the hands of voluntary agencies, which also provided the bulk of residential child care services. It was not until after the passing of the Social Work (Scotland) Act 1968 and the Local Authority Social Services Act (England and Wales) 1970 that statutory social services were on a level that seriously undermined voluntary ones. New generic Social Work and Social Service Departments brought together the previously disparate services under one roof, offering universal personal social services for all; 'through one door on which to knock' (Seebohm Committee, 1968). The voluntary sector's task was confirmed as being 'to supplement local authority work' and 'a stimulus to further progress', in the words of the Social Work (Scotland) Act. These developments have been described as the 'high tide' of social work (Langan, 1993).

There is a paradox in the expansion of the state's responsibilities. While voluntary agencies in the nineteenth century had, at least in part, seen their role as one of restraining state interference in the lives of citizens, voluntary agencies in the twentieth century became increasingly supportive of a greater role for the state. Those who campaigned for the passing of the Children Act in 1948 included representatives from powerful voluntary organizations that worked with children. The same was true of the later 1968 and 1970 Acts. In practice, voluntary social work agencies did unprecedentedly well out of the expansion of statutory social work, as local authorities, strapped for cash and resources, turned to the voluntary sector to meet requirements of the new legislation.

The driving force behind the developments that took place in both statutory and voluntary social work can be found in the intersection between the needs of the growing welfare state and the demands of social workers themselves. The state needed professional workers to staff its new departments. At the same time, the 'would-be professions' benefited from the occupational and organizational base provided by the state (J. Clarke, 1993, p. 15). The 'bureau professionalism' that became the pattern in local authority social work departments (and in many of the larger voluntary agencies) guaranteed social work its service-user base and its continuing legitimacy. But it also restricted the kind of activity that social work could be involved in, and the autonomy and discretion that social workers could exercise. Commentators have been critical of the self-serving nature of professions and the social work profession in particular. It is argued that professionalization encouraged social workers to give up their claims to change society (Hugman, 1991), led to a diminishing of the authority of women's voices in social work (Dominelli, 1997), and an abandonment of social work's traditional commitment to the poor (Jones, 1997).

Whichever is the case, the old arguments against the growing dominance of the state did not vanish. In the 1970s and 1980s in the UK, the welfare state in general, and social work in particular, came under increasing attack from both the right and the left. Challenges came from a number of distinct, and at times overlapping areas:

- A decline in the UK's economic competitiveness and a reorientation of fiscal and monetary regimes led to the welfare state becoming a target for radical change (Clark and Cree, 2001).
- Black and anti-racist groups drew attention to the deep-seated racism within social work ideology and practice (Dominelli, 1988).
- Child abuse tragedies from the early 1970s onwards highlighted statutory social work's powerlessness to prevent abuse from taking place, either at home or in the very institutions set up to protect vulnerable children (Hill and Aldgate, 1996).
- Feminists pointed out that state services, while claiming to support women, reinforced gender stereotypes and confirmed women's oppression (Langan and Day, 1992).

- Disabled people campaigned against the paternalism of state provision, and fought for a measure of control over how services were to be delivered (Campbell and Oliver, 1996).
- Key voluntary agencies pushed for an increased role for the voluntary sector in 'welfare pluralism' (Gladstone, 1979).
- Radical social workers drew attention to the structural causes of service users' problems and sought to form political alliances through trade unions (Langan, 1993).
- A New Right agenda was promoting the role of the family and voluntary provision in preference to the 'nanny state' (Pinkney, 1998).

The consequences of the disillusionment with the welfare state included a retrenchment of the state in terms of its provision of welfare services. The idea that the state could not – and should not – provide all social welfare began again to gain ascendency. But although the rhetoric of the 1980s may have been about reducing state involvement, the reality was the introduction of new and ever more stringent mechanisms for regulating and controlling social services, in statutory, voluntary and private sectors. The result has been greater, not less power for the state.

International comparisons make it evident that there is no 'right answer' to the questions of who should provide social work services, and of what kind. In many European countries, social workers are state employees with wide responsibilities in relation to employment and social insurance. In contrast, social services in Australia rest firmly with the voluntary sector, while in the USA most qualified social workers are either self-employed or working for private agencies as counsellors and therapists. In Latin America, social workers attached to churches play a key role in working with groups to tackle poverty. Moreover, some of the largest non-governmental organizations (NGOs), for example, the Red Cross, Age Concern and Oxfam, play a major role in the organization of welfare services throughout the world during times of trauma such as wars and civil conflicts (Dominelli, 2000, p. 32).

Social Work and 'Postmodern' Society

It is impossible to say when the 'modern' period in social work ended and the 'postmodern' began, supposing that it exists at all. But whatever we think about 'postmodernity', we can be certain that the world of the twenty-first century has changed and is continuing to change rapidly. The structure and organization of social work in the UK has been transformed; 'modern' assumptions about the role of social work are open to question; it is uncertain what form social work will take in the future.

As we have seen, the relationship between social work and society has been shaped by a number of different processes, historical, social, economic and political. Factors beyond our geographical boundaries are of even greater significance for social work and postmodern society. The impact of economic organization on an international scale (globalization) has been that individual countries can no longer function as closed societies, if this was ever truly possible. Smart (1993) argues that social life and social relations, identity and experience can no longer be limited in scope to 'society', particularly where society is envisaged in terms of the boundaries of the nation-state. For many countries, globalization has been experienced as a kind of colonization of local cultures and customs; a 'Westernization' or even 'Americanization'. Yet globalization has also opened up so-called marginalized and 'peripheral' communities throughout the world, bringing the potential for greater awareness of diverse cultures that may challenge the hegemony of Western ideas (Allahar, 1995).

Globalization has already begun to have a direct influence on social work in the UK. As the transnational nature of economic organization has undermined the power of nation-states (Bauman, 1998), old defensive barriers between countries have broken down and new alliances formed. Agreements reached at European level (such as the European Convention on Human Rights) are today reshaping policy and practice in all the member countries in the European Union, just as international treaties (such as the UN Convention on the Rights of the Child) are having an impact on adults and children across statutory, voluntary and private agencies. Whilst some systems of government have become larger, there has been a cross-Europe movement towards the devolution of responsibilities away from governments to smaller units of power. In the UK, the Scottish Parliament and the Welsh and Northern Irish Assemblies have brought increasing disparities in the relationship between social work and society across England and Wales, Scotland and Northern Ireland, as demonstrated in the different countries' approaches to the question of provision of social care for older people.

Globalization has been accompanied by attempts across advanced industrialized societies to cut public expenditure and introduce new ways of managing welfare. In most countries, this has meant an increase in social inequalities. In the UK, the mechanism of the market has been introduced throughout public sector agencies. Statutory social work agencies have seen the creation of a split between purchaser and provider roles, and the introduction of charges for services, the contracting out of services and the promotion of competition between the statutory, voluntary and private sectors. Clients have become 'customers', and social workers budget-holders, with little control over the resources which they must purchase in the 'market' of care. Social workers are experiencing high levels of anxiety and pressure, as they strive to maintain the social work role in the face of challenges from other care professionals, such as occupational therapists, district nurses and community psychiatric nurses.

Some commentators propose that the defining characteristic of the post-industrial society is information – it is information that produces and sustains contemporary society and makes globalization possible (Kumar, 1995). By bringing together ever faster and cleverer computers with worldwide telecommunications systems, knowledge and information can be shared instantaneously, and people can build social networks and communities of support across societies and countries. This has clear advantages for social workers and service users. But critics have pointed out that information technology (IT) is only really available to certain groups in society, leading to an increase in social exclusion for those who have no access to it. Information technology has also brought with it the capacity for surveillance and control to a degree unthinkable in the past. Networked computer systems, DNA screening and electronic 'tagging' bring ever more sophisticated ways in which the 'disciplinary society' can 'police' its members (Foucault, 1977).

Globalization and information are not the only reasons for the changes taking place in social work. Postmodern society is also a 'risk society' (Beck, 1992). Our lives are affected by global risks beyond our control; the speed at which change is taking place makes us feel insecure and vulnerable. Social work in the UK has sought to cope with (and manage) the idea of risk and uncertainty by introducing new systems for organizing professional practice and new mechanisms for predicting future risks and their potential negative outcomes. How far management of risk is ever truly achievable remains an open question, but Cree and Wallace (2005) argue that social workers must nevertheless seek to behave in a professional, ethical manner, working alongside service users and other professionals to share the responsibilities and challenges that real life brings.

Useful websites

- http://www.gcal.ac.uk/heatherbank/index.html – the Heatherbank Museum of Social Work, founded in 1975, is the only museum of social work in Europe.
- http://www.workhouses.org.uk/ – contains interesting materials about workhouses and poorhouses across the UK.
- http://www.idbsu.edu/socwork/dhuff/XX.htm/ – outlines American social work history.

Conclusion

The relationship between social work and society is a dynamic and highly contested one. As society 'modernized', so social work shifted from the informal to the formal sphere, from voluntary to statutory agencies. Social work became a key mechanism of the new 'disciplinary society', positioned, as Donzelot (1980) and others have claimed, at a midway point between the individual and the state. In more recent years, disciplinary power has continued to grow, as the state has increased its regulatory and inspectorial role in a new 'mixed economy' of care.

But the story of the changing relationship between social work and society is not one of 'caring' voluntary agencies versus 'controlling' statutory services. On the contrary, the motivations of those involved in the nineteenth century voluntary agencies were as much about controlling and re-educating the working classes as they were about humanitarian concern or social reform. They worked hand-in-hand with statutory (poor law) agencies to manage the social consequences of industrialization and urbanization. At the same time, the emergence of 'the social' provided a gateway for middle-class women to enter the public arena and the world of professional work.

Today the lines between voluntary and statutory agencies have become increasingly blurred. Most voluntary agencies rely heavily on local and central government funding for their activities. Meanwhile statutory agencies depend on informal networks of caring to meet most social need. There is a general acceptance (again) that the state cannot provide all social welfare needs: that statutory social work must inevitably remain a 'last resort service', rationed by tests of income and need (Hill, 2000). The 'undeserving poor' of the past are today's 'socially excluded' or 'underclass', and they are the major users of statutory social work services.

So what of social work and society in the future? Realistically, social work will continue to be more about helping people to fit into society than about changing society; it will be concerned with maintenance rather than social revolution (Davies, 1994). But given its breadth of scope, its complexities and its diversities, social work can do more than this. Social work has privileged access to the lives of individuals and the workings of society. Through this, it holds the possibility of exerting a positive influence on both. If it is to achieve this, it will have to align itself more completely with those it sets out to mediate on behalf of – the poor, the socially excluded and the less powerful in society. And it will have to show courage to speak out about the structural causes of people's problems and the extraordinary resilience of their lives.

Five Key Points

- Social work is situated midway between the individual and society, between the powerful and the excluded, negotiating, and at times in conflict, with both.
- Historical analyses demonstrate that social work has always been subject to competing claims of definition and practice – there is no essential social work task.
- Modern social work emerged as a deliberate strategy to ameliorate the worst effects of rapid industrialization and urbanization.
- The professionalization of social work in the UK meant that social work (statutory and voluntary) increasingly looked to the state to provide its 'clients' and regulate its activities.
- The postmodern world brings new opportunities for creativity and diversities in social work, as well as dangers of increased surveillance and control of social work's subjects.

Three Questions

? How far is social work a class-specific activity?
? What does it mean to say that social work is a 'women's profession'?
? What is the role of the voluntary sector in social work today?

Further reading

1 Cree, V. E. (2000) *Sociology for Social Workers and Probation Officers*. London: Routledge.
2 Fraser, D. (2003) *The Evolution of the British Welfare State: A History of Social Policy since the Industrial Revolution*, 3rd edn. Basingstoke: Palgrave Macmillan.
3 Payne, M. (2005b) *The Origins of Social Work: Continuity and Change*. Basingstoke: Palgrave Macmillan.

CHAPTER 4.2

Social Work and Politics

Mark Drakeford

What is the rationale for a chapter on politics in a text which is all about social work? Surely, social welfare is one of those rare topics which closes rather than widens political differences? Who could be against the proposition that help should be offered to those who need it the most? Well, as this chapter aims to demonstrate, almost all the apparently straightforward ideas which these questions contain turn out, on closer examination, to be more complicated and more contested than a casual observer might have imagined. Far from it being ground upon which differences are merged, social welfare and social work have become policy and practice areas in which some of the most fundamentally different ways of thinking about society are fought out.

The social worker who claims to be above or beyond politics is one who has denied her or himself access to a set of conceptual tools which are directly necessary to a properly informed conduct in today's complex world of practice. The claim to be 'unpolitical' is itself a political stance which tells us much about the organizations or individuals who make such declarations.

This chapter takes a broad view of what is meant by 'politics'. At root, the material discussed here is about *ideology*. It is concerned with basic questions about the organization of society, the relationship between individuals and the state, the ways in which some behaviours are deemed lawful and others unlawful, the sorts of policy choices which governments make, the actual services which are provided, and so on. In the practical world of social workers, these ideological questions are rarely faced in such a basic form. Instead they emerge in more everyday clothing, lurking, for example, behind the rules which govern the treatment of young people before the courts, decisions about charging for community care services, or the powers to detain an individual on the grounds of mental illness.

Moreover, all such day-by-day decisions are taken in particular organizational contexts. It may be difficult to generate much heat in a discussion about local government committee structures or drawing the boundary between health and social services, yet from the resolution of such political questions a whole range of direct consequences flow for social workers and their clients.

The relationship between social work and politics is thus a complex one and one which operates at very many different levels. To begin with, social welfare services are shaped and delivered within directly political milieux. Policy is formed in the different political settings of the UK's devolved administrations – the National Assembly in Wales, the Executive of the Scottish Parliament, the Northern Ireland Assembly, when operating, and the Houses of Parliament in London. Political decisions at such institutions bring different approaches which shape the policies which flow from them.

Secondly, statutory services, at least, are delivered in the political context of local councils. Decisions about the allocation of resources, the location of services, the organization of particular functions and so on, are arrived at as the result of the political preferences and composition of local authority councillors, operating within the strategic frameworks which have been laid down by central government in its different guises. This chapter argues that the day-to-day practice of on-the-ground social work is highly influenced by this local political context, and that the level and nature of services provided to individual users is similarly affected.

Thirdly, it will be suggested here that social work is an inherently political activity, concerned fundamentally with a series of power relationships and conducted according to competing sets of notions as to how such relationships ought best to be resolved. Social workers spend a good deal of time inside families where power relations – between parents and children, for example – are fundamental to the issues which have produced a call upon social services in the first instance. The same individuals are likely to be engaged in a series of other relationships with the outside world, all of which have a formative power dimension. The social-worker-as-broker spends huge amounts of time in mediating between the individual and the school, or the doctor, or the housing department. In all those encounters, the social worker is anything but power-neutral. Statutory social workers in child welfare or mental health, for example, exercise direct and substantial powers on behalf of the state. Such powers reflect a view of social relations which is fundamentally political in its determination.

Ideology and Central Government

One of the most consistent dangers which face contemporary actors in social welfare – policy-makers and practitioners alike – is that *novelty*, in the sense of immediate change, always appears more pressing and important than *continuity*, in the sense of longer-term trends and ideas which are more slow-moving or submerged. For the purposes of the discussion here, I want to suggest that the activities in which social workers are engaged take place at the intersection of a number of interlinked and long-term ideological disputes in which the boundary between one side and another moves backwards and forwards, like some never-ending contest between two evenly matched tug-of-war teams. These disputes include:

- *Government: help or hindrance?* For more than 150 years – and some would argue for a lot longer – social policy in Britain and Ireland has been fundamentally contested between those who believe that the state is essentially benign and ought to work actively to assist the lives of its citizens, and those who believe that the state is essentially malign, more likely to do harm than good and has a tendency ever to encroach upon the lives of private individuals which ought vigorously to be resisted. In modern times, the Welfare State of the post-1945 period most clearly demonstrates the first approach, while the ambitions of the Thatcher governments of the 1980s to 'roll back the frontiers of the state' belong to the second tradition.

- *Private or public welfare?* A linked ideological divide emerges between those who believe that the best social welfare is privately provided and those who believe that public provision has greater advantages. Believers in private welfare emphasize the role of the family and the locality. They remind us that most 'care' provided in our society is the result of families, neighbours and friends looking after one another. Where needs cannot be met in that way, such thinkers argue, individuals ought to have as much choice as possible in identifying and obtaining the sort of services which they would prefer. In this sort of analysis, the market emerges as the only place where such choice can effectively be delivered. Here, it is argued, a plethora of private providers will compete to attract purchasers on the basis of price and customer care.

  On the other side are those who believe that reliance on private welfare simply replicates and reinforces existing inequalities in society. The ability to choose private child care, for example, will depend wholly upon having the money to pay for such services. Those who have stable families and access to financial resources will be able to use such private advantages to their own benefit. Those without either will find their disadvantages exaggerated still further. In these circumstances, such analysts suggest, public provision is much to be preferred because such services can be made genuinely available to all in a way which can guarantee access and quality.

These fundamentally different ways of thinking about government and services mean that the impact of politics, in the sense of ideology, has been directly felt in social work throughout its history. At different periods the practical effect has been sharper or less apparent, as ideological tides ebb and flow. The community care arrangements of the last 50 years provide a direct example of the way in which underlying political philosophies can come to the surface, impacting upon the services which social workers provide and the daily activities in which they are engaged.

Community care is a policy which, at the outset, received a good deal of bipartisan support in the political arena. The phrase 'community care' was first used by Sir Derek Walker-Smith, a Conservative Health Minister, on introducing the House of Commons Bill which was eventually to become the Mental Health Act 1959. During the 1960s, a series of scandals in mental health hospitals produced an added impetus to the policy of transferring care from an institutional to a community base. The Ely Hospital Inquiry of 1969 was chaired by an up-and-coming Conservative lawyer, Geoffrey Howe, and reported to the Labour Secretary of State, Richard Crossman. Crossman's response laid the foundations for the 1972 White Paper, *Better Services for the Mentally Handicapped*, introduced by his Tory successor, Sir Keith Joseph. In 1976, with Labour back in power again, the follow-up

White Paper, *Better Services for the Mentally Ill*, was published by Barbara Castle.

The plans of the 1960s and 1970s, by both Parties, were written essentially from within the model of the 1945 welfare state in which governments were thought able to plan, over a considerable time horizon, and to set out policies and programmes which others – in this case primarily health and social services – would be charged to implement. As Parton (1994b, p. 97) suggests, such a view rested upon a belief that, 'the interests of the social worker, and hence the state were similar to, if not the same as, the people they were trying to help.'

Much of this ideological quiescence was to change during the 1980s. The Thatcher governments of that decade embraced a very different notion of the proper role and capacity of the state itself and of its agents. A new emphasis was placed upon the role of the family, and of voluntary and informal networks, in the provision of care. Local authority departments were to be reorganized to reflect this new arrangement. Councils were to be essentially *purchasers* of services *provided* by others. The nature of that provision was to be determined in a new *market*, in which voluntary and private sector organizations would compete for contracts with the local authorities in order to carry out the work. For social workers, it is important to understand the implications of this change, for at its root lay a distrust of both their profession and their professionalism. The New Right distrusted the public servants and public services in general, but in welfare matters the political edge of this ideological position was particularly acute, dealing as it does with individuals and families who are, very often, economically inactive and net consumers of, rather than contributors to, the public purse.

Under New Labour, the politics of welfare moved away from the neo-liberal certainties of the Thatcher and Major years. Instead, the 1997 government made a positive virtue of what it claimed to be an absence of ideological dogma in its approach to social policy matters generally and the social services in particular. Rather than privileging one ideological position above others, the Blair Government preferred a pragmatic 'what works' approach to policy-making. As Iatridis suggests, however, the apparent retreat from politics and ideology is itself an ideology. The apparent neutrality which a 'what works' approach provides, however, allows politicians an elegant means of dealing with some difficult moral or financial questions – by passing such problems on to 'experts' for solution. As Harrison (1998, p. 21) describes this in the field of health, 'Not only does evidence-based medicine offer a solution, but a solution which diffuses the responsibility for potentially unpopular decisions by their delegation to doctors. This is important for the political acceptability of rationing.'

In social work, the 'what works' movement has also gathered considerable pace. Here, the ideological side-step involved is less concerned with rationing than with ethics. If a solution 'works' then arguments over issues such as freedom and individual rights can be portrayed as minor or peripheral. The then-Home Secretary, Jack Straw, for example, in announcing the extension of electronic tagging to children as young as ten years of age, justified this course of action by reference to the 'successful trials' of such methods which had already been conducted and fended off criticism not by any reference to the ethical and ideological questions posed, but by citing an 'evaluation report of the trials' which the Home Office itself had conducted (Hansard House of Commons Written Answers, 20 November 2000, Column 100W).

As the New Labour years moved on, however, the Westminster model for social work generally located it either as a simple hand-maiden to its health policy (absorbing social workers into Primary Care Trusts, for example) or as a tool in the authoritarian axis of its social policy-making. If Blairism involved dividing the population into those who play by the rules and those who do not (Blair, 1997), then social workers spend their time amongst the latter: neighbours who cause difficulties to others; parents who cannot look after their own children; young people who fall foul of the law and so on. Even in areas where blameworthiness is more difficult to mobilize, such as mental health, the part mapped out for social work has fallen on the policing part of the social services spectrum, as in successive drafts of the long-promised, ill-fated Mental Health Bill.

Such a cast of mind is not confined to ministers. There are social workers, as well as governments, who profess to regard their activities as somehow untouched by politics. The view of social work as a set of techniques, validated by 'evidence' has gathered substantial ground in recent years. As Kilty and Meenaghan (1995, p. 446) point out, however, the technocratic and managerial view can have the effect of disguising the essential point that social work activity is activity with a *purpose*, and that purpose involves the promotion of change. As they suggest, the direction of change is an expression of the values which social work espouses and 'it is also influenced by the political context in which it operates'. The preference for social work as a radical, emancipatory and transformative activity is not one based on the efficiency of one set of techniques over another. It is an *ideological* stance, and one which positions social work as a political rather than simply a practical activity (see Butler and Drakeford, 2001, 2005 for a fuller exploration of these issues). The next section turns to consider the connection between politics, administrative context and social work practice by looking at the impact of devolution on social services and the place where most social work in Britain and Ireland still takes place – within the framework of local government.

Administration, Devolution and Local Government

Devolution in the post-1997 United Kingdom has been the most radical departure in constitutional politics since the completion of universal suffrage in the last century. It means that policies and practices in social work will vary, perhaps increasingly, between the four nations of the UK. There is no space here to go beyond a small number of indicative examples of the differences which devolution brings. In England, Children's Trusts will radically alter patterns of political accountability, while in Wales social services for children will remain a direct responsibility of local government. The difficulties in bringing forward new mental health legislation at Westminster, noted above, have been avoided in Scotland where the Scottish Executive has already successfully reformed the legal framework in this area, in a way which has commanded broad-based support. As, over time, different political parties come to power in different parts of the UK, the 'living laboratory' of devolution,

A case example

Politics and social work remain intrinsically linked at the front line of service delivery as much as in wider debates. Look at this case example and consider it in the light of the issues discussed in this chapter. How do you make sense of the link between ideology and action in social work practice?

A potential user comes to a social work office, complaining that her children keep falling ill because her home suffers badly from damp. As a result, they have missed a good deal of school and are falling behind others in education and other sorts of development. She has received letters from the local education authority, threatening her with prosecution. The house has central heating but, your client explains, she cannot afford to use it. Do you:

- put her in touch with a campaigning group in her local area which is lobbying the local council for new investment in structural improvement;
- make a series of appointments in which you will offer advice on better budgeting;
- make a referral to the local welfare rights team, to ensure that your client is receiving all the income to which she is entitled;
- contact the education office to make sure that all the information about the family is pooled and coordinated action can be taken;
- advise her that, in your view, the children may be at risk and that a fuller examination of her ability to look after them properly will have to be undertaken.

Think about the basis upon which you came to your chosen course of action. Did your decision emerge from a view of social work which is about changing the individual to fit society, or society to fit the individual? Was your understanding of social work one which regards the profession as one dedicated to keeping families together, or one which starts from a belief that children sometimes need protecting from their parents? The point of these questions is to bring to the surface those political and ideological roots, which lie behind the resolution of the most everyday social work encounters.

in which each nation applies its own solutions to suit local circumstances, will be increasingly felt in social work.

One of the most important ways in which devolved administrations shape the politics of social services lies in the changes which it can bring about in the structure of *local* government. Central authorities, in all the countries of Britain, are policy-makers. No such authority delivers meals-on-wheels, plays with vulnerable children in a nursery or works with a mentally ill person on survival skills. The *delivery* of services rests with local government; but the *terms* of that delivery and the *capacity* to do so are shaped by actions of central administrations. In that delivery, the political character of local authorities has a real impact upon the design and delivery of social services in each area. Indeed, as Parton (1994b, p. 107) suggests, the connection between changes in social services and wider political change needs to be understood far more broadly than in simply organizational terms. The thrust of the 1980s and 1990s towards a reduced role for directly provided services, and a greater emphasis upon the market, paralleled 'a general shift away from corporatist centralism towards a more decentralised and fragmented minimal state'. Yet, the degree to which pluralism has been embraced in practice has varied between authorities, as has the level of investment provided. Both these variations, in form and funding, reflect political decisions which produce a very direct impact on street-level social work.

Social Services

So far, this chapter has considered social welfare in relation to the directly political contexts of ideology, government and administration in which social work services are designed and directed. What, however, about the *delivery* of services? In what sense can on-the-ground social work be described and understood as a political activity?

In the argument developed here, the different purposes to which social work might be directed have always been highly ideological and, as a consequence, highly contested. The denial of ideology, on the basis of an appeal to some 'scientific neutrality', has always been consistent with an attempt to by-pass the inherent tensions of social welfare provision, by defining them out of debate. In the American context, where the social-worker-as-technician has been widely promoted, Mills (1996, p. 394) suggests that some New Right advocates, including some from within social work, have argued for a care management strategy in which such individuals are 'deliberately driven' to 'hopeless desperation', in order to bring about greater efforts to free themselves from the fetters of state support and welfare dependency. In such circumstances, Mills (1996, p. 395) argues, social workers are not simply caught in an ideological field, they are *players* on that field, whose actions either support or resist the prevailing orthodoxies.

In the context of Britain and Ireland, Harris (1997, p. 28) makes the same point when he notes that 'social work entails applying social and political theory to a multitude of complex and sometimes insoluble problems', and speaks of social work as 'the child of contemporary politics'. Two contemporary examples of this linear relationship must suffice to illustrate the wider picture.

The first and most basic example lies in the perennial tension which exists in social work between its duty to individuals and its duty to society. Simplifying radically, it could be said that social workers might be divided between those who see their primary task as changing the individual to meet the needs of society and those who see themselves as changing society to meet the needs of the individual. The reality, as in so much practical social welfare, lies more in the messy middle of these polar opposites, but, even if caricatured, the division does describe a basic fault-line around which different forms of practice can be distinguished. In the immediate post-war period, with a belief that, with the advent of the welfare state, the problems of poverty and of access to basic services had been solved, so social work appeared to be dominated by an approach which looked for ways in which 'sad, bad or mad' people might be better 'adjusted' to an essentially beneficent society. During the 1960s, with the 'rediscovery' of poverty, and rising trends towards radicalism in politics and liberalism in personal morality, so the dominant outlook in social work changed too. 'Radical social work', essentially Marxist in persuasion, suggested that alliances could be formed between workers and clients in social welfare which would allow for vested interests to be challenged and authority to be redistributed from the powerful to the powerless. Even in less *avant-garde* circles, the nature of social work was moved from the margins of the maladjusted to the mainstream. The Seebohm Committee of 1968 proposed a 'universal' social work service which ordinary citizens would use as normally as a visit to the doctor or the school. The spirit of the times emphasized the rights of individuals to a service which was to mobilize resources on their behalf, rather than simply aid their accommodation to their circumstances.

The Seebohm reforms of the early 1970s represent what is arguably the high-water mark of social services in the second half of the twentieth century. A second example of the linear relationship between politics and social work took place in just that period. In 1973 one of those landmark events, which colour the long-term public perception of an issue or a profession, occurred in social work, when the death of Maria Colwell led to a public inquiry in which blame for the child's fate was laid firmly at the door of the profession. The view which was taken from the inquiry was of a social work service which had alternated between incompetence on the one hand, and a doctrinaire adherence to a particular theoretical model on the other. As a result, Maria had been returned to her natural mother, despite her own wishes and what was presented at the inquiry as the weight of 'common-sense' evidence. Once at that home, the warnings of neighbours and others had appeared to have been ignored or overlooked until the tragedy – which, with hindsight, the inquiry glossed as avoidable – occurred.

While the handling of the Colwell inquiry was not 'political' in the party sense, it was highly so in relation to the contest which ensued for understanding of what had taken place. Sir Keith Joseph, the then Secretary of State for Social Services, was a Conservative and an adherent of the 'transmission' theory of intergenerational deprivation. According to this perspective, the explanation for the enduring nature of much disadvantage and inequality in society was to be found not in large-scale forces – such as economic inequality, unemployment, poor housing – but in the child-rearing practices of certain social classes which passed, from generation to generation, the faults and inadequacies of one to the next. The purpose of social work, according to this view of the world, was to focus upon individuals, rather than structures, helping – or obliging – those whose own way of life had proved inimical to progress to mend their ways, or risk losing the care of their own children.

While the Colwell case thus promoted a further turn in the wheel of social work's ideological focus, its greater legacy was to be found in the enduring reputation which now clung to the profession for what, in the 1980s and 1990s, came to be known as 'political correctness'. During the Thatcher era social work training and practice had come to place particular emphasis upon what was known as 'anti-discriminatory' or 'anti-oppressive' practice. Social workers were enjoined to 'confront' prejudice – on the grounds of race, gender, sexuality, disability and so on – wherever it threatened to stand in the way of client progress. While these practices became an easy target for right-wing media commentators, the paradox of their appearance at a time of New Right domination can be explained by their close allegiance to neo-liberal preoccupations with equality of *opportunity*. According to this doctrine, society makes most progress when competition for success amongst its members is conducted according to individual effort and merit. Questions of race, gender and so on ought to play no independent part in the valuing of individuals who should be assessed according to their actions rather than their appearance. Close reading of the documents of official government bodies of the period, such as those coming out of the Central Council for Education and Training in Social Work, show a close affinity between this prevailing emphasis and the anti-discriminatory actions expected of social workers. In other hands, however, these tenets were either criticized or were found capable of being stretched to accommodate a very different sort of equality, that of *outcome* rather than opportunity. From this chapter's perspective, the important point to emerge is just how closely the connection between politics and social work emerges across time, and between issues.

Conclusion

This chapter has focused on the political impact of external agencies upon the nature of the duties which social workers are called upon to perform and the ways in which such duties can be carried out. Of course, there is a different form of politics which also has an important impact upon practice, the internal politics of the profession itself. Social work is rightly characterized by debates and disputes amongst practitioners and academics about the nature of the job itself – whether social work is a 'profession' at all, or whether it can just be reduced to a set of mechanical 'competencies' through which the requirements of employing organizations can be implemented. Equally different views are debated as to the *techniques* of social work, those courses of actions which might best be followed in particular cases, and by arguments even about the nature of evidence itself.

The connecting thread between these internal debates and the concerns of the external world is that while these discussions can appear to be arcane or learned most are ideological in character, shaped by fundamental views about the nature of the society in which we live and are, in that essential sense, *political*. Moreover, the outcome of such discussions is political, in the sense that they represent changes in power distribution, between workers and employers, between different service providers or between service providers and users. In all the activities in which social work is engaged, in other words, political considerations shape both the context and the results. Establishing the critical need for an understanding of that formative process, and its direct impact upon the sort of social work we wish to pursue, and the sort of social workers we wish to be, has been the central purpose of this chapter.

Five Key Points

- Social work stands upon some of the most ideologically contested terrain of modern politics.
- Claims that social welfare is 'above' or 'beyond' politics, by governments, organizations or individuals disguises a set of assumptions which are themselves ideological.
- Organizational forms, as well as policy decisions, have political consequences which translate directly into decisions made at individual user level.
- Face-to-face social work always involves power relationships which have an impact upon even the most apparently mundane encounters.
- Social work is characterized by internal political debates about the nature of professionalism and the purpose of action which are linked to wider political forces, by considerations of both ideology and power.

Three Questions

? How does the basic ideological divide between state-as-force-for-good and state-as-source-of-harm have an impact upon social work?

? The framework for social work is set by national and devolved governments, but social work is mainly delivered through local government. How does this political relationship make a difference to services on the ground?

? In what ways can the power differences between providers and users of social work services be described as *political*?

Further reading

1 Jones, C. (2001) Voices from the front line: state social workers and New Labour. *British Journal of Social Work*, 31(4), 547–62.

2 Butler, I. and Drakeford, M. (2005) Trusting in social work. *British Journal of Social Work*, 35(5), 639–53.

3 Powell, F. W. (2005) *The Politics of Social Work*. London: Sage.

CHAPTER 4.3

Gendering the Social Work Agenda

Audrey Mullender

It is not possible to understand the personal or social world without taking a gendered perspective. We cannot intervene appropriately in people's lives unless we see how women remain disadvantaged in contemporary society, and how both men and women are expected to play over-rigid and falsely dichotomized roles. At the same time, it is important both to recognize diversity (bearing in mind the charge that early feminism focused on the interests of middle-class, middle-aged, white, able-bodied, heterosexual women) and to see women as social actors in their own lives, not as passive victims.

Despite major advances, underpinned by sex discrimination and other legislation, women in Britain still lack equal access to social influence – and women who are black, lesbian, disabled, poor or older find their choices doubly or multiply constrained. Women suffer discrimination in relation to education, employment, income, domestic responsibilities, support for caring, and social attitudes and expectations throughout all stages of life. Women are also frequently in danger both in public spaces and in the privacy of their own homes from sexual violence. These are realities that social work must encompass.

Social work itself is far from free of gender discrimination. The majority of service users, informal carers, and staff in the lower grades are female, while the majority of senior managers are men. Social work agencies, like society, are run within operational systems that favour the interests, lifestyles and coping strategies of men (Coulshed and Mullender, 2006). Practitioners, given the chance, can look beyond the pressures of day-to-day work to identify underpinning gender issues that their employing organizations typically ignore (White, 2006).

Child Care

Social work perceives women predominantly in terms of child rearing and yet leaves mothers poorly supported. The majority of lone parents are women and women disproportionately live in poverty, which in turn causes health problems. One in three women experiences domestic violence (Mooney, 2000). Lesbian mothers and disabled women, especially those with learning difficulties, may still have to fight to prove themselves as competent parents. Social work intervention can add to the problems, rather than providing much-needed practical and emotional assistance or routes to safety.

In some respects, women's position is worsening. Prevailing political attitudes condemn teenage mothers, especially those who lack money and a partner. Increased concern about children living with domestic violence has not been accompanied by social work help to make women safer and there is still a presumption that contact with absent fathers is good for children, even where there is a grave danger from post-separation violence (Humphreys and Stanley, 2006).

The recognition that most sexual violence is perpetrated by men alerts us to the threat posed by some male practitioners. A gendered analysis suggests that male workers may be less appropriately able to work with survivors, that male-dominated authorities will be threatened by revelations of the scale of sexual abuse, and that investigative approaches are unlikely to name or tackle abuses of patriarchal power, whether in the family or in the child protection agencies themselves. The avoidance of challenge to male abuse can be seen in family dysfunction theories which deflect responsibility, in accusations that mothers 'fail to protect', and in expecting children to keep themselves safe. Meanwhile, therapeutic work with survivors remains under-resourced, and mothers of abused children are blamed rather than supported.

Community Care

Women have particular needs in the adult care field, in every specialism from AIDS care to substance misuse. An overview of gender issues in the community care context is provided by Orme (2000).

Women as carers

Considerations of gender in community care began with a focus on women as carers which remains real, even today. Although there are also substantial numbers of male carers, they are mainly husbands and mainly elderly. The person who gives up work, leisure or health to care for a dependant is far more likely to be a woman. Minority ethnic carers and lesbian and gay partners who care remain amongst the most neglected groups. The idea that informal carers should have attention paid to their own needs is only slowly influencing practice.

Carers in residential settings are almost all female. The assumption that this automatically makes them suitable for the work blocks access to training, support and promotion. Many black women carry a double burden of caring, acting both as low-paid care or nursing staff and as key family and community supports.

Women and mental health

Women use mental health services more than men, yet diagnostic practice frequently ignores gender issues including ethnic context, treatments can be inappropriate, and psychiatric hospitals too often still lack child care facilities. Amongst the largest groups of women patients are survivors of abuse, but virtually all histories of childhood and adult sexual and physical assaults are missed by psychiatrists.

Women have begun to reject traditional labels and inadequate responses and to name widespread sexual abuse by male therapists and male service users in mixed institutions. Women are setting their own standards and finding their own solutions to psychological distress both within and outside mainstream services. Workshops on agoraphobia or tranquillizer use, eating disorders or depression, groups to develop creativity or empowerment, and alternative therapies all offer healing in a postmodern society where expertise is questioned and individuals seek to become experts about their own needs and health.

Disabled women

Disabled women have particular needs as women, over and above those they have as disabled people. Double oppression can compound feelings of powerlessness, rejection and invisibility. Whereas women are generally stereotyped as wives and mothers, disabled women struggle to be regarded as sexual beings and as capable of parenting. Women with learning difficulties have traditionally been denied sexual knowledge, sexual choices and reproductive rights. Not recognized as being at risk of sexual violence, disabled women may actually be more vulnerable, both in their own homes, where partners and other carers may be abusive, and in care and educational settings. In one disability equality group, every member had had experiences of abuse; one had regularly been indecently assaulted by the driver who transported her to school as he lifted her in and out of the taxi.

Disabled women are increasingly organizing themselves for change, for example through the women's group of the British Council of Disabled People and the Women's Committee of the UK Disability Forum. Organizations like Powerhouse help learning disabled women speak out, whilst Beverly Lewis House in London offers refuge to women with learning difficulties who have been threatened or abused.

Older women

Older women, though growing in numbers, are doubly marginalized on grounds of age and gender. Our youth-orientated society considers their domestic, sexual and economic roles to be over, rendering them socially invisible. Poverty disproportionately results from gendered inequities in pay and pensions, while physical and mental frailty add negative connotations of dependence for some. All social workers can help oppose such ageist attitudes. An exciting innovation would be to run women-only groups in residential settings and day centres for older people, where women predominate. They might well have current issues of discrimination or abuse to share, as well as hugely interesting life stories of changing gender politics in family and society.

Criminal Justice

Male-dominated criminal justice services do little to challenge the conceptualizations of masculinity that are implicated in most crime, despite examples in the probation service of gender awareness and of agendas voiced by women staff. Women's offending is perceived as doubly deviant because it is statistically so much lower than men's and because it is measured in relation to norms of domestic and sexual roles and behaviour, rather than poverty or male coercion. This can have an impact on sentencing, which also pays too little attention to women's responsibilities as mothers. One area of real progress, though, is practice with male perpetrators of sexual violence, who are at last beginning to be held accountable for their behaviour.

Methods and Settings of Intervention

Women are most easily empowered through women-only groups which focus on lived experiences of socially constructed inequalities and ways to challenge them (Cohen and Mullender, 2003). Such groups free women from taking responsibility for men's feelings and communication difficulties. Discussion starts from individual narratives and moves on to draw out broader institutional, cultural and social control and denial of choice. Women recognize, together, that abuse and exploitation are not their personal fault but are endemic in a society dominated by male agendas, which devalues women and their contribution. This leads to decisions to take relevant action for change. Similar principles have been applied to modes of organizing women-only work settings and support for women at work (Coulshed and Mullender, 2006). There are also individual approaches to intervention that recognize women as women (Milner, 2001) and all social work practice can be rooted in principles that strive not to oppress women as mothers, carers, service users or low-paid staff.

Challenges to Men

It is not only women who need to change. The challenge to men is arguably greater as they have more status and power to lose. In social work education and practice, men can usefully come together in groups to work on the emotional barriers to the feminine in themselves – to feelings and vulnerabilities – which drive them towards aggressive competitiveness and, at the same time, keep women and gay men oppressed. Men need to consider how they can better support women colleagues – at every level from campaigning for crèches and sharing the care of dependants, to tackling sexual harassment and violence – and be part of a more appropriate service for women and children and a more confrontational practice with abusive or exploitative men.

Conclusion

We live in a society where there is no such thing as gender balance. Achieving equality in numbers – in organizations, on committees, between group members or facilitators – cannot of itself achieve equity since women carry less social influence, and often less organizationally ascribed authority than men. There is no form of social work intervention and no setting for social work practice where gender does not have a central relevance. Women-only organizations have led the way in helping women feel more in control of their lives and more able to make choices. Women's agendas have posed a challenge to men, too, to stop being the problem and become part of the solution. Gendering the agenda in social work will improve both the employment context and the commissioning and delivery of every type of service.

Five Key Points

- Gender must be on the agenda in every aspect of the organization and practice of social work.
- Women have traditionally been discriminated against by society and its institutions, including social work.
- Women's needs and experiences of life are different from men's.
- Groups and organizations established by women for women and run to women's agendas are the best means of empowering women.
- Men, too, both as professionals and as service users, need to be challenged to rethink their traditional roles and assumptions.

Three Questions

? In relation to your social work practice or your reading about social work practice, ask yourself: What is the gender power analysis of what you are doing? Are there men or male-dominated institutions wielding personal, organizational or social power unfairly over women? How does this integrate with your understanding of other oppressions?

? What difference does it make, to you and to them, that the person or people you are working with is/are male or female, and that you are male or female?

? What can you do to empower women colleagues and service users to have greater safety, more choices and higher self-esteem, and to challenge men to take responsibility for their own actions and feelings and the impact these have on other people?

Further reading

1 Orme, J. (2000) *Gender and Community Care: Social Work and Social Care Perspectives*. Basingstoke: Palgrave.

2 Humphreys, C. and Stanley, N. (2006) *Domestic Violence and Child Protection*. London: Jessica Kingsley.

3 White, V. (2006) *The State of Feminist Social Work*. London: Routledge.

CHAPTER 4.4

Culture, Ethnicity and Identity

Kwame Owusu-Bempah

Due to Western nations' plundering and exploitation of the rest of the world, now euphemistically termed 'globalization', coupled with the USA's unrelenting quest for global dominance (Chomsky, 2004), modern migratory patterns have ensured that every culture, with its language, artefacts and practices, is represented in the UK, as elsewhere. Professional practice in today's multi-cultural, multi-ethnic and multi-faith world must, therefore, reflect this diversity. This chapter examines the influence of beliefs and assumptions about culture, ethnicity and identity on professional practice with black clients. The emphasis is on children and families.

Culture and Ethnicity

A generally accepted definition of culture is that it is a composite structure of the real and the symbolic: beliefs, mythology, religion, ideas, sentiments, institutions and objects of a given group transmitted generationally and internalized in varying degrees by its members. It includes child-rearing practices, kinship patterns and the ethics governing interpersonal relationships. It includes also ideas about personhood: personal identity and group identity.

Although both *culture* and *ethnicity* are frequently used synonymously, there is a conceptual distinction between the two, as the following definitions of *ethnicity* illustrate:

> one of a number of [human] populations . . . which individually maintain their differences . . . by means of isolating mechanisms such as geographic and social barriers . . . an ethnic group may be a nation, a people, a language or a [religion]. (Montagu, 1997, p. 186)

> a distinct category of the population in a larger society whose culture is usually different from its own . . . the members of such a group are, or feel themselves, or are thought to be bound together by common ties of race or nationality or culture. (Morris, 1968, p. 167)

These definitions indicate that there is no single criterion by which *ethnic group* can be defined. They show also that everyone has multiple ethnicity in terms of geographical region, religion, social class, and so forth. Notwithstanding, ethnicity and culture are frequently used by professionals, politicians, the mass media and even the academic community not only interchangeably, but also to connote, and often denote, 'race', 'immigrant' or 'otherness'.

Self-identity

We derive our self-concept from our culture. In Western European cultures, children are socialized to see themselves as autonomous, free from all external control. The child is taught not only to possess mastery of him/herself, but also of everyone and everything, including even time. This conception of the self is alien to most cultures outside the West. Other cultures emphasize interdependence, and so prepare their children for reciprocal relationships in adulthood with the social, physical and spiritual worlds (Wiredu, 1998).

Various investigators inform us that, within the context of world cultures, an actualized person is one who is most deeply connected to others and society as a whole. For example, there are Pacific Island groups who view themselves not as bounded, distinct entities, but as integral pieces of an eternal life scheme (Lesser, 1996); there are Indian cultures where the deep inner self, upon maturity, is not seen as achieving unbridled autonomy, but as merging with the social and spiritual worlds (Roland, 1988); there are African cultures where one is less than human without 'Us', or where the individual seeks the answer to the question 'Who am I?' not only in the question 'Who are we?' but also in the question 'Who were we?' (Owusu-Bempah and Howitt, 2000). In the extreme, there is the Innu (Eskimo) culture that does not even have a word for self-reference (Page and Berkow, 1991). In other words, every culture is a different world with its own idiosyncrasies; meaning that there are as many conceptions of the self as there are cultures. The implications of this for professional interventions which claim to enhance the self-esteem of ethnic minority children in British society, children of diverse and radically different cultural, ethnic and social backgrounds to the therapist's, are clear. It also renders such social work rhetoric as 'black culture' or 'black perspective' nonsensical.

Culture, Ethnicity and Identity: An Interplay

Foster (1998) poses a number of questions to illustrate the fatuity of any attempt to generalize Western theoretical assumptions about culture, ethnicity, identity and psychotherapy. This is one such question:

> How do we figure out the deep self-experience of a Middle Eastern man from a religious sect, who feels that without the tribe he was trained to lead, his self-esteem is unformed, non-existent? Do we view this client through the American self-psychological terms of a narcissistically derailed self, through the Ego Psychology lens of a poorly differentiated self? Or rather, as a person centred in the ensembled self-experience of his Eastern

> culture, where bonding to family and group kinship renders individuals who throughout life are deeply identified with others? (Foster, 1998, pp. 259–60)

Trying to face the hard clinical or practice-related questions posed by such clients forces us to re-examine our assumptions, theory and practice. A good start will be an acknowledgement that we can understand people only by respecting and studying how they understand themselves. People of every nationality, culture or ethnicity seek to understand themselves – their own character, their ways and peculiarities that differentiate them from other peoples.

It is ironic that despite the emphasis on ethnic and cultural restitution as a solution to the structural difficulties facing ethnic minority children in Britain, what passes for and is recommended as culture might best be described as a pastiche of a culture. Perhaps this is unsurprising given the miscomprehension about the nature of culture and ethnicity amongst practitioners. The simple truth is that the culture which practitioners see as a lifeline for their black and ethnic minority children has little or nothing to do with any indigenous culture. These interventions implicitly assume a monolithic culture for ethnic minority groups in British society. This is far from the truth.

Self-identity and Practice with Ethnic Minority Children

Practitioners very often conflate personal, 'racial', cultural and ethnic identities. This is quite apparent in social work where the issue concerning these terms has been hotly contested in recent years. The literature in the area of fostering/adoption is replete with claims that black children in the public care system as well as those fostered or adopted by white families experience more psychosocial developmental problems than other children, including their white counterparts. These problems are routinely ascribed to the children's lack of awareness of their 'black culture' (e.g. Small, 1991). For obvious reasons, this explanation, rather than racism, is favoured by the Children Act.

Although institutional racism is a more plausible explanation for the children's psychosocial developmental difficulties, the accepted solution is to 'work on' the children's self-identity. Many casually accept this practice. Others even advocate it as a necessary anti-racist strategy for social work with black adults as well. Some social services departments have taken these damaging assumptions seriously and have established special clinics to 'repair the damaged self-identity' of black children in their care. Briefly, social work and educational establishments increasingly refer black children to therapists to improve their racial identity or self-concept. Coward and Dattani (1993) drew attention to how child protection case conferences and statutory child care reviews routinely result in requests for professional involvement to improve black youngsters' self-image. Mullender (1991) also described a project designed to improve their self-confidence ostensibly because they are confused about their 'racial identity' as a consequence of being adopted or fostered by white families. Such an approach ignores obvious alternative causal factors, for example separation and loss (Owusu-Bempah, 2006), and attributes the youngsters' difficulties to their colour.

Unsurprisingly, programmes used to achieve this are ethnicity- or culture-based. They include providing the children with information about their 'black cultural background', including information about black historical figures and/or counselling them to identify with 'the black community' and to take pride in their 'blackness' (e.g. Banks, 1992; Maximé, 1994). Such programmes are guilty of victim-blaming (Owusu-Bempah, 1994). Conventionally, biological factors have been evoked to justify the plight of black people. Today psychological (self-identity) and social anthropological factors (culture/ethnicity) provide the excuse. It is no comfort to the children whatever is adduced to justify their difficulties if it remains at the level of the individual (the child or the family) and fails to tackle the structural barriers facing them in the larger society; it matters not a hoot the skin-colour of its proponents, or their intentions.

The programmes assume also that the children experience 'identity-crises' because they have favourable attitudes to the white community. For example, Maximé (1991, p. 103) described a 10-year-old black girl as psychologically disturbed, simply because she preferred 'a white family placement as black ones were all too poor'. Describing this girl's choice as astute, based upon reality, would be more meaningful. However, because of its policy and resource implications, such an interpretation would not be welcome. It would also seriously implicate black practitioners; it would challenge them to work toward dismantling the structural barriers which preclude black communities from providing homes and support to their young members who need such help and support, instead of colluding with the system by rationing and administering palliative measures to these children, including psychotherapy. As such, one must be forgiven for suspecting an (unwitting) coalition of conspiracy or interests (Owusu-Bempah, 2003).

As the above case (Maximé, 1991) shows, the programmes also equate 'non-affiliation' with one's ethnic group with psychological damage warranting intervention. It may be rather helpful to regard such behaviour as an example of 'negative identification'. Erikson (1968) saw negative identification as neither always nor necessarily harmful; and so must not be interfered with unnecessarily. Furthermore, it suggests that the identity crises (personal, ethnic or cultural) which black children are presumed to experience may be caused by adults' (notably social workers' and therapists') preconceptions and over-reaction to their exploration of aspects of different cultures to their own. This type of exploration or experimentation must be seen as a normal developmental process, given the variety of ways of life they are exposed to, as a result of growing up in a 'global village'.

Because 'race', culture and ethnicity are endemic in these programmes they confuse self-identity with ethnic/cultural identity. There is a distinction between the two concepts.

- Self-identity refers to an individual's sense of uniqueness, a unique personal property – what sets person A apart from person B; although a culture is shared by all its members, each member experiences it in a unique way, resulting in individual personalities.
- Ethnic or cultural identity relates to group identity, a 'racial', ethnic, cultural or social reference-group.

Owing to the confusion surrounding these concepts, ethnic minority groups are often presented as culturally homogenous, belonging to a single, monolithic culture shared by all ethnic minorities, regardless of their national or geographical origins. This illusory posture is likely to diminish the efficacy of programmes and practices in meeting clients' individual needs, or even harm them. Social workers' handling of Victoria Climbié's case is a crystalline example (Owusu-Bempah, 2003).

Negating the Other's Self-definition

The offspring of black and white unions are particularly singled out for pathologizing by helping professionals. The popular belief that identity crises are endemic to children of black and white unions is obviously no more than a racist assumption (Owusu-Bempah, 1994, 2005; Owusu-Bempah and Howitt, 1999). It is the ghost of the 'marginal man' evoked to haunt these children, to justify our unfair treatment of them. The notion of the 'marginal man' holds that they owe their marginal status in a racist society, and its concomitant social, economic and psychological disadvantages, to their inability to integrate their 'racial', ethnic and cultural identities. In modern British society, it is claimed that their psychological salvation lies only in identifying with the so-called black community (Maximé, 1994; Small, 1991). Is this not a reification of the 'one drop rule'? (Owusu-Bempah, 2005)

Systematic activities to deal with this putative psychological disturbance involve, explicitly or implicitly, denying their white side, a process which many of the children find emotionally painful, damaging and undesirable (Tizard and Phoenix, 1993/2002). The underlying assumption is equally paralogistical, as well as bizarre: if it is acceptable for these children to identify with their black side, what is problematic about their identification with their white side? Who should decide which aspects of their heritage should be significant to them, the children or those who want them to see themselves as 'black'? Briefly, which 'racial', ethnic or cultural side of their inheritance they feel comfortable with is largely determined by their own experiences and the subjective meanings of those experiences to them; denial of the 'black' label, or group-rejection, is not necessarily symptomatic of a personality disturbance. Numerous empirical studies using a wide variety of procedures over the last several decades support this view (e.g. Cross, 1991; Wilson, 1987). It is an irony that those professionals who try to foreclose these children's identity at the same time claim to subscribe to human diversity, ethnic and cultural diversity.

Allen (1997) argues that identity, like 'race', ethnicity/culture, continues to loom large in the practitioner–ethnic-minority-client relationship, to the virtual exclusion of structural factors because:

> The [Western] concept of the self as a separate, atomistic, private, autonomous individual has been constituted by specific, complex, social, economic, historical, cultural and psychological relations . . not only is [it] philosophically inadequate, but also serves neo-colonial and imperial goals of domination. (Allen, 1997, p. 9)

Bhavnani (1994) agrees with this view in describing the concept of intelligence as a psychological tool of subjugation, domination and control. In social work, as in other social institutions, 'race'/ethnicity has historically served this purpose. It is now unacceptable to espouse overt racist theories to justify the provision of second-class services to ethnic minority clients. Invoking 'black inferiority' under the guise of ethnicity, culture or identity serves this purpose safely. It does so more expediently and effectively because, as the literature reveals, it has the support and cooperation of ethnic minority professionals, particularly social workers, teachers and therapists.

Black Culture, Black Perspectives

What social work model is needed to provide appropriate services to diverse populations? One common way of dealing with this is to highlight practitioners' poor knowledge and understanding of the cultures of ethnic minority clients. This offers the expedient solution of establishing units of ethnic minority 'experts' to service ethnic minority communities; black-on-black practice is an obvious example (Owusu-Bempah, 2003). Apart from holding ethnic minority workers responsible for solutions to the structural problems facing ethnic minority clients, it is deskilling. Owing to modern migratory patterns, the population of the UK (like that of any nation) comprises numerous ethnic and cultural groupings. The excessive demands (implicit in the Children Act) that would be placed on any practitioner wishing to be competent to know something of the cultures of all sectors of society can be illustrated, for example, by briefly examining language – one of the key elements of any culture. Knappert (1995) estimates that over a thousand different languages (discounting dialects) are spoken in Africa alone. No practitioner could be expected to understand even the beliefs and practices relating to health, illness and psychological functioning of so many different cultures. It is, therefore, not surprising that issues of race, culture and ethnicity often cause anxiety both in everyday social exchanges and in the activities of practitioners.

Is cultural or ethnic/colour match a solution to the difficulty? Although a practitioner may be knowledgeable about a particular culture or language, factors such as social class and status differential may also militate against professional effectiveness. The use of ethnic/cultural match does not automatically ensure effective outcomes. We saw the dire consequence of this in Victoria Climbé's case. The practitioners' professional background and training, based on Western values and assumptions, such as those regarding the 'normal' individual or 'healthy' family, may offset any gains from ethnic/colour match (see Owusu-Bempah, 2003). Furthermore, the sharing of ethnicity by professionals and their clients does not always exclude the intrusion of stereotypes. Hall (1997, p. 645) argues that 'not all the perpetrators of cultural errors are white'. Again, this reminds us of the cultural misjudgement by Climbié's key social worker.

Of course, there are training models designed to prepare practitioners for effective work with ethnic minority clients. Characteristically, however, such training has been dominated by issues of 'race', ethnicity and culture (and 'political correctness'). It must be stressed that this can easily lead to feelings of insecurity amongst practitioners whose sense of a lack of competence in matters of ethnicity and culture can make them feel deskilled; it may also serve as an excuse for professional inertia.

This emerged in the Victoria Climbié Inquiry (Laming, 2003). Additionally, training programmes and practices which over-emphasize ethnic/cultural issues can be criticized for lacking a clear conceptual framework or for trying to use simplistic and formulaic methods to solve complex structural problems. Cacas (1984, p. 465) called such models and practices 'cultural *generalizations*, when the practitioner assumes that all presenting problems are related to the client's culture/ethnicity rather than to other factors'.

Conclusion: Closing Gaps

The UN Convention on the Rights of the Child emphasizes that the goal of child care practice should be to achieve equality for *all* children, whoever, whatever and wherever they may be; that it should aim at closing social, educational and economic gaps; an important goal of child care practice must be to reduce social inequalities; the removal of discriminations, especially normative discriminations which are covertly institutionalized. Ascribing ethnic minority children and their families' difficulties to their colour, ethnicity, culture or psychological functioning, and dealing with them through psychological means is an admission of institutional racism, of 'racial' inequality in society.

The focus of social services departments has been on describing and explaining ethnic-minority-service-users' 'pathology'. Pollard (1989) has suggested an 'empowering' two-pronged approach to work with ethnic minority children and families, and other disadvantaged families. The approach distinguishes between 'alterable' and 'static' variables. 'Alterable variables' relate to factors in a person or the environment which can be manipulated somehow to enhance their functioning. 'Static variables' represent factors that are not easily changed, but only classify or label people; ethnicity, culture and self-identity are examples. In the case of children in care, for example, the 'alterable variables' approach seeks to:

- identify those children who seem to be thriving in the system and determine what factors are associated with their resilience;
- identify those factors within the system or environment which deleteriously affect, as well as those which enhance, their functioning.

This framework requires a positive attitude towards ethnic minority families, such as identifying, fostering and encouraging their strengths. It is similar to Wakefield's (1996) eco-systems approach to the social work assessment process. Both approaches are different from the problem-family/client model which pathologizes even the strengths of these families, such as the extended family structure, and adoption/fostering within the community.

While it is unlikely that few practitioners would assume a monocausality to problems in black childhood, for instance, their failure to identify clearly what distinguishes a racial/ethnic or cultural identity problem from any other causes means that the boundaries are fuzzy and that culture, ethnicity or identity may be blamed unnecessarily. A preoccupation with skin tone, ethnicity/culture is likely to obscure the assessment process resulting in misinterpretations of ethnic minority clients' needs and the provision of inappropriate services to them.

Five Key Points

- Assumptions about 'race' culture, ethnicity and identity have a negative impact on service-provision for ethnic minorities in British society.
- British society is a complex web of cultures.
- Conceptually as well as in practice, 'black culture' is a nonentity.
- Providing effective services to diverse populations requires cultural competence more than cultural knowledge.
- Helping professionals face a formidable task in a world in constant flux.

Three Questions

? There is no empirical foundation to own-race adoption and fostering policies and practices. Discuss.

? What is the relationship between 'race', culture, ethnicity and self-identity?

? An important goal of social work must be to reduce social inequalities. Discuss with reference to ethnic minority clients.

Further reading

1 Owusu-Bempah, K. and Howitt, D. (2000) *Psychology beyond Western Perspectives*. Oxford: Blackwell.

2 O'Hagan, K. (2001). *Cultural Competence in the Caring Professions*. London: Jessica Kingsley.

3 Okitikpi, T. (ed.) (2005). *Working with Children of Mixed Parentage*. Lyme Regis: Russell House.

CHAPTER 4.5

Families

Graham Allan

Since the early days of industrialization, the decline of family life has regularly been lamented. Throughout this time, pleas to 'strengthen the family', to preserve 'family values' and to ensure that the next generation is properly socialized have been ever-present. Such moral and political rhetoric can undoubtedly be influential in shaping legislative action which directly affects the welfare of different families. For example, the state's actions in 'policing' and monitoring the behaviour of families through its various agencies, including social work, health visiting and other services, help to shape the boundaries of what constitutes acceptable family relationships. So too, regulations governing welfare benefits and tax advantages have a noticeable impact on family well-being. Yet claims made about the demise of family life have generally misrepresented the real character of the changes occurring. Not only has historical analysis demonstrated that contemporary family dilemmas – domestic violence, child abuse or family dissolution – are not new, but as importantly, families continue to be seen by those involved as arenas in which personal security and emotional satisfaction can be expected, if not always achieved.

Confusion often arises within popular discourses because change in family organization is frequently viewed as inherently negative. Romantic visions of the past are glorified, so that almost any change gets defined as damaging. Yet precisely because family relationships are both personally and socially significant, family organization cannot be expected to remain static. Any social institution which is central to the workings of a society is necessarily integrated with other key aspects of economic and social structure. Consequently, that institution must itself alter as these other aspects are modified under new social and economic conditions. In this regard, dominant family forms cannot remain constant and still be institutionally significant. They must change to reflect transformations in other spheres of social and economic activity. From a sociological angle, this is the key to understanding family life: family organization is inevitably patterned by the wider social and economic formation, even if ideologically the family is presented as being separate and apart – a cosy private domain located in an increasingly threatening public world.

Changing Families and Households

In Britain over the last thirty years, as elsewhere in the Western world, there have been radical changes in the demography of family life (Allan and Crow, 2001; Lewis, 2001b). While debate continues about whether these changes reflect a genuine reordering of family relationships – between parents and children, husbands and wives, and wider kin – three areas of change can be identified as particularly significant.

First, there have been major changes in patterns of coupledom and family formation. Aside from gay couples now being more accepted, the growth in cohabitation has been particularly remarkable. According to the data available, relatively few people cohabited outside of marriage until the early 1970s. The typical pattern was one of youthful marriage following a formal engagement which often involved elements of a sexual relationship but stopped well short of living together. Currently, cohabitation has not only become the dominant form of engagement in that most couples now do cohabit prior to marriage, but as importantly, increasing numbers of couples now cohabit whether or not they are planning to marry. For example, only 11 per cent of non-married women aged between 18 and 49 were cohabiting in 1979; by 2002, the figure was 29 per cent (General Household Survey, 2004). From being a stigmatized form of coupledom, cohabitation has become a normal phase, receiving social approval rather than opprobrium. Moreover as cohabitation has increased, it is now becoming evident that there has been a concomitant decline in marriage. This is not just an issue of later marriage but also one of people choosing not to marry at all. Officially it is estimated that by 2031 some 46 per cent of the adult male population and 39 per cent of the adult female population will never have married, compared to 35 per cent of adult men and 28 per cent of adult women in 2003 (Government Actuary's Department, 2005). The figures were far lower a generation or so ago when roughly 90 per cent of people married.

The second major change has been the growth in levels of partnership separation and divorce. While legislative change has clearly facilitated increased divorce, the

Table 1 *Selected family changes in England and Wales, 1971–2001*

	1971	*1986*	*2001*
Number of first marriages	320,347	220,372	148,642
Women's average age at first marriage	21.4	23.1	27.7
Number of second marriages	84,390	127,552	100,585
Rate of divorce per 1,000 marriages	5.9	12.9	13.0
Children under 16 of divorcing parents	82,304	151,964	146,914
Number of lone-parent families[a]	570,000	1,010,000	1,750,000[b]
Percentage of all births to unmarried mothers	9.2	21.4	40.0
Percentage of teenage births to unmarried mothers	25.8	68.9	89.4

[a] These figures are for Great Britain.
[b] This figure is for the year 2000.
Sources: http://www.statistics.gov.uk/ (Birth Statistics Series FM1; Marriage, Divorce and Adoption Statistics Series FM2); Haskey, (1998); Haskey, (2002).

root causes go far deeper, reflecting – and in turn encouraging – fundamental shifts in the ways people define a satisfactory and acceptable marriage. Over time, there has been considerable movement in what Cancian (1987) usefully terms 'marital blueprints'. These have developed to emphasize the expectation of intimacy and mutual fulfilment through the quality of the couple relationship itself. A failure in this regard within a relationship is increasingly recognized as grounds for reconsidering its future (Jamieson, 1998). The result is that some 40 per cent of those marrying this year will divorce – more if the divorce rate continues to increase as it has been doing. Moreover each year, some 150,000 children under the age of 16 experience their parents' divorce. In addition, increasing numbers of children whose parents cohabit are also experiencing parental separation without this being officially recorded. Debates continue about how children's interests can be best protected during the process of parental separation and divorce (Richards, 1999).

Third, there have been major changes in patterns of child-bearing. As well as women having children later, there is far less expectation that mothers should be married. In 1973, only 9 per cent of all mothers, and 28 per cent of teenage mothers, were unmarried. Thirty years later, these figures had risen to 41 per cent and 90 per cent respectively (Office of Population and Census Surveys, 1974; Office for National Statistics, 2004c). While some 63 per cent of unmarried mothers are cohabiting with their child's father at the time of the birth, this is by any standards a mammoth demographic shift in a single generation. It reflects the changed social vision about the place of marriage (and divorce) within society and altered images of what individuals, and especially women, should be striving for in constructing their personal lives. Together with increased levels of partnership separation and divorce, it has contributed to major increases in the number of lone-parent families.

Because of these and other associated changes in family patterns – including increased numbers of remarriages, repartnering and stepfamilies – new approaches to analysing family life have needed to be developed (Silva and Smart, 1999; Lewis, 2001b). In the past, social science discourses were often based around some notion of 'the normal family'. While the relationships, domestic roles and kinship responsibilities of these 'normal' families were not static, they were nonetheless characterized by what now seems a curious sense of uniformity. This was best captured by the notion of the family or domestic cycle through which families typically passed: marriage; child-bearing; child-rearing; the 'denuded' family once children had left home; and the death of one of the spouses. At the beginning of the twenty-first century, such images of 'normal' families have become increasingly problematic. What has emerged is a higher degree of diversity in family patterns and a greater variation in the pathways different families follow. This has repercussions for how 'normal' families are defined (Allan and Crow, 2001).

With increases in cohabitation, in childbirth outside marriage, in divorce, and in remarriage and stepfamily formation, there can be no assumed or standard familial pathway. Recognizing that these factors can affect people's experiences in both childhood and adulthood, it is evident that over the course of their lives different people follow quite distinct family pathways. So it is reasonable to talk of 'family course' or 'family pathway' but it is not sensible to think in terms of structured, patterned family careers that are common for the majority of people in the way that the notion of 'family cycle' implies. Yet in recognizing this, it is important to be aware that different pathways have implications for the family issues and problems which people face and which influence family decisions. There is no suggestion of randomness in this; family life may not follow a tidy schema, but earlier household and family structures still impact on later experiences.

Because 'the family' appears at nearly all times to be seen as under threat and in need of protection and strengthening, many of the issues which have rightly concerned social workers should be recognized as matters which indicate less a fall in public and private standards and more the emergence of new discourses and practices about the ways family relationships should be ordered (Morgan, 2004). In analysing the emergence of these 'problems', it becomes apparent that demographic change and family organization are only part of the process. What also matters is the interplay of moral, political and professional responses to the difficulties families of different forms face.

Many of the 'family problems' with which social workers have to grapple – child abuse, marital breakdown, domestic violence, family support for elderly people – are discussed elsewhere in this book, so will not be considered here. Instead the focus is on one particular 'issue': the growth of lone-parent families and the development of different understandings of these families. Examining the 'social construction' of lone-parent families illustrates some of the means by which aspects of family life become problematized within public discourses and highlights the dangers of too readily generalizing about the consequences of particular family and household structures.

Lone-parent Families

The numbers of lone-parent families have increased substantially from 0.6 million in 1971 to nearly 1.8 million in 2000. In 1971 there were approximately one million dependent children in lone-parent families, but by 2000 this had increased to 2.9 million (Haskey, 2002). It is probable that these trends will continue for some time. This represents more than a quarter of all households with dependent children living in them, compared to 8 per cent in 1971 (General Household Survey, 2004). Of course, these figures are 'snap-shots': they represent the number of adults and children in lone-parent families at a given time. Others will have experienced living in lone-parent families, but now be independent or part of stepfamilies through cohabitation or (re-)marriage.

Just as family life in general has become more diverse, so the experiences of lone-parent families are also varied (Rowlingson and McKay, 2002). Many factors influence the circumstances in which they operate. However, the single most common characteristic of such families remains poverty; despite significant changes in policy, material disadvantage is the norm. Only a minority of lone-parent families has sufficient resources to manage comfortably. In particular, female-headed lone-parent families, which comprise 90 per cent of all such families, are especially likely to be experiencing financial hardship. In 2002 Bradshaw reported that nearly three-fifths of all children in lone-parent families were living in poverty (Bradshaw, 2002, p. 135), with children in these families comprising half of all children in poverty (see also Rowlingson and McKay, 2002). The reasons for this include the low level of women's earnings, especially for those women with few qualifications; the pattern of mothers in Britain re-entering the labour force in a part-time capacity; and the difficulties of securing adequate child-care provision, despite important policy initiatives since the late 1990s. Thus even though there has been an increase since 1997 in the number of lone parents in employment – 56 per cent in 2005 – this employment is often low paid and insecure. Moreover in 2005, there were 1.2 million children living with lone parents where the parent was not in employment, the vast majority of whom were dependent on benefits (Department of Work and Pensions, 2005; Evans et al., 2004).

Lone-parent families tend also to be disadvantaged in terms of housing. One indicator of this is the disproportionate number living in rented accommodation rather than owner-occupation. In 2002, nearly two-thirds of lone-parent families lived in rented housing compared to less than a quarter of other families (General Household Survey, 2004). Similarly, lone-parent families are three times as likely as other families to be living in flats rather than houses (22 per cent and 7 per cent respectively). They are also generally likely to have less space and fewer household amenities than do two-parent families. Moreover many of those with least resources live in more run-down urban areas with poorer schooling, health care and other services (Rowlingson and McKay, 2005).

Social concern for lone-parent families has a long history, much of it less than progressive. The welfare of children in such families is a recurring theme, but so too is the burden of support which the state bears. In the mid-twentieth century, welfare measures aimed at increasing social participation and citizenship rights, including the development of health, education and income support services, covered lone-parent families just as much as any other family and household forms. However, there was at this time a sense in which lone-parent families were seen as pathological and in need of extra support. A metaphorical red light flashed in the minds of social welfare professionals in their dealings with lone-parent families, warning them that special provision might be necessary.

As the number of lone-parent families increased, this potentially stigmatizing professional benevolence became less marked. The red light no longer flashed, certainly not as brightly. Instead there was greater acceptance of the 'normality' of lone-parent families and a recognition that many of their problems were caused by poverty rather than family disorganization or personality disorders. Yet concern with reducing state expenditure since the 1980s has led to the 'problem' of lone-parent families being redefined. The high dependence of lone mothers on state benefits and state housing, the increasing numbers of divorces and births to single mothers, and the apparent failure of non-married fathers to accept financial responsibility for their children resulted in the state seeking ways to limit its commitments. Policies have been developed, especially since 1997, to encourage more lone mothers to find employment and greater pressure has been placed on non-residential fathers to make adequate financial contributions to their children's needs. The Child Support Agency was created in 1993 to police this and enforce compliance by aberrant fathers, in an effort to reduce the costs which the state bore in providing financial support to lone-parent families.

By the beginning of the twenty-first century, continuing concerns over social exclusion and inadequate socialization had 'politicized' lone-parent family issues further. For a period in the mid-1990s, the idea of 'underclass' captured popular concerns about the interplay between individual pathology and social divisions. Although the underclass was not restricted to lone-parent families, some, in particular young unmarried mothers and those who had been dependent on state support long-term, were certainly seen as core to it. Like earlier notions of 'cultures of poverty' and 'cycles of deprivation', the concept of 'underclass' highlighted the idea that children lacking the benefits of a 'normal' family environment come to be socialized into dysfunctional patterns of behaviour and hold sub-cultural values at odds with those of the mainstream. These discrepant values and behavioural patterns, instilled into the next generation thereby supposedly perpetuating the underclass, are then seen as a principal cause of poverty. While such views – not least the idea of lone mothers rejecting values associated with the material and other benefits of coupledom – have been heavily criticized in academic research, the main issue concerns the ways in which public visions of particular family forms and particular family problems are modified within a changing socio-political climate.

The emphasis on 'social exclusion' introduced by New Labour governments since 1997 focuses more on structural issues and personalizes social disadvantage rather less. Moreover, with the continuing demographic changes there have been in family life, lone-parent families are now culturally accepted more as a variant rather than deviant family form. Yet a tension nonetheless remains, especially with regard to those lone-parent families headed by young mothers with fewest resources. These mothers are often still portrayed as feckless and irresponsible, and as playing a 'welfare state' game for the housing and other material benefits they can accrue. Yet it is evident that these families experience significant hardship, constantly struggling to manage on inadequate resources. This has clear consequences for the well-being of both the women and children involved. Not only are they effectively excluded from many of the activities defined as socially normative, they are also disadvantaged in a range of other ways which exacerbate their more immediate problems of coping with economic deprivation. For example, the correlation between poverty and poor health is firmly established, as is the link between educational underachievement and deprived material background. It is not surprising then that these families are likely to be defined as 'problem families' and to require disproportionate amounts of support from health and welfare agencies.

Conclusion

As the social and economic basis of society alters so too does the structure and organization of domestic and reproductive relations. With the increasing separation of sex, marriage and child-rearing, the complexity of family relationships has undoubtedly increased. This in turn is reflected in popular imagery and language about family patterns. New ideas evolve about what is appropriate for families and what is problematic. However, not all the new complexities of family life attract the same public concern. While some lone-parent families have continued to be problematized, other family matters which generate equal levels of personal concern and potentially have an impact on children's development are left largely outside public action.

Consider particularly the increasing number of stepfamilies. Research has pointed to the complex dynamics inherent in these families. Certainly for children the advent of a new 'parent' can raise all manner of emotional tensions, resentment and ambiguity. To develop successfully, these relationships require considerable investment and understanding. Yet the state apparently regards the formation of stepfamilies as unproblematic, if anything viewing them as 'solutions' to the problems of divorce and lone-parenthood. Thus there are relatively few official services provided for people entering stepfamilies, even at the level of protecting the interests of children. These families are defined as 'normal' and as quite capable of meeting their own needs without additional support. In many respects the 'problem families' continue to be defined as those in poverty who rely on state welfare benefits and public housing. Caught in a vortex of material disadvantage, there is an ever-present tendency to redefine their problems in terms of their own personal inadequacies, despite all that is known about the difficulties of sustaining family well-being with inadequate resources.

Five Key Points

- In recent years the diversity of family life has increased.
- There have been radical shifts in patterns of family formation and dissolution.
- Changes in family and domestic relationships need to be understood in the context of other social and economic changes.
- Poverty continues to be a common experience for the increasing numbers of lone-parent families.
- Economic and political factors influence the processes through which 'families with problems' become defined as 'problem families'.

Three Questions

? How can the processes of divorce and stepfamily formation be best managed from the viewpoint of children?

? What role does state action, including the activities of social welfare professionals, play in shaping domestic life?

? What impact has the decline of marriage had on social work practice?

Further reading

1 Allan, G. and Crow, G. (2001) *Families, Households and Society*. Basingstoke: Palgrave.
2 Lewis, J. (2001) *The End of Marriage? Individualism and Intimate Relations*. Cheltenham: Edward Elgar.
3 Rowlingson, K. and McKay, S. (2002) *Lone-Parent Families: Gender, Class and State*. Harlow: Prentice Hall.

CHAPTER 4.6

Sexuality and Sexual Relationships

Siobhan Canavan and Seamus Prior

Sexuality issues in social work practice are legion. We may quickly identify a wide range of areas of social work practice where sexuality issues arise. For example:

- the loss of intimacy for an older person who loses a partner either because of bereavement or admission to residential care;
- the sexuality of vulnerable adults living in the community;
- the sexual abuse of vulnerable adults in residential settings;
- sexual behaviour between children and young people;
- inappropriate sexual behaviour of some people with dementia;
- the sexuality of social workers and the impact of this on their practice;
- the exposure of children to parental sexual behaviour;
- the sexual abuse of children by trusted adults, including care workers;
- the housing of sex offenders in local communities;
- the placing of adults in mixed sex wards or care establishments at a time of psychological or physical vulnerability.

Sexuality presents one of the most complex and emotive areas in which social work professionals are required to make assessments and decisions. The general proliferation of sexual expressiveness in the media has not necessarily been matched by an increased individual capacity to reflect on and discuss sexual thoughts, feelings and behaviours. Although issues relating to sexuality are rarely the main reason for people coming into contact with social work agencies, they are often inherent and implicit in direct practice with service users. While sexuality issues evoke taboos and provoke anxiety, service users require of their social workers the facility to engage in the contemplation and discussion of sexual issues both to promote the service user's healthy sexual development and to protect them and others from harm. Service users may look to their social workers to initiate conversations on sexuality and workers need to develop the requisite skills to engage in these issues without being intrusive or causing unnecessary anxiety. There are four main areas in which social workers need to be aware of issues relating to sexuality and sexual relationships: first, they have a role in supporting service users in their sexual choices and preferences; secondly, they have a statutory role in protecting vulnerable people from sexual exploitation; thirdly, they need to be aware of not making assumptions regarding sexuality or sexual activity; and fourthly, they are required to demonstrate cultural sensitivity in this terrain.

Recent years have seen the construction of a more comprehensive body of knowledge on topics relating to sexuality and related aspects of social work practice. This may be a consequence of better training, publicity relating to sexual exploitation and a more open society in which matters relating to sexuality are more widely debated. The worker's own sexuality is also significant, as is the organizational context in which social work practice is carried out. With a professional commitment to practice which addresses issues of power, difference and diversity and the requirement for a sound knowledge base for practice, the imperative for an individual worker to address issues relating to sexuality is considerable. Here, we offer an overview of some issues which might be considered when thinking about sexuality and social work practice, starting with a consideration of the complexities of the issue.

Defining the Territory

Sexuality is a significant part of our lives although we may want to debate the usefulness of assuming that there is a common set of ideas about sexuality when the concept is so differently expressed between cultures, from one person to another and at various points in history and in a person's life course. The emergence of social movements concerned with sex and sexuality – the gay movement in particular – have challenged ideas about sexual preference, identity and choice. Feminism too has exposed the multiple forms of domination of women in the sexual arena – sexual violence and harassment, the language of sexual denigration and abuse. It has also posed questions about reproductive rights, sexual desire and pleasure. In all of this we are challenged to rethink the nature of our understanding about sexuality and the interconnectedness of influences and forces that shape our emotions, needs, desires and relationships.

Irrespective of their sexual orientation, young people in their teenage years have common issues relating to being in relationships, making informed choices about choosing whether to become sexually active or not, and practising safer sex. Many young people feel coerced into sexual activity because of peer pressure and they will need support if they make different choices from their peers. Others may go through a process of questioning their sexual orientation. For example, young people who have difficulty in acknowledging a sexual orientation other than straight, may have behavioural problems which lead to them coming into care. If the young person has experienced same-sex feelings or relationships they will need sensitive work and support. They may experience victimization by other children, compounding an already fragile sexual identity. If staff have not looked at the issue in training they may believe that there is something wrong with being lesbian or gay and pathologize the young person rather than offer them the support which they need. Social workers need to recognize that many adolescents question their sexual orientation and may need support in this process. If a young person identifies as gay or lesbian, for example, they may need support if faced with family disapproval or rejection. They may also need help in developing a social network.

There are four different, but related themes which are helpful in locating sexuality and its relationship to sex and gender. First, there is its biological and physical base. It includes sexual arousal, the act of having sex, responding to sexual stimuli and fantasy and relating to other people. As such, the sexual response is physiological, located in the body's reactions. Secondly, there is the question of the function of sexual activity in any relationship, whether it is a casual encounter, a long-term partnership, consensual or not. Not only can it be a way of expressing intimacy, love and affection, it can also be used as a way of exerting power or inflicting pain. This takes us into the arena of sexual abuse and exploitation. Thirdly, there is the question of the way in which feelings are managed in sexual relationships. A knowledge of psychology and human relationships can help here, as can the knowledge about the effect of childhood experiences on adult sexual behaviour. Fourthly, there is a need for an understanding of the relationship between sexuality, power and gender.

Self-awareness, Sexuality and Gender

The confidence and competence with which social workers are able to address issues of sexuality are largely dependent on the extent to which they have worked on their own issues around sex, sexuality and sexual relationships. It is essential that they have an understanding of their own sexuality, no matter how confused or unsettled this feels. This means recognizing the extent to which their sexuality has been affected by their history and the personal significance of gender, class, faith beliefs, age and ethnicity. Understanding ourselves is vital to the process of understanding others and in the area of sexuality this has particular significance when social workers are called on by their clients to respond to a range of issues including sexual preference, sex education, sexual exploitation, sexual violence, problem pregnancies and choosing whether or not to be sexually active.

Sexuality issues cannot be understood or appreciated without reference to gender. The increasing public awareness of child sexual abuse perpetrated by male care workers has had the cumulative effect of inhibiting male social workers from addressing sexual issues which arise in their practice. Men may be concerned that raising sexual matters with managers or colleagues will be judged inappropriate or indicative of a sexual motive on their part. In direct work with service users, men are rightly cautious that references to sexuality may be misinterpreted by service users, especially those with a history of sexual abuse. Anxiety in relation to sexuality may leave male workers feeling professionally deskilled and personally vulnerable, especially when their work involves providing intimate personal care. At the same time there is an unquestioned assumption that women are comfortable with providing personal care for men. A failure to grapple with, and find a way through, this discomfort and anxiety may result in traditional gender roles being reinforced, leaving women with the burden of personal care and the responsibility for addressing issues relating to sexuality or the body, further perpetuating the anxiety that men are not to be trusted in these areas.

Workers need to be clear about how their personal value base in relation to sexual issues may converge with or diverge from ethical and responsible practice. For example, when it comes to light that a 15-year-old boy in care is accessing Internet pornography, the worker's own attitude to pornography may affect what is regarded as an appropriate professional response. A male social worker who uses pornography unquestioningly in his private life may minimize the potential harm of this activity to the young person, advocating for the young man's rights to privacy, autonomy and freedom of expression, based on an unarticulated assumption that pornography is both ubiquitous and a normal part of male adolescent sexual development. This worker may not be able to undertake the assessment required in this situation to gauge the nature, content, frequency and circumstances of the young person's use of pornography and its consequential impact on his thinking, feelings, attitudes and behaviour.

Social workers with strong faith beliefs which condemn homosexuality need to address how they can promote the healthy sexual development of their lesbian, gay, bisexual or transgender (LGBT) service users. From another perspective, social workers who are personally very committed to LGBT equality issues need to be cautious that they do not inadvertently encourage service users who are questioning their sexual orientation to 'come out' when they are not ready to do so, when they may be exploring the possibility of same-sex attraction rather than identifying themselves as LGBT.

Social work, Sexuality and Vulnerable Adults

While, previously, vulnerable adults were cared for in institutions, where sexual behaviour could be prevented or minimized through prohibition, punishment and supervision, or covered up in an organizational culture of denial and silence, community care has now placed the sexuality of vulnerable adults under the public and professional spotlight. Social workers face ethical and moral dilemmas in balancing an adult's right to freedom of sexual expression with their responsibility to protect vulnerable people from exploitation. These dilemmas are highlighted in the situation of a sexually active adult woman with a learning disability living in the community. While she may be content in what she regards as a fulfilling and consensual relationship, others may see her as being ruthlessly exploited for the sexual gratification of another. If this is a heterosexual relationship, there is the further complication of potential pregnancy, raising issues of the service user's right to parenthood, their parenting capacity and the protection of a child born into such a situation. These circumstances have led some social work departments to seek permission through the courts for sexually active women with learning disabilities to be forcibly sterilized. The rationale offered in defence of these actions is that it offers protection to the women from the trauma of pregnancy and the responsibilities of child-rearing and that it is an effective form of contraception. So here the granting of rights in two areas – integration into the community and the right to have intimate relationships – is paid for by the denial of rights to reproduce and to parent.

Sexuality and Young People

One of the most sensitive areas for children and family social workers is the assessment of sexual behaviour between children. Research has shown that children and young people are as likely to be abused by other young people as by adults, calling into question the common assumption that sexual behaviour among young people may be regarded as playful or developmentally appropriate, a normal part of growing up (Cawson et al., 2000). Social workers need to be able to distinguish between sexual behaviour which is mutually consenting, exploratory and age-appropriate and that which is coercive, exploitative and abusive. Key to such assessment is the capacity to discuss sexual behaviour and feelings with children, young people, their parents and carers, and to evaluate the subjective meanings which young people attribute to sexual incidents in which they are involved. Assessment and intervention need to balance the rights of the young person to privacy and freedom of sexual expression and the responsibility invested in social workers to protect children from harm. Young people also need to learn to be responsible in their sexual behaviour and to know that they have the right to choose not to be sexually active, when peer and media pressure make this difficult.

The complexity of this area is seen in the provision of residential care where young women who may be accommodated on account of their vulnerability to sexual exploitation are placed in settings with young men who may pose a significant risk to them. A natural tendency to regard young people in the care system as casualties of troubled family histories may result in professional reluctance to make a realistic assessment of the risks that they might pose to other vulnerable young people. Workers may be torn between the desire to protect young people from the further stigmatization that the label 'a potential risk to others' might impose and their duty to ensure that others are adequately protected. This dilemma, reflected in the ongoing care versus control debate, may be acute in relation to young people with learning disabilities who exhibit concerning sexual behaviours.

Social workers seeking care placements for children have to make careful judgements in relation to how much information about a young person is passed on to other professionals. They need to balance the young person's right to privacy in relation to sexual behaviour or abuse and the placement family's or residential unit's right to be fully informed of potential care needs and risks. These decisions are often made in the context of placement scarcity and the reluctance carers may have to accommodate children and young people with a history of sexual behaviour or abuse. The anxiety which is provoked in adults by children's sexuality is often managed through silence and denial. Social workers, practising within a legal framework, need to be able to contemplate and discuss young people's sexual thoughts, feelings and behaviours, while teams and managers need to provide an environment where these taboo-laden subjects may be aired in order that appropriate assessments and decisions are made.

Sexuality and Older People

Despite a significant increase in the older population, there is still a reluctance to consider older people as sexual beings, with specific sexual and intimacy needs.

Older people who come into residential care may have partners who are still living in the couple's home. In this situation both people are facing significant losses which need to be taken on board as one person is admitted to residential care. The loss of separation, physical ability, independence, company, social networks and privacy are all present and will have implications for the way in which both people in the couple manage the transition. Residential care and nursing homes have few facilities for couples, whether the relationship is part of a person's life already or has developed within the care home. Admission to residential care also poses challenges for privacy in relation to personal care, the meeting of intimate sexual needs and control of private space. The personal and professional attitudes of care staff in relation to older people as sexual beings who are of a different generation with its own social mores further complicates this dynamic.

Working with people with dementia poses challenges as some people may begin to display sexually uninhibited behaviour towards staff and other residents. Not only does this cause distress in the living environment but family members and friends will need support in witnessing these unexpected and often shocking interactions.

Sexual Abuse and Residential Care

There are three reasons for service users to expect the highest of standards in these contexts of care. First, when children or vulnerable adults are entrusted to care provided or purchased for their safety, they have an undeniable right to an assurance that they will be as safe as humanly possible. Secondly, care systems should alleviate the adversity already experienced by service users, not compound it. Thirdly, service users in residential settings are particularly vulnerable, as an abuser operating in this context is likely to gain access to large numbers of children or vulnerable adults to abuse, and some abusers may deliberately gravitate to social care work for this reason. Police checks will identify only a small number of abusers since, in common with sexual abuse in other contexts, the abuse is more likely to go unreported and the abuser undetected.

Social Work with Sex Offenders

Social work with alleged and convicted sex offenders is a particularly challenging area of practice in which practitioners need to be highly aware of their motivations and the potential impact of the work on themselves. The persistent topicality of sex offender-focused stories in the media, epitomized by 'naming and shaming' campaigns, highlights the extent to which the sex offender has become the predominant 'other' in the public mind. People quickly take up polarized positions in relation to the risks offenders may pose: for some, offenders should be given the benefit of the doubt, regarded as humans who had lapsed and should be forgiven, or are even seen as the victims of malicious false accusers; for others, all offenders pose ongoing extreme risks such that their rights and freedoms should be significantly curtailed. Social workers are required to work on a daily basis with the risks inherent in the assessment, care and rehabilitation of sex offenders. They have to relate in a meaningful and helpful way to a person who is entitled to respect and consideration, yet who has also committed (or allegedly committed) deeply disturbing acts against vulnerable others and may continue to be dangerous in this respect. Managing the anxieties associated with the risks, uncertainties and dual responsibilities in this situation, without resort to stereotyping, punitive thinking or emotional dissociation, is no mean feat.

Sexuality in Social Work Training and Organizations

Within the social work training context, the learning environment needs to address both process and content – not only what is taught about sexuality but how it is taught. The creation of a safe, boundaried yet challenging learning environment is crucial, so that both tutors and students can develop their self-awareness on this topic of significance for personal identity and professional practice. Decisions that tutors and students make about how open they are about their sexual orientation, for example, raise important questions. The assumption of heterosexuality is pervasive. To be out at work as a gay, lesbian or bisexual tutor or student is both a personal decision and a political act. Some would argue that not to come out is colluding with the oppression which is being challenged through anti-oppressive practice and is itself a form of internalized homophobia. A counterargument is that uncertainty caused by not revealing sexual preference might be more effective in challenging expectations and assumptions.

Since December 2003 an individual is now protected from discrimination on the grounds of their sexual orientation under the Employment Equality (Sexual Orientation) Regulations 2003. Previous equality acts did not address this type of discrimination specifically. In recent years, as it has become more acceptable for LGBT social workers to be open about their sexual orientation in the workplace, an unspoken assumption has emerged in some teams that LGBT staff are more confident in dealing with sexual issues because of their personal development in coming to terms with their own sexuality. An unequal division of labour may occur where the service users for whom sexuality issues are more prominent are allocated to the lesbian and gay social workers who are seen to be, and may see themselves as, more comfortable dealing with sexual issues. The potential for ghettoization, discrimination and reinforcement of stereotypes is evident.

A healthy social work team in a practice setting or in the academic context is one where gender and sexuality issues can be addressed, not only in relation to the service users, but also in relation to the dynamics of the team itself, providing opportunities to address the unspoken assumptions and possible taboos which may underlie the team's day-to-day operation.

Conclusion

Although not explicit in the new professional standards and codes of practice, social workers have a personal and professional responsibility to work on their own issues around sex, sexual relationships and sexuality if they are to practise in a responsible and ethical way. This demands a high level of self-awareness, being comfortable with the language of sexual expression and being able to talk explicitly about sex. This will inevitably mean that long-held views may be challenged but, equally importantly, it means that the social worker will be more open to others who are struggling to express doubt, distress and anxiety in relation to sexual matters. None of this is easy. It is likely to be fraught and messy at times. It will, however, go a long way towards ensuring that social work clients and social workers themselves are understood and supported in matters relating to their sexuality and sexual relationships.

Five Key Points

- Training on issues relating to sex, sexuality and sexual relationships is crucial for ethical social work practice.
- A high level of self-awareness in relation to sexuality is important for ethical social work practice.
- Social workers need to consider sexuality issues in different contexts and across the life course.
- Sexuality offers an important arena for discussion and exploration of issues of difference, diversity and power.
- Sexually abusive behaviour occurs in a myriad of ways in social work organizations.

Three Questions

? What personal work are you aware you need to do in the area of sex, sexuality and sexual relationships in order to enable you to practise more effectively?

? How might social work practice around sexuality and sexual relationships take into account issues relating to difference, power and diversity?

? What professional boundaries in relation to sexuality have you encountered in your practice? How have these been addressed by you by the organization in which your work took place?

Further reading

1 Richardson, D. (2000) *Rethinking Sexuality*. London: Sage.

2 Wilton, T. (2000) *Sexualities in Social Care: A Textbook*. Buckingham: Open University Press.

3 Dominelli, L. (2002b) *Anti-Oppressive Social Work Theory and Practice*. London: Palgrave Macmillan.

CHAPTER 4.7

Psychology and Social Work

Brigid Daniel

Psychology is often defined as 'the scientific study of behaviour'. It is essentially a discipline or field of study that uses scientific methods to develop a body of knowledge about human behaviour. This knowledge is then applied by clinical, educational and occupational psychologists.

The spread of subdisciplines and theoretical strands can be bewildering but what does characterize psychology, is the emphasis upon an empirical approach that involves systematic, scientific and objective observations. Such observations may be obtained in many different ways that can be broadly classified into three types:

- Non-experimental methods that obtain correlational data to help find patterns of behaviour and include, for example, interviews, surveys and case studies.
- Experimental methods that look for causes of behaviour by varying one or more independent variable.
- Quasi-experimental methods that also explore causation by measuring variables that cannot be directly manipulated, for example by comparing younger and older people's memory skills.

Whatever the method, psychology aims to be rigorous. In this respect it has much to offer the current social work endeavour to move towards evidence-based practice.

Social workers are people who work with people. At the very heart of their work lies the ability to use interpersonal skills, based upon their knowledge of human functioning, to help, support, protect and empower people in distress. Therefore, psychology is fundamental, both as a tool for practice and for understanding the dynamics of practice. Consider the following:

> A social worker visits a household after an anonymous referral alleging that the mother of the children is a drug addict and that the children are neglected. At the house three generations of the family are encountered: two children who appear undernourished,

to have very limited language skills and to be out of parental control; the father, who is known to have a criminal record for violent behaviour, who looks deeply unhappy and says nothing; the mother who speaks to the social worker, but whose speech is very slurred; the father's mother who is very unkempt and appears confused.

From the first contact a number of questions might go through the social worker's mind:

- Are the children developmentally delayed?
- Has the mother a problem with drugs?
- Is the father depressed?
- Is the father's mother showing signs of senile dementia?
- What is the motivation of the anonymous caller?

Psychology can offer information about each of these issues. The broad academic subdivisions that offer most to social work include developmental psychology, social psychology and abnormal psychology. Most social workers will be uncomfortable with the term 'abnormal' psychology and may prefer to use the operational term 'clinical' psychology.

A different set of questions relate to the areas that would be most useful for the social worker to explore when making the assessment and deciding how to intervene:

- Is the mother physiologically addicted to drugs?
- Are there ways in which the parental environment maintains the children's difficult behaviour?
- Is the father's depression related to negative thoughts and beliefs?
- Could the mother's own childhood have affected her current behaviour?
- Would it be helpful to allow the grandmother space to describe her views about her situation?

Psychology has developed five main theoretical approaches to the study of behaviour: biological, behaviourist, cognitive, psychodynamic and humanist. All five of these theoretical approaches have influenced social work and all are associated with particular methods of intervention. The subdisciplines already described have all, to a greater or lesser degree, been approached from each of these five theoretical directions. It is this complex interweaving of broad areas of study and different approaches to study that can make psychology a rather bewildering discipline from which to garner clear messages for practice. The situation is further complicated by the fact that a different theoretical approach can be used to guide intervention than was used to understand the reason for the problem.

A final set of questions is:

- What impact will the social worker's first impressions have upon future decisions and actions?
- Do the parents have any particular stereotype of, or prejudice against, social workers?

- How will the social worker and other professionals interact at any subsequent meetings?

Social psychology can help provide insight into these questions that relate to the underlying factors impinging upon the process of social work.

In summary, therefore, psychology underpins social work in three main ways:

1. It provides a wealth of information about human functioning, including development across the lifespan, social interactions and psychopathology.
2. It offers a number of theoretical strands that can be used both to guide assessment and to plan intervention.
3. It illuminates the kind of common psychological errors that can impinge upon, and undermine, effective practice.

The Biological Approach

The biological approach is based upon materialism, that is, the view that the mind and body cannot be split. The assumption is that all behaviour has a physiological basis and that the key to understanding human behaviour lies in studying human biology. Physiological psychologists study all aspects of human biology, but the primary focus has been upon the study of the central nervous system and related systems.

Different areas of the brain that relate to particular functions have been mapped. The effects of head injuries that damage specific areas of the brain provide further evidence of the links between brain activity and behaviour. The effects of different drugs on mood and behaviour help with the understanding of chemical processes in the brain. It may seem that such information is relevant only to the medical profession, but for example, it can help the social worker in the above scenario to know that the grandparent's confusion may have a physiological basis so that appropriate referral for further assessment can be made. Similarly, an understanding of the physiological effects of addiction to and withdrawal from drugs can guide the provision of appropriate support.

The effects of the mind on the body can be illustrated by the work on the physiological impact of stressful life events. There is a significant link between the number of life events a person experiences and the likelihood of developing some form of physical illness. The current view is that a range of social and environmental factors impact upon the body's immune functions in a way that increases vulnerability to illness.

People with a history of childhood abuse have a higher risk of developing post-traumatic stress disorder in response to trauma in adulthood, perhaps due to the physiological effects of childhood trauma. Social workers are not in a position to diagnose or treat physiological effects but the knowledge that these processes occur can help the planning of prompt intervention to reduce trauma in childhood and in the recognition of the potential need for support for adult survivors of childhood trauma. The social worker in the case scenario can be helped by the knowledge that severe childhood neglect can lead to developmental abnormalities in the neuronal pathways in the brain.

Much clinical psychology is underpinned by advances in drug treatments for mental disorders such as depression and schizophrenia. The efficacy of such drug treatments attests to the biological underpinnings of some mental disorders although the details of the physiological aspects are not fully understood.

The 'nature–nurture' debate about the relative impact of inherited characteristics and of environmental influences has a long history. A range of methods have been used to study genetic influences including twin studies that allow comparisons of variations in characteristics between identical and non-identical twins; and the comparison of characteristics between twins reared together and reared apart.

This area of study has been associated with vigorous and, at times, acrimonious debate because of the ways that genetic arguments have been (and, in some cases, continue to be) used to justify classist, sexist and racist views. There is now a general consensus amongst psychologists with the interactionist view that both genetic and environmental factors affect behaviour.

The notion that behaviour such as criminal behaviour has a genetic component is a highly influential one. Eysenck (1977), for example, believed that much of personality is due to variations along two innate personality dimensions, neuroticism and extraversion, and that people who score highly on both are most likely to become involved in criminal activity because they are impulsive and do not respond well to reward and punishment. The belief that criminal behaviour has a strong genetic component leads to the view that the best response is containment but it is a theoretical approach that is not drawn upon heavily within criminal justice social work.

Behaviourist Approach

The behaviourist approach is based upon the assumption that behaviour is learnt and shaped as a result of environmental circumstances. This approach attempts to explain behaviour by studying observable responses rather than by looking for internal processes. Those practitioners who work from behaviourist beliefs apply the principles of learning when trying to change behaviour patterns. Two main strands of empirical work have contributed to the current state of knowledge about learning. One springs from Pavlov's work on classical conditioning and the other from Skinner's work on operant conditioning.

Pavlov's ground-breaking work began in the early 1900s. He was initially studying digestive processes in dogs and showed that salivation was a reflex response to the arrival of food. He then tried ringing a bell every time the food was presented. In subsequent tests the dog would salivate at the sound of the bell, without the presence of food. In behavioural terms, the dog normally shows an unconditioned response (salivation) to an unconditioned stimulus (food), in the presence of a neutral stimulus. Subsequently, after the process of classical conditioning the dog shows a conditioned response (salivation) to the conditioned stimulus (bell ringing). From this very simple paradigm have sprung a myriad of variations and an explanation for the development of phobias. Wolpe (1973) developed a treatment for phobias that is still widely used. Based on the fact that two reflexes cannot co-exist, systematic desensitization aims to replace the fear reflex (conditioned response) to the feared object with a relaxation reflex.

Operant conditioning describes the way in which voluntary behaviour (as opposed to reflex behaviour) changes as a result of environmental consequences. On the basis of his experiments on cats Skinner (1958) proposed that the probability of a voluntary response increasing depends upon it being reinforced by some type of reinforcer. This is now known as the ABC approach, in which Antecedents cue the start of Behaviour that has a Consequence that reinforces it. Skinner believed that all behaviour could be understood by looking in detail at the contingency of reinforcement, that is, the way in which behaviour depends on the reinforcer. The system of reinforcers is quite complex and is frequently misunderstood or simplified. The simplest types are a reward to increase behaviour (positive reinforcer) or a punishment to decrease behaviour (negative reinforcer).

Operant conditioning techniques have been applied in many ways in social work. Behaviour that appears bizarre can often be understood when a careful analysis of the consequences is carried out. For example, the children in the scenario may be receiving positive reinforcement for demanding behaviour in the form of additional attention from the parents. The most effective intervention is not to remove attention, but to increase the amount of attention during times when behaviour is more desirable.

Cognitive Approach

The cognitive approach seeks to describe the processes that mediate between external stimuli and behaviour. It grew from a sense that behaviourism could not fully explain phenomena such as insight. It is a disparate theoretical approach that includes the study of memory, perception, language, problem-solving, social cognitions and so on.

The study of memory has distinguished between the processes of recognition of previously seen information and recall of previously stored information. Memory is currently understood to consist of three stages, sensory memory, that is an initial buffer; short-term memory, which only has a short retention span; and long-term memory. Such concepts are used in clinical psychology to help identify the type of memory loss in brain damage or dementia. Such knowledge will also be helpful for the social worker planning care for a client with memory problems.

Memory recall occurs by a combination of retrieval and reconstruction. The study of such processes and the ways that context and suggestion can affect them are useful for social workers. For example, there is a considerable body of work on the reliability of child witness testimony that is crucial for child abuse cases. Such evidence suggests that in some circumstances children's memories may be better than adults' for information that is very familiar or distinctive to them. Younger children tend to provide less detail and less information about events, but as they get older their accounts become similar to adult levels of free-recall. Children rarely report something that has not happened but younger, especially pre-school children, can be more susceptible to suggestion.

It is suggested by cognitive theorists that language development is based on an innate language acquisition device (Chomsky, 1972). The study of language development shows children actively working out the rules of grammar. Clinical and educational psychologists are skilled in assessing language skills; however, it would be helpful for the social worker in the scenario to have an overview of the stages of language development.

One of the most well-known cognitive theories in developmental psychology is Piaget's stage theory of cognitive development. He proposed that two processes drive development with the aim of achieving equilibrium between the world and mental representations. These are assimilation, by which new information is integrated, and accommodation, where existing representations are changed to incorporate new information. Piaget (1952) described four stages of cognitive development that culminate in the ability to think abstractly. Despite challenges to details of the theory, it remains conceptually helpful.

Kohlberg (1969) also used the cognitive approach to help with the understanding of moral reasoning. His six-stage theory proposes that children move from morality based upon obedience to those in authority towards reasoning based upon the recognition of the role of intention and of laws. Some people move towards reasoning based upon values that transcend laws. There is evidence that some young people who become involved in delinquency and aggression show immature types of moral reasoning.

Social psychology has also benefited from the cognitive approach. With a series of experiments on aggression Bandura (1973) set out to explain the role of modelling in learning. He hypothesized that imitation influenced behaviour and tested this by creating situations whereby children observed an adult acting either aggressively or non-aggressively towards a large doll. When the children were subsequently frustrated by removal of some toys, those who had observed the aggressive behaviour were more likely to behave aggressively themselves. He therefore suggested that learning can be influenced by modelling. People are more likely to imitate people they like, respect and see as successful.

Modelling is seen as one of the key factors in the development of prosocial behaviour; children whose parents act kindly are more likely to be kind themselves. Social workers can make extensive use of the theory, both to understand how some behaviour has developed and for intervention. They can, at times, themselves act as models for appropriate behaviour (Howe, 1987).

The cognitive approach to the understanding of behaviour has led to cognitive behavioural theory, one that is becoming very significant for psychologists and social workers. Researchers such as Ellis (1962) hold that behaviour is influenced by the way people perceive and think about themselves and the world. He uses an ABC approach, where the Activating event triggers a faulty Belief, that in turn triggers an emotional Consequence and problems arise from faulty cognitions. He developed rational-emotive therapy in which faulty cognitions are replaced with rational ones. Intervention based upon these principles is used in clinical psychology, especially for the treatment of depression, and increasingly in social work. The approach is also helpful for understanding low self-esteem and self-efficacy in children who have been abused or neglected. If children are convinced by perpetrators that they are to blame for the abuse they are likely to develop faulty cognitions about being bad and guilty. Intervention can focus on changing these cognitions.

Psychodynamic Approach

To many, psychology is equated with the psychodynamic approach, so powerful has its influence been (Freud, 1910). It was also the first psychological theory that social workers drew upon. Fundamental to Freud's approach was the attempt to explain the internal processes that motivate behaviour. Freud's belief was one of psychic determinism, that is, that all behaviour has a cause that is to be found in the mind. As a result of his work with patients with hysteria he postulated that the mind has a conscious aspect which contains all the thoughts and feelings that we are aware of; and a subconscious part that has two levels: the preconscious from which thoughts and feelings can be accessed by choice, and the unconscious that holds repressed thoughts and feelings. According to Freud, the personality consists of three parts. The id, largely in the subconscious, is the source of the basic drives of libido and aggression and is governed by the pleasure principle. The superego, most of which is conscious, holds the internalized views of authority figures and acts as the 'conscience' trying to inhibit the id's drives. The ego, largely conscious, mediates between the id, the superego and the outer world. In order to cope with the tensions resulting from competing demands of the id, superego and outer world, the ego deploys a range of defence mechanisms. Anna Freud developed the notion of defence mechanisms further (1958).

Freud located adult pathology within faulty psychosexual development. He delineated five stages in the development of the expression of sexual drive energy: the oral, anal, phallic, latency and genital. At each stage the child has to resolve conflicts between the id, ego, superego and outer world. The way that the parent responds to the child is crucial to the successful resolution of conflicts. Problems of development are the result of the maladaptive use of defence mechanisms.

The psychodynamic approach has influenced all disciplines of psychology. Developmental psychologists have used Freud's theories to explore the impact of early experiences upon the development of adult personality. The theory that aggression is an innate drive has been employed by social psychologists attempting to understand conflict. Clinical psychology has drawn upon the view that dysfunction is due to unhealthy defence mechanisms.

Two main other strands of psychodynamic theorizing have affected social work. One strand, known as ego psychology, is represented by Erikson. He incorporated cultural factors and devised eight psychosocial stages characterized by conflicts, beginning with the trust versus mistrust conflict in the first year. Many social workers find Erikson's (1959) stages helpful in guiding their practice. For example, the worker in the scenario might consider whether the grandparent has problems with the final conflict of integrity versus despair.

The other strand, known as object relations, focused on the early development of the ego in personal relationships with significant others. Bowlby's attachment theory is from this tradition and has been hugely influential in social work theory and practice (Bowlby, 1969, 1971). Although his initial emphasis upon the primacy of the mother has since been challenged, the idea that children need a secure attachment for healthy development underpins much child care and protection work. It is highly unlikely that the social worker in the scenario would not be beginning to assess the children's relationships with the parents.

Yelloly (1980) provides a detailed account of the influence of psychoanalysis upon social work. She asserts that psychoanalytical thinking led to a more compassionate approach to mental illness and criminal behaviour because it challenged the Victorian view of people as morally autonomous that was associated with a culture of blame and censure. It also underpinned the development of case work, a technique that is still used. Yelloly (1980, pp. 121–2) lists six ways in which the social work value system was affected:

1 the primacy given to affective (rather than cognitive) elements of behaviour;
2 the central role ascribed to unconscious psychological determinants of behaviour;
3 the greater emphasis given to inner psychological processes than to social factors in explaining behaviour;
4 the stress on infantile life and its importance for the development of a personality;
5 a heightened sensitivity to psychopathology;
6 a belief in rationality, and a reliance on insight as a major strategy of intervention in therapeutic change.

Humanist Approach

In contrast to Freud's theory, the humanist approach is optimistic. It is also phenomenological in that it states that to understand behaviour it is necessary to understand the person's individual subjective experience. Behaviour is not determined purely by biology or by past experiences, rather people have a sense of purpose, are free and act intentionally. The empirical evidence to support this approach is largely gathered from case studies.

Rogers (1951) and Maslow (1954) are two of the best known humanist psychologists. Rogers identified the actualizing tendency which is the human drive for growth and self-enhancement. Each individual has cognitive structures for the 'self' and for an 'ideal self' that represents what one aspires to be. When the self and the ideal self are similar the individual experiences a state of congruence, but when they are very different the experience is of incongruence. The development of congruence is supported by social factors:

- the need for positive regard;
- conditions of worth – self or other imposed conditions for the earning of positive regard;
- introjection of values – incorporation of conditions imposed by others into the ideal self.

The best conditions for growth are:

- unconditional positive regard;
- openness (or warmth);
- empathy.

These concepts are applied in clinical practice. Rogers developed client-centred practice (later person-centred) based on the premise that the client knows what is wrong and what needs to change. The helping process hinges upon developing a relationship of equals and by aiming to provide the conditions of worth.

The concept of respect for the person and understanding of the subjective experience is a helpful model for practice, for example with people with disabilities, because it is based on a partnership rather than paternalistic model. It is also a common model for play therapy with abused and neglected children.

Maslow's focus was upon healthy rather than pathological personality development. He suggested that people's behaviour is motivated by a hierarchy of needs. First, there are those that drive behaviour by their absence. These deficiency motives are:

- physiological;
- safety;
- love and belongingness;
- esteem.

Overlaid on these are metaneeds for growth that impel the individual on a path of *self-actualization*.

Within social psychology both Roger's and Maslow's theories propose that violent behaviour is neither an innate drive, nor a simple behavioural response, but is the result of making a choice to respond aggressively. Maslow's theory has been applied to the understanding of the role of unmet needs in both victim and perpetrator psychology in criminal justice (Ainsworth, 2000).

Table 1 maps out the interactions between the different theoretical approaches and the different disciplines, with some practice examples.

Process of Social Work

Precisely because social workers are people working with people, their own psychological make-up affects the process of social work. The cognitive approach to social psychology has shown that in any human interaction people make cognitive shortcuts. Whilst helpful in allowing quicker information processing, such shortcuts undermine objectivity. They include:

- selective attention;
- group polarization;
- stereotyping.

Another is the fundamental attributional error: the tendency to underestimate the influence of situational factors when interpreting other people's behaviour and to overestimate the importance of internal factors.

In a study of the reports of enquiries into child deaths, Munro (1999) found a number of common psychological errors of evaluation that can have potentially fatal consequences:

Table 1 *Theoretical approaches and disciplines*

Approach	*Causes of behaviour*	*Treatment*	*Examples*		
			Developmental	*Social*	*Clinical*
Biological	Physiological	Treat physiological causes	Appreciate physiological effects of childhood trauma	Contain criminals	Refer those with mental health problems for drug treatment
Behaviourist	Environmental reinforcement	Create an environment where reinforcers support required behaviour	Use behaviour management for conduct disorder in children	Use positive reinforcement to encourage pro-social behaviour	Behaviour modification for phobias
Cognitive	Cognitive processes	Replace negative automatic thoughts with rational reasoning	Change thoughts and beliefs underlying low self-esteem in abused children	Guard against attribution errors of assessment	Help a person with depression to overcome negative thoughts
Psychodynamic	Unhealthy defence mechanisms due to problems of psychosexual development	Develop insight into causes of behaviour	Ensure that a child has the opportunity to develop at least one secure attachment	Help a violent criminal to sublimate aggressive drive through art	Help an anxious person to gain insight into the impact of childhood trauma
Humanist	Incongruence between what people feel they are and what they feel they should be; unmet needs	Provide conditions for growth; ensuring needs are met	Provide non-directive therapy for a traumatized child	Help a criminal to find appropriate ways to meet needs	Help a person with low self-esteem to become self-confident

- being resistant to changing one's mind, and failing to revise risk assessments;
- paying greater attention to evidence that supports one's own beliefs;
- looking for evidence to support one's beliefs;
- being less critical of supporting evidence than of challenging evidence.

Thus, social work can benefit from psychological insights into the ways that human functioning can impact upon professional functioning.

Pitfalls of Drawing Exclusively upon Psychology

Although it is clear that psychology has much to offer social work, the wholesale adoption of psychological theory is not without potential problems. For example, there is a tendency to individualize problems and locate them within the person, whilst not paying sufficient attention to wider factors. This tendency has been described by Rose (1985) as the 'psy complex'. So, a further set of questions that the social worker could ask about the family in the scenario is:

- Is the family's income adequate to clothe and feed two children?
- Is the accommodation suitable for their needs?
- What access do the parents have to formal and informal support services?
- Do the family members feel integrated into the community?

Because psychology is based heavily upon the construction of norms, there is a danger that people who deviate from the norm are considered to be 'abnormal', even though a norm is only an average of the spread of possibilities. When the norm becomes that which is desired and normative there is a danger of labelling people as deviant, even when they represent part of the natural diversity of human beings.

This has particularly been the case when it comes to the understanding of the psychology of black people (Robinson, 1995). The flourishing of a black perspective in psychology is one attempt to address this problem, and the challenge for social workers is to ensure that they draw upon this material and avoid perpetuating institutional racism.

Potential

Psychology does, clearly, offer a huge amount to social work, but the potential is probably not fully realized. Training in social work covers some psychology, but it is such a vast subject that only some of the basic principles of psychology and some areas such as human development can be addressed. However, it can be guaranteed that for every human problem the social worker encounters there will be a body of relevant psychological research.

Five Key Points

- Psychology is the scientific study of behaviour and is characterized by empirical research.
- Social work can make use of three main disciplines of developmental, social and cognitive psychology.
- Psychology underpins social work in three ways: by providing evidence-based knowledge, by offering theoretical approaches and by helping with the understanding of the process of practice.
- The five main theoretical approaches are biological, behaviourist, cognitive, psychodynamic and humanist.
- The use of a psychological approach must be balanced by knowledge from sociology.

Three Questions

? What arguments are there to support and refute Nicolson and Bayne's (1990) statement that 'social work is a branch of applied psychology'?

? How can social workers ensure that their use of psychological theory does not lead them to individualize problems to the exclusion of consideration of wider ecological influences?

? There is no doubt about the lessons that social work can learn from psychology, but in what ways could social work influence the direction of psychological research?

Further reading

1 Milner, J. and O'Byrne, P. (2002) *Assessment in Social Work*. Basingstoke: Palgrave Macmillan.

2 Glassman, W. E. and Hadad, M. (2004) *Approaches to Psychology*. Buckingham: Open University Press.

3 Nicolson, P., Bayne, R. and Owen, J. (2006) *Applied Psychology for Social Workers*, 3rd edn. Basingstoke: Palgrave Macmillan.

PART 5

The Human Life Cycle

CHAPTER 5.1

Infancy

Gillian Harris

The period of infancy is usually defined by developmental psychologists as being the first two years of life. There are many focal points of study in this field, but perhaps one of the most interesting questions we can ask about infants is: How and when do they become social beings? When do they begin to recognize others? And when does the first relationship form between the infant and caregiver?

One of the main problems with studying infants is that it is difficult to measure their skills and preferences. We cannot rely on verbal response or even upon controlled motor movements in the early months. Research carried out on early developmental preferences has, therefore, to rely upon certain assumptions. These are: that the infant will turn or orient towards pleasing or familiar stimuli; that the infant will preferentially look at pleasing or familiar stimuli; that the infant will modify its sucking response to experience pleasant or familiar stimuli; and that when the infant is bored with (or has habituated to) a known stimulus, it will preferentially respond to a novel stimulus. Most studies of newborn infants rely upon these methodologies.

Early Development

The infant is born with certain innate preferences which are usually for salient stimuli within the environment that have survival value. The most salient stimuli are those that are linked with other humans, in that infants are relatively helpless for many years and must attract another to care for them. Newborn infants have specific perceptual preferences for speech-type sounds and for visual stimuli which, if grouped together, comprise face-type configurations. Newborn infants also prefer sweet-tasting solutions. This means that the neonate prefers stimuli associated with the caregiver: human speech, the human face and, of course, breast milk – which is sweet.

Following birth, and even in some cases prior to birth, there is a period of very rapid learning in which the infant learns to identify known tastes, smells, sounds and faces. The newborn infant shows a preference for the mother's voice, the mother's face, and the smell of the mother's milk. This does not mean that the infant recognizes the mother, but that the infant prefers things that are familiar. Innate neonatal preferences can also be modified very rapidly by learning if this modification has survival value. If an infant is given bitter-tasting milk from birth, then because the bitter taste is associated with a positive calorie intake, the infant will learn to like it, even though infants usually find bitter tastes aversive.

Although the infant seems to prefer the known properties of the mother, this does not mean that a relationship has formed. There is no evidence to support the idea of early 'bonding' between infant and mother, despite the findings by Klaus et al. (1972) which seemed to support the 'bonding' hypothesis. More recent studies do not support the idea that early contact between infant and mother has a beneficial effect upon mothering behaviour in the long term (Svejda et al., 1980).

Given the dangers of the birth process it would give the infant no advantage to become attached to the biological mother at or immediately after birth. In fact, the newborn infant does not appear to show any signs of specific pleasure in the mother's presence or distress at separation from her. This absence of early attachment means that the first relationship does not have to be with the biological mother; it does not even have to be with a female adult. Research has shown that men can and do react to and interact with infants in the same manner as women, especially where they have had experience in caregiving (Field, 1978). Infants can form an attachment to their fathers even if they do not form an attachment to their mothers. In extended families, infants might form an attachment to family members other than the main care provider. The early preference shown by the infant for the caregiver seems to give the appearance of social intent and makes the caregiver feel that the infant recognizes them. As a result, the caregiver is more likely to feel attached to the infant, and to provide care.

Social Cognition and Attachment Formation

In order to decide whether or not an attachment has formed between infant and caregiver we must observe and measure infant behaviours; but which behaviours are likely to indicate that an attachment has formed?

One affiliative behaviour, smiling, is present from birth. The neonate will smile in response to various internal and external stimuli that are found pleasing. The smile gradually becomes more discriminatory until it is only observed as a response to social stimuli – that is, other people. Eventually, the smile is reserved only for familiar people. This only tells us, however, that the infant can discriminate between those who are known and those not known.

A better indicator of attachment is thought to be distress at separation, a behaviour not observed until about 6 months, when the infant will cry if left by the primary caregiver. Similarly, discriminatory responses, which are fear responses directed towards a stranger, are not usually observed until around 10 months. This 'fear of strangers' response is less marked if the 'stranger' looks familiar to known caregivers, behaves in a positive manner to the infant or if the caregiver behaves in a positive manner towards the 'stranger'. This is possibly because the infant is able, at this age, to match internal representations of known adults with the external representation of the stranger, and find a mismatch. We could say that, at this age, the infant is able not only to recognize but to recall images of absent caregivers. In effect the infant has achieved *person permanence:* the child is aware that the caregiver continues to exist when out of the sight of the infant, and has an existence separate from that of the infant.

We would expect that the concept of person permanence would be attained at about the same age as *object permanence* – the understanding that objects continue to exist when out of sight of the infant. It was thought by Piaget (1952) that infants did not attain object permanence until the age of 18 months. But the task that infants were asked to do in his studies was quite complex and mapped onto other abilities that possibly do not develop until the second year. If we look at research studies carried out on purely perceptual tasks (Baillargeon et al., 1985) then the infant seems to be able to understand that objects continue to exist even though they can no longer be seen, and that the objects have certain immutable properties in that one cannot pass through another. In a far simpler task (Hood and Willets, 1986), 6-month-old infants were observed to reach out for objects in the dark that they had observed in the light. Infants do then seem to develop concepts of object and person permanence at around the same time. We might also say that to be able to form an attachment to someone it is necessary to be able to sustain a memory of them in their absence. Research studies certainly suggest that infants retain some memory for events which are experienced as early as 10 months (Fivush, 1994).

Infants of 10 months are able not only to recognize familiar caregivers (including siblings) but to remember sustained patterns of interaction specific to each caregiver. Infants can play elaborate social games with familiar others: games of 'give and take', games of 'hide and look'. During these games, the infant is able to predict the partner's behaviour, to attempt to elicit such behaviour and to respond to it appropriately. Caregivers usually also respond in quite a specific way to infants. Not only do they engage in specific 'games', but all adults and 'experienced' children use a unique form of speech and behavioural mannerism when interacting with infants and young children. The speech style, sometimes termed 'motherese', uses lots of exaggerations of pitch and speed, with questions, imitations, repetitions and extensions of the infant's own utterances. This speech style acts mainly as an attentional marker for the infant. When someone uses such a speech style the infant is more likely to react to them and interact with them. The behaviours which accompany this speech style, such as exaggerated facial expression and extensive eye contact, also serve to engage and maintain the infant's attention within the dyadic interaction. In this way the infant learns not how to talk, for that ability is innate, but how to structure social interactions with others and what to expect from others. When strange adults use this familiar style of interaction infants are less wary of them; if strangers address or behave towards them in the usual 'adult' style of interaction then the infant will be more wary. The infant is also able, from the age of 10 months, to use the caregiver as a source of information – they can engage in social referencing (Feinman and Lewis, 1983). And although we might say that an infant of this age is not fully aware of another's mind state, infants are able to interpret the adult's emotional expression. If an adult smiles at, or behaves positively towards, a stranger then the infant will be less wary of that stranger.

Attachment Classifications

Infants of 10 months or so show separation distress, are more discriminatory in affect, smile more at the people with whom they are familiar and are more wary of strangers; and these are all behaviours which we would expect to observe between adults where an emotional bond has formed. It is assumed, therefore, that by this age infants are likely to have formed attachments, and that attachment behaviour between infant and caregiver can be measured. There is one standardized measure of infant–adult attachment that is most frequently used in research studies; the procedure is called the 'strange situation', and was first devised by Mary Ainsworth (Ainsworth et al., 1978). It is usually carried out when the infant is mobile, at about 14 months, and entails monitoring the infant's behaviour during a series of manoeuvres in which the mother (or father) and a 'stranger' alternately leave the room and return. The infant is left at one point with the stranger, and at a second point, entirely alone. Separation, reunion and exploratory behaviours are specifically noted. The infant's behaviour in this situation tends to fall into one of three categories; two of which are deemed insecurely attached, one of which is deemed securely attached. The securely attached infants explore the strange environment with some confidence, and there is a difference between the ways in which they respond to the parent and to the stranger. The secure infant shows some distress on separation, and shows pleasure at reunion with the parent; but not so with the stranger. Insecure avoidant infants tend to ignore the parent. Insecure anxious infants, however, tend to be very clingy towards the parent in the strange situation and do not explore the environment. They also become extremely distressed at separation from the parent and rather ambivalent and angry upon reunion.

In the original studies approximately 66 per cent of a sample of children were observed to be securely attached, 20 per cent avoidantly attached, and 12 per cent ambivalently attached, when observed with the mother.

It has been suggested that this behaviour, shown by the infant, merely reflects differences in infant temperament. However, an infant can display insecure behaviour with one parent but secure behaviour with the other. This is not to say that infant temperament does not play any part in determining the relationship between infant and caregiver, but it does not explain all the behavioural differences observed in the 'strange situation'. Cultural differences have, however, been observed in the percentages of infants who fall into the three categories. Therefore, differences in child-rearing methods or expectations about the achievement of autonomy will affect the mode of interaction in the infant–parent dyad and hence the attachment category attributed to that relationship.

We can gain some insight into how and when this first attachment relationship is formed, by observing the behaviour of the parents towards infants who are given different attachment classifications. Observations carried out in the home showed that a mother's behaviour towards her infant could explain the infant's responses to her. Mothers of infants that were rated as securely attached behaved in a consistent and sensitively responsive manner towards their infants. Mothers of insecurely attached children behaved in either a rejecting or an inconsistent fashion towards their infants. It could be said then, that infants respond to the mothers' behaviour towards them. Those infants who are treated consistently and responsively become securely attached. Those infants whose mothers reject them show avoidant behaviour (an absence of overt attachment behaviours). Those mothers who are inconsistent in their behaviour to their infants have anxiously attached children, children who cannot predict the attachment figure's likely behaviour towards them.

Attachment formation, infant to caregiver, would seem to depend upon consistent and reciprocal interactions which occur across time. The process does not seem to start before the age of 3 months, and is possibly complete by the end of the first year. It has been suggested, most notably by Bowlby (1953), that an attachment to a primary caregiver must form within the first 2 years of life for the subsequent optimal mental health of the child. However, in single case studies of children deprived of the opportunity to form attachments in the first 6 years of life (Clarke and Clarke, 1976), subsequent attachments have been observed to foster parents. If there is a critical period for attachment formation then it would appear to be a long one. In normal family life, infants usually form a hierarchy of attachments to available family members or caregivers; and this hierarchy seems to serve a protective function for the infant. The availability of multiple caregivers also means that the likelihood of forming a secure attachment with at least one available caregiver is increased.

We might conclude then, that infants do not become truly social beings until the end of the first year of life, and that the ability to form attachments is based upon the acquisition of specific stages in cognitive development, and upon the availability of a consistent reciprocal interaction with another.

Five Key Points

- Following birth, there is a period of very rapid learning.
- There is no evidence to support the idea of early 'bonding' between infant and mother.
- A 'fear of strangers' response is not usually observed before about 10 months. At the same age the child can remember sustained patterns of interaction specific to each caregiver.
- Infants of 10 months show separation distress, are more discriminatory in affect, smile more at the people with whom they are familiar and are more wary of strangers. They are social beings.
- Attachment formation, infant to caregiver, is dependent on consistent and reciprocal interactions occurring across time – usually between 3 and 12 months.

Three Questions

? How and when do attachments form?
? What methods have developmental psychologists used to observe infant behaviour?
? How do patterns of attachment appear to affect infant behaviour?

Further reading

1 Mehler, J. and Dupoux, E. (1994) *What Infants Know: New Cognitive Science of Early Development*. Oxford: Blackwell.
2 Schaffer, H. R. (1998) *Making Decisions about Children*. Oxford: Blackwell.
3 Goldberg, S. (2000) *Attachment and Development*. London: Arnold.

CHAPTER 5.2

Childhood

Gillian Schofield

When social workers think about childhood from infancy to adolescence, they need to be aware of the specific features of the period which tend to mark certain stages. But they also need to be aware of the continuous tasks, such as building self-esteem or defining an identity, which flow from birth through infancy, childhood, adolescence and continue to evolve in adult life. Although social workers must be familiar with all kinds of evidence of healthy development, it is often the relationship-based areas of development which social workers are best placed to observe and assess because of their perspective on the child in her social context – the family, the playgroup, the school and the community.

Dependency and Autonomy in Pre-school Children

The early attachment relationships which are established during infancy form the basis of development during the toddler and pre-school years. In the first year of life the available and sensitive parent needs to do whatever will build the child's *trust*. Understanding this process is helpful in thinking about how the development of a secure attachment leads to the child's experience of the attachment figure as a secure base for exploration (Bowlby, 1969). During the second year, in the context of the child's experience of security, the parent needs to respond in whatever way will make the child feel more *capable* (Fahlberg 1991). The task of this period is to begin the move from the *dependency* of infancy to a gradual sense of *autonomy*. This development is a challenge to both the child and the parent. The toddler often goes through a phase of assertive or oppositional behaviour as she learns the power of saying 'mine' and 'no'. Assertiveness can be associated with pleasure and also with anxiety. As the sense of a *psychological* separation from the parent develops, the child can become anxious and apprehensive about *physical* separation. Behaviour at this stage is neither consistent nor apparently rational. The child who one day is demanding the freedom to put on her own shoes and gaining obvious pleasure from her new-found abilities, the next day may be refusing to walk and be demanding to be spoon-fed. The lesson to be learned most vividly from toddlers, but which is relevant throughout childhood, is that although children's development may be seen as broadly following in stages, a child's anxiety and uncertainty about the implications of progress are likely to mean frequent regressions before the drive to move forward reasserts itself. The challenge for parents in this period is to allow the child some flexibility and regression while giving appropriate encouragement to the child to enjoy and develop new skills.

Parents who get into difficulties at this stage have often been unable to cope with the challenge to their authority which a toddler or pre-schooler may represent. Dunn's research (1988) showed that the majority of 2- to 3-year-olds persisted in demands or did what they had just been told not to do. What is more, although many children were simply angry and defiant, a good number would be actually smiling at the parent and teasing them as they defied them. For most parents, such behaviour is immediately recognizable as part of a common and temporary phase, but some children may be at risk because of what parents attribute to the child and to the behaviour. The impact of parental attributions may mean that defiant behaviour is seen as confirmation that a child is responsible for parenting failure and is *constitutionally* a bad or difficult child. In this context, normal developmental processes of assertiveness are seen as *persecutory* and as beyond the influence or control of the parent. If the behaviour is perhaps further linked, for example, with an absent parent whom the child is felt to resemble, then the *meaning* of the child's behaviour will contribute to a further distortion in the parental response.

Although defiant behaviour is usually an important expression of the child's growing ability to see themselves as a separate person, there is evidence that serious behaviour problems, or *conduct disorders,* in pre-school children may persist into middle childhood. Behaviour, therefore, needs to be examined in the light of the other important processes of this period in order to distinguish between normal development, of which there is a wide range, and the problems which need to be recognized and helped.

Development of Social Understanding

From birth, the child is learning lessons about how the world works. Early connections are made which help the child feel safe and allow her to postpone satisfaction. Even young babies are able to learn after a while that they can stop crying as soon as they hear the parent's footsteps on the stairs, because they can predict that a cuddle or a bottle or both is going to happen next. Looking for patterns in relationships and social behaviour, starting to learn the rules, is a critical part of the early experiences of children. The sound of the footstep starts to represent in a symbolic sense the beginning of the feed. This predictability, the reciprocity between parent and child and the development of trust in symbols are important elements in developing language. The likelihood that events follow each other also starts the child on the way to understanding that two and two always make four, that life has patterns which can be relied on. Predictability in the young child's world enables her to develop that feeling of competence which emerges from a capacity to produce

Attachment patterns

In their efforts to adapt defensively to their caregiving relationship, children develop one of four basic internal working models which give rise to distinct attachment patterns.

1 *Secure* attachment patterns: children experience their caregiver as available and themselves as lovable and effective.
2 *Ambivalent* patterns: children experience their caregiver as inconsistently responsive and themselves as dependent and poorly valued.
3 *Avoidant* patterns: children experience their caregivers as consistently rejecting and themselves as insecure but compulsively self-reliant.
4 *Disorganized* patterns (often associated with children who have suffered severe maltreatment): children experience their caregivers as either frightening or frightened and themselves as either helpless or angry and controlling.

Each pattern is associated with a characteristic strategy for managing anxiety and relationships:

1 *Secure*: approach, confident in the availability of others and worth of the self.
2 *Ambivalent*: maximize attachment behaviour, rely on emotion.
3 *Avoidant*: minimize attachment behaviour and shows of emotion; rely on reason.
4 *Disorganized:* incoherent, mix of avoidance and approach, helpless in infancy, controlling in older children.

Source: Adapted from David Howe (2000) Attachment theory. In M. Davies (ed.), *The Blackwell Encyclopaedia of Social Work*. Oxford: Blackwell, p. 27.

an impact on her world. But predictability also brings mastery of her feelings. Secure attachment leads to a capacity to reflect and to regulate feelings.

A key part of what we think of as the secure base effect of attachment (Bowlby, 1969) is the way in which the child is freed to *think*, to explore and to find out about her environment. In everyday life, the child who is preoccupied about getting emotional needs met and fears separation, will find it hard to be interested in the leaf which floats by or the sound of the rain. The child has a natural awareness of stimuli from birth which, if needs are met in a way which can be described as 'good enough' to use Winnicott's expression (Winnicott, 1965), will continue through childhood and will lead to learning. To a large extent the environment merely has to facilitate that process. This facilitative environment depends on the nature of the available relationships more than it does on the nature of the available toys. When children learn to role play the parent who feeds the baby or gets cross, she safely explores social situations which give pleasure or cause anxiety and develops her ability to see the world through the eyes of others.

Learning about the social world initially requires the child to learn from the patterns of relationships which she, herself, experiences; the impact others have on her and the impact she has on them. But a sophisticated operator within the social world needs also to learn about *how other people feel and how other people think*. Young children's capacity to comprehend the subtleties of 'other minds' has emerged as far more sophisticated than had been thought. This sophistication has important survival value for the child since communication of needs, practical and emotional, relies on some degree of understanding of how certain kinds of communications will be received and an ability to predict reactions. These lessons are learned with parents, grandparents, brothers and sisters. Increasingly, children start to become skilled observers of relationships *between* other family members and to learn lessons from them. The child is then likely to move into relationships with other children. Within the peer group, the child learns a whole new set of rules and the skills needed to establish relationships and negotiate within them.

Judy Dunn found that within what she called 'the drama of their everyday world', young children are highly motivated and emotionally involved, and therefore much more skilled in negotiating and learning about how the world works than had been thought by writers like Piaget who emphasized the 'egocentrism' of young children. In her research, Dunn found that by the age of three, children were demonstrating an *understanding of other's feelings*, 'the causes of pain, distress, anger, pleasure and displeasure, comfort and fear in others as well as in themselves. They joke, play with, and tell stories about these feeling states in self and other' (1988, p. 170). Out of this early responsiveness, she suggests, comes 'the foundations for the *moral* virtues of caring, considerateness and kindness'.

Children of this age are also demonstrating an *understanding of others' goals and intentions*. Dunn suggests that an understanding of feelings and intentions leads to 'an interest in transgressions of acceptable or expected behaviour and an understanding of social rules and family relationships'. Children's use of humour, jokes and teasing can be seen in this context as important evidence of the child's growing ability to use their understanding of adults and other children to anticipate and have an impact on other people in their lives.

Dunn and other researchers have made a case for rejecting Piaget's suggestion that young children are egocentric, in that by 3 years of age children are quite sophisticated in their ability to understand the feelings and goals of others. However, it is the case that children, and particularly children facing stressful situations, are often egocentric in the sense of holding themselves responsible for much of what happens to them. *Magical thinking*, as it is often called, or a sense of omnipotence can be particularly striking in children between the ages of four and seven or eight, who are still trying to make sense of their world. Social workers need to be constantly alert to the ways in which children blame themselves for the separation of parents, for parental illness and, most commonly, for the abuse which they have experienced.

Developing and Refining a Sense of Self

Much of the process of social learning derives from and contributes to the child's developing sense of self. The emotional significance of secure attachment to parents and the tension which follows between dependence and autonomy in a world of more powerful and more competent others, motivate the child to find a place for herself in the social world. The child's sense of 'self-efficacy' (Dunn, 1988) develops as the child finds the skills to operate within relationships. The child learns to oppose others where necessary, negotiate where necessary and cooperate where necessary. The *self-esteem* which is derived from early secure attachments should during this phase evolve through increasing competence, both socially and in playing with objects, toys and games.

For children whose experience of early relationships has not included developing a sense of trust and attachment which provides a secure base, self-esteem may be fragile. Children who live in families where there are frequent changes either in the physical environment or in the relationships and the emotional climate, do not experience the reassuring and predictable patterns which encourage them to go on to the next stage and develop a sense of self-efficacy. Maltreated children are particularly vulnerable. This becomes important when we consider what is needed for the child to make a successful transition to school.

The primary-school years from five to eleven have often been seen as a relatively quiet phase developmentally compared with the dramatic changes from birth to five and during adolescence. This is also reflected in Freud's labelling of this period as 'latency' within his psychosexual model of development. More recently, it has come to be seen as a period of *consolidation* but also further development of much of the learning about *self* and *relationships* which we know has been initiated in the pre-school years.

The emphasis on developing a sense of self has important implications for much of social work practice with the middle-childhood age group. We know, for example, from research on the psychology of adoption, that adopted children are particularly curious about their origins around the age of eight or nine. Children in foster care also need to make sense of where they fit and can feel very unsettled by change of home and change in school. Children in middle childhood are often well able to talk about their situation and they need to have their feelings about their situation listened to carefully if their hopes, fears and anxieties are to be recognized. But insecure fostered and adopted children who have had to construct defensive strategies to manage stresses and fear in their birth families communicate in rather different ways – for example, shutting down on their feelings or displaying feelings but in ways that miscue caregivers and social workers (Schofield and Beek, 2006).

In middle childhood, the impact of the school environment, the increasing distance from parental control of day-to-day life and the intensity of peer group relationships during this period create a significant shift in the child's development. Specifically, they require the child to move even further towards understanding what is required and expected by the wider society. What is more, they place the emphasis on the child understanding the standards of others and then establishing her own. The exact nature of these standards and expectations will inevitably be very culturally specific. Some societies, for example, encourage individualism, expect children to express their individual needs and are inclined to favour children who are assertive. In others, the most important lesson for children to learn is that where there is a conflict, what is in the best interests of the family or the village or the community must take priority over the child's individual wishes. What is important is for a child to learn the rules which are appropriate to their particular culture. Of course, children are regularly exposed to conflicting cultures, most obviously children from ethnic minority families or minority religions. For many of these children, the challenge will be the need to understand both social worlds, learn to operate in both and to that extent incorporate both identities. Although adolescence is regularly seen as the stage of establishing identity, it is during the period from seven to twelve that children are developing an understanding of the psychosocial meaning of their racial identity.

Sense of self during this period will also include significant areas such as the development of gender identity. We know that by the age of two, children are choosing stereotypical toys and are already associating certain tasks with men and women. Given the child's need to register patterns in the social world, this is not perhaps so surprising (Bee and Boyd, 2004). Cross-cultural research has found that stereotyping by gender on certain characteristics, such as aggression, strength and cruelty for men and weakness, gentleness and appreciativeness for women, is almost universal and that for many children these stereotypes become more fixed between the ages of five and eight.

When we think of the psychosocial skills required to enable a child to make friends, the ability to be appropriately assertive while also being appropriately concerned for the other child's feelings, the ability to negotiate and cooperate, it is not hard to see the complex interconnections between cognitive skills, emotional qualities and the child's behaviour. Within the child's close relationships it is also possible to think in terms of increased complexity of family and peer group as children develop a more varied hierarchy of attachments that may include figures outside the family (Kearns and Richardson, 2005).

Conclusion

This account of childhood has focused on some of the key processes of emotional, social and cognitive development, knowledge of which enables the social worker to go beyond the description of a child's behaviour and to acquire an understanding of the meanings behind it. Working sensitively with children in order to understand their needs and take into account their wishes and feelings would not be possible without developing an ability to see the world through the child's eyes.

Five Key Points

- Pre-school children need to gradually move from the dependency of infancy to a sense of autonomy and self-efficacy.
- By the age of three, secure children have a sophisticated understanding of others' feelings and are already learning about the social world but insecure children are less reflective about their own or other minds. .
- By the time children start school, they need to have many social as well as cognitive skills.
- Between the ages of five and eleven, children refine their sense of self, expand their knowledge of the social world and develop standards of behaviour.
- Cognitive, emotional, behavioural and social development proceed together and affect each other. Problem behaviour in one area of development must be put in the context of all areas of development if the behaviour is to be understood.

Three Questions

? What might be the impact of abuse and neglect in early childhood on a child's secure base, self-esteem and identity?
? What is the importance of peer group relationships for healthy development in childhood?
? What are the factors which might enable the child to be resilient and to make good developmental progress at home and at school in spite of adversity?

Further reading

1 Bee, H. and Boyd, D. (2004) *The Developing Child*. New York: HarperCollins.
2 Kearns, K. A. and Richardson, R. A. (2005) *Attachment in Middle Childhood*. New York: Guilford Press.
3 Schofield, G. and Beek, M. (2006) *Attachment Handbook for Foster Care and Adoption*. London: British Association for Adoption and Fostering.

CHAPTER 5.3

Adolescence

Martin Herbert

Somewhere between the immaturity of childhood and the hoped-for maturity of adulthood lie the six or seven years referred to as adolescence. That there is a stage of transition from 'irresponsibility' to 'responsibility' has been widely, but not universally, accepted. Some cultures, notably pre-literate ones, had 'rites of passage' that took children directly from their childhood to adult status.

Some theorists reject the notion of adolescence as a distinct stage of development. They repudiate the idea that at puberty every child somehow takes on a qualitatively different personality or engages in radically different developmental tasks more or less overnight. Rather the child grows by imperceptible degrees into a teenager, and the adolescent turns by degrees into an adult.

Others disagree. The confusion over the boundaries defining adolescence is revealed by the metaphors applied to it: the 'in-between stage', and 'that no-man's land between childhood and adulthood'. It has also been referred to as a 'tunnel' into which young people disappear, displaying certain kinds of character. They are then 'lost to sight' for a few years. According to this metaphor you never know what is going to emerge at the other end – a daunting prospect for parents and teachers (if true) when they have put so much time, effort and affection, into preparing the children in their care for adulthood.

It is generally agreed that adolescence begins in biology (the variable time of onset of puberty) and ends in culture (the even more variable point at which young people are deemed 'responsible' and 'independent' by society). Whatever the boundaries, the fact is that many parents anticipate the adolescent years as something to be endured rather than enjoyed. It is often the case that they are apprehensive that they may 'lose' the closeness, the affection and the degree of parental control they feel to be important in the relationship with their son or daughter. If parents expect the worst they are quite likely to get it – indeed, they contribute unwittingly to a self-fulfilling prophecy.

Of course, adolescence can be traumatic for some young individuals and disruptive for their parents, but it is by no means necessarily so. The fact is that adolescence does not deserve its gloomy reputation. The popular notion that adolescence is different from the whole of development which precedes it and the whole of development which follows it is of relatively recent origin. Among the early proponents of this view was G. Stanley Hall in 1904. His belief, that adolescence is necessarily a stage of development associated with emotional turmoil and psychic disturbance, was to become so deeply rooted, reinforced by a succession of psychoanalytically orientated writers, that it persists to this day. This 'storm and stress' conceptualization (built on eagerly by journalists in sensational items about teenage hooligans and vandals) has filtered down to street level as a veritable 'demonological' theory of adolescence. Certainly the psychiatric profession – with its biased sample of clinic-attending youngsters – has tended to take a jaundiced view of adolescence. Attention was drawn to neurotic- or psychotic-like features: hysteria, regression, mood swings and disintegration.

Hutter in the 1930s described adolescence in Alice in Wonderland terms as a period of development 'in which normally abnormalities so often happen it is abnormal that everything passes normally'. Anna Freud writing in the 1950s said it was 'abnormal' if a child kept a 'steady equilibrium during the adolescent period . . . The adolescent manifestations come close to symptom formation of the neurotic, psychotic or dissocial order and merge almost imperceptibly into . . . almost all the mental illnesses.' As a final illustration of the medical view of adolescence as pathology, we have van Krevelen writing in the 1970s that 'adolescence is a period of life, which by its disintegrative character may seem a psychosis in itself . . . it is difficult to discern in this stage a pathological process from normal development'.

The evidence based on studies of 'run-of-the-mill' adolescents rather than only the impressions of clinicians who mainly see disturbed or deviant young people (Rutter, 1979; Coleman, 1980; Herbert, 1987a; Nielsen, 1987) is that adolescence, while not without its difficulties, can be negotiated by children with intuitive, sensible parents and reasonably benign socio-economic backgrounds with relatively little fuss. If approached in the right frame of mind, adolescence can be a period of relatively harmonious relationships – or at least as harmonious as any other stage of development. This requires an acceptance of the essential continuity of important aspects of the personality from childhood, through adolescence, and onto adulthood. The 'changeling' phenomenon – in the sense of some radical transformation – is highly unusual. Nevertheless, transition and change are features of adolescence, and an understanding of these processes can be of benefit to harassed young people and their parents, especially if they 'normalize' the adolescent context by repudiating some of the popular myths – especially the notion that the problems necessarily exist because the client is a member of a distinct and potentially dangerous species.

Take the 'storm and stress' view of adolescence: this phase, while certainly not immune from its share of pain for those growing up is not disproportionately characterized by severe emotional disturbance. Psychological problems are probably a little commoner during adolescence than during middle childhood, but the difference is not great: some 10–15 per cent of adolescents experience significant psychological problems, but these figures are close to rates at other stages of development (Graham and Rutter, 1973).

The generation gap is another popular conception that does not live up to expectations. What, in any event, constitutes a gap? Labels are misleading and even dangerous because they suggest distinctions that are absolute rather than matters of degree. If anything, it could be said that the generations are drawing together rather than apart. Adolescents and their parents tend to agree on the important issues more than do parents and their parents (grandparents). People have been led to believe that the 'distancing' of young adults from their parents means that they may not be able to communicate with their children when they get older. Distancing is not, however, a typical pattern. Most adolescents are still attached to their homes in a positive way, and they continue to depend upon the emotional support, goodwill and approval of their parents.

The family continues to be of critical importance to them as it was in earlier, less mature years; indeed, concern and supervision (as long as it is not oppressive, or too intrusive) can be demonstrated to be vital during a phase when youngsters are experimenting with life. Emotional support is important as the young person deals with changes in body image (during the 'growth spurt'), changes in hormonal activity and the increasing challenge of more complex developmental tasks (see Herbert, 1987b).

It is exceptional for teenagers to feel torn between their two 'worlds' of parents and peers, certainly on the more important issues of life. There are most likely to be differences of opinion on minor issues such as hairstyle, fashion, social habits and privileges, where parental views are likely to be rejected in favour of the standards of friends. Where major issues are concerned, it seems that only a minority of adolescents radically depart from their parents' views; there is little evidence that secondary or higher education in itself causes dramatic changes in the political attitudes that young people absorb from their parents. A majority of adolescents share their parents' attitudes towards moral and political issues, and are prepared, by and large, to accept their parents' guidance on academic, career and personal issues.

Another popular belief about adolescence is that a crisis over personal identity occurs, producing all or some of the symptoms of stress: anxiety, depression, a sense of frustration, conflict and defeatism. The development of identity does not always proceed smoothly, but what evidence we have calls into question the belief of Erikson, that adolescents usually suffer a crisis over their identity. Most teenagers have a positive but not unrealistically inflated self-image and this view of themselves tends to be fairly stable over the years (Coleman et al., 1977).

Although adolescents have become more accepting in their attitudes to pre-marital sex, this does not imply, as the media like to suggest, a massive rise in casual sexual relationships. Young people, and particularly girls, continue to emphasize the importance of love and stable emotional attachment in pre-marital sex, although intended marriage or an engagement is not so often seen as a prerequisite of such relationships. The emphasis tends to be on a stable relationship with one sexual partner at a time (Rutter, 1979). Girls do, however, display more conservative attitudes to these issues than boys. Most youngsters wish to get married and have children. Certainly a committed relationship is generally thought to be essential for the rearing of children and, although a majority would wish such a long-standing commitment to take the form of marriage, a substantial minority reject such a view

(Schofield, 1973; Rutter, 1979). An American study, by Sorensen in 1973, indicated that a majority of teenagers expect sexual fidelity after marriage, even though they do not expect it before then. There is no evidence that this view has changed.

It is important to remember that children do not face the 'hurdles' of adolescent development all at once. Different challenges (sexuality, new relationships, changes in body and self-image, identity and independence issues) are spread out over several years. Children have strengths; they generally bring forward into maturity their positive attributes. They do not suddenly lose these characteristics which most parents have so assiduously nurtured. They also develop new intellectual, social and emotional capacities. They are capable of more flexible, abstract problem solving. Of course, they may wish to flex their intellectual 'muscles' and give their parents an argument. Their idealism may cause them to make unflattering comments about their parents' world-weary opinions.

Having said all this, it is obvious to anyone working in the social, health or educational services that there are some very real problems in adolescence, as there are for every other stage of development. Fortunately, the serious, as opposed to day-to-day difficulties, affect a relatively small minority. At that day-to-day level parents are going to face difficulties prompted by the child's reactions to the new demands of rapid physical change and sexual maturity. There is also the challenge (often an ambiguous one in our society) to be 'grown up'. What puts particular pressure on parents is their perception of some of the awful risks their children may confront at this age: unwanted pregnancies, the exploitation of *naïveté* and innocent emotions, sexually transmitted disease, not least AIDS. Then there are the dangers of experimenting with drugs or the implications of youthful showing off (such as reckless driving in cars or motor bikes). But parents who have fostered a good relationship and honest lines of communication with their children are best placed to sensitize them to danger and strengthen their resolve not to overstep the bounds of reasonable behaviour and risk taking (Herbert, 1987b).

Having emphasized the need to 'normalize' the concept of adolescence (a lengthy stage of life best differentiated in casework into early, middle and late adolescence because of the different changes and challenges arising) there are particular age-related problems which may beset the young person, his/her parents and the social worker who may become involved.

Emotional and Behavioural Problems

Contrary to received wisdom, adolescence is not usually characterized by severe emotional disturbance. Still there is a substantial minority of parents who will need to help their children themselves, and if the problems show no signs of being alleviated they should seek expert guidance. There is a paradox in all of this in the sense that, just as it was being appreciated that most adolescents did not suffer from psychological disorders, the evidence began to accumulate that since the late 1940s there has been a dramatic rise in psychosocial problems in teenagers. These include suicidal behaviour, delinquent activities, alcohol and substance abuse, depression and eating disorders, and they have occurred at a time of general improvements in living conditions and physical health. A closer look at the nature of psychological disorders is required.

The term 'psychological disorder' refers collectively to a large and mixed bag of disorders ranging from depression, anxiety, inhibition and shyness to non-compliance, destructiveness, stealing and aggression. In essence, these problems represent exaggerations, deficits (deficiencies) or disabling combinations of feelings, attitudes and behaviours common, at one time or the other, to most young people. Aggression, shyness and a combination of low self-esteem and poor concentration are examples of each category.

There is a distinction between those difficulties which primarily lead to emotional disturbance or distress for the young people themselves (anxiety, phobic fear, shyness, depression, feelings of inferiority and timidity) and those which mainly involve the kinds of anti-social behaviour (aggression, lying, stealing and disobedience) which disrupt the well-being of others, notably those in frequent contact with the young person.

The first category, referred to by psychologists as 'emotional disorders', are manifested by about 2.5 per cent of pre-adolescent children. Their prevalence increases somewhat by adolescence, and we find that boys and girls are about equally prone to them. For most children these kinds of problems manifest themselves briefly at certain periods and then become minimal or disappear completely. We know from research that, for the most part, young people who suffer from emotional disorders become reasonably well-adjusted adults. In a sense these difficulties are the emotional equivalent of 'growing pains'. They come and go; nevertheless they sometimes persist, and can reach levels of intensity which cause all-round suffering.

At the age of 11 children exhibit an increase in fear. Among 11- and 12-year olds, worries connected with school are nearly half as many again as worries about home matters. In Britain, 11 is that awkward age in a youngster's life when the change from junior to senior school is being made. It may not be coincidental that it is also the age at which phobias about school are at a peak. Abnormal fears (phobias) involve an intense dread in the presence of an object or situation often amounting to panic; and although the object may be individual to the adolescent, certain forms are common, for example, dread of open or closed spaces, height, water and so on. Some definitions of phobia emphasize the incapacitating or restrictive effect of a phobia, in contrast to the more common fears which most of us endure.

There are various types of phobia. For example, some teenagers have a persistent fear of, and compelling desire to avoid, a social situation (say, a party) in which they are exposed to possible scrutiny by others and fear that they may act in a manner that will cause embarrassment or humiliation. In the case of agoraphobia, the young person has an intense fear of, and thus avoids, being alone or in public places. Behavioural psychotherapy is particularly effective in treating fear-based problems.

There are children and teenagers whose behaviour is notable for their fundamental inability or unwillingness to adhere to the codes of conduct prescribed by society. Conduct problems cover a lot of territory, including as they do seriously anti-social acts as well as what is only moderately troublesome behaviour. Although conduct problems can create misery for everyone concerned with the younger child, the disturbance can often be contained within the home or classroom – although often at great cost. As children grow older those problems that involve a persistent defiance of authority, together with a refusal or inability to show self-restraint, become more serious in their implications. They extend beyond the confines of the child's life at home and school, and the reverberations of the child's misdemeanours may eventually lead to the child not only being labelled 'conduct-disordered', but also of earning the designation 'juvenile delinquent' if he or she infringes the law, is apprehended and found guilty.

The number of young people committing detected and adjudicated crimes in the UK and the USA has increased markedly. What was once an almost completely male preserve now includes substantial numbers of female offenders. The average age for the first court appearance of juveniles is lower, and there is a marked trend towards more violent offences.

It has to be recognized that relatively minor delinquent activities (petty thefts, vandalism) are surprisingly common in adolescence and tend to be transitory. However, there is a small but hard core of adolescents who habitually break the law. Delinquency is perhaps the most noteworthy of all activities as an adolescent manifestation, reaching a peak at 15 years for boys and 14 years for girls. By their twenties most of the former offenders have become broadly law-abiding members of the community. Behavioural cognitive methods (individual and group) have had an encouraging success rate with conduct and delinquent disorders (see Hollin, 1991; Webster-Stratton and Herbert, 1994).

Psychiatric Disorders

There are serious but relatively rare psychiatric disorders, such as schizophrenia and anorexia or bulimia nervosa, whose onset is particularly associated with the teenage years. It is fairly typical, in the transition from childhood to adulthood, to experience an upsurge of moodiness and feelings of misery. Adolescents are often tormented by low self-esteem, worries about the future, and fears about such matters as attending school or participating in social activities. These problems are usually relatively mild and might be viewed as developmental problems.

Depression and suicide

However, the feelings of misery and inner turmoil give way, in some adolescents, to more serious moods of depression – a sense of helplessness and powerlessness, of events being out of control. Some teenagers even entertain ideas about committing suicide. The milder form of depression may show itself as a lack of physical energy and well-being. In its more severe manifestations, adolescents tend to be irritable and bad-tempered, and, when it is at its worst, they sleep poorly, show a lack of appetite, and are always dejected, apathetic and lifeless. They cease to strive and to use their full effectiveness in whatever sphere of activity they find themselves.

The apathy of a young person with poor health is often mistaken for laziness. If a child is to be successful at school, good health is vital; it provides the basis for the stamina demanded by hours of concentration in the classroom. Regular attendance at school depends upon it, and effective learning, in turn, depends upon reasonably consistent presence at lessons. High rates of non-attendance at school are often a significant indicator that all is not well with the young person.

Depression is a common feature of suicide, which, in adolescents, is usually associated with emotional and behavioural problems related to psychological and social stress. Suicide rates rise sharply during the teens so that it comes to rank among the half-dozen most common causes of death among older adolescents (the figures are still well below those for adults, and only a minute fraction of the suicide rate in old age). Attempted suicide is very much a late adolescent phenomenon, the peak being among 15- to 19-year-olds. There has been a tenfold increase in such incidents since the 1960s among adolescent boys and a fivefold rise for girls. Nevertheless, the rate of attempted suicides for adolescent girls far exceeds that for boys. No-one seems able to explain the surge in the statistics. It does not seem to be related to drug abuse or to too liberal prescribing of tablets by doctors. It may be associated with increased use of alcohol, and is most likely linked in some way with the increasing prevalence of marital discord, childhood separations, unemployment and criminality.

Teenagers sometimes have fantasies about their own death which involve their 'ending it all' and yet surviving the event by 'attending' their own funeral where they are able to savour the grief and guilt displayed by errant parents or boyfriends/girlfriends. These fantasies indicate how, in some adolescents, the finality of death is not fully appreciated, or at least not while in a depressed or hysterical state, and not at the time when the gesture (and, often, more than a gesture) of suicide is contemplated. The cliché that suicide is often a cry for help is true despite its banality. Threats of suicide should not be treated lightly. Many individuals who have threatened to commit suicide do in the end carry out their threat. In cases of adolescent depression the disorder may be masked and sometimes the outward and visible sign of the problems takes the form of 'acting out' delinquent activity.

Anorexia nervosa

A problem particularly (but not only) associated with adolescent girls – it also occurs in pre-pubertal children – is anorexia nervosa. The anorexic girl deliberately restricts her food intake; indeed, she does not want to eat at all, because she believes she is fat and wishes to lose weight. The word 'anorexia' means loss of appetite. However, the absence of hunger or appetite is not a crucial feature of anorexia nervosa. Nevertheless, the teenager will characteristically act as if she had lost her appetite.

Anorexia nervosa is essentially about weight rather than eating. The really central feature of the disorder is a body weight which is abnormally low for the age, height and sex of the person accompanied by a distorted perception by the sufferer of her body. There is a further crucial feature: the individual's attitude to her weight. What makes life difficult for parents and other would-be helpers is that someone with anorexia nervosa will not always be open or truthful about her feelings and will frequently resist help. If she is, she is likely to say that she is ashamed of her body and very frightened of the thoughts of being heavier. She may suffer in various ways through being thin, but compared with putting on weight it is seen as the lesser evil.

Drug Misuse and Abuse

Drug abuse is relatively infrequent among younger schoolchildren, but not as rare as it used to be; it certainly becomes more common during the years of adolescence. Fortunately, most youngsters who try drugs or misuse substances out of curiosity do not continue to use or misuse them regularly. Those who take drugs tend to do so infrequently and give them up altogether after a year or so. The key factor in drug taking is opportunity – the availability of drugs and people to tempt and 'prompt'. Users have generally been exposed to drugs by their peers or by people (not infrequently family members) whose values incline towards non-conformity or even deviance. Rebelliousness, low self-esteem, a poor sense of psychological well-being (including depression) and low academic aspirations are among characteristics commonly found in adolescent drug users. The boredom and hopelessness of unemployment also play their part.

Educational Failure

Mass formal education has created serious problems for the life goals of adolescents with educational disabilities. For academically successful adolescents, school is a bridge between the world of childhood and the world of adulthood. For children unwilling or unable to learn, school is a place where the battle against society is likely to begin. Failure in a success-orientated world has significant consequences for the well-being of adolescents, not only at school, but in other facets of their lives. There is a strong association between emotional disturbance and under-achievement at school. Emotionally disturbed adolescents tend to distract and harass their teachers, and disrupt and anger their more conscientious fellow students.

A sense of failure often manifests itself in an obstinate façade behind which the student hides. There is a vicious circle of self-fulfilling prophecy at work. Tell teenagers often enough that they are fools, criticize them whatever they do, even if it is commendable within their own capabilities, and in the end they are likely to become extremely demoralized and even give up. Their confidence will be destroyed and they may retreat behind a mask of stupidity and 'don't care' laziness – signs of what, clinically, is referred to as 'learned helplessness'.

Young people who do well at school tend to enjoy good health, have average or above-average intelligence and well-developed social skills. They are likely to have a good opinion of themselves, the ability to gauge accurately their effect on others, and to perceive correctly the quality of others' approaches and responses to themselves. Early-maturing boys and girls also have many advantages in terms of capability and self-confidence.

Doubtless there will be times when parents' assistance is brushed aside, their advice resisted, and their guidance interpreted as interference. But times of rapid transition *are* recognized as times when people are open to help. Contrary to widely held myths about adolescence, teenagers *are* susceptible to the right sort of intervention despite their famous reticence and prickliness. Their minds, at this age, are probably as open as they will ever be. But, are parents' minds open or closed?

Wise parents have no wish to emerge as victors of battles of will or confrontations with their children. Rather they wish to *win through*, in the task of supporting them in their journey through adolescence to maturity. A realistic, and optimistic view of adolescence *plus* a sound knowledge of what is happening physically and emotionally to teenagers, will allow parents to remain rock-solid while their youngster finds his or her adult status. Parents can survive, indeed, enjoy adolescence, by letting the occasional waves of discontent, criticism and rebellion break around them – without breaking them!

Five Key Points

- Adolescence, while not without its difficulties, can be negotiated by children with intuitive, sensible parents and reasonably benign socio-economic backgrounds with relatively little fuss.
- Most adolescents are attached to their homes, and continue to depend on the emotional support, goodwill and approval of their parents.
- The serious problems of adolescence affect only a small minority.
- Some 10–15 per cent experience serious psychological problems. Although relatively minor delinquent activities are common in adolescence, they are also transitory.
- Failure at school has significant consequences for the well-being of adolescents.

Three Questions

1. When does adolescence begin and end?
2. How does adolescence differ for males and females?
3. Why has the incidence of attempted suicide in adolescence risen so much?

Further reading

1. Coleman, J. and Hendry, L. (1999) *The Nature of Adolescence,* 3rd edn. London: Routledge.
2. Herbert, M. (2002) *Typical and Atypical Development: From Conception to Adolescence.* Oxford: Blackwell.
3. Herbert, M. (2004) *Developmental Problems of Childhood and Adolescence: Prevention Treatment and Training.* Oxford: Blackwell.

CHAPTER 5.4

Partnership and Parenting

Janet Walker

At night returning, every labour sped,
He sits him down the monarch of a shed;
Smiles by his chearful fire, and round surveys
His childrens looks, that brighten at the blaze:
While his lov'd partner, boastful of her hoard,
Displays her cleanly platter on the board . . .
The Traveller, *Oliver Goldsmith, 1728–74*

Writing in the eighteenth century, Goldsmith captured a vision of partnership and parenting in which paternal and maternal roles are complementary, clearly defined and delineated, within an economic union which creates a supportive adult alliance and kinship networks. It constitutes a powerful image of stability and permanence, but it is a deceptively simple portrayal of complex intimate bonds between adults and between parents and their children. It is doubtful whether this idealized construction of warmth, well-being and contentment has ever realistically reflected family life, yet parents today are often judged against it.

Traditionally, marriage, parenting and family have been regarded as 'a package deal' (Struening, 2002), but changing patterns of partnership and parenting since the middle of the twentieth century have provoked concerns about its demise, and fears that families are fundamentally unstable and family values are being rejected, leading to increases in juvenile crime, antisocial behaviour, drug use and behavioural disorders in children. As a consequence, the policy agenda in the early years of the twenty-first century has been dominated by a plethora of initiatives spanning child and family services, child protection, criminal justice and family law, designed to ensure that children at risk are identified as early as possible and that their parents are supported in fulfilling their responsibilities. Particular emphasis has been placed on involving fathers more in their children's education and upbringing, and on finding the right balance between working and caring.

Let us consider four questions:

1 What demographic, social and economic changes have impacted on family life?
2 What are the realities of modern partnerships?
3 How do these influence patterns of parenting and the obligations it implies?
4 What are the concerns and how are they relevant to social work practice?

Dramatic social changes since the 1970s have resulted in greater ethnic and cultural diversity, and huge variations in family living arrangements through a declining fertility rate and increases in cohabitation, parental separation and divorce, single parenthood, same-sex partnerships, stepfamilies, people living alone, and the employment of women.

By 2011, the proportion of people aged over 64 is expected to outweigh that of children under 16 (Barratt, 2004). Generally, people are living longer, are healthier, although health improvements are not evenly distributed across classes and cultures, and spend longer periods of their lives outside the conventional family unit (Roseneil and Budgeon, 2004). In 2004–5:

- 42 per cent of all births occurred outside marriage, as against just 12 per cent in 1980;
- 76 per cent of dependent children lived in family units headed by a couple, as against 92 per cent in 1972;
- 24 per cent of children lived in a lone-parent family (90 per cent of which were headed by a mother), as against just 7 per cent in 1972;
- 67 per cent of all working-age mothers with dependent children were in employment, and 67 per cent of lone fathers and 53 per cent of lone mothers were combining employment with child care;
- 24 per cent of men and 25 per cent of women under 60 were cohabiting, as against 11 per cent and 13 per cent respectively in 1986 (Office for National Statistics, 2006).

While married couples still represent the main type of adult couple partnership, the age at which people marry has continued to rise since 1970: in 2003, the average age was 31 for men and 29 for women. Most couples now enter marriage having experienced earlier sexual relationships: an upward trend which has been evident for over a hundred years. Despite a liberal attitude towards sexual behaviour outside marriage, facilitated by vastly improved methods of birth control, paradoxically, marriage appears to demand a far greater commitment to sexual exclusivity and fidelity than was evident in more traditional marital partnerships. As a consequence deep tensions emerge: sexual freedom prior to marriage is not only tolerated but frequently encouraged, while monogamy is emphasized as the distinguishing feature of the marital relationship. Expectations of marriage are substantially greater than in the past, affording more opportunity for pursuing personal interests and other friendships. Yet, adulterous relationships are more likely to threaten the stability and durability of marriage since tolerance of such behaviour has substantially diminished.

Until the industrial revolution, although the connection between romantic love and lifelong partnership through the institution of marriage was acknowledged, love and companionship were secondary considerations. The 'traditional' marriage has been described as 'differentiated' and 'complementary'. Modern partnerships, by contrast, are described as 'symmetrical' or 'companionate': a strong emotional bond from which personal emotional benefits are derived is no longer viewed as a bonus, but as the key aspiration. The emphasis in the 1980s and 1990s on achieving personal fulfilment changed the ways in which young adults view and form partnerships and approach parenthood. By the late 1980s, 40 per cent of marriages were preceded by cohabitation, but by 1996 this had increased to 77 per cent of first marriages and almost all second marriages. If these trends continue, by 2021 more than one in five partnerships will consist of cohabiting couples and it will be increasingly common for children to be born to never-marrying couples (Haskey, 2001). Of course, cohabitation is not new: before divorce was an option, people left unhappy marriages and lived with new partners. However, cohabitation, either as a prelude to marriage or as a chosen alternative to it, is new.

Marriage today embodies a basic conundrum: mutual dependence, intimacy and sexual exclusivity have to be balanced within a culture which emphasizes personal growth and getting ahead – the 'we'/'me' dilemma. There is renewed emphasis on privacy, increased expectation of emotional companionship and equality, and a positive focus on sexuality beyond its function in procreation. In 2000, a British Social Attitudes survey (Barlow et al., 2002) found little support for the view that 'married couples make better parents than unmarried ones', and young people were considerably less likely to believe that 'people who want children ought to get married'. Although the quality of personal relationships is more important than their legal status, parenting and caring are still central elements in modern family life. Moreover, research indicates that there is no loss of commitment in modern partnerships: people seek to sustain the relationships they value. In order to understand connectedness and the moral texture of commitment, it is necessary to look beyond marriage as the ideal foundation for family life.

It is clear that the sexual and gender order that has underpinned family life is weakening (Roseneil, 2005), thereby stretching the conventional boundaries of partnership and parenting and rendering them infinitely flexible and permeable (McKie et al., 2005). The Adoption and Children Act 2002 enabled gay men and lesbians to adopt children and, in 2005, the Civil Partnership Act 2004 allowed same-sex couples in the UK to register their partnership, according them rights and responsibilities similar to those of married couples. These newly acknowledged intimacies require policy-makers and practitioners to move beyond traditional heteronormative conceptualizations of family life and parenting practices.

The change in family living arrangements which has caused the most widespread concern, however, relates to the huge increase in parental separation and divorce. Between 1958 and 1969 the number of divorces in Great Britain doubled, and it doubled again by 1971. The number increased until 1993, fell slightly up to 2000, and increased again between 2000 and 2004. Although more marriages survive than end in divorce, around 40 per cent of children experience parental divorce by their sixteenth birthday and others experience the breakdown of a cohabiting relationship. A fifth of children affected by divorce in 2004 were under five and just under two-thirds were aged 10 or under (Office for National Statistics, 2006). Although the median length of marriages which end in divorce is around 11 years, the modal length is closer to between 3 and 6 years. This, of course, is the period in which couples are most likely to become parents. Since many parents remarry quite quickly, and second marriages are even more likely to end in divorce, increasing numbers of children face repeated disruptions and the loss of several parental figures from the household. Such children are especially vulnerable and the most adversely affected by family transitions.

Until the twentieth century, divorce was not a feature of daily life although there were probably just as many unhappy marriages. Economic, social and emotional constraints locked couples into intensely unsatisfactory and often violent relationships, with death as the only release. In the nineteenth century, two in every five children lost their father by the age of 15, and almost the same proportion their mother. Some 25 per cent lost both. Step-parents were as much a feature of Victorian life as they are today, as was living in a lone-parent household. The loss of a parent was absolute, however, and the complexities of post-divorce parenting arrangements unknown. Divorce, by contrast, has profound effects on parenting. In assessing the consequences of parental separation for children, the following factors demand consideration:

- the way in which children are prepared for parental separation and divorce (most are not);
- arrangements for continued contact with each parent and day-to-day living arrangements.;
- the transition from a two-parent to a lone-parent (or step-parent) household;
- the number of disruptions;
- the quality of relationships between the parents, and between them and their children.

It is impossible and unwise to generalize about the effects, but the most distressed children are those caught up in their parents' battles. While most children experience short-term distress at the time of separation, only a minority suffer long-term adverse outcomes (Pryor and Rodgers, 2001). Child poverty, enduring parental conflict and father absence are the three outcomes of parental separation of most concern, and the latter has put the role of fathers into sharp perspective. Disentangling the emotional ties associated with the marital relationship while reformulating parental ties represents a hugely demanding and difficult transition for parents, making the ongoing obligations of parental responsibility particularly fraught (Walker et al., 2004). Many non-resident fathers struggle to remain involved in their children's lives and some lose contact with their children over time, particularly when conflict between the parents is unresolved.

Parents often form new relationships quite quickly. In 2003, remarriages accounted for 40 per cent of all marriages. In the 2001 census, 38 per cent of cohabiting couples with dependent children were stepfamilies. An analysis of calls to Parentline Plus (2005) has shown that stepfamily life can be very complex and highly stressful: divided loyalties, feelings of rejection, anxieties about favouritism, resentment and anger are common. Since post-divorce family relationships are dynamic and subject to change, new parental relationships have to integrate with new forms of old relationships. The absence of clear cultural norms defining appropriate step-parent (particularly stepfather) responsibilities contributes to the difficulties 'blended' families experience. Fathers and mothers have to renegotiate and redefine parental roles when parenting does not go hand in hand with marital partnerships, and their roles are open to a complex set of influences.

Postmodern living arrangements 'are diverse, fluid and unresolved, constantly chosen and rechosen' (Roseneil, 2005). Koschorke (2004) has argued that modern partnership demands a high degree of personal maturity, communication and negotiation skills, and he described it as a difficult art. Pahl (2000) has suggested that people are constantly in the process of refashioning relationships into new 'confluent' associations in which 'men and women are gradually learning to talk to one another as equals'. Starting a family, however, appears to present a particularly important challenge to notions of equality in companionate partnerships. Although men and women can contract an equal partnership in cohabitation or marriage while they have only themselves to consider, when there are children the situation alters radically and the allocation of parenting tasks tends to be far from equal. While psychological literature has moved away from a belief in the exclusivity of the mother–child relationship, accepting that children can and do form multiple attachments, responsibilities for child care fall primarily on mothers, even though the majority go out to work. Fathers spend less time than mothers with their children and are less likely to take responsibility for their children's daily lives and care (Clarke and O'Brien, 2004). The resulting parental role strain can have a detrimental impact on family relationships as increased freedoms in conjugal arrangements often conflict with the constraints inherent in parenthood.

Whereas having a baby inevitably disrupts mothers' working patterns, few men can or do shift their work routines to accommodate children. Since 2003, parents who have completed at least one year's service with their employer have been entitled to 13 weeks of unpaid parental leave to care for children under five, and family-friendly working practices have enabled parents to work more flexibly. Relatively few fathers are pursuing their rights under these provisions, however: in 2004, only 1 in 10 fathers was asking for flexible working time (Hewitt, 2004). Most parents, and fathers in particular, view providing an income for the family as the central aspect of fathering.

While parenthood requires no particular form of relationship or family structure, parenting denotes expectations about behaviours, tasks and commitments, and is a challenging task. In recent decades the meaning of parenthood has been transformed alongside the reconstruction of marital relationships. What has emerged is parenting based less on authority, gender division and marital status, and more on the quality of relationships between adults and between parents and children. Increasingly, the obligations of parenthood are not related to marriage but to the fact of being a parent. Moreover, children appear to have an accepting, inclusive view of what counts as family: their definitions and expectations do not centre on biological relatedness. While there are concerns for children who are brought up in seriously adverse environments, poor outcomes are not inevitable: many children show considerable resilience and manage to overcome stress and disruption in their lives. The task for policy-makers and welfare practitioners is to ensure that risk factors can be minimized and protective factors increased, whatever models of partnership and parenting children experience.

Although the twenty-first century has seen greater acceptance of diverse family forms, anxieties continue about the stability of family life and the well-being of children. These prompted the New Labour Government to institute a variety of initiatives from the late 1990s to redress the perceived deficit in parenting, emphasizing that the processes of welfare reform and moral reordering go together. The appointment in 2003 of a Minister for Children, Young People and Families signalled the emergence of a new, explicitly child-centred family policy with the eradication of child poverty by 2020 as the central goal. Policies have stopped short of promoting marriage as the preferred family form, but there is a clear belief that children do better if they are cared for by two parents within a stable household. Data from the Millennium Cohort Study (Kiernan, 2004) suggest that the child-raising environment provided by cohabiting mothers may be less good for children than that provided by married mothers: mothers in cohabiting relationships are more likely to have had an unplanned pregnancy, live in a disadvantaged neighbourhood, have lower incomes and smoke more heavily. Cohabiting fathers are just as involved in child care as married fathers, however, and both cohabiting and married mothers score higher on all health and social indices than mothers who live alone.

The Government's proposals for promoting its 'every child matters' agenda set out five key outcomes for every child irrespective of family structures:

- being healthy;
- staying safe;
- enjoying and achieving;
- making a positive contribution;
- experiencing economic well-being (Department for Education and Skills, 2003).

In order to achieve these outcomes when parents separate, the Government's agenda for change emphasized that:

- the child's welfare must be the paramount consideration in any help, support or intervention given;
- this is usually best promoted by a continuing and constructive relationship with both parents;
- both parents have a responsibility to ensure their child has constructive contact with each parent;
- help, advice and support for parents and children should be readily available;
- collaborative agreements between parents are likely to work better than those imposed by courts;
- the wishes and feelings of children should be considered and taken into account (Department for Education and Skills, 2003).

This agenda and reforms in youth justice have given courts powers to refer parents to parenting programmes, to make parenting and child safety orders, and to imprison parents for failing to ensure that a child goes to school or for breaching a parenting order. Poor parenting and lack of care and supervision are important influences on youth offending and antisocial behaviour, and parental obligations to bring up children as competent, responsible citizens are both encouraged and enforced.

The evidence suggests that families do benefit, and that parenting programmes can improve parent–child interaction and child behaviour (Quinton, 2004): universal services seek to support families at the key stages of vulnerability and change in a child's life, while targeted services aim to meet specific needs, for example during the break-up of parental relationships, when children get into trouble or through periods of mental or physical ill health. To be effective, 'parenting programmes need to ensure that they do not stigmatize or create dependency and last long enough for changes to be sustained rather than for false hopes and negative reactions to be evoked' (Barratt, 2003, p. 204). Nevertheless, the considerable growth in family and parenting services has been so marked that the role of the state in both supporting and regulating families is being questioned. The Commission on Families and the Wellbeing of Children (2005) identified the need for greater consistency in the degree to which a supportive approach informs public policy towards families, but argued for caution in terms of the expectations placed on family services to deliver social change and to support families in the upbringing of children. It is usually mothers who participate in parenting programmes despite the widespread acceptance that fathers have a crucial role to play in their children's upbringing: fathers' involvement in their children's training and education is 'associated with better educational, social and emotional outcomes for children, including better exam results, better school attendance and behaviour, and higher educational expectations' (Goldman, 2005, p. 269). Contemporary fathers, however, are a diverse group and fathering has multiple dimensions within a diversity of styles and relationships (O'Brien, 2004). Fathering normally involves interaction with mothers, but when parents live apart that interaction can be damaged, disrupted or non-existent, thereby changing the ways in which fathering can take place. In order to promote a positive change in fathering practices, there is a need to:

- challenge traditional gender roles associated with child-raising and childcare;
- encourage more flexible social attitudes to masculinity and fatherhood;
- facilitate more widespread family-friendly employment practices;
- encourage fathers' involvement in parenting activities and family learning programmes.

As patterns of partnership change so do patterns of parenting. Practitioners face a considerable challenge in supporting parents across a variety of family forms, particularly those in which men have a weak investment. The modern family is faced with a paradox: on the one hand, partnership formation and couple relationships are increasingly private and diversity is acknowledged; on the other, parents are expected to meet high expectations and their functioning is increasingly regulated. Social workers have to work at the interface between family autonomy and the state's expectations of parents.

Today's families perform a variety of functions, including meeting the daily material needs of their members, caring for and raising children, caring for dependent and independent adults, and meeting the intimacy needs of partners. Clearly, there is a potential conflict between adults' need for intimacy and children's need for stability. Struening (2002) has argued that the voluntary nature of modern adult partnerships has made them both fragile and strong: fragile because feelings are notoriously changeable, but strong because freely chosen relationships have an integrity and dignity which those based on economic dependence or coercion do not. She also advocated that the welfare of fragile families must be a state interest because it is difficult for parents to do well unless they receive support.

Parents in the twenty-first century face a harder task than ever before. However, although family forms are diverse, research shows that people are usually committed to their relationships, and, in particular, to the generally loving relationships between parents and children. Despite social flux, there are strong emotional and caring bonds within today's families, most of which provide children with an upbringing that is conducive to good physical and mental health, education, life opportunities, fulfilment and enjoyment (Williams, 2004).

Five Key Points

- Marriage, parenting and family have been regarded as 'a package deal', but the reality is rather different.
- Modern partnerships put a strong focus on companionship and strong emotional bonds.
- The boundaries of partnership and parenting are infinitely flexible, permeable and diverse.
- Parental separation and divorce have a profound influence on parenting, with potentially detrimental consequences for children.
- Fathers play a very important role in children's lives: traditional gender roles therefore need to be challenged and more flexible attitudes towards fatherhood encouraged.

Three Questions

? How does your experience of childhood, partnership and parenting measure up?

? Should all parents have to attend parenting classes (a) when they have children and (b) if they split up?

? How can fathers be encouraged to play a more central role in their children's upbringing?

Further reading

1 Jenson, A. M. and McKee, L. (eds.) (2003) *Children and the Changing Family: Between Transformation and Negotiation*. The Future of Childhood series. London: Routledge/Farmer.
2 Lamb, M. (ed.) (2004) *The Role of the Father in Child Development*, 4th edn. New Jersey: Wiley.
3 Duncombe, J., Harrison, K., Allan, G. and Marsden, D. (eds.) (2004) *The State of Affairs*. Hillsdale, NJ: Erlbaum.

CHAPTER 5.5

Late Life Ageing

Ian Philp

Late life ageing is shaped by the accumulation of life events and the proximity of death.

Although it is tempting to consider late life ageing as that which occurs towards the end of life, it is becoming increasingly recognized that late life ageing is profoundly influenced by earlier life experience. For example, a substantial body of research from the Medical Research Council Epidemiology Unit in Southampton suggests that early life nutritional experience, including as an embryo, affects health status in late life (Barker, 1992). Therefore, late life ageing needs to be considered as part of the complete life course.

Rembrandt's self-portraits in late life reflect this. His method of building up the foreground from the background until a clear and unique portrait emerges is one reason why his paintings of old age resonate. His method is analogous to late life ageing; the production of a complex and unique individual emerging from layer upon layer of background experience.

As long life increases exposure to life events, there is a tendency for late life ageing to be characterized by increasing diversity amongst individuals in relation to their health, functioning, relationships, standards of living, attitudes and perceived quality of life.

Although death is the ultimate leveller, late life ageing is not. We need, therefore, to avoid the temptation to make general assumptions which are too simplistic to explain late life ageing.

Furthermore, the world is changing at an accelerating pace, so the 80-year olds of 20 years from now will have lived in very different times from the 80-year olds of today, or 10 years ago, whose lives were dominated by the cataclysmic events of the Second World War. One of the most obvious changes is the greying of the population which is occurring in both the developed and developing worlds. However, the expectations of older people for improved material and health status may have as much impact on late life as the proportionate increase in the number of older people in the population.

Societies are also becoming more heterogeneous with widening differences (sometimes referred to as inequalities) in health and income which persist into later life.

To a large extent, then, late life ageing reflects the life-long influence of many external events on the individual. This process is described as extrinsic ageing.

Intrinsic ageing, on the other hand, refers to the ageing processes which are independent of external events which, to a large extent, are programmed by genetic control. The genetic basis of ageing is illustrated by the 'disposable soma' theory (Kirkwood, 1995). This states that the human body is simply a vehicle for the transmission of genetic material. Ultimately, the human body is disposable, having served its role in the transmission of genetic material. In late life, it is of greater evolutionary advantage for the human to support 25 per cent of his or her gene pool in his or her grandchild, than 50 per cent in his or her child. Much human attitude and behaviour can, therefore, be explained from this perspective, including differing societal attitudes to old age which, on the one hand, include idealized views of old people in grandparenting roles and, on the other hand, discrimination against old people in relation to life-saving interventions (Giallombardo and Homer, 1994). The most graphic illustration of an ambiguous attitude to old age is the apocryphal tale of a native American tribe which, in times of plenty, venerates its elders and, in times of famine, eats them (Eric Midwinter, personal communication).

An important determinant of intrinsic ageing is the limitation of the number of times different cells of the body can replicate. This is referred to as the 'Hayflick Limit', although the theory can be traced back to the nineteenth century (Weismann, 1891). Replication is necessary to repair worn out cells. In theory, it may be possible to alter the mechanisms which limit cell division, creating immortal cells, and extending life expectancy. However, interference with intrinsic ageing may extend life of poor quality if other ageing changes persist. Put simply, we could live for 700 years, but the last 600 might be spent in a state of advanced dementia.

In fact, advances in medical science are increasing our ability to modify extrinsic rather than intrinsic ageing, but there remains the prospect of molecular and genetic treatments becoming available which would fundamentally alter late life ageing.

The overall impact of recent health and social care systems on late life ageing is debated. Some have argued that the net effect has been the 'survival of the unfittest' (Isaacs, 1972), whereby people who would otherwise have died are saved for a life of disability. Others argue that the net effect has been to extend healthy active life which could lead to the compression of the period of disability into the last few years of life, prior to natural death from old age (Fries, 1980).

The balance of epidemiological evidence suggests that modern health and social care systems are helping to extend both healthy active life and disability-associated life prior to death. The combined effect, therefore, extends overall life expectancy.

Perhaps because extrinsic factors are dominant in the ageing process, we have yet to see life expectancy increase to the extent that compression of morbidity can occur as we get close to the limit of human life. Life expectancy for humans limited by intrinsic ageing is reckoned to be about 120 years.

A common misperception about ageing is that ill health and disability in later life are an inevitable feature of growing old. Although some features, such as deafness, poor vision, arthritis, a decline in fitness, failing memory and loss of teeth are common, they are not inevitable in old age. The phenomenon of 'successful' ageing has been described, based on studies of cohorts of middle-aged people who have been followed over time into later life (Rowe and Kahn, 1987). Most of these people experience 'usual' ageing, characterized by a decline in a number of body functions, but some experience very little age-associated decline. Others experience greater than usual decline, described as 'pathological' ageing.

The importance of these studies is that they point to the challenge for disease prevention which could modify usual ageing towards successful ageing for future cohorts of elderly people. These studies also show that usual ageing changes are less dramatic than popular conceptions of ageing, which, for example, equate ageing with dementia. Only about 20 per cent of people aged 85 plus experience dementia, an example of pathological ageing, although most experience mild memory loss (usual ageing) and a small proportion experience no memory loss (successful ageing). These clinical findings are corroborated by autopsy examination of the brains of older people where a minority have extensive numbers of neurofibrillary tangles and plaques (the hallmark of Alzheimer's Disease); most have a few, and a minority have none.

Public health goals may be directed towards promoting successful ageing, but health and social care practitioners will continue to work with older people whose ageing process is usual or pathological. A preoccupation with successful ageing could lead to discrimination against older people with disease and disability.

Disease in late life often comes to attention in non-specific ways including falls, confusion, immobility and failure to thrive. These presentations can be precipitated by a wide range of events, from a urinary infection to a change of environment, but there is usually a background of longer-term problems and a complex interplay of physical, psychological and social factors. Treatment strategies themselves may add to the problem. The term 'iatrogenesis' is used to describe illness induced by treatment and is fairly common in older people. The physiological reserve of the older person may be small, so that he or she may function adequately most of the time, but with a minimal threat a critical threshold may be breached causing dysfunction. A chain reaction may be set up where dysfunction in one area leads to multiple failures of organs, systems, overall functioning and perhaps death.

For these reasons, rapid response to crises in older people may be rewarded by restoration of the older person to a state of acceptable health and functioning. However, repeated crises will reduce physiological reserve further and create a vicious cycle of increasing frequency of crisis and further decline in physiological reserve.

Much of health and social care practice is, therefore, concerned with caring for this type of frail older person, living close to the edge of incapacity. Fragmentation of health and social care systems, and exclusion of older people from access to acute care services undermines our ability to respond to the dynamic needs of older people, and leads to an increased reliance on long-term care services or family care to support an increasingly disabled population of older people.

A medical model of ageing which embraces the concepts of disability and disease inevitably reinforces the perception of ageing as a process of decline. A perception of decline in late life extends to the psychological and social as well as physical features of late life ageing, characterized by loss of health, autonomy, financial status and the comfort of family, friendship and marital relations. Yet the experience of late life ageing for many people is not dominated by decline, but by accomplishment and satisfaction with life.

A theoretical basis for a positive view of late life ageing is provided by the work of Eric Erikson on psychological ageing.

Each stage of life, from infancy to old age is characterized by a psychological battle between successful and unsuccessful ageing. In old age, the battle is between integrity and despair. Integrity is characterized by a sense that life was worthwhile, life's mission is complete, and death, while not welcome, is not feared. Despair is accompanied by a fear of death, or death may be desired because life is seen as worthless.

With increasing longevity, there may be a stage beyond integrity, given that years of life may follow the milestone when life's mission is perceived to have been accomplished (Erikson et al., 1986). In spite of the many losses which accompany late life ageing, many, perhaps most, older people achieve a sense of integrity. Perhaps the fundamental task of social work with old people should be to promote this goal. Recent work on 'life strengths' (Kivnic, 1991) provides a systematic approach for doing so.

There is much still to be studied about late life ageing, and how it is changing with time, and amongst individuals and cultures of great diversity. New horizons from genetics to psychology are appearing, which could change the course of late life ageing. We can be sure of very little, except that the challenge to better understand late life ageing will remain a fascinating and worthwhile endeavour.

Five Key Points

- Late life ageing is shaped by the accumulation of life events and the proximity of death.
- Old people vary in health, functioning, relationships, standards of living, attitudes and their perceived quality of life.
- Advances in medical science are increasing our ability to modify extrinsic rather than intrinsic ageing.
- Life expectancy for humans limited by intrinsic ageing is reckoned to be about 120 years.
- Despite the many losses which accompany late life ageing, many older people achieve a sense of integrity.

Three Questions

? What ethical concerns are raised by the potential of genetic therapy to intervene in the ageing process?

? If the goals of public health are to reduce disability-associated life prior to death, would resources be withdrawn from disabled older people?

? How will social work for older people change when the 'me' generation reach old age?

Further reading

1 Walker, A. and Hagan Hennessy, C. (eds.) (2004) *Growing Older: Quality of Life in Old Age*. Buckingham: Open University Press.
2 Harper, S. (2005) *Ageing Societies*. London: Hodder.
3 Victor, C. R. (2005) The epidemiology of ageing. In M. Johnson (ed.), *The Cambridge Handbook of Age and Ageing*. Cambridge: Cambridge University Press.

PART 6

Perspectives on Social Work

CHAPTER 6.1

Service Users' Perspectives

Suzy Croft and Peter Beresford

This discussion is concerned with the key critique of social work which is emerging from its recipients. Long hidden and largely ignored, it has grown in strength, visibility and impact in recent years. Three of the key questions it raises are:

- What part have service users played in the development of social work?
- What part do they want to play?
- What kind of social work, if any, does this point to for the future?

The Dominant Social Work Discourse

In some ways, in the early years of the twenty-first century, social work might seem to be set fair. Domestically, the professional qualification is now set at degree level, numbers of students in training have risen and social work posts have increased considerably in number. Yet in 2006, a high profile manifesto argued that social work in Britain had lost direction, was dominated by managerialism, and undermined by financial restrictions, increased bureaucracy, privatization and mechanical care management approaches (Jones et al., 2006).

Concern has continued that social work and social services are being used to implement authoritarian welfare policies and that social work education is under tightening bureaucratic control (Jones, 1998). Commentators fear that social work has itself internalized the market-led political ideologies which are associated with the increasing poverty, social injustice and division which it is meant to counter (Jordan and Jordan, 2000). At the same time, social work is seen as under constant attack from the media and the political right (Neate and Douglas, 2000). It is not difficult to see the reasons for social work's anxiety and loss of confidence. The Griffiths Report (1988), which underpinned the reshaping of community care, made no reference to social work. The new arrangements which it heralded restructured social work tasks as 'care management' and a wide range of other professionals, including nurses and occupational therapists, were seen as equally qualified to undertake them. There was little detailed discussion of social work in the 2006 government White Paper on social care and health (Department of Health, 2006a). Its talk of the role of social worker as 'navigator' seems like a restatement of care management, without recognition of the particular professional contribution of social work practice. Its emphasis on integration looks likely further to subordinate social care to health and social approaches to the medical model. *Every Child Matters*, (Department for Education and Skills, 2003) has resulted in the radical reorganization of children's services, but whether this will overcome shortages of resources and increasing bureaucratization to prevent another tragic death like that of Victoria Climbié, remains open to question. Social work's preoccupation with child protection has been challenged by official research (Department of Health, 1995a) and in the area of fostering and adoption, social work's competence and philosophy have both continued to be heavily challenged by politicians and the media.

There has been a search for a new direction for social work, away from market-led practice, to a more humane and humanistic model (Smale et al., 2000; Parton and O'Byrne, 2000), but no clear route maps have been offered to show how social work is to reach these different destinations, or from where the support for them is to come. At the same time, the idea of *empowerment* has come to the fore in social work, as it has in other human service professions, as a basis for increasing people's control over their lives (Shera and Wells, 1999). But critics have raised fundamental questions about it, suggesting that its dominant definition by professionals reflects their agendas rather than those of service users (Jack, 1995) and that it may have regulatory as well as liberatory implications, focusing narrowly on people taking responsibility for their own lives, instead of recognizing and challenging the constraints operating upon them.

New Labour overlaid social work with a new vocabulary, ideological framework and structures. These have made for a changed context, role, regulation and objectives for social work. Government highlights 'quality', 'partnership', 'participation', 'modernization', 'social inclusion', 'communitarianism' and personal 'responsibility'. All these terms are contentious and ill-defined. Probably most important for social work is the prioritizing of labour market based interpretations of 'social exclusion' based on people's assimilation into employment, rather than reliance on state welfare, wherever possible. Service users have had little involvement in welfare reform, although the official rhetoric is of service users being at the centre of policy and practice development.

New structures have been established to define and regulate social work and social care standards, staff, practice and training, but already the status of these is uncertain, with one, the Commission for Social Care Inspection, scheduled for absorption into the Health Care Commission. There is also a strong and continuing commitment to the increased application of compulsion in mental health policy and practice.

What Service Users Have to Say about Social Work

Service users have raised serious concerns about social work. They have highlighted its failings and expressed fundamental reservations about it. They have spotlighted the frequent failure of social work to safeguard service users' rights or meet their needs. Psychiatric system survivors report additional problems, with social work as part of a system based on a medicalized model of madness and distress and the restriction rather than the protection of people's rights. Moreover, the more that social work is associated with regulation and control, the less service users are likely to want to turn to it and the more public hostility we can expect it to incur.

However, it is not only where social work's powers to restrict people's rights are applied that these difficulties arise. People's experience has been equally problematic where social work is intended to provide support. Social work has traditionally given low priority to work with older people, people with learning difficulties and disabled people. It has been part of a system of social services based on a model which segregates and congregates disabled people, reinforcing their economic dependence rather than ensuring equal opportunities, access, choices and rights (Oliver and Barnes, 1999). For most adult service users, contact with social care staff is restricted to low-paid unqualified workers (Beresford et al., 2005). In a survey of disabled people, a disabled researcher concluded that most received little help from social workers in moving out of residential services or organizing housing and personal assistance (Morris, 1993, p. 69). There is little evidence of the situation improving since then.

Recipients of social work generally report little choice in practitioner or in the professional practice they experience. Conventional research reinforces this discouraging picture. Assessments are clouded by judgementalism, workers' preconceptions and overwhelmingly by budgetary constraints. Despite the introduction of formal complaints procedures, there continue to be many problems in making a complaint and service users remain reluctant to complain (Simons, 1995).

Social work has continuing difficulties ensuring equal access, opportunities and outcomes for women, black people and members of minority ethnic groups as both service users and workers (Dominelli, 1988; Hanmer and Statham, 1999). There does not seem to have been the pre-market golden age of social work for service users to which some expert commentators seem anxious to retreat. Instead the dominant pattern has been one of exclusion and paternalism, which Bill Jordan summed up more than a quarter-century ago as the 'giving of second hand goods and second hand sympathy' (Jordan, 1975).

The Role of Service Users in Social Work

So far service users have played little part in the development of social work. They have been allocated two overlapping roles.

The first role follows from the tradition epitomized and established by *The Client Speaks* (Mayer and Timms, 1970). This study was not, as has sometimes been assumed, a plea for more accountable or democratic social work. It was less 'the client' than the authors of the study who spoke. They were mainly interested in clients as a *data source* for researchers (Beresford and Croft, 1987). This tradition still thrives. More than three decades later, the role of service users in evaluating social work effectiveness is still seen mainly as one of providing information rather than helping to define or measure effectiveness (Williams et al., 1999).

Since *The Client Speaks*, there has been an attempt to extend the role of service users in social work through the idea of 'partnership' (Marsh and Fisher, 1992), which has also been encouraged by government. But this has been undermined by a lack of clarity and agreement about the meaning and definition of partnership. The failure of its advocates to take sufficient account of conflict and inequalities of power and control has resulted in it carrying little credence among service users. Other critics argue that: 'even more curious is the notion that parents or carers accused of abusing a child are expected to relate as "partners" with those investigating the allegation' (Shemmings and Shemmings, 1995).

The second role offered to service users in social work and social services is that of 'getting involved'. The 1990s saw the beginning of a new emphasis on 'user involvement'. This followed from:

- the commitment of Conservative governments to a mixed economy of care and consumerist welfare;
- legislation such as the Children Act 1989 and the NHS and Community Care Act 1990 including provision for the involvement of service users;
- pressure from service users and their organizations for more say in and control over their lives and services affecting them.

It has subsequently been encouraged by political commitment to managerialist and regulatory approaches to the construction of social care. User involvement has mainly focused on planning and management rather than on social work practice itself. Service users have typically been drawn into formal consultative structures concerned with bureaucratic and administrative functions. The indications from service users and independent research findings are that user involvement has been patchy and qualified and its gains limited and rarely evaluated (Carr, 2004). Instead of social work practice being more explicitly participative, competing government priorities of 'value for money', 'best value' and 'needs-led provision' have resulted in budget-driven rather than the promised user-centred services. Service users have more often experienced user involvement as stressful, diversionary and unproductive. While it has generally failed to include black people and members of minority ethnic groups on equal terms, service users and their organizations can expect to be criticized as 'unrepresentative' (Bewley and Glendinning, 1994; Shemmings and Shemmings, 1995; Campbell, 1996, 1999).

Policy and practice for user involvement have mainly been concerned with consultation and market research exercises, rather than with any shift in decision-making or power. Service users have been expected to feed into professional debates and developments. Thus service users' main role in the development of modern social work has remained essentially unchanged – to provide information – first for researchers and subsequently for social work agencies, policy-makers and professionals.

This is a role with which users of social services have expressed increasing dissatisfaction. It is based on a narrow, service-led approach to involvement which abstracts the contribution of service users. The conceptualization of user involvement has become heavily contested, reflecting the competing concerns of service providers and users. Service providers are primarily concerned with meeting the political, economic and managerial requirements of their agencies and services. The concerns of service users are at once more personal and broader: they are committed to improving the *quality of their lives*, rejecting inappropriate provision which restricts what they can do and seeking appropriate support to live as they want to.

Service users have shown an increasing frustration with demands to comment on the detail of existing arrangements. There is now a strong and growing sense of 'consultation fatigue' and distrust of agency initiatives for involvement among service users and their organizations. They do not see themselves in narrow terms as 'consumers' of social work or 'users' of social services.

Service Users' Perspectives on Social Work

Service users have a different starting point. Disabled people and other social care service users have established their own powerful movements. They have their own democratically constituted local, regional, national and international organizations. They have developed their own discussions, writings, arts, culture and forms of political action. In their struggle for anti-discrimination legislation in the UK, disabled people showed that they had become far more powerful politically than the social work profession which traditionally intervened to shape their individual lives (Beresford, 1999).

Social work's commentators continue to look for solutions to social work's ills from among their own ranks (Coulshed and Orme, 1998). But so far their track record for halting social work's decline is poor. Social care service users, on the other hand, are changing the terms of the social work debate. They are asking fundamental and important questions: Why social work? What is it for? How is it to be accountable? What should it look like?

And they are beginning to offer their own answers to these questions. They are developing demands, models and theories which are having a growing impact on public policy and which point to the reconception and reconstruction of social work and social services. They place an emphasis on people's civil rights and the relation between the individual and society and the service system and society.

Disabled people's social model of disability draws a distinction between people's *impairment* – the functional limitations which affect their bodies, and their *disability* – the oppression, barriers and discrimination they experience as a result of society's reaction to impairment. The social model of madness and distress emerging from psychiatric system survivors validates people's experience, feelings and perceptions and highlights the social causes of people's distress and the damaging and discriminatory psychiatric and social response to it (Beresford, 2000).

In their discussions, social care service users constantly return to three key themes and priorities: *autonomy*, *participation* and *inclusion*. The disabled people's movement places an emphasis on independent living, but it has turned conventional ideas of independence – meaning 'to stand on your own two feet' – on their head. It has transformed 'independence' to mean autonomy instead of individualism – to have appropriate support to ensure people equal rights, choices and opportunities. Participation, the idea of speaking and acting for yourself and being part of mainstream society, lies at the heart of the social care service user movements. Service users have highlighted the limitations of personal social services policy from both the political left and right. They have reported the failure of market solutions to meet need and of paternalistic state prescriptions to ensure choice and equal opportunities and pressed instead for *user-led* policy and provision. To ensure inclusion, they have stressed the need for:

- support for service users to be able to participate on equal terms;
- equity in the treatment of service users, regardless of age, class, 'race', disability, sexual identity and gender;
- recognition of diversity, for example, people's different ways of communicating – non-verbally, in pictures, by signing, or in minority ethnic languages.

Service users argue for social work and social services which:

- are concerned with enabling people to be independent rather than maintaining them in dependence, focusing on people's abilities rather than their incapacities, and supporting people to be autonomous;
- do not serve as a palliative for the failure of mainstream policies but instead are systematically related to broader rights and needs-led social and economic policies which include rather than marginalize groups like disabled people, lone parents and psychiatric system survivors, ensuring their access to education, training, child care and employment;
- provide support rather than direction and are fully participative.

Service users also highlight the skills that are needed to achieve these objectives. In one development project they identified a wide range of skills which they felt were needed for helpful practice. Significantly, there was considerable agreement between different 'user groups' about these skills. They included: seeing the individual as a whole person, not as a set of symptoms or problems; treating people as individuals, not as an anonymous group or class; treating people with respect; acknowledging the validity of their experience and views; providing them with full and accessible information; listening to what they say and asking them what they want; recognizing the need to meet them on their own terms and if possible on their own ground where they would feel more comfortable and relaxed (Beresford and Trevillion, 1995). Service users emphasize the importance of social workers having positive human qualities as well as learned skills and at the heart of everything they put the quality of the relationship of the service user with the social worker (Beresford et al., 2007).

The standards which service users have begun to identify for social services workers reflect similar priorities and concerns and again there is great consistency from a wide range of service users. They stress:

> courtesy and respect, being treated as equals and as individuals, and as people who make their own decisions; they value people who are experienced and well informed, able to explain things clearly and without condescension and who 'really listen'; and they value people who are able to act effectively and make practical things happen. (Harding and Beresford, 1996, p. 1)

Service users argue that they need to play a greater part in both the *socialization* and *practice* of social workers to achieve these skills, standards and objectives. Strategies for the first include service users' involvement in social workers' selection and recruitment; the increased and systematic involvement of service user trainers and service user organizations in social work education and training (Beresford, 1994; National Institute for Social Work, 1999) and the increased recruitment of disabled people and other service users as social workers (National Institute for Social Work, 2000). There is already considerable experience to show the effectiveness and feasibility of all three.

The social work degree introduced in 2003 requires user involvement in all stages and aspects of students' learning (Levin, 2004). While progress on this is patchy, this development does offer real hope for progress for the future (Branfield et al., 2005). Routes to increasing service users' involvement in practice range from schemes ensuring service users an effective say in assessment, planning, recording and review, through to service users defining their own needs, putting together their own 'package of support' with the support of user-led advocacy and information services, and monitoring and evaluating the service they receive.

The direct payments schemes 'created, designed, established and developed by disabled people' to achieve the goals of the independent living movement have perhaps been the ultimate expression of the latter (Evans, 1995). Such schemes are self-operated and self-directed and enable people to choose and control the support they want. They have been demonstrated to be cost-effective and to increase the quality of disabled people's lives and the control they have over them (Zarb et al., 1996) The government is now expressing interest in extending both direct payments and individualized budget schemes which put service users in charge of different streams of funding to which they are entitled. If these schemes are to be successful, though it is crucial that they are based on the empowerment model developed by the disabled people's movement, rather than the consumerist approach which government seems to favour.

The same desire for more appropriate, more participatory provision is embodied in the idea of collective 'user-led alternatives'. These are now being established by disabled people, psychiatric system survivors, people living with HIV/AIDS and

The Human Rights Act

- Right to life
- Prohibition of torture
- Right to a fair trial
- Right to respect for private and family life
- Freedom of thought, conscience and religion
- Freedom of expression
- Freedom of assembly and association
- Right to marry
- Prohibition of discrimination

other groups in many parts of the world. They offer training, employment, accommodation, counselling, information, crisis support, advocacy, drop-in, asylum and other support services. They are rooted in the values and beliefs of service users rather than within traditional medical and professional frameworks.

We can expect the Human Rights Act, which reflects the commitment of the disabled people's and social care service users' movements to a rights approach to the meeting of their needs, to have a profound effect on social work, which has operated as part of a social care system that has often denied service users these rights actively or through neglect.

Towards User-led Social Work

Service users' ideas, initiatives and demands add up to a coherent paradigm for social work, but how does it relate to social work's own agendas and aspirations? What distinguishes social work is that it operates at the junction of our personal lives and civil status. It is concerned with our selves and our personal relationships. It addresses both our psyche and our understanding of and dealings with the social world we inhabit. Thus it is concerned with the social and personal; the psychological and the public, the individual and the collective; with the self and agencies affecting it. The social worker deals with the benefits agency and the housing department, as well as addressing people's innermost fears and desires. She is concerned with the social, economic, sexual, political and cultural aspects of people's lives, as well as the politics of welfare and of the state. The key recurring themes and goals of social work have been to enable people to live their lives independently, to negotiate conflict and safeguard people's rights.

This closely coincides with service users' concerns. Their agenda comes close to restoring social work to its original inspiration and challenging the narrow bureaucratic and regulatory role to which both its proponents and the political right have increasingly confined it. The latter have ignored valued and innovative areas of social work, like work with people living with HIV/AIDS and in palliative care.

Service users challenge the view of social work as a marginal special service for a separate 'disadvantaged' group and instead emphasize its relevance to all in those times and conditions of loss, impairment, distress, abuse and illness that are an inherent part of the human condition. The vision of social work which service users offer – as a universalist support service – not only represents a return to first principles. It also unifies the concerns of social work and service users. By doing this, it offers both a positive prospect for the future.

Five Key Points

- Social work continues to be marginalized publicly and politically, amid continuing professional fears that it is tied to authoritarian welfare policies.
- Social work service users have traditionally played little part in the development of social work.
- Social work service users and their organizations highlight fundamental failings in social work policy and practice.
- Social work service users highlight three themes and priorities for policy and practice: autonomy, participation and inclusion.
- User-led social work, based on social work service users' priorities, provides a practical basis to restore social work to its traditional commitment to uphold service users' independence, rights and choices.

Three Questions

? What part have service users played in the development of social work?
? What part do they want to play?
? What kind of social work, if any, does this point to for the future?

Further reading

1 Beresford, P., Shamash, O., Forrest, V., Turner, M. and Branfield, F. (2005) *Developing Social Care: Service Users' Vision for Adult Support* (Report of a consultation on the future of adult social care), Adult Services Report 07. London: Social Care Institute for Excellence in association with Shaping Our Lives.
2 Tew, J. (ed.) (2005) *Social Perspectives in Mental Health: Developing Social Models to Understand and Work with Mental Distress*. London: Jessica Kingsley.
3 Barnes, C. and Mercer, G. (2006) *Independent Futures: Creating User Led Disability Services in a Disabling Society*. Bristol: Policy Press.

CHAPTER 6.2

The Perspective of the Disabled People's Movement

Sally French and John Swain

New ways of knowing disability, essentially generated by disabled people themselves, have increasingly informed debates amongst theorists, policy-makers and practitioners. Disablism, in all its diverse and pernicious manifestations, is being challenged. It is becoming recognized that the policies and practices of social work and social care can compound disablism but can also challenge the discrimination experienced by disabled people. Here we summarize the new ways of knowing disability and their implications for social work practice.

The Social Model of Disability

The crucial development in theories of disability in recent years has been the establishment of the social model of disability. The first clear and principled statement of the social model is generally thought to have been that presented by the Union of the Physically Impaired against Segregation (UPIAS) in 1976. It took the form, centrally, of two definitions:

1 *Impairment*: lacking part of or all of a limb, or having a defective limb, organ or mechanism of the body.
2 *Disability*: the disadvantage or restriction of activity caused by a contemporary social organisation which takes no or little account of people who have physical impairments and thus excludes them from participation in the mainstream of social activities. Physical disability is therefore a particular form of social oppression. (Union of the Physically Impaired against Segregation, 1976, p. 14)

The word 'physical' is now frequently excluded from this definition so as to include people with learning difficulties and survivors of the mental health system.

The social model has been significant in a number of ways. First, it stands in direct opposition to the dominant individual models of disability which include tragedy and medical models. In particular, the dominant medical model assumes that the difficulties faced by disabled people are a direct result of their individual impairments. As Mercer and Barnes (2000, p. 85) state, 'the medical approach concentrates on a set of discrete functional limitations requiring technical intervention and individual adjustment'. The social model of disability, on the other hand, recognizes the social origins of disability in a society geared by and for non-disabled people. The disadvantages or restrictions experienced by disabled people, often referred to as barriers, permeate every aspect of the physical and social environment: attitudes, institutions, language and culture, organization and delivery of support services, and the power relations and structures of which society is constructed.

Second, the social model of disability promotes the personal and political empowerment of disabled people. The social model engenders self-confidence and pride, rather than the guilt and shame associated with the individual tragedy model. The political implications of the social model, often explicitly stated, are to promote the collective struggle by disabled people for social change, equality, social justice and the rights of full participative citizenship. The model has gained some acceptance by social workers although Gibbs (2004) doubts that this has had very much impact on professional practice.

Third, this model of disability is borne out of the collective experience of disabled people as they have challenged the ways in which 'experts' have defined and controlled them (Charlton, 2000; Davis, 2004). It is no coincidence that the Disabled People's Movement and the social model of disability have developed together.

As a collective, dynamic theory, the social model is undergoing continued development (Swain et al., 2003). Disabled people have voiced criticisms on a number of grounds, though it is crucial to recognize that all such critics accept the basic principles of the social model and are arguing for its development, extension or renewal. The fundamental point to be made about these debates is that they reflect the voices of disabled people as they attempt to generate a new discourse about themselves, and take control of the development of theory (Barnes and Mercer, 2003).

The Disabled People's Movement

A strong Disabled People's Movement has emerged in Britain in the face of the discriminatory barriers and oppression experienced by disabled people (Campbell and Oliver, 1996). The Movement consists of organizations of disabled people – that is, those that are controlled by disabled people themselves. The British Council of Disabled People (BCODP) was formed as an umbrella group for such organizations in 1981. By 2005, it represented over 120 organizations with membership also open to individual disabled people. It articulates its demands through formal political channels and lobbies and advises both central and local government. It also undertakes research, organizes demonstrations and campaigns of direct action, and promotes disability equality training (you can access its website at www.bcodp.org.uk).

The Movement continues to develop in a number of ways. *Disability Arts* is a relatively recent, though well-established, branch of the Disabled People's

Movement. A wide diversity of activities are encompassed within Disability Arts. There are a growing number of examples of the work of individual disabled artists expressing their experiences and communicating their thoughts and feelings as disabled people (Swain et al., 2003). A central feature of Disability Arts, however, is collective experience. Disabled people are increasingly coming together to help each other express themselves in music, drama, poetry, forms of visual art and comedy. Through Disability Arts many disabled people have regular opportunities to share ideas and information with each other (Goodley and Moore, 2002; Vasey, 2004). The magazine *Disability Arts in London* (DAIL) is one way in which ideas are generated and shared.

Disability Arts is a political as well as an artistic forum and, as such, has four major functions.

1 It involves making the implicit theories of disability explicit, exposing the derogatory nature of negative images and stereotypes of disabled people.
2 Disability Arts has also, often through humour, lampooned and challenged disabling attitudes, and forms of discrimination and oppression.
3 Through their writing, visual and performing arts disabled people are also promoting very different images of disability which celebrate difference among people and promote the value of all people. Disability Arts, then, has furthered the exploration of a social model of disability.
4 The active participation of disabled people in Disability Arts in itself combats images of passivity and dependence.

A significant development in social movements generally has been the growth of international networks of activists. *Disabled People's International* (DPI) is an umbrella group of organizations of disabled people which was established in 1981. It has member organizations of disabled people, including BCODP, in over 110 countries and is recognized by the United Nations as the representative voice of disabled people internationally (www.dpi.org/uk). *Disability Awareness in Action*, for instance, is an organization led by disabled people to increase networking among them and their organizations throughout the world (www.daa.org/uk). In the globalized world in which we live there is a pressing need to analyse disability in an international context. This is slowly being reflected in the disability literature (Barnes and Mercer, 2005; Lawson and Gooding, 2005).

The Disability Discrimination Act 1995

A major concern of the Disabled People's Movement in Britain over the past 20 years has been the passing of disability discrimination legislation. The first attempt was made in 1982 by Jack Ashley, a deaf MP, who introduced the Disabled People's Bill. This, and the following 12 attempts, were, however, defeated and it was not until November 1995 that the Disability Discrimination Act (DDA) finally reached the statute books.

The DDA gives disabled people limited rights in many areas including education, employment, transport, housing and the provision of goods facilities and services.

The legislation is, however, weak when compared with the Sex Discrimination Act 1975 and the Race Relations Act 1976. It is full of loopholes and phrases such as 'if it is reasonable' and ill-defined words like 'substantial' which, in effect, tell people when it is lawful to discriminate and when discrimination can be justified. Cost and health and safety regulations can, for example, be taken into account when measures to combat discrimination are considered. There have been long delays in the implementation of parts of it: for example, the requirement that landlords must apply 'reasonable adjustments' to rented property only became operational in December 2006.

The report *Improving the Life Chances of Disabled People* (2005) is an important statement of government strategy covering such things as independent living; early years and family support; and transition to adulthood. Though there are significant criticisms, it is generally recognized as having the social model of disability as its starting point.

It would be naive to believe that any piece of legislation or an exclusive emphasis on rights will end discrimination. This has been shown very clearly in the case of the Sex Discrimination Act 1975 and Race Relations Act 1976 where discrimination against women and ethnic minorities is still rife. Oliver (1996, p. 25) warns that: 'as disabled people we need to recognise that the law will not do it for us . . . we will still have to force the politicians and the lawyers to take our concerns seriously. We will still have to go out on the streets. The road to liberation is one that we can only take for ourselves.'

Implications for Social Work Practice

Oliver and Sapey (2006) believe that social workers, like all other health and welfare professionals, have operated with inappropriate models of disability. This has been intensified by the imposition of a competency-based paradigm upon education and training. Values which are central to the practice of social work have also been under attack, with a change of emphasis from social justice and anti-oppressive practice to a softer 'equal opportunities' approach to discrimination.

These developments are associated with the individualization of problems and interventions which is antithetical to that of the social model of disability which promotes collective action against oppression and the fight for civil rights. Some developments in social work thus represent a serious threat to the goals of disabled people and social workers who wish to work in partnership with them.

While social workers may feel constrained by their agency role or the administrative procedures required in carrying out assessments, there usually remains some degree of flexibility in which they can work in partnership with disabled people. For example, they can share power by sharing 'expert' knowledge and information, and they can encourage clients to participate actively in the writing of reports and case files so that their voices are heard and their viewpoints represented in 'official' documents. Information about services can also be put into accessible formats.

Awareness of disability by all those who work in social care can be encouraged and developed through disability equality training run by skilled disabled people. Disability equality training is primarily about changing the meaning of disability from individual tragedy to social oppression; it emphasizes the politics of disability, the social and physical barriers that disabled people face, and the links with other oppressed groups.

Principles for social work practice with disabled people

1. Heighten self-awareness of disability from the perspective of disabled people.
2. Work in partnership with disabled people to remove disabling barriers.
3. Recognize the expertise of disabled people and use professional power to assist disabled people in their fight for full citizenship.

Another way in which social workers can work in partnership is by recognizing and acknowledging the disabled person's expertise in relation to the meaning and experience of being disabled. This means encouraging disabled people to exercise choice of services appropriate to their desired lifestyles. Two quotations from disabled women (French, 2004, pp. 103–4) illustrate the conflicting perspectives disabled people and professional workers frequently have:

> What concerns me most of all is this focus on trying to make me 'normal' . . . I get a lot of referrals of 'this may help' and 'that may help'. They had a massive case conference before the adaptations – it was a case of 'how normal can we make her first? Are the adaptations necessary?'

> The biggest thing is about asking and not telling. They need to get into the habit of asking what would be helpful. They don't seem to enter into a dialogue – we respect them far more if we can have an equal partnership in the challenge we're both facing. I would expect a person to be trained to the task and have an excellent knowledge base, and I would expect to have an exchange of knowledge – theirs would be knowledge from their training and mine would be about my own body, and my lifestyle.

Social workers can work in partnership with disabled people by regarding themselves as a resource (expertise, information, advocacy) so that disabled people can work towards achieving their own goals. This would include:

- clarifying the goals to which the disabled person aspires;
- identifying the barriers which may prevent the realization of those goals;
- working towards removing the barriers.

Counselling skills may also be employed in the service of enabling disabled people to overcome disabling barriers or to counteract painful and oppressive experiences at the hands of a disabling society. However, counselling disabled people to 'come to terms' with the 'limitations' of their impairments or with the lack of resources to achieve a desired lifestyle is inappropriate if social workers wish to practise within the social model of disability (Swain et al., 2005).

Social workers and managers can actively encourage disabled people to become involved in forums where they can influence the development of relevant services. This includes ensuring that meetings are held in accessible venues and that disabled people are not excluded by lack of transport or inappropriate methods of communication (Carr, 2004).

From the perspective of the social model of disability, professional power can be used to highlight the shortfall in resources for disabled people, to ensure that the subjugated voices of disabled people are heard and responded to, and to encourage and support disabled people to assert themselves so that their expertise about disability is at the centre of the development of services and support. It is important that social workers and all other staff in social services departments make a conscious decision to heighten their awareness of disability as an area of enquiry.

Conclusion

Professionals, and all who work with disabled people, need to become informed about disability in its widest sense and about the many factors which constitute discrimination. Anti-oppressive practice requires social workers to move away from the traditional casework approach to 'helping', to become 'politically literate' with regard to disability, and to work with a much broader brief. They need to join forces with the Disabled People's Movement and to use their professional power in collaboration and partnership with disabled people to dismantle every aspect of disablism and to further the fight for full citizenship for all disabled people.

Five Key Points

- The social model of disability conceptualizes disability in terms of external physical and social barriers.
- The social model of disability has arisen from the experiences of disabled people themselves and promotes their personal and political empowerment.
- The Disabled People's Movement is international and consists of organizations *of* disabled people, that is organizations that are controlled by disabled people themselves.
- The Disability Discrimination Act 1995 is weak legislation and there have been delays in its implementation. It gives disabled people limited rights in many areas including employment, the provision of goods, facilities and services, education, transport and housing. It may or may not be strengthened by emergent government policy, such as that outlined in the report *Improving the Life Chances of Disabled People* (Cabinet Office, 2005).
- In order to work within the social model of disability social workers need to collaborate fully with disabled people in their fight for full citizenship.

Three Questions

? How is disability defined within the social model and how did this model of disability arise?

? What is the significance of the social model of disability, the Disability Discrimination Act 1995 and more recent developments in government policy to social work practice?

? What steps can social workers take to work within the social model of disability?

Further reading

1 Barnes, C. and Mercer, G. (eds.) (2004) *Disability Policy and Practice: Applying the Social Model.* Leeds: The Disability Press.

2 Swain, J., French, S., Barnes, C. and Thomas, C. (eds.) (2004) *Disabling Barriers – Enabling Environments* (2nd edn). London: Sage.

3 Oliver, M. and Sapey, B. (2006) *Social Work with Disabled People* (3rd edn). Basingstoke: Macmillan.

CHAPTER 6.3

The Carer's Perspective

Rose Barton

Carers provide support for relatives, neighbours or friends who need extra help as a result of illness, disability, mental health problems, substance misuse or frailty associated with ageing. The support provided often relates to personal care, home care, management of money, communication, emotional support or medication. Although informal care is a universal phenomenon carers are not a homogeneous group. They may be men, women or children living with those they care for, or at a distance. Care responsibilities may be voluntary or involuntary, individual or joint, temporary or lifelong. The caring role may be the carer's main form of work or it may be carried out alongside education, training or employment. The terms *informal carer*, *family carer, parent carer* and *unpaid carer* are sometimes used to avoid confusion with paid care workers. The 2001 census showed that in England and Wales there were 5.2 million carers; equivalent to one in ten of the population.

Carers moved centre stage in UK health and social care policy towards the end of the twentieth century. Their emergence from the shadows was driven by two main factors: increasing pressure on government from campaigning groups, and rapid expansion of community-based health and social care. The Carers (Recognition and Services) Act 1995 introduced assessment for carers providing regular and substantial care but implementation was patchy and the need for more flexible powers soon became apparent. The Carers and Disabled Children Act 2000, which came into force in April 2001, enabled:

- assessment of the carer where the cared-for person refuses an assessment;
- innovative and creative services for carers based on outcomes that they value;
- the extension of direct payments (Department of Health, 2000f, p. 2).

The Carers (Equal Opportunities) Act 2004, which came into force in July 2004, introduced three principal changes, further strengthening carers' rights:

- a duty on local authorities to inform carers that they may be entitled to an assessment;

- a requirement that assessors consider carers' employment, education, training and leisure needs and commitments;
- a requirement on public authorities to cooperate with requests from local authorities to assist in planning services for individual carers.

Sometimes carers remain hidden from service providers because of mistaken assumptions about 'who cares' based on gender, ethnicity, sexual orientation or age. Some people supporting relatives or close friends reject the term 'carer' because they see the help that they provide as a natural part of their relationship. Other carers may be reluctant to come forward because of the stigma still attached to conditions such as HIV/AIDS and mental health problems, or because they fear being burdened with responsibilities they are not able to take on. Young carers are a particularly invisible and hard to reach group; and the extent to which children provide care, and their thoughts and feelings about this, have only recently begun to be explored (Morgan, 2006). And in all types of informal care relationship lack of insight into specific needs of minority ethnic groups can exacerbate the failure to deliver effective and appropriate support.

Carers are involved in a wide range of tasks including personal care, emotional support and assistance with activities outside the home. Carers' experiences are individual and varied, and it is difficult for workers to provide adequate support unless it is clear which aspects of caring can be easily accommodated, which are causing problems and which are proving unmanageable. Carers need time to build trusting relationships with professionals and they need to feel confident that the difficulties they describe will be taken seriously. Acknowledging the expertise of the carer is an important part of the assessment process. Taken together with the service user's perspective, the carer is well placed to provide a comprehensive and intimate account of the situation and to describe how it developed. Sharing personal insights and memories can be painful, though, and carers need to be treated with sensitivity and respect:

> Sophie last spoke to me nearly seven years ago. Until then, she had opinions on everything and voiced them freely. Unfortunately, she contracted encephalitis lethargica, an infection of the brain.
>
> Now tetraplegic, and with no reliable means of communication apart from moans and groans, Sophie requires care day and night. Along with boredom and loneliness, another ongoing problem is that I still miss her desperately. I miss the 17-year-old daughter I lost. I miss the arguments, the sassiness and the hugs. (Cameron, 2006)

The power differential between carers and health and social care professionals means that the carer's perspective can easily be overlooked. Carers often resent the fact that they are not encouraged to play an active part in the process of assessment, care planning and review for the person they support. This perceived lack of involvement assumes particular significance when potentially life changing decisions are being made. This account of a multi-agency case conference was given by the mother of a severely disabled child:

> They called a case conference . . . because the situation was getting quite serious – we were really suffering – at the meeting there were 14 professional people . . . and [only

three of them] knew my daughter . . . They were deciding what I needed – I'd sit there and try to ask one of the professionals who actually knew her what they thought and I'd be told: 'Please don't interrupt'. At the end of the meeting a couple of social workers said they thought they could give me long-term foster care, but I didn't want long-term foster care, we never wanted long-term foster care at all . . . when they said that to me, I felt they hadn't listened to a word I'd said . . . (Barton, unpublished research)

Four dimensions of outcomes that are important to carers

A *Quality of life for the person they care for*
- Personally clean, comfortable and well turned-out.
- Maintain maximum independence.
- Personal safety and security.
- To be in social contact with others (apart from the carer).
- To have meaningful activity/stimulation.
- Maintain dignity.
- Improve mobility, morale.

B *Quality of life for carer*
- Physical health or well-being.
- Emotional/mental health.
- Peace of mind (freedom from excessive anxiety re person cared for).
- Ability to have a life of their own (i.e. to work if they choose, pursue interests).
- To avoid social isolation.
- To maintain a positive relationship with person cared for.
- Adequate material circumstances (income/housing).

C *Recognition and support in the caring role*
- Able to define the limits of their role (level of involvement and nature of task).
- Feeling skilled, confident and knowledgeable.
- A sense of satisfaction or achievement in caring.
- Sense of shared responsibility/being emotionally supported.
- Able to manage the physical/practical tasks of caring.

D *Process outcomes (impacts of the way help is provided)*
- Valued/respected as an individual.
- Expertise as a carer recognized.
- Having a say in the way care is provided.
- A 'good fit' with existing life routines and care giving.
- Value for money.

Source: Department of Health (2000f, pp. 26–7).

The caring role is not confined to set working hours and is carried out alongside other commitments such as housework, childcare, education and paid work. Outside interests in the form of employment, education or leisure may prolong a carer's ability to cope but can be difficult to sustain and may create extra pressure. Unsurprisingly, carers are susceptible to poverty, physical and mental ill health and social exclusion. And although caring has many positive aspects, physical and emotional demands can be intense and long lasting. Many carers have little time to attend to their own needs:

> This world mainly consists of mundane chores within the home, hospital visits, and medication. It's not very interesting and not much fun. Neither is it a chosen occupation. Any other role I have undertaken in my life has been chosen by me, whether as wife or mother, or a job I have applied for.
>
> Carers get a job that is persistent, tedious and boring. No matter how much you love someone, having to look after their every need daily and always putting those needs above your own is wearisome. (Cameron, 2005)

Care can break down in a number of ways and both the carer and the person they support may be vulnerable to neglect or abuse. This raises important issues that are difficult to explore (Brechin et al., 2002). In assessing the sustainability of the caring role it is essential for workers to ask the right questions and to listen carefully to what carers, and those they support, say. A Department of Health Guide (2000f, p. 7) suggested the following key questions:

- How long has the carer been caring?
- How much help does the carer get?
- How often does the carer get a full night's sleep?
- How much physical impact does the caring role have?
- How much emotional impact does the caring role have?
- Does the carer understand the nature of the cared-for person's condition?
- How much time does the carer have when they feel 'off duty'?
- How appropriate is the role for someone of the carer's culture, religion, gender?
- How many other roles (parent, employee, carer for someone else) impact on the carer?
- How does the caring role impact on the carer's other relationships and community networks?
- How sustainable does the carer's role appear?
- Does the cared-for person want the carer to continue in this role?
- How far does the carer gain any sense of satisfaction/reward from caring?

Even if carers who are assessed for services refuse support or fail to meet eligibility criteria the assessment process can still result in:

- recognition of the carer's role;
- peace of mind for the carer who knows how to make contact in future;
- a chance for the carer to talk through the issues and consider their own needs;
- an opportunity to provide the carer with information on other sources of support;

- the chance for carer and worker to develop a sense of shared responsibility;
- increased confidence that may eventually lead to the carer accepting support.

Carers consistently comment on the difficulty of accessing services, and sometimes describe dealing with health, social care and other agencies as like being in a maze. The systems designed to support them can be confusing and they are often dependent on professionals to guide them through. The modernizing agenda for health and social care aims to make information on services and resources more easily accessible to carers. And standards have been set to assure the quality and effectiveness of local carer support services in:

- giving information to carers;
- providing a break for carers;
- offering emotional support to carers;
- supporting care and helping carers to maintain their own health;
- ensuring that carers have a voice (Blunden, 2002).

Five Key Points

- Labelling people as carers is not straightforward. Relatives, neighbours and friends who provide support may not identify themselves as carers and some disabled people resent the suggestion that they need to be 'cared for'.
- Informal care arrangements are diverse and individual and cannot be understood without reference to the past and present relationships, social and economic circumstances, culture and beliefs of those involved.
- Carers carry out many of the same tasks as health and social care workers without support from colleagues, training or financial reward. They are usually motivated by love, duty and a sense of enduring commitment but are sometimes compelled to take on this role against their wishes.
- Although many carers derive satisfaction from caring they are at increased risk of poverty, physical or mental ill health and social exclusion. Carers and those they care for may be vulnerable to neglect and abuse.
- The concept of partnership between carers and social care workers has proved easier to put into policy than to put into practice.

Three Questions

? What are some of the key similarities and differences between the role of a carer and the role of a paid care worker?

? Identify some of the main factors that promote or inhibit joint working between social workers and carers.

? To what extent are carers' experiences universal and to what extent are they linked to the time, place, culture and context within which support is provided?

Further reading

1 Department of Health (2000f) *A Practitioner's Guide to Carers' Assessments under the Carers and Disabled Children Act 2000*. London: Department of Health; also at www.dh.gov.uk/carers
2 Blunden, R. (2002) *How Good Is Your Service to Carers? A Guide to Checking Quality Standards for Local Carer Support Services*. London: King's Fund.
3 Stalker, K. (ed.) (2002) *Reconceptualising Work with 'Carers': New Directions for Policy and Practice*. Research Highlights in Social Work No. 43. London: Jessica Kingsley.
4 Department of Health (2005d) *Carers and Disabled Children Act 2000 and Carers Equal Opportunities Act 2004) Combined Policy Guidance*. London: Department of Health.

CHAPTER 6.4

Black Perspectives

Beverley Prevatt Goldstein

'Black' is an adjective which has been given meaning by the racism of society and responses to that racism. It is an adjective initially used in a derogatory way to apply to certain groups and subsequently reclaimed by them as an expression of solidarity and resistance. 'Black' has been used as a political umbrella encompassing diverse cultures and religions but with a common core, the experience of colour-based racism and pride in the strategies and cultures developed to resist it (Brah, 1992). In Britain the term 'black' has been used to refer 'to Africans (continental and of the diaspora) and Asians (primarily of Indian sub-continental descent) . . . All have a shared history of British colonialism and oppression' (Mama, 1984, p. 23). This inclusive meaning in Britain has latterly been challenged as not meeting the needs of South Asians or those who are black with a white parent. 'Black' is therefore increasingly being used to refer only to those of African ancestry. But as racism continues to be endemic in Britain (Macpherson, 1999), including in social work institutions (Butt and Davey, 1998), black as an inclusive political term is invaluable. It is this inclusive political use of 'black' that underpins *black perspectives.* The concept of *black perspectives* refers to a particular way of viewing the world and of prioritizing actions and goals, a way that is rooted in the experience of and the struggle against racism.

Black perspectives is not any perspective held by any black person, or any one geographical or cultural group: it is rooted in the collective experiences of black people and directed towards ethical and political outcomes for all (West, 1994). In *black perspectives* (Ahmad, 1990; hooks, 1991; Shukra, 1995) four central interlocking features can be identified:

- valuing black people (individually and collectively) and their right to self-define and determine their agendas;
- recognizing the strengths, commonality and diversity of black people;
- struggling against racism in its daily manifestations;
- valuing the multiple ways of constructing and understanding the world that black people have developed.

These elements can be balanced in different ways, expressed in different forms and combined with multiple other perspectives, for example, feminism, lesbian and gay, a Muslim perspective. Working with others to eradicate all oppressions has been a deep tradition in black perspectives (Cooper, 1893; hooks, 1991; John, 1991; Lorde, 1984; Moraga and Andalzua, 1981; Sivanandan, 1990; West; 1994).

The Impact of Black Perspectives

Black perspectives has initiated challenges to racism in immigration, employment, education, housing, policing and has facilitated alternative and complementary structures in education, welfare, politics and services which challenge oppression within black communities (Sivanandan, 1990). Challenges to racism and racist or ethnocentric services have been mounted from other perspectives (Thoburn et al., 2005) but black perspectives provide a particular impetus and ethos.

Valuing black people

The belief that black people matter has been the motivating and maintaining force behind the black-led concern with appropriate services and working conditions for black people, as highlighted in Butt and Mirza (1995) and Ahmad and Atkin (1996).

Valuing black people has led to specific innovations in social work practice. For instance, it has emphasized that black children should be offered the care most likely to encourage a positive black identity, buffer them from and prepare them to withstand racism, that is, quality care by conscious black care-givers; has challenged the lack of consideration of the interlocking needs of black disabled children (Flynn, 2002) and has carefully explored the parameters of culture in assessing need and protecting black children (Dutt and Phillips, 1996; Dutt and Phillips, 2000).

Black perspectives has advocated culturally appropriate and safe services for older people and survivors of domestic violence. It has valued the black-led community services because they provide these, are directed by black agendas and maintain reciprocal links within communities (Ahmad, 1990). Nevertheless, it has also identified the inequity in the needs of black people being left solely to underfunded voluntary groups or to an 'extended family' that is excluded or impoverished by immigration and economic policies (Patel, 1990). It has identified the ways ignorance of the expressions of black cultures and religions have led to misdiagnoses in mental health services, and challenged the focus on cultural miscommunication which has obscured inappropriate and racist services and structures (Fernando, 1995; Kelleher and Hillier, 1996). It has also challenged the ethnocentric/racist basis of normalization theories: 'What is culturally normative is dictated by the values of white society and white service users' (Northern Curriculum Development Project, 1993).

Black perspectives has contributed to the well-being of service users generally. For example:

- Issues of race, culture, language and religion must now be considered for every child.

- Issues of identity are integral to significant social work frameworks.
- Single carers are acceptable as foster carers and adopters (in part) due to the pioneering work of those attempting to increase the numbers of black carers (Small and Prevatt Goldstein, 2000)
- The concept of empowerment, first introduced by Solomon (1976) is now embedded in social work theory.

Recognizing strengths, commonality and diversity

The *black perspectives'* focus on the strengths of black people and communities has influenced social work practice with mixed outcomes for the welfare of black people. It has challenged the pathologization of black people as prone to identity problems (Owusu-Bempah and Howitt, 1999; Prevatt Goldstein, 1999a) and has enabled black voluntary organizations to demonstrate their expertise at identifying unmet needs of black people. However, it has led to children being left unprotected due to inadequate services being offered to those stereotyped as strong and resourceful (London Borough of Lambeth, 1987) and to inadequate resources being offered to communities stereotyped as 'looking after their own'.

Black perspectives emphasizes the commonality between black people based on their experience of racism. This has led to a recognition in social work practice of the validity of group work with black service users, black students and black workers, though an essential element of *black perspectives* – that these groups should have influence – has been harder to realize (Prevatt Goldstein, 1996, 2002).

This tension between strengths, commonality and diversity is critical to an ethical black perspective. Not all black people are strong and not all black people experience racism and interpret that experience similarly. A recognition of strength needs to be combined with a recognition of accountability and of support needs. A recognition of commonality needs to be combined with a recognition of differences, between black workers and service users, amongst black workers, amongst black service users. In the words of Audre Lorde, 'in order to work together we do not have to . . . resemble a vat of homogenised chocolate milk' (1984, p. 136).

The contradictory effect of these aspects of *black perspectives* on social work is not only due to the inherent tensions within them but also to the context of racism and other oppressive structures. For example, the strength of black families may be assumed on the basis of stereotypes and to ration resources, or be denied in order to place children elsewhere. Differences between black individuals and communities may be exaggerated to counteract a solid oppositional power base or denied to provide a one size fits all solution. Black families may be stereotyped as sexist because of racism or sexism overlooked because of narrow anti-racism. A black perspective arises from an insider position with a knowledge of complexity and contradiction (Prevatt Goldstein, 2003).

Struggling against racism

Black perspectives has significantly altered the value base of social work by inserting into it a focus on recognizing and challenging racism and oppression, initially with the Central Council for Education and Training in Social Work (CCETSW) Anti-Racist Statement and latterly with the General Social Care Council (GSCC) Code for social care workers on 'challeng[ing] dangerous, abusive, discriminatory or exploitative behaviour and practice' (General Social Care Council, 2002, 3.2). This is a development of the original principles of social work as described by Biestek (1961) and was partly due to the struggles of the Black Perspectives committee of the CCETSW, supported by anti-racist black and white colleagues and activists.

Black perspectives has also struggled to challenge (its own and others') simplistic and personalized ways of understanding anti-racism (John, 1991) and:

- insists that anti-racist activity is a practical struggle against diverse manifestations of racism and will take different forms to suit different local and national circumstances;
- links the local struggles against anti-racism with international struggles;
- locates racism in the structures of an oppressive society rather than individual pathology;
- acknowledges that black people subvert, challenge as well as experience racism and that racism does not define black people;
- challenges cultural explanations being used as a diversion from identifying and challenging racism.

This political and structural perspective on anti-racism does not fit easily with the individualistic focus of social work nor its role in the state. Yet there have been concerted efforts to promote this via social work education (Northern Curriculum Development, 1991) and this has helped create the space for other oppressions to be named.

Valuing the world that black people have developed

One aspect of *black perspectives* which has been recognized by social work is its valuing of black cultures. However, *black perspectives* is not an ethnic, cultural or religious perspective but an ethical and political perspective. *Black perspectives:*

- challenges devaluation of the cultural and religious expressions of black people that arise from racism and ethnocentricism;
- recognizes that aspects of black cultures can be enriching for some black (and white) people (Hylton, 1997);
- recognizes the dangers of an over-reliance on cultural, religious interpretations which can assume cultures are static and homogenous and overlook the individual, condone oppressive elements within cultures and religions, and substitute cultural solutions for challenging oppressive interactions and structures.

Black perspectives both values and critically appraises the cultural expressions of black people, insisting on the fluidity and hybridity of cultures. *Black perspectives* treads a line between valuing the individual and the collective; focusing on difference and on commonality; challenging both racism towards the cultures of black people and the culturalization of racism; challenging both the practice of racism and the

A black perspective on the death of Victoria Climbié and the Laming Inquiry

Valuing black people

- The extent to which an African child, homeless, transient, not speaking English, with unclear legal status was not visible or valued.
- The extent to which black staff were homogenized and assumed to have cultural expertise, not provided with adequate training and support, not monitored yet scapegoated for the tragedy.

Recognizing strengths, commonality and diversity

- Assuming strengths within the family and failing to monitor and provide resources.
- Relying on general cultural and medical assumptions without checking.
- Assuming adults and children from the same country and family do not have conflicting needs.

Struggling against racism

- The institutional racism against perceived asylum seekers/immigrants.
- The differential impact of the Inquiry on white and black staff.
- Valuing the world that black people have developed.
- That an individual's murderous behaviour is not necessarily due to the group culture.
- That black family and church patterns are not dysfunctional but likely to be negatively stereotyped by the media and professionals.

Source: Prevatt Goldstein (2006).

discourse of anti-racism being viewed as the only defining parameter of black people. It thus has much to offer a profession which tends to focus on black people as problems or victims rather than responsible agents, which is more comfortable with meeting cultural needs than challenging racist structures and which finds it difficult to accept expertise of black workers without exploiting them as experts (Prevatt Goldstein, 2002).

Developing Black Perspectives . . .

. . . *by black people*

To arrive at a black identity is a complex, shifting phenomenon, not dependent solely on skin-tone or experience of racism, subject to internal and external dynamics

(Mama, 1995). To arrive at a black perspective is to add a particular ethical and political lens to that black identity. The balance of elements of the perspective may differ over time, the perspective may be combined with others or may be abandoned if it is no longer internally satisfying or externally viable. The development of *black perspectives* begins with the personal valuing of black people (self and others). This achievement encompasses a redefinition of self against racist labelling and an appreciation of different black experiences. It also requires a willingness to identify and name racism. This naming of the daily experiences of racism and the powerful structures of racism can be demoralizing and disempowering if it is situated only in negative experiences of being black and in a context where racism is being experienced or challenged in isolation. The implications for social work practice include challenging all forms of racism as well as the placement of black children where they will not be isolated in their experience, a reduction of the isolation of black people in day care, residential provision, service delivery, decision-making forums and the development of groups for black service users and workers.

Increasing identification of some black people with Islam, perhaps due to Islamophobia or disillusionment with current civil and political society, may be perceived as a challenge to a black identity, black perspective and anti-racism (O'Hagan, 2001) or as one identity and one perspective that co-exists with others (Brah, 1992). A black perspective and a Muslim perspective can mutually reinforce each other. A black perspective must challenge the devaluation of Islam, recognize its enriching aspects while being cognizant of the dangers of an over-reliance on interpretations that can assume religious practice and understandings are static and homogenous and of condoning or colluding with any oppressive practices. A black perspective encompasses challenging all racisms including Islamophobia.

There is currently a growing movement to recognize mixed racialized people as a distinct racialized group (Okitikpi, 2005). But people with one black minority ethnic and one white parent can experience racism to a similar extent as those with two black parents (Tizard and Phoenix, 1993) and their way of viewing the world can be similarly rooted in the experience of and struggle against racism (EYTARN, 1995, p. 59). There may be differences in the experience of racism and interpretation of the experience due to early intimate white relationships, ability to pass for white or/and experiences of exclusion, harassment by black people (Prevatt Goldstein, 1999b). Wilson's (1987) and Fatimlehin's (1999) research indicates how this can lead to both perspectives, black and 'mixed racialized', being comfortably combined.

. . . by white people

The appreciation and advocacy of *black perspectives* requires a decentring of white experience and white perspectives, and 'an empathic sense of outrage' against racism (Husband, 1995, p. 95). It may also be facilitated by close positive relationships with black people or making links between a personal experience of oppression and racism. While this need not entail a loss of other perspectives, any decentring can be experienced as loss and it is important that this is not compensated for by taking the lead in *black perspectives*. The ability to value difference without appropriating it is critical, as a key aspect of black perspectives is the space for black self-definition and agenda setting. White workers need allies (black and white) in order to be advocates for *black perspectives* while black workers need to 'develop alliances with non-blacks without compromising our own priorities, self-reliance and needs' (Small, 1995, p. 7).

Working together from and with a black perspective is one route towards social justice.

> You do not have to be me in order for us to fight alongside each other. I do not have to be you to recognise that our wars are the same. What we must do is commit ourselves to some future that can include each other and to work towards that future with the particular strengths of our individual identities. And in order to do this we must allow each other our differences at the same time as we recognise our sameness . . . (Lorde, 1984, p. 142).

Five Key Points

- *Black perspectives* derives from the experiences of black people (broadly defined) and is directed towards the advancement and liberation of black people in the context of social justice for all.
- *Black perspectives* incorporates:
  (a) valuing black people and their right to self-define and determine their agendas;
  (b) recognizing the strengths, commonality and diversity of black people;
  (c) struggling against racism in its daily manifestations;
  (d) valuing the multiple ways of constructing and understanding the world that black people have developed.
- *Black perspectives* can be interlinked with, influence and be influenced by a range of other perspectives, for example, feminist, Muslim.
- Working from *black perspectives*, working with *black perspectives* can be achieved by black and white individuals respectively.
- *Black perspectives* in social work has benefited both black and white service users.

Three Questions

? Explore the impact of your racialized experiences on your priorities in social work.

? How could a *black perspective* benefit service users in your area of work?

? Analyse one policy or new initiative in social work from a *black perspective*.

Further reading

1 Williams, C. (1999) Connecting anti-racist and anti-oppressive theory and practice: Retrenchment or reappraisal? *British Journal of Social Work,* 29, 211–30.

2 Maitra, B. and Miller, A. (2002) Children, families and therapists. In K. N. Dwivedi (ed.), *Meeting the Needs of Ethnic Minority Children.* London: Jessica Kingsley.

3 Prevatt Goldstein, B. (2003) Black families and survival strategies. In L. Jamieson and S. Cunningham-Burley (eds.), *Families and the State: Changing Relationships.* London: Palgrave Macmillan.

CHAPTER 6.5

The Research Perspective

Nick Gould

The assertion that social work is a scientific activity that should be underpinned by knowledge derived from empirical research is not a proposition that is universally upheld. For example, from time to time it has been proposed that doing social work is better understood as a form of artistic endeavour that should be informed by the cultivation of aesthetic sensibilities (England, 1986). More recently, social work has been influenced by arguments that it is fundamentally a practical-moral project and should derive its purpose and expression from moral and ethical discourse (Webb, 2006). Sometimes these debates are distorted by misrepresentation of the nature of science as a rigid set of procedures when it actually encompasses a diverse set of social practices. In the social sciences it is well established that although some problems can be addressed by experimental research designs adapted from the natural sciences, human beings as conscious and self-aware creatures are also appropriately studied using methods that depend on interpretation, dialogue and cooperative inquiry.

Social work is a practical activity directed at the improvement of the circumstances of the client, but those circumstances are shaped by the social environment of individuals and families, and the institutional processes which impact on their problems or disempowerment. All of these domains, the resilience and vulnerabilities of people, the impact on their circumstances of social formations such as gender, class or disability, and the way in which these factors are mediated by the intervention of institutions, are capable of systematic investigation. Subsequently, social work is an intellectually vibrant research field where many of the controversies that lie at the core of the social sciences about method, agency and structure are reflected and played out. Any generalizations that purport to be about 'normal science' in social work need to be heavily qualified by the observation that this is a contested domain (Dominelli, 2005) which indeed derives vitality from debate and controversy.

Various commentators have remarked on (and sometimes exaggerated) the close comparisons between the practice of research and the practice of social work in their mutual concern with problem formulation, investigation, accumulation and synthesis of evidence and analysis. Above all, research seeks answers to questions, and the form of the question asked has direct implications for the way that a piece of research is designed and executed. This chapter considers the main kinds of question asked in social work research and the repertoire of methods used to answer them. It then goes on to consider further the relationship between doing research and doing social work practice, the possibilities of research promoting emancipatory outcomes and, finally, the factors constraining or promoting the development of capacity for future development of social work research.

Social Work Research – Mapping the Field

As a research discipline, social work is defined by its field of inquiry rather than by any research method that is unique to it. Social work research draws on a wide range of social science methods. This is not to say that it is not a discipline within which methodological innovation has taken place and subsequently influenced other disciplines (for instance research undertaken by social work researchers to elicit the voice of the child and its influence within the 'new' sociology of childhood). To the rather mundane question, 'What are social work researchers most interested in?', a descriptive answer can be provided, for Britain at least, by examining the results of the 'Research Assessment Exercise', an occasional audit of research activity within universities. When undertaken in 2001 it reported eight themes of social work research in order of their prevalence (Research Assessment Exercise, 2002):

- children, youth and families;
- social work practice;
- health and social care;
- theory and methodology;
- race and diversity;
- criminal justice;
- social justice;
- organization studies.

Such a list gives a sense of the range of social work research interests. However, closer scrutiny of the list reveals that such classificatory systems obscure more than they reveal – the categories are not mutually exclusive and seem to represent overlapping analytical categories. Another approach to mapping research starts from the premise that research seeks to answer questions, and the logic and design of research flows from the selection of the method best able to provide answers to those questions (Gould, 2006a). This section therefore suggests that research methods can be surveyed from the position of formulating the main kinds of questions asked in social research, and matching them to research methods and their combination. Thus we shall consider the following questions as a way into capturing the core repertoire of research methods in social work:

- What is the effectiveness of specified interventions? (Experimental approaches)
- What are the factors associated with the social problems of service users and carers? (Survey research)

- What are the experiences of individuals or groups? (Qualitative research)
- How can we research organizational processes and programmes? (Case study and mixed methods research)

Experimental Approaches

It is arguable that the only way to scientifically establish a process of causation is through research that follows an experimental design; it is not possible to establish whether a social work intervention is effective if it is not clear what causes what effects. The experimental method has a long tradition in the Western sciences and has been adapted for the purposes of the social sciences, particularly in psychology. The fundamental principle of experimental design is that an artificial (though not necessarily laboratory-based) situation can be established whereby multiple causes of phenomena can be controlled by excluding some influences, standardizing others, while allowing others to vary. The logic of experimental design can be concisely captured through the acronym *PICO*. This is achieved by identifying the *population (P)* of people for whom the intervention is relevant, specifying the *intervention (I)* that is to be evaluated, randomly assigning members of the research population to an experimental group that receives the intervention and a control group that receives no intervention or some other *comparator (C)* such as 'normal treatment', and to compare the *outcomes (O)* between the group receiving the intervention and the control groups. If there is significant improvement in the outcomes for the experimental group then the cause can be attributed to the intervention, as the random assignment of subjects to the experimental or control group should cancel out any other so-called 'confounding' variables. This research design is usually described as a 'randomized controlled trial' or RCT.

Axford and colleagues (2005) have noted some of the progress that has been made in evaluating children's services using experimental methods, and draw attention to challenges in using this approach in social work. There is not a tradition in British social work research of segmenting the potential population into categories that can be known to have similar trajectories or outcomes. For instance, the needs of a child being fostered for a few days while a parent is hospitalized are very different from the needs of a child accommodated because they have been abused by parents. An evaluation of a fostering programme that makes no differentiation of needs but lumps all fostered children regardless into the study, is unlikely to be able to identify any meaningful findings of outcomes. Similarly, unless the characteristics of the fostering programme can be precisely specified and operationalized, it will not be unambiguously clear that the research findings are attributable to any specific intervention.

Critics of the experimental research approach argue that in real world situations met by social workers the circumstances and needs of service users are too diverse, and social work interventions and outcomes too complex, to permit experimental research methods to be meaningfully applied to the everyday realities of practice. However, the growth of political expectations that interventions should be evidence-based is pressing social work researchers to be more ambitious in adopting experimental methods into evaluations. The concern that social work and social care research lack appropriate measures of outcomes has been addressed in adult care through the Outcome for Social Care for Adults (OSCA) programme, a linked series of research programmes to develop measures of outcome that have relevance to practitioners and service users and carers but are robust enough for the purposes of researchers (Henwood and Waddington, 2002).

Often practitioners wishing to research innovative interventions do not have the resources or access to large numbers of service users to make a controlled experiment feasible. Alternative research approaches seek to incorporate a rigorous approach to the evaluation of practice through so-called single-system designs where the before and after effects of the intervention are evaluated (Bloom, 1999). Kazi and Wilson (1996, cited in Bloom, 1999) give an example of researching whether a counselling approach was effective in helping a girl settle into a new school. The outcome measure was frequency of crying at school, which was measured before the counselling programme began, and after. Follow-up was later undertaken to see whether the improvement was sustained. This is a relatively simple example of single-system evaluation but can be elaborated to accommodate evaluation of more complex measurements and outcomes, for instance so-called ABAB designs where an intervention is alternately introduced and withdrawn to assess whether the problem intensity or frequency reoccurs accordingly.

In the USA there is a stronger tradition of such experimental evaluations represented by the empirical practice movement, probably best known in the UK through William Reid's work on task-centred practice (Kirk and Reid, 2002). In the UK there has been an emergence of this perspective through the influence on social work of evidence-based medicine and the work of protagonists in social work such as Macdonald and Sheldon (1992). An aspiration has been that social work should generate sufficient experimentally based evidence for the effectiveness of interventions so that systematic reviews of that evidence can then support evidence-based guidelines for practice (Macdonald, 2003; Rosen and Proctor, 2003). This has remained a contestable issue in social work, with antagonists concerned that experimental research designs such as randomized controlled trials are closely associated with managerial agendas, cost effectiveness and performance measurement, to the exclusion of other legitimate interests such as service user preferences and other forms of knowledge production such as qualitative research (Powell, 2002).

Survey Research

Surveys may have two main purposes – to describe and to explain. Even non-social scientists will have some grasp of the procedure of survey methods from their experiences as respondents to market research questionnaires. Some confusion may arise in integrated health and social care services for social workers, as there is a tradition in health research of referring to surveys as 'observational studies'. Typically the strategy of a survey involves drawing up a representative sample of the population to be studied, using a questionnaire or similar instrument to elicit responses relevant to the research question from the sample, analysing statistically the distribution of responses to items in the questionnaire and associations between them. Descriptive surveys may be used to elicit the patterns of take-up of services, to measure the needs of service users, or to capture users' satisfaction with services they receive. When this is undertaken at one point in time it is referred to as a 'cross-sectional' survey; when the same respondents are interviewed at intervals over time this is a 'longitudinal' panel survey. An explanatory survey follows the same steps as a descriptive survey to capture a data-set, but then uses more advanced statistical measurements of the relationship between variables to test hypotheses about the nature of the relationships between variables and possible causal relationships (though see below).

Social inclusion has become an important perspective within mental health social work and this can be attributed in part to the accumulation of survey evidence relating to the lack of social participation as citizens by people with mental health problems (Gould, 2006b). The UK Social Exclusion Unit report, *Mental Health and Social Exclusion* (Office of the Deputy Prime Minister, 2004) draws extensively on the Office for National Statistics psychiatric morbidity surveys to demonstrate the large range of social indicators relating to issues such as employment, income, housing, education and leisure, where people with mental health problems are disadvantaged. In social work surveys are probably most extensively used in the evaluation of user satisfaction with services, for instance as part of audits. These small-scale surveys can provide useful feedback to service providers but often fall short of meeting the more exacting standards of valid and reliable research. Larger surveys are expensive, often requiring the logistical support of private research agencies and consequently are often limited to large-scale, well-funded research programmes. E-mail and the Internet have created the possibilities of cheaper, opportunistic surveys, and these may be appropriate, for instance for researching professionals who have ready access to technology, but are biased in their lack of reach to more disadvantaged and marginalized groups.

Of increasing influence in social sciences, and appearing on the horizon of social work, are the methods of epidemiology, which studies factors influencing well-being and illness at a population level. Epidemiology has become a dominant methodological approach within public health, and as preventative approaches also become more prioritized within social care, so epidemiological research may gain more purchase within social work. Research into the social ecology of child abuse, identifying neighbourhood and familial factors associated with harm to children, demonstrates some of the possibilities (Jack, 2000).

A social worker seeking to use survey evidence to inform their practice needs to be aware of some of the basic technical issues that have a bearing on whether the findings can be used appropriately. There needs to be sufficient care in the sampling to ensure that it is representative of the population and that bias has not been introduced inadvertently. The survey needs to be large enough in order to have enough statistical power so that there is confidence that any differences between sub-groups of the sample do not arise simply from chance. Also, that there is a statistically significant correlation between two variables measured in a survey should not be confused with a finding of causation between them. In order to determine that one event or factor causes another the research usually needs to have a longitudinal element, that is, data needs to be collected from the same respondents on at least two occasions. Last, but not least, the 'ecological fallacy' has to be avoided; this is the error committed by making assumptions about the behaviour or characteristics of individuals on the basis of the characteristics of the geographical area from which they come.

Qualitative Research

Qualitative research can be defined as research that is not expressed in numbers. Usually it involves the collection and analysis of text, either derived from notes made from direct observation in the field, from the transcriptions of interviews or from documentary evidence, although it can also include the study of audio or video recordings. The term qualitative research refers to a family of approaches with, as Riessman observed, 'a loose and extended kinship, even divorces' (quoted in Shaw and Gould, 2001, p. 8). Terms such as 'symbolic interactionism' (studying individual meanings and the ascription of meaning) and ethnomethodology (addressing how people create reality through social interaction) are but two instances of qualitative approaches drawing upon distinct theoretical and methodological pedigrees. Sherman and Reid (1994), amongst others, have suggested that social work has a natural affinity for qualitative research because of the profession's dependence on description in words: words and the interactive processes that generate shared meanings for words and actions are the media of social work practice. For a profession that is concerned with the voice of the marginalized and disempowered, qualitative research also holds out the possibility of methods that restore voice to those people.

There is an orthodoxy in the USA that qualitative research is a minority perspective in the mainstream of social work research, mainly because the research culture of social work is dominated by quantitative methods derived primarily from psychology. The publication of several US and international edited collections of qualitative social work research (Riessman, 1993; Sherman and Reid, 1994), and a dedicated journal – *Qualitative Social Work* – suggests a more complex and changing picture. Certainly in Europe and Australia it is arguable that qualitative research has the ascendancy, with strong interconnections with theoretical approaches to social work grounded in philosophical positions such as hermeneutics, critical theory and postmodernism. A key feature of qualitative research is the notion of 'reflexivity'; in contrast to the quantitative and experimental traditions where the researcher claims neutrality and invisibility, qualitative researchers often position themselves autobiographically within the research account, treating their own standpoint and reaction as part of the process and, often, the findings. In his chapter, 'Interviewing Interviewers and Knowing about Knowledge', Scourfield writes about his experiences as a male researcher interviewing social workers about investigating sexual abuse of children:

> As well as presenting as a young, educated, middle-class white man, I presented as married and as a father. Within a few days of starting fieldwork, in the course of small talk with social workers, these aspects of my life had come to light. (Scourfield, 2001, pp. 62–3)

The complexity of the shifting perspective between insider and outsider has been treated as a creative tension in qualitative research; White (2001) has used her dual role as social work team leader and ethnographic researcher to produce a rich series of studies exploring the nuanced processes of decision-making in children's services. While qualitative social work derives its justification from the detailed unpacking of dense narratives, fieldwork notes and transcripts, often based on small samples, this 'localism' has also been the basis of scepticism from some policy-makers as to whether qualitative research can be sufficiently generalizable to inform service development and practice improvement. This has generated extensive debate within the methodological literature about the distinction between 'generalizability' in quantitative research, justified in terms of representative and large sample sizes, as contrasted with 'transferability' in qualitative research, the more tentative possibility that findings can be applied elsewhere on the basis of comparability of the context of the research. Thus, social workers considering the applicability of qualitative research findings to their own situation need to consider the relevance to it of the setting in which the research was undertaken.

Case Study and Mixed Methods Research

On occasion a researcher might wish to study an individual, programme or event in some depth over a specified period of time, and this is usually described as a 'case study'. As Hakim (1987) comments, a distinctive feature of the case study as a research method is the focus on analytical social units and social processes, and as such it lends itself to mixing methods to capture both qualitative and quantitative data. A not untypical linkage may be between qualitative analysis and survey research. For example, a case study of organizational change, such as health and social care service integration within a particular service, might use in-depth interviews with people identified as key players in the process and analysis of key policy documents, with statistical analysis derived from a survey of the wider workforce. In social work research this is likely to incorporate interviews with or a survey of service users to identify impacts of change on them. The policy lessons of case study research can be important; for instance, the study of service integration in an English mental health service by Peck et al. (2002) found that the service as experienced by service users worsened before it improved. Whether the lessons of a case study can be generalized by social workers to inform their practice in other contexts raises similar considerations as for qualitative research; there needs to be sufficient detail in the description of the case study to inform judgements by research users as to transferability of findings to other settings. Multiple case studies, based on careful sampling of the cases, may overcome some of these difficulties.

In constructing a case study a fundamental design issue is to decide the sequencing of the various components of the case study. For example, some preliminary qualitative evidence from interviews may be used to inform the subsequent design of a survey and quantitative analysis. Conversely, an initial survey may be undertaken to identify the issues that need to be pursued in qualitative interviews. Another possibility is that the different strands of the research run concurrently with interim analyses informing the ongoing process of the research. This notion of ongoing iteration of the analysis and research design is a particular feature of 'action research' where the interim research findings act as feedback loops into the organization and are acted upon (Kemmis, 1997); such research challenges the orthodox conception of research as detached and neutral, but is aligned with more radical conceptions of research as committed to progressive social change. A case study of a national voluntary organization providing children's services (Gould, 2000), researching the endeavours of the agency to transform itself into a 'learning organization', illustrates some of the characteristics of an action research process where reflections emerging from the research process informed the emergence of strategies to become a learning organization.

Practitioner Research

An important but often overlooked source of research evidence comes from 'practitioner research'. This is defined in an oft-cited source as, 'research carried out by practitioners for the purposes of advancing their own practice' (McLeod, 1999, p. 8). This definition certainly applies to some research undertaken by practitioners but fails to do justice to the full diversity of this field. An audit undertaken by Keane et al. (2003) estimated that the hidden nature of practitioner research disguises the probability that there are more practitioners engaged in social work research than professional researchers. In an article drawing on that audit, Shaw (2005) suggested that practitioner research can be categorized on a continuum from personal curiosity-driven inquiry to participation in more formalized, larger research programmes. Though generalizations are risky, it seems broadly the case that in the USA practitioner research is equated with quantitative and experimental research, with single system evaluations as discussed above to the fore. In the UK the orientation of practitioner research appears to be more toward case study evaluations of programme innovations, or small qualitative studies of practitioner or service user experiences.

Although the encouragement of practitioner research is often cited as a good thing in promoting research-mindedness amongst practitioners – supporting an evidence-based culture in organizations and adding to the accumulation of knowledge for practice – there are also important critiques relating to its strategic purpose and methodological adequacy. The supporters of practitioner research argue that the research process is analogous to practice itself with their shared concern with problem formulation, collection and interpretation of information, and prescription for effective intervention. This position is often aligned with advocacy for qualitative research as the preferred approach for practitioner research, with interpretative and inductive methods, in the famous phrase of Jane Gilgun (1994), 'fitting practice like a glove'. The sceptics have pointed out the fundamental differences between research and practice, for instance that there are very different circumstances determining the beginning and end points of research and social work intervention and, not least, there are different ethical and power implications pertaining to the service users' withdrawal of permission to continue collaboration with research or practice (Padgett, 1998).

There are also intensive debates concerning the possibility of practitioners achieving the neutrality and detachment necessary for good research. On one side are aligned those who argue that practitioner research is often methodologically naive and flawed in its appropriation of methods developed in other social science fields (Hammersley, 1993), while its defenders assert the possibility of 'defamiliarizing' oneself within the context within which one practises and that research can be enriched by alternating the perspective of being both 'insider and 'outsider' (White, 2001). Given that practitioner researchers are also to be found in many other professions, it is clear that these challenges are not unique to social work. It is likely that practitioner research will continue to develop as part of overall aspirations for evidence-based practice, but that the quality of such research is dependent upon having a supportive organizational climate for research, effective partnerships with universities to enhance methodological rigour, and mechanisms for dissemination that ensure that findings add cumulatively to the knowledge base.

Emancipatory Research

It is frequently asserted that social work's distinctive character as a profession lies in its value base, rather than any particular claim to uniqueness of method of intervention. Within the research field this orientation towards moral purpose and values finds expression through the development of interest in the project of emancipatory research. This perspective is strongly indebted to the work of activist researchers within the disability movement (particularly those researchers who have identified themselves as disabled and users of services), and also from some of the theoretical and methodological standpoint positions developed within feminism and anti-racism. Drawing upon the wider traditions of social and political struggle, some service users who are also researchers have argued that the purpose of social research should be explicitly emancipatory, rather than seeking legitimacy through claims to scientific neutrality. This perspective critiques professional researchers who are perceived to be pursuing knowledge to enhance their professional careers or to generate knowledge that may not contribute to the advancement of the interests of disadvantaged or socially marginalized individuals or groups. Emancipatory research, expressed at its broadest conception, is committed to the prioritization of research that addresses the empowerment of service users, often linked to implications for broader social and political change. However, more than other research traditions it also foregrounds matters relating to the power relations that exist between researchers, and between researchers and the 'subjects' of research. The so-called 'Toronto group', a network of researchers within which social work has always been strongly represented, has suggested that in order to be deemed 'emancipatory', research should be controlled by service users throughout the whole research process although 'researchers who are not service users may be involved' (Hanley, 2005, p. 40).

This orientation to research which explicitly fuses the relationship between moral purpose of research and the politics of research production, can also be seen as closely connected to the debates within social research concerning epistemology, that is the evidential and truth basis on which something can be known. Beresford, a social work researcher and user of mental health services, has argued strongly that the validity and reliability of knowledge is determined by the distance between the researcher and the object of his or her research, and that the closer the lived experience of the researcher is to the phenomena being researched the more dependable the knowledge that has been derived (Beresford, 2003, 2005). This challenges the traditional assumption of science that truth and objectivity are best served by the independence of the researcher to insulate them from bias and subjectivity. Emancipatory research resonates strongly with the approach of social work researchers who believe that social work as a critical activity is best served by a research approach that democratizes the relations of production of research and empowers the service user as the controlling agent in the research process.

Building Capacity for the Future of Social Work Research

There is increasing awareness within the research community that the resources available to social work research fall considerably short of what is needed to support the modernization of services and the establishment of a truly knowledge-based approach to practice (Marsh and Fisher, 2005). Aspects of this resource shortfall include: the volume of money available to support social work research projects; the limited supply of adequately trained researchers; and the educational gap in preparing practitioners to be equipped as critical appraisers of research relevant to their practice. Historically, the primary funders of social work research in the UK have been government departments. Though this has supported important research, it has also shaped the content of that research towards supporting politically determined agendas. Researchers wishing to pursue curiosity-driven primary research have either had to find a charitable source that happens to have a policy interest in the researcher's ideas, or seek research council funding under the Trojan horse of some other academic discipline, for example social policy, psychology or sociology. Significant progress has now been made with the main UK research council for social science research, the Economic and Social Research Council, in 2005 recognizing social work as a research discipline in its own right. This means that social work researchers can submit proposals which will be reviewed by social work peers, and not under the flag of convenience of another discipline. This innovation is an important marker of the development of social work as a fully-fledged research discipline.

This recognition also begins to unlock a further barrier to building capacity for social work research, the training of an adequate number of researchers. In most academic disciplines the pathway to becoming a professional researcher is through obtaining a first degree and then by completing a PhD. For social workers there have always been barriers to following this route. As in other applied disciplines, there has been an expectation of accumulating sufficient experience of practice before having the credibility to become an educator of student social workers, leaving individuals little opportunity within their personal development to also accumulate the credentials to become established researchers. Recognition by the research council of social work as a bona fide discipline opens the way to the development of accredited Masters degree level research training for social workers, studentships to help support those undertaking a doctoral programme, and some opportunities for post-doctoral fellowships, all of which are milestones towards converting from practice to a research career.

The utilization of research in practice also depends upon the education of future generations of practitioners who are aware of the contribution research makes to practice and who are critical consumers of research findings. The establishment of social work as an all-graduate profession provides the basis for the development of a curriculum that is research-based, and for educating students to appreciate some of the fundamental aspects of research design. The future realization of a research-minded workforce then depends not only on the delivery by universities of a research-oriented curriculum, but also the support within employing agencies of a learning culture which promotes opportunities for staff to apprise themselves of and reflect on current research output.

Five Key Points

- Whether social work is an activity that can be researched using scientific methods or whether it is a moral-practical activity remains contested.
- Social work research is defined by its fields of interest rather than by distinct methodological contributions; it draws eclectically on the repertoire of research methods employed in the social sciences.
- Practitioner research is an important constituent within social work research though there is debate about the nature of the contribution it makes best to knowledge-creation.
- There are important synergies between some areas of social work research and the emancipatory approaches developed within feminism, anti-racism and the disability movement.
- There remains a need to develop greater capacity in social work research, but there are important indicators of its maturation as a research discipline.

Three Questions

? Select a real life piece of research that interests you and analyse how the research questions relate to the design and methods used in the study.
? What are the advantages and disadvantages of practitioner research in social work?
? What steps should be taken to make social workers more research-minded?

Further reading

1 Gomm, R., Needham, G. and Bullman, A. (2000) *Evaluating Research in Health and Social Care*. London: The Open University in association with Sage Publications.

2 Shaw, I. and Gould, N. (2001) *Qualitative Research in Social Work*. London: Sage Publications.
3 Kirk, S. A. and Reid, W. J. (2002) *Science and Social Work: A Critical Appraisal*. New York: Columbia University Press.

CHAPTER 6.6

The Evidence-based Perspective

Geraldine Macdonald

The underpinning principle of evidence-based practice appears relatively uncontroversial. It is that when professionals intervene in people's lives they should do so on the basis of the best available evidence regarding the likely consequences of their actions. Put simply, they should be as confident as possible that what they do will (1) bring about the changes sought, and (2) will do so without adverse consequences.

Evidence-based practice denotes an approach to decision-making which is transparent, accountable and based on a consideration of current best evidence about the effects of particular interventions on the welfare of individuals, groups and communities. It relates to the decisions both of individual practitioners and policy-makers. The impetus to adopt an evidence-based approach to social work came from outside of the profession: 'The commitment to evidence-based medicine increasingly pervades modern medical practice. This kind of commitment should be extended to the social services world' (Steven Dorrell, Conservative politician, 1996). New Labour followed suit, endeavouring to place its policy initiatives on a consideration of best evidence. This simple and intuitively appealing maxim is now widely accepted. How people interpret the term is, however, highly variable and contentious.

Not *Just* Evidence

At its heart, evidence-based practice is about using evidence from research into the effectiveness of interventions – outcome research. This has led to concerns that research evidence will be inappropriately privileged over other factors that are important in decision-making. This is not so. Evidence-based practice is not, for example, advocated as a substitute for professional judgement. It does not suggest that resources do not matter, or that the accumulated wisdom of individual practitioners, teams or agencies is not important. And for sound, evidence-based reasons it does not negate the importance of process variables which we know to be important in securing good outcomes. What evidence-based practice *is* advocating, however, is a reconsideration of the relationship between these factors. In particular, it advocates that we should pay more attention than has been paid in the past to outcome research, give it more prominence in our decision-making and become much more critical consumers of what passes for evidence in the research world.

Even when knowing which of a number of available interventions is effective, and which interventions are more effective than others, decision-makers still have to make choices based on available resources, values (not everything that is effective is acceptable, either to service users or to professionals) and public opinion. The erroneous idea that proponents of evidence-based practice are happy to ignore other sources of legitimate influence on decision-making resulted in some critics arguing for alternative concepts such as 'research-mindedness' (Harrison and Humphries, 1998), 'knowledge-based practice' (see Fisher, 1998), and 'research-informed' practice (Orme, 2001). These terms steer thinking away from two central tenets of evidence-based practice: first, knowing 'what works' for whom and in what circumstances has not been taken sufficiently seriously by professionals, and needs to be; second, that some research designs are better than others for answering questions about effectiveness.

Finding Out What Works

The proposal that not all research designs are equally fit for purpose in assessing the effectiveness of social interventions is probably the most hotly contested issue. Here are the arguments in favour of this proposition.

The challenge, when we are endeavouring to assess the effectiveness of an intervention – whether it is community sentencing or treatment foster care – is to be sure that any changes that occur are attributable to our intervention and not to something else. Very often other things are happening at the same time that we are working with people which provide equally plausible explanations for any improvements that may occur: people may acquire a new partner or a new job; relationships may improve; financial problems be resolved, and so on. Thus, if a parent-training group appears to be effective, then before recommending it to others we need to be able to rule out competing accounts of why the parents might have improved. We also need to separate out the effects of the programme itself from other related factors, such as getting the parents out of their homes, or socializing with other parents. Such alternative explanations are known as threats to internal validity. They threaten the certainty with which we can attribute changes to the intervention we have deployed.

The *only* way we can be reasonably confident that an intervention is responsible for bringing about a particular set of changes is by controlling for other possible sources of influence. The best way to do this is to compare the progress of a group of people who are receiving a particular intervention with another similar group who are not. If we can be confident that the two groups are broadly similar in all respects except that only one is receiving our intervention, then we can also be confident that if that group improves and the other does not (or improves less) then it is our intervention that is responsible. This is because nothing else relates *only* to that group.

It is not easy to ensure comparability. Even if we match people on what we think are important characteristics (age, gender, ethnicity, duration of problem, etc.) we cannot be sure we have second-guessed every potential influence. This is why one research design *randomly* allocates participants to each of the groups. This way, if the groups are large enough, researchers can reasonably assume that if something other than the intervention is influencing outcomes in the intervention group, it is also operating in the control group; we can therefore rule it out as a causal effect. In essence, this is the design of studies known as randomized controlled trials (RCTs). RCTs can also be used to compare the relative effectiveness of two interventions.

Methodological Democrats

In health, RCTs are almost always used to determine the effectiveness of new drugs, and many other health interventions. Other approaches to evaluation are ranked in terms of their descending ability to control for the competing explanations for patterns of outcome (CRD, 2001).

Such talk of 'hierarchies of evidence' has not been greeted with enthusiasm within the more democratic profession of social work. First, it is argued that the promotion of one methodological approach may entail, by implication, the disparaging of others. This does not follow. There are different hierarchies of appropriateness for different kinds of research question. It is only in relation to evaluations of the *effects of interventions* that one might wish to argue for the 'in principle' superiority of controlled trials over others. If we want to improve our understanding of how it feels to be a child looked-after then a survey of children using in-depth qualitative interviews is much more appropriate.

A second concern is that people and social interventions are too complex for what seems, to some, the rather mechanistic approach of controlled trials and similar designs. But it is precisely the complexities that we are dealing with that make controlled studies in general and RCTs in particular so useful. Undoubtedly the implementation of controlled trials in social work is immensely challenging, but this is a technical challenge, rather than an epistemological one.

Third, some are concerned that controlled trials (whether randomized or not) ignore the individuality of people who use services, and reduce important dimensions of helping to meaningless numbers. This is a legacy of the tendency to divide research and researchers into two camps: the qualitative and the quantitative. So-called quantitative researchers are said to ignore subjective experience and to be interested only in things which can be counted and analysed statistically. This may be true of some social scientists, but it is a gross caricature of the history of experimental research within social science (see Oakley, 2000). The earliest RCTs in social work were rich in qualitative data (Macdonald, 1997). Without qualitative data we cannot move beyond ascertaining whether or not something works to why and how it works, what it is like to be on the receiving end of such help and whether or not people find different approaches more or less helpful. The converse is, however, also true: the history of social work research warns us against the assumption that a positive report of services by those on the receiving end is a guarantee that change has occurred and is attributable to the intervention in question. The crucial issue is whether or not the research design we are proposing, together with the outcomes selected (whether 'quantitative' or qualitative), is capable of answering the question it is seeking to address.

Another set of concerns is ethical in nature. When researchers make a proposal to allocate research participants to one of two or more groups, only one of which will receive the intervention being evaluated, they are often challenged about the ethics of withholding services from people in need. This worry rather misses the point of evaluation studies – to find out whether or not an intervention produces the benefits we intend, and to ensure that there are no unintended harms. We assume that 'helping' is a good thing but the history of social work bears testimony to the fact that well-trained, well-supported, well-resourced and well-intentioned people doing what appear to be perfectly sensible things can do more harm than good (Petrosino et al., 2003). An equally serious – but rarely discussed – concern would be the ethical propriety of asking people to participate in a study that, by definition, could not answer the question it sought to address (see Macdonald and Macdonald, 1995). Such studies may well be appropriate as a 'first step' in an evaluative process: they can help to identify promising approaches; provide information about interventions; shed light on issues around delivery and reception, and so on. As a general rule, however, they should not be regarded as a secure source of evidence about the effectiveness of policy or practice decisions.

Finally, there are situations in which controlled trials are not appropriate (for ethical reasons) or not possible (for financial or technical reasons). An evidence-based approach does not insist that controlled trials are the *only* research designs on which decisions should be made, but it does suggest that, when other designs are necessary, researchers should be mindful of the problems that RCTs are designed to address and exercise appropriate caution in the conduct of studies and the interpretation of the findings.

Those who advocate evidence-based practice are undeniably urging more than the closer linkage of research with practice. Unwelcome though the idea may be to some, it is suggested that *some* research might lead to a poorer quality of service to people in relatively powerless positions. An evidence-based approach to decision-making does *not* regard all research as equally 'fit for purpose' and holds that – all things being equal – some research designs *are* better than others for addressing the question 'what works?'

Beyond the Single Study

An evidence-based approach takes us beyond the single study as a source of evidence. It is always possible to find a study that supports one's preferred way of working, particularly if one takes a democratic approach to research design. Ascertaining an accurate picture of the effectiveness of an intervention requires a rigorous appraisal of *all* appropriate evidence, and this usually involves a review of the relevant literature. Unfortunately, just as individual studies can be undermined if they are not carefully conducted, so too can reviews. The traditional review process – now referred to as *narrative reviews* – involves reviewers gathering together as many studies as they could (or chose to), reviewing each of them and writing an account of the state of play as they perceive it. Such an approach can introduce a number of sources of bias which can invalidate any conclusions reached.

Systematic Reviews and Meta-analyses

Methods are now available which enable reviewers to apply scientific principles to the synthesis of research. Reviews produced in this way are generically referred to as *systematic reviews*. When augmented with statistical analyses, they are typically referred to as *meta-analyses*.

Systematic reviews seek to minimize bias and error by requiring reviewers to state clearly their decision-making rules for each stage of the process, before they embark on the review itself. Reviewers are expected to indicate:

- *The precise question the review is setting out to answer.*
- *The criteria by which studies will be included.* Minimally, these will include the types of research design, and a clear definition of the kinds of participants (gender, age, setting, 'problem' or situation), and of the intervention. Systematic reviews do not have to set standards of evidence at the level of the RCT, but reviewers would be expected to state clearly the reasons why the thresholds of evidence had been set where they were. This requirement to 'pin one's methodological colours to the mast' is important. In a less rigorous and transparent process it is all too tempting to relax one's original methodological criteria when faced with a dearth of qualifying studies. If reviewers find there are no studies which meet what they deem to be minimally acceptable standards of evidence, then we know something important.
- *The outcomes of interest.* Specifying these counters the temptation to find something that appears to have changed as a result of an intervention, and to use this as evidence of the intervention's effectiveness. It also ensures that reviewers identify relevant outcomes, rather than simply reporting those that researchers may have focused on. For example, studies of interventions designed to prevent abuse and neglect only rarely assess this directly (Barlow et al., 2006).
- *The search strategy* – or how the reviewers intend to identify potential studies. This ensures that reviews are not biased by the way in which studies are identified, for example, by limiting searches to electronic databases (thereby missing uncatalogued studies) or to papers published in English.
- *The criteria used to judge methodological quality.* Personal experience, views and preferences can influence decisions about which studies to include in a review and what weight to accord them. It is perfectly human, but wrong, to be methodologically 'picky' when faced with studies whose conclusions we do not much care for, and methodologically 'forgiving' with those whose conclusions appeal to us.

- *The ways in which information (data) will be extracted and managed.* Wherever possible, at least two people are needed to select studies, extract and enter data for a review, in order to minimize the risk of error.
- *How data from different studies will be analysed.* The sample sizes of many contemporary outcome studies are not big enough to detect the changes the intervention is designed to bring about. In other words, they have insufficient statistical power. Combining data from more than one study (where these are sufficiently similar) can overcome this problem, and this is essentially what meta-analysis seeks to do. It is not always appropriate to combine data in this way, and, when it is appropriate, reviewers have to make a series of decisions about how best to do this (see Egger et al., 2000; Petticrew and Roberts, 2005).

Recent Developments

There are still relatively few systematic reviews of the effectiveness of interventions used by social workers, although these are beginning to come on stream. It is important to fill this gap if busy practitioners are to be able to make evidence-based decisions. A number of organizational developments that will assist in this endeavour:

1 The international Cochrane Collaboration prepares, maintains and makes accessible systematic reviews of the effects of health care interventions (www.cochrane.org). Over 50 review groups take responsibility for synthesizing research relevant to the particular areas with which they are concerned. Reviews are published on an electronic platform known as the Cochrane Library, which includes a UK 'user interface' (www.nelh.nhs.uk). Many of its reviews are relevant to social work and social care.
2. In February 2000 the Campbell Collaboration was established to prepare, maintain and make accessible systematic reviews of the effects of social interventions in the fields of social welfare, crime and justice, and education (www.campbellcollaboration.org).
3. The Social Care Institute for Excellence was established in 2001 'as part of the Government's drive to improve social care'. Some of the Institute's work seeks to incorporate an approach to research synthesis of the kind outlined here (www.scie.org.uk).

The success of these initiatives in establishing evidence-based practice will, to a large extent, depend on the choices made about standards of evidence. Decision makers need access to relevant, high quality systematic reviews. To ensure relevance, practitioners and people who use services need to become actively involved in prioritizing topics and helping to decide on standards of evidence and how the review should be conducted. Finally, an evidence-based approach requires that practising social workers should have a basic competence in the skills necessary critically to appraise research studies and to distinguish between poor quality and high quality reviews. This has obvious implications for the curricula of qualifying and post-qualifying training programmes.

Five Key Points

- Evidence-based practice is concerned to help practitioners use the most effective interventions when they intervene in people's lives.
- Evidence-based practice recognizes that effectiveness research is only one factor that needs to be taken into consideration when making decisions about policy or practice, but argues for a more central role for such research.
- Evidence-based practice involves more than 'research mindedness' or being 'research-informed', for not all research merits integration into practice. Some research designs are better than others for answering questions about effectiveness.
- Practitioners need access to relevant, high quality systematic reviews of the effects of interventions. Such reviews need to be updated as new studies come on line.
- Qualifying training should equip social workers with the skills to appraise research and with a preparedness to change their minds when the evidence changes.

Three Questions

? Given two studies of the same intervention which have reached different conclusions about its effectiveness, how would you decide between them?

? You are working in a family centre and have developed your expertise in a particular method of working. What would it take to persuade you to consider an alternative approach?

? For one group and/or one issue (e.g. adults with depression; parents who are physically abusing their children) what do you know about the evidence base for the following interventions: family therapy, Rogerian counselling, cognitive–behavioural therapy or therapeutic groupwork?

Further reading

1 Oakley, A. (2000) *Experiments in Knowing: Gender and Methods in the Social Sciences*. Cambridge: Polity Press.

2 Macdonald, G. (2003) *Using Systematic Reviews to Improve Social Care*. London: Social Care Institute for Excellence.

3 Petticrew, M. and Roberts, H. (2006) *Systematic Reviews in the Social Sciences*. Oxford: Blackwell.

CHAPTER 6.7

An Ethical Perspective on Social Work

Richard Hugman

In recent years there has been a renewed and steadily growing interest in social work ethics (Congress, 1999; Clark, 2000; Reamer, 2001; Banks, 2006). Ethics is the branch of philosophy that considers the formation and operation of moral values. In other words, it is the explicit deliberation about what is good or bad and what is right or wrong. Social work attends to core aspects of our society, often focusing on people who are excluded, marginalized, disadvantaged or who lack access to the resources needed to resolve their own problems. Such people include children and their parents, people with disabilities, older people, people with mental health difficulties, people struggling with poverty and lack of access to social infrastructure such as reasonable housing, and so on. These are areas of our lives about which we all tend to hold strong and sometimes conflicting values. So how could ethics not always be at the forefront of our thinking about social work?

The main reason why interest in social work ethics can be said to have grown *again* is that in the 1950s and 1960s the influence of an individualist perspective on ethics tended to predominate. Indeed, I would argue that for a generation of social workers the writing of Biestek (1961) on the principles of casework was the main ethical point of reference. That Biestek's work is not primarily an ethical work as such, but is concerned with principles of a particular practice, is something that appears often to escape both his supporters and detractors. With the development in the 1970s of a greater awareness of the social structural, and hence political, roots of the problems which the service users of social work faced in their lives, questions of ethics (seen as the 'correct actions of individual practitioners') became supplanted by concerns with the politics of practice (for example, Bailey and Brake, 1975; Galper, 1975). The more recent 'return' to ethics as a focus of attention is coterminous with the rise of neo-liberalism in the political sphere that, among other things, has sought to delegitimize the overt political actions of professions. Social work, perhaps more than some other occupations, has responded by looking again at the ethical basis of its values, because ethics is something that cannot be said to be beyond the concern of professions.

A separation of ethics and politics would have made no sense to the early moral philosophers whose work continues to be foundational, either in the Western tradition of Socrates and Plato (around 400 BCE), or in the Eastern tradition of Confucius (around 500 BCE). For all these ancient thinkers ethics and politics were not separate but inherently bound together. Questions about the good person and the good society are two sides of the same coin. For example, we might imagine them asking how social workers who are unjust in their personal relationships can work effectively for social justice, or how just social workers cannot be concerned about social injustices around them. Thus ethics cannot be confined to questions of personal responsibility. Yet at the same time we must be concerned with personal responsibility – professionals exercise considerable power with respect to service users through their knowledge and skills and their access to resources. Failing to take account of this reality does not make it go away. Without a conscious engagement with ethics social workers are poorly equipped to deal with such responsibilities and to act accountably to service users or, indeed, to address issues of injustice, exclusion or disadvantage.

Ethical Principles and Core Approaches

The ethics of social work is, in many ways, actually very similar to that of other caring professions. That is, whether or not social workers may consider themselves to have unique values, the formal statements of ethical principles of the profession are often either identical or very close to those of medicine, nursing, occupational therapy, physiotherapy, school teaching and so on (Hugman, 2005). This is because all such statements are derived from the same stock of concepts in moral philosophy and the wider values of the societies in which these professions have developed. Furthermore, although the formal ethical statements or codes of social workers in various countries differ from each other in detail (Banks, 2006), almost all of them share core characteristics. This is because the professionalization of social work globally has tended to follow a similar pattern, which reflects the emergence of contemporary professionalism as an aspect of modernized, industrialized, urbanized society.

There are two philosophical concepts in particular that underpin almost all social work ethics (and the ethics of other caring professions). The first of these is 'deontology'. This term is derived from the Greek word 'deon', meaning 'duty'. It refers to ways of understanding what is good and what is right by considering what duties each person has towards other people and the world around them. For example, it may be argued that all human beings should be treated with respect, simply because they are human beings and therefore are all moral entities. So in these terms 'telling a lie' is morally wrong because it treats another person as less than fully human, irrespective of the consequences of telling the truth. (The origins of deontology understood in this way is usually attributed to the work of Emmanuel Kant [1724–1804].)

In contrast to deontology, professional ethics in social work also embodies the principles of 'teleology'. This term also comes from a Greek word 'telos' meaning 'the end' and it is the approach that considers something to be good or right by looking at what follows from it. Thus some writers also refer to it as 'consequentialism'. So, for example, whether it is good or right to tell a lie will depend on what are the ends of doing so: the classic example is that of using a lie to protect someone from serious physical harm. Teleology often appears in social work ethics in the form of 'utilitarianism', which is a particular form of the approach. 'Utility' in this sense refers to the way in which something contributes to the greatest possible well-being for the greatest possible number of people. (The origins of utilitarianism are usually seen in the work of Jeremy Bentham [1748–1832] and J. S. Mill [1806–73].)

As these two approaches are inherently in conflict with each other, but both influence professional practice, they have tended to be moderated by taking core principles from them and combining these in a way that downplays their differences. This third approach is sometimes referred to as 'principlism' and is most highly developed in bio-medical and health ethics (Beauchamp and Childress, 2001). The principles that appear in this approach are: respect for people; beneficence (seeking to do good); non-maleficence (seeking not to do harm); justice. As Beauchamp and Childress themselves, among others, have acknowledged, the bringing together of principles from different approaches still leaves it to professions and their individual members to make sense of how these ideas are constituted in practice and how to develop a shared sense of what is good and what is right.

Ethics, Professionalism and Accountability

As I have already stated, the importance of ethics in a profession such as social work is that all professionals exercise power in relation to the users of their services. While the experience of a junior member of a profession may not always be experienced as 'powerful', the impact of all practice on service users can be said to be powerful in that it has the capacity to affect human lives in profound ways. Indeed, if it does not we perhaps should ask what is the purpose of undertaking such work.

Power does not have to be overt or equated with force. It can take the form of influence or persuasion, for example. The power of a therapist or counsellor would often take such forms, as would the pronouncements of a community development worker. Because of the expertise that professionals are seen to have, their words 'carry weight' and this is often the most effective sort of power in contemporary society.

The sense of responsibility on which professional ethics is based comes from recognizing power while at the same time holding values that emphasize the moral (including the political) standing of service users as equal to that of professionals. The ethical documents of professions thus serve as guidance, which is sometimes quite firm, about the 'good' in practice. Moreover, they also constitute a declaration to the wider society, including service users, about what can be expected of the 'good' practitioner. On these two grounds, taken together, codes of ethics and similar statements can provide an explicit vehicle for accountability (Banks, 2004). In a society such as the USA the implications of a code of ethics may even be seen as contractual, forming the basis by which service users can seek legal redress for actions that breach the terms of a code (Reamer, 2001). In many other countries codes of ethics provide a mechanism for redress that falls short of litigation but in which a professional body may hold practitioners to account for failures to conform to the terms of a code.

Codes of Ethics

In the contemporary globalized world it is difficult to think of a profession that does not have a code of ethics. These are the formal statements that represent the values of the professional community. Some national associations, such as those in Australia and in the UK, state that the core values are: human dignity and worth; social justice; service to humanity; integrity; competence (Australian Association of Social Workers [AASW], 2002, p. 8; British Association of Social Workers [BASW], 2002, p. 2). To these, the national association in the USA adds 'the importance of human relationships' (National Association of Social Workers [NASW], 1999, p. 1).

In addition, codes usually – but not always – contain quite detailed guidance or instruction on how values and principles are to be interpreted in specific aspects of practice (Banks, 2006). For example, in the Australian Association of Social Workers *Code of Ethics (1999)*, each clause in the section on 'ethical practice' begins with or includes the phrase 'social workers will . . .' (AASW, 2002, pp. 11–21). Similar phrasing is used in the codes of the British Association of Social Workers (2002), the New Zealand/Aotearoa Association of Social Workers (1993) and the National Association of Social Workers (1999). Sometimes such statements are concrete, as in:

> 4.2.6 [. . .] (f) Social workers will protect clients' records, store them securely and, where applicable, retain them for any statutory period. (AASW, 2002, p. 17);

or:

> 1.04 [. . .] (a) Social workers should provide services and represent themselves as competent only within the boundaries of their education, training, license, certification, consultation received, supervised experience, or other relevant professional experience (NASW, 1999, p. 4).

At other times the statements of codes can appear to be quite general or abstract:

> 4.1.6 [. . .] Social workers will: (a) Acknowledge the significance of culture in their practice, will recognise the diversity within and among cultures and will recognise the impact of their own ethnic and cultural identity (BASW, 2002, p. 9);

or:

> 4.1.3 [. . .] (a) Social workers will provide a competent and humane service to clients, mindful of fulfilling their duty of care and observing the principles of natural justice (AASW, 2002, p. 11).

Some codes, such as those of the AASW and NASW provide additional support for practitioners through discursive advice on the interpretation of the code in specific situations (AASW, 2002, pp. 22–4; NASW, 1999, pp. 1–2).

Furthermore, these instructions are given the force of requirements through their role in sanctions that can be exercised against individual practitioners. In some states of the USA and in some provinces of Canada someone who is held to have breached professional ethics may have their registration or licence removed. More recently registration has been introduced in the UK and in New Zealand giving ethics similar importance. In Australia, as yet, the sanction remains that of exclusion from the professional association.

The problem for individual practitioners is that many statements in codes of ethics may at times be open to interpretation, despite the guidance provided for individual application. Although an injunction to 'protect client's records' may be relatively easy to apply, a statement such as 'social workers will acknowledge the significance of culture in their practice' requires a greater degree of interpretation, while the injunction to 'provide a competent and humane service to clients, mindful of fulfilling their duty of care and observing the principles of natural justice' necessitates a sophisticated grasp of ethical concepts by a practitioner.

The IFSW/IASSW Joint Statement on Ethical Principles

In 2004 the International Federation of Social Workers (IFSW) and the International Association of Schools of Social Work (IASSW) approved a joint statement on ethical principles in social work that replaces previous ethical documents of the two bodies (IFSW/IASSW, 2004). As the global peak organizations for social work, this statement serves as the basis for national social work associations around the world in the formation of their codes or statements of ethics. The IFSW/IASSW document is not intended to form a blue-print, but rather to act as a guide and as a starting point.

Compared with the previous 'codes' of the two bodies, the 2004 *Statement of Principles* is simplified. It discusses in detail, but briefly, just two core values which are asserted as being core to professional social work: human rights and human dignity, and social justice. These values (which roughly map onto the twin approaches of deontology and teleology) are a reflection of the United Nations and related documents that are cited as the point of reference for social work internationally (such as the UN Declaration on Human Rights). This list is considerably shorter than those of the national associations cited above. Moreover, the implications of the values, and the broad principles that are derived from them, are spelled out succinctly. Human rights and dignity are seen in terms of self-determination, participation, treating each person as a whole and focusing on people's strengths. Social justice is considered to include challenging discrimination, recognizing diversity, seeking equity, challenging unjust policies and working in solidarity (IFSW/IASSW, 2004). Thus the international associations' document does not include the other principles to which national association documents may refer, such as service, integrity or competence. It could be argued that these latter notions are themselves either explicable in relation to the foundational ideas of human rights and dignity or social justice, or else are to be understood as derived from a different approach to ethics as a whole – integrity, for example, is perhaps more accurately seen as a virtue, which is an approach that has a very different dynamic to those of either deontology or utilitarianism.

The other point of interest about the IFSW/IASSW *Statement of Principles* is that the document is quite specifically not intended to be a 'code'. This task is left to national associations (who are required to have a code of ethics as part of the conditions of membership of IFSW, for example) (IFSW/IASSW, 2004). This approach recognizes that although there are some core values and principles in social work, such as human rights and social justice, it is appropriate that variations between countries are reflected in specific codes of ethics, for example embodying cultural differences. Nonetheless, the *Statement of Principles* does contain a brief list of short prescriptions of 'good social work', such as not using social work skills to support torture or terrorism, where these were seen to be helpful to defend the core values (personal communication). The point remains that this list is neither exhaustive nor is it enforceable at the local or individual levels of practice by either international organization.

The Challenge of 'Different' Ethics in Diverse Societies

Although I have indicated that there are some similarities between the ancient ethical traditions of Eastern and Western societies, in the centuries since Confucius and Socrates a greater divergence has opened up. The dominant approaches in professional ethics that have been described, namely deontology, teleology and principlism, are Western. They reflect the impact of scientific thought and what is called 'modernization'. Thus the values expressed in the United Nations documents to which the IFSW/IASSW ethical statement refers, with their foundational principles of human rights and social justice, have been criticized as inherently Western in their outlook. In particular, the concept of 'rights' that exists in Eastern approaches to ethics is somewhat different to that of the West, especially in so far as Eastern ethics tends to prioritize the harmony of the family and the community over the interests of individuals (Wong, 2004). Similar observations may be made about the core values of indigenous societies, such as Aboriginal Australians or Native Americans, and about post-colonial communities such as traditional Muslim communities in Western countries. Thus some critics have argued that professional ethics as presented by the IFSW and IASSW are not international, but represent an imposition of values from one cultural perspective onto all others (Azmi, 1997).

It is also the case that the approaches of deontology, teleology and principlism do not represent all the possibilities in Western ethical thought. Recent ideas have included the 'ethics of care' (in which the nurturing of caring relationships is a primary value), ethics grounded in the intelligent use of emotions (in which 'compassion' is a primary value) or 'postmodern ethics' (in which, I would argue, an appeal to the Socratic idea of virtue is a very strong element) (Hugman, 2005). However, as Banks (2006) argues, although these approaches provide many useful ideas that can inform how principles may be operationalized in specific situations, they do not provide a firm foundation for the ethics of *a profession*. That is, where membership of an occupation is the one common factor between all social workers (who may be from many different cultures, both men and women, with different identities and experiences) it is insufficient to rely on each individual person applying their own values. Service users should be able to expect something in common between practitioners, so that they can rely on knowing that social workers should protect the privacy of service users, should not exploit service users (for example, sexually or financially) and so on, rather than having to negotiate each of the aspects that are covered by a code of ethics.

Perhaps, then, the solution to diversity is to regard ethical statements, at both the national and international level, as living traditions in the manner of an on-going conversation (Hugman, 2005). At any specific time there will be a written statement on ethics, probably in the form of a code, which applies to the professional community. But this is open to continual debate and reconsideration. The task for each social worker is to be prepared to take part in the conversation and to ensure that the ethical tradition of social work remains alive and continues to grow.

Five Key Points

- Ethics is the way we understand moral values, what is good and bad or right and wrong in our society.
- Professional ethics is important because of the power that social workers can exercise in relation to service users.
- The primary values of social work have been defined by the profession internationally as 'human rights and human dignity' and 'social justice'.
- In many countries, social work associations have 'codes of ethics', which are often written as 'rules for good practice'.
- Recognizing cultural diversity in beliefs and values creates a challenge for contemporary professional ethics.

Three Questions

? What do you consider to be the core values of social work?
? Read your national social work code of ethics – how can you apply it in your everyday practice?
? Can there be an effective, over-arching code of professional ethics if all our values are grounded in different cultures and personal beliefs?

Further reading

1 International Federation of Social Workers/International Association of Schools of Social Work (2004) *Ethics in Social Work: Statement of Principles*. Berne: IFSW (available online at: http:/www.ifsw.org/en/p38000325.html).

2 Hugman, R. (2005) *New Approaches in Ethics for the Caring Professions*. Basingstoke: Palgrave.

3 Banks, S. (2006) *Ethics and Values in Social Work*, 3rd edn. Basingstoke: Palgrave.

CHAPTER 6.8

Inspection: A Quality-control Perspective

Ian Sinclair

This chapter is about inspection. At first sight this may seem a rather restricted field. Inspection, however, is only one of a large number of provisions intended to prevent scandal and drive up performance. Complaints procedures, performance assessment frameworks, children's rights officers, independent reviewing officers, methods for checking on the histories and qualities of staff, and much guidance on the involvement of service users are all part of related efforts. The task of this chapter is to consider inspection within this context.

There is a still wider context that we must also consider. Public services are intimately bound up with economics and it is not surprising that they are increasingly influenced by its ideas. So throughout government there is an increasing emphasis on driving up the quality of services through mechanisms that rely on the economic concepts of choice, incentives and competition. This trend has been labelled New Public Management. It is not confined to the UK. Many of the ideas have been developed in New Zealand, Australia or the USA. Developing countries too are starting to implement them either as a requirement of their donors or out of a genuine belief in their efficacy.

In this new philosophy functions are devolved to relatively small organizations (for example, hospitals and schools rather than health and education authorities). Private providers, their operations honed by the rigours of the market, and innovative, committed voluntary providers compete with the public sector. The public and their advisers are able to 'shop around' choosing the better provision. Funding follows choice concentrating the minds of professionals. The better institutions survive. Worse ones go to the wall or are taken over. Public authorities provide strategic oversight, commission and monitor services and generally hold the ring. They are not expected to take part in the hurly-burly of competition themselves.

This general philosophy provides the context for the analysis of inspection and other methods of assuring quality. The hope is that the new emphasis on competition will drive up quality. Inspection is needed to provide information, a yardstick according to which choices can be made and agencies judged and called to account.

This information comes variously from inspections and the measurement of agreed targets – figures on waiting lists or the number of placements for looked after children, for example. Those funding services can take account of this information and so, in certain circumstances, can those using them. The pressure to maintain funding and to keep their 'customers' will therefore ensure that agencies improve their own performance.

This chapter considers inspection within this context. It asks the following questions:

- What is inspection?
- What is the case for inspection?
- What are the difficulties facing inspection?
- What is the evidence that inspection works?
- How might inspection be improved?

What Is Inspection?

According to the *Oxford English Dictionary* an inspection is an 'official investigation or oversight'. In this chapter I am thinking of inspection of agencies or operating units by outside inspectors. I also take it for granted that they will inspect against defined standards and have powers to demand changes, publish reports and, if necessary, take action to close establishments. Inspection of this kind has a long history in social services but has been delivered in a variety of ways. At present the key body in the UK is known as the 'Commission for Social Care Inspection'. This arrangement will change but the activity itself will, as before, persist.

The activity of inspection generally involves an attempt to gain an overview of the operation of what is inspected. This may require surveys and the collection of routine data. Following this overview an inspector may decide to focus on particular issues suggested by the overview. Previous inspections or general policy concerns at the time may also serve to direct the inspection. Whatever the focus the inspection is likely to involve a number of detailed activities – reading documents, tracking cases, looking at records, talking to key staff and those using the service, and perhaps observing practice.

Inspections can take place at levels varying from a department, to a service (e.g. the fostering service) to a unit (e.g. an elderly person's home). Particularly at the higher levels inspectors are likely to be concerned with Performance Assessment and with the measurement that implies. In the case of Social Services this involves a wide variety of measures (for example, the proportion of looked after children who are fostered). There are also two summary ratings for the quality of service that departments provide for children on the one hand and adults on the other. Finally, there is, at present, an overall star rating that has implications for the department's prestige and freedom of action. However much the details of these arrangements may change, the basic idea will continue.

One purpose of this activity is to ensure that the activities inspected are legal and conform to regulation. A second purpose is to anticipate and prevent gross abuse or bad practice. A third, and rhetorically at least, increasingly important purpose is to drive up standards through a focus on outcomes. The latter are broadly defined and include what researchers would call intermediate as well as final outcomes. So in children's homes there is a concern to see whether young people feel they can easily turn to staff, have experienced bullying and take part in education. These are undoubtedly key issues for the young people, even if they are not the same as more 'final' outcomes such as whether they turn out to have happy and fulfilled lives.

What Is the Case for Inspection?

Inspection seems clearly an idea whose time has come. The clientele of social services include the most vulnerable in society. Market forces seem unlikely to protect them. The private market in care provides itself a strong argument for inspection – for how else are we to be satisfied that public money is being well spent and that providers compete on quality as well as price? The logic of inspection with its insistence on goals, explicit standards and a credible feedback mechanism relating performance to change seems impeccable. And an increase in inspectors seems as natural an answer to a scandal as an increase in police to a rise in crime.

What Are the Difficulties Facing Inspection?

The judgements of inspectors are expected to be:

- *appropriate* so that they concentrate on key rather than irrelevant issues;
- *well founded* in the sense that they are accurate and based on evidence;
- *transparent* so that they command public confidence and, if need be, surmount legal challenge;
- *influential* so that they prevent scandal and improve practice.

In all these respects there are severe difficulties.

It is hard for inspectors to make judgements that are *widely agreed to be appropriate*. The values against which they assess services conflict. The need to consult parents may conflict with the need to protect children. The need to provide choice of provision conflicts with the need to make full use of scarce resources. Improvements in one service may often require an increase in expenditure that can only be achieved at cost to another service. There is uncertainty about what are the key features of provision. For example, authorities place much store on the proportion of staff in, for example, children's homes and foster homes who are trained when at the moment there is no evidence that current training improves outcomes for children.

It is hard to make *well-founded judgements* when much that goes on in social welfare – the transactions of the social worker with her client or of the residential staff with an elderly person – are effectively invisible to outside parties. The more powerless the user, the less they may wish to draw attention to malpractice. It is often the case that crucial social processes – the relationship of foster carer with her charges or of home carers with their elderly clients – are widely dispersed and weakly influenced by the overall agency or service that the inspectors judge. So the reasonably favourable report on the management of Haringey social services department proved no protection against the subsequent scandal surrounding the death of Victoria Climbié.

It is hard to make *transparent judgements*. Standards are hard to measure. Much that is key in social provision is elusive. Attempts to concentrate on the measurable lead to long lists which themselves generate unreliability. Inspectors are willing to commit themselves to judgements of quality but one study suggests that their witness agrees very weakly with that of another inspector assessing the same home (Gibbs and Sinclair, 1992).

It is hard to make *influential decisions*. Resources are often the key to performance but outside the control of the service providers they assess. Even where this is not the case, authorities may themselves be uncertain what actions will, for example, reduce the extent of movement in the care system. And if strong action needs to be taken, there are often formidable reasons for not taking it – partly because of the difficulty of getting evidence which stands up against legal challenge, and partly for practical reasons such as lack of time and the need to ensure alternative arrangements for clients. Sometimes there is no alternative to what has been inspected. Inspections of councils cannot simply close the council down.

All these problems apply equally to the particular case of performance measures. There are criticisms of the technical quality of the measures, the degree to which they do enable choice or competition, and the degree to which they focus on the measurable rather than the important. In addition it is hard to obtain useful feedback in a situation where managers are uncertain how to effect the measures or where the staff, on whom performance depends, have a more complex agenda. In this field complexity comes with the territory. Social services pursue a variety of goals, have to satisfy a variety of audiences, and are influenced by differing professional and managerial values. They have to do this in situations where they have to account for their activities, compete for funds, and collaborate with others without whom they cannot successfully achieve their ends. In this situation neither the measurement nor the management of performance is easy.

Finally there is the issue of time. An inspector does not have much of it. He or she may have, for example, six days in which to cover an entire fostering service. Faced with the kind of problems outlined above they do not have an easy job. What evidence is there that they have much of an impact?

What Is the Evidence that Inspection Works?

Inspection is intended to improve quality and prevent scandal and abuse. The inspection of agencies or units should result in higher average quality and less extreme variation in the quality of operating units. How far is this the case?

My own interest in variations in quality was sparked by the first piece of social research in which I was involved. This focused on probation hostels for young men aged 15 to 21 and generally required by the courts to live in the hostels for a year (Sinclair, 1971). In many ways the most striking thing about these establishments was the extraordinary variation in the degree to which the young people were involved in delinquent activities. Under different wardens (the places were run by husband and wife teams), the proportion of young men leaving prematurely as a result of an absconding or offence varied from 14 to 78 per cent.

These percentages were calculated on routine information available on over 4,000 young men over a period of 10 years. Interestingly, the variations were not explained by differences in intake, or by the location, size, physical characteristics, or any other aspect associated with the hostel other than its staff. Differences in the failure rates between successive wardens in the same hostel were as great as those between different wardens in different hostels. In short, these differences in outcome all seemed to boil down to the characteristics of the husband and wife teams who ran the hostels, together with a 'random effect' whereby waves of trouble could occur in even the best ordered establishment.

These findings on the importance of individuals in shaping the welfare of small residential establishments were complemented by other studies of residential care for young people carried out at around the same time. Recent evidence suggests that they continue unabated. So establishments vary in the percentages of their young people who feel supported, in the numbers who are bullied or run away, in the quality of talk between staff and young children, in the degree to which the rules are humane and child-centred, and indeed in almost every aspect of the regimes and outcome which can be studied. There is now abundant evidence that these variations reflect differences in regime at least as much as, indeed probably more than differences in the residents.

An interesting feature of these variations is that they persist despite inspection and regulation. Residential care for children has a long tradition of both. The probation hostels given as an example were subject to a detailed set of regulations and received regular inspections from both the probation and the then Children's Inspectorate. Despite this, examples of bad practice persisted for years. I interviewed the warden who ran the hostel with a 'failure rate' of 78 per cent. He happily remarked 'each boy has his breaking point and I find it'. Later he left to run a children's home. More recently my colleagues and I studied a children's home in which bullying and sexual intimidation amounting virtually to rape were endemic. The home had recently passed an external inspection.

These observations are not unique. There is now a large literature on abuse in children's homes. From this it does not appear that inspection has played a large part in detecting the abuse. This does not, of course, mean that other abuses may not have been prevented either by closing homes or by producing improvements. It does, however, suggest that there is a need for evidence that this is the case. At present this positive evidence is lacking. Indeed the persistence of the variations discussed above is evidence against the idea that inspection either prevents abuse or improves practice.

I have focused on residential care for children since this is an area where there is a long history of inspection. In other areas inspection is either relatively new or less intense or non-existent. In general there is enthusiasm for spreading the benefits of inspection to these areas. It has to be said, however, that there is remarkably little if any evidence that inspection has improved practice in any of the areas covered by social services.

Quality features in children's homes

What size is the home?	Research suggests: the smaller, the better.
How does the ratio of staff to residents compare with other homes?	There is no evidence that higher staffing ratios yield better results.
Is the home manager properly supported in her or his post?	Evidence suggests that managers who are, for example, acting up have greater difficulty in exercising effective leadership.
Are the home's objectives clear and agreed with the management, head and staff?	There is evidence that clarity and such agreement are crucial.
Is the head of the home able to articulate a clear approach in key areas of behaviour and education? Are the staff united behind this approach?	There is evidence that this influences long-term success.
Is there a functioning *key worker* system?	This probably relates to the satisfaction of the children.
Are key measures of poor performance (running away, school non-attendance, cautions/convictions, reports of bullying, misery and harassment) low?	Evidence suggests that there are wide variations between homes.
Do children have constructive agreed plans which are actively implemented?	This probably tests the implementation of shared vision.

How Might Inspection Be Improved?

One response to the difficulties outlined above would be to do away with inspection. No one has proposed this and it will not happen. A more constructive response would be to seek improvements. These are likely to depend on three factors: improvements in the knowledge base on which inspection is based, the practice of inspection, and the role inspection plays in relation to other provisions.

Improvements in knowledge will help at a variety of levels. First, it will help in identifying key areas on which inspection can concentrate. At present there is a desire for inspection to focus on 'outcomes'. Inevitably, however, these outcomes are often remote from what is inspected. The inspector can see the children's home: the ultimate outcome is in the child's future life. The inspector judges the quality of management in a department the fruits of which are or are not apparent in day-to-day operations of which the inspector can only have a hazy picture. By making clearer the connections between the immediate and the distant research can assist inspection, enabling it to concentrate on essentials and making it more transparent and defensible.

In terms of practice part of the solution is likely to lie in the scheduling and operation of inspections. Common sense would suggest that guarding against malpractice is more likely to be successful if 'risky' services are inspected more frequently than less risky ones. In identifying 'risk', lessons could perhaps be learnt from the field of child protection in that the difficulty may be less one of identifying bad practice than of ensuring that concerns about a situation are brought together in one place so that a pattern begins to emerge. In order for this to happen it would be necessary for the wide variety of those in contact with the service – users, relatives, staff, GPs, social workers and so on – to know what they can expect and where they can take their concerns.

In carrying out inspections inspectors would then need to concentrate on key points (for research suggests that they get lost if standards are too numerous), to solicit a wide range of user opinion using postal questionnaires if necessary, to visit at times without appointment and to pursue initial concerns in a systematic manner. (For example, a high runaway rate from a children's home may simply suggest that the young people are particularly difficult or it may indicate a deeper malaise. To determine which applies an inspector would need to examine the intake, and to talk to the young people and staff about what was going on.)

If difficulties are identified, they have to be tackled. Ideally this takes place against a common framework in which all sides have agreed on the standards that are to be applied and that things are not going well. In practice there may well be differences of opinion on such matters. Successful action is then more likely if the inspector has been able to identify allies (e.g., external managers), if he or she has been even handed – not attributing to staff failures that arise through lack of resources – if there is a timetable for implementation and review, and if there are penalties for non-compliance which stop short of the draconian action of closure. Success must also be more likely if there is a coherence between inspection, management, training, registration and complaints. For it is unlikely that a single inspection will succeed, if the messages given by other parts of the organization differ from the inspector's report, or if their proposals for extra resources or training cannot be followed up.

In this respect it is particularly important that external inspection dovetails with internal mechanisms for quality control. Authorities have a wide variety of methods of quality assurance available to them: complaints procedures, children's rights officers, independent reviewing officers, independent visitors, annual appraisals, exit interviews, visits by councillors to name but some. In addition they should have detailed information from their own social workers on the quality of many of the placements they use and they have aggregated information from their information systems and sometimes consumer surveys. Systematically and carefully used this has the potential to offer a much more grounded and wide-ranging view of practice than is available for an inspector in six days. Inspections might do well to concentrate on assessing the appropriateness and accuracy of this system and on the degree to which agencies and councils take the results on board and respond to them.

More widely, it is important that inspection plays its role in enhancing both the operation of the market and the system of incentives. Councils, relatives, old people and others who choose provision need information. Without this the market cannot operate efficiently. Professionals need to know what counts as good practice and that they are judged fairly against this. Inspection can play its part by ensuring that there are appropriate systems for operating a market, providing information and judging performance. They can try and ensure that the standards and information required for this process to operate are accurate and appropriate. In this way again they achieve their ends not as a separate lever of power but rather by working with the grain of processes that operate in any event.

For, finally, what is important is that inspection resembles policing and indeed government more generally: it depends on the consent of those subjected to it.

Conclusion

Inspection is one of a large number of provisions designed to prevent scandal in public services and improve standards. It has a respectable logic and occupies a key role within the new philosophy of public management. Unfortunately it faces numerous difficulties and there is little evidence that it has been effective in the past. Improvements for the future will depend on improvements in the knowledge base for inspection, developments in both the practice of inspection and in the degree of coherence achieved between inspection and other aspects of social services.

Five Key Points

- Research has shown wide variations in the effectiveness of individual staff and units in social services.
- Strangely, these findings have rarely been pursued: little further attempt has been made to determine how a more consistent performance might be achieved.
- But we know that consumers are clear about the kind of social workers, residential staff and carers they want; and we know, also from consumer studies, that social workers do differ from each other – for example, in their reliability.
- The various mechanisms designed to 'even up' performance (for example, market forces and inspections) typically fail to do so.
- Inspection is one mechanism that may help to do this but for this to happen it needs to 'dovetail' with other mechanisms designed to the same end.

Three Questions

? What are the appropriate criteria for judging a particular service?
? What mechanisms are likely to ensure that these criteria are met?
? How can systems of management and inspection contribute to this process rather than leading to defensive actions by staff and the diversion of scarce resources?

Further reading

Much of the most important writing on inspection quickly becomes out of date. The best way to access current thinking is by using the web. As I write, for example, a Google search based on 'Commission for Social Care Inspection' and 'principles of inspection' turns up key material. The search term 'Commission for Social Care Inspection' will in due course become out of date, but the need to use the web will remain and students are strongly urged to use a search engine to access up-to-date and relevant information.

CHAPTER 6.9

The Legal Perspective

Teresa Munby

Law regulates social work practice, informs it, and provides a framework within which social workers operate. It suggests that the discretion and flexibility inherent within social work be actively moderated *externally* through the courts and the legal system and *internally* through workers' awareness of human rights issues.

Why Social Workers Need to Know About the Law

The legal knowledge that social workers need is determined by the range of their practice and responsibilities. For example, in their work with children and families they must know about the Children Act 1989, Adoption and Children Act 2002, Children Act 2004 and Children and Adoption Act 2006. They must understand the relevance of law to child protection and the provision of family support. In their work with mentally ill people the statutory powers under the Mental Health Act 1983 and the specific legal responsibilities of Approved Social Workers have to be absorbed. This knowledge and understanding is significantly different from that required by a solicitor specializing in care proceedings or in mental health or of a community worker striving to secure resources for a drop-in centre.

In broad terms, social workers need legal knowledge in order to:

- discharge their statutory responsibilities;
- offer advice and assistance;
- protect the rights of individuals as service users of social services;
- practise in an anti-oppressive and anti-discriminatory manner;
- protect their own position as employees.

To discharge their statutory responsibilities

Most social workers have statutory duties which require them to have knowledge of substantive law, process and procedure as it relates to practice. They need to understand the application of law within the court and tribunal system and to develop an awareness of key issues.

Social workers must understand the legal foundations of their own professional role: a working knowledge of the statutory basis for practice under the Local Authority and Social Services Act 1970 and an understanding of local and central government organization. Through the establishment of the General Social Care Council (GSCC) by the Care Standards Act 2000 and the issuing of standards devised by the Training Organization for the Personal Social Services (TOPSS) there is a regulatory framework for practice. The GSCC lays down a Code of Conduct and Practice for social care workers, and TOPSS has published the *National Occupational Standards for Social Work* (2003a) and a *Statement of Expectations from Individuals, Families, Carers, Groups and Communities* (2003b). By this means, a comprehensive standard for practice has been established.

To offer advice and assistance

Fundamental to the welfare rights of service users is knowledge of the comprehensive body of literature encompassing welfare benefits, tax credits and related matters. The Child Poverty Action Group regularly produces a detailed annually updated guide to these benefits (Osborne, 2006; www.cpag.org.uk).

Other questions around law may arise tangentially when working with service users. Access to advice is readily available electronically from either www.adviceguide.org.uk or the Federation of Law Centres (www.lawcentres.org.uk). For example, a social worker working with a family with children considered to be at risk may need to be able to advise on issues such as debts, housing, immigration and asylum, or divorce and separation in addition to being clear about her legal role and responsibilities.

The social worker must be able to help service users by referring them to agencies best placed to help them. This depends on the worker having a good knowledge of which agencies can meet service users' needs, how to access the services and how to meet the cost where this applies. It requires knowledge of the Community Legal Service (CLS) which was established in 2000 under the Access to Justice Act 1999 and is managed by the Legal Services Commission (www.legalservices.gov.uk). The CLS is responsible for civil legal aid and was designed to ensure improved access to information and advice about legal rights. It produces leaflets on key areas of law – available on the Internet at www.clsdirect.org.uk. In 2006, the Carter Report, following a major review of legal aid delivery, proposed a new structure of publicly funded legal services.

To protect the rights of individuals as service users of social services

Rights of service users have increased with the introduction of complaints procedures required by specific statutes governing particular areas of social work. Legislation gives right of access to personal information held by social workers under the Access to Personal Files Act 1987, Access to Health Records Act 1990, Data Protection Act 1998 and general information held by local authorities and public bodies under the Freedom of Information Act 2000.

There are issues particular to the independent and not-for-profit sectors – a network of advice centres, Citizens' Advice Bureaus, law centres and other specialist operations.

Social workers need to develop an understanding of rights and balance this with their responsibilities. In the context of the allocation of resources, they must consider whether social work decisions have legal implications. It is only with knowledge about previous legal challenges – for example, in the field of community care – that social workers become aware of the implications of their practice. Maintaining their knowledge base ensures good practice (Clements, 2004, 2005).

To practise in an anti-oppressive and anti-discriminatory manner

Issues around discrimination – whether on grounds of race, class, gender, sexuality, disability, religion and belief or age – can only be tackled effectively where social workers have had a good grounding in the legislation and are aware of its extent and application in practice. Knowledge about and an understanding of the structure of the legislation is important (McColgan, 2005; Connolly 2006).

Key discrimination legislation

Legislation relevant to issues of discrimination in the UK has developed considerably. The key statutes comprise:

- Race Relations Act 1976
- Race Relations (Amendment) Act 2000
- Race Relations Act 1976 (Amendment) Regulations 2003
- Racial and Religious Hatred Act 2006
- Equal Pay Act 1970
- Sex Discrimination Act 1975
- Sex Discrimination Act 1986
- Sex Discrimination (Gender Reassignment) Regulations 1999
- Sex Discrimination Act 1975 (Amendment) Regulations 2003
- Disability Discrimination Act 1995
- Disability Rights Commission Act 1999
- Disability Discrimination Act 1995 (Amendment) Regulations 2003
- Special Educational Needs and Disability Act 2001
- Disability Discrimination Act 2005
- Employment Equality (Sexual Orientation) Regulations 2003
- Employment Equality (Religion or Belief) Regulations 2003
- Human Rights Act 1998
- Gender Recognition Act 2004
- Civil Partnership Act 2004
- Equality Act 2006
- Age Regulations 2006

It is crucial for social workers to understand the duties placed upon local authorities under section 71 of the Race Relations Act to eliminate unlawful racial discrimination and promote equality of opportunity. It is equally important to recognize how this has been enhanced and extended to all public authorities under the Race Relations (Amendment) Act 2000 along with the duty to develop Race Equality schemes. Mirroring this is a new 'Gender Duty' placed upon public bodies under the Equality Act 2006 requiring them to promote equality of opportunity for women and men. Social workers should make themselves aware of the bodies covered by the legislation and develop an understanding of their functions, powers and limitations – the Commission for Racial Equality (CRE) www.cre.gov.uk, the Equal Opportunities Commission (EOC) www.eoc.org.uk and the Disability Rights Commission (DRC) www.drc.org.uk. Under the Equality Act 2006 all three bodies will by 2009 be incorporated into a Commission for Equality and Human Rights (CEHR).

The Disability Discrimination Acts 1995 and 2005 offer a significantly different formula for addressing direct discrimination of and making reasonable adjustments for disabled people. In the burgeoning case law since their implementation important principles have been established that strengthen their impact. The extent to which 'reasonable adjustments' should be made to avoid discrimination against a person with disabilities in employment has been strongly reinforced by the House of Lords in the case of *Archibald* v *Fife Council Scotland* [2004] UKHL 32. The use of a non-disabled comparator when considering whether direct discrimination has taken place (crucial to the impact of the Act) was established by the House of Lords in the case of *Clark* v *TDG Ltd t-a Novacold* [1999] EWCA Civ 1091. This case confirmed that to decide whether a person with a disability has been treated less favourably requires a comparison with someone who *does not* suffer from the disability; this allows an answer to the question 'But for the disability would the person have been so treated?'

In contrast, other discrimination legislation is based on the concept of discrimination occurring where a person is treated less favourably (on grounds, for example, related to their sex or their race or another's race) than a person of the opposite sex or of a different racial group. The practical effect of this is that for sex, race, religion or belief, sexuality or age discrimination to occur there must have been an absence of *equal* treatment between the person being discriminated against and other persons – which then fails to take account of meaningful differences that *may* exist. The fact that pregnancy occurs only in women is a clear difference between men and women. Yet it took nearly 20 years (and the European Court of Justice in the case of *Webb* v *EMO Air Cargo (UK) Ltd* [1995] 4 All ER 577) to remedy the effect of the equal treatment provisions within the Sex Discrimination Act 1975 which *prevented* women from taking cases of discrimination on pregnancy-related grounds as an appropriate male comparator (not surprisingly) could not be found. Pregnancy now constitutes a *prima facie* ground for sex discrimination under the amended Sex Discrimination Act 1975.

Learning about the limited statutory definitions of discrimination and the recent efforts to expand these through case law and developments in European Union law enhances a social worker's understanding of the legal system's failure to resolve problems of race, gender and sexuality discrimination. In this way students can begin to build up an understanding of the processes by which individuals, groups and communities feel discriminated against by state institutions – including local authority social workers. The reports of the Scarman Inquiry (1981), which reviewed inner city policing policies following riots in London, and the Macpherson Inquiry (1999), which examined the circumstances surrounding the murder of Stephen Lawrence, both illustrated how the lack of adequate legal redress can give rise to a frustrated and bitter community response. The Macpherson Inquiry led directly to amendment of the Race Relations Act in 2000.

European Union Directives transposed into domestic legislation have introduced new protection for people on the grounds of sexual orientation, religion or belief and age. Under these directives, people cannot be discriminated against in employment by virtue of their sexual orientation, age, religion or belief (but not political belief). The UK government has extended the right not to be discriminated against on the grounds of sexual orientation and religion or belief in the provision of 'goods and services'. *Stonewall* is a campaigning organization for gays and lesbians which identifies, monitors and documents discrimination in employment and other areas of life (www.stonewall.org.uk).

Outlawing discrimination on the grounds of age was introduced into English law in 2006 by virtue of the EU Employment Equality directive. It applies to all aspects of employment from recruitment to retirement and in respect of both younger and older workers (www.dti.gov.uk/employment/discrimination/age-discrimination/index.html).

To protect their own position as employees

Any acquisition of knowledge in substantive areas of law, procedures and legal process will necessarily enhance a social worker's awareness of their own position as an employee. This is beneficial in a profession where there are issues around personal safety working with vulnerable service users and broader health and safety concerns involving working conditions and occupational hazards related to the nature of the work itself. Neither should employee rights, whistle blowing, trade unionism, pay and general terms and conditions of employment be overlooked (Slade, 2004; Lewis, 2005).

The regulatory and licensing requirements of the GSCC require social workers to be alive to their professional standards of practice and the possibility of refusal of initial registration or subsequent removal from the register (www.gscc.org.uk). As the private sector comes to play an increasing role in the delivery of personal social services, the legal position of social workers as employees becomes ever more important as does the need both to understand the role and purpose of a trade union and to become an active member.

How the Law Regulates Social Work Practice

An understanding of law and the legal system is fundamental to grasping how the law regulates practice and provides a legal basis for social work intervention:

- how law is made;
- where law comes from;
- how law is administered;
- what the process of law is, in terms of courts, tribunals and access to the law;
- what public funding is available to cover the costs of litigation;
- what assistance is available from the legal profession and the voluntary advice sector.

Accessible texts are Quinn and Elliott (2006) and, with particular reference to social workers, Brayne and Carr (2005), Brammer (2006) and Johns (2005).

Sources of English law

English law, unlike the continental legal system, has developed through the common law, which is law made by the decisions of courts or judges. With the demise of the political role of the monarchy and the growth of Parliament, a chief source of law became statutes or Acts of Parliament. These are generally applicable in England and Wales with separate legislative provision for Scotland and Northern Ireland. Statutes or Acts pass into the law following a parliamentary debating and voting process. 'Delegated' or secondary legislation comes about where primary legislation (an Act) specifies that delegated powers are to be given to government ministers, Secretaries of State or other bodies (often local authorities) to introduce regulations and detailed provisions at a later date without having to submit to the full scrutiny of a parliamentary process. Delegated legislation can take the form of statutory instruments, orders in council, local authority by-laws or the rules of professional bodies governing the conduct of doctors, lawyers and social workers.

In order to understand the different types of legislation and how it is made, it is necessary to appreciate their status. Regulations in the form of Statutory Instruments, for example, issued under powers granted by Act of Parliament, will be binding in law. By contrast, guidance issued by a government department will not normally have the status of law. Nonetheless, section 7 of the Local Authority Social Services Act 1970 specifies that local authorities *must* act under guidance issued by the Secretary of State, and failure to do so could result in a court decision that a local authority had acted unlawfully.

There are numerous examples of regulations and guidance relevant to social workers issued under the Children Act 1989 and 2004 and associated court rules. Initially, ten volumes of guidance were issued under the Children Act 1989. Department of Health and further guidance has been issued since (Department of Health, 1989b, 1991b, 1991c, 2000b; Department of Health et al., 1998b) and under the 2004 Act similarly (Department of Health, 2006b). Under community care legislation extensive guidance has been issued (Department of Health 1990b, 1991d, 2000d, 2002a, 2003a, 2003b, 2005b).

The EU Dimension

With the UK's membership of the European Union, social work and its practitioners are subject to EU legislation. A comprehensive website is www.europa.eu. The

European Community Act 1972 specifically makes EU law applicable and effective in the UK and requires the UK courts to interpret English law in accordance with EU law. Articles are agreed by member states at the point of signing treaties and are directly and automatically applicable to the member state's law. According to Article 249 of the Treaty of Rome (formally Article 189) Regulations are 'binding in their entirety and directly applicable' whereas Directives are 'binding as to the result to be achieved . . . but shall leave to the national authorities the choice of form and methods'. Directives are transposed by the introduction of legislation in each member state to bring about the result set out in the Directive within a time period. In contrast, Regulations are immediately effective in the form they are made.

The process for making EU secondary legislation involves a proposal being put to the European Commission, after it has been suggested by the European Parliament, an individual member state or a pressure group. The Commission forwards it to the Council of Ministers who, in consultation with the Parliament, the Economic and Social Committee and, where relevant, the Committee of the Regions, frames the legislation and approves it. It is then passed into law (sometimes being first subject to ratification by all member states) where it is immediately binding if it is a Regulation, or if a Directive effective once domestic legislation has been passed.

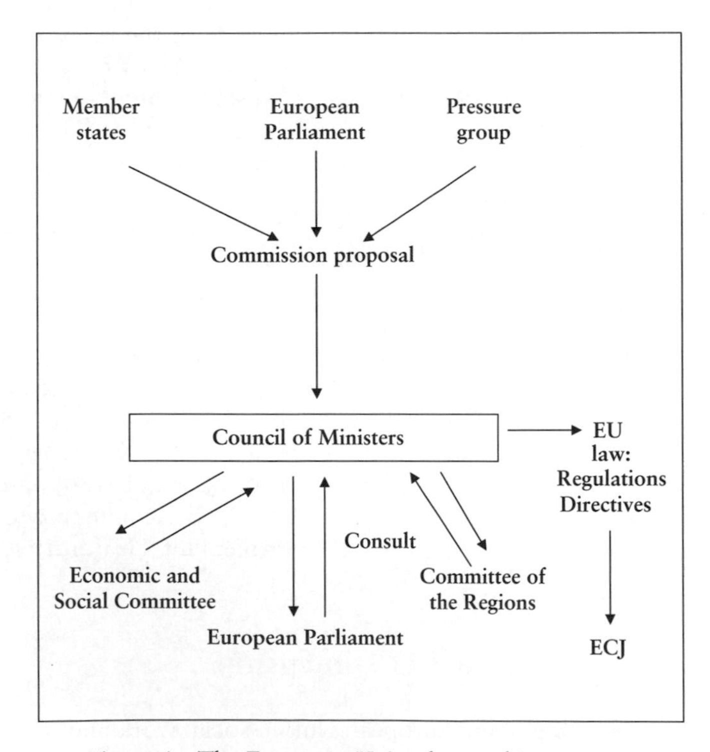

Figure 1 The European Union law-making process

An example of primary legislation is Article 141 which provides for equal pay for equal work. Two examples of secondary legislation are the Equal Pay Directive 75/117 and the Equal Treatment Directive 76/207. Three anti-discrimination Directives which establish a general framework for equal treatment in employment and occupation (2000/78/EC), implement the principle of equal treatment between people irrespective of race and ethnic origin (2000/43/EC) and establish a community action programme to combat discrimination (2000/750/EC), were proposed by the European Commission in November 1999, adopted in 2000 and came into force in 2006.

The legal framework for social work intervention

The Local Authority Social Services Act 1970 included a requirement in section 2 that every local authority 'shall' establish a Social Services Committee to have responsibility for all functions under legislation listed in a Schedule to the Act. The Social Services Committee is ultimately responsible for the operation of a social services department set up under the Act, and social workers are governed and their statutory framework delineated by legislation listed in the Schedule including Acts concerning children, adoption, community care, mental health, housing and various miscellaneous provisions such as the registration of homes. The statutory framework is amended as new legislation is introduced. New arrangements for the organization of childcare social work services, under the Children Act 2004, bring about an integration of children's services under local Children Services Directorates and a national Children's Commissioner at the Department for Education and Skills (Department for Education and Skills, 2003; Department for Education and Skills and Department of Health, 2004; www.everychildmatters.gov.uk/socialcare/). Corresponding developments are anticipated to take effect in respect of social and health care provision and financing for adult service users through care trusts and, ultimately, fully integrated services (Department of Health, 2005b).

Under the Local Authority Social Services Act 1970 there is a requirement on each local authority to establish complaints procedures. Additionally, statutory rights to bring a complaint exist under various social welfare legislation – for example, under section 26 of the Children Act 1989 and section 50 of the NHS and Community Care Act 1990. Social services complaints related to health care have undergone reform following implementation of the Health and Social Care (Community Health and Standards) Act 2003 in September 2006, obliging health and social services authorities to cooperate with one another where complaints relate to both services.

In carrying out their functions prescribed by legislation, social workers have both *powers* and *duties*. A *power* may be described as being permissive and will be identified in legislation by use of the word 'may'. Examples of this include section 29 (1) of the National Assistance Act 1948, which gives a power to promote the welfare of disabled people. A *duty* is obligatory and will be identified in legislation by the words 'must' or 'shall'. Examples include section 47 of the Children Act 1989 which imposes a duty to protect children, and section 47 of the NHS and Community Care Act 1990 which imposes a duty to carry out community care assessments.

As well as knowledge of areas of statutory responsibility, social workers need a wider knowledge and awareness of the law. For example, having an awareness of rights under immigration and nationality legislation or in relation to the treatment of asylum seekers applying for refugee status will help a social worker understand why certain groups may not readily accept the offer of service or may be hostile to them in anticipation of them acting in a discriminatory manner.

Similarly, understanding the legal remedies for domestic violence as enshrined in the Family Law Act 1996 and positive developments since with the Domestic Violence, Crime and Victims Act 2004, is important for social workers.

A rapidly developing area of law concerns human rights and the effect of the Human Rights Act (HRA) 1998, in force since October 2000. This Act, through its incorporation into English law of the rights contained in the European Convention on Human Rights 1950, requires public bodies to act and make decisions in a way that is compatible with these rights (Wadham and Mountfield, 2000). As a 'living instrument' the original convention and the body of case law built up in the Court of Human Rights in Strasbourg provides the UK courts and practitioners in social and health care with a body of new concepts and solutions to address legal and related problems and will continue to have a major impact on social work practice.

Social workers and their employers need to ensure that their practice is consistent with the rights covered by the HRA and be aware of cases that have successfully challenged practice and obtained remedies to correct infringement of rights. Examples include:

- *R (Howard League for Penal Reform)* v *Secretary of State for the Home Department* [2002] EWHC 2497 (Admin) where Article 8 rights were held to apply to vulnerable children in young offender institutions;
- *R (A, B, X and Y)* v *East Sussex County Council (No. 2)* [2003] EWHC 167 (Admin) where positive obligations on local authorities to provide services in the home to vulnerable adults were held to exist under Article 8;
- *P, C and S* v *UK* [2002] 35 EHHR 1075 where the European Court of Human Rights ruled that removal of a child from its mother shortly after birth was not justified by relevant and sufficient reasons and thereby breached Article 8, right to family life.

A debate continues as to how effective the HRA is in promoting and protecting rights – especially for those living in poverty or in conditions of social exclusion (Clements and Thomas, 2005). In the wake of terrorist attacks and serious crime, the Act has been criticized for benefiting the human rights of the perpetrators of such acts rather than their victims. A more balanced view has been promoted by organizations, lawyers and academics seeking both to understand and develop a framework for protecting and balancing competing rights (Edmundson, 2006).

Relevant for social workers is understanding how a culture of human rights awareness can be equally beneficial in developing practice and responding to service users' needs in a sensitive and appropriate manner without the need for litigation. Examples include:

- a local authority providing support workers for disabled people in residential care to enable them to go to social venues (Article 8, right to respect for private life);
- a mental health befriending scheme challenging a hospital which repeatedly sectioned asylum seekers with little English for failing to provide interpreters (Article 5, right to liberty; Article 14, right to freedom from discrimination);
- a disabled man who had stopped attending hospital appointments due to the humiliation of being examined in front of a large group of people including students, successfully challenging this practice so that he was examined by just one doctor (Article 3, prohibition of inhuman or degrading treatment) (www.bihr.org).

In Conclusion

Legal challenges to social work practice and decision-making have increased in recent years. Some have resulted in legislative changes – such as the provision made by the Adoption and Children Act 2002 for courts to consider a care plan before making a care order and an obligation on the local authority to review the plan once in place.

Constraints – especially financial constraints – pose difficulties in decision-making for social workers and local authorities alike. This has generated a significant body of case law, particularly in respect of the allocation of resources by local authorities in meeting their responsibilities under community care legislation (Clements, 2004, 2005).

A number of cases – as a result of decisions made by the European Court of Human Rights – have shaped the exercise of professional social work discretion through a finding of negligence where initially the highest English court (the House of Lords) had not wished to interfere – *X (Minors)* v *Bedfordshire CC* [1995] 3 All ER 353. Thus, cases once thought better left to the discretion of social workers (free from defensive litigation considerations) have been brought firmly within the ambit of court decision-making. The significance of this is that the courts have recognized the liability of social services where they fail in their common law duty of care to their clients in the same way that doctors, lawyers and other professionals have long been liable.

Social workers need to develop practice which respects and is sensitive to the rights of clients without compromising the protection of those within their statutory care and responsibility. They need to develop practices which are capable of offering protection and support to those vulnerable by virtue of age, infirmity, or mental incapacity without infringing their rights or those of their relatives or carers.

Social work and its practice has increasingly been affected by legislative changes, the development of human rights and the regulation and standard setting in relation both to the profession itself and the agencies with which it works and provides services. Social work students and practitioners therefore need to have a clear focus upon and interest in the law and an awareness of how it affects them.

Five Key Points

- Social workers need to know about law.
- Law regulates social work practice.
- Law provides a framework for social work intervention.
- Knowledge of the law informs and enhances anti-discriminatory and anti-oppressive practice.
- The courts are playing an increasingly significant role in determining the rights of service users, the legality of social work decisions and the legality of the exercise of discretion in social work practice.

Three Questions

? Why do social workers need to know about the law?
? How important are human rights in the practice of social work?
? Can the law help in balancing the rights of service users with the powers and duties of social workers?

Further reading

1 Cull, L-A. and Roche, J. (eds.) (2001) *The Law and Social Work*. Basingstoke: Palgrave.
2 Brayne, H. and Carr, H. (2005) *Law for Social Workers,* 9th edn. Oxford: Oxford University Press.
3 Quinn, F. and Elliott, C. (2006) *The English Legal System,* 7th edn. London: Longman.

Bibliography

ACE Bulletin (2000) Children who need champions. *ACE Bulletin*, 95 (June). London: Advisory Centre for Education.

Acton, R. G. (2001) *Angry Parents: A Group Psychotherapy Manual for Aggression Management Training*. Calgary: Acton House.

Adams, R., Dominelli, L. and Payne, M. (eds.) (2002) *Social Work, Themes, Issues and Critical Debates*. Basingstoke: Palgrave.

Advisory Council on the Misuse of Drugs (2003) *Hidden Harm: Responding to the Needs of Children of Problem Drug Users*. London: Home Office.

Ahmad, B. (1990) *Black Perspectives in Social Work*. Birmingham: Venture Press.

Ahmad, B. (1992) *A Dictionary of Black Managers in White Organizations*. London: National Institute of Social Work.

Ahmad, W. I. U. and Atkin, K. (eds.) (1996) *'Race' and Community Care*. Buckingham: Open University Press.

Ainsworth, M. D. S., Blehar, M. and Waters, E. (1978) *Patterns of Attachment*. Hillsdale, NJ: Erlbaum.

Ainsworth, P. B. (2000) *Psychology and Crime: Myths and Reality*. Harlow: Pearson Education.

Alcock, C., Payne, S. and Sullivan, M. (2004) *Introducing Social Policy*. Harlow: Pearson.

Alcohol Concern (2002) Alcohol misuse among older people. *Acquire*. London: Alcohol Concern.

Alderson, P. (1996) *What Works? Effective Social Interventions in Child Welfare*. Ilford: Barnados.

Aldgate, J. and Bradley, M. (1999) *Supporting Families through Short Term Fostering*. London: The Stationery Office.

Alford, B. A. and Beck, A. T. (1997) *The Integrative Power of Cognitive Therapy*. New York: Guilford Press.

Allahar, A.L. (1995) *Sociology and the Periphery*. Toronto: Garramond Press.

Allan, G. and Crow, G. (2001), *Families, Households and Society*. London: Palgrave.

Allard, A., Fry, E. and Sufian, J. (2004) *Setting the Agenda: What's Left to Do in Leaving Care?* London: Action on Aftercare Consortium.

Allen, D. (1997). Social construction of self: Some Asian, Marxist, and feminist critiques of dominant Western views of self. In D. Allen (ed.), *Culture and the Self: Philosophical and Religious Perspectives, East and West*. Boulder, CO: Westview Press, pp. 3–26.

Allen-Meares, P. (ed.) (2004) *Social Work Services in Schools*, 4th edn. Boston: Pearson.

American Psychiatric Association (1994) *Diagnostic and Statistical Manual of Mental Disorders-IV*. Washington, DC: American Psychiatric Association.

Amnesty International (2000) *Most Vulnerable of All: The Treatment of Unaccompanied Refugee Children in the UK*. London: Amnesty International UK.

Anderson, T. (1987), *Reflecting Teams: Dialogues and Dialogues about the Dialogues*. Broadstairs: Borgmann.

Arber, S. and Ginn, J. (1995) *Connecting Gender and Ageing*. Buckingham: Open University Press.

Asthana, S. and Halliday, J. (2006) *What Works in Tackling Health Inequalities? Pathways, Policies and Practice through the Life Course*. Bristol: Policy Press.

Atkinson, J. and Coia, D. (1995) *Families Coping with Schizophrenia*. Chichester: Wiley.

Atkinson, M., Halsey, K., Wilkin, A. and Kinder, K. (2000a) *Raising Attendance: Working Practices and Current Initiatives within Education Welfare Service*. Slough: NFER.

Atkinson, M., Halsey, K., Wilkin, A. and Kinder, K. (2000b) *Raising Attendance: A Detailed Study of Education Welfare Service*. Slough: NFER.

Audit Commission (2000) *The Way to Go Home: Rehabilitation and Remedial Services for Older People*. London: Audit Commission.

Australian Association of Social Workers [AASW] (2002) *Code of Ethics (1999)*, 2nd edn. Canberra: AASW.

Averill, J. R. (1982) *Anger and Aggression: An Essay on Emotion*. New York: Springer Verlag.

Axford, N., Little, M., Morpeth, L. and Weyts, A. (2005) Evaluating children's services: Recent conceptual and methodological developments. *British Journal of Social Work*, 35 (1), 73–88.

Azmi, S. (1997) Professionalism and social diversity. In R. Hugman, M. Peelo and K. Soothill (eds.), *Concepts of Care*. London: Edward Arnold.

BACP (2006) *www.bacp.co.uk*, accessed 5 February 2006.

Bailey, R. and Brake, M. (eds.) (1975) *Radical Social Work*. London: Edward Arnold.

Bailey-Dempsey, C. and Reid, W. J. (1996) Intervention design and development: A case study. *Research on Social Work Practice*, 6(2), 208–28.

Baillargeon, R., Spelke, E. S. and Wasserman, S. (1985) Object permanence in 5-month-old infants. *Cognition*, 20, 191–208.

Bainham, A., Lindley, B., Richards, M. and Trinder, L. (eds.) (2003) *Children and their Families: Contact, Rights and Welfare*. Oxford: Hart.

Bandura, A. (1969) *Principles of Behavior Modification*. New York: Holt, Rinehart and Winston.

Bandura, A. (1973) *Aggression: A Social Learning Analysis*. Englewood Cliffs, NJ: Prentice Hall.

Bandura, A. (1997) *Self-efficacy: The Exercise of Control*. New York: W. H. Freeman.

Bank, L., Marlowe, J. H., Reid, J. B., Patterson, G. R. and Weinrott, M. R. (1991) A comparative evaluation of parent training interventions for families of chronic delinquents. *Journal of Abnormal Child Psychology*, 19, 15–34.

Bank, L., Patterson, G. R. and Reid, J. B. (1987) Delinquency prevention through training parents in family management. *The Behaviour Analyst*, 10, 75–82.

Banks, N. (1992) Some considerations of 'racial' identity and self esteem when working with mixed ethnicity and their mothers as social services clients. *Social Services Review*, 3, 32–41.

Banks, S. (2004) *Ethics, Accountability and the Social Professions*. Basingstoke: Palgrave.
Banks, S. (2006) *Ethics and Values in Social Work*, 3rd edn. Basingstoke: Palgrave.
Baraclough, J., Dedman, G., Osborn, H. and Willmott, P. (1996) *One Hundred Years of Health Related Social Work 1895–1995: Then, Now, Onwards*. Birmingham: Venture Press.
Barber, J. (2002) *Social Work with Addictions*, 2nd edn. Basingstoke: Palgrave Macmillan.
Barker, D. J. P. (ed.) (1992) *Fetal and Infant Origins of Adult Disease*. London: British Medical Journal.
Barlow, A., Duncan, S., James, G. and Park, A. (2002) Just a piece of paper? Marriage and cohabitation. In A. Park, J. Curtice, K. Thomson, L. Jarvis and C. Bromley (eds.), *British Social Attitudes: Public Policy, Social Ties: The 19th Report*. London: Sage.
Barlow, J., Johnston, I., Kendrick, D., Polnay, L. and Stewart-Brown, S. (2006) Individual and group-based parenting programmes for the treatment of physical child abuse and neglect. *The Cochrane Database of Systematic Reviews*, Issue 3, Art. No. CD005463.
Barnes, C. and Mercer, G. (eds.) (1996) *Exploring the Divide: Illness and Disability*. Leeds: The Disability Press.
Barnes, C. and Mercer, G. (eds.) (2003) *Implementing the Social Model: Disability and Research*. Leeds: The Disability Press.
Barnes, C. and Mercer, G. (eds.) (2004) *Disability Policy and Practice: Applying the Social Model*. Leeds: The Disability Press.
Barnes, C. and Mercer, G. (eds.) (2005) *The Social Model of Disability: Europe and the Majority World*. Leeds: The Disability Press.
Barnes, C. and Mercer, G. (2006) *Independent Futures: Creating User-led Disability Services in a Disabling Society*. Bristol: Policy Press.
Barnes, C., Oliver, M. and Barton, L. (eds.) (2002) *Disability Studies Today*. Cambridge: Polity Press.
Barnes, M. (1997) *Care, Communities and Citizens*. London: Longman.
Barnes, M. and Maple, N. (1992) *Women and Mental Health: Challenging the Stereotypes*. Birmingham: Venture Press.
Barnes, M., Bauld, L., Benzeval, M., Judge, K., Mackenzie, M. and Sullivan, H. (2005) *Health Action Zones: Partnership for Health Equity*. London: Routledge.
Barratt, H. (2003) *Parenting Programmes for Families at Risk: A Source Book*. London: National Family and Parenting Institute.
Barratt, H. (2004) *Social Trends 1994–2004*. London: National Family and Parenting Institute.
Bateman, N. (2000) *Advocacy Skills for Health and Social Care Professionals*. London. Jessica Kingsley.
Bateman, N. (2005) *Practising Welfare Rights*. London: Routledge.
Bateson, G., Jackson, D. and Haley, J. (1956) Towards a theory of schizophrenia. *Behavioural Science*, 1, 251–64.
Bauman, Z. (1998) *Globalization: The Human Consequences*. Oxford: Blackwell.
Baumgardner, J. and Richards, A. (2000) *Manifesta: Young Women, Feminism and the Future*. New York: Farrar, Strauss and Giroux.
Beauchamp, T. L. and Childress, J. F. (2001) *Principles of Biomedical Ethics*. 5th edn. Oxford: Oxford University Press.
Beck, A. (1976) *Cognitive Therapy and the Emotional Disorders*. New York: International University Press.
Beck, A. T. (1999) *Prisoners of Hate: The Cognitive Basis of Anger, Hostility and Violence*. New York: Harper Collins.
Beck, A. T., Rush, A. J., Shaw, B. F. and Emery, G. (1979) *Cognitive Therapy of Depression*. New York: Guilford.

Beck, U. (1992) *Risk Society: Towards a New Modernity*. London: Sage.

Becker, S. (1997) *Responding to Poverty. The Politics of Cash and Care*. Harlow: Addison Wesley Longman.

Beckett, C. (2003) *Child Protection: An Introduction*. London: Sage.

Beckett, C. (2006) *Essential Theory for Social Work Practice*. London: Sage.

Bee, H. and Boyd, D. (2004) *The Developing Child*. New York: HarperCollins.

Beek, M. and Schofield, G. (2004) *Providing a Secure Base in Long-Term Foster Care*. London: BAAF Adoption and Fostering.

Belsky, J. (1993) Etiology of child maltreatment: A developmental-ecological analysis. *Psychological Bulletin*, 114, 413–34.

Benson, B. A., Rice, J. C. and Miranti, S. V. (1986) Men working with men in groups: masculinity and crime. *Groupwork*, 7(1), 37–49.

Beresford, P. (1994) *Changing the Culture: Involving Service Users in Social Work Education*, Paper 32.2. London: Central Council for Education and Training in Social Work.

Beresford, P. (1999) Making participation possible: Movements of disabled people and psychiatric survivors. In T. Jordan and A. Lent (eds.), *Storming the Millennium*. London: Lawrence and Wishart, pp. 35–50.

Beresford, P. (2000) What have madness and psychiatric system survivors got to do with disability and disability studies? *Disability & Society*, 15 (1), 167–72.

Beresford, P. (2003) *It's our Lives: A Short Theory of Knowledge, Distance and Experience*. London: Citizen Press.

Beresford, P. (2005) Developing the theoretical basis for service user/survivor-led research and equal involvement in research. *Epidemiologia e Psichiatria Sociale*, 14(1), 4–9.

Beresford, P., Adshead, L. and Croft, S. (2007) *Palliative Care, Social Work and Service Users Making Life Possible*. London: Jessica Kingsley.

Beresford, P. and Campbell, J. (1994) Disabled people, service users, user involvement and representation. *Disability and Society*, 9(3), 315–26.

Beresford, P. and Croft, S. (1987) Are we really listening. In T. Philpot (ed.), *On Second Thoughts: Reassessments of the Literature of Social Work*. London: Community Care.

Beresford, P., Shamash, O., Forrest, V., Turner, M. and Branfield, F. (2005) *Developing Social Care: Service Users' Vision for Adult Support* (Report of a consultation on the future of adult social care), Adult Services Report 07. London: Social Care Institute for Excellence in association with Shaping Our Lives.

Beresford, P. and Trevillion, S. (1995) *Developing Skills for Community Care: A Collaborative Approach*. Aldershot: Arena.

Bewley, C. and Glendinning, C. (1994) *Involving Disabled People in Community Care Planning*. York: Joseph Rowntree Foundation and Community Care.

Bhavnani, K. (1994) Shifting identities, shifting racism: An introduction. In K. Bhavnani and A. Phoenix (eds.), *Shifting Identities Shifting Racism: A Feminism and Psychology Reader*. London: Sage, pp. 5–18.

Biestek, F. P. (1961) *The Casework Relationship*. London: George Allen and Unwin.

Biggs, S., Kingston, P. and Phillipson, C. (1995) *Elder Abuse in Perspective*. Buckingham: Open University Press.

Birmingham Voice (2000) Pensioners claim £2.4M. *Birmingham Voice,* 174 (23 February), 1.

Blair, T. (1997) Speech at Stockwell Park School, Lambeth, 8 December. (http://www.open.gov.uk/co/seu.more.html/speech by the Prime Minister).

Blakemore, K. and Boneham, B. (1994) *Age, Race and Ethnicity: A Comparative Approach*. Buckingham: Open University Press.

Blom-Cooper, L., Hally, H. and Murphy, E. (1995) *The Falling Shadow: One Patient's Mental Health Care*. London: Duckworth.

Bloom, M. (1999) Single-system evaluation. In I. Shaw and J. Lishman (eds.), *Evaluation and Social Work Practice*. London: Sage, pp. 198–218.

Blunden, R. (2002) *How Good Is Your Service to Carers? A Guide to Checking Quality Standards for Local Carer Support Services*. London: King's Fund.

Blyth, E. and Milner, J. (eds.) (1999) *Improving School Attendance*. London: Routledge.

Bond, J. and Coleman, P. (1993) Ageing into the twenty-first century. In J. Bond, P. Coleman and S. Peace (eds.), *Ageing in Society: An Introduction to Social Gerontology*. London: Sage, pp. 333–50.

Bornat, J. (ed.) (1994) *Reminiscence Reviewed*. Buckingham: Open University Press.

Bosanquet, H. (1902) *The Strength of the People*. London: Macmillan.

Bourne, J. (1999) A mixed approach to education. *Professional Social Work*, 9, 16–17.

Bowl, R. (1985), *Changing the Nature of Masculinity: A Task for Social Work*. Norwich: Social Work Monographs.

Bowlby, J. (1953) *Child Care and the Growth of Love*. Harmondsworth: Penguin Books.

Bowlby, J. (1969) *Attachment and Loss: Volume 1, Attachment*. New York: Basic Books.

Bowlby, J. (1971) *Attachment and Loss*. London: Penguin.

Boyd Report, Steering Committee of the Confidential Inquiry into Homicides and Suicides by Mentally Ill Persons (1994) *A Preliminary Report on Homicide*. London: Steering Committee of the Confidential Inquiry into Homicides and Suicides by Mentally Ill Persons.

Boyd-Franklin, N. (1989) *Black Families in Therapy*. New York: Guilford Press.

Boyes, M. and Allen, S. (1993) Patterns of parent child interactions and socio moral reasoning in adolescent and young adulthood. *Merrill-Palmer Quarterly*, 39(4), 551–570.

Boylan, J. and Ing, P. (2005) Seen but not heard: Children and young people's experiences of advocacy. *International Journal of Social Welfare*, 14, 2–12.

Bradley, G. and Manthorpe, J. (eds.) (2000) *Working on the Faultline*. Birmingham: Venture Press.

Bradshaw, J. (2002) Child poverty and child outcomes. *Children and Society*, 16, 131–40.

Bradshaw, J., Stimson, C., Skinner, C. and Williams, J. (1999) *Absent Fathers*. London: Routledge.

Brah, A. (1992) Difference, diversity and differentiation. In J. Donald and A. Rattinsi (eds.), *Race, Culture and Difference*. London: Sage.

Brammer, A. (2006) *Social Work Law*, 2nd edn. Harlow: Longmans.

Brandon, M., Thoburn, J., Lewis, A. and Way, A. (1999) *Safeguarding Children with the Children Act 1989*. London: The Stationery Office.

Branfield, F., Beresford, P. and Levin, E. (2005) *Common Aims: A Strategy to Support Service User Involvement in Social Work Education*. London: Social Care Institute for Excellence.

Braye, S. and Preston-Shoot, M. (1995) *Empowering Practice in Social Care*. Buckingham: Open University Press.

Brayne, H. and Carr, H. (2005) *Law for Social Workers*, 9th edn. Oxford: Oxford University Press.

Brearley, J. (1991) *Counselling and Social Work*. Buckingham: Open University Press.

Brechin, A., Barton, R. and Stein, J. (2002) Getting to grips with poor care. In K. Stalker (ed.), *Reconceptualising Work with 'Carers': New Directions for Policy and Practice*, Research Highlights in Social Work No. 43. London: Jessica Kingsley.

Bricker-Jenkins, M. (1990) Another approach to practice and training: Clients must be considered the primary experts. *Public Welfare*, Spring, 11–16.

British Association of Social Workers [BASW] (2002) *The Code of Ethics for Social Work*. Birmingham: BASW.

British Gas and Help the Aged (2004) *Older and Colder: The Views of Older People Experiencing Difficulties Keeping Warm in Winter*. London: Help the Aged.

Broad, B. (2005) *Improving the Health and Well-being of Young People Leaving Care*. Lyme Regis: Russell House.

Brown, A. (1992) *Groupwork*, 3rd edn. Aldershot: Ashgate.

Brown, A. and Mistry, T. (1994) Groupwork with 'mixed' membership groups: Issues of race and gender. *Social Work with Groups*, 17(3), 5–21. Reprinted in T. Mistry and A. Brown (eds.) (1994) *Race and Groupwork*. London: Whiting and Birch.

Brown, C. (1986) *Child Abuse Parents Speaking: A Consumer Study*. Bristol: School for Advanced Urban Studies, University of Bristol.

Brown, C. (1997) *Religion and Society in Scotland since 1701*. Edinburgh: Edinburgh University Press.

Brown, G. W. (1996) Life events, loss and depressive disorders. In T. Heller, J. Reynolds, R. Gomm, R. Muston and S. Pattison (1996) *Mental Health Matters: A Reader*. Basingstoke: Palgrave Macmillan.

Brown, G. W. and Harris, T. H. (1978) *Social Origins of Depression*. London: Tavistock.

Browne, K. D. (1988) The naturalistic context of family violence and child abuse. In J. Archer and K. D. Browne (eds.), *Human Aggression: Naturalistic Approaches*. London: Routledge.

Bruegal, I. (1989) Sex and race in the labour market. *Feminist Review*, 32(Summer), 49–68.

Burbach, F. and Stanbridge, R. (1998) A family interventions in psychosis service: Integrating the systemic and family management approaches. *Journal of Family Therapy*, 20, 311–25.

Butler, I. and Drakeford, M. (2001) Which Blair Project? Communitarianism, social authoritarianism and social work. *Journal of Social Work*, 31(1), 1–19.

Butler, I. and Drakeford, M. (2005) Trusting in social work. *British Journal of Social Work*, 35(5), 639–53.

Butler, I., Scanlan, L., Robinson, M., Douglas, G. and Murch, M. (2003) *Divorcing Children: Children's Experience of their Parents' Divorce*. London: Jessica Kingsley.

Butt, J. and Davey, B. (1998) The experience of black workers in the social care workforce. *Social Policy Review*, 9, 140–61.

Butt, J. and Mirza, K. (1995) *Social Care and Black Communities*. London: HMSO.

Byng-Hall, J. (1995) *Rewriting Family Scripts*. London: Guilford Press.

Bytheway, B. (1994) *Ageism*. Buckingham: Open University Press.

Bytheway, B., Bacigalupo, V., Bornat, J., Johnson, J. and Spurr, S. (2002) *Understanding Care, Welfare and Community: A Reader*. London: Routledge.

Bywaters, P. (1986) Social work and the medical profession: Arguments against unconditional collaboration, *British Journal of Social Work*, 16(4), 661–67.

Bywaters, P. and McLeod, E. (2001) The impact of new labour health policy on social services: A new deal for service users' health? *British Journal of Social Work*, 31(94), 579–94.

Cacas, J. M. (1984) Policy, training, and research in counselling psychology: The racial/ethnic minority perspective. In S. D. Brown and R. W. Lent (eds.), *Handbook of Counselling Psychology*. New York: Wiley, pp. 785–831.

Caddick, B. and Watson, D. (1999) Rehabilitation and the distribution of risk. In P. Parsloe (ed.), *Risk Assessment in Social Care and Social Work*. London: Jessica Kingsley, pp. 53–68.

Calder, M. (2005) *Children Living with Domestic Violence: Towards a Framework for Assessment and Intervention*. Lyme Regis: Russell House.

Cameron, J. (2005) Who cares? *The Guardian*, Society, 7 December.

Cameron, J. (2006) Who cares? *The Guardian*, Society, 1 March.

Campbell, A., Converse, P. and Rogers, W. L. (1976) *The Quality of American Life: Perceptions, Evaluations and Satisfactions*. New York: Russell Sage.

Campbell, J. and Oliver, M. (1996) *Disability Politics: Understanding our Past, Changing our Future*. London: Routledge.

Campbell, P. (1996) The history of the user movement in the United Kingdom. In T. Heller, J. Reynolds, R. Gomm, R. Muston and S. Pattison (eds.), *Mental Health Matters*. Basingstoke: Macmillan.

Campbell, P. (1999) The service user/survivor movement. In C. Newnes, G. Holmes and C. Dunn (eds.), *This Is Madness: A Critical Look at Psychiatry and the Future of Mental Health Services*. Ross-on-Wye: PCCS Books, pp. 195–209.

Cancian, F. (1987) *Love in America: Gender and Self-Development*. Cambridge: Cambridge University Press.

Carers UK (2004) *In Poor Health: The Impact of Caring on Health*. London: Carers UK.

Carr, A. (2000) *Family Therapy: Concepts, Process and Practice*. Chichester: Wiley.

Carr, S. (2004) *Has Service User Participation Made a Difference to Social Care Services?* Position Paper 3. London: Social Care Institute for Excellence.

Carson, D. (1996) Risking legal repercussions. In H. Kemshall and J. Pritchard (eds.), *Good Practice in Risk Assessment and Risk Management*. London: Jessica Kingsley, pp. 3–12.

Carter, Lord (2006) *Legal Aid: A Market-based Approach to Reform*. London: Department for Constitutional Affairs.

Cassell, P. (ed.) (1993) *The Giddens Reader*. London: Macmillan.

Castles, S. and Davidson, A. (2000) *Citizenship and Migration*. Basingstoke: Palgrave.

Cavadino, M. and Dignan, J. (2007) *The Penal System: An Introduction*, 4th edn. London: Sage.

Cavanagh, K. and Cree, V. (eds.) (1996), *Working with Men: Feminism and Social Work*. London: Routledge.

Cawson, P., Wattam, C., Brooker, S. and Kelly, G. (2000) *Child Maltreatment in the United Kingdom*. London: NSPCC.

Challis, D., Darton, R., Hughes, J., Stewart, K. and Waines, K. (1998) *Care Management Study: Report on National Data; Mapping and Evaluation of Care Management Arrangements for Older People and Those with Mental Health Problems*. London: Department of Health.

Chappell, A., Goodley, D. and Lawthorn, R. (2001) Making connections: The relevance of the social model of disability to people with learning disabilities. *British Journal of Learning Disabilities*, 29, 45–50.

Charity Commission (2000) *The Promotion of Community Capacity Building*. http://www.charity-commission.gov.uk/publications/rr5.asp

Charlton J. I. (2000) *Nothing about Us without Us: Disability Oppression and Empowerment*. Berkeley: University of California Press.

Cheesbrough, S. (2003) Young motherhood: Family transmission or family transition? In G. Allan and G. Jones (eds.), *Social Relations and the Life Course*. London: Palgrave Macmillan.

Child Poverty Action Group (published annually) *Welfare Benefits Handbook*. London: CPAG.

Chomsky, N. (1972). *Language and Mind*. New York: Harcourt Brace Jovanivich.

Chomsky, N. (2004). *Hegemony or Survival? America's Quest for Global Dominance*. London: Penguin.

Cigno, K. and Bourn, D. (1998) *Cognitive-Behavioural Social Work in Practice*. Aldershot: Ashgate/Arena.

Clark, C. (2000) *Social Work Ethics: Politics, Principles and Practice*. Basingstoke: Macmillan.

Clark, C. and Cree, V. E. (2001) The voluntary sector: No time like the present. In I. Martin and M. Shaw (eds.), *Educational Resources for Renewing Democracy in Scotland*. Edinburgh: University of Edinburgh.

Clark, H., Dyer, S. and Horwood, J. (1998) *'That Bit of Help': The High Value of low Level Preventative Services for Older People*. Bristol: Policy Press; York: Joseph Rowntree Foundation.

Clarke, A. M. and Clarke, A. D. (1976) *Early Experience: Myth and Evidence*. London: Open Books.

Clarke, C. and O'Brien, M. (2004) Fathers' involvement in Britain: The research and policy evidence. In R. Day and M. Lamb (eds.), *Reconceptualising and Measuring Fatherhood*. Hillsdale, NJ: Erlbaum.

Clarke, J. (1993) *A Crisis in Care? Challenges to Social Work*. London: Sage, in association with the Open University.

Clarke, R. (1993) Discrimination in child protection services. In L. Waterhouse (ed.), *Child Abuse and Child Abusers: Protection and Prevention*. London: Jessica Kingsley.

Cleaver, H. (2000) *Fostering Family Contact*. London: The Stationery Office.

Cleaver, H. and Freeman, D. (1995) *Parental Perspectives in Cases of Suspected Child Abuse*. London: HMSO.

Clements, L. (2004) *Community Care and the Law*, 3rd edn. London: Legal Action Group.

Clements, L. (2005) *Carers and their Rights: The Law Relating to Carers*. London: Carers UK.

Clements, L. and Thomas, P. A. (2005) *Human Rights Act: A Success Story?* Oxford: Blackwell.

Cockerham, W. (2000) *Sociology of Mental Disorder*. London: Prentice Hall.

Cohen, M. B. and Mullender, A. (eds.) (2003) *Gender and Groupwork*. London: Routledge.

Cohen, S., Humphries, B. and Mynott, E. (eds.) (2002) *From Immigration Controls to Welfare Controls*. London: Routledge.

Coleman, J. C. (1980) *The Nature of Adolescence*. London: Methuen.

Coleman, J. and Hendry, L. (1999) *The Nature of Adolescence*, 3rd edn. London: Routledge.

Coleman, J. C., Herzberg, J. and Morris, M. (1977) Identity in adolescence: Present and future self-concepts. *Journal of Youth and Adolescence*, 6, 63–75.

Collingwood, P. (2005) Integrating theory and practice: The three-stage theory framework. *Journal of Practice Teaching in Health and Social Work*, 6 (12), 6–23.

Collins, P. H. (2000) *Black Feminist Thought: Knowledge, Consciousness and the Politics of Empowerment*, 2nd edn. London: Routledge.

Commission on Families and the Wellbeing of Children (2005) *Families and the State: Two-way Support and Responsibilities*. Bristol: Policy Press.

Congress, E. (1999) *Social Work Values and Ethics*. Belmont CA, Wadsworth.

Connell, R. W. (1995) *Masculinities*. Cambridge: Polity Press.

Connolly, M. (2006) *Discrimination Law*. London: Sweet and Maxwell.

Connor, A. and Tibbitt, J. E. (1988) *Social Workers and Health Care in Hospitals*. London: HMSO.

Coote, A., Harman, H. and Hewitt, H. (1994) Changing patterns of family life. In J. Eekelaar and M. Maclean (eds.), *A Reader on Family Law*. Oxford: Oxford University Press.

Cooper, A. (1893) The intellectual progress of the coloured woman in the United States since the emancipation proclamation. In B. Loewenberg and R. Bogin (eds.), *Black Women in 19th Century America: Their Words, Their Thoughts, Their Feelings, 1976*. University Park, PA: Penn State University Press.

Copello, A., Templeton, L., Krishnan, M., Orford, J. and Velleman, R. (2000) A treatment package to improve primary care services for relatives of people with alcohol and drug problems. *Addiction Research*, 8, 471–84.

Copello, A., Williamson, E., Orford, J. and Day, E. (2006) Implementing and evaluating social behaviour and network therapy in drug treatment practice in the UK: A feasibility study. *Addictive Behaviors*, 31(5), 802–10.

Corby, B. (1996) *Child Abuse*. Buckingham: Open University.

Corey, G. (1997) *Theory and Practice of Counselling and Psychotherapy*. Pacific Grove, CA: Brooks/Cole.

Corney, R. (1984) The mental and physical health of clients referred to social workers in a local authority department and a general practice attachment scheme. *Psychological Medicine*, 14, 137–44.

Coulshed, V. and Mullender, A. with Jones, D. N. and Thompson, N. (2006) *Management in Social Work*, 3rd edn. Basingstoke: Palgrave.

Coulshed, V. and Orme, J. (1998) *Social Work Practice: An Introduction*, 3rd edn. Basingstoke: Macmillan.

Coulshed, V. and Orme, J. (2006) *Social Work Practice: An Introduction*, 4th edn. Basingstoke: Palgrave Macmillan.

Coward, B., and Dattani, P. (1993). Race, identity and culture. In K. N. Dwivedi (ed.), *Group Work with Children and Adolescents: A Handbook*. London: Jessica Kingsley, pp. 245–61.

Cowburn, M. and Dominelli, L. (2001) Masking hegemonic masculinity: Deconstructing the paedophile as the dangerous stranger. *British Journal of Social Work*, 31(3), 399–415.

Cox, S. (ed.) (1998) *Home Solutions: Housing and Support for People with Dementia*. London: Housing Associations Charitable Trust.

Craig, G. (2006) *The Social Fund and Local Government*. London: Local Government Association. www.lga.org.uk.

Crawford, A. and Newburn, T. (2003) *Youth Offending and Restorative Justice*. Devon: Willan.

CRD (2001) *Undertaking Systematic Reviews of Research on Effectiveness: CRD's Guidance for Those Carrying out or Commissioning Reviews,* 2nd edn. University of York: NHS Centre for Reviews and Dissemination. http://www.york.ac.uk/inst/crd/report4.htm.

Cree, V. E. (1995) *From Public Streets to Private Lives: The Changing Task of Social Work*. Aldershot: Avebury.

Cree, V. E. (2000) *Sociology for Social Workers and Probation Officers*. London: Routledge.

Cree, V. E. and Wallace, S. J. (2005) Risk and protection. In R. Adams, L. Dominelli and M. Payne (eds.), *Social Work Futures: Crossing Boundaries, Transforming Practice*. Basingstoke: Palgrave Macmillan, pp. 115–27.

Creighton, S. J. (1994) The incidence of child abuse and neglect. In K. Browne, C. Davies and P. Stratton (eds.), *Early Prediction and Prevention of Child Abuse*. Chichester: John Wiley and Sons.

Cretney, S. (2005) *Family Law in the Twentieth Century: A History*. Oxford: Oxford University Press.

Crighton, D. and Towl, G. (eds.) (2005) *Psychology in Probation*. Oxford: Blackwell.

Cross, W. E. (1991) *Shades of Black: Diversity in African American Identity*. Philadelphia: Temple University Press.

Cull, L-A. and Roche, J. (eds.) (2001) *The Law and Social Work*. Basingstoke: Palgrave.

Curtice, L., McCormack, C. and Petch, A. with Hallam, A. and Knapp, M. (2001) *Over the Threshold? An Exploration of Intensive Domiciliary Support for Older People*. Edinburgh: The Stationery Office.

Curtis, Z. (1993) On being a woman in the pensioners movement. In J. Johnson and R. Slater (eds.), *Ageing and Later Life*. London: Sage.

Dale, P., Davies, M., Morrisson, T. and Waters, J. (1986) *Dangerous Families*. London. Tavistock.

Dallos, R. and Draper, R. (2000) *An Introduction to Family Therapy: Systemic Theory and Practice*. Milton Keynes: Open University Press.

David, M. and New, C. (1985) *For the Children's Sake: Making Childcare more than Women's Business*. London: Penguin.

Davies, D. and Neale, C. (1996) *Pink Therapy*. Buckingham: Open University Press.

Davies, M. (1994) *The Essential Social Worker*, 3rd edn. Aldershot: Arena.

Davies, M. (ed.) (2000) *The Blackwell Encyclopaedia of Social Work*. Oxford: Blackwell.

Davies, M. and Connolly, J. (1995) Hospital social work and discharge planning: An exploratory study in East Anglia. *Health and Social Care in the Community*, 3(6), 363–71.

Davies, N. and Duff, M. (2001) Breast cancer screening for older women with intellectual disability living in community group homes. *Journal of Intellectual Disability Research*, 45(3), 253–7.

Davis, K. (2004) On the movement. In J. Swain, S. French, C. Barnes and C. Thomas (eds.), *Disabling Barriers – Enabling Environments*. London: Sage.

Day Sclater, S. and Piper, C. (eds.) (1999) *Undercurrents of Divorce*. Aldershot: Ashgate.

Denicola, J. and Sandler, J. (1980) Training abusive parents in cognitive-behavioural techniques. *Behaviour Therapy*, 11, 263–70.

Department for Constitutional Affairs, Department for Education and Skills and Department for Trade and Industry (2005) *Parental Separation: Children's Needs and Parents' Responsibilities: Next Steps*, Cm 6452. Norwich: The Stationery Office.

Department for Education and Skills (2003) *Every Child Matters*, presented to Parliament by the Chief Secretary to the Treasury, Cm 5860. Norwich: The Stationery Office.

Department for Education and Skills (2004) *Every Child Matters – Next Steps*. London: DfES.

Department for Education and Skills (2005) *Implementing Sure Start Local Programmes: An In-depth Study*. London: DfES.

Department for Education and Skills (2006a) *Common Assessment Framework for Children and Young People*. London: The Stationery Office. http://www.everychildmatters.gov.uk/deliveringservices/caf/

Department for Education and Skills (2006b) *Information Sharing: Practitioners' Guide*. http://www.everychildmatters.gov.uk/deliveringservices/informationsharing/

Department for Education and Skills (2006c) *Working Together to Safeguard Children*, London: DfES.

Department for Education and Skills and Department of Health (2004) *The National Service Framework for Children and Maternity Services*. London: DfES/DH.

Department for Work and Pensions (2005) *Opportunities for All: 7th Annual Report*. London: The Stationery Office.

Department for Work and Pensions Decision Making Standards Committee (2005) *Annual Report April 2003–March 2004*. London: DWP.

Department of Health (1989a) *Caring for People: Community Care in the Next Decade and Beyond*, Cm 849. London: HMSO.

Department of Health (1989b) *The Children Act 1989: Principles and Practice in Guidance and Regulations*. London: HMSO.

Department of Health (1990a) *National Health Service and Community Care Act 1990*. London: HMSO.

Department of Health (1990b) *Caring for People: Community Care in the Next Decade and Beyond, Policy Guidance*. London: HMSO.

Department of Health (1991a) *Patterns and Outcomes in Child Placement*. London: HMSO.

Department of Health (1991b) *The Children Act 1989: Regulations and Guidance*. London: HMSO.

Department of Health (1991c) *Working Together under the Children Act 1989*. London: HMSO.

Department of Health (1991d) *Care Management and Assessment: A Practitioners Guide*. London: HMSO.

Department of Health (1992) *Implementing Caring for People,* CI (92) 30. London: HMSO.

Department of Health (1993) *Social Services for Hospital Patients 3: Users' and Carers' Perspective*. London: HMSO.

Department of Health (1994a) *A Wider Strategy for Research and Development Relating to Personal Social Services: A Report to the Director of Research and Development, Department of Health, by an Independent Review Group*. London: HMSO.

Department of Health (1994b) *Research and the Personal Social Services*. London: HMSO.

Department of Health (1995a) *Child Protection: Messages from Research*. London: HMSO.

Department of Health (1995b) *Moving On: National Inspection of SSD Arrangements for the Discharge of Older People from Hospital to Residential or Nursing Home Care*. London: The Stationery Office.

Department of Health (1996) *Disabled Persons (Services, Consultation and Representation) Act 1986*. London: HMSO.

Department of Health (1997) *The New NHS: Modern, Dependable,* Cm 3807. London: Department of Health.

Department of Health (1998a) *Getting Better: Inspection of Hospital Discharge (Care Management) Arrangements*. London: The Stationery Office.

Department of Health (1998b) *Modernising Health and Social Services: National Priorities Guidance 1999–2002*. London: The Stationery Office.

Department of Health (1998c) *Modernising Social Services*. London: The Stationery Office.

Department of Health (1998d) *Partnership in Action: New Opportunities for Joint Working between Health and Social Services*. London: The Stationery Office.

Department of Health (1999a) *Open all hours? An Inspection of Local Authorities Social Services Emergency Out of Hours Arrangements: Key Messages for Practitioners and Managers*, London: The Stationery Office.

Department of Health (1999b) *Assessment Framework*. London: The Stationery Office.

Department of Health (1999c) *Residential Child Care: Messages from Research*. London: The Stationery Office.

Department of Health (1999d) *Working in Partnership: Joint Working between Health and Social Services in Primary Care Groups*. London: The Stationery Office.

Department of Health (2000a) *The Community Care (Direct Payments) Act 1996: Policy and Practice Guidance*. London: The Stationery Office.

Department of Health (with the Department for Education and Employment, Home Office) (2000b) *Framework for the Assessment of Children in Need and their Families*. London: The Stationery Office.

Department of Health (2000c) *A Health Service for All the Talents: developing the NHS workforce*. London: Department of Health

Department of Health (2000d) *The NHS Plan,* Cm 4818-1. London: The Stationery Office.

Department of Health (2000e) *Working Together to Safeguard Children: A Guide to Inter-agency Working to Safeguard and Promote the Welfare of Children*. London: The Stationery Office.

Department of Health (2000f) *A Practitioner's Guide to Carers' Assessments under the Carers and Disabled Children Act 2000*. London: Department of Health. Also at: www.dh.gov.uk/carers

Department of Health (2001a) *Fair Access to Care Services, Statutory Guidance*. London: Department of Health.

Department of Health (2001b) *The Children Act Now: Messages from Research*. London: The Stationery Office.

Department of Health (2001c) *The National Service Framework for Older People*. London: Department of Health.

Department of Health (2001d) *National Service Framework for Older People*. London: Department of Health.

Department of Health (2001e) *Valuing People: A New Strategy for Learning Disability in the 21st Century*, London: The Stationery Office. http://www.archive.official-documents.co.uk/document/cm50/5086/5086.htm

Department of Health (2002a) *Fair Access to Care Services, Policy Guidance*. London: The Stationery Office.

Department of Health (2002b) *Fairer Charging Policies for Home Care and Other Non-residential Social Services – Practice Guidance*. London: Department of Health.

Department of Health (2002c) *The National Suicide Prevention Strategy for England*. London: Department of Health.

Department of Health (2003a) *CCDDA Guidance for Implementation ('Delayed Discharge Guidance')*. London: The Stationery Office.

Department of Health (2003b) *Community Care, Services for Carers and Children's Services (Direct Payments) Guidance*. London: The Stationery Office.

Department of Health (2003c) *Fair Access to Care Services: Guidance on Eligibility Criteria for Adult Social Care*. London: Department of Health.

Department of Health (2005a) *Evaluation of the Exemplar Programme for Integrated Out-of-hours Care: Final Report*. London: The Stationery Office.

Department of Health (2005b) *Independence, Well-being and Choice: Our Vision for the Future of Social Care for Adults in England: Social Care Green Paper*. London: The Stationery Office. http:// www.dh.gov.uk/socialcare

Department of Health (2005c) *National Service Framework for Children and Young People*. London: Department of Health.

Department of Health (2005d) *Carers and Disabled Children Act 2000 and Carers Equal Opportunities Act 2004: Combined Policy Guidance*. London: Department of Health.

Department of Health (2006a), *Our Health, Our Care, Our Say: A New Direction for Community Services*, White Paper. London: The Stationery Office.

Department of Health (2006b) *Working Together Guidance*. London: The Stationery Office.

Department of Health, Home Office, Lord Chancellor's Department and the Welsh Office (1998a) *Support Services in Family Proceedings – Future Organisation of Court Welfare Services: Consultation Paper*. London: Department of Health.

Department of Health, Home Office and the Department for Education and Employment (1998b) *Working Together to Safeguard Children*. London: The Stationery Office.

Department of Health and Social Security (1948) *The National Assistance Act 1948*. London: HMSO.

Department of Health and Social Security (1970) *Chronically Sick and Disabled Persons' Act 1970*. London: HMSO.

Department of Health and Social Security (1973) *Report of the Working Party on Collaboration between the NHS and Local Government*. London: HMSO.
Department of Health and Social Security (1976) *Joint Care Planning*. HC76.18, LAC 76.6. London: DHSS.
Department of Health and Social Security (1979) *Royal Commission on the National Health Service*, Cmnd. 7615/ London: HMSO.
Department of Health and Social Security (1982) *Child Abuse: A Study of Inquiry Reports*. London: HMSO.
Department of Health and Social Security (1983) *Mental Health Act 1983*. London: HMSO.
Department of Health and Social Security (1984) *Mental Health (Scotland) Act*. Edinburgh: HMSO.
Department of Health and Social Security (NI) (1986) *Mental Health (Northern Ireland) Order*. Belfast: HMSO.
Dickens, J. (2006) Care, control and change in child care proceedings: Dilemmas for social workers, managers and lawyers. *Child and Family Social Work*, 11, 23–32.
Digby, A. and Stewart, J. (eds.) (1996) *Gender, Health and Welfare*. London: Routledge.
Dimmock, B. and Dungworth, D. (1985) Beyond the family: Using network meetings with statutory child care cases. *Journal of Family Therapy*, 7, 45–68.
Disability Alliance (published annually) *Disability Rights Handbook*. London: Disability Alliance Educational & Research Association.
Dobash, R. E. and Dobash, R. P. (1979) *Violence against Wives: A Case against the Patriarchy*. London: Open Books.
Dodge, K. A. and Frame, C. L. (1982) Social cognitive biases and deficits in aggressive boys. *Child Development*, 53, 620–35.
Doel, M. (2006) *Using Groupwork*. London: Routledge/Community Care.
Doel, M. and Marsh, P. (1992) *Task-centred Social Work*. Aldershot: Ashgate.
Doel, M. and Sawdon, C. (1999) *The Essential Groupworker*. London: Jessica Kingsley.
Dominelli, L. (1986) Father–daughter incest: Patriarchy's shameful secret. *Critical Social Policy*, 16, 8–22.
Dominelli, L. (1988) *Anti-Racist Social Work*. Basingstoke: Macmillan.
Dominelli, L. (1989) Betrayal of trust: A feminist analysis of power relationships in incest abuse and its relevance for social work practice. *British Journal of Social Work*, 19, 291–307.
Dominelli, L. (1991a) *Gender, Sex Offenders and Probation Practice*. Norwich: Novata Press.
Dominelli, L. (1991b) *Women across Continents: Feminist Comparative Social Policy*. London: Harvester Wheatsheaf.
Dominelli, L. (1992) An uncaring profession? An examination of racism in social work. In P. Braham, A. Rattansi and R. Skellington (eds.), *Racism and Antiracism: Inequalities, Opportunities and Policies*. London: Sage Publications.
Dominelli, L. (1997) *Sociology for Social Work*. Basingstoke: Macmillan.
Dominelli, L. (ed.) (1999) *Community Approaches to Child Welfare: International Perspectives*. Aldershot: Ashgate.
Dominelli, L. (2000) International comparisons in social work. In R. Pierce and J. Weinstein (eds.), *Innovative Education and Training for Care Professionals*. London: Jessica Kingsley.
Dominelli, L. (2002a) *Feminist Social Work Theory and Practice*. London: Palgrave/ Macmillan.
Dominelli, L. (2002b) *Anti-Oppressive Social Work: Theory and Practice*. London: Palgrave Macmillan.

Dominelli, L. (2005) Social work research: Contested knowledge for practice. In R. Adams, L. Dominelli and M. Payne (eds.), *Social Work Futures: Crossing Boundaries, Transforming Practice*. Basingstoke: Palgrave Macmillan.

Dominelli, L. and McLeod, E. (1989) *Feminist Social Work*. London: Macmillan.

Donzelot, J. (1980) *The Policing of Families*. London: Hutchinson.

Dorrell, S. (1996) *The Guardian*, 19 June.

Dowling, M. (1999) *Social Work and Poverty: Attitudes and Actions*. Aldershot: Ashgate.

Duffy, S. (2005) Individual budgets: Transforming the allocation of resources for care. *Journal of Integrated Care*, 13(1), 8–16.

Dunant, S. (ed.) (1994) *The War of the Words: The Political Correctness Debate*. London: Virago.

Duncombe, J., Harrison, K., Allan, G. and Marsden, D. (eds.) (2004) *The State of Affairs*. Hillsdale, NJ: Erlbaum.

Dunn, J. (1988) *The Beginnings of Social Understanding*. Oxford: Blackwell.

Dunning, A. (1995) *Citizen Advocacy with Older People*. London: Centre for Policy on Ageing.

Dutt, R. and Phillips, M. C. (1996) Race, culture and the prevention of child abuse. In *Childhood Matters: Report of National Commission of Inquiry into the Prevention of Child Abuse*, Vol. 2, Background Papers, pp. 149–21. London: The Stationery Office.

Dutt, R. and Phillips, M. C. (2000) Assessing black children in need and their families. In Department of Health, *Assessing Children in Need and their Families*. London: The Stationery Office.

Eastman, M. (1984) *Old Age Abuse*. London: Age Concern England.

Edleson, J. (2001) Studying the co-occurrence of child maltreatment and domestic violence in families. In S. Graham-Bermann and J. Edleson (eds.), *Domestic Violence in the Lives of Children: The Future of Research, Intervention and Social Policy*. Washington, DC: American Psychological Association.

Edmundson, A. (2006) In defence of the Human Rights Act. *Legal Action Bulletin*, July, 6–7.

Egan, G. (1990) *The Skilled Helper*. Pacific Grove, CA: Brooks/Cole.

Egger, M., Davey-Smith, G. and Altman, D. G. (2001) *Systematic Reviews in Health Care: Meta-analysis in Context*. London: BMJ Publishing.

Ellis, A. (1962). *Reason and Emotion in Psychotherapy*. New York: Lyle Stuart.

Ellis, A. (1973) *Humanistic Psychotherapy: The Rational-Emotive Approach*. New York: McGraw-Hill.

Ellis, A., Gordon, J., Neenan, M. and Palmer, S. (1997) *Stress Counselling: A Rational Emotive, Behaviour Approach*. London: Cassell.

England, H. (1986) *Social Work as Art: Making Sense for Good Practice*. London: Allen and Unwin.

Erikson, E. H. (1959). *Identity and the Life Cycle*. New York: International Universities Press.

Erikson, E. H. (1968). *Identity: Youth and Crisis*. London: Faber.

Erikson, E. H., Erikson, J. M. and Kivnic, H. Q. (1986) *Vital Involvement in Old Age: The Experience of Old Age in Our Time*. New York: Norton.

Evandrou, M., Arber, S., Dale, A. and Gilbert, N. (1986) Who cares for the elderly: Family care provision and receipt of statutory services. In C. Phillipson, M. Bernard and P. Strang (eds.), *Dependency and Interdependency in Old Age*. London: Croom Helm, pp. 150–66.

Evans, J. (1995) Direct payments and why they are important: from being dependent on inappropriate services to becoming an employer. Presentation to the Association of Metropolitan Authorities, London, 16 February.

Evans, M., Harkness, S. and Ortiz, R. (2004) *Lone Parents Cycling Between Work and Benefits*. London: Department for Work and Pensions, HMSO.

Everitt, A., Hardiker, P., Littlewood, J. and Mullender, A. (1993) *Applied Research for Better Practice*. London: BASW/Macmillan.

Eysenck, H. J. (1977). *Crime and Personality*. London: RKP.

EYTARN (Early Years Trainers Anti-Racist Network) (1994) *The Best of Both Worlds: Celebrating Mixed Parentage*. London: EYTARN.

Fahlberg, V. (1991) *A Child's Journey through Placement*. London: British Agencies for Adoption and Fostering.

Farmer, E. (1995) *Child Protection Practice*. London: HMSO.

Farmer, E. and Pollock, S. (1998) *Sexually Abused and Abusing Children in Substitute Care*. Chichester: Wiley.

Farrall, S. (2002) *Rethinking What Works with Offenders*. Devon: Willan.

Fatimlehin, I. A. (1999) Of jewel heritage: Racial socialisation and racial identity attitudes amongst adolescents of mixed African-Caribbean/White parentage. *Journal of Adolescence*, 22, 303–18.

Feindler, E. L. (1979) Cognitive and behavioural approaches to anger control training in explosive adolescents. Unpublished doctoral dissertation, West Virginia University.

Feindler, E. L. and Ecton, R. B. (1986) *Adolescent Anger Control: Cognitive-Behavioural Techniques*. New York: Pergamon Press.

Feindler, E. L., Ecton, R. B., Kingsley, D. and Dubery, D. (1986) Group anger control training of institutionalised psychiatric male adolescents. *Behaviour Therapy*, 17, 109–23.

Feindler, E. L. and Fremouw, W. J. (1983) Stress inoculation training for adolescent anger problems. In D. Meichenbaum and M. E. Jaremko (eds.), *Stress Reduction and Prevention*. New York: Plenum Press.

Feindler, E. L., Marriot, S. A. and Iwata, M. (1984) Group anger management training for junior high school delinquents. *Cognitive Therapy and Research*, 8(3), 299–311.

Feinman, S. and Lewis, M. (1983) Social referencing at ten-months: A second order effect on infants' responses to strangers. *Child Development*, 54, 753–71.

Fernando, S. (ed.) (1995) *Mental Health in a Multi-ethnic Society*. London: Routledge.

Fernando, S. (2003) *Cultural Diversity, Mental Health and Psychiatry: The Struggle against Racism*. London: Routledge.

Field, T. (1978) Interaction behaviours of primary versus secondary caretaker fathers. *Developmental Psychology*, 14, 183–4.

Fisher, M. (1998) Research, knowledge and practice in community care. *Issues in Social Work Education*, 17(2), 1–14.

Fisher, T., Bingley-Miller, L. and Sinclair, I. (1995) Which children are registered at case conferences? *British Journal of Social Work*, 25, 191–207.

Fivush, R. (ed.) (1994) *A Special Issue of Memory: Long Term Retention of Infant Memories*. Hove: LEA.

Flynn, R. (2002) *Short Breaks: Providing Better Access and More Choice for Black Disabled Children and their Parents*. Bristol: Policy Press.

Foster, R. M. P. (1998) The clinician's cultural countertransference: The psychodynamics of culturally competent practice. *Clinical Social Work Journal*, 26(3), 253–70.

Foucault, M. (1977) *Discipline and Punish*. London: Allen Lane.

Foundation for People with Learning Disabilities (2003) *Statistics on Learning Disabilities*, Fact Sheet. www.learningdisabilities.org.uk

Fraser, D. (1984) *The Evolution of the British Welfare State*, 2nd edn. Basingstoke: Macmillan.

Fraser, D. (2003) *The Evolution of the British Welfare State: A History of Social Policy since the Industrial Revolution*, 3rd edn. Basingstoke: Palgrave Macmillan.

Fratter, J., Rowe, J., Sapsford, D. and Thoburn, J. (1991) *Permanent Family Placement: A Decade of Experience*. London: British Agencies for Adoption and Fostering.

French, S. (2004) Enabling relationships in therapy practice. In J. Swain, J. Clark, S. French, F. Reynolds and K. Parry (eds.), *Enabling Relationships in Health and Social Care*. Oxford. Butterworth-Heinemann.

Freud, A. (1958) *Adolescence: Psychoanalytic Study of the Child*. New York: International Universities Press.

Freud, S. (1910) The future prospects of psycho-analytic therapy. In *The Standard Edition of the Complete Psychological Works of Sigmund Freud, Volume 11*. London: Hogarth Press.

Fries, J. F. (1980) Ageing, natural death and the compression of morbidity. *New England Journal of Medicine*, 303, 130–5.

From Margin to Mainstream (1995) *Social Care Summary Three*. York: Joseph Rowntree Foundation.

Galper, J. (1975) *The Politics of Social Services*. Englewood Cliffs, NJ: Prentice-Hall.

Galvani, S. (2001) The role of alcohol in violence against women: Why should we care? *Practice,* 13(2), 5–20.

Galvani, S. and Humphreys, C. (2005) The impact of violence and abuse on engagement and retention rates for women in substance use treatment: A feasibility study. Final report to the National Treatment Agency for Substance Misuse. London: NTA.

Gambrill, E. (1983) *Casework: A Competency Based Approach*. Englewood Cliffs, NJ: Prentice Hall.

Gambrill, E. (1990) *Critical Thinking in Clinical Approach*. San Francisco: Jossey-Bass.

Gambrill, E. D., Thomas, E. J. and Carter, R. D. (1971) Procedure for sociobehavioral practice in open settings. *Social Work*, 16, 51–62.

Gardner, J. and Gray, M. (1982) Violence towards children. In M.P. Feldman (ed.), *Developments in the Study of Criminal Behaviour: Volume 2, Violence*. Chichester: Wiley.

Gardner, W. I. and Cole, C. L. (1987) Managing aggressive behaviour: A behavioural diagnostic approach. *Psychiatric Aspects of Mental Retardation Reviews,* 6, 21–5.

Garland, D. (1985) *Punishment and Welfare*. Aldershot: Gower.

Garland, D. (2001) *The Culture of Control*. Oxford: Oxford University Press.

Garvin, C. D., Gutiérrez, L. M. and Galinsky, M. J. (eds.) (2004) *Handbook of Social Work with Groups*. New York: Guilford Press.

Gelles, R. J. (1987) *Family Violence*, 2nd edn, Sage Library of Social Research No. 84. Beverly Hills, CA: Sage.

General Household Survey (2004) *Living in Britain: The General Household Survey, 2002*. London: HMSO. http://www.statistics.gov.uk/CCI/nugget.asp?ID=824&Pos=2&ColRank=2&Rank=224

General Social Care Council (GSCC) (2002) *Codes of Practice for Social Care Workers*. London: GSCC.

General Social Care Council (GSCC) (2004) *Code of Practice for Social Care Workers*. London: GSCC.

Ghate, D. and Hazel, N. (2002) *Parenting in Poor Environments: Stress, Support and Coping*. London: Jessica Kingsley.

Giallombardo, E. and Homer, A. (1994) Resuscitation: A survey of policies. *Journal of the British Society of Gerontology, Generations Review*, 4(3), 5–7.

Gibbons, J., Conroy, S. and Bell, C. (1995) *Operating the Child Protection System: A Study of Child Protection Practice in English Local Authorities*. London: HMSO.

Gibbons, J., Thorpe, S. and Wilkinson, P. (1990) *Family Support and Prevention*. London: HMSO.

Gibbs, D. (2004) Social model services: An oxymoron. In C. Barnes and G. Mercer (eds.), *Disability Policy and Practice: Applying the Social Model*. Leeds: The Disability Press.

Gibbs, I. and Sinclair, I. (1992) Consistency: A prerequisite for inspecting residential homes for elderly people? *British Journal of Social Work*, 22, 535–50.

Gibbs, J. (2003) *Beyond the Theories of Kohlberg and Hoffman: Moral Development and Reality*. Thousand Oaks, CA: Sage.

Gibbs, J. C., Potter, G. B. and Goldstein, A. P. (1995) *The EQUIP Program: Teaching Youth to Think and Act Responsibly through a Peer-helping Approach*. Champaign, IL: Research Press.

Gibson, C. (1994) *Dissolving Wedlock*. London: Routledge.

Giddens, A. (1977) *Studies in Social and Political Theory*. London: Hutchinson.

Giddens, A. (1987) *Social Theory and Modern Sociology*. Oxford: Blackwell.

Giddens, A. (1991) *Modernity and Self-Identity: Self and Society in the Late Modern Age*. Cambridge: Polity Press.

Gil, D. (1970) *Violence against Children*. Cambridge, MA: Harvard University Press.

Gilgun, J. (1994) Hand in glove: The grounded theory approach and social work practice research. In E. Sherman and W. Reid (eds.), *Qualitative Research in Social Work*. New York: Columbia University Press.

Gladstone, F. J. (1979) *Voluntary Action in a Changing World*. London: Bedford Square Press.

Glasby, J. and Littlechild, R. (2000) *The Health and Social Care Divide*. Birmingham: Pepar Publications.

Glassman, W. E. and Hadad, M. (2004) *Approaches to Psychology*. Buckingham: Open University Press.

Goldberg, D. P. and Gater, R. (1991) Estimates of need. *Psychiatric Bulletin*, 15, 593–5.

Goldberg, D. and Goodyer, I. (2005) *The Origins of Common Mental Disorders*. London: Routledge.

Goldberg, D. P. and Huxley, P. J. (1980) *Mental Illness in the Community: The Pathway to Psychiatric Care*. London: Tavistock.

Goldberg, D. P. and Huxley, P. J. (1992) *Common Mental Disorder: A Biosocial Model*. London: Routledge.

Goldberg, S. (2000) *Attachment and Development*. London: Arnold.

Goldman, R. (2005) *Fathers' Involvement in their Children's Education*. London: National Family and Parenting Institute.

Goldner, V., Penn, P. and Steinberg, M. (1990) Love and violence: Gender paradoxes in volatile attachments. *Family Process*, 29, 343–64.

Goldstein, A. P., Glick, B., and Gibbs, J. C. (1998) *Aggression Replacement Training: A Comprehensive Intervention for Aggressive Youth*. Champaign, IL: Research Press.

Goldstein, A. P. and Keller, H. (1987) *Aggressive Behaviour, Assessment and Intervention*. New York: Pergamon Press.

Gomm, R., Needham, G. and Bullman, A. (2000) *Evaluating Research in Health and Social Care*. London: The Open University in association with Sage Publications.

Goodley, D. (2004) Who is disabled? Exploring the scope of the social model of disability. In J. Swain, S. French, C. Barnes and C. Thomas (eds.), *Disabling Barriers – Enabling Environments*. London: Sage.

Goodley, D. and Moore, M. (2002) *Disability Arts against Exclusion: People with Learning Difficulties and their Performing Arts*. Kidderminster: British Institute of Learning Disabilities.

Gordon, L. (1986) Feminism and social control: The case of child abuse and neglect. In J. Mitchell and A. Oakley (eds.), *What Is Feminism*? Oxford: Basil Blackwell.

Gough, D. (1993) *Child Abuse Interventions: A Review of the Literature*. London: HMSO.

Gould, N. (2000) Becoming a learning organisation: A social work example. *Social Work Education*, 19(6), 585–6.

Gould, N. (2006a) An inclusive approach to knowledge for mental health social work practice and policy. *British Journal of Social Work*, 36(1) 109–25.

Gould, N. (2006b) Social inclusion and UK mental health policy: A new deal for mental health social work? *Journal of Policy Practice*, 5(2–3), 77–90.

Government Actuary's Department (2005) *Marital Status Projections for England and Wales*. London: Government Actuary's Department. http://www.gad.gov.uk/marital_status_projections/background.htm

Graham, H. (1999) *Complementary Therapies in Context: The Psychology of Healing*. London: Jessica Kingsley.

Graham, H. (2000) Introduction. *Health Variations*, Issue 6, 2–3. Lancaster: Economic and Social Research Council Health Variations Programme, Department of Applied Social Science, University of Lancaster.

Graham, P. and Rutter, M. (1973) Psychiatric disorders in the young adolescent: A follow-up study. *Proceedings of the Royal Society of Medicine*, 66, 1226–9.

Grant, G., Goward, G., Richardson, M. and Ramcharan, P. (eds.) (2005) *Learning Disability: A Life Cycle Approach to Valuing People*. Maidenhead: Open University Press.

Gray, P. (2005) The politics of risk and young offenders' experiences of social exclusion and restorative justice. *British Journal of Criminology*, 45, 938–57.

Green, C. R. (2003) The unequal burden of pain: Confronting racial and ethnic disparities in pain. *Pain Medicine*, 4(3), 277–94.

Green, R. (2000) Applying a community needs profiling approach to tackling service user poverty. *British Journal of Social Work*, 30(3), 287–303.

Griffiths, R. (1988) *Community Care: Agenda for Action*. London: HMSO.

Groth, A. N (1979) *Men Who Rape*. New York: Plenum Press.

Groves, D. and McLean, M. (1991) *Women and Social Policy*. London: Routledge.

Hakim, C. (1987) *Research Design: Strategies and Choices in the Design of Social Research*. London: Allen and Unwin.

Haley, J. (1980) *Leaving Home*. New York: McGraw-Hill.

Hall, C. (1997) Cultural malpractice: The growing obsolescence of psychology with the changing US population. *American Psychologist*, 52, 642–51.

Hall, G. S. (1904) *Adolescence*. New York: Appleton.

Hallett, C. (1990) *Women in Social Work*. London: Sage.

Hammersley, M. (1993) On the teacher as researcher. *Educational Action Research*, 1(3), 425–45.

Hammersley, R., Marsland, L. and Reid, M. (2003) *Substance Use by Young Offenders: The Impact of the Normalisation of Drug Use in the Early Years of the 21st Century*. London: Home Office.

Hanley, B. (2005) *Research as Empowerment? The Report of a Series of Seminars Organised by the Toronto Group*. York: Joseph Rowntree Foundation.

Hanmer, J. and Statham, D. (1988) *Women and Social Work: Woman Centered Practice*. London: Macmillan.

Hanmer, J. and Statham, D. (1999) *Women and Social Work*, 2nd edn. Basingstoke: Macmillan.

Harding, J. (2000) *The Uninvited: Refugees at the Rich Man's Gate*. London: Profile.

Harding, T. and Beresford, P. (eds.), (1996) *The Standards We Expect: What Service Users and Carers Want from Social Services Workers*. London: National Institute for Social Work.

Harker, R. M., Dobel-Ober, D., Berridge, D. and Sinclair, R. (2003) More than the sum of its parts? Interprofessional working in the education of looked after children. *Children and Society*, 18(3), 179–93.

Harper, S. (2005) *Ageing Societies*. London: Hodder.

Harris, J. (2003) Let's talk business. *Community Care*, 21–27 August, 36–7.

Harris, R. (1997) Power. In M. Davies (ed.), *The Blackwell Companion to Social Work*, 1st edn. Oxford: Blackwell, pp. 28–33.

Harris, T., Brown, G. W. and Robinson, R. (1999) Befriending as an intervention for chronic depression among women in an inner city. 1: Randomised controlled trial. *British Journal of Psychiatry*, 174, 219–24.

Harrison, C. and Humphries, C. (1998) *Keeping Research in Mind: Final Report and Recommendations for Future Developments in Social Work Education and Training*. London: CCETSW.

Harrison, S. (1998) The politics of evidence-based medicine in the United Kingdom. *Policy and Politics*, 26(1), 15–31.

Haskey, J. (1998) One-parent families and their dependent children in Great Britain. *Population Trends*, 91, 5–14.

Haskey, J. (2001) Cohabitation in Great Britain: Past, present and future trends – and attitudes. *Population Trends*, 103, 4–25.

Haskey, J. (2002) One-parent families – and the dependent children living in them – in Great Britain. *Population Trends*, 109, 46–57.

Hatton, C., Emerson, C. and Lobb, C. (2005)_*Evaluating the Impact of Valuing People: Report of Phase 1: A Review of National Datasets*. Institute of Health Research, Lancaster University. http://www.lancs.ac.uk/fass/ihr/publications/chrishatton/eivp_1_review_of_existing_data.pdf

Hayden, C. (2004) Parental substance misuse and child care social work: Research in a city social work department in England. *Child Abuse Review*, 13(1), 18–30.

Hayes, D. (2002) From aliens to asylum seekers: A history of immigration control and welfare in Britain. In S. Cohen, B. Humphries and E. Mynott (eds.), *From Immigration Controls to Welfare Controls*. London: Routledge.

Hayes, D. and Humphries, B. (forthcoming) *Social Work with Asylum Seekers and Refugees*. Cambridge: Polity Press.

Hayes, S. C., Follette, V. M. and Linehan, M. M. (2004). *Mindfulness and Acceptance: Expanding the Cognitive Behavioral Tradition*. New York: Guilford Press.

Hayes, S. C., Strosahl, K. D. and Wilson, K. G. (1999). *Acceptance and Commitment Therapy: An Experiential Approach to Behavior Change*. New York: Guilford Press.

Hayter, T (2000) *Open Borders: The Case against Immigration Controls*. London: Pluto Press.

Henkel, M. (1994) Social work: An incorrigibly marginal profession? In T. Belcher (ed.), *Governments and Professional Education*. Buckingham: SRHE and Open University Press.

Henkel, M. (1995) Conceptions of knowledge and social work education. In M. Yelloly and M. Henkel (eds.), *Learning and Teaching in Social Work: Towards Reflective Practice*. London: Jessica Kingsley.

Henry, S. (1992) *Group Skills in Social Work*, 2nd edn. Pacific Grove, CA: Brooks/Cole.

Henwood, M., Lewis, H. and Waddington, E. (1998) *Listening to Users of Domiciliary Care Services: Developing and Monitoring Quality Standards*. Leeds: Nuffield Institute for Health/UKHCA.

Henwood, M. and Waddington, E. (2002) *Messages and Findings from the Outcomes of Social Care for Adults (OSCA) Programme*. Leeds: Nuffield Institute for Health.

Herbert, M. (1987a) *Conduct Disorders of Childhood and Adolescence*. Chichester: Wiley.

Herbert, M. (1987b) *Living with Teenagers*. Oxford: Blackwell.

Herbert, M. (2002) *Typical and Atypical Development: From Conception to Adolescence*. Oxford: Blackwell.

Herbert, M. (2004) *Developmental Problems of Childhood and Adolescence: A Guide to Preventive, Remedial and Therapeutic Interventions*. Oxford: Blackwell.

Heron, J. (1997) *Helping the Client*. London: Sage.

Hester, M. (2006) Asking about domestic violence: Implications for practice. In C. Humphreys and N. Stanley (eds.), *Domestic Violence and Child Protection: Directions for Good Practice*. London: Jessica Kingsley.

Hewitt, P. (2004) Keynote speech, 'Working with Fathers', Fathers' Direct Conference, London, 5 April. Available at: http://www.dti.gov.uk/ministers/speeches/hewitt050404.html (accessed August 2004).

Heyman, B. (ed.) (1998) *Risk, Health and Health Care: A Qualitative Approach*. London: Arnold.

Hill, M. (ed.) (2000) *Local Authority Social Services. An Introduction*. Oxford: Blackwell.

Hill, M. (ed.) (2001) *Effective Ways of Working with Children and their Families*. London: Jessica Kingsley.

Hill, M. and Aldgate, J. (1996) *Child Welfare Services*. London: Jessica Kingsley.

Hill, M. and Tisdall, K. (1997) *Children and Society*. London: Longman.

Hill, O. (1884) *Homes of the London Poor*. London: Macmillan.

Hills, J. (1995) *Joseph Rowntree Foundation Inquiry into Income and Wealth: Volume 2, A Summary of the Evidence*. York: Joseph Rowntree Foundation.

Hirschfeld, R. and Cross, C. (1982) Epidemiology of affective disorders: Psycho-social risk factors. *Archives of General Psychiatry*, 3935, 46–50.

HM Government (2006) *Working Together to Safeguard Children*. London: The Stationery Office.

HM Inspectorate of Probation (1998) *Evidence Based Practice: A Guide to Effective Practice*. London: Home Office Publications Unit.

HMSO (1942) *Report on Social Insurance and Allied Services*, Cmd 6404. London: HMSO.

HMSO (1995) *Disability Discrimination Act 1995*. http://www.opsi.gov.uk/acts/acts1995/1995050.htm

HMSO (1998) *Human Rights Act 1998*. http://www.opsi.gov.uk/acts/acts1998/19980042.htm

HMSO (2005) *Disability Discrimination Act 2005*. http://www.opsi.gov.uk/acts/acts2005/20050013.htm

Hockenberry, J. (1996) *Declarations of Independence: War Zones and Wheelchairs*. London: Viking.

Hoffman, L. (1981) *Foundations of Family Therapy: A Conceptual Framework for Systems Change*. New York: Basic Books.

Hogan, D. M. (1998) Annotation: The psychological development and welfare of children of opiate and cocaine users: Review and research needs. *Journal of Child Psychology and Psychiatry*, 39(5), 609–20.

Hollin, C. R. (1991) Cognitive behaviour modification with delinquents. In M. Herbert (ed.), *Clinical Child Psychology: Behaviour, Social Learning and Development*. Chichester: John Wiley.

Hollis, F. (1964) *Casework: A Psycho-Social Therapy*. New York, Random House.

Holloway, K. and Bennett. T. (2004) *The Results of the First Two Years of the NEW-ADAM Programme*. Home Office online report 19/4. Available at: http://www.homeoffice.gov.uk/rds/pdfs04/r179.pdf (accessed 28 July 2006).

Holman, B. (1988) *Putting Families First: Prevention and Child Care*. London: Macmillan.

Home Office (1999) *Managing Dangerous People with Severe Personality Disorder: Proposals for Policy Development*. London: Home Office.

Home Office (2000) *Probation Statistics, England and Wales, 1999*. London: Home Office.

Home Office (2006) *Respect Action Plan*. London: Home Office.

Home Office, Department of Health, Department of Transport, Department of Education and Science, and Welsh Office (1991) *Working Together under the Children Act 1989: A Guide to the Arrangements for Inter-agency Co-operation for the Protection of Children from Abuse*. London: HMSO.

Hood, B. and Willets, P. (1986) Reaching in the dark to an object's remembered position: Evidence for object permanence in 5-month-old infants. *British Journal of Developmental Psychology*, 4, 57–66.

hooks, b. (1991) *Yearning*. London: Turnaround.

Hopper, J. (1993) The rhetoric of motives in divorce. *Journal of Marriage and the Family*, 55, 801–13.

Hopper, J. (2001) The symbolic origins of conflict in divorce. *Journal of Marriage and the Family*, 63, 430–45.

House of Commons (1977) *Violence to Children: First Report for the Select Committee on Violence in the Family, Session 1976–7*. London: HMSO.

House of Commons Committee on the Lord Chancellor's Department (2003) *Children and Family Court Advisory and Support Service: Third Report of Session 2002–3*. London: The Stationery Office.

Howe, D. (1986) The segregation of women and their work in the personal social services. *Critical Social Policy*, 15, 21–36.

Howe, D. (1987) *An Introduction to Social Work Theory*. Aldershot: Gower.

Howe, D. (1996) Surface and depth in social work practice. In N. Parton (ed.), *Social Theory, Social Change and Social Work*. London: Routledge.

Howells, K. (1982) Aggression: Clinical approaches to treatment. Paper presented to the symposium for Broadmoor Psychology Department's 21st birthday. In D. Black (ed.), *Criminological and Legal Psychology, 2*. Leicester: British Psychological Society.

Hoyle, C., Young, R. and Hill, R. (2002) *Proceed with Caution: An Evaluation of the Thames Valley Police Initiative in Restorative Cautioning*. York: Joseph Rowntree Foundation.

Hughes, B. and Mtezuka, M. (1992) Social work and older women: Where have older women gone? In M. Langan and L. Day (eds.), *Women, Oppression and Social Work: Issues in Anti-Discriminatory Practice*. London: Routledge.

Hugman, R. (1991) *Power in Caring Professions*. Basingstoke: Macmillan.

Hugman, R. (2005) *New Approaches in Ethics for the Caring Professions*. Basingstoke: Palgrave.

Humphreys, C. (2000) *Social Work, Domestic Violence and Child Protection: Challenging Practice*. Bristol: Policy Press.

Humphreys, C., Hague, G., Hester, M., Mullender, A. Abrahams, H. and Lowe, P. (2000). *From Good Intentions to Good Practice: Working with Families where There Is Domestic Violence*. Bristol: Policy Press.

Humphreys, C. and Stanley, N. (eds.) (2006) *Domestic Violence and Child Protection: Directions for Good Practice*. London: Jessica Kingsley.

Humphreys, C. and Thiara, R. (2003) Domestic violence and mental health: 'I call it symptoms of abuse'. *British Journal of Social Work*, 33(2), 209–26.

Humphries, B. (2002) From welfare to authoritarianism: The role of social work in immigration controls. In S. Cohen, B. Humphries and E. Mynott (eds.), *From Immigration Controls to Welfare Controls*. London: Routledge.

Humphries, B. (2006) Immigration in the UK. In U. Segal (ed.), *Immigration Worldwide*. New York: Haworth Press.

Humphries, B., Khan, F., David, P. and Rose, N. (2004) *Labour Lost: Refugees and Employment.* North West Regional Development Agency, Refugee Action and Lancaster University.

Huntington, J. (1981) *Social Work and General Medical Practice.* London: Allen and Unwin.

Husband, C. (1995) The morally active practitioner and the ethics of anti-racist social work. In R. Hugman and D. Smith, *Ethical Issues in Social Work.* London: Routledge.

Hutter, A. (1938) Endogene en functionelle psychosen bei kindern in den pubertatscjahren. *A. Kinderpsychiat*, 5, 97–102.

Huxley, P. J. and Evans, S. (2000) Recent evidence in quality of life research in mental health. Paper presented to the ISQOL Conference, Girona, Spain, July, for future publication.

Huxley, P. J., Evans, S., Munroe, M. and Cestari, C. (2006) Fair access to care services in integrated health and social care teams. Draft final report to the DH. London: Institute of Psychiatry.

Huxley, P., Korer, J., Raval, H. and Jacob, C. (1988) Psychiatric morbidity in the clients of social workers. *Journal of Psychiatric Research*, 22(1), 57–67.

Huxley, P. J., Mohamad, H., Korer, J., Jacob, C., Raval, H. and Anthony, P. (1989) Psychiatric morbidity in social workers' clients: Social outcome. *Social Psychiatry and Psychiatric Epidemiology*, 24, 258–65.

Huxtable, M. and Blyth, E. (eds.) (2000) *School Social Work Worldwide.* Washington: National Association of Social Work.

Hylton, C. (1997) *Black Families' Survival Strategies: Ways of Coping in UK Society.* York: Joseph Rowntree Foundation.

The Information Centre (2006) *Statistics on Young People and Drug Misuse: England, 2006.* Leeds: The Information Centre. Available at: http://www.ic.nhs.uk/pubs/youngpeopledrugmisuse2006/youngpeopledrugmisusefull/file (accessed 28 July 2006).

Institute of Alcohol Studies (2006) *Adolescents and Alcohol.* IAS Factsheet. Available at: http://www.ias.org.uk/resources/factsheets/ adolescents.pdf (accessed 28 July 2006).

International Federation of Social Workers [IFSW]/International Association of Schools of Social Work [IASSW] (2004) *Ethics in Social Work: Statement of Principles.* Berne: IFSW.

Isaac, B., Minty, E. B., and Morrison, R. M. (1986) Children in care: The association with mental disorder in the parents. *British Journal of Social Work*, 16, 325–39.

Isaacs, B. (1972) *Survival of the Unfittest: A Study of Geriatric Patients in Glasgow.* London: Routledge & Kegan Paul.

Iwaniec, D., Larkin, E. and Higgins, S. (2006) Research review: Risk and resilience in cases of emotional abuse. *Child and Family Social Work*, 11, 65–72.

Jack, G. (2000) Ecological influences on parenting and child development. *British Journal of Social Work*, 30, 703–20.

Jack, R. (ed.) (1995) *Empowerment in Community Care.* London: Chapman & Hall.

Jackson, S. (1998) Educational success for looked after children: The social worker's responsibility. *Practice* 10(4), 47–57.

Jacobs, M. (1988) *Psychodynamic Counselling in Action.* London: Sage.

Jacobs, M. (1991) *Insight and Experience.* Buckingham: Open University Press.

Jacobs, M. (1993) *Still Small Voice.* London: SPCK.

Jacobs, M. (ed.) (1995a) *Charlie, an Unwanted Child?* Buckingham: Open University Press.

Jacobs, M. (ed.) (1995b) *Jitendra, Lost Connections.* Buckingham: Open University Press.

Jacobs, M. (1998) *The Presenting Past.* Buckingham: Open University Press.

James, A. (1995) Social work in divorce: Welfare, mediation and justice. *International Journal of Law and the Family*, 9, 256–74.

James, A. (2003) Squaring the circle – the social, legal and welfare organisation of contact. In A. Bainham, B. Lindley, M. Richards and L. Trinder (eds.), *Children and their Families: Contact, Rights and Welfare*. Oxford: Hart.

James, A. and Hay, W. (1993) *Court Welfare in Action: Practice and theory*. London: Harvester Wheatsheaf.

James, A. L., James, A. and McNamee, S. (2004) Turn down the volume? Not hearing children in family proceedings. *Child and Family Law Quarterly*, 16(2), 189–202.

James, A. and Prout, A. (1997) *Constructing and Reconstructing Childhood*. London: Falmer Press.

Jamieson, L. (1998) *Intimacy*. Cambridge: Polity Press.

Janssens, J. and Dekovic, M. (1997) Pro social moral reasoning and pro social behaviour. *International Journal of Behavioural Development*, 20(3), 509–27.

Jenkins, R. (1985) Sex differences in psychiatric morbidity. *Psychological Medicine Monograph Supplements*, 12.

Jenkins, R., Lewis, G., Bebbington, P., Brugha, T., Farrell, M., Gill, B. and Meltzer, H. (2003) The National Psychiatric Morbidity Surveys of Great Britain – Initial findings from the household survey. *International Review of Psychiatry*, 15(1–2), 29–42.

Jenson, A. M. and McKee, L. (eds.) (2003) *Children and the Changing Family: Between Transformation and Negotiation*, The Future of Childhood series. London: Routledge/Farmer.

JM Consulting (1999) *Review of the Diploma in Social Work*. Bristol: JM Consulting.

John, G. (1991). Taking sides: Objectives and strategies in the development of anti-racist work in Britain. In Northern Curriculum Development Project (ed.), *Setting the Context for Change*. London: CCETSW.

Johns, R. (2005) *Using the Law in Social Work*, 2nd edn. Exeter: Learning Matters.

Jones, C. (1997) British social work and the classless society: The failure of a profession. In H. Jones (ed.), *Towards a Classless Society?* London: Routledge.

Jones, C. (1998) Social work and society. In R. Adams, L. Dominelli and M. Payne (eds.), *Social Work: Themes, Issues and Critical Debates*. Basingstoke: Macmillan, pp. 34–43.

Jones, C. (2001) Voices from the front line: State social workers and New Labour. *British Journal of Social Work*, 31(4), 547–62.

Jones, C., Ferguson, I., Lavalette, M. and Penketh, L. (2006) *Social Work and Social Justice: A Manifesto for a New Engaged Practice*. Liverpool: Liverpool University Press.

Jones, D. (2002) *Myths, Madness and the Family*. Basingstoke: Palgrave Macmillan.

Jones, E. (1993) *Family Systems Therapy*. Chichester: Wiley.

Jordan, B. (1975) Is the client a fellow citizen? *Social Work Today*, 30 October.

Jordan, B. (1990) *Social Work in an Unjust Society*. London: Harvester Wheatsheaf.

Jordan, B. and Jordan, C. (2000), *Social Work and the Third Way*. London: Sage.

Jorm, A. (1990) *The Epidemiology of Alzheimer's Disease and Related Disorders*. London: Chapman & Hall.

Judge, S. (1993) Feminist counselling: A private practice. Paper given at the Social Work Seminar, Sheffield University, 26 May.

Kanfer, F. H. and Schefft, B. K. (1988) *Guiding the Process of Therapeutic Change*. Champaign, IL: Research Press.

Karlsen, S. and Nazroo, J. (2000) The relationship between racism, social class and health among minority ethnic groups. *Health Variations: Official newsletter of the ESRC Health Variations Programme*, Issue 5, 8–9.

Kazi, M. and Wilson, J. (1996) Applying single-case evaluation methodology in a British social work agency. *Research on Social Work Practice*, 6(1), 5–26.

Keane, S., Shaw, I. and Faulkner, A. (2003) *Practitioner Research in Social Work and Social Care: An Audit and Case Study Analysis*. Cardiff: Wales Office for Research and Development.

Kearney, K., Levin, E. and Rosen, G. (2000) *Alcohol, Drug and Mental Health Problems: Working with Families*. London: National Institute for Social Work.

Kearns, K. A. and Richardson, R. A. (2005) *Attachment in Middle Childhood*. New York: Guilford Press.

Kelleher, D. and Hillier, S. (eds.) (1996) *Researching Cultural Differences in Health*. London: Routledge.

Kelly, L. (1988) *Surviving Sexual Violence*. Cambridge: Polity Press.

Kemmis, S. (1997) Action research. In J. Keeves (ed.), *Educational Research, Methodology and Measurement: An International Handbook*, 2nd edn. Oxford: Elsevier.

Kemshall, H. (1998) Defensible decisions for risk: Or it's the doers wot get the blame. *Probation Journal*, 45(2), 67–72.

Kemshall, H. (2001) *Risk Assessment and Management of Known Sexual and Violent Offenders: The Current Issues*. London: Home Office, Police Research Series Paper 140. Available at: www.homeoffice.gov.uk/rds/prgpdfs/prs140.pdf

Kemshall, H. (2002) *Risk, Social Policy and Welfare*. Buckingham: Open University Press.

Kemshall, H. (2003) *Understanding Risk in Criminal Justice*. Buckingham: Open University Press.

Kemshall, H. and Littlechild, R. (eds.) (2000) *User Involvement and Participation in Social Care*. London: Jessica Kingsley.

Kemshall, H., Mackenzie, G., Wood, J., Bailey, R. and Yates, J. (2005) *Strengthening Multi-Agency Public Protection Arrangements (MAPPA)*. London: Home Office, Development and Practice Report 45.

Kerr, M. (1998) Primary health care and health gain for people with a learning disability. *Learning Disability Review*, 3, 6–14.

Kessell, N. (1986) Communication between doctors and social workers. In J. Walton and G. McLachlan, *Partnership or Prejudice: Communication between Doctors and Those in the Other Caring Professions*. London: Nuffield Provincial Hospital Trust.

Kestenbaum, A. (1996) *Independent Living: A Review*. York: Joseph Rowntree Foundation.

Kiernan, K. (2004) Redrawing the boundaries of marriage: The rise of cohabitation and unmarried parenthood. Paper presented at the Parent and Child 2004 Family Futures Conference, London, 18 June.

Kiernan, K., Land, H. and Lewis, J. (1998) *Lone Motherhood in Twentieth-Century Britain*. Oxford: Clarendon Press.

Kilty, K. M. and Meenaghan, T. M. (1995) Social work and the convergence of politics and science. *Social Work*, 40(4), 445–53.

Kirk, S. and Reid, W. (2002) *Science and Social Work: A Critical Appraisal*. New York: Columbia University Press.

Kirkwood, T. B. L. (1995) The evolution of ageing. *Reviews in Clinical Gerontology*, 5, 3–9.

Kivnic, H. Q. (1991) *Living with Care, Caring for Life: The Inventory of Life Strengths*. Minneapolis: School of Social Work, University of Minnesota.

Klaus, M. H., Jerauld, R., Kreger, N., McAlpine, W., Steffa, M. and Kennel, J. H. (1972) Maternal attachment: Importance of the first post-partum days. *New England Journal of Medicine*, 286, 460–3.

Knappert, J. (1995). *African Mythology: An Encyclopedia of Myth and Legend*. London: Diamond Books.

Kohlberg, L. (1969) Stage and sequence: The cognitive-developmental approach to socialisation. In D. A. Goslin (ed.), *Handbook of Socialisation Theory and Research*. Chicago: Rand McNally.

Koschorke, M. (2004) Who has power in today's families? A Western perspective. In International Commission on Couple and Family Relations (ed.), *Never the Same Again? Families and their Relationships Ten Years after the Year of the Family*. Proceedings of the 51st Annual International Conference, Tallinn, Estonia: ICCFR.

Kroll, B. (1994) *Chasing Rainbows: Children, Divorce and Loss*. Dorset: Russell House.

Kumar, K. (1995) *From Post-Industrial to Post-Modern Society*. Oxford: Blackwell.

Lago, C. with Thompson, J. (1996) *Race, Culture and Counselling*. Buckingham: Open University Press.

Lamb, M. (ed.) (2004) *The Role of the Father in Child Development*, 4th edn. New Jersey: Wiley.

Laming, Lord (2003) *The Victoria Climbié Inquiry Report,* Cm 5730, Department of Health and Home Office. Norwich: The Stationery Office.

Langan, M. (1993) The rise and fall of social work. In J. Clarke (ed.), *A Crisis in Care? Challenges to Social Work*. London: Sage.

Langan, M. and Day, L. (eds.) (1992) *Women, Oppression and Social Work*. London: Routledge.

Law Commission (1990) *Family Law: Ground for Divorce*, Law Com. No. 192. London: HMSO.

Lawson, A. and Gooding, C. (2005) *Disability Rights in Europe: From Theory to Practice*. Oxford: Hart.

Leat, D. and Perkins, E. (1998) Juggling and dealing: The creative work of care package purchasing. *Social Policy and Administration*, 32, 166–81.

Leathard, A. (ed.) (2003) *Interprofessional Collaboration: From Policy to Practice in Health and Social Care*. Hove: Brunner-Routledge.

Lee, J. (1991) Empowerment through mutual aid groups: A practice grounded practice framework. *Groupwork*, 4(1), 5–21.

Lee, N. (2001) *Childhood and Society: Growing Up in an Age of Uncertainty*. Buckingham: Open University Press.

Leece, J. and Bornat, J. (eds.) (2006) *Developments in Direct Payments*. Bristol: Policy Press.

Lefley, H. (1996) *Family Caregiving in Mental Illness*. London: Sage.

Lesser, R. C. (1996) All that's solid melts into air: Deconstructing some psychoanalytic facts. *Contemporary Psychoanalysis*, 32, 5–23.

Lester, H. and Glasby, J. (2006) *Mental Health Policy and Practice*. Basingstoke: Palgrave Macmillan.

Levin, E. (2004) *Involving Service Users and Carers in Social Work Education*, Social Care Institute for Excellence. Bristol: Policy Press.

Levin, E., Sinclair, I. and Gorbach, P. (1989) *Families, Services and Confusion in Old Age*. Aldershot: Avebury.

Levitt, I. (1988) *Poverty and Welfare in Scotland 1890–1948*. Edinburgh: Edinburgh University Press.

Levy, J. and Payne, M. (2006) Welfare rights advocacy in a specialist health and social care setting: A service audit. *British Journal of Social Work,* 36, 323–31.

Lewis, J. (1996) Women, social work and social welfare in twentieth century Britain. In M. Daunton (ed.), *Charity, Self-Interest and Welfare in the English Past*. London: UCL Press.

Lewis, J. (2001a) Older people and the health-social care boundary in the UK: Half a century of hidden social policy conflict. *Social Policy and Administration,* 35(4), 343–59.

Lewis, J. (2001b) *The End of Marriage? Individualism and Intimate Relations*. Cheltenham: Edward Elgar.

Lewis, J. and Glennerster, H. (1996) *Implementing the New Community Care*. Buckingham: Open University Press.

Lewis, J. and Meredith, B. (1988) *Daughters Who Care: Daughters Caring for Mothers at Home*. London: Routledge.

Lewis, T. (2005) *Employment Law: An Advisers' Handbook*, 6th edn. London: Legal Action Group.

Lindow, V. and Morris, J. (1995) *Service User Involvement: Synthesis of Findings and Experience in the Field of Community Care*. York: Joseph Rowntree Foundation.

Little, V. L. and Kendall, P. C. (1979) Cognitive behavioural interventions with delinquents: Problem solving, role taking and self control. In P. C. Kendall and S. D Hollan (eds.), *Cognitive Behavioural Interventions*. New York: Academic Press.

Lloyd, M. (2000) Where has all the care management gone? The challenge of Parkinson's disease to the health and social care interface. *British Journal of Social Work*, 30, 737–54.

Lloyd, M. and Taylor, C. (1995) From Hollis to the Orange Book: Developing a holistic model of social work assessment in the 1990s. *British Journal of Social Work*, 25, 691–710.

Lochman, J. E. (1984) Psychological characteristics and assessment of aggressive adolescents. In C. Keith and R. Keith (eds.), *The Aggressive Adolescent: Clinical Perspectives*. New York: The Free Press.

London Borough of Brent (1985) *A Child in Trust: Report of the Panel of Inquiry Investigating the Circumstances Surrounding the Death of Jasmine Beckford*. London: London Borough of Brent.

London Borough of Lambeth (1987) *Whose Child? A Report of the Public Inquiry into the Death of Tyra Henry*. London: Borough of Lambeth.

Long, J. (2000) Who's crying for whom? Setting up an under five's counselling service in a social services family centre. *Journal of Social Work Practice*, 14(1), 51–61.

Lord Chancellor's Department (1993) *Looking to the Future: Mediation and the Ground for Divorce*, Cm 2424. London: HMSO.

Lord Chancellor's Department (1995) *Looking to the Future: Mediation and the Ground for Divorce – The Government's Proposals*, Cm 2799. London: HMSO.

Lorde, A. (1984), *Sister Outsider*. Freedom, CA: The Crossing Press.

Lorenz, W. (1991) Social work practice in Europe. In M. Hill (ed.), *Social Work and the European Community*. London: Jessica Kingsley.

Low, H. and Weinstein, J. (2000) Interprofessional education. In R. Pierce and J. Weinstein (eds.), *Innovative Education and Training for Care Professionals: A Providers' Guide*. London: Jessica Kingsley, ch. 13.

Loxley, A. (1997) *Collaboration in Health and Welfare: Working with Difference*. London: Jessica Kingsley.

Luria, A. R. (1961) *The Role of Speech in the Regulation of Normal and Abnormal Behaviour*. New York: Liveright.

Lymbery, M. (2005) *Social Work with Older People*. London: Sage.

Lymbery, M. and Millward, A. (2000) The primary health care interface. In G. Bradley and J. Manthorpe (eds.), *Working on the Faultline*. Birmingham: Venture Press.

Macdonald, G. M. (1997) Social work: Beyond control? In A. Maynard and I. Chalmers (eds.), *Non-random Reflections on Health Services Research. On the 25th Anniversary of Archie Cochrane's Effectiveness and Efficiency*. Plymouth: BMJ Publishing.

Macdonald, G. M. (2003) *Using Systematic Reviews to Improve Social Care: SCIE Report No. 4*. London: Social Care Institute for Excellence.

Macdonald, G. M. and Macdonald, K. I. (1995) Ethical issues in social work research. In R. Hugman and D. Smith (eds.), *Ethical Issues in Social Work*. London: Routledge.

Macdonald, G. and Sheldon, B. (1992) Contemporary studies of the effectiveness of social work. *British Journal of Social Work*, 22, 615–43.

Macdonald, G. and Sheldon, B. (1998) Changing one's mind: The final frontier? *Issues in Social Work Education,* 18(1), 3–25.

Macpherson, Sir W. (1999) *The Stephen Lawrence Inquiry*. London: The Stationery Office.

Maitra, B. and Miller, A. (2002) Children, families and therapists. In K. N. Dwivedi (ed.), *Meeting the Needs of Ethnic Minority Children*. London: Jessica Kingsley.

Magura, S. and Moses, B. S. (1984) Clients as evaluators in child protective services. *Child Welfare*, 53(2), 99–112.

Mahoney, M. J. (2003). *Constructive Psychotherapy: A Practical Guide*. New York: Guilford Press.

Maluccio, A. N., Ainsworth, F. and Thoburn, J. (2000) *Child Welfare Outcome Research in the United States, the United Kingdom and Australia*. Washington DC: Child Welfare League of America.

Mama, A. (1984) Black women, the economic crisis and the British state. *Feminist Review*, 17, 21–35.

Mama, A. (1989) *Hidden Struggle: Statutory and Voluntary Responses to Violence against Black Women in the Home*. London: London Race and Housing Unit.

Mama, A. (1995) *Behind the Mask*. London: Routledge.

Mandelstam, M. (2005) *Community Care Practice and the Law,* 3rd edn. London: Jessica Kingsley.

Manktelow, R. (1994a) *My Brother's Keeper? The Community Response to the Resettlement of Former Long-stay Psychiatric Patients in a Small Town in Northern Ireland*. Norwich: Social Work Monographs.

Manktelow, R. (1994b) *Paths to Psychiatric Hospitalisation: A Sociological Analysis*. Aldershot: Avebury.

Manktelow, R. (1998a) The social inclusion of individuals with psychiatric disabilities. In J. Campbell and R. Manktelow (eds.), *Mental Health Social Work in Ireland*. Aldershot: Avebury.

Manktelow, R. (1998b) Political conflict, mental ill-health and social work. In CCETSW (ed.), *Social Work and Social Change in Northern Ireland*. Belfast: CCETSW.

Manktelow, R., Hughes, P., Britton, F., Campbell, J., Hamilton, B. and Wilson, G. (2002) The experience and practice of approved social workers in Northern Ireland. *British Journal of Social Work,* 32, 43–61.

Marchant, H. and Wearing, B. (eds.) (1986) *Gender Reclaimed*. Sydney: Hale and Iremonger.

Marks, D. (1999) *Disability: Controversial Debates and Psychosocial Perspectives*. London: Routledge.

Marks, D., Burman, E., Burman, L. and Parker, I. (1995) Collaborative research and reflective practice in educational decision-making. *Educational Psychology in Practice,* 11(1), 41–8.

Marlow, A. and Loveday, M. (eds.) (2000) *After MacPherson: Reflections on Policing after the Stephen Lawrence Inquiry*. Lyme Regis: Russell House.

Marsh, P. (1991) Task-centred practice. In J. Lishman (ed.), *Handbook of Theory for Practice Teachers in Social Work*. London: Jessica Kingsley, pp. 157–72.

Marsh, P. and Crow, G. (1998) *Family Group Conferences in Child Welfare*. Oxford: Blackwell Science.

Marsh, P. and Doel, M. (2005) *The Task-centred Book*. London: Routledge.

Marsh, P. and Fisher, M. (1992) *Good Intentions: Developing Partnership in Social Services*. York: Joseph Rowntree Foundation.

Marsh, P. and Fisher, M. (2005) *Developing the Evidence Base for Social Work and Social Care Practice*. London: Social Care Institute for Excellence.

Marsh, P. and Peel, M. (1999) *Leaving Care in Partnership*. Norwich: The Stationery Office.

Marsh, P. and Triseliotis, J. (1996) *Ready to Practise?* Aldershot: Avebury.

Maslow, A. H. (1954) *Motivation and Personality*. New York: Harper.

Mason, M. (1992) Internalised oppression. In R. Rieser and M. Mason (eds.), *Disability Equality in the Classroom: A Human Rights Issue*. London: Disability Equality in Education.

Massachusetts Citizens for Children (MCC) (2001) *A State Call to Action: Working to End Child Abuse and Neglect in Massachusetts*. Boston: MCC, Kids Count Publication.

Masson, J., Harrison, C. and Pavlovic, A. (eds.) (1999) *Lost and Found: Making and Remaking Working Partnerships with Parents of Children in the Care System*. Aldershot: Ashgate.

Maximé, J. E. (1991) Some psychological models of black self-concept. In S. Ahmed, J. Cheetham and J. Small (eds.), *Social Work with Black Children and their Families*. London: B.T. Batsford, pp. 100–16.

Maximé, J. (1994) *Mixed Parentage: Workbook Three. Black Like Me Series*. London: Emani Publications.

May, J. R. and Johnston, H. J. (1973) Physiological activity to internally elicited arousal and inhibitory thoughts. *Journal of Abnormal Psychology,* 82, 239–45.

Mayer, J. and Timms, N. (1970) *The Client Speaks*. London: Routledge & Kegan Paul.

McCarthy, T. and Galvani, S. (2004) SCARS: A new model for social work with substance users. *Practice,* 16(2), 85–97.

McColgan, A. (2005) *Discrimination Law: Text, Cases and Materials,* 2nd edn. Oxford: Hart.

McConkey, R., Slevin, E. and Barr, O. (2004) *Audit of Learning Disability in Northern Ireland,* The University of Ulster http://www.science.ulster.ac.uk/inr/ddch/audit/audit_of_learning_disability_research_in_northern_ireland.pdf

McDonald, A. (1999) *Understanding Community Care: A Guide for Social Workers*. Basingstoke: Macmillan.

McGuire, J. (ed.) (1995a) *What Works: Reducing Reoffending – Guidelines from Research and Practice*. Chichester: Wiley.

McGuire, J. (1995b) Assessing self control loss in violent offences committed by juveniles. Paper presented at the 5th European Conference on Psychology and Law, Budapest, September.

McGuire, J. (1997) Psycho-social approaches to the understanding and reduction of violence in young people. In V. Varma (ed.), *Violence in Children and Adolescents*. London: Jessica Kingsley.

McIvor, G. and Raynor, P. (2007) *Developments in Social Work with Offenders,* Research Highlights in Social Work. London: Jessica Kingsley.

McKie, L., Cunningham-Burley, S. and McKendrick, J. H. (2005) Families and relationships: boundaries and bridges. In L. McKie and S. Cunningham-Burley (eds.), *Families in Society: Boundaries and Relationships*. Bristol: Policy Press.

McLeod, E. (1987) Some lessons from teaching feminist social work. *Issues in Social Work Education*, 3(2), 131–43.

McLeod, E. and Bywaters, P. (2000) *Social Work, Health and Equality*. London: Routledge.

McLeod, E., Bywaters, P. and Cooke, M. (2003) Social work in accident and emergency departments: A better deal for older patients' health? *British Journal of Social Work,* 33(6), 787–802.

McLeod, E. and Sanden Eriksson, B. (2002) Hospital social work in Sweden and the UK. *European Journal of Social Work,* 5(2), 171–86.

McLeod, J. (1999) *Practitioner Research in Counselling.* London: Sage.

McLeod, J. (2003) *An Introduction to Counselling.* Buckingham: Open University Press.

Meads, G. and Ashcroft, J. (2005) *The Case for Interprofessional Education in Health and Social Care.* London: Blackwell.

Means, R., Richards, S. and Smith, R. (2003) *Community Care Policy and Practice,* 3rd edn. Basingstoke: Palgrave Macmillan.

Mearns, D. and Thorne, B. (1999) *Person Centred Counselling in Action.* London: Sage.

Mearns, D. and Thorne, B. (2000) *Person-centred Therapy Today: New Frontiers in Theory and Practice.* London: Sage.

Mehler, J. and Dupoux, E. (1994) *What Infants Know: New Cognitive Science of Early Development.* Oxford: Blackwell.

Meichenbaum, D. (1971) Training impulsive children to talk to themselves. *Journal of Abnormal Psychology,* 77, 115–26.

Meichenbaum, D. (1977) *Cognitive Behavioural Modification.* New York: Plenum Press.

Mercer, G. and Barnes, C. (2000) Disability: From medical needs to social rights. In P. Tovey (ed.), *Contemporary Primary Care: The Challenges for Change.* Buckingham: Open University Press.

Middleton, L. (1997) *The Art of Assessment.* Birmingham: Venture Press.

Middleton, M. (1998) Services for disabled children, integrating the perspective of social workers. *Child and Family Social Work,* 3(4), 239–46.

Mills, C. W. (1959) *The Sociological Imagination.* Oxford: Oxford University Press.

Mills, F. (1996) The ideology of welfare reform: Deconstructing stigma. *Social Work,* 41(4), 391–5.

Milner, J. (2001) *Women and Social Work: Narrative Approaches.* Basingstoke: Palgrave.

Milner, J. S. and Campbell, J. C. (1995) Prediction issues for practitioners. In J. Campbell (eds.), *Assessing Dangerousness: Violence by Sexual Offenders, Batterers, and Child Abusers.* London: Sage.

Milner, J. and O'Byrne, P. (2002) *Assessment in Social Work.* Basingstoke: Palgrave Macmillan.

Minuchin, S. (1974) *Families and Family Therapy.* London: Tavistock.

Minuchin, S., Montalvo, B., Gurney, B. and Schumer, H. (1967) *Families of the Slums: An Exploration of their Structure and Treatment.* New York: Basic Books.

Mirrlees-Black, C. (1999) *Domestic Violence: Findings from a New British Crime Survey Self-Completion Questionnaire 1996.* London: HMSO.

Monahan, J. (1993) Limiting therapist exposure to Tarasoff Liability: Guidelines for risk containment. *American Psychologist,* 48, 242–50.

Monahan, J. and Steadman, H. (1994) *Violence and Mental Disorder: Developments in Risk Assessment.* Chicago: University of Chicago Press.

Montagu, A. (1997) *Man's Most Dangerous Myth: The Fallacy of Race,* 6th edn. Wallnut Creek: Alta Maria Press.

Mooney, G. (1998) 'Remoralizing' the poor? Gender, class and philanthropy in Victorian Britain. In G. Lewis (ed.), *Forming Nation, Framing Welfare.* London: Routledge.

Mooney, J. (2000) *Gender, Violence and the Social Order.* Basingstoke: Palgrave Macmillan.

Moraga, C. and Anzaldua, G. (eds.) (1981) *This Bridge Called my Back.* Watertown, MA: Persephone Press.

Moran, D. and Wilson, M. (1997) *Men Who Are Violent to Women*. Lyme Regis: Russell House.

Morgan, D. H. J. (2004) Everyday life and family practices. In E. B. Silva and T. Bennett (eds.), *Contemporary Culture and Everyday Life*. Durham: SociologyPress.

Morgan, R. (2006) *Being a Young Carer: Views from a Young Carers Workshop*. Newcastle Upon Tyne: Office of the Children Rights Director. Commission for Social Care Inspection. www.rights4me.org

Morris, H. S. (1968) Ethnic groups. In D. L. Skill (ed.), *International Encyclopedia of the Social Sciences, Volume 5*. New York: Macmillan, pp. 167–72.

Morris, J. (1993), *Independent Lives? Community Care and Disabled People*. Basingstoke: Macmillan.

Moss, B. (2006) *Values*. Lyme Regis: Russell House.

Mullender, A. (1991) The Ebony Project: Bicultural group work with transracial foster parents. *Social Work with Groups,* 13, 34–41.

Mullender, A. and Humphreys, C. (1998) *Domestic Violence and Child Abuse: Policy and Practice Issues for Local Authorities and Other Agencies*. London: Local Government Association.

Mullender, A., Kelly, L., Hague, G., Malos, E. and Iman, U. (2002) *Children's Perspectives on Domestic Violence*. London: Routledge

Munro, E. (1999) Common errors of reasoning in child protection work. *Child Abuse and Neglect*, 23(8), 745–58.

Naleppa, M. J. and Reid, W. J. (1998) Task-centred case management for the elderly: Developing a practice model. *Research on Social Work Practice*, 8(1), 63–85.

Naseby, W., Hatyden, B. and DePaulo, B. M (1980) Attributional bias among aggressive boys to interpret unambiguous social stimuli as displays of hostility. *Journal of Abnormal Psychology,* 98, 459–68.

NASW (National Association of Social Workers) (1999) *Code of Ethics of the National Association of Social Workers*. Washington DC: NASW.

National Assembly for Wales (2003) Statistics for Wales: A Statistical Focus on Wales. *Disability and Long Term Illness in Wales*. Available at: www.wales.gov.uk/keypubstatisticsforwales/content/publication/health/2003/fod2003/fodw2003-ment.pdf

National Assembly for Wales (2004) *Learning Disabilities Strategy*, Cardiff: Welsh Assembly. Available at: http://www.wales.gov.uk/subisocialpolicy/content/guidance/sp-response-guide-e.pdf

National Association of Social Workers (NASW) (1999) Code of Ethics of the National Association of Social Workers. Washington DC: NASW.

National Audit Office (2005) *Dealing with the Complexity of the Benefits System*. London: National Audit Office.

National Health Service Executive (1996) *Primary Care: The Future*. London: HMSO.

National Institute for Social Work (1999) *National Debate on the Future of Social Work: Creating a New Agenda*, NISW Briefing Paper No. 28. London: National Institute for Social Work.

National Institute for Social Work (2000) *Modernising Social Work: Social Work in the Modernising Agenda*, NISW Briefing Paper No. 29. London: National Institute for Social Work.

National Treatment Agency (2006) *Performance Information*. Available at: http://www.nta.nhs.uk/frameset.asp?u=http://www.nta.nhs.uk/programme/national/monitoring.htm (accessed 28 July 2006).

NCH (2005) Close the gap for children in care. Available at: www.nch.org.uk (accessed December 2005).

Neate, P. and Douglas, A. (2000) Take control of your future: Launch of *Community Care*'s Speak Out Campaign. *Community Care*, 13 January, 16.

Neil, E. and Howe, D. (eds.) (2004) *Contact in Adoption and Permanent Foster Care*. London: BAAF.

Nevins, J. (2002) *Operation Gatekeeper: The Rise of the 'Illegal-Alien' and the Making of the US-Mexico Boundary*. New York: Routledge.

Newton, C. and Marsh, P. (1993) *Training in Partnership: Translating Intentions into Practice in Social Services*. York: Joseph Rowntree Foundation.

New Zealand/Aotearoa Association of Social Workers (1993) *Code of Ethics*. Dunedin: NZASW.

Nicolson, P. and Bayne, R. (1990) *Applied Psychology for Social Workers*. London: Macmillan.

Nicolson, P., Bayne, R. and Owen, J. (2006) *Applied Psychology for Social Workers*, 3rd edn. Basingstoke: Palgrave Macmillan.

Nielsen, L. (1987) *Adolescent Psychology: A Contemporary View*. London: Holt, Rinehart and Winston.

Nirje, B. (1980) The normalisation principle. In R. J. Flynn and K. E. Nitsch (eds.), *Normalisation, Social Integration and Community Services*. Baltimore: University Park Press.

Noble, M., Platt, L., Smith, G. and Daly, M. (1997) The spread of disability living allowance. *Disability & Society*, 12(5), 741–51.

Norman, A. (1985) *Triple Jeopardy: Growing Old in a Second Homeland*. London: Centre for Policy on Ageing.

Northern Curriculum Development Project (1991) *Setting the Context for Change*. London: CCETSW.

Northern Curriculum Development Project (1993) *Improving Practice with Learning Difficulties*. London: CCETSW.

Northern Ireland Department of Health, Social Services and Public Safety (2005a) *Community Statistics*. Available at: www.dhsspsni.gov.uk/master_community_statistics_(2004-05).pdf

Northern Ireland Department of Health, Social Services and Public Safety (2005b) *Equal Lives: A Review of Policy and Services for People with a Learning Disability in Northern Ireland*. Available at: www.rmhldni.gov.uk

Novaco, R. W. (1975) *Anger Control: The Development and Evaluation of an Experimental Treatment*. Lexington, MA: D.C. Heath.

Novaco, R. W. (1976) The function and regulation of the arousal of anger. *American Journal of Psychiatry*, 133, 1124–8.

Novaco, R. W. (1977) A stress inoculation approach to anger management in the training of law enforcement officers. *American Journal of Community Psychology*, 5, 327–46.

Oakley, A. (2000) *Experiments in Knowing: Gender and Methods in the Social Sciences*. Cambridge: Polity Press.

Obholzer, A. and Roberts, Z. (1994) *The Unconscious at Work: Individual and Organisational Stress in the Human Services*. London: Routledge.

O'Brien, J. (1987) A guide to lifestyle planning: Using the activities catalogue to integrate services and natural support systems. In B. W. Wilcox and G. T. Bellamy (eds.), *The Activities Catalogue: An Alternative Curriculum for Youth and Adults with Severe Disabilities*. Baltimore: Brookes.

O'Brien, J. and Lovett, H. (1992) *Finding a Way towards Ordinary Lives: The Contribution of Person Centred Planning*. Harrisburg: Pennsylvania Office of Mental Retardation.

O'Brien, M. (2004) *Fathers and Family Support: Promoting Involvement and Evaluating Impact*. London: National Family and Parenting Institute.

Office for National Statistics (ONS) (2001) *Trends in Life Expectancy by Social Class 1972–1999*. London: Office for National Statistics.

Office for National Statistics (ONS) (2004a) *Focus on Health Inequalities*. London: Office for National Statistics.

Office for National Statistics (2004b) *Population Size*. London: Office for National Statistics.

Office for National Statistics (2004c), *Birth Statistics*. London: The Stationery Office.

Office for National Statistics (ONS) (2005a) Healthy life expectancy by area deprivation: magnitude and trends in England, 1994–1999. *Health Statistics Quarterly*, 25, 19–27. http://www.statistics.gov.uk/down;loads/theme_health/HSQ25.pdf

Office for National Statistics (2005b) *General Household Survey 2004/5*. London: ONS Available at: http://www.statistics.gov.uk/CCI/ nugget.asp?ID=1027&Pos=2&ColRank=2&Rank=448 (accessed 28 July 2006).

Office for National Statistics (2006) *Social Trends No. 36*. London: Palgrave Macmillan.

Office of the Deputy Prime Minister – Social Exclusion Unit (2004) *Mental Health and Social Exclusion*. London: Office of the Deputy Prime Minister.

Office of Population and Census Surveys (1974) *Birth Statistics*, Series FM1, No. 1. London: HMSO.

O'Hagan, K. (2001) *Cultural Competence in the Caring Professions*. London: Jessica Kingsley.

Okitikpi, T. (ed.) (2005) *Working with Children of Mixed Parentage*. Lyme Regis: Russell House.

Oldman, C. (2000), *Blurring the Boundaries: A Fresh Look at Housing and Care Provision for Older People*. Brighton: Pavilion/Joseph Rowntree Foundation.

Oliver, M. (1990) *The Politics of Disablement*. Basingstoke: Macmillan.

Oliver, M. (1996) *Understanding Disability: From Theory to Practice*. Basingstoke: Macmillan.

Oliver, M. and Barnes, C. (1999) *Disabled People and Social Policy: From Exclusion to Inclusion*. Longman: London.

Oliver, M. and Sapey, B. (2006) *Social Work with Disabled People,* 3rd edn. Basingstoke: Macmillan.

Olkin, R. (1999) *What Psychotherapists Should Know About Disability*. New York: Guildford Press.

Orme, J. (2000) *Gender and Community Care: Social Work and Social Care Perspectives*. Basingstoke: Palgrave.

Orme, J. (2001) Hail the education of social work. *The Guardian*, 30 March.

Orme, J., Dominelli, L. and Mullender, A. (2000) Working with perpetrators of domestic violence: A feminist approach. *International Social Work*, 43, 89–106.

Osborne, S. (2006) *Welfare Benefits Handbook 2006/2007*. London: Child Poverty Action Group.

Owusu-Bempah, J. (1994) Race, self-identity and social work. *British Journal of Social Work*, 24, 123–36.

Owusu-Bempah, K. (2003) Political correctness: In the interest of the child? *Educational and Child Psychology*, 20, 53–63.

Owusu-Bempah, K. (2005) Mulato, marginal man, half-caste, mixed race: The one drop rule in professional practice. In T. Okitikpi (ed.), *Working with Children of Mixed Parentage*. Lyme Regis: Russell House, pp. 27–44.

Owusu-Bempah, K. (2006) Socio-genealogical connectedness: Knowledge and identity. In J. Aldgate, D. Jones, W. Rose and C. Jeffery (eds.), *The Developing World of the Child*. London: Jessica Kingsley.

Owusu-Bempah, J. and Howitt, D. (1999) Even their soul is defective. *The Psychologist,* 12(3), 126–30.

Owusu-Bempah, K. and Howitt, D. (2000) *Psychology beyond Western Perspectives*. Leicester: British Psychological Society.

Packman, J. and Hall, C. (1998) *From Care to Accommodation: Support, Protection and Care in Child Care Services*. London: The Stationery Office.

Padgett, D. (1998) Does the glove really fit? Qualitative research and clinical social work practice. *Social Work*, 43(4) 373–81.

Page, R. C. and Berkow, D. N. (1991) Concepts of the self: Western and Eastern perspectives. *Journal of Multicultural Counselling and Development*, 19, 83–93.

Pahl, R. (2000) *On Friendship*. Cambridge: Polity Press.

Palazzoli, M., Boscolo, L., Cecchin, E. and Prata, G. (1978) *Paradox and Counter-Paradox*. New York: Jason Aronson.

Palmer, E. J. (2003) *Offending Behaviour, Moral Reasoning, Criminal Conduct and the Rehabilitation of Offenders*. Devon: Willan Publishing.

Palmer E. J. (2005) The relationship between moral reasoning and aggression, and the implications for practice. *Psychology, Crime and Law*, 11, 353–61.

Palmer, E. J. and Hollin, C. R. (1996) Socio moral reasoning, perceptions of own parenting and self reported delinquency. *Personality and Individual Differences*, 21, 175–82.

Palmer, E. J. and Hollin, C. R. (1997) The influence of own parenting on socio-moral reasoning, attributions for criminal behaviour and self reported delinquency. *Personality and Individual Differences*, 23, 193–7.

Papell, C. and Rothman, B. (1980) Relating the mainstream model of social work with groups to group psychotherapy and the structured group. *Social Work with Groups*, 3(2), 5–23.

Parentline Plus (2005) *Stepfamilies: New Relationships, New Challenges*. London: Parentline Plus.

Parker, J. (2007) The social work process: Assessment, planning, intervention and review. In M. Lymbery and K. Postle (eds.), *Social Work: A Companion for Learning*. London: Sage.

Parker, J. and Bradley, G. (2003) *Social Work Practice: Assessment, Planning, Intervention and Review*. Exeter: Learning Matters.

Parkinson, L. (1997) *Family Mediation*. London: Sweet and Maxwell.

Parry, M. (1994) Children's welfare and the law: The Children Act 1989 and recent developments – Part 2. *Panel News*, 7(3), 4–11.

Parsloe, P. (ed.) (1999) *Risk Assessment in Social Care and Social Work*, Research Highlights 36. London: Jessica Kingsley.

Parton, N. (1985) *The Politics of Child Abuse*. London: Macmillan.

Parton, N. (1994a) Modernity, postmodernity and social work. *British Journal of Social Work*, 24, 513–32.

Parton, N. (1994b) The nature of social work under conditions of (post) modernity. *Social Work and Social Sciences Review*, 5(2), 93–112.

Parton, N. and O'Byrne, P. (2000) *Constructive Social Work*. Basingstoke: Macmillan.

Patel, N. (1990) *A Race against Time? Social Services Provision to Black Elders*. London: Runneymede Trust.

Patterson, K. and Hughes, B. (1997) The social model of disability and the disappearing body: Towards a sociology of impairment. *Disability and Society*, 12(3), 325–40.

Pavlov, I. P. (1927) *Conditioning Reflexes* (trans.G. V. Anrep). New York: Liveright.

Payne, M. (2000) *Teamwork in Multidisciplinary Care*. Basingstoke: Palgrave Macmillan.

Payne, M. (2005a) *Modern Social Work Theory*, 3rd edn. Basingstoke: Palgrave Macmillan.

Payne, M. (2005b) *The Origins of Social Work: Continuity and Change*. Basingstoke: Palgrave Macmillan.

Payne, M. (2006) *What Is Professional Social Work?* Oxford: Policy Press.

Peck, E., Gulliver, P. and Towell, D. (2002) *Modernising Partnerships: An Evaluation of Somerset's Innovations In the Commissioning and Organisation of Mental Health Services: Final Report*. London: Institute for Applied Health and Social Policy.

Petch, A., Cheetham, J. Fuller, R., MacDonald, C., Myers, F. with Hallam, A. and Knapp, M. (1996) *Delivering Community Care: Initial Implementation of Care Management in Scotland*. Edinburgh: HMSO.

Petersen, T. and McBride, A. (2002) *Working with Substance Misusers: A Guide to Theory and Practice*. London: Routledge.

Petrosino, A., Turpin-Petrosino, C. and Beuhler, J. (2003) 'Scared straight' and other juvenile awareness programs for preventing juvenile delinquency (Updated C2 review). In *The Campbell Collaboration Reviews of Intervention and Policy Evaluations (C2-RIPE)* November 2003. Philadelphia: Pennsylvania: Campbell Collaboration.

Petticrew, M. and Roberts, H. (2005) *Systematic Reviews in the Social Sciences*. Oxford: Blackwell.

Phillipson, C., Bernard, M., Phillips, J. and Ogg, J. (2001) *The Family and Community Life of Older People*. London: Routledge.

Philo, G. (1997) *Media and Mental Distress*. London: Longmans.

Piaget, J. (1952) *The Origin of Intelligence in the Child*. New York: Basic Books.

Pierce, R. and Weinstein, J. (2000) *Innovative Education and Training for Care Professionals: A Providers' Guide*. London: Jessica Kingsley.

Pinkney, S. (1998) The reshaping of social work and social care. In G. Hughes and G. Lewis (eds.), *Unsettling Welfare: The Reconstruction of Social Policy*. London: Routledge.

Piper, C. (1993) *The Responsible Parent: A Study in Divorce Mediation*. London: Harvester Wheatsheaf.

Pitcairn, T. and Waterhouse, L. (1993) Evaluating parenting in child physical abuse. In L. Waterhouse (ed.), *Child Abuse and Child Abusers: Protection and Prevention*. London: Jessica Kingsley.

Pollard, D. S. (1989). Against the odds: A profile of academic achievers from the urban underclass. *The Journal of Negro Education,* 58, 297–309.

Powell, F. W. (2005) *The Politics of Social Work*. London: Sage.

Powell, J. (2002) The changing conditions of social work research. *British Journal of Social Work*, 32, 17–33.

Prevatt Goldstein, B. (1996) The role of a black student group. *Practice*, 8(4), 15–24.

Prevatt Goldstein, B. (1999a) Black with one parent: A positive and achievable identity. *British Journal of Social Work,* 29, 285–301.

Prevatt Goldstein, B. (1999b) Direct work with black children with a white parent. In R. Barn (ed.), *Working with Black Children and Adolescents in Need*. London: BAAF.

Prevatt Goldstein, B. (2002) Catch 22: Black workers' role in equal opportunities for black service users. *British Journal of Social Work,* 32, 765–78.

Prevatt Goldstein, B. (2003) Black families and survival strategies. In L. Jamieson and S. Cunningham-Burley (eds.), *Families and the State: Changing Relationships*. London: Palgrave Macmillan.

Prevatt Goldstein, B. (2006) A study of the barriers in translating 'race' related research into policy. *Research Policy and Planning,* 24(1), 24–38.

Priebe, S., Huxley, P., Knight, S. and Evans, S. (1999) Application and results of the Manchester Short Assessment of Quality of Life (MANSA). *International Journal of Social Psychiatry*, 45(1), 7–12.

Prime Minister's Strategy Unit, Department of Work and Pensions, Department of Health, Department for Education and Skills, Office of the Deputy Prime Minister (2005) *Improving the Life Chances of Disabled People,* London: Cabinet Office. Available at: http://www.strategy.gov.uk/work_areas/disability/

Pringle, K. (1995) *Men, Masculinities and Social Welfare*. London: University College London Press.

Prior, P. (1999) *Gender and Mental Health*. Basingstoke: Macmillan.

Prior, P., Lynch, M. A. and Glaser, D. (1999) Responding to child sexual abuse: An evaluation of social work by children and their carers. *Child and Family Social Work*, 4, 131–43.

Pritchard, C. (2006) *Mental Health Social Work: Evidence-based Practice*. Abingdon: Routledge.

Pritchard, J. (1996) Risk and older people. In H. Kemshall and J. Pritchard (eds.), *Good Practice in Risk Assessment and Risk Management*. London: Jessica Kingsley, pp. 68–79.

Prochaska, F. K. (1980) *Women and Philanthropy in Nineteenth Century England*. Oxford: Oxford University Press.

Pryor, J. and Rodgers, B. (2001) *Children in Changing Families: Life after Parental Separation*. Oxford: Basil Blackwell.

Quinn, F. and Elliott, C. (2006) *English Legal System*, 7th edn. London: Longman.

Quinton, D. (2004) *Supporting Parents: Messages from Research*. London: Jessica Kingsley.

Rachman, R. (1993) The role of social work in discharge planning. *Health and Social Care in the Community*, 1(1), 105–13.

Rachman, R. (1995) Community care: Changing the role of hospital social work. *Health and Social Care in the Community,* 3(3), 163–72.

Rankin, J. (2005) *Mental Health and Social Inclusion*. London: Institute for Public Policy Research.

Raynor, P. and Robinson, G. (2005) *Rehabilitation, Crime and Justice*. Basingstoke: Palgrave Macmillan.

Reamer, F. R. (2001) *Ethics Education in Social Work*. Alexandria, VA: NASW.

Redl, F. (1951) Art of group composition. In S. Shulze (ed.), *Creative Living in a Children's Institution*. New York: Association Press.

Reed, J. (1993) The relationship between semi-professions in acute and long-term care of elderly patients. *Journal of Clinical Nursing*, 2, 81–7.

Refugee Council and Oxfam (2002) *Poverty and Asylum in the UK*. London: Oxfam and Refugee Council.

Reid, K. (2004) A long term strategic approach to tackling truancy and absenteeism from schools: the SSTG scheme. *British Journal of Guidance and Counselling,* 32(1), 57–74.

Reid, W. J. (1963) *An Experimental Study of Methods Used in Casework Treatment*. New York: Department of Social Work, Columbia University.

Reid, W. J. (1975) A test of task-centred approach. *Social Work*, 20(January), 3–9.

Reid, W. J. (1992) *Task Strategies*. New York: Columbia University Press.

Reid, W. J. (2000) *The Task Planner: An Intervention Resource for Human Service Professionals*. New York: Columbia University Press.

Reid, W. J. and Beard, C. (1980) An evaluation of in-service training in a public welfare setting. *Administration in Social Work*, 4(Spring), 71–85.

Reid, W. J. and Helmer, K. (1985) *Session Tasks in Family Treatment*. Albany, NY: State University of New York, School of Social Welfare.

Reid, W. J. and Shyne, A. W. (1969) *Brief and Extended Casework*. New York: Columbia University Press.

Reimers, S. and Treacher, A. (1995) *Introducing User-Friendly Family Therapy*. London: Routledge.

Research Assessment Exercise 2001 (2002) *Overview Report on UOA41 Social Work*. Available at: www.hero.rae.ac.uk

Research in Practice (n.d.) http://www.rip.org.uk

Reynolds, J. (1994) Introducing gender issues into social work education: Is this just women's work?, *Issues in Social Work Education*, 9, 3–20.

Richards, M. (1999) The interests of children at divorce. In G. Allan (ed.), *The Sociology of the Family: A Reader*. Oxford: Blackwell.

Richardson, D. (2000) *Rethinking Sexuality*. London: Sage.

Richardson, A., Jackson, C. and Sykes, W. (1990) *Taking Research Seriously: Means of Improving and Assessing the Use and Dissemination of Research*. London: HMSO.

Richman, N., Stevenson, J. and Graham, P. J. (1984) Pre-school to school: A behavioural study. In R. Schaffer (ed.), *Behavioural Development: A Series of Monographs*. London: Academic Press.

Riessman, C. (ed.) (1993) *Qualitative Studies in Social Work Research*. Thousand Oaks, CA: Sage.

Rimm, D. C. and Masters, J. C. (1979) *Behaviour Therapy*. New York: Academic Press.

Roberts, J. and Taylor, C. (1993) Sexually abused children and young people speak out. In L. Waterhouse (ed.), *Child Abuse and Child Abusers: Protection and Prevention*. London: Jessica Kingsley.

Roberts, G. and Wolfson, P. (2004) The rediscovery of recovery: Open to all. *Advances in Psychiatric Treatment*, 10, 37–49.

Robinson, L. (1995) *Psychology for Social Workers: Black Perspectives*. London: Routledge.

Rodgers, B. and Pryor, J. (1998) *Divorce and Separation: The Outcomes for Children*. York: Joseph Rowntree Foundation.

Roe, S. (2005) *Drug Misuse Declared: Findings from the 2004/5 British Crime Survey. England and Wales*. London: Home Office.

Rogers, A., Pilgrim, D. and Lacey, R. (1993) *Experiencing Psychiatry: Users' Views of Services*. London: Macmillan.

Rogers, A. and Pilgrim, D. (2005) *A Sociology of Mental Health and Illness*, 3rd edn. Buckingham: Open University Press.

Rogers, C. R. (1951) *Client-centred Therapy*. Boston: Houghton Mifflin.

Rogers, C. R. (1961) *On Becoming a Person*. Boston: Houghton Mifflin.

Roland, A. (1988). *In Search of Self in India and Japan: Towards a Cross-cultural Psychology*. Princeton, NJ: Princeton University Press.

Ronen, T. (1994) Cognitive-behavioural social work with children. *The British Journal of Social Work*, 24, 273–85.

Ronen, T. (1997) *Cognitive Developmental Therapy with Children*. Chichester: Wiley.

Ronen, T. (1998) Direct clinical work with children. In K. Cigno and D. Bourn (eds.), *Cognitive and Behavioural Social Work in Practice*. Aldershot: Ashgate/Arena, pp. 39–59.

Ronen, T. (2003) *Cognitive Constructivist Psychotherapy with Children and Adolescents*. New York: Kluwer/Plenum.

Ronen, T. (2005) Students' evidence-based practice intervention for children with oppositional defiant disorder. *Research in Social Work Practice,* 15, 165–79.

Ronen, T. and Freeman, A. (2007) *Cognitive Behavior Therapy in Clinical Social Work Practice*. New York: Springer.

Ronen, T. and Rosenbaum, M. (2001) Helping children to help themselves: A case study of enuresis and nail biting. *Research in Social Work Practice,* 11, 338–56.

Rooney, R. H. (1985) Does in-service training make a difference? Results of a pilot study of task-centred dissemination in a public social service setting. *Journal of Social Service Research*, 8(3), 33–50.

Rooney, R. H. (1988) Measuring task-centred training effects on practice: Results of an audiotape study in a public agency. *Journal of Continuing Social Work Education*, 4(4), 2–7.

Rose, N. (1985). *The Psychological Complex: Psychology, Politics and Society in England 1869–1939,* London: Routledge & Kegan Paul.

Rosen A. and Proctor, E. (eds.) (2003) *Developing Practice Guidelines for Social Work Intervention.* New York: Columbia University Press.

Rosenbaum, M. (1990) The role of learned resourcefulness in self-control of health behavior. In M. Rosenbaum (ed.), *Learned Resourcefulness: On Coping Skills, Self-Control and Adaptive Behavior.* New York: Springer, pp. 3–30.

Rosenbaum, M. (1998). Learned resourcefulness, stress, and self-regulation. In S. Fisher and J. Reason (eds.), *Handbook of Life Stress, Cognition and Health.* Chichester: Wiley, pp. 483–96.

Rosenbaum, M. (1999) The self-regulation of experience: openness and construction. In D. Dewe, T. Cox and A.M. Leiter (eds.), *Coping, Health and Organizations.* London: Taylor and Francis, pp. 51–67.

Rosenbaum, M. and Ronen, T. (1998) Clinical supervision from the standpoint of cognitive-behavior therapy. *Psychotherapy*, 35, 220–29.

Roseneil, S. (2005) Living and loving beyond the boundaries of the heteronorm: Personal relationships in the 21st century. In L. McKie and S. Cunningham-Burley (eds.), *Families in Society: Boundaries and Relationships.* Bristol: Policy Press.

Roseneil, S. and Budgeon, S. (2004) Cultures of intimacy and care beyond 'the family': Personal life and social change in the early 21st century. *Current Sociology*, 52(2), 135–59.

Rossman, B. (2001) Longer term effects of children's exposure to domestic violence. In S. Graham-Bermann and J. Edleson (eds.), *Domestic Violence in the Lives of Children: The Future of Research, Intervention and Social Policy.* Washington, DC: American Psychological Association.

Rowe, J. W. and Kahn, R. L. (1987) Human ageing: Usual and successful. *Science*, 237, 143–9.

Rowland, O. and Parker, G. (1998) *Informal Carers: 1995 General Household Survey.* London: Office for National Statistics.

Rowlingson, K. and McKay, S. (2002) *Lone-Parent Families: Gender, Class and State.* Harlow: Prentice Hall.

Rowlingson, K. and McKay, S. (2005) Lone-motherhood and socio-economic disadvantage. *Sociological Review*, 53, 30–49.

Royal Commission on Long Term Care (1999) *With Respect to Old Age: Long Term Care – Rights and Responsibilities.* London: The Stationery Office.

Rummery, K. and Coleman, A. (2003) Primary health and social care services in the UK: Progress toward partnership? *Social Science and Medicine*, 56(8), 1773–82.

Rushton, A. and Davies, P. (1984) *Social Work and Health Care.* London: Heinemann.

Rustin, M. (2005) Conceptual analysis of critical moments in Victoria Climbié's life. *Child and Family Social Work*, 10, 11–19.

Rutter, M. (1967) A child behaviour questionnaire for completion by teachers: Preliminary findings. *Journal of Child Psychology and Psychiatry*, 8, 1–11.

Rutter, M. (1979) *Changing Youth in a Changing Society.* London: The Nuffield Provincial Hospitals Trust.

Safran, J. D. and Segal, Z. V. (1990) *Interpersonal Process in Cognitive Therapy.* New York: Basic Books.

Scarman, Lord (1981) *The Brixton Disorders: The Report of an Enquiry.* London: HMSO.

Schaffer, H. R. (1998) *Making Decisions about Children.* Oxford: Blackwell.

Schlichter, K. J. and Horan, J. J. (1981) Effects of stress inoculation on the anger and aggression management skills of institutionalised juvenile delinquents. *Cognitive Therapy and Research*, 5, 359–65.

Schofield, G. and Beek, M. (2006) *Attachment Handbook for Foster Care and Adoption*. London: BAAF.

Schofield, M. (1973) *The Sexual Behaviour of Young Adults*. London: Allen Lane.

Schön, D. A. (1983) *The Reflective Practitioner*. New York: Basic Books.

Scottish Executive (2000a) *Community Care: A Joint Future – Report of the Joint Future Group*. Edinburgh: The Scottish Executive.

Scottish Executive (2000b) *The Same as You? A Review of Services to People with Learning Disabilities*. Edinburgh: The Stationery Office.

Scottish Executive (2002a) *Plan for Action on Alcohol Abuse*. Edinburgh: Scottish Executive.

Scottish Executive (2002b) *Report of the Child Protection Audit and Review: 'It's Everyone's Job to Make Sure I'm alright'*. Edinburgh: Scottish Executive.

Scottish Executive (2005) *Statistics Release: Adults with Learning Disabilities. Implementation of The Same as You? Scotland 2004*. Available at: www.scotland.gov.uk/publications/2005/05/23160344/03472.

Scott Peck, M. (1990) *The Road Less Travelled: A New Psychology of Love, Traditional Values and Spiritual Growth*. London: Arrow.

Scourfield, J. (2001) Interviewing interviewers and knowing about knowledge. In I. Shaw and N. Gould (eds.), *Qualitative Research in Social Work*. London: Sage.

Sears, R., Maccoby, E. and Levin, H. (1957) *Patterns of Child Rearing*. New York: Harper & Row.

Secretary of State for Social Services (1988) *Report of the Inquiry into Child Abuse in Cleveland 1987*, Cmnd. 412. London: HMSO.

Seden, J. (2005) *Counselling Skills in Social Work Practice*. Maidenhead: Open University Press and McGraw Hill Education.

Seden, J. and Katz, J. (2003) Managing significant life events. In J. Seden and J. Reynolds (eds.), *Managing Care in Practice*. London: Routledge.

Seebohm Committee (1968) *Report of the Committee on Local Authority and Allied Social Services*, Cmnd 3703. London: HMSO.

Seeley, A. and Lobstein, T. (2004) *Going Hungry: The Struggle to Eat Healthily on a Low Income*. London: NCH.

Segal, U. (ed.) (2006) *Immigration Worldwide*. New York: Haworth Press.

Sellars, C. (2002) *Risk Assessment in People with Learning Disabilities*. Oxford: Blackwell.

Sellick, C. and Howell, D. (2004) A description and analysis of multi-sectoral fostering practice in the United Kingdom. *British Journal of Social Work*, 34, 481–99.

Sellick, C., Thoburn, J. and Philpot, T. (2004) *What Works in Adoption and Foster Care?* Barkingside: Barnardos.

Shakespeare, T. and Corker, M. (eds.) (2002) *Disability/Postmodernity: Embodying Disability Theory*. London: Continuum.

Shaw, I. (2005) Practitioner research: Evidence or critique?, *British Journal of Social Work*, 35, 1231–47.

Shaw, I. and Gould, N. (2001) *Qualitative Research in Social Work*. London: Sage.

Sheldon, B. (1987) Implementing findings from social work effectiveness research. *British Journal of Social Work*, 17, 573–86.

Shelley, E. L. V. and Toch, H. H. (1968) The perception of violence as an indicator of adjustment in institutionalized offenders. In H. Toch and H. C. Smith (eds.), *Social Perception: The Development of Internalized Impressions. An Enduring Problem in Psychology*. Princeton, NJ: D. Van Nostrand.

Shemmings, Y. and Shemmings, D. (1995) Defining participative practice in health and welfare. In R. Jack (ed.), *Empowerment in Community Care*. Hampshire: Chapman & Hall.

Sheppard, M. (1997) Social work practice in family and child care: A study of maternal depression. *British Journal of Social Work*, 27, 815–45.
Shera, W. and Wells, L. M. (eds.) (1999) *Empowerment Practice in Social Work*. Toronto: Canadian Scholars' Press.
Sherman, E. and Reid, W. (eds.) (1994) *Qualitative Research in Social Work*. New York: Columbia University Press.
Shukra, K. (1995) From black power to black perspectives: The reconstruction of a black political identity. *Youth and Policy*, 45, 5–20.
Sibeon, R. (1991) *Towards a Sociology of Social Work*. Aldershot: Avebury.
Siddell, M. (1995) *Health in Old Age*. Buckingham: Open University Press.
Silva, E. and Smart, C. (eds.) (1999) *The New Family?* London: Sage.
Simons, K. (1995), *I'm Not Complaining but . . . Complaints Procedures in Social Services Departments*. York: Joseph Rowntree Foundation/Community Care.
Simpson, B. (1998) *Changing Families*. Oxford: Berg.
Sinclair, I. (1971) *Hostels for Probationers*. London: HMSO.
Sinclair, I. (2005) *Fostering Now: Messages from Research*. London: Jessica Kingsley.
Sivanandan, A. (1990) *Communities of Resistance*. London: Verso.
Skinner, B. F. (1938) *The Behavior of Organism*. New York: Appleton-Century-Crofts.
Skinner, B. F. (1958). Reinforcement theory. *American Psychologist*, 13, 94–9.
Slade, E. (2004) *Tolley's Employment Handbook*, 18th edn. Croydon: LexisNexis Butterworths.
Sloan, D. (2003) *Children in Need Census 2003*, Social Factors Survey, Domestic Violence Analysis. Available at: www.cheshire.gov.
Smale, G., Tuson, G. and Statham, D. (2000) *Social Work and Social Problems: Working towards Social Inclusion and Social Change*. Basingstoke: Palgrave.
Small, J. (1991) Transracial placements: Conflicts and contradictions. In S. Ahmed, J. Cheetham, and J. Small (eds.), *Social Work with Black Children and their Families*. London: Batsford/BAAF, pp. 81–99.
Small, J. and Prevatt Goldstein, B. (2000) Ethnicity and placement: Beginning the debate. *Adoption and Fostering*, 24(1), 9–15.
Small, S. (1995) The black family in us. In D. Crosskill (ed.), *The Black Family in Us*. London: CCETSW.
Smart, B. (1993) *Postmodernity*. London: Routledge.
Smart, C. and Neale, B. (1999) *Family Fragments?* Cambridge: Polity Press.
Smith, M., Lees, D. and Clymo, K. (2003) The readiness is all: Planning and training for post-disaster support work. *Social Work Education*, 22(5), 517–28.
Social Exclusion Unit (1998) *Truancy and School Exclusion*. London: Cabinet Office.
Social Exclusion Unit (2004) *Mental Health and Social Inclusion*. London: Office of the Deputy Prime Minister.
Social Services Inspectorate, Department of Health (1991) *Women in Social Services: A Neglected Resource*. London: HMSO.
Social Services Inspectorate (1995) *The Challenge of Partnership in Child Protection: Practice Guide*. London: HMSO.
Solomon, B. B. (1976) *Black Empowerment: Social Work in Oppressed Communities*. New York: Columbia University Press.
Sorensen, R. C. (1973) *Adolescent Sexuality in Contemporary America*. New York: World Publishing.
Speicher, B. (1992) Adolescent moral judgement and perceptions of family interaction. *Journal of Family Psychology*, 6(2), 128–39.
Spender, D. (1980) *Man Made Language*. London: Routledge & Kegan Paul.
Staffordshire County Council (1991) *The Pindown Experience and the Protection of Children*. Stoke: Staffordshire County Council.

Stainton, T. (2002) Learning disability. In R. Adams, L. Dominelli and M. Payne (eds.), *Critical Practice in Social Work*. London: Palgrave.

Stalker, K. (ed.) (2002) *Reconceptualising Work with 'Carers': New Directions for Policy and Practice*. Research Highlights in Social Work No. 43. London: Jessica Kingsley.

Stalker, K., Cadogan, L., Petrie, M., Jones, C. and Murray, J. (1999) *'If You Don't Ask, You Don't Get': Review of Services to People with Learning Disabilities: The Views of People Who Use Services and their Carers*. Edinburgh: Scottish Executive Central Research Unit.

Stanley, K. (2001) *Cold Comfort: Young Separated Refugees in England*. London: Save the Children.

Stanley, N. and Manthorpe, J. (2001) Reading mental health inquiries: Messages for social work. *Journal of Social Work*, 1(1), 77–99.

Stark, E. and Flitcraft, A. (1996) *Women at Risk: Domestic Violence and Women's Health*. London: Sage.

Stein, M. (1997) *What Works in Leaving Care?* Barkingside: Barnardos.

Stewart, J. (1999) The twentieth century: An overview. In R. M. Page and R. Silburn (eds.), *British Social Welfare in the Twentieth Century*. Basingstoke: Macmillan.

Stockwell, T., Greunewald, P., Toumbourou, J. and Loxley, W. (eds.) (2005) *Preventing Harmful Substance Use: The Evidence Base for Policy and Practice*. Chichester: John Wiley and Sons.

Struening, K. (2002) *New Family Values: Liberty, Equality and Diversity*. Lanham, MD: Rowman and Littlefield.

Summers, A. (1979) A home from home: Women's philanthropic work in the nineteenth century. In S. Burnam (ed.), *Fit Work for Women*. London: Croom Helm.

Svejda, M. J., Campos, J. J. and Emde, R. N. (1980) Mother–infant 'bonding': A failure to generalize. *Child Development*, 51, 775–9.

Swain, J., French, S. and Cameron, C. (2003) *Controversial Issues in a Disabling Society*. Buckingham: Open University Press.

Swain, J., French, S., Barnes, C. and Thomas, C. (eds.) (2004) *Disabling Barriers – Enabling Environments*. London: Sage.

Swain, J., Griffiths, C. and French, S. (2005) Counselling with the social model: Challenging therapy's pathologies. In D. Goodley and R. Lawthorn (eds.), *Disability and Psychology: Critical Introductions and Reflections*. Basingstoke: Palgrave Macmillan.

Taylor. J. (2000) Welfare in the wilderness. *ACE Bulletin*, 93, 8–9.

Taylor, S. (1992) How prevalent is it? In W. Stainton Rogers, D. Hevey, J. Roche and E. Ash (eds.), *Child Abuse and Neglect: Facing the Challenge*. London: B.T. Batsford in Association with the Open University.

Taylor-Gooby, P. and Lawson, R. (eds.) (1993) *Markets and Managers: New Issues in the Delivery of Welfare*. Buckingham: Open University Press.

Thoburn, J. (1994) *Child Placement: Principles and Practice*. Aldershot: Arena.

Thoburn, J., Chand, A. and Procter, J. (2005) *Child Welfare Services for Minority Ethnic Families: The Research Reviewed*. London: Jessica Kingsley.

Thoburn, J., Wilding, J. and Watson, J. (1999) *Family Support in Cases of Emotional Maltreatment and Neglect*. London: The Stationery Office.

Thomas, A. and Chess, S. (1977) *Temperament and Development*. New York: Bruner/Mazel.

Thomas, D. and Woods, H. (2003) *Working with People with Learning Disabilities: Theory and Practice*. London: Jessica Kingsley.

Thomas, N. (2005) *Social Work with Young People in Care: Looking After Children in Theory and Practice*. London: Palgrave Macmillan.

Thompson, N. (1992) *Existentialism and Social Work*. Aldershot: Avebury.

Thompson, N. (2002) *People Skills*, 2nd edn. Basingstoke: Palgrave Macmillan.
Thompson, N. (2003) *Promoting Equality: Tackling Discrimination and Oppression*, 2nd edn. Basingstoke: Palgrave Macmillan.
Thompson, N. (2005) *Understanding Social Work*. Basingstoke: Palgrave.
Thompson, N. (2006a) *Power and Empowerment*. Lyme Regis: Russell House.
Thompson, N. (2006b) *Anti-Discriminatory Practice*, 4th edn. Basingstoke: Palgrave Macmillan.
Thompson, N. (2006c) *Promoting Workplace Learning*. Bristol: Policy Press.
Thompson, N. and Thompson, S. (2005) *Community Care*. Lyme Regis: Russell House.
Thompson, S. (2005) *Age Discrimination*. Lyme Regis: Russell House.
Titterton, M. (2005) *Risk and Risk Taking in Health and Social Welfare*. London: Jessica Kingsley.
Tizard, B. and Phoenix, A. (1993/2002). *Black, White or Mixed Race? Race and Racism in the Lives of Young People of Mixed Parentage*. London: Routledge.
Tolson, E. R. (1985) Teaching and measuring task-centred skills: The skill assessment teaching model. In A. E. Fortune (ed.), *Task-centred Practice with Families and Groups*. New York: Springer.
Tolson, E., Reid, W. J. and Garvin, C. (eds.) (1994) *Generalist Practice: A Task-centered Approach*. New York: Columbia University Press.
Tong, R. (1989) *Feminist Thought: A Comprehensive Introduction*. San Francisco: Westview Press.
TOPSS (2003a) *The National Occupational Standards for Social Work*. Available at: www.topss.org.uk (accessed 1 December 2003).
TOPSS (2003b) *Statement of Expectations from Individuals, Families, Carers, Groups and Communities Who Use Services*. Available at: www.topss.org.uk (accessed 1 December 2003).
TOPSS (2003c) *Academic Standards for Social Work*. Available at: www.topss.org.uk (accessed 1 December 2003).
Treacher, A. and Carpenter, J. (1983) *Using Family Therapy*. Oxford: Blackwell.
Trevithick, P. (2005) *Social Work Skills*. Maidenhead: Open University Press and McGraw Hill Education.
Trinder, L. (ed.) (2000) *Evidence Based Practice: A Critical Appraisal*. Oxford: Blackwell.
Triseliotis, J., Sellick, C. and Short, R. (1995) *Foster Care: Theory and Practice*. London: Batsford.
Trotter, C., Cox, D., Crawford, K. (2002) Family problem solving: A case study. *Australian Social Work*, 55(2), 119–27.
Tunnard, J. and Atherton, K. (1996) *Family Group Conferences*. London: National Children's Bureau.
Tunstill, J., Aldgate, J. and Hughes, M. (2006) *Improving Children's Services Networks: Lessons from Family Centres*. London: Jessica Kingsley.
Turnell, A. and Edwards, S. (1999) *Signs of Safety: A Solution and Safety Oriented Approach to Child Protection Casework*. London: Norton.
Turner, Francis J. (ed.) (1996) *Differential Diagnosis and Treatment in Social Work*, 4th edn. New York: Free Press.
Tyrer, P. and Steinburg, D. (2003) *Models for Mental Disorder: Conceptual Models in Psychiatry,* 2nd edn. Chichester: Wiley.
UKATT Research Team (2005) Effectiveness of treatment of alcohol problems: Findings of the randomized United Kingdom Alcohol Treatment Trial (UKATT). *British Medical Journal*, 331, 541–4.
Ungerson, C. (1987) *Policy is Personal: Sex, Gender and Informal Care*. London: Tavistock.

Union of the Physically Impaired against Segregation (1976) *Fundamental Principles of Disability*. London: UPIAS.

University of Glasgow (2002) Centre for Drug Misuse Research, *Parental Drug Misuse in Scotland*. Glasgow: University of Glasgow.

Utting, D. (1995) *Families and Parenthood: Supporting Families, Preventing Breakdown*. York: Joseph Rowntree Foundation.

Utting, W. (1991) *Children in the Public Care*. London: HMSO.

Utting, W. (1997) *People Like Us*. London: The Stationery Office.

Vallelly, S., Evans, S., Fear, T. and Means, R. (2006) *Opening Doors to Independence*. London: Housing 21.

Valios, N. (2000) Vanishing act. Available at: www.community care.co.uk (accessed 5 January 2006).

van Krevelen, D. A. (1971) Psychoses in adolescence. In J. G. Howells (ed.), *Modern Perspectives in Adolescent Psychiatry*. Edinburgh: Oliver and Boyd.

Vasey, S. (2004) Disability culture: The story so far. In J. Swain, S. French, C. Barnes and C. Thomas (eds.), *Disabling Barriers – Enabling Environments,* 2nd edn. London: Sage.

Vernon, J. and Fruin, D. (1986) *In Care: A Study of Social Work Decision-Making*. London: National Children's Bureau.

Victor, C. (1992) From pillow to post. *Health Service Journal,* 102 (5315) 20–2.

Victor, C. R. (2005) The epidemiology of ageing. In M. Johnson (ed.), *The Cambridge Handbook of Age and Ageing*. Cambridge: Cambridge University Press.

Wadham, J. and Mountfield, H. (2000) *Guide to the Human Rights Act 1998,* 2nd edn. London: Blackstone.

Waine, B. and Henderson, J. (2003) Managers, managing and managerialism. In J. Henderson and D. Atkinson (eds.), *Managing Care in Context*. London: Routledge.

Wake, I., Wilmott, I., Fairweather, P. and Birkett, J. (1999) *Breaking the Chain of Hate: A National Survey Examining Levels of Homophobic Crime and Community Confidence Towards the Police Service*. London: Stonewall.

Wakefield, J. C. (1996). Does social work need the eco-systems perspective? Part 1. Is the perspective clinically useful? *Social Service Review*, 70, 1–32.

Walby, S. (1990) *Theorizing Patriarchy*. Oxford: Basil Blackwell.

Walby, S. and Allen, J. (2004) *Domestic Violence, Sexual Assault and Stalking: Findings from the British Crime Survey*, Home Office Research Study 276. London: Home Office Research, Development and Statistics Directorate.

Walker, A. and Hagan Hennessy, C. (eds.) (2004) *Growing Older: Quality of Life in Old Age*. Buckingham: Open University Press.

Walker, J., McCarthy, P., Stark, C. and Laing, K. (2004) *Picking Up the Pieces: Marriage and Divorce Two Years after Information Provision*. London: Department for Constitutional Affairs.

Walker, M. (ed.) (1995a) *Peta, A Feminist's Problem with Men*. Buckingham: Open University Press.

Walker, M. (ed.) (1995b), *Morag, Myself or Mother Hen?* Buckingham: Open University Press.

Walker, N. (1996) *Dangerous People*. London: Blackstone Press.

Walker, S. and Akister, J. (2005) *Applying Family Therapy*. Lyme Regis: Russell House.

Wallace, K. and Henderson, G. (2004) *Social Backgrounds of Children Referred to the Reporter: A Pilot Study*. Stirling: Scottish Children's Reporter Administration.

Walsh, E. (1998) *Working in the Family Justice System: A Guide for Professionals*. Bristol: Family Law/Jordans.

Walters, M. (1988) *The Invisible Web; Gender Patterns in Family Relationships*. New York: Guilford.

Walton, R. (1975) *Women in Social Work*. London: Routledge & Kegan Paul.

Warner, R. (2004) *Recovery from Schizophrenia: Psychiatry and Political Economy*, 3rd edn. London: Routledge.

Waterhouse, L., Dobash, R. and Carnie, J. (1994) *Child Sexual Abusers*. Edinburgh: The Scottish Office.

Waterson, J. (1999) Redefining community care social work: Needs or risks led? *Health and Social Care in the Community*, 7, 276–9.

Watson, J. B. (1970) *Behaviorism*. New York: Norton.

Weaver, T., Madden, P., Charles, V., Stimson, G., Renton, A., Tyrer, P., Barnes, T., Bench, C., Middleton, H., Wright, N., Paterson, S., Shanahan, W., Seivewright, N. and Ford, C. (2003) Comorbidity of substance misuse and mental illness in community mental health and substance misuse services. *British Journal of Psychiatry*, 183, 304–13.

Webb, S. A. (2006) *Social Work in a Risk Society: Social and Political Perspectives*. Basingstoke: Palgrave.

Webster-Stratton, C. and Herbert, M. (1994) *Troubled Families: Problem Children*. Chichester: John Wiley.

Weismann, A. (1891) *Essays upon Heredity and Kindred Biological Problems, Volume 1*. Oxford: Clarendon Press.

Welsh Office (1983) *All Wales Strategy for the Development of Services for Mentally Handicapped People*. Available at: http://www.wales.gov.uk/subisocialpolicy/content/mentalhealth/handicap/contents-e.htm

Wenger, C. (1984) *The Supportive Network*. London: George Allen and Unwin.

Wenger, C. (1992) *Help in Old Age*. Liverpool: Liverpool University Press.

West, C. (1994) *Race Matters*. New York: Vintage Press.

Whelan, E. and Speake, B. (1977) *Adult Training Centres in England and Wales: Report of the First National Survey*. Manchester: NATMH.

Whelan, R. (1998) *Octavia Hill and the Social Housing Debate*. London: IEA Health and Welfare Unit.

White, M. (1995) *Re-Authoring Lives*. Adelaide: Dulwich Press.

White, S. (2001) Auto-ethnography as reflexive inquiry: The research act as self-surveillance. In I. Shaw and N. Gould (eds.), *Qualitative Research in Social Work*. London: Sage.

White, V. (2006) *The State of Feminist Social Work*. London: Routledge.

Whitehead, A. (2002) Rethinking masculinity: Observations of men's relationships with men and women in a British prison. Unpublished PhD thesis, University of Southampton, Southampton.

Whitney, B. (1998) Child employment legislation: Changing the focus. In B. Pettit (ed.), *Children and Work in the UK: Reassessing the Issues*. London: Child Poverty Action Group.

Whittington, C. and Bell, L. (2001) Learning for interprofessional and inter-agency practice in the new social work curriculum. *Journal of Interprofessional Care* 15(2), 153–69.

Wiggan, J. and Talbot, C. (2006) *The Benefits of Welfare Rights Advice: A Review of the Literature*. London: National Association of Welfare Rights Advisers. www.nawra.org

Wijsen, F. (1999) Beyond the fatal impact theory: Globalization and its cultural underpinnings. In M. Amaladoss (ed.), *Globalization and its Victims: As Seen by the Victims*. Delhi: Cambridge University Press, pp. 122–31.

Williams, C. (1999) Connecting anti-racist and anti-oppressive theory and practice: Retrenchment or reappraisal? *British Journal of Social Work*, 29, 211–30.

Williams, F. (2004) *Rethinking Families*. London: Calouste Gulbenkian Foundation.

Williams, J., Popay, J. and Oakley, A. (eds.) (1999) *Welfare Research: A Critical Review*. London: UCL Press.

Willis, P. (1977) *Learning to Labour: How Working Class Kids Get Working Class Jobs*, Farnborough: Saxon House.

Willmott, P. (1996) 1895–1945: The first 50 years. In J. Baraclough, G. Dedman, H. Osborn and P. Willmott (eds.), *One Hundred Years of Health Related Social Work 1895–1995: Then, Now, Onwards*. Birmingham: Venture Press.

Wilson, A. (1987). *Mixed Race Children: A Study of Identity*. London: Allen and Unwin.

Wilson, M. (1993) *Crossing the Boundary: Black Women Survive Incest*. London: Virago.

Wilton, T. (2000) *Sexualities in Social Care: A Textbook*. Buckingham: Open University Press.

Winnicott, D. (1965) *The Maturational Processes and the Facilitating Environment*. New York: International Universities Press.

Wiredu, K. (1998) Moral foundations of an African culture. In P. H. Coetzee and A. P. J. Roux (eds.), *The African Philosophy Reader*. London: Routledge, pp. 306–16.

Wolfensberger, W. (1972) *The Principle of Normalisation in Human Services*. Toronto: National Institute on Mental Retardation.

Wolfensberger, W. (1983) Social role valorisation: A proposed new term for the principle of normalization. *Mental Retardation*, 21(6), 234–9.

Wolpe, J. (1973). *The Practice of Behavior Therapy*. New York: Pergamon Press.

Wolpe, J. (1982) *The Practice of Behavior Therapy*, 3rd edn. New York: Pergamon Press.

Wong, D. B. (2004) Rights and community in Confucianism. In K.-L. Shun and D. B. Wong (eds.), *Confucian Ethics*. Cambridge: Cambridge University Press.

Wood, D. (1988) Dangerous offenders and the morality of protective sentencing. *Criminal Law Review*, 424–33.

World Health Organisation (1992) *Mental Disorders: Glossary and Guide to the Classification in accordance with the Ninth Revision of the International Classification of Diseases ICD 10*. Geneva: WHO.

Yeandle, S., Escott, K., Grant, L. and Batty, E. (2003) *Women and Men Talking about Poverty*, Working Paper Series No. 7. London: Equal Opportunities Commission.

Yelloly, M. A. (1980) *Social Work Theory and Psychoanalysis*. New York: Van Nostrand Reinhold.

Zarb, G., Nadash, P. and Berthoud, R. (1996) *Direct Payments for Personal Assistance: Comparing the Costs and Benefits of Cash Services for Meeting Disabled People's Support Needs*. London: Policy Studies Institute for British Council of Disabled People.

Ziguras, S. J. and Stuart, G. W. (2000) A meta-analysis of the effectiveness of mental health care management over 20 years. *Psychiatric Services*, 51, 1410–21.

Legislation and Related Matters Index

Name Index

Subject Index